SPECIAL EDITION

USING

Microsoft®

SharePoint
Portal Server

Robert Ferguson, et al.

CONTENTS A

800 East 96th Street
Indianapolis, Indiana 46240

Special Edition Using Microsoft® SharePoint Portal Server

Copyright © 2003 by Que

International Standard Book Number: 0-7897-2570-3

Library of Congress Catalog Card Number: 2002103973

Printed in the United States of America

First Printing: August 2002

05 04   4   3

Trademarks

Warning and Disclaimer

Associate Publisher
Greg Wiegand

Acquisitions Editor
Stephanie J. McComb

Development Editor
Mark Cierzniak

Managing Editor
Thomas F. Hayes

Project Editor
Carol Bowers

Production Editor
Benjamin Berg

Indexer
Mandie Frank

Proofreader
Leslie Joseph

Technical Editor
Andy Ball

Team Coordinator
Sharry Lee Gregory

Interior Designer
Anne Jones

Cover Designers
Anne Jones

Page Layout
Brad Lenser

TABLE OF CONTENTS

VI Troubleshooting

ABOUT THE AUTHORS

Robert Ferguson has more than 15 years experience in the computer industry, having worked extensively with legacy technologies such as Banyan Vines, Novell NetWare, and Microsoft BackOffice. Robert is currently a Windows 2000 MCSE, NetWare MCNE, and a Compaq ASE, and works for Compaq Global Services as a client principal. His role at Compaq is to provide tip-of-the-spear technical sales expertise for professional services solutions for several of Compaq's largest accounts within North America. While Robert's focus is on delivering solutions across all Global Services practices, his core strength is with Microsoft-based technologies such as Windows 2000, Exchange 2000, and SharePoint Portal Server. Robert also participated as part of a core team for authoring Que's *Special Edition Using Microsoft Exchange 2000 Server* (ISBN 0-7897-2278-X).

During the evenings and on weekends, Robert enjoys spending time with his soul mate (Wendy) and two children, Courtney and Michael. Whenever possible, his goal is to spend as much time as possible at the family lake house playing in the sun. From time to time, Robert also finds a moment or two to explore his new hobby, which is stock trending technical analysis.

Robert can be reached at `robert.ferguson@hp.com`.

George W. Anderson, MCSE, PMP, MBA, is a senior enterprise project manager and technical consultant. George spends his time at work designing, deploying, and managing large enterprise integration, collaboration, eBusiness, and supply chain projects. Outside of work, George is an active member of his church, an avid guitarist, and an enthusiastic follower of emerging technologies. He may be reached at `george.anderson@hp.com`.

Jan Cirpka is a senior technology consultant within Compaq Global Services, designing collaborative solutions for more than a decade now. Within Compaq's Microsoft Business Solutions practice, these days he works extensively with Exchange 2000 and SharePoint Portal Server. Raised in Germany, Jan now lives happily in The Netherlands.

Reza Dianat is a technical consultant for Compaq Global Services—.NET Solutions Practice who has deployed and implemented Microsoft SharePoint Portal solutions for many customers. For more than 18 years, he has been providing solutions for commercial and government sectors on IBM and Microsoft technologies. He is fascinated with and very optimistic about the future of Web Services and its impact on services and the software industry in general. He holds a master's degree in computer science from The Johns Hopkins University, and can be reached at `reza.dianat@hp.com`.

Jennifer Heiliger is a senior program manager employed by Compaq Global Services, with a focus on designing and implementing deployment technologies and projects. She is a member of Compaq's Microsoft Windows and Messaging team, consulting with large enterprise customers to achieve success with their deployments and migrations. She currently resides in Houston, Texas.

Richard Kuhlmann is the founder of an e-commerce company specializing in business-to-business needs. His IT career has developed from a variety of technical skills, including sales. A strong background in IT has allowed this lateral move, creating the opportunity for helping his customers' economic growth.

Jared Walker is a technology consultant within Compaq Global Services' Windows and Messaging Practice, and has been delivering IT services and solutions for more than 10 years. He earned an MBA in decision and information sciences from the University of Houston, and possesses numerous certifications, including his MCSE for Windows 2000. Born in California, Mr. Walker was raised in El Paso, Texas, and currently resides in Irving, Texas.

ABOUT THE TECHNICAL EDITOR

Andy Ball is an MCSE and MVP with 12 years experience in the IT industry. He runs his own UK-based consultancy firm, Greenfell Computing, whose clients vary from small dot coms to large multinational investment banks. He has recently evaluated and deployed SharePoint Portal Server–based solutions for several of these clients. He owns and runs `http://www.sharepointcode.com`, which provides code samples and Web Parts for SharePoint Portal Server. While not at work, Andy enjoys cycling up steep hills and sampling New World wines.

ACKNOWLEDGMENTS

First and foremost, I would like to thank my darling wife (Wendy) for putting up with me during the authoring of this book. You will always be the love of my life and my one and only soul mate. It is difficult to give up even a moment of time away from you and the kids to embark on personal endeavors such as writing a technical publication. Although we can never recover this time lost, I personally want to thank you for being a good sport and making sure the kids never missed a beat. You are a great woman and I am so blessed to be your husband.

I would also like to thank my mother (Adeline Ferguson) for supporting me during my most challenging times, teaching me to hold my head high, and helping me to believe that anything is possible in life. To my father (Orville Vaudie "Mike" Ferguson), I look forward to sometime in the future when I will join you in heaven and we can spend quality time together. Growing up without you is not easy but I dare not question God's good will.

I would sincerely like to thank the following co-authors who stepped up to help me complete this publication: Wendy Ferguson, Jennifer Haliger, Jared Walker, Reza Dianat, Richard Kuhlmann, Jan Cirpka, and especially George Anderson. Many of you stepped up in a short amount of time and pulled through to produce high-quality content. In addition, you are all from different walks of life, which allows your various real-world experiences to be leveraged throughout the book.

Thank you to Kent Goshi for inviting me to co-author the *Special Edition Microsoft Using Exchange 2000 Server* publication last year and recommending me to Que for the SharePoint effort. To Michelle Newcomb at Sams, thanks for having the confidence in me to lead the effort and bring the right resource to the table.

Finally, I would like to thank other key mentors in my life such as Eddie Frequez, Sonny Fresquez, Darryl Mastin, Beth Gibson, George Anderson, Michael Oubre, and Mark Rizzo.

WE WANT TO HEAR FROM YOU!

As the reader of this book, *you* are our most important critic and commentator. We value your opinion and want to know what we're doing right, what we could do better, what areas you'd like to see us publish in, and any other words of wisdom you're willing to pass our way.

As an associate publisher for Que Publishing, I welcome your comments. You can email or write me directly to let me know what you did or didn't like about this book—as well as what we can do to make our books better.

Please note that I cannot help you with technical problems related to the *topic* of this book. We do have a User Services group, however, where I will forward specific technical questions related to the book.

When you write, please be sure to include this book's title and author as well as your name, email address, and phone number. I will carefully review your comments and share them with the author and editors who worked on the book.

Email: feedback@quepublishing.com
Mail: Greg Wiegand
        Associate Publisher
        Que Publishing
        800 East 96th Street
        Indianapolis, IN 46240 USA

For more information about this book or another Que title, visit our Web site at www.quepublishing.com. Type the ISBN (excluding hyphens) or the title of a book in the Search field to find the page you're looking for.

INTRODUCTION

HOW THIS BOOK WAS AUTHORED

Many readers follow the *Special Edition* series by Que. If you have read the recent edition on Exchange 2000, you probably noticed that it was authored by a large team of distinguished consultants from companies such as Compaq, Lucent, and Software Spectrum. I was a co-author on this Exchange 2000 publication, and part of the core team under the leadership of the respected lead author of the messaging industry (Kent Joshi). Thanks to a referral from Kent, this co-authoring opportunity resulted in an chance for me to become the lead author of this *Special Edition Using SharePoint Portal Server* publication.

As lead author for a new product in the Microsoft family, I wanted to start a new tradition. I wanted to continue to leverage real-world consulting expertise from the field. However, this time I wanted to keep the authoring team within Compaq Global Services, which was recently acquired by Hewlett Packard. Compaq Global Services is a world-class consulting organization with a core focus, and when it comes to Microsoft technology, it is obvious that Microsoft technology is a core competency.

Senior consultants from Compaq Global Services have been hand-chosen to provide their collective experience to produce a world-class publication on SharePoint Portal Server. While reading this book, you may find the co-authors added specific input leveraged from their own experiences in implementing real-world solutions implementation experiences. These anecdotes have been added with various types of audiences in mind. The goal for each chapter is to discuss a feature or capability at a conceptual level, and then drill down into detail and provide instructions for how to perform specific planning, design, and implementation tasks.

Compaq Global Services has been working with SharePoint Portal Server since the early beta versions. In addition, Compaq Global Services has implemented enterprise portals based on SharePoint Portal Server for many medium and large organizations across the globe. Using a standard methodology of Planning, Design, Implementation, and Support, Compaq has capabilities to assist at any stage of your portal project lifecycle. In addition, Compaq is using SharePoint internally within many business units across the organization. For example, Global Services is using SharePoint as a single portal for various types of intellectual capital. Consultants from around the world have access to the portal site and are encouraged to contribute and reciprocate knowledge. I personally have set up *subscriptions* to various types of information. Several times a day I get subscription *notifications* as an email within my Microsoft Exchange inbox. As of date of this publication, Compaq has also deployed more than eight million seats of Exchange 5.x, three million seats of Exchange 2000, and more than three million seats of Windows 2000. Compaq was recently selected as

Microsoft's Global Services Partner of the year, and we are also the only Microsoft partner with the unique status of Prime Integrator for Windows 2000, Exchange 2000, and BizTalk 2000. We fully expect to lead the industry with SharePoint Portal Server as well. We currently do not have an accurate count of the number of deployed SharePoint Portal Server seats, but we fully expect to lead the industry for number of seats deployed and managed. To find out more information about Compaq services, visit `http://www.compaq.com/services`. Now that we have discussed how the book was authored, we can begin to discuss the details on features and real-world benefits of the product.

OVERVIEW AND SYNOPSIS

The book is broken down into six parts, as follows:

- Part I—Overview
- Part II —SharePoint Planning, Design, and Administration
- Part III—Customizing SharePoint
- Part IV—Planning and Managing Indexing
- Part V—Real World Scenarios
- Part VI—Troubleshooting

PART I, OVERVIEW

In Part I, the authoring team provides a high-level overview of SharePoint Portal Server features and benefits. This part consists of five chapters, each with a specific focus. Chapter 1 provides a high-level introduction to SharePoint. We do not attempt to start discussing how-to's in Chapter 1, as we want to provide a high-level conceptual overview. Chapter 2 discusses the core features and capabilities of SharePoint, and exposes the reader to a variety of key terms that will be discussed throughout the book. Again, we intentionally do not provide how-to steps in Chapter 2, as we drill into detailed walk-through steps later within each individual chapter. Chapters 3 through 5 discuss what we feel are the three core features of SharePoint Portal Server: using the workspace and dashboard, document management, and using indexing to allow efficient searches for your content. Our goal in Part I is to introduce the key concepts of SharePoint, while providing just enough detail to allow our readers to increasingly learn more about SharePoint as chapters progress in a linear fashion. Upon completion of Chapter 1, you will have a very good overview of SharePoint and its core features and capabilities. Reading this part first is important, as the following sections drill into more detail about the key concepts introduced in Part I.

PART II, PLANNING, DESIGN, AND ADMINISTRATION

In Part II, the authoring team commences to provide granular details about planning, design, and administration requirements. We discuss the requirements for capacity planning for small, medium, and large sites. We provide detailed instructions on how to install SharePoint, as well as common troubleshooting techniques to be aware of. Common administrative tasks are discussed for managing a server, managing the workspace, and managing folders. As we begin to discuss managing folders, we then need to clearly understand SharePoint security, and how security is integrated with Windows 2000 security. We then end the part with details on creating categories, processes, and procedures for backup, restore, and duplication.

PART III, CUSTOMIZING SHAREPOINT

Part III begins to explore advanced topics on how to customize SharePoint. Key authors with extensive development expertise teach the reader how to customize dashboards, as well as how to create Web Parts using ASP, COM+, SQL Server, and WebDAV. In addition, the authors share their expertise for how to customize SharePoint using XML and XLST.

PART IV, PLANNING AND MANAGING INDEXING

Part IV is dedicated to the key features of planning and managing indexing. We felt a dedicated part was necessary due to the importance of these topics. Detailed processes and procedures are articulated for how to configure SharePoint to crawl a variety of other content sources. Configuring content sources then becomes extremely important for how to set up and manage indexes.

PART V, REAL WORLD SCENARIOS

In this part, many of the concepts and detailed tasks come together to articulate a methodical approach to planning a real-world deployment. Detailed scenarios are provided for small and large sites.

PART VI, TROUBLESHOOTING

Part VI provides a detailed list of troubleshooting tips and techniques that are sorted in a logical manner. The format of this section allows the reader to drill down into a variety of troubleshooting threads according to problems they may be having at any given time of the SharePoint Portal Server lifecycle.

CONVENTIONS USED IN THIS BOOK

Que, as well as all of Pearson Technology Group's various imprints, has more than 10 years' experience creating the most popular and effective computer reference books available. From trainers to programmers, Que's authors have invaluable experience using—and most importantly—explaining computer and software concepts. From basic to advanced topics, Que's publishing experience, and its authors' expertise and communication skills, combine to create a highly readable and easily navigable book.

TIP

> Liberally sprinkled throughout the text, tips are places where we share insights that we've gained after using and writing about SharePoint Portal Server.

NOTE

> Notes contain extra information or alternative techniques for performing tasks that we feel will enhance your use and/or understanding of the current topic.

CAUTION

> If we want to warn you about a potential problem, you'll see that information in a caution.

 This element is designed to call your attention to areas where you are likely to get into trouble. When you see a Troubleshooting note, you can skip to the Troubleshooting at the end of the chapter to learn how to solve (or avoid) a problem.

CROSS-REFERENCES

Cross-references are used whenever possible to direct you to other sections of the book that give complementary or supportive information.

BUTTONS

Whenever a button is referred to in an explanatory paragraph or step-by-step procedure, the button will appear in the left margin, next to the paragraph or step that mentions it. This visual reminder helps you quickly locate the button on the toolbar so that you can remember it for future use.

KEYBOARD SHORTCUTS

Whenever a combination of keys can be pressed to execute a command, they'll appear paired by a plus sign, as in Ctrl+Home (to move to the top of a document) or Ctrl+P (to open the Print dialog box). When using a keyboard shortcut, press the first key, and while that key is depressed, tap the second key, and then release the first key.

TYPEFACES

Throughout this book, a variety of typefaces are used, each designed to draw your attention to specific text:

Typeface	Description
Monospace	Screen messages, text you type, and Internet addresses appear in this special typeface.
Italic	New terminology and emphasized text will appear in italic.

END-OF-CHAPTER EXAMPLES

Every chapter ends with a Troubleshooting section, where you'll find answers to frequently encountered problems. We've addressed more than just the simplest problems and solutions here—we cover the pitfalls you're likely to encounter when you push SharePoint Portal to the limit.

PART I

OVERVIEW

CHAPTER 1

INTRODUCING SHAREPOINT

In this chapter

UNDERSTANDING SHAREPOINT PORTAL SERVER BENEFITS

The history of the personal computer has presented many challenges to managing and accessing information for end users. In addition, since organizations began using the Internet, they have become increasingly interested in a single site that provides organized views of their corporate information. This concept is known as a *portal*. This portal concept has become an extremely powerful tool that allows users to aggregate content and applications from a variety of information sources, while at the same time providing meaningful sorting and classification of the knowledge. Simply stated, information can be logically consolidated such that users can utilize a standard Web browser to access a single Web site to access to content that resides in various locations across the organization. With SharePoint Portal Server, Microsoft offers a breakthrough solution designed to integrate the two closely related issues of managing documents and simplifying how users find, share, and publish information.

The power of Microsoft Office 2000 and SharePoint Portal Server seamlessly connects people, content, and data in enterprise systems through a single set of familiar tools, thereby making this combination of products the core of any document management solution.

CURRENT CHALLENGES

Over the years, companies of all sizes have accumulated important intellectual capital. Administrators spend a great deal of time organizing and managing the information in an effort to make it available and easy to find. Yet, the end users within the organization spend countless hours searching for specific information that is relevant to their daily tasks and responsibilities.

Take some time to review your intranet site and interview users or other administrators within your environment. After browsing through intranet sites, you may consider asking the following questions:

1. How familiar are you with the content on your intranet site?

2. How easy or difficult is it to find the information you are looking for when your intranet site is accessed?

3. When you access the site, do you have to search for information, or is the site set up in a way that allows you to browse through a list of categories or topics to quickly access relevant information?

4. If you do have to search for information, does the search engine return relevant results, or do you find yourself having to scroll through many different links to verify whether the results meet your needs?

The preceding questions are just a small example of the types of questions you will want to ask. When these questions are asked, you will likely discover your end user community is not fully aware of the types of information available. In addition, you will likely find that end users have attempted to search for key information at some point in the past, and became frustrated due to not being able to find what they were looking for.

Furthermore, once these end users do become aware of the locations for discrete pockets of information, they often become less likely to return, as the value of the data is not fully comprehended within their day-to-day activities.

→ To learn more about the types of questions to ask your end users and other planning requirements that should be considered prior to implementing SharePoint Portal Server, **see** "Planning a Deployment for ABC Company," **p. 520**.

It is important to discover where information resides today within most organizations, as well as how this information is currently accessed. Administrators and end users place content on file servers, database servers, and within public folder shares on your messaging server. On a file server, the administrator must enable a hierarchical share and expose it in a manner such that the data can be securely accessed by required end users. Many times this is done by establishing a top-level folder with a series of subfolders which categorize the content according to relevance of data or security access to the data. Public folders on your messaging server are established in the same manner, and exposed through the Outlook client. While information sharing in this manner was sufficient over the last few years, the problem is that end users have to navigate through various hierarchical folders to locate desired content. This process is time-consuming and often frustrates the end users. We will discuss the concept of *Categories*, which allows administrators to logically group data for timely and efficient access when a search is made.

SHAREPOINT PORTAL SERVER AS A SOLUTION

SharePoint Portal Server can be used in a variety of scenarios and can by used by many different types of users. For example, an IT director may be considering introducing SharePoint Portal Server within the organization to provide a consistent enterprise portal interface for providing information as a solution. A second example might be an IT administrator looking for better methods for managing and publishing information for the end user community. A third example might find that a power user is looking for a quick community solution for a departmental or line of business within an enterprise. SharePoint Portal Server can provide document management, content and index search services, and a collaborative applications platform for a customizable out-of-the-box dashboard site that can be accessed with a Web browser.

The primary benefit SharePoint Portal Server provides is the ability to find, analyze, and organize information of all types. The view that is ultimately presented to the user can be specifically tailored to the needs of that particular end user or group of users, such that information is presented as a solution according to the way the user works. This customization for the end user is done by customizing the workspace according to groups of users. If end users need individual customization, you can enable additional levels of personalization using personal dashboards.

→ For more details on customizing personal dashboards to meet specific end user requirements, **see** "Customizing Dashboards," **p. 343**.

1

SharePoint Portal Server allows you to present a customized workspace view of key information to your readers no matter where the information physically resides, while filtering unnecessary information from the reader's immediate view. It is about managing information and creating a custom view of key information that fits the business needs for the way your organization needs to work. It's about presenting information in a way that creates order out of chaos.

- Microsoft BackOffice—SharePoint Portal Server is one of the newest additions to the Microsoft BackOffice family that integrates document management and search capabilities with standard Microsoft Office tools that you probably use every day.

- Dashboard—The flexible Web-based dashboard site allows documents to be easily found, shared, and published.

- Explorer and Office—SharePoint Portal Server was designed to work well with Web browsers, Windows Explorer, and Microsoft Office applications for creating, managing, and sharing your organization or individual business unit's content. The product integrates document management capabilities such as check-in, checkout, document profiles, and document publishing. The functionality can be implemented using a variety of interfaces, which will be described in greater detail throughout this book.

- Wizards—SharePoint Portal Server is also designed for departmental professionals who are not necessarily a part of the IT organization. The "all-defaults" four-screen setup wizard allows for a rapid installation with a fully operational departmental server that can be immediately used to provide value to a particular department. The dashboard site offers a single customizable foundation for accessing information drawn from a wide variety of content sources while maintaining the security of the documents. Additional wizards can be used to register data sources for an out-of-box initial dashboard site that potentially could be structured to crawl parts of an Internet, intranet, Exchange 5.5 and Exchange 2000 server public folder hierarchies, Lotus Notes 4.6a+ and R5 databases, local file systems, and networked file servers within a few short hours of installation.

While we discussed a few solution examples, Part V of this book discusses several real-world scenarios. The chapters within Part V provide much more detail on using SharePoint as a solution.

ARCHITECTURAL FRAMEWORK

SharePoint Portal Server is closely coupled with existing key Microsoft technologies such as Digital Dashboards, Windows, Office, Microsoft Internet Explorer, the Microsoft Web Storage System, and the Microsoft Search Service. In addition, external content can be integrated to add additional value to the end user experience. Figure 1.1 provides a visual representation of this integrated architecture.

Figure 1.1
All the components are closely coupled to make a SharePoint Portal Server Solution.

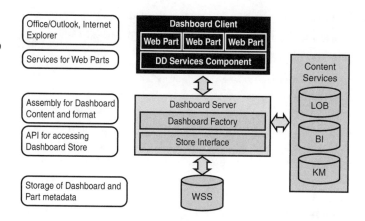

PLANNING DESIGN GOALS

The SharePoint Portal Server team relies on three key design goals during the development of this new addition to the Microsoft BackOffice family that would allow users to easily find, share, and publish information.

Specifically, the SharePoint Portal Server's development team design goals are

1. Create easy access to business-critical information
2. Create the premier document management application for Office users
3. Create the best place to organize and communicate around projects

The following sections provide additional details about the design goals.

CREATE EASY ACCESS TO BUSINESS-CRITICAL INFORMATION

The first design goal for SharePoint Portal Server is to create easy access to business-critical information. Many companies of all sizes have the problem of inheriting extensive amounts of corporate information, and they need to make this information available to knowledge workers through Web sites, Exchange public folders, Lotus Notes databases, documents, presentations, and so on. The challenge to the development team was to figure out how to allow end users to obtain the full benefit of all organization information, while making sure it is easy to locate. The answer was the portal dashboard, made up of Web Parts that could be easily custom-tailored to meet your needs using the Microsoft Office Developer's Kit or the SharePoint Portal Server SDK, which is located at http://www.microsoft.com/ sharepoint/doanloads/tools/sdk.asp.

NOTE

A Web Part is a reusable component that contains Web-based content. SharePoint enables administrators to assemble various Web Parts to make up a digital dashboard framework. Several Web Parts are shipped with SharePoint Portal Server, and custom Web Parts can be developed.

→ To learn more dashboards, **see** " Dashboard Overview," **p. 42**.

The digital Dashboard technology is used within SharePoint Portal Server to display and manage end user data.

This concept of centralized content and end user data based on the Web Storage System can be integrated with SQL Server and other key information sources. To speed the development of applications, application developers can build on this set of core services. SharePoint Portal Server allows end users to centralize desired content from within the organization as well as from external data sources into one single portal. If necessary, SharePoint Portal Server allows users to utilize a *"subscription"* feature to be notified when desired documents, content, and topics are made available. A feature called *"best bets"* can be used to assist end users with targeted searches to ensure that when searches are made, the most relevant material is retrieved as a result.

→ To learn more about Web Storage System, **see** "Web Storage System," **p. 400**.

CREATE THE PREMIER DOCUMENT MANAGEMENT APPLICATION FOR OFFICE

SharePoint Portal Server integration with Microsoft Office programs is essential, considering that most end users today spend a tremendous amount of time working with Office. A key integration point is to allow the document management functionality to be enabled through both Microsoft Office and Internet Explorer. Now end users can use one software application to create as well as manage their documents.

With SharePoint Portal Server, end users can easily create, review, and publish documents. This is done through the core set of services such as check in, check out, versioning, and document profiling. During the document creation lifecycle, SharePoint Portal Server allows granular security and access control. Once the document is created, an approval process can be automatically initiated, and once approved, the document can be published to the desired final destination.

SharePoint Portal Server utilizes a document profile feature to classify documents using a common process. This concept of a document profile is essential to provide the details that are required so end users can find key information that is stored throughout the enterprise, regardless of its location. The document profile information becomes the essential metadata that is associated with the document.

ORGANIZING INFORMATION

SharePoint Portal Server was designed to take advantage of the features and benefits of Microsoft Office. Users of SharePoint Portal Server can have administrators build departmental portal sites that are logically linked as a single enterprise portal solution.

SharePoint Portal Server can be used to create high-performance native Web applications based on your specific business needs. Data is accessed by using Extensible Markup Language (XML) support, which enables developers to leverage existing skills sets.

→ To learn more about XML, **see** "XML and XSL," **p. 428**.

SHAREPOINT PORTAL SERVER AND SHAREPOINT TEAM SERVICES

The new Office XP includes SharePoint Team Services, which allows end users to create and add content to team, departmental, or project-based Web sites.

If your organization is currently using SharePoint Team Services, it may be beneficial to allow the index of a SharePoint Portal Server workspace to include documents that are stored in the existing SharePoint Team Services Web Site document libraries. After this indexing capability is enabled, the SharePoint Team Services content is then available to be searched directly from within the SharePoint Portal Server workspace.

NOTE

> You must have SharePoint Portal Server 2001 Service Pack 1 installed for access to the protocol handler that enables searches for SharePoint Team Services document libraries.

If your organization has a need for teams to work together within a business unit or across multiple business units, SharePoint Team Services is a great product that enables this to happen through a simple Web-based solution. The product can be used to perform basic tasks such as teams efficiently managing their tasks from a Web browser. In addition, SharePoint Team Services can be used to provide a rich collaborative Web solution, which can be closely coupled with features and capabilities of Office XP.

Table 1.1 illustrates the similarities and differences between SharePoint Portal Server and SharePoint Team Services:

TABLE 1.1   CORE FEATURES OF SHAREPOINT PORTAL SERVER VERSUS SHAREPOINT TEAM SERVICES

Feature	SharePoint Portal Server	SharePoint Team Services
Enterprise search	X	
Rich document management functionality	X	
Customized with Digital Dashboards and Web Parts	X	
Based on Web Storage System for custom collaboration solutions	X	
Extensible with Visual Studio and common programming interfaces such as OLEDB, ADO, and CDO	X	
Departmental/enterprise information portals	X	X
Team collaborative Web sites	X	X

TABLE 1.1   CONTINUED

Feature	SharePoint Portal Server	SharePoint Team Services
Easy document sharing and team organization	X	X
Available for intranets and for extranets via ISPs	X	X
Integrated Office XP user experience	X	X
Customized using Microsoft FrontPage		X
Team templates for easy Web site creation		X
Can be used to create Internet sites as well as intranet		X

NOTE   To learn more about the detailed list of features and capabilities of SharePoint Team Services, visit the Microsoft site located at `http://www.microsoft.com/sharepoint/`.

By now you are aware that Office XP can be used along with SharePoint Team Services to set up and manage small team- and project-based Web sites. When you factor in the use of SharePoint Portal Server, you are then exploiting the product's capabilities to provide a variety of content types throughout the enterprise. Later in this book we will discuss how SharePoint Portal Server can be used as the corporate portal within the enterprise.

→ To learn more about using SharePoint as a corporate portal, **see** "Example Scenario 3 - Enterprise Wide Solution," **p. 577**.

This single portal concept will also be the central document management library with categories set up according to the way your end users work on a daily basis. Organizations of all sizes can benefit when both SharePoint Team Services and SharePoint Portal Server are used to provide the level of flexibility that your company requires.

Consider the possibilities of allowing small workgroups the ability to collaborate with each other with little or no IT resource support requirements. You then add the robust enterprise search and document management features of SharePoint Portal Server, and the result is an aggregated enterprise corporate knowledge forum. The enterprise portal could consist of a single workspace with access to SharePoint Team Services Web sites, intranet sites, file servers, Notes databases, public folders, and external Internet sites.

SharePoint Portal Server exists in several language versions such as English, Spanish, French, Italian, German, and Japanese. SharePoint Portal Server includes both the server and client components, but does not include a specific client graphical users interface. However, functionality is enabled through tight integration with Office, Windows, and your Web browser.

FINDING THE RIGHT DOCUMENT

Organizations today are constantly looking for ways to reduce operational costs for managing important information. Clearly, with the advent of the Internet, it is now easier than ever to publish and locate important information. However, many corporate knowledge workers still struggle daily to find the right document within their own intranet or document library system. Finding the right document has always been a challenge. However, it is not just about finding a document. Knowledge that exists within a document can be used to implement standard business processes.

Users need to be able to access documents, track changes, manage approvals, classify documents, and keep documents private to a specific group until they are ready to be shared with a broader audience. Users also struggle to collaborate when creating documents. The technology required to let ad hoc groups collaborate often requires the complex integration of a Web server, a file server, and other sophisticated technologies.

Many document management products exist on the market today. These tools can be used to solve a number of specific business problems. However, these products are not used by too many companies because the products cost too much, deployment costs are high, learning the products introduces great challenges, and often the products require a separate post-implementation management infrastructure.

UNDERSTANDING THE SHAREPOINT SEARCH ENGINE

In order to understand how to make documents easy to find, it is important to realize the importance of the search engine within SharePoint Portal Server. Once you understand the search engine, you can then plan for linking metadata within the document profiles of each of your documents.

→ To learn more document profiles, **see** "Document Profiles," **p. 26.**

You can use categories to help you find the right documents. SharePoint was designed so that end users could do the same function several different ways.

→ To learn more about Categories, **see** "Creating Categories," **p. 299**.

Categories can be used for the visual end users that prefer to browse down through the workspace to find exactly what they are looking for. One of the best practices in the early stages of the planning process is to interview your end user community within the various business units. Plan and design SharePoint Portal Server categories according to the way your end users need to work.

TIP

> Create a questionnaire for your end users and involve them in the planning process. This is very important and will ensure that they understand how categories and metadata can be used to make sure their information is easy to find. This will also help end users to embrace the portal after it is made available to your reader's community.

1

AUTOMATIC ROUTING AND APPROVAL

One of SharePoint Portal Server's greatest features is document management and the automatic routing and approval process that can be used. Consider the following manual business processes for document approval that exists today: A document is created by an author and saved as a draft. The draft document is either saved in a public share or saved on an internal hard drive and sent via email to a set of reviewers for additional feedback. The reviewers make appropriate manual changes and comments to the document, and either save the document within the public share with a revised version or save the document on their hard drives with a different version. Whether the document is saved on their internal hard drives or on a public share, a separate notification process must take place to inform the original author of the status of the review and revision process. The notification could require phone calls to be made, emails to be sent, or even manually having to track individuals down to ensure next steps are taken on the document.

Even with this simple example, at least two separate versions of the document exist in two separate places. Once the notification happens, the original author reviews the changes to the document made by the reviewer, and if acceptable, saves the document as a final version. Most often, important documents that several individuals are working on require multiple iterations before the document can be saved as a final draft. Nevertheless, the document is then either published to a public share or sent via email to the final destination.

SharePoint Portal Server was designed to streamline the document approval process while ensuring the process is much more efficient and transparent to authors and editors.

PLANNING DOCUMENT APPROVAL

Before you can develop an efficient approval process solution, it is very important to get answers to the following questions:

1. Who needs to be involved with the creation of the document?
2. Who must review the document before it can be saved as final draft?
3. Where is the final destination for the document and what process will be required to get the document to this final location?

CAUTION

Be aware that if the approval process relies on a single user, and the user is out of the office, your approval process will be delayed. In this case, an administrator can override the approval process.

→ To learn more about the approval process, **see** " Approval Process Types," **p. 51**.

1

Once you have the answers to the preceding questions, you can then use native SharePoint Portal Server functionality to enable access to a document share so several users can collaborate on a document. You can then setup granular control and specify who can do what to a document by specifying authors and editors one of the three security access permissions (Reader, Author, and Coordinator). Within the document profile, the Coordinator can specify the approval process (see Figure 1.2) for how the document is routed and whether the document is automatically published upon acceptance of the final reviewer.

→ To learn more about Security roles, **see** "Permissions," **p. 281**.

Figure 1.2
Illustration of the Sales folder, with restrictions set so that documents must be approved before they can be published. All documents placed in the folder will require this approval process.

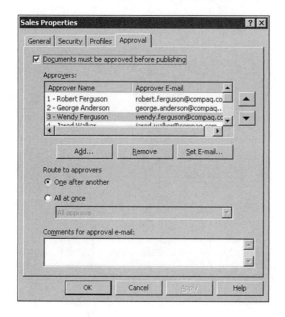

→ To learn more routing and approval, **see** "Approval Process Types," **p. 51**.

AGGREGATING INFORMATION SOURCES

SharePoint Portal Server enables the use of integrated searchable indexes for all content in the workspace, as well as specific information from the content sources that you specify. *Content sources* refer to a location outside the workspace where content is stored. Once content sources are configured, the aggregate view allows end users to search for and view information from the extended workspace, which now includes the content sources. *Aggregated content* can include information within different workspaces or file systems on the same server, workspace or file systems on another server on your network, databases, or information from Web sites or file shares across the Internet.

NOTE

When content sources are used, only the URL for the external content source is stored in the workspace. When setting up a content source, a username and password can be included for remote sites, if required.

→ To learn more about setting up and configuring content sources, **see** "The Crawling Process," **p. 455**.

Figure 1.3 shows a visual diagram of how SharePoint Portal Server is used and linked to a variety of additional information sources.

Figure 1.3
The diagram shows a visual representation of some of the content sources that can be integrated with SharePoint Portal Server.

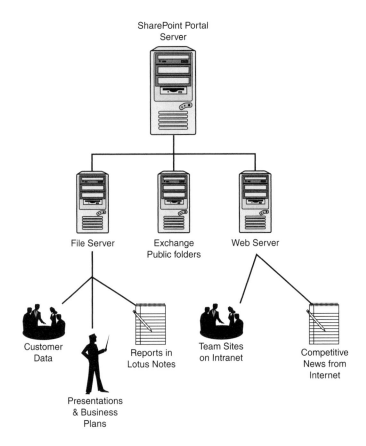

SharePoint Portal Server allows the following content source types:

- File shares
- Web sites
- Microsoft Exchange 5.5 public folders
- Microsoft Exchange 2000 public folders

- Lotus Notes databases
- Other SharePoint Portal Server workspace
- STS with SP1
- FTP with Resource Kit add in

NOTE
> Check-in/check-out functionality is not possible with content sources. Within the Management folder of the workspace, the Content Sources Folder exists for stored content. You must be designated as a Coordinator of the Management folder in order to create and manage content sources. Once you have the appropriate security, the Add Content Source wizard can be used to add desired content sources.

TIP
> Consider creating and providing an end user survey to determine what content exists and what type of information is needed for individual users or groups of users. This ensures that content sources are customized for the way the end users need to work.

Portals operate by searching (also known as crawling) content stored locally as well as on remote systems. A set of rules (known as a *taxonomy*) allows information to be then indexed and sorted. This taxonomy enables your end users to organize key business information around concepts that are closely related to the way your business operates. The information can then be searched upon and custom views can be created according to the way your users need to think about the data.

SharePoint Portal Server allows document management, personalization, and discussions, which are document-centric.

However, the most pervasive feature is the ability to crawl, analyze, and sort large quantities of information. In this way, the portal becomes a gateway into a vast array of information available on the intranet and Internet. No matter how many various information sources are crawled, the view of the portal is only as valuable as the structure that applies to this view. In other words, the more detailed the taxonomy, the less generic the results. If the taxonomy is not utilized, the portal becomes little more than a search engine. We all have had the experience of performing an Internet search only to return several hundred hits for a relatively simple search.

In most cases, the departmental or business unit information that the corporate portal will need to crawl and index will need to be created and maintained by the department or business unit. These groups within the organization will have a much clearer understanding of the required subject matter at a more detailed, topic-specific level. As stated earlier, you need to interview your users and clearly understand their business requirements.

1

SUMMARY

Microsoft's SharePoint Portal Server is well suited to meet the needs of most enterprises. SharePoint Portal Server provides both document management and search functions, accessible either from a Web browser or the Windows desktop. The integration with Microsoft Office and your Web browser allows SharePoint Portal Server to be used at all levels of the enterprise, from a departmental collaboration server to a robust enterprise search engine. Important content and enterprise intellectual capital resides within multiple data repositories within the environment. SharePoint Portal Server can be used to manage and display this knowledge to your end user community. SharePoint Portal Server can be used as a single departmental solution or at the center of the core for enterprise knowledge management portal solution.

SharePoint Portal Server Features and Capabilities

In this chapter

THREE MAIN FEATURES

As discussed in Chapter 1, three distinct design goals were established during the development of SharePoint Portal Server. To review, the design goals were

- To offer easy access to business-critical information.
- To create the premier document management application for Office users.
- To create the best place to communicate about and organize projects.

After working with the product for some time, you will find that these goals are closely embedded within the three main features of SharePoint Portal Server. These three main features are

- Rich enterprise search

→ To learn more about enterprise search capabilities with SharePoint, **see** "The End User Experience," **p. 94**.

- Integrated document management

→ To learn more about document management, **see** "The Document Management Process," **p. 70**.

- Robust intranet portals based on digital dashboard technology

→ For more information on digital dashboard functionality, **see** "Understanding Digital Dashboard," **p. 42**.

SEAMLESS ADMINISTRATION

The SharePoint Portal Server workspace concept allows multiple teams' document libraries to be enabled from a single server. The Microsoft Management Console (MMC) snap-in, called SharePoint Portal Server Administration, will allow administrators to utilize standard administrative tools for server management.

NOTE

> SharePoint Portal Server runs on a Windows 2000 platform, and does not require Microsoft Active Directory. The MMC on the local server must be used for administration, as you cannot administrate remotely without enabling terminal services.

All SharePoint Portal Server events are logged to the NT event log, and the Windows 2000 Performance Monitor is used to track specific load-tracking counters.

→ To learn more about Performance Monitor counters for SharePoint, **see** "Monitoring Using Standard Performance Counters," **p. 136**.

SharePoint Portal Server was designed for non-information technology (IT) professionals to install and use in a departmental setting. The "all-defaults" four-screen setup wizard allows non-technical professionals to set up a fully operational server within minutes.

RICH ENTERPRISE SEARCH

Users of SharePoint Portal Server will find that an out-of-the-box intranet installation includes a full text search engine. The focus of including this search engine was to allow groups of users, large or small, to be able to locate information no matter where it actually resides within the enterprise. This could mean all users within the enterprise could access a Human Resources site to search for the latest HR related documents, or you could have a specific business unit such as Marketing that needs specific information from the Marketing intranet. The robust search capabilities allow full text and Boolean searching in order to find the information that is desired. In addition, *metadata* attributes can be embedded in the document profile to ensure that specific information is located according to the way you want it located.

NOTE

> Metadata is defined as the properties and associated values of a document. Examples of system-defined metadata include the size of the file or the last date a document was modified. Documents can also have user-defined metadata, such as name of author and title of document.

SEARCHING BASED ON BEST BETS

The new search capability now allows for the option to search based on relevance. The SharePoint Portal Server search engine ensures that the most relevant hits are retrieved. Additional customization and the use of *best bets* can be enabled to associate documents with specific categories. Best bets is a feature that allows individual documents to be associated with a category, series of categories, or series of keywords. This process ensures that specific documents are returned as the most relevant when a search is performed on the category or keyword criteria. See Figure 2.1 for an overview of a search with a best bet keyword defined.

Figure 2.1
This example utilizes a best bet associating the keyword briefing with a particular document called Briefing Overview. When a user searches for "briefing", the Briefing Overview document will be displayed at the top of the list.

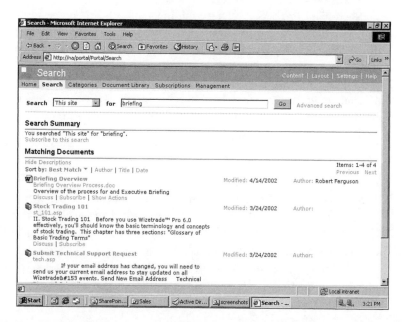

This capability allows you to customize your portal, and tune the way you want documents to be retrieved according to the particular searches that are executed. As you can see, this will require careful planning when planning your corporate portal.

DOCUMENT MANAGEMENT LIFECYCLE

The value of SharePoint Portal Server is that it allows efficient management of documents through the document lifecycle continuum. Whether you are working on the first draft of a document, working with other authors and editors to make required modifications, or in the process of publishing documents to the final destination of choice, SharePoint Portal Server has management options to manage documents through the entire document management lifecycle. An additional document discussion feature enables authors and editors to collaborate on document revisions while the original version remains accessible to existing workspace readers. The document discussion option is only possible once the first version of a document has been published.

THE DRAFT PHASE

With SharePoint Portal Server, authors can designate documents as Drafts. When specified as a Draft, the document can be shared with other authors and editors. However, this Draft option ensures documents are not published to the intended audience until the author specifies that the document is ready. Once the document is ready for the intended audience, it can then be manually published. After publication, the document and all associated metadata become part of the search index. Users could then manually search for documents or navigate through predefined categories to locate required documents.

THE PUBLISHING AND APPROVAL PHASE

With SharePoint Portal Server, the publishing and approval process can be automated. The application supports enabling an automated routing and approval process from within the properties page of an enhanced folder. The Coordinator specifies a set of Approvers who have access to approve or reject documents as part of the approval process. The author then submits a document for review; the Approver examines the document and approves or rejects the document based on approval or rejection criteria. After the document has been approved by all designated Approvers, the automated approval process proceeds and the document is published.

The publishing and approval methods that can be specified are

- Serial—With this method, Approvers are designated and approval or rejection is decided in a one-after-another fashion. Once the last Approver in the chain completes the approval process, the document is then published and made available to the intended audience. The document will remain in a checked-in state until published.

- Parallel (Everyone)—With this method, Approvers are designated and notified in parallel that a document is ready for their approval. Once all Approvers agree, the document is then published and made available to the intended audience.

- Parallel (Anyone)—With this method, Approvers are designated and notified in parallel that a document is ready for their approval. The difference is that with this approval method, it only takes one approval and the document is then published and made available to the intended audience.

SharePoint Portal Server leverages the Microsoft Digital Dashboard technology to allow efficient dashboard site development. Information from a variety of information sources across the enterprise is brought together in one context as an efficient way to manage information.

INTEGRATED DOCUMENT MANAGEMENT

In this section we will provide a high-level overview of the key features of document management. We will discuss check-in and check-out, versioning, security, document profiles, and integration with Microsoft Office. If you think about the traditional lifecycle of a document, you may agree that document creation is rarely an activity that involves just a single author. For example, an author creates a document, and often an additional individual will act as editor and collaborate on the document to provide feedback and review. Multiple versions of the document are created, until consensus is reached that the document is approved and ready to be sent or posted to the final destination. SharePoint Portal Server was designed to address this tedious manual document management challenge. The document management capabilities within SharePoint Portal Server are likely to be the single most important set of capabilities within the product. The core capabilities within the document library integrated services are document version control, document security, document profiling, and history tracking. These features are described in more detail in the following sections.

CHECK-IN/CHECK-OUT

SharePoint Portal Server allows an efficient process for authors and editors to check-in and check-out documents. When a document is checked out, other authors and editors cannot make any changes to the document. Administrators have the option to enable the check-in/check-out feature on a per-folder basis. By default, folders are set up as "Standard," and SharePoint Administrators must specify a folder as "Enhanced" in order to enable the check-in/check-out capabilities.

VERSION CONTROL

The version control feature within SharePoint Portal Server enables tracking of the history of a document, which can determine who changed the document, when it was changed, and more importantly which changes were made. This audit feature is one of the two main benefits of version control. The second component of version control is recovery, which allows a user to revert back to a previous version of a document. Additional features of version control are

- Version Numbering Scheme—The version method that is used is a [Major.Minor] numeric versioning scheme. The number on the left of the decimal point refers to the major version; in the examples 1.0 and 2.0, the major versions are 1 and 2, respectively.

The number on the right of the decimal point refers to the minor version of the document; in the examples 1.1 and 1.2, the minor versions are 1 and 2. Version retention is a parameter that is established by the SharePoint Portal Server administrator.

- Version comments—This allows comments to be associated with each version of a document. A sample comment may be "Revised Letter of Intent to include subcontractor responsibilities." These comments associated with each version of the document are important. The comments can be leveraged by an author or editor to allow browsing through a historical view of all changes made to the document.

- Auditing—The auditing capability tracks changes to documents as well as changes to metadata (document profiles) associated with the documents. This tracking is done by security account (for example, CPQNA\robertf) to show not only who made the changes, but also what changes were made.

DOCUMENT PROFILES

The *document profile* is a form that is completed when documents are published to the portal site. The form allows the author to specify which information is optional and which is required in order for the document to be published. This metadata embedded within the document profile is used to allow for efficient search results, and to ensure that documents can be easily found and organized within SharePoint Portal Server. Figure 2.2 provides visual representation of a document profile.

Figure 2.2
Sample illustration of a base document profile. This particular example shows four base properties: Title, Author, Keywords, and Description.

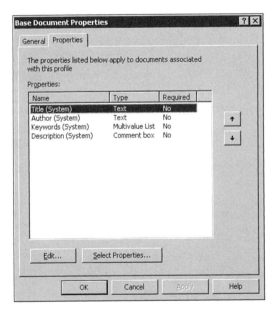

The search services within SharePoint Portal Server allows searching for documents according to content, keywords within the content, the state of a particular attribute, or matching value of a particular attribute. The workspace Coordinator can specify that all authors and editors posting documents to a particular folder complete a document profile form prior to allowing any documents to be checked in. This form will need to be completed no matter if the document is being checked-in from Microsoft Office, Windows Explorer, or from Internet Explorer through the Web. Within the document profile form, the Coordinator can specify document profile attributes as required or optional.

→ For a more in-depth description of the Coordinator role, **see** "Workspace Coordinator role," **p. 49**.

Document Profiles can be accessed by navigating to Document Profiles through the Management Workspace. A Coordinator has the option of using one of the default profiles, or setting up a custom profile. This Document Profile location is where all document profiles are stored. You have the option to select the profile on a per-folder basis. In Figure 2.3, a base document profile is being used. However, the illustration shows how to change the field from Optional to Required. Once a field is specified as Required, the end user cannot check-in the document until the field values are properly populated. In our example, the end user must specify a document title.

Figure 2.3
SharePoint allows you to customize the document profile and specify which properties are specified as "required." In this example, the Title field can be changed from Optional to Required by clicking on the box titled Require users to enter a value for this property.

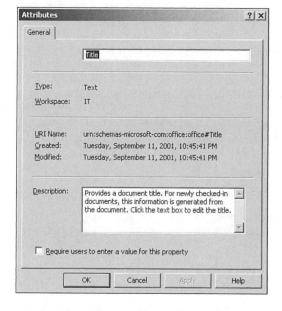

→ To learn more about the document profiles, **see** "Document Profiles," **p. 264**.

The Document Profile allows users to create custom document types to group by document intent. For example, a document type called Field Sales Report could always include a Sales attribute. This is also an example of associating metadata with a document, which can streamline the search for this data type.

In addition to these features, the profile creation process utilizes a wizard-based setup so attributes can be specified, additional vocabularies can be used, the order can be modified, and coordinators can specify attributes as required or optional.

INTEGRATED SECURITY

SharePoint Portal Server relies heavily on the existing native Windows NT Access Control List (ACL) and NT user-IDs. Additional functional administrative control can be used to ease security administration. The security is compatible with Microsoft Windows NT version 4 as well as Windows 2000 file-based security.

> **NOTE**
>
> Even though Windows NT version 4 and Windows 2000 directory security can be leveraged, remember that SharePoint Portal Server can only be installed on a Windows 2000 server.

This security control is essential to ensure that workspace readers can only see and access documents in which they have the appropriate security context. The integrated functionality within SharePoint Portal Server also ensures that Coordinators do not have to administer security utilizing multiple security tools across multiple locations.

SharePoint Portal Server utilizes a concept of security roles based on how authors and editors will work within a workspace. The three security roles that are used are Reader, Author, and Coordinator. Granular access is controlled through assigning users one of these three roles. If users are not assigned one of the three roles, they will not have access to view data within the workspace. Administrators can add NT users and groups to the role to provide the required level of access.

In addition to roles, granular access can be further controlled by specifying security at the workspace level, folder level within the workspace, or on a per-document level within the folder.

To simplify administration, inheritance rules enable workspaces and folders to inherit security access control by default. These changes can be easily modified according to your organization's context-level security business requirements.

→ To learn more about the security within SharePoint, **see** "SharePoint Security Concepts," **p. 280**.

INDEXING ENGINE

Data is easily managed and organized, as SharePoint Portal Server allows content to be indexed from a variety of information sources. Today, information exists in a variety of formats and languages. In addition, information often resides in multiple locations, which introduces challenges with traditional intranet tools as end users have to follow links and jump back and forth from site to site.

The indexing engine shipped with SharePoint Portal Server is an extremely mature technology. This is a technology that evolved from other existing Microsoft products such as MSSQL, Index Server, and Commerce Server, and includes the following benefits:

- Protection against invalid and incorrectly formatted documents
- Protection against network problems and faulty Web servers
- Multi-thread data source access and document crawling

SharePoint Portal Server was designed to withstand crawling documents that are incorrectly formatted or even potentially corrupt. In addition, SharePoint Portal Server will not halt or crash due to interruption while accessing content due to local/wide area network issues or problematic Web servers. Since SharePoint is CPU bound, not I/O bound, the scalability and performance of SharePoint Portal Server allow efficient performance even when network latency is an issue. Furthermore, SharePoint Portal Server allows multiple processors to be added to address CPU utilization. Lastly, when you consider how SharePoint optimizes crawling throughput by indexing many documents at once, the latency is further reduced.

→ To learn more about the crawling process, **see** "The Crawling Process," **p. 455**.

STANDARD CRAWLING TECHNOLOGY

SharePoint Portal Server keeps indexes up to date by using existing industry standard crawling technology. This technology crawls and updates, indexing in the background so that users do not have the real-time latency involved with refreshing an index. SharePoint Portal Server updates and indexes as documents match search criteria, which ensures optimal search performance. SharePoint Portal Server includes the required tools to manage indexes for a variety of information sources and data repositories.

The crawling options allow for the following index updates:

- Scheduled or on-demand—The crawling options, managed by the Windows Task Scheduler, can be configured to be on a scheduled basis or initiated on-demand.
- Incremental—Incremental updates involve data sources being interrogated by SharePoint Portal Server to compare the delta of change since the last crawl activity. This capability allows the rapid incremental index update process.
- Notification-based— Servers can be configured to launch a crawl process when a crawling event exists. Windows 2000, Exchange 2000 Public Folder servers, and other SharePoint Portal Servers are all examples of data sources that can be specified to notify a specific SharePoint Portal Server to execute a crawl event. As a result of the notification and crawl event, the index is then updated for optimized use for your end users.
- Adaptive—Similar to the incremental index update, adaptive crawling only allows crawling of content changed since the last update. The difference between incremental and adaptive is that adaptive uses complex historical analysis for documents that are likely to have changed.

INDEXED FILE TYPES

SharePoint Portal Server allows the inclusion of a variety of file types within an index. In addition, an *IFilter* can be used to include other file types. An IFilter is a component exposed by the Platform SDK (SDK) and is used by the Index Server.

→ For information on IFilters, **see** "Configuring IFilters," **p. 213**.

SharePoint Portal Server includes indexing the following file types out of the box:

- Office 95, Office 97, and Office 2000
- HTML files
- Text files
- TIFF files
- Adobe Acrobat files
- Corel documents
- Other custom formats

The index includes multi-file HTML-format documents as well as document discussions for Office 2000–specific documents. For HTML files, the index includes the files and meta tags. Text files can be indexed. For TIFF files, SharePoint Portal Server includes an optical character recognition (OCR) package that incorporates document images within an index based on the words the images contain.

NOTE

> For Adobe Acrobat files and Corel documents, it is required that an IFilter be installed. Both of these filters need to be obtained from their respective companies. You can access the manufacturer's Web site, such as http://www.adobe.com, and search for "ifilter".

→ For information on how to register TIFF files, **see** "Advanced Topics," **p. 212**.

Additional custom file formats are supported through the Windows 2000 IFilter interface. Third parties and customers will continue to develop and publicly share custom IFilters.

CONTENT SOURCE TYPES

We know that data resides in multiple locations and across multiple types of data sources. This section provides details on the types of data sources that can be accessed with SharePoint Portal Server. When we use the term *content source*, we refer to a location where data resides within or outside your environment. Figure 2.4 displays the content source types. The benefit of using SharePoint Portal Server is that administrators can leave information in its current location, while creating a robust search capability to provide a single search portal to search multiple data repositories. SharePoint Portal Server allows access to the following content sources:

- Microsoft Windows NT 4.x/Windows 2000
- Microsoft Exchange 5.x/2000 Public Folders
- Lotus Notes databases
- Intranet/Internet sites

Figure 2.4
Graphic showing available content sources within SharePoint Portal Server.

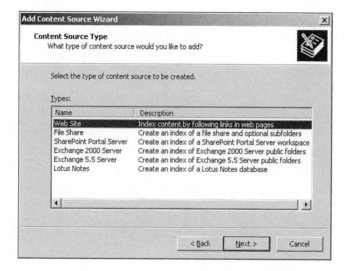

Indexing maintains existing security, so if an end user does not have the appropriate access through the Windows file system or Exchange public folder, they will not have the access from within the workspace. In other words, depending on the end user's rights, a series of documents may be returned in their search, but they may not be able to access the documents.

It is important to note that the index includes attributes, attachments, and embedded documents, and SharePoint Portal Server allows both intranet and Internet servers to be accessed and indexed. When Lotus Notes databases are indexed, Notes database security is also maintained.

ADJUSTING WEIGHT

Within a document, certain properties contain the most relevant information. Examples of these types of properties are Title, Subject, and so on. With SharePoint Portal Server, Coordinators can adjust the weight of certain properties so that when searches are made according to a criteria set, a relevance match ensures that documents are returned during a search.

PRESERVING EXISTING SECURITY

Even though several documents may be returned within a given search, SharePoint Portal Server ensures that only documents which an individual user has rights to open can be opened. This is a key security feature of SharePoint as it leverages the existing NT file system security model.

INTEGRATING THIRD-PARTY CONTENT

SharePoint Portal Server search engine can be integrated with third-party content, performed as follows:

- IFilter—Using an IFilter allows end users and third-party providers to integrate with custom document formats.
- Protocol Handler—Using the protocol handler allows end users and third-party solution providers to develop custom protocol handlers to integrate additional content sources with the existing search engine. An example of an integrated third-party solution is Lotus Notes.
- SQL-based query language—Custom search and dashboard site applications are easier to develop due to SharePoint Portal Server being based on extensions to industry-standard SQL. This also minimizes your required investment and training.

DASHBOARD SITE SCALABILITY

Dashboards can be developed in a variety of sizes. SharePoint Portal Server will scale from small workgroup-based solutions to medium-sized solutions, from a business unit up to enterprise dashboard solutions for an entire corporation.

→ For more information on Dashboard Sites, **see** "Dashboards and Web Parts," **p. 344**.

CATEGORY INTEGRATION

Content within SharePoint Portal Server utilizes the concept of categories to enable users to navigate through a classification system to find desired information. The categories used are completely up to the Coordinator, and organizational taxonomies can be planned and integrated according to the business requirements. This classification system is closely coupled with the SharePoint Portal Server document management system to allow an efficient management process. Within the dashboard, end users can navigate through and search for categories.

When categories are established, it is a good idea to have a description, an owner, a picture, a set of best bets, and the associated documents. Managed through the Windows Explorer, categories are presented through the dashboard site.

NOTE

It is important to note the importance of getting the design of category taxonomy correct, as moving subscriptions around is currently not an easy and efficient process.

→ For information on categories, **see** "Categories—A Different View on Information," **p. 108**.

SUBSCRIPTIONS

With SharePoint Portal Server, users can now utilize a key feature called *subscriptions* to subscribe to search criteria, and can request to be notified when changes occur or when specific information becomes available. This feature within SharePoint Portal Server expands on the current Office 2000 Server Extensions subscription feature, and the following additional subscription types are enabled:

- Search-Based Subscriptions—From the dashboard site, users can subscribe to interest-based searches. For example, a user can search for all documents of type "Services" authored by "Robert Ferguson". If the search does not return the desired results, the end user can then set up a subscription to be notified if these criteria become available in the future. See Figures 2.5 and 2.6.

Figure 2.5
In this example, we searched for "Services", and only for documents created by the author "Robert Ferguson".

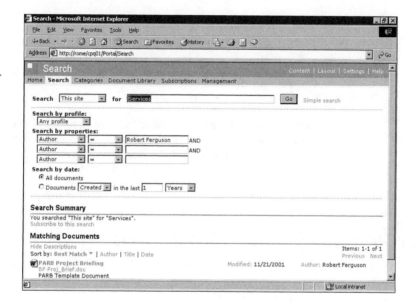

- Documents and Directory-Based Subscriptions —SharePoint Portal Server allows users to subscribe to changes that may occur for documents and folders. Notifications can be provided through a personalized Web Part or via Simple Mail Transport Protocol (SMTP) email. Furthermore, end users can choose from notification intervals such as when a change occurs, daily, or weekly.

- Category-Based Subscriptions —The last subscription option allows users to subscribe to changes for document management categories. For example, a reader could navigate through a list of categories from the Categories menu option within the workspace. The user could then click on Subscribe to this category.

Figure 2.6
An end user could potentially click on the search summary to set up a subscription to the search, and request intervals for how often they want to be notified when new information is posted related to their search.

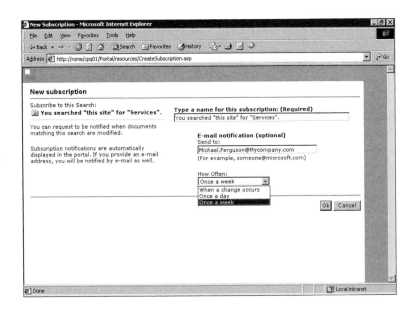

NOTE

Once the subscription is enabled, the end user will be notified when content is added to the category. The notification will occur through email or personalized dashboard site, according to the notification route and interval that was specified during the subscription.

A default Web Part provides a counter for the pending notifications.

DASHBOARD SITE AND WEB PARTS

SharePoint Portal Server provides robust dashboard functionality out of the box. In addition, the SharePoint Portal Server dashboard site can be customized to include a variety of existing or custom Web Parts.

For example, Outlook can be integrated with the SharePoint Portal Server dashboard to provided integrated email functionality according to the way your end users need to work. Additional Web Parts such as stock tickers, traffic maps, custom reporting, and query results can be integrated into the dashboard to provide value to the end user. These custom Web Parts can be added and linked together without having to purchase or maintain a full custom Web site application.

SharePoint Portal Server allows further customization to allow Web Parts such as document folder views, news details, subscription notifications, and even the search box to be registered with several digital dashboard sites, and many of the capabilities within SharePoint Portal Server are scriptable using Microsoft Active Data Objects (ADO) and OLE DB, SQL full-text search queries, or Collaborative Data Objects (CDO) extensions. An example of this type of customization may be a personal dashboard that includes a custom Web Part for an Internet search engine such as Alta Vista, integrated with CNN news.

AN INTEGRATED SOLUTION

The real value of SharePoint Portal Server is realized when several of the key features—like the search engine and document management—are closely integrated with your organization's categorization taxonomy and other custom Web Parts to provide a solution-based business application. The following section provides a couple sample solution scenarios that further describe the potential of SharePoint Portal Server.

CLIENT EXTENSIONS

From an end user perspective, the SharePoint Portal Server features are enabled through extended client capabilities. Once installed, Microsoft Office, Windows Explorer, and Internet Explorer allow specific SharePoint Portal Server features to be exposed through these familiar tools.

WINDOWS EXPLORER EXTENSIONS

Within Windows Explorer, extended SharePoint Portal Server capabilities expose document libraries as a Web folder. The interface (see Figure 2.7) provides a traditional view to document folders and an enhanced context level view to metadata (profile) details. All SharePoint Portal Server documents have extended property pages that includes metadata, security settings, version history, and so on. Additional right-click functionality allows documents to be easily checked in and checked out. Logical category-based views allow Coordinators to organize in a nontraditional logical manner.

Figure 2.7
SharePoint Portal Server extends the familiar Windows Explorer interface to include key metadata associated with documents. Clicking on the document from within Windows Explorer exposes all metadata associated with the document.

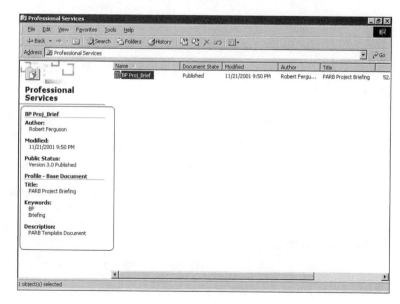

OFFICE 2000 EXTENSIONS

With SharePoint Portal Server, COM (Component Object Model) add-ins are utilized to allow enhanced menu extensions from within Office 2000 to enable the document management process. This allows documents to be checked in, checked out, and submitted for publication without having to leave the Microsoft Office application. (See Figure 2.8.) End users can navigate and save directly to the core document management library from traditional Open/Save dialog boxes. Additional collaboration within the Office 2000 toolbar exists that enables integrated document level collaboration.

NOTE

> Office 2000 client extensions are enabled by installing a separate client extensions installation script. The client extensions are natively present in Office XP.

Figure 2.8
SharePoint Portal Server document management features such as check-in, check-out, and publish are tightly integrated into the Microsoft Office menu once the office extensions are installed.

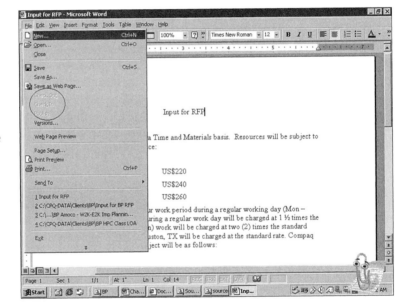

REQUIREMENTS AND LIMITATIONS

The following sections provide a high-level overview of requirements for the client, the server, and the network. In addition, limitations are discussed.

SYSTEM REQUIREMENTS FOR SERVER

Each server running SharePoint Portal Server requires the following:

- Processor—Intel Pentium III–compatible.
- RAM—256 megabytes (MB).

- Disk space—550MB, formatted on a drive with NTFS file system.

- Operating system—Microsoft Windows 2000 Server or Windows 2000 Advanced Server with Windows 2000 Service Pack 1 (SP1) or later.

- Additional Services—Internet Information Services (IIS) 5.0 and the Simple Mail Transfer Protocol (SMTP) service.

NETWORK REQUIREMENTS

- Directory Services—It is possible to install SharePoint Portal Server in a Windows NT 4.0 or Windows 2000 environment.

- Network Protocol—Requires Transmission Control Protocol/Internet Protocol (TCP/IP).

- Proxy Changes—A proxy server enhances performance as it caches Web pages and protects against unauthorized individuals from the Internet. SharePoint Portal Server uses the Hypertext Transfer Protocol (HTTP) verbs, the Distributed Authoring and Versioning (DAV) set of HTTP extensions, and a custom SharePoint Portal Server verb called INVOKE. You will need to make the appropriate changes to your proxy server to pass the required verbs. By default, SharePoint Portal Server uses the proxy server settings of the default content access account, taken from the current proxy server settings in Internet Explorer. Changes to the proxy settings for the SharePoint Portal Server computer do not affect other applications on the server. For example, you can configure the SharePoint Portal Server computer to use a specific proxy server without affecting Internet Explorer. HTTP is used by clients in an effort to communicate with the SharePoint Portal Server dashboard site. Improper configuration of proxy settings for Internet Explorer at the client may impact a user's ability to interact with the SharePoint Portal Server dashboard site.

- Firewall Requirements—If your organization uses firewalls, plan where the firewalls and SharePoint Portal Server will be located. Since index propagation uses the standard Windows file sharing protocol, if you desire to take advantage of index propagation, ensure that you do not have a firewall between the server dedicated to indexing and the search server. If a firewall does exist between the index server and search server, you will need to make sure that Windows file share capabilities are allowed.

SYSTEM REQUIREMENTS FOR CLIENTS

The system requirements for running the SharePoint Portal Server client components are described below:

- Processor—Intel Pentium-compatible 200 megahertz (MHz) or higher processor.
- RAM—64 megabytes (MB).
- Disk space—30MB on Windows 2000 systems; 50MB on all other systems.

- Operating system—Microsoft Windows 98; Microsoft Windows Millennium Edition; Microsoft Windows NT version 4.0 with SP6A; or Windows 2000 Professional, Server, or Advanced Server.

NOTE

To utilize the SharePoint Portal Server Coordinator security functions, you must have Windows 2000 Professional, Server, or Advanced Server installed.

- Messaging client—Microsoft Outlook Express 5.01 or later.
- Office extensions—SharePoint Portal Server Office extensions require Microsoft Office 2000 or later.
- Web browser—Microsoft Internet Explorer 5 or later with Visual Basic Scripting support.

TIP

SharePoint Portal Server Office extensions are installed by default when you install Microsoft Office 2000. If you are using previous versions of Microsoft Office, you will need to manually install the Office extensions to get the SharePoint Portal Server functionality through Windows.

DASHBOARD SITE REQUIREMENTS

End users do not have to install the client components to access the SharePoint Portal Server dashboard site. The site can be accessed using one of the following Web browsers:

- Microsoft Internet Explorer 4.01 or later.
- Netscape Navigator 4.51 or later (for Italian and Spanish versions of SharePoint Portal Server).
- Netscape Navigator 4.75 or later (for English, French, German, and Japanese versions of SharePoint Portal Server).

NOTE

The Macintosh and Solaris operating systems are not supported. You will also need to enable Microsoft JScript or Netscape JavaScript support within your browser for proper dashboard site functionality.

SHAREPOINT PORTAL SERVER LIMITATIONS

SharePoint Portal Server does not coexist with the following software:

- Microsoft Office Server Extensions
- Microsoft Exchange Server version 5.5 and earlier
- Exchange 2000 Server
- Microsoft Site Server (all versions)

- Microsoft Windows 2000 cluster service
- Microsoft SharePoint Team Services

Summary

In this chapter, we discussed the three main features of SharePoint Portal Server, which are rich enterprise search, integrated document management, and the robust portal capabilities that can be accomplished using the digital dashboard technology. We expanded on the core capabilities at a high level, in an effort to prepare you for the in-depth discussions on how these features are utilized and referenced throughout the book. In addition to the core capabilities, we also discussed client and server requirements and limitations. The next three chapters will explore these three main features in more detail. Our goal is to provide an increasingly more in-depth understanding of these features and capabilities, and put it all together with the real world scenarios and troubleshooting chapters toward the end of the book.

2

CHAPTER **3**

OVERVIEW OF THE WORKSPACE AND DASHBOARD

In this chapter

DASHBOARD OVERVIEW

SharePoint Portal Server automatically creates a workspace and corresponding dashboard site during the initial installation. In this chapter, we will discuss both the workspace and dashboard, including how they are accessed, configured, and used.

The workspace may be described as a Web folder or a Network Place. As such, it may be thought of as an organized compilation of data, distributed and managed by Document, Management, Category, and Portal Content folders, including a Web page with links to Help files and configuration wizards. The workspace simply affords access to data—views, content, and shortcuts to content—and includes organized data categories as well.

The dashboard site, on the other hand, is a Web-based view of the workspace. Using a Web browser, the dashboard site becomes a Web-based portal for users with appropriate security to be able to search for and manage documents, as well as access other key information both internally and externally.

3

NOTE

Using the Web browser for access to the dashboard site has certain end user requirements. If you are using a Windows operating system, you can use Internet Explorer version 4.0, Internet Explorer version 5.0, or Netscape Navigator version 4.75. Lastly, for the dashboard site to function properly, you must enable Microsoft JScript or Netscape JavaScript.

At the dashboard, users can search for information, browse through information by categories, check in and check out documents, subscribe to new documents and changes to existing documents, review a document version history, approve documents ready to be published, and publish documents.

UNDERSTANDING THE DIGITAL DASHBOARD

The dashboard site uses Microsoft Digital Dashboard (MDD) technology to organize and display information. A digital dashboard consists of reusable, customizable Web Parts such as Search, Categories, News, and Announcements. You can easily add or remove Web Parts to customize the dashboard site for your organization. SharePoint Portal Server includes quite a few default Web Parts, which are covered briefly later in this chapter, and in more detail in Chapter 9. Microsoft Digital Dashboard technology also supports roles, creating custom Web Parts, and more. MDD is all about flexibility. The dashboard site leverages default and custom Web Parts to ultimately create a more useful and efficient portal site. Custom Web Parts, for example, can be used to represent or organize specific content within a portion of the dashboard. For additional information on MDD, check out the Digital Dashboard Resource Kit (DDRK) .

Figure 3.1
This is a basic dashboard site with a few basic categories.

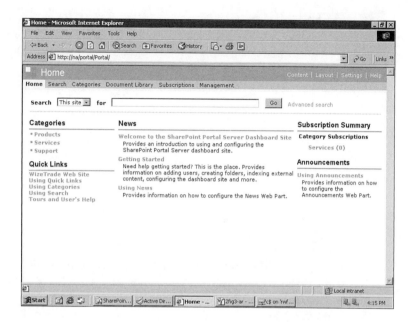

The dashboard consists of upper and lower sections. The top section contains the following components:

- Title bar that can be customized.
- Search bar with a drop-down menu that allows users to specify the scope of the search. In addition, a text box allows entry for the specific search criteria.

The lower section contains the following components:

- Logo that can be customized
- Site navigation buttons as follows:
  - Home
  - Search
  - Categories
  - Document Library
  - Subscriptions
  - Management

ADDING DEFAULT WEB PARTS

The default SharePoint Portal Server installation includes four default Web Parts that can be used to quickly add value to an out-of-the-box installation scenario. These four default Web Parts are

- News—A News Web Part can provide details that may be of particular interest to your end users. Examples of the data that can be displayed through this News Web Part include company news, departmental or business unit news, competitors' news or press releases, and so on.

- Announcements —An Announcements Web Part can provide details about company related announcements, departmental activities or events, and so forth. For example, the Announcements Web Part for a human resources site may contain specific details related to updates for an upcoming annual employee benefits enrollment process.

- Quick Links —A Quick Links Web Part provides links to other important key content within the environment. For example, a human resources dashboard site could use Quick Links to important employee information and benefit details. Quick Links may also point to HTTP content outside of the portal, assuming that Internet access is available from the SPS server.

- Subscription Summary —A summary of the current user's subscription notifications can be viewed through the default Subscriptions Summary Web Part. This Web Part provides details about the two most current subscription notifications and links to the actual documents that can be viewed. The user leverages this subscription page to terminate a subscription, too. For example, a user on a special project might subscribe to the results of a particular query, and once the project has ended, would then terminate his subscription to this subscription by again leveraging this Web Part.

Within the actual workspace, a Portal Content folder exists that includes subfolders for the default Web Parts above. The subfolders are the physical location for content of the actual Web Part. If the individual viewing the dashboard site has active subscriptions, the Subscription Summary Web part would display the status of these notifications.

The Coordinator at the workspace level is the individual who is allowed to add information to the News, Announcements, and Quick Links Web Parts. This Coordinator has little control over the Subscriptions Web Part, though, since this is tied to subscriptions for each individual user. However, an administrator feature from the dashboard allows the Coordinator to delete subscriptions for specific users. In the Manage Subscriptions section (see Figure 3.2), type in the name of the user for the subscription you want to manage, and then click Go.

Once you click Go, SharePoint Portal Server will return a list of all subscriptions (see Figure 3.3) and pending notifications for the user as requested.

Other Web Parts may be built, customized, and included in the workspace as well. Some of the more commonly created Web Parts involve those that display business information such as news headlines and stock tickers, or facilitate collaboration using tools like Microsoft NetMeeting. Other Web Parts might be configured to display information specific to a certain subset of users, for example a special "Search" Web Part for the site.

Figure 3.2
As Workspace Coordinator, click on Management from he main menu, noting the self-documenting straightforward approach that Micro-soft has taken in regard to these every-day management tasks.

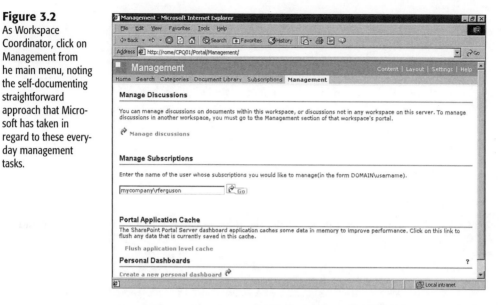

Figure 3.3
Here, all current sub-scriptions may be noted. It's a good idea to occasionally review these, and unsubscribe as appropriate. Too much information is only too much of a good thing.

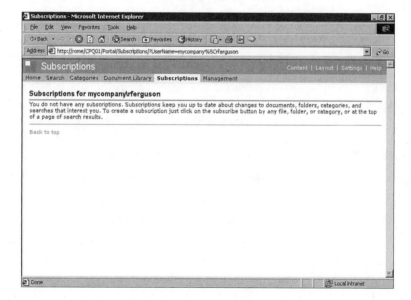

→ For additional detail on adding and managing Web Parts, **see** "Managing the Subscription and Other Web Parts," **p. 225** in Chapter 9.

ADDING CONTENT TO THE NEWS WEB PART

To modify or add data to the default News Web Part, do the following:

1. Using Explorer, navigate to the document or object that you would like to ultimately add to your News Web Part, right-click it, and select the option to Copy.

2. Next, open the Portal Content folder from within the workspace.

3. Open the News folder by double-clicking it.

4. Finally, paste the document that you want to appear in the News Web Part into the News folder. As is obvious by now, this whole process is easily accomplished by using normal cut-and-paste functionality found in Microsoft's products.

5. Once you have placed the document in the News folder, right-click the document, and click Edit Profile, noting that the document profile appears.

6. Within the Title field, type the title you want to show up for the news item. This title text will appear on the News Web Part as a link within your dashboard.

7. Within the Description field, enter a brief description about the news item. This will be displayed directly below the title, which serves as the link.

8. After you enter the description, click OK. Refresh your dashboard to view the updated News Web Part.

TIP

> Deleting a news document is even simpler than adding one—within the News folder, highlight the document to be deleted, right-click it, and select the Delete option. The News item has now been removed from the News Web Part.

Analogous to the News Web Part, which typically features announcements or events of an "external-to-the-company" nature, is the Announcements Web Part. Information and features found within this Web Part tend to highlight areas of "internal" interest, therefore representing the internal functional equivalent of what is provided by the News Web Part. They are equally simple to manage and make the most of.

ADDING CONTENT TO THE ANNOUNCEMENT WEB PART

To modify or add data to the default Announcement Web Part, do the following:

1. Open the Portal Content folder from within the workspace.

2. Open the Announcements folder.

3. Place the document that you want to appear in the Announcement Web Part in the Announcements folder—leverage the same approach as detailed previously for the News Web Part.

4. Once you have placed the document in the Announcements folder, right-click the document, click Edit Profile, and the document profile appears.

5. Within the Title field, type the title you want to show up for the Announcements item. This title text will appear on the Announcements Web Part as a link within your dashboard.

6. Within the Description field, type a brief description about the news item. This will be displayed directly below the title, which serves as the link.

7. After you enter a description, click OK. Refresh your dashboard to view the updated Announcement Web Part.

3

TIP

> Deleting the Announcements document within the Announcement folder removes the Announcements item from the Announcement Web Part.

To clarify a bit more on the differences between the News and Announcement Web Parts, consider the following. The Announcements Web Part, seeking to share data of a "company- or department-internal" nature, might announce the promotion of a new employee, or describe an upcoming department-wide team-building exercise. The News Web Part, on the other hand, might feature company-wide press releases, or point to external news services like the Associated Press.

ADDING CONTENT TO THE QUICK LINK WEB PART

To modify or add data to the default Quick Link Web Part, do the following:

1. Open the Portal Content folder from within the workspace.
2. Open the Quick Links folder.
3. Create your document and save this document to the Quick Links folder with the name that describes the link you are adding. It is not necessary to add text to the document yet.
4. Once you have placed the document in the Quick Links folder, right-click the document, click Edit Profile, and the document profile appears.
5. Enter the address in the Link field for the desired link you are trying to add in Uniform Resource Locator (URL) format (for example, http://www.compaq.com).
6. Within the Title field, type the title you want to show up for the Quick Link item. This title text will appear on the Quick Links Web Part as a link within your dashboard.
7. Click OK.

TIP

> Deleting the Quick Links document within the Quick Links folder removes the item from the Quick Links Web Part.

It is clear that the Quick Links Web Part contains handy links to other content of interest to the organization. For example, the Quick Links Web Part in the dashboard site of a product support organization might contain links to engineering diagrams, most-frequently-asked-questions, contact data for technical resources, and so on. If a document or resource is commonly used by an organization, consider adding a quick link to it.

ADDING CONTENT TO THE SUBSCRIPTIONS WEB PART

The last default Web Part used in an SPS implementation is the Subscriptions Summary Web Part, which provides a summary of the current user's subscription notifications. A user can quickly view his two most current subscription notifications in this manner, along with links to any relevant documents. If the user has no active subscriptions, the associated folder is empty. What a shame! Many SharePoint Portal Server users obtain great value from subscribing to highly job-relevant content like specific documents, folders, categories, or a set of search results. Subscriptions are simple to set up, and SharePoint Portal Server automatically notifies you of changes to the areas for which you have subscribed. Use this Web Part, and it will quickly become apparent how valuable such a service can become. Caution, though—as we said before, subscribing to too much information will only hamper your productivity.

WORKSPACE OVERVIEW

A workspace is a Web folder or a Network Place created by an administrator in your group. The workspace contains the *document library*, where documents are stored on the server, along with management tools, the category structure, dashboard site content, and a searchable index of information. A workspace can store any type of file, including spreadsheets, faxes, graphics, audio files, Web pages, presentations, and scripts. A workspace can also contain links to content stored on network file servers, Web sites, Microsoft Exchange servers, Lotus Notes databases, and other SharePoint Portal Server workspaces. An organization can have a single workspace or multiple workspaces, depending on its needs. A single server can host up to 15 workspaces.

ACCESSING THE WORKSPACE

Web folders and My Network Places are utilized by end users for accessing the workspace. In addition, users can utilize a Web browser for access to the workspace through the dashboard site. As mentioned earlier, SharePoint Portal Server automatically creates a dashboard site and an associated workspace during the initial installation. Web folders are covered in greater detail later in this chapter.

Assuming end users have the appropriate rights, the initial site provides a Web view of the workspace and enables users to view, manage, and search for desired documents in the workspace as well as from other content sources. Using Microsoft Word with Office extensions enabled, for example, provides an additional access method for certain document management features.

The SharePoint Portal Server workspace is capable of storing documents of all types. Assuming the appropriate roles are enabled, Readers, Authors, and Coordinators can access and manage these documents from within the workspace. SharePoint Portal Server was designed to allow Microsoft Office 2000 and Office XP applications such as Word, Excel, and PowerPoint native integration with SPS through drop-down menus.

Depending on the features enabled by the workspace or folder Coordinator, certain document management features are available from the workspace, the dashboard site, and within integrated menus from Microsoft Office applications.

Examples of this access include the ability to check in, check out, and publish documents; view document version history; review and approve documents; view document profiles; categorize documents; and participate in Web discussions. SharePoint Portal Server users should become at least familiar with the features and capabilities of the workspace and dashboard site in order to take full advantage of the product in their day-to-day work life.

The way you will use the workspace depends on your role within SharePoint Portal Server. As alluded to previously, the three roles are Coordinator, Author, and Reader. Note that these roles are actually predefined SPS Groups that are populated by NT User objects— that is, groups and users. No other roles exist or may be added.

WORKSPACE COORDINATOR ROLE

If you are assigned Coordinator privileges at the workspace level, you have the ability to configure and manage workspace settings, document profiles, categories, and index options. This is the SPS equivalent of "Administrator-level" access found in Microsoft's OS products.

If you are assigned Coordinator privileges at the folder level, the workspace can be used to specify settings for the specific folder. A few examples of the tasks that can be performed at the folder level include configuring access by enabling the appropriate security roles, and setting up publishing and approval processes.

Specific folders and subfolders are configured and managed by the Coordinator at the folder level. When subfolders are created, the Coordinator must choose between specifying the folder type as Standard or Enhanced. The difference between these two folders will be discussed later in this chapter. However, some examples of the tasks that can be performed on standard versus enhanced folders include

STANDARD FOLDERS

- creating folders and subfolders
- applying document profiles to folders
- editing and deleting documents
- assigning roles
- managing multipart documents (such as an Excel document linking to another document)

ENHANCED FOLDERS

- creating folders and subfolders
- applying document profiles to folders
- editing and deleting documents
- assigning roles
- applying approval processes to allow document publishing (approval routing)
- maintaining a private "draft" version of a document
- document management features, like check-in, check-out, and versioning of documents residing in the folder

NOTE

> The Coordinator role has the ability to deny access at a very granular level. For example, a specific user may be denied access to a particular folder, or even a specific document within the folder.

Within a folder, documents cannot be accessed by Authors and Readers, which have the Deny Access setting enabled. You can modify workspace settings only if you are an administrator or assigned to the Coordinator role.

WORKSPACE AUTHOR ROLE

The Author security role can use the workspace to save, manage, and search for documents and indexed content associated with content sources. The goal of the Author role is to enable and facilitate collaboration and co-authoring with other users assigned the Author role. Authors have the ability to add, edit, delete, or read documents within a folder. Authors also have the ability to create, delete, and rename their own folders. When new folders are created, the security roles and approval policies are inherited from the parent folder. If these inherited policies are not sufficient, the Coordinator will need to make manual adjustments according to the folder level security requirements.

WORKSPACE READER ROLE

If you are a Reader within SharePoint Portal Server, you can use the workspace and dashboard site to browse and search for published documents and indexed content associated with content sources. By default, all folder users have reader permissions. A reader can search for and read documents but cannot add them to the workspace. They are also unable to check out, edit, or delete documents.

NOTE

> Readers do not have the ability to view documents that are in the approval process. That is, a Reader cannot "see" a document until it is published (in other words, officially posted to the portal after being checked in for the last time by its author or the final Approver) .

→ To learn more about publishing, **see** "Managing Documents Within the Workspace," **p. 263** in Ch 10.

THE WORKSPACE APPROVER ROLE

When an Author publishes a document, if you are specified as an Approver of that document, you will be sent an email notification with a link to the document. Your role is to view the document and approve or reject it depending on approve or rejection criteria.

NOTE

The Approver role is a special role only associated with specific tasks on a per-folder basis for enhanced folders. It is important to note that this role is not a formal role similar to the three main security roles (Coordinator, Author, or Reader). This role is only associated with enhanced folders, obviously, since the SharePoint Portal Server approval process is not supported on standard folders.

During the approval process, documents cannot be checked out or edited. Authors can collaborate on documents during the approval process by using the Web discussion feature or simply sending emails back and forth. All Web discussions are retained until removed by a Coordinator.

CAUTION

Web discussions are viewable and searchable by everyone—this may be an issue for documents named "staff reduction plan.doc" or similar such disquieting documents or titles of a sensitive nature.

Upon approval of a given document, the document is published to the workspace or dashboard. It is then available to be accessed or searched upon by readers with access to this document.

APPROVAL PROCESS TYPES

Two different approval processes are possible within SharePoint Portal Server: serial and parallel. The *serial process* requires Approvers to approve documents one after another. The *parallel process* sends notifications of a required approval to all Approvers at the same time. If you are specified as an Approver, you will participate in the approval process and will receive an email notification (see Figure 3.4) with details of the particular approval process.

Figure 3.4
Visual representation of a pending document approval request.

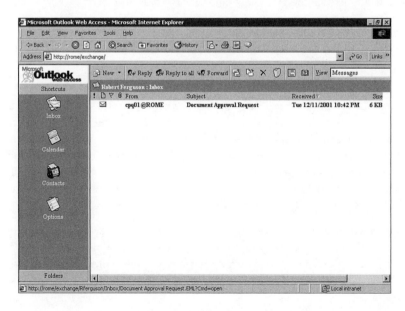

The notification provides basic information about the document requiring approval and asks for you to click to approve or reject this document. Once you click on the link (shown in Figure 3.5), a Document Inspection page pops up to provide more details about the document.

Figure 3.5
Here, the link that must be clicked to approve or reject a document is illustrated.

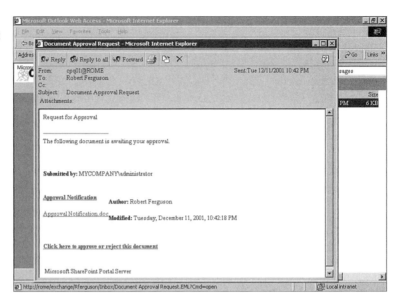

Regardless of the method used to approve a document for publishing, the process is similar:

1. Via Windows Explorer, open the enhanced folder containing the documents to be published. For our example, we will be working with the HR folder.
2. Right-click the HR folder, and select Properties.
3. The HR Properties dialog box is displayed. At this point, note the two approval process types available under the Route to Approvers section. This is also displayed in Figure 3.6.

In the first of the approval process types, the "one after another" or "serial" process, when a document is sent to be published, then the approval process is initiated. The first Approver specified in the approval list is sent a Document Approval Request notification by SharePoint Portal Server. Upon approving the document, the SharePoint Portal Server automatically sends a Document Approval Request to the second person specified in the approval list. The process will continue for all Approvers specified on your approval list. If all Approvers within your list approve the document, the document will be published to the specified destination. If any one of the Approvers rejects the document, a rejection notice is sent and the document returns to the previous checked-in status.

The second approval process is called *All At Once*, which sends approval request notifications to all Approvers at the same time. For an example of what this selection might entail, see Figure 3.7, noting that the steps illustrated previously to get to the HR properties screen still apply. This process is very similar to voting, which allows folder Coordinators to specify whether a single Approver or all Approvers must have consensus before the document can be published. The document profile form allows Coordinators and Authors to specify whether you want to allow SharePoint Portal Server to continue the process and actually publish the document once approved. Otherwise, a Coordinator must manually publish the document.

Figure 3.6
Viewing the properties of the HR folder yields the following display, where the selection of the approval routing type is clearly shown. Note that the One After Another (serial) approval process has been selected in this case.

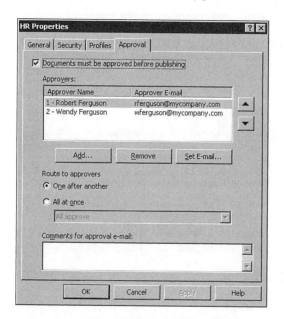

Figure 3.7
You can also specify whether all Approvers must approve this document, or if the document can be published with just one approval.

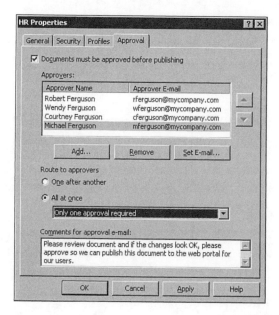

NOTE

> Think carefully about the serial versus parallel choice, depending on how soon you want your Approvers to be notified about a required approval. If you need quick approval, parallel is probably the best choice, as Approvers send an approval notification request to all users at the same time. You can then manage the Approvers to ensure a rapid approval process.

During the approval process, Approvers have two options: Approve and Reject. The options are available from within the approval request notification email, the workspace, or the dashboard site. These are discussed in detail next.

APPROVING AND REJECTING DOCUMENTS

Documents can be approved or rejected in a variety of ways. Once an approval process is in progress, the Coordinator role can also bypass or cancel the entire document publishing process, thereby ending the approval routine. Bypassing or canceling the publishing process might be valuable in cases where circumstances or timelines dictate rapidly disseminating information (even at the risk of publishing imperfect data). It might also prove useful in cases where an Approver is simply no longer available, for example if they're sick, placed on another assignment, or let go from the company altogether. In any case, these approval and rejection/canceling processes are defined in more detail in the following sections.

APPROVING WITHIN AN EMAIL REQUEST

To approve or reject a document from within an email approval notification request, do the following:

1. Click on Click here to approve or reject this document.
2. A Document Inspection page is opened by the dashboard site.
3. Select the correct document and click on Approve or Reject.
4. Click OK.

APPROVING DOCUMENTS FROM WITHIN THE WORKSPACE

To approve or reject a document from within the workspace, do the following:

1. From within the workspace, locate the document you are trying to approve or reject.
2. Right-click the document, and then click Approve or Reject.

APPROVING DOCUMENTS FROM THE DASHBOARD

To approve or reject a document from within the dashboard site, do the following:

1. Click Document Library from the navigation bar within the dashboard site.
2. Once the Document Library page appears, browse through the subfolders to locate the document that requires approval.

3. Once you locate the document, click the Show Actions link, and the dashboard will open the Document Inspection page (see Figure 3.9).

4. Validate that the correct document is selected, and then click Approve or Reject.

5. Click OK.

Figure 3.8
The request provides all the details about the document, including the list of Approvers. In the left pane of the dialog box, you are given options to approve or reject the document.

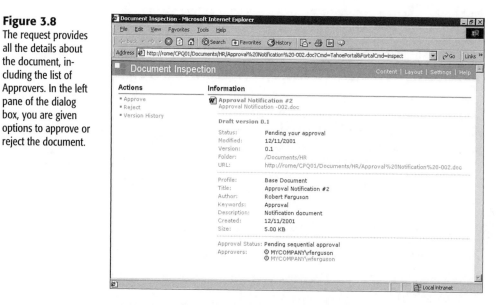

Figure 3.9
Note the options for document approval and rejection from the dashboard site, including the additional metadata available as well.

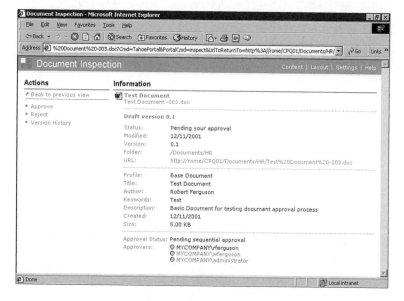

Using the dashboard site may be the best way to go, in that multiple methods are available. While the previous process works quite well, it is interesting to note that a Web Part available via Microsoft's Web Part Gallery may be leveraged in this case, too. Called the Document Status Web Part, this represents an easy way for authors and Approvers to manage the status of documents for which they are responsible in one form or another. For example, this Web Part displays status information like "Documents awaiting my approval," "Documents checked out by me," and more.

BYPASSING AND CANCELING THE APPROVAL PROCESS

If you are specified as the Coordinator for a folder, you have the ability to bypass or cancel the approval process. Selecting Bypass or Cancel has different implications, but either option ends the approval process. Bypass will automatically skip all remaining Approvers within the Approvers list and immediately approve the document for publishing. This feature can be used as an override when your Approvers are not being as responsive as your business requires. The Cancel process, on the other hand, immediately ends the approval process and returns the document back to checked-in status.

BYPASSING APPROVAL FROM THE WORKSPACE

To bypass the approval process, perform the following:

1. From within the workspace, locate the desired document for which the approval process will be bypassed.
2. Right-click the document, and then click Bypass Approval.

NOTE

> You must have workspace Coordinator role privileges to bypass the approval process.

BYPASSING APPROVAL WITHIN AN EMAIL APPROVAL REQUEST

If you are a Coordinator for a folder, the email-based approval request will also include the Bypass Approval and Cancel Publishing commands in addition to the standard options for Approve and Reject.

1. From within the email notification request, click Bypass Approval.
2. Click OK to bypass approval and complete the approval process.

If you are a Coordinator for a folder, the email document approval request will also include the Bypass Approval and Cancel Publishing commands in addition to the standard options for Approve and Reject.

CANCELING THE APPROVAL PROCESS FROM THE WORKSPACE OR DASHBOARD SITE

It might become necessary to cancel the approval process, for example if a document needs to be completely reworked by the author (perhaps based on initial feedback from other Approvers). In this case

1. In the workspace, locate the desired document.
2. Right-click the document and then click Cancel Publishing.
3. Click Yes.

Within an email approval request, you can do the following to cancel the approval process.

1. From within the email notification request, click Cancel Publishing.
2. Click OK to end the approval process and return the document back to an unpublished status.

Now that we have covered the various methods of approving and rejecting or canceling documents to be published, we are ready to discuss in greater depth how to configure the workspace.

CONFIGURING THE WORKSPACE

One of the first things that should be considered after installing SharePoint Portal Server and creating the default workspace is to create and customize an efficient document folder hierarchy under the Documents folder within the workspace. After creating the document folder hierarchy, the next step is to assign security roles to allow access to the workspace and subfolders within the document folder. Once security is enabled on a folder, all subfolders inherit the parent's existing security by default. The folder Coordinator has the ability to set folder security to allow subfolders to dynamically change as security settings are modified. Alternatively, the Coordinator can allow subfolders to retain existing security settings even when security for the parent is modified.

The default view of the workspace shows the four top-level folders: Documents, Management, Categories, and Portal Content (see Figure 3.10).

In the next few pages, we will drill down into each of these four top-level folders.

→ For great detail on configuring and managing the major components of the workspace, **see** "Introduction to the Workspace," **p. 220** in Chapter 9.

Figure 3.10
Default workspace
folder hierarchy.

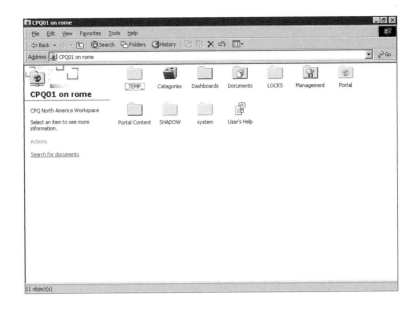

THE DOCUMENTS FOLDER

The Documents folder is used to provide a document location within the workspace or dashboard site for end users. Additional subfolders can be created for organizing and managing documents. SharePoint Portal Server allows you to create two types of folders within the workspace: standard and enhanced.

> NOTE   Only files stored in the Documents or Portal Content folders will be included in the index, which will allow users to search for these documents from the dashboard site.

By default, the Documents folder is specified as an enhanced folder, and unless specified otherwise, all subfolders created underneath the Documents folder inherit all parent folder enhanced settings (see Figure 3.11).

The only way to create a standard folder beneath an enhanced folder is to manually modify the properties page within the new folder, as illustrated in Figure 3.12. Click on the General tab of the document properties page, and then click the check box indicating Enhanced to enable enhanced folders.

Standard folders provide only limited document management features and benefits of SharePoint Portal Server. For example, all documents that are placed in standard folders are automatically published, and all users have the ability to view and search for documents residing in a standard folder.

Only enhanced folders allow private views of documents based on security, as well as check in and check out, version tracking, automated approvals, and so on.

Figure 3.11
Notice the difference in the icon for standard folder vs. enhanced folders.

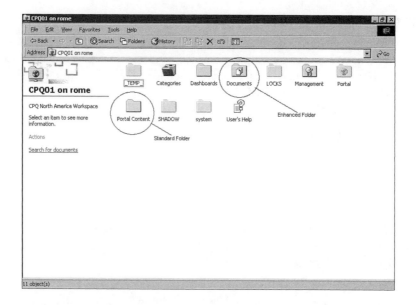

Figure 3.12
SharePoint Portal Server makes it easy to change the status of a folder from Standard to Enhanced.

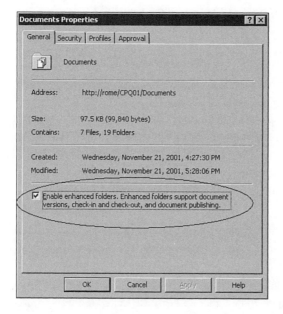

3

→ Creating and managing enhanced and standard folders are covered in greater depth in "Comparing Standard to Enhanced folders," **p. 71** in Chapter 4.

THE MANAGEMENT FOLDER

The Management folder is used to configure and manage the workspace, document profiles, and content sources. It includes various tools and folders that Coordinators can use to manage the portal's data, and to configure the workspace, document profiles, and content sources. While other tools, Web Parts, and so on exist to manage data, this folder allows specifically for managing the following:

- Document Profiles
- Content Sources
- Subscriptions
- Discussions

These are each discussed in more detail in the following sections.

DOCUMENT PROFILES

Within the Management folder, a subfolder exists called Document Profiles. This folder is used to create and store document profiles for the entire workspace. When you create subfolders within the workspace, you associate one of the document management profiles with the folder.

> **TIP** All documents within the workspace must be associated with a document profile that contains a set of properties. This association of the metadata specified within the document profile is what users use to easily search for and locate documents.

SharePoint Portal Server includes a document profile base document template which includes general properties that can be applicable to all documents or individual documents. Examples of these properties are title and keywords. The properties included within this base template can be configured to be included on other customized document profiles you create. Alternatively, inclusion of these properties can be overridden.

To configure the properties, double-click Management, then Document Profiles, then Base Document. Once you pull up the Base Document template, click on the Properties tab. Make changes as required. Note that Document Profiles are associated with a folder.

CONTENT SOURCES

Within the Management folder, a subfolder exists called Content Sources. The content source represents a location for documents outside the workspace that can be accessed and included within a SharePoint Portal Server index. Content sources are represented by location and specified by a URL. Since one server can house several workspaces, the content source location could point to content outside of the workspace but on the same server, on another server on your intranet, or to locations on the Internet. Once content sources are configured, an index for the content is created and updated regularly, based on index settings enabled. Users with appropriate roles can then search for and view desired content from the SharePoint Portal Server dashboard through a Web browser.

Figure 3.13
Note the various properties that may be associated with a Document Profile.

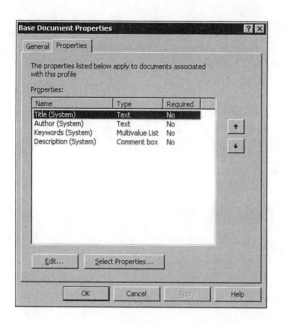

NOTE

Native SharePoint Portal Server document management functionality such as checking out or editing documents is not possible for data exposed through content sources.

You can then search for and display content source information through the workspace. Content sources are added by running the Add Content Source Wizard (see Figure 3.14), which can be accessed from within the Content Sources folder beneath the Management folder within the workspace.

Figure 3.14
View of Content Sources Web Folder from within the workspace.

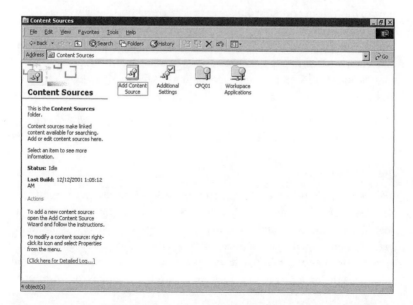

TIP

> The Content Sources folder cannot be accessed using a computer running Microsoft Windows 98 or Windows NT. To create and manage content sources, you must have Windows 2000 installed on your computer.

The following content sources can be created within SharePoint Portal Server:

- Web links—such as http://www.compaq.com/sharepoint.
- Web folders—Folders located in another workspace.
- File share—such as file://server/share/folder_name.
- Microsoft Exchange 5.5 public folders—such as exch://Exchange_Server_Name/.
- Microsoft Exchange 2000 public folders—such as http://server/Public/Public Folders/folder_name/.
- Lotus Notes databases.

NOTE

> If you configure a content source in a Lotus Notes Server, you will need to install a Lotus Notes client on SharePoint Portal Server. In addition, you will need to configure the server with a Lotus Notes utility called NotesSetup. Notes Server integration is discussed in more detail in Chapter 18, "Configuring SharePoint Portal Server to Crawl Other Content Sources."

CATEGORIES FOLDER

Another top-level folder within the root of the workspace is the Categories folder. In contrast to the Documents folder, the Categories folder permits special subfolders to be created which are organized into a logical hierarchy based on topics and subtopics. Categories are used to enable your end users to efficiently locate content, and can contain documents and information from content sources that are external to the workspace. Categories can be used to sort documents into a hierarchy of groups under different headings according to subject matter, and they can include an easy-to-manage set of terms that helps users consistently characterize documents. Categories are not mandatory, but provide an extremely useful way to logically classify and organize documents. The use of categories can help make sure your end users can search for and locate documents based on document relevance.

Categories are configured as a workspace setting, so only the Coordinator role within the workspace can create and modify categories within the hierarchy. Coordinators can configure a dedicated category contact for each category, or a single contact to be responsible for multiple categories.

The contact can become a focal point for end user feedback for required category changes that may help to further classify your content. Since categories provide a link to documents regardless of location, multiple categories can be associated with a single document. This may be useful when a single document includes topics that are related to a variety of categories. For example, you may have a document that has both benefits and payroll information. This document could be associated with both the Payroll and Benefits categories.

Adding documents to categories, as opposed to creating or modifying them, can be done by the author of the document, a category contact, or the Coordinator of the workspace.

THE CATEGORY ASSISTANT

The Category Assistant is an automated categorization tool that can be used within the workspace. It can be used to reduce the amount of time required to implement categories and categorize documents. This feature is accessed through the properties page of the Categories folder.

→ The Category Assistant will be discussed in more depth in Chapter 12, "Configuring the Category Assistant," **p. 310**.

To access the Category Assistant, right-click on the Categories folder within the workspace, and then click on Properties (see Figure 3.15).

Figure 3.15
Accessing the Category Assistant is easily performed by right-clicking the Categories folder and then clicking Properties.

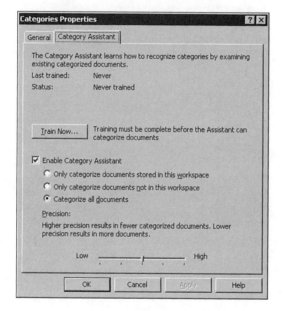

Document categorization can be done through use of the document profile form, as well through use of the Search and Categories tab, which is accessed from the Properties page of the document. The Search and Categories option is illustrated in Figure 3.16. Browse down through the Documents folder to the subfolder that contains the document you want to manage. Right-click on the document, and then click Properties. Click the Search and Categories tab to bring up the dialog box.

Figure 3.16
Note that the Search and Categories tab is one of a number of tabs associated with the properties of a document.

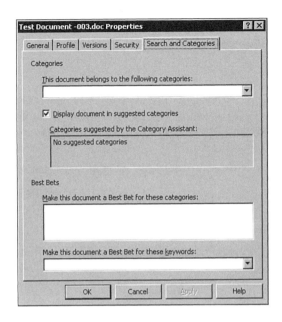

Once categories are enabled, your end users can begin to browse through and search the category hierarchy to learn how content is logically organized.

PORTAL CONTENT FOLDER

The fourth and final top-level folder is called Portal Content. The purpose of this folder is to store default folders, which are used to configure and manage the information displayed within the default Web Parts displayed through the SharePoint Portal Server dashboard site.

Default portal content such as News, Announcements, and Quick Links (see Figure 3.17) are configured as required by a workspace level Coordinator. This is done by adding documents to the News, Announcements, and Quick Links subfolders within the workspace. These are in fact default Web Parts, and can be either removed or not shown as required.

USING WEB FOLDERS

Web folders can be set up to enable shortcuts to Web servers. If your server supports Web folders, folder taxonomies can be created to save and publish documents. These documents can then be exposed through the portal dashboard site via Web Folders or My Network Places, or accessed by your end users' standard Web browser. Files and folders can be displayed from Web servers as well as network file servers and local drives. The key difference between Web folders and other folders, of course, is that the Web folders reside on a Web server and not on a user's local hard drive or mapped drive.

Figure 3.17
View of the default
subfolders within the
Portal Content folder.

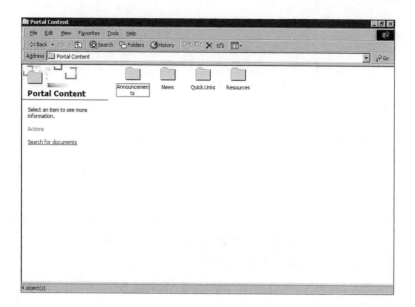

This difference between the Web folder and other folders is realized during the save process. When you save files on a Web folder, the file is saved directly to the Web server rather than the local personal computer or network-based file share. Assuming you have the appropriate security, you can easily view the contents of a Web folder. Files saved on a local drive or network file server, on the other hand, are not as easily accessed by or shared with others.

TIP

> Web folders and My Network Places are essentially the same thing. PCs running Windows 2000 will use My Network Places for access to SharePoint Portal Server. PCs running Windows 98 or Windows NT 4.0 utilize Web folders for access to SharePoint Portal Server.

CREATING A WEB FOLDER

A Web folder (or network place) must be created for access to the workspace. To create a Web folder, perform the following:

1. Double-click Add Network Place from within My Network Places.
2. Proceed through the instructions in the Add Network Place Wizard.
3. Files can be saved to the network place by dragging files and folders to this new network place.

Note that a Network Place shortcut to the new workspace specified at installation time is created for you. A network place can be just as easily deleted, too, if you do not want the network place to appear on your computer any longer.

To delete a network place, do the following:

1. Open My Network Places.
2. Right-click the target network place that you wish to delete.
3. Click Delete.
4. Click Yes.

Web folders can be used to store and manage files from within the workspace. Files can be added by using Windows Explorer or by using the Open or Save As dialog boxes within Microsoft Word. Once you run the Add Web folder wizard and create the Web folder, you can then save files and folders to the new location.

To create and then use a Web folder from My Computer, do the following:

1. Double-click My Network Places from My Computer.
2. Double-click Add Network Place.
3. Proceed through the instructions in the Add Network Place Wizard.
4. Files can be saved to the Web server by dragging files and folders to this new Web folder.

To create a Web folder from Microsoft Word, do the following:

1. Click File, and then Open from within Word.
2. Within the Open dialog box, click Web Folders on the Look In bar.
3. Click the New Folder icon in the toolbar, and then follow the instructions in the Add Web Folder Wizard.

To create a new Web folder from an existing Web server location, do the following:

1. Click File, and then click Save As from within Word.
2. In the Save As dialog box, click Web Folders on the Save In bar.
3. Type the Web address (such as //MyServer/) in the File name box, and then click OK.

Web folders can also be easily deleted if you do not want the Web folder to appear on your computer any longer. To delete a Web folder, do the following:

1. Double-click Web Folders from within My Computer.
2. Right-click the desired Web folder that you want to delete.
3. Click Delete.
4. Click Yes.

ACCESSING SHAREPOINT PORTAL SERVER THROUGH WEB FOLDERS

The workspace is actually a Web folder on the SharePoint Portal Server with unique properties and a dashboard site. Basic Web folder document management functions can be performed. For example, as we have seen, the Web folder view allows documents to be checked in, checked out, published, approved, or rejected.

This content becomes part of an enterprise index that allows efficient searches for information stored within and outside your organization. Categories can be accessed, which enables end users to browse through a hierarchical view of how documents are classified. Lastly, per-folder settings can be enabled for role based security, document publishing, and document version control.

THREE METHODS OF ACCESSING WEB FOLDERS

File and folders within a Web folder can be viewed and managed in several ways, as follows:

- Web Browser—Once Microsoft Office Server extensions are enabled on a Web server, a Web browser allows users to browse Web Folder Content as well as file system properties.
- Microsoft Office—Allows users to view, open, save, and create new Web folders.
- Windows Explorer—The Explorer view allows users to see a detailed list of files and folders. The files and folders can be renamed, moved, copied, or deleted. This view also allows files and folders to be dragged from Web server to Web server, as well as between Web servers and traditional network file servers.

3

SUMMARY

A workspace consists of document folders, management tools, and a searchable index of information. Each workspace initially contains four main folders: Documents, Management, Portal Content, and Categories. In addition, Web page links to Help files and configuration wizards are also available.

Within SharePoint Portal Server, documents are stored and managed within the Documents folder of the workspace. The Documents folder is the root of the document management library. Configuration of the Documents folder represents the major task in preparing the workspace for document management and group collaboration within your environment. The Management folder provides the necessary tools and subfolders that enable workspace Coordinators to manage and configure the workspace, content sources, and document profiles. The Categories folder allows categories to be set up, which allow data to be efficiently organized according to topics and subtopics. The Portal Content folder contains a set of default folders that workspace Coordinators can use to manage and configure default Web parts.

In addition to the workspace, users can access and search for content through a Web site called the dashboard site. The dashboard site, which could represent data from within and outside your organization, can be accessed using a Web browser. This dashboard site enables users to locate and share documents regardless of location or format. Furthermore, the dashboard site allows you to customize the home page using Web Parts to display organizational news and other important information. The ability to search for information, browse through information by categories, subscribe to new or changing information, check documents in and out, approve documents for publication, publish documents, and review a document's version history is also facilitated via the dashboard site.

In the next chapter, we build upon what has been covered here and provide an overview of document management, certainly one of the most compelling features of SharePoint Portal Server.

3

CHAPTER 4

OVERVIEW OF DOCUMENT MANAGEMENT

In this chapter

THE DOCUMENT MANAGEMENT PROCESS

A document's lifecycle begins with the initial creation of the document by an end user, and is often extended as it is reviewed and approved by others. SharePoint Portal Server provides a unique way of managing the stages of the document's lifecycle. Some of the key features that will be discussed in this chapter are check in and check out, routing approval, and document profiles. In addition, we will discuss folder-level Coordinator procedures that use and manage other key document management features of SharePoint Portal Server.

In Chapter 2, "Features and Capabilities," we learned that SharePoint Portal Server could be used to help users manage the creation, preparation, and publication of documents. As a document matures within the document management lifecycle, SharePoint Portal Server helps the necessary individuals edit or review a document while maintaining the document's integrity. We have not talked in great detail about additional collaboration capabilities. However, after a document version is published, SharePoint Portal Server can be used to enable Authors and Editors to collaborate on a document and update as necessary. All this can be done while the original version of the document can be seen by Readers.

USING DRAFTS

The earliest stage of the document lifecycle is a *Draft*. With SharePoint Portal Server, Authors control whether a document is made available for public view. The initial document is created and saved as a draft. The draft can be shared with an Author or group of Authors. Readers are not yet aware of documents that are in draft state, and it is not until the state is changed to *publish* that users can then view and modify the document based on the security access level granted.

Upon being published, Readers can search for the document or navigate to it through the use of categories. Document versioning is used to update the document while preserving the previous published document. A single SharePoint Portal Server can store up to one million document versions. The maximum number of documents per server is dependent on the number of document versions. With the assumption of an average of two versions per document, the maximum documents per server is 500,000. If the average versions per document were eight, the recommended maximum would be 125,000.

ADMINISTRATION BASED ON FOLDER TYPE

In Chapter 3, "Overview of Using the Workspace and Dashboard," we discussed the Coordinator role within the workspace. A folder-level Coordinator is a subordinate role that can be delegated by the workspace Coordinator. While this could be the same person, often a different person within a department or business unit is assigned to manage a top-level folder and subfolders beneath it. There are two types of folders that can be managed: enhanced and standard. The folder-level Coordinator will perform various tasks which depend on the type of folder they are responsible for managing. For example, within a standard folder, the assigned folder Coordinator can assign roles, edit and delete documents, create folders and subfolders, and apply pre-established document profiles to folders.

4

TIP

> It is recommended to use standard folders when working with documents that will not require group interaction tasks. If a document requires editing and approval from several individuals, you probably should be using enhanced folders.

NOTE

> All documents placed within a standard folder are automatically published to the dashboard site. Once a file is placed in a standard folder, all users that have the Reader role assigned will have the ability to browse and search for these documents. Document management features such as check in and check out, public and private views, version control, and approval routing can only be done within an enhanced folder.

Within an enhanced folder, the folder-level Coordinator can do all the same tasks as stated above within a standard folder. In addition, Coordinators of enhanced folders can enable appropriate approval processes, which allow documents to be published to the dashboard site for the end user community. Since the top-level Documents folder is an enhanced folder, any subfolders created within this folder will inherit the enhanced folder settings. In addition, when you drag a folder from your computer to the workspace, folder inheritance will apply. For example, if you drag a folder into an enhanced folder within the workspace, the folder you drag into the workspace inherits the parent folder settings and also becomes an enhanced folder. If you need to create a standard folder within an enhanced folder, you must manually uncheck the Enable Enhanced folders setting within the properties page of the new folder that you create.

4

COMPARING STANDARD TO ENHANCED FOLDERS

Table 4.1 below compares key features supported within standard and enhanced folders.

TABLE 4.1   COMPARISON MATRIX

Feature Supported?	Standard Folders	Enhanced Folders
Role-based security	Yes	Yes
Document categories	Yes	Yes
Document indexing	Yes	Yes
Document profiles (metadata)	Yes	Yes
Version control	No	Yes
Check-in/check-out	No	Yes
Private draft versions	No	Yes
Approval routing	No	Yes

CORE DOCUMENT MANAGEMENT COMPONENTS

Within SharePoint Portal Server, a document library exists that enables the key components of document management functionality. Examples of this functionality include check in and check out, document version control, history tracking, document profiling with the use of metadata, and granular document security access control. Some of these features were discussed at a high level in Chapter 2. For example, check in and check Out, can be enabled or disabled on individual folders. Coordinators will need to determine the folders that require an Author or Editor to have exclusive access over the document by checking the document out. When a document is checked out, other users cannot modify the document.

VERSION CONTROL

As discussed at a high level in Chapter 2, version control within SharePoint Portal Server is extremely important and allows for audit and recovery. Auditing is used to provide history tracking of a document. Many Authors and Editors find it helpful to know when a document has been changed, exactly what was changed within the document, and who made the change. A recovery option can be used when a document needs to be rolled back to a previous version. Versioning within SharePoint Portal Server is handled as follows:

- Versioning scheme—Documents are referred to using a Major.Minor numeric versioning scheme. An example of this scheme is as follows: 1.0, 1.1, 1.2, 2.0, 2,1, and so on. The first numeric in the versioning scheme (for example, 1.) refers to the major version. The second numeric (for example, .1) refers to the minor version.

  To view a previous version of a document, right-click on the document from within the workspace. Click the Versions tab (see Figure 4.1), select the version you want to work with, and click View Document.

NOTE

> The main difference between a major version and a minor version is the fact that minor versions are incremented when checked in, and major version are incremented when published.

→ For additional details about document versions, **see** "Document Properties and Settings," **p. 266**.

- Version comments—Authors and Editors can create comments for each version of a document. Version comments allow Authors and Editors to see deltas within various versions of the document over time. They also enable Authors and Editors to browse specifically to a desired version by simply cycling through the changes that have taken place.

- An example of version comments within a document might be "Latest revision with changes according to customer feedback" (see Figure 4.2).

Figure 4.1
Within the Version tab, all previous document versions are displayed and readily accessible.

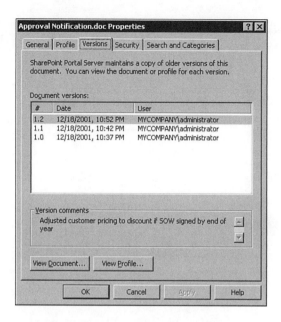

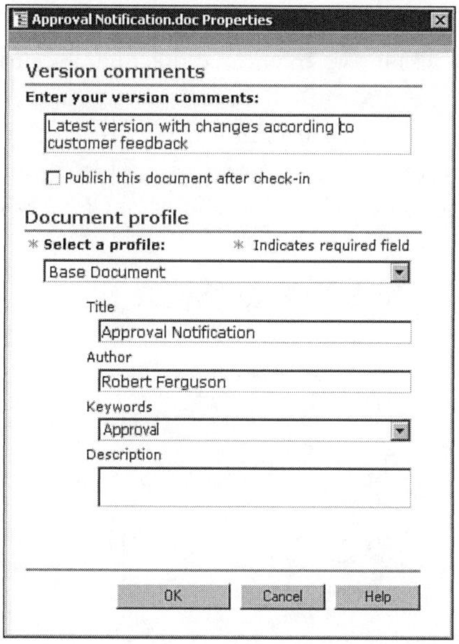

After a document is published, right-click the document, click Properties, and select the Versions tab (see Figure 4.3). Click on the version number and the version comments will be displayed in the Version Comments window.

Figure 4.2
Version comments are added as part of the document profile form completion process.

4

Figure 4.3
As you can see, users can utilize the version comments feature to navigate through various versions of the document according to changes that were made.

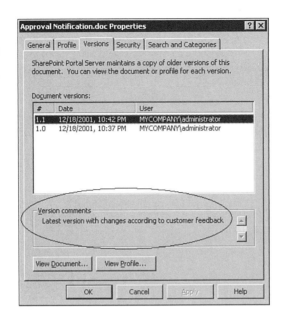

■ Auditing—This feature within version control is used to track exactly who made a change and when the change was made. Integrated document security enables each edit of the document to be tracked and identified by security account. An administrator has to initially grant access using document level role-based security within SharePoint Portal Server. The security account is what is used to track and identify the Editor's changes, and is displayed as follows: ("DOMAINNAME\USERNAME").

Figure 4.4
In this example, the administrator made the changes to all three versions of the document. As you can see, having the ability to view the current version and who made the changes, as well as when the changes were made, is a very helpful feature.

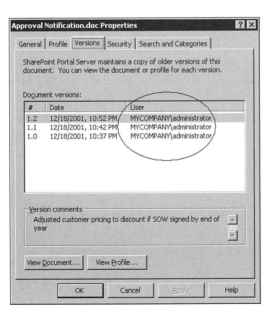

- Metadata change tracking—Another important tracking mechanism is the changes to the metadata information. If an Author or Editor makes changes to the metadata (document profile) associated with a document, the version control feature tracks previous versions of the document and all changes to the metadata linked to the document.

ASSOCIATING METADATA WITH DOCUMENTS

Authors can simplify the document management process by associating logical attributes to documents. As previously discussed at a high level in Chapter 3, this association is done by associating metadata to documents within a document profile, which will allow documents to be easily searched for and located within the document management library. As stated in Chapter 1, many organizations have a similar problem: that desired content is too difficult to locate within their traditional intranet. Within a SharePoint Portal Server site, this problem is addressed by having a Coordinator use a document profile to apply metadata to documents.

→ For more details about associating metadata with documents, along with additional examples, **see** "The Document Library," **p. 262**.

SharePoint Portal Server gives various levels of administrative control for a Coordinator to configure specific settings on a per-folder basis. The Coordinator can require that all new documents placed within a particular folder must have a profile form completed by the Author or Editor before they can be checked in. This is done by applying a document profile to a folder and mandating that certain fields are populated. When document profiles are used, the Author or Editor is presented with a form that may contain optional or required fields. The Coordinator specifies which fields are required; all other fields are optional. This document profile is then presented, whether the document is checked in using Microsoft Office, Windows Explorer, or through the Web-based SharePoint Portal Server workspace.

4

For an example of required versus optional fields within the document profile, see Figure 4.5. Within the document profile form for an Author or Editor, a red asterisk indicates required fields. Failure to complete a required field will result in a Document Profile dialog box that indicates which field must be completed.

Metadata enables you to associate additional details about a document. In most cases, the descriptive metadata associated includes additional search keywords which do not exist within the body of the document. During a search, both the document's metadata and the text of a document are searched. Metadata enables a Coordinator to match properties to values. An example might be that you associate several metadata values, such as Armada or Deskpro, with a property called Computers. A document profile provides a consistent way to describe and classify documents using a set of properties. This metadata component can also be used for multicategorization of the document. Associating metadata in this manner is extremely powerful and provides a much greater value over using the traditional file directory structure for organizing and grouping documents for your end users.

Figure 4.5
In this example, a dialog box is indicating that keyword values must be entered in order to complete the check-in process.

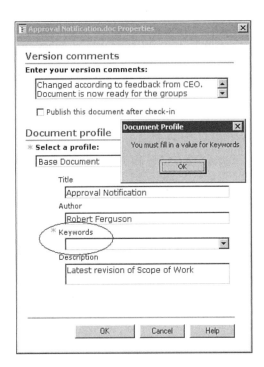

USING CUSTOM PROPERTIES

Within a document profile, you can include custom properties such as color, accessories, and partners. A workspace can contain multiple document profiles. Once a document profile is created and added to the workspace, click on the properties of the document, click the Profiles tab, and assign the document profile.

An example of using custom properties might be that an end user named John creates a comparison white paper on all portal products in the marketplace today. This comparison matrix details all the key features and capabilities, but does not actually use the word "comparison" within the body of the text. Although John does not mention "comparison" in the document, he decides to include this word as a keyword property value. Once the document is published, a dashboard site Reader named Susan can initiate a search query on the word "comparison" within the dashboard site and the search results will return John's comparison matrix document. The reason the search found the comparison data is because the keyword property value was matched within the document's metadata by the search query.

NOTE All documents must have a document profile associated.

USING DOCUMENT TYPES

Document types can be used to indicate the document objective. Documents that are specified to have the same type can have the same attribute. Search speeds can be increased and searches are more efficient when metadata is associated with the document type. A document type called Sales Report (see Figure 4.6) could contain a specific keyword attribute called forecast.

Figure 4.6
Users could search for the document type of forecast and Sales Report would be returned as a result of the search.

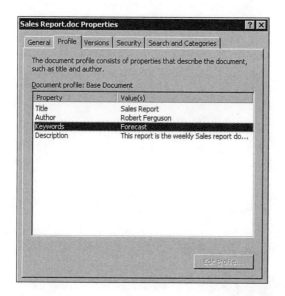

As you can see, there are many ways to customize how documents are returned when specific searches are made. It is highly recommended that you plan and document how this feature will be utilized to ensure the most effective portal experience for your end users.

USING THE WIZARD TO CREATE A PROFILE

With SharePoint Portal Server, the use of the wizard can be utilized to provide high levels of consistency, while ensuring that specific attributes are used throughout a variety of documents. The administrative functionality provided by the Coordinator allows custom attributes to be specified: The order can be selected and fields can be specified as either required or optional.

Within the workspace, double-click on the Management folder and double-click on the Document Profiles folder. Double-click on Add Document Profile to launch the Add Documents Profile Wizard.

Figure 4.7
View of the Document
Profiles folder.

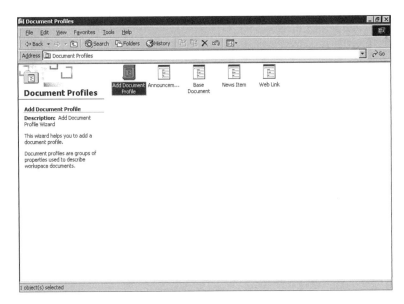

Click Next at the Add Document Profile Wizard dialog box.

4

Figure 4.8
View of Add Docu-
ment Profile dialog
box that is launched
after you click on Add
Document Profile,
as displayed in Fig-
ure 4.7.

Provide a name for your document profile. Click Next.

Figure 4.9
Example of changing a document profile's name to Customer Orders.

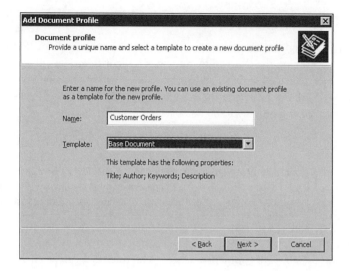

Click the property and click Edit. Select or deselect this field depending on whether you want fields enabled or disabled within the document management profile.

Figure 4.10
Only selected property names will be displayed within the new document management profile.

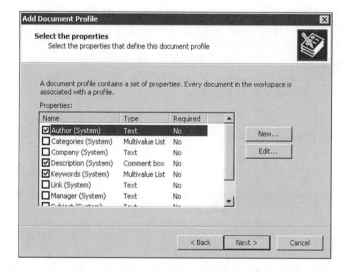

As illustrated in Figures 4.7–4.10, creating document profiles is a simple process. All documents must be associated with a document management profile, and their use allows for you to control what information needs to be provided as documents are checked in and published.

ROLE-BASED SECURITY

As discussed at a high level in Chapter 3, security within SharePoint Portal Server is achieved by leveraging the existing Windows NT security model. The security component provides granular security control and simplified security management. While integrating with existing Windows NT Security is important, additional role-based security allows documents to be accessed only by individuals who are granted access through SharePoint Portal Server security specific roles.

NOTE

> SharePoint Portal Server uses existing NT user-IDs and native Windows NT–based Access Control Lists (ACLs). SharePoint Portal Server must be run on a Windows 2000 Server platform. However, both NT and Windows 2000 directory security can be used.

SharePoint Portal Server allows role-based security for managing what users can do within the workspace or subfolders of the workspace. The roles that can be enabled are Coordinator, Author, and Reader. The roles have different authority and the role assigned will determine the level of authority within the workspace.

→ To learn more role based security and how it is used, **see** "Permissions," **p. 281**.

Roles are used to logically group end userswith similar access, but the role-based membership is not stored within Active Directory. Rather, the roles are stored within individual folders, and each folder could potentially contain a different set of users and groups for each role. A workspace Coordinator or Coordinators for specific folders can assign roles. Workspace Coordinators can assign roles at the workspace or for folders within the workspace. Coordinators for specific folders can only assign roles within the assigned folder. When the Coordinator assigns a user to a role, the user is granted specific permissions to perform specific tasks.

NOTE

> Permissions are assigned to roles and cannot be changed.

To enable security, a Coordinator assigns a user or a group to a security role. To change security, right-click the folder, click Properties, and click Security. Select an existing user and change the role or add a new user or group (see Figure 4.11).

It is best practice to set up NT groups, assign users to the groups, and associate the security role to the group rather than an individual user. In addition, you should not use a combination of individual and group assignments. When assigning security at multiple levels, the most permissive role applies.

NOTE

> If an Author creates new folders, the new folder automatically inherits the folder level policies from the parent folder, which was configured by the Coordinator of the parent folder. The Author role does not have the ability to modify the roles or approval policies on any folders which they create.

Figure 4.11
Notice the three roles you can select from when assigning rights to a user or group.

NOTE

> All users are assigned to the Reader role by default. This means that everyone in your domain can read published documents. This is possible because within Windows NT and Windows 2000, the Everyone group is assigned to the Reader role. This default assignment is performed on all folders within the workspace during the creation of the workspace.

Within a standard folder, Readers have the ability to view all documents within the folder. Within an enhanced folder, Readers can only view folders and public documents. A Reader cannot check out, edit, or delete documents, and cannot view draft versions of documents.

ROLE-BASED ACTIVITIES

SharePoint Portal Server allows Coordinators to perform the following role-based functions:

- Assigning users or groups to a role
- Adding a user or a group to a folder
- Removing a user or a group from a folder
- Configuring folder-level inheritance

Step-by step processes and procedures for how to perform these role-based functions are documented in great detail within SharePoint Portal Server's Help.

ADDITIONAL SECURITY

In addition to the three main security roles, an additional document level setting of Deny Access, as well as a folder level setting of Approver, can be used to provide additional security granularity.

Deny Access is not a core security role. However, this feature allows an additional level of granular document-based security restrictions. Not available within the folder level, Deny Access can be enabled on individual documents within a folder. Access can be denied for individual users as well as for a group of users not allowed to view the document.

It is possible that some end users might have the appropriate security role that would normally allow access to documents within a folder. However, the Author of a document could still block access using the Deny Access feature.

The Approver role is a special role only associated with specific tasks on a per-folder basis for enhanced folders. This role is not a formal role similar to the three main security roles (Coordinator, Author, or Reader). A Coordinator for an enhanced folder can add a user as an Approver within the Approval tab on the Properties page of the folder.

The reason this role is only associated with enhanced folders is because a SharePoint Portal Server approval process cannot be set up on standard folders. Coordinators can assign Approvers only to folders which have approval routing enabled.

Right-click an enhanced folder, click Properties, click the Approval tab, and then click Document must be approved before publishing. Add desired Approvers and select the approval route type. Input to the "Comments for the approval email" section will be passed through in the document approval notification email.

Figure 4.12
All routing and approval configuration is done within the Approval tab of a folder.

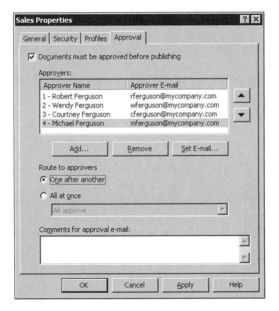

TIP

> You can select local users and groups, or users from your existing Windows NT or Windows 2000 domain, and assign them to roles. You can define these users and groups locally on the server, or on the domain of which the server is a member. However, since SharePoint Portal Server does not recognize local user server accounts located on another server, it is best practice to use domain user and group accounts when assigning a role to a user.

USERS WITH MULTIPLE ROLES

It is possible that a user can have several roles within different folders in a single workspace. For example, in the Sales folder a user might be assigned to the Coordinator role, while in another folder the same user might only be assigned to the Reader role.

NOTE

> Assigning a group to a role within a folder allows all members of the group (such as Sales) to have the same role-based access to the folder. Let's assume that a role is assigned to one specific individual of the Sales group. The most permissive combination of the two roles combined then applies. Only the Deny Access role can limit the access of a particular document. If this role is specified within a document for a specific group or individual user, the group or user cannot access the document. This role takes priority over all other roles, even Coordinator.

GRANULAR ACCESS CONTROL

Specifying access control within SharePoint Portal Server can be done at multiple levels. Access can be specified at the workspace level and allow specific inheritance rules to apply. The Coordinator can provide more granular access control by specifying access at the folder level within the workspace. In addition, extreme granular control can be provided by controlling further access within the folder on a per document basis.

NOTE

> Using document-level access will likely increase the amount of required administration. One should carefully evaluate the inclusion of this feature to prevent an unnecessary substantial increase in administration costs.

SECURITY INHERITANCE

To ease administration, workspace and folders can be configured such that subfolders automatically inherit access control settings from their parent folder.

Right-click your folder and click Properties. Select the Security tab and click Use parent folder's security settings (see Figure 4.13). All subdirectories will inherit this security structure unless manually changed.

Figure 4.13
Click on Use parents folder's security settings to enable the new folder to automatically inherit the security from the parent folder.

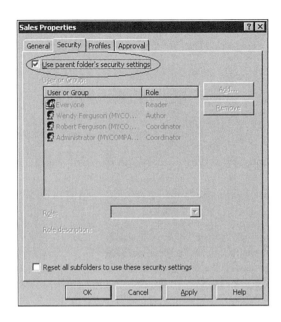

When working with document management, it is important to be able to restrict and control access to specific information. SharePoint Portal Server role based security allows you to control access to a document and make it available only to a selected group of individuals who need to edit it or approve it. Once the document is edited or approved, the document can then automatically be published to the final destination and made available to a larger audience.

ADDITIONAL DOCUMENT MANAGEMENT KEY FEATURES

The SharePoint Portal Server user interface is designed around Microsoft Office, Windows, and a Web browser. SharePoint Portal Server features are exposed through extensions to these familiar user interface elements.

WINDOWS INTEGRATION

SharePoint Portal Server exposes document libraries as Web folders within Windows Explorer using the universal folders and documents interface. Users can easily sort and organize documents based on specific business purpose. This is accomplished through the use of enhanced document folders, which show metadata (document profile) details.

Windows integration features are as follows:

■ Properties pages—Extended property pages exist within SharePoint Portal Server documents to show version history, security settings, and metadata.

Figure 4.14
The standard Explorer view is extended to display additional Metadata information.

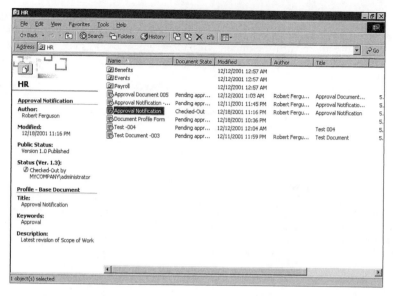

Right-click functionality—SharePoint Portal Server enhancements allow context menu functionality for checking in, checking out, and so on. Right-click the document to expose the available options. Our example shows a document that was already checked in and published. The only option on this document is check out.

Figure 4.15
Illustration of the options for a document that is currently checked in.

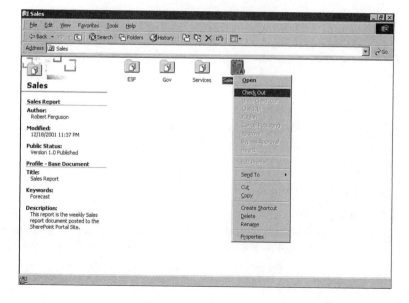

4

This example (see Figure 4.16) shows a document during the approval route process. The Coordinator can cancel the publishing process, which would end the approval route and return the document back to a checked in state. The Bypass Approval option enables a Coordinator to bypass the approval process and force the document to be published.

Figure 4.16
Notice that the metadata displays the current version, which is pending. The Coordinator can cancel the publishing process or bypass approval, which would publish the document immediately.

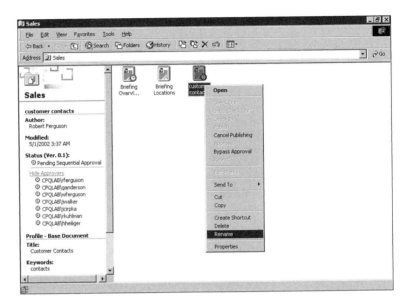

■ Explorer-based view—The folder view allows the metadata to be viewed so documents can now be viewed according to context. Figure 4.18 shows an example of the Explorer-based view.

■ Category-based views —Categories allow documents that may exist in different physical locations to be represented as a single logical view.

Figure 4.17 shows how you can view documents by category using the dashboard view. From the Dashboard home site, click on Categories and then click on the category that includes the documents that you want to view.

OFFICE 2000 INTEGRATION

COM (Component Object Model) add-ins are used within SharePoint Portal Server to enable document library menu extensions to be utilized within the application where documents are created and modified. Key features of Office 2000 are as follows:

■ Collaboration toolbar—The Office 2000 collaboration toolbar allows for document-level team interaction.

- File menu additions —With Office 2000, the enhanced capabilities allow you to natively check in, check out, and submit a document to be published without having to launch any additional tools. From within the File drop-down menu of Office 2000, document libraries can be directly viewed and navigated.

- Property promotion —Document properties within a document are synchronized with the document profile. An example might be an Author property within a document. When changes are made to the document profile, changes are made to the actual properties within the document.

Figure 4.17
Readers can browse through Categories within the Dashboard.

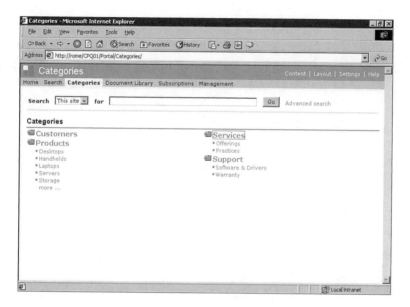

Figure 4.18
Document check in, check out, and publishing can be done directly from a drop-down menu within Microsoft Office.

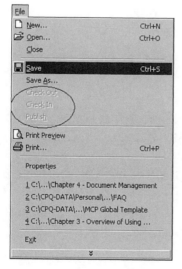

The ability to check in, check out, and publish documents using this integrated functionality provides end users with a seamless document management process.

BROWSER-BASED INTEGRATION

All Author and Reader functionality is available through a Web-based interface for users who do not use Office or Windows. Internet Explorer or Netscape Navigator version 4.x or later is required. With the browser, users can access the dashboard site. An example of the dashboard site is illustrated in Figure 4.19.

Figure 4.19
Dashboard site exposed through the Web browser.

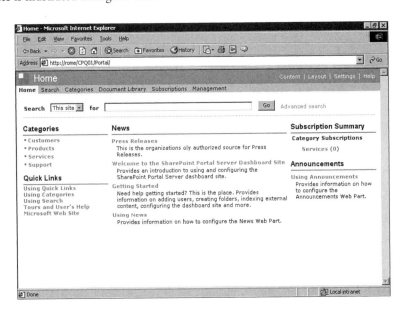

DOCUMENT MANAGEMENT EXTENSIONS

To ease migration, management, and integration into line-of-business applications, SharePoint Portal Server supports programmatic access to document library functions through OLE DB, ActiveX Data Objects (ADO), and extensions to Collaborative Data Objects (CDO). Customizing SharePoint Portal Server using ASP, COM+, and SQL is discussed in more detail in Chapter 15.

WEB STORAGE SYSTEM FOR CUSTOM APPLICATION DEVELOPMENT

The Web Storage System supports a large variety of collaborative application development options through OLE DB and ActiveX Data Objects (ADO), SQL, Internet file system (IFS), and Hypertext Transfer Protocol (HTTP).

ACCESSING WEB DISCUSSIONS

A key feature that enables users to add remarks about a document without modifying the actual document is called Web discussions. Web discussions within the workspace are enabled by default. However, a workspace Coordinator can disable Web discussions to prevent users from accessing this feature. Since all input appears as a threaded discussion, this feature can provide an efficient method for remote groups to collaborate on a particular document. For example, a group in the UK might create a document and start a discussion thread. Another set of users within the US might share the responsibility to edit and approve revisions of a particular document. Due to the time zone difference and the high long distance costs for direct communication, the Web discussions feature can be used to provide the required document-level collaboration.

Browse down through the Documents folder within the dashboard. Once you locate your document, click Discuss. You can then click on Insert Discussion and complete a discussion thread by entering text in the dialog box that appears.

Figure 4.20
Discussions can be initiated from the Document Library view of the Dashboard.

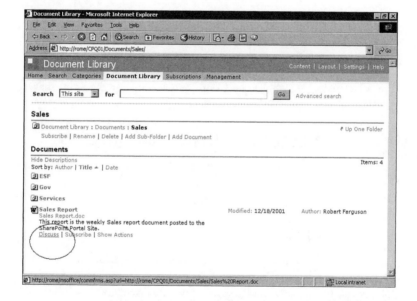

Even though version control may be enabled, which allows several versions of a document to exist, only one set of discussions is maintained for each document. Contrary to what you may think, discussions are not stored within the actual document. They are stored separately from the document, which they reference. A document can be deleted and the discussions will continue to remain within the workspace until manually deleted by the workspace Coordinator.

Web discussions can be accessed from within the collaboration toolbar in Office 2000, or from within Microsoft Internet Explorer at the dashboard site.

USING THE DASHBOARD SITE TO DISCUSS A DOCUMENT

1. Browse through the folder hierarchy within the dashboard site to locate the document you want to discuss.

2. Within the title of the document, click the Discuss link.

3. The desired document is opened along with a discussion thread set of dialog options.

The Insert Discussion dialog is where an Author or Editor will launch a dialog box to enter a discussion on a document.

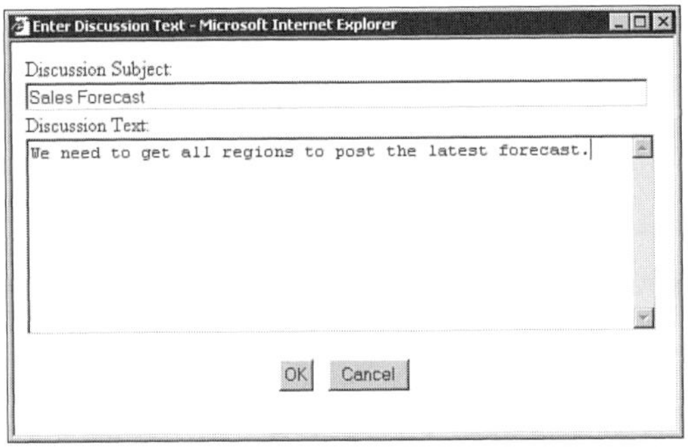

Figure 4.21
Example of discussion thread initiated on a document called Sales Forecast.

The View dialog box allows the Coordinator to specify the fields that will be enabled within the Web-based discussions window.

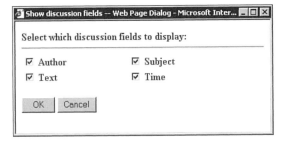

Figure 4.22
Select or deselect the required fields you want to have displayed.

The Filter dialog box allows you to show only discussion based on a filtered view. Figure 4.23 shows how you can filter discussion threads based on an individual, or find threads created within the last 24 hours, 2 days, 7 days, 30 days, 2 months, or 6 months.

Once the document discussion filter criteria is specified, you can click on the Close button to close the dialog boxes.

Figure 4.23
Specify the filter criteria according to your needs.

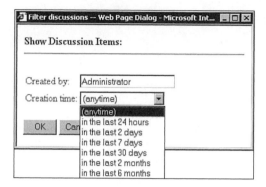

INDEXING WEB DISCUSSIONS

The search feature for discussion can be enabled, which then includes discussion items in search results. Once Web discussions are enabled, the index will include existing document discussions. Users with the proper role-based security can search the dashboard site for a specific desired discussion.

We learned earlier in this chapter that SharePoint Portal Server uses integrated NT security to control access to documents. If end users do not have the appropriate NT file-based security for a document, these files will be filtered out during a search. However, Web discussions associated with a document are not linked to NT-based Access Control Lists (ACLs) for the document.

NOTE

> Indexing Web discussions could present a potential security risk for secure documents within a portal. Users could uncover important details about secure documents through exposed document-based Web discussions.

SUMMARY

In this chapter we discussed the key features of the core document management capabilities within SharePoint Portal Server. The key features discussed were check in, check Out, and version control. We discussed how document profiles can be used to associate metadata with documents, as well as how document types can be used to allow for more efficient searches for desired content. We discussed the differences between standard and enhanced folders, and which features are supported within each folder. The publishing and approval process was discussed to highlight the approval methods, such as One After Another and All At Once. We provided a high-level overview of role-based security, the roles that exist, and how users are assigned to roles within a workspace or folder. Lastly, we discussed how Web discussions could be used to conduct threaded Web-based discussions about a document, even though an end user might not have appropriate access to the document itself.

CHAPTER **5**

OVERVIEW OF INDEXING AND SEARCHING CONTENT

In this chapter

THE END-USER EXPERIENCE

SharePoint Portal Server is an excellent example of a knowledge discovery tool based on the combination of a portal and a rich index. The portal provides a single point of contact targeted to the knowledge worker; the index maintains information about documents present in the department, throughout the organization, and even beyond. Indexing such a variety of content in one place prevents users from needing to physically search or browse all the various content repositories for information. As you will see, SharePoint Portal Server can be used to make employees more effective, because they have timely and accurate access to information that is relevant for their business.

SharePoint Portal Server augments this environment as outlined in the earlier chapters with its own place to store documents, something that comes in handy once employees recognize the value of a more structured approach to filing their documents. This chapter will outline the core architecture and principles of the search engine and index.

Before we discuss the search and indexing capabilities, let's take a look at the end-user experience. Through each of the three environments that SharePoint interacts with—the Web Browser, Explorer using Web Folders, and Office XP applications such as Word—search capabilities are available.

SEARCHING THOUGH THE BROWSER

If you are using a browser (see Figure 5.1), the search is dominantly present on each dashboard through a dedicated search Web Part.

Figure 5.1
This is a dashboard site with the Search Web Part on top.

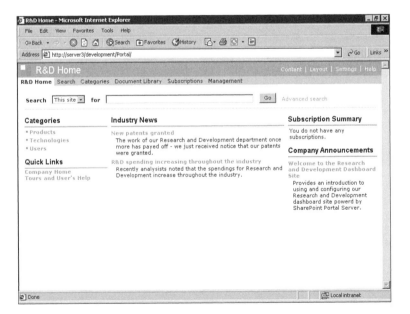

This Web Part can be toggled between two modes: Simple Search and Advanced Search.

SIMPLE SEARCH

In a simple search, the end user has the capability to specify a *Search Scope* and to type text that should be found in the document or its properties. Note that text matches are not case sensitive. Search Scopes can be defined by the Coordinator to classify the source of the data. You might for example use *External Content* to indicate information that is crawled from competitors' Web sites.

NOTE

> The default "This Site" Search Scope does not only refer to the current workspace or server; it actually refers to all content indexed by that workspace, so it also includes any content sources pointing to external Web Sites or Web Links with external URLs.

Later in this chapter, we'll discuss more details on the algorithms that are used to return the most appropriate results for a text search. As users typically type in only a little information, just a simple search for words would not be too useful.

ADVANCED SEARCH

SharePoint Portal Server addresses this problem with some advanced technologies that originated from Microsoft's research work and experience in developing Index Server, Site Server, and to some extent even Exchange 2000. Of course, the user can give the system a helping hand, opening the Advanced search (see Figure 5.2). Here you see the search capabilities for specific properties, which should help you to narrow the search results. If you type multiple words in the text search box, any word will match. That is, in logical terms, an OR is implemented. Any property conditions that are specified in the advanced search must be met; this is a logical AND.

Figure 5.2
Using the Advanced Search, a query is constructed to search for all documents with more than 20,000 bytes created in the last 14 days that contain the word "Portal" and have the keyword "Microsoft" specified.

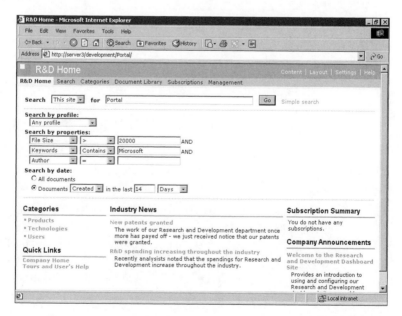

NOTE

The SharePoint Portal Server Query engine is far more flexible than the built-in user inter-face. In fact, the Advanced Search is still a very rudimentary user interface. For date type properties, one could think of comparisons with terms such as "last week." Another fre-quently heard request is to allow that only one of the property conditions must be met. These are not possible in the default Advanced Search, but all of this can be implemented, by modifying the user interface of the Search Web Part to build up the query in a more flexible manner.

→ See Chapter 17 for more details on building custom Web Parts.

Once the search query is executed, and the results determined, the search dashboard is opened to display the search results.

In fact, you may notice in Figure 5.3 that the results are shown in up to four different Web Parts which illustrate some of the features that are provided with SharePoint Portal Server. These Web Parts will be discussed later in this chapter.

Figure 5.3
The search dash-board displays four new Web Parts as a result of a previous search for "Portal".

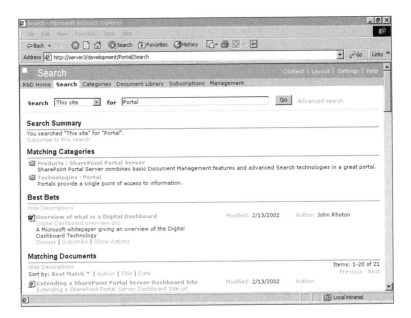

The four Web Parts of the Search Dashboard include the Search Summary, Matching Categories, Best Bets, and Matching Documents. Details regarding each of these include

■ The *Search Summary* Web Part summarizes the search request. Most importantly, note the ability to *subscribe* to the search. Subscribing to a search will register your search request, such that for any future updates of the index, your search will be updated again if the document causing the update matches your request. In other words—through subscriptions you can search the future. Paired with the My Subscriptions Web Part, this is indeed a powerful tool.

- The *Matching Categories* Web Part illustrates another concept that has been introduced with SharePoint Portal Server: *Categories*. Categories allow for classification of documents in such a manner that users can browse through a virtual folder hierarchy.

- The *Best Bets* Web Part shows documents that have been specifically marked by the author to match a particular term used in the query.

- The *Matching Documents* Web Part displays all documents and folders that match your query. The documents are shown in such an order that more relevant results are on top of the list. *Relevance ranking* is another important feature of SharePoint Portal Server's search technology.

You may not always see all four Web Parts discussed above. If there are not matching categories or best bets, these Web Parts will be hidden to improve the end-user experience.

SEARCHING IN WEB FOLDERS

Searching is also possible if you have an open Web Folder that points to SharePoint. In that case, you simply right-click in the Web Folder pane so the Actions menu shows up on the right side. Clicking Searching for Documents will then redirect you to the Web browser interface of the same folder. Now all the options discussed previously are available for you.

> **TIP**
> The SharePoint Search functions are not integrated with the Windows Start menu. That is, Start, Search, For Files and Folders or Start, Find, For Files and Folders (depending on your operating system) will only search in regular folders or folders within a file share. Web folders are unfortunately not included.

SEARCHING IN OFFICE XP

Office XP is tightly integrated with SharePoint Portal Server, and thus it should come as no surprise that you can search the SharePoint Portal Server workspace from within the Office applications. To do so

1. Select File, Search from the menu to open on the left side of the search pane.
2. Make sure that your workspace is included in "Selected Locations," for example by selecting "Everywhere" or your workspace under "My Network Places."
3. Enter the text you want to search for and click "Search."
4. The results will be presented in the left pane, where you can then open them directly.

This feature enables users that primarily work within Word or Excel to remain in their favorite environment, instead of switching to their Web browser.

Next to the Basic Search, you can toggle to an Advanced Search pane, in which you can use AND or OR conditions based on properties.

5

DESIGN GOALS

Knowledge discovery, as the term alludes to, is based on searching for information. For a good implementation of SharePoint Portal Server, the following major design goals must be kept in mind:

- **Timely** Unless users get their search results relatively quickly, they will not use the tool. You likely know from your own experience how annoying it is to wait for the results of a query.

- **Accurate** Search results should contain the specific information that has been searched for. That is, if you wonder why a specific document was included in the search results, you likely will not trust any of the results. Another example of inaccurate results would be references to documents that cannot be read by the user due to security constraints. Revealing the existence of information, even though the user is not allowed to see it, can have some serious business implications and must be avoided.

- **Relevant** Users will likely look at the top results first. Therefore, it is important that the most likely expected results—or what one may call the best matches—are returned first. Knowing what is relevant and what is not in the end will be determined by the user who is searching for documents. But as you will see, SharePoint Portal Server uses some advanced heuristics that generally work very well.

- **Comprehensive** If a document does match a specific search request, it must be shown as a search result. Imagine that an author is searching for his document on imaging, for example, and his document does not show up in the results! This will certainly affect his confidence in any search results returned by SharePoint Portal Server.

To these four "common sense" design goals, another three have been added that make SharePoint Portal Server a very rich, flexible, and easy to use tool within an organization:

- **Extensible** Many of the documents one would like to search for might be dispersed across the enterprise. They might be stored for example on a Web site, a file share, an Exchange Public Folder, or in a Lotus Notes Document Library. And while the place where information resides may vary, the format in which the information is provided may also be different. Providing flexible and extensible architecture therefore is essential.

- **Self-serviceable** While a typical systems administrator has excellent skills to maintain a system, this person likely will not know which information is relevant for a specific department. That is much more expected from the end-user community, the folks who understand the business. Such business information, for example, includes knowledge of the competition, or the end-user community's most frequently visited sites. It is much more efficient, and thus more cost effective, if the end-user community can directly define the information that should get indexed.

5

- **Scalable** Searching for information is done at all levels of an organization: on an individual desktop, within the department, or throughout the enterprise. Providing a scalable architecture that allows the reuse of the same technology for department and enterprise is a clear benefit.

BUILDING THE INDEX

Obviously, when dealing with documents that may reside in different places, it saves time to have a local copy of the data contained in these documents to search. This data originates from different document formats, such as Microsoft Word or HTML. Storing this data in a common, optimized format will further improve the times necessary to search. This local copy is called an index, which in effect is a database optimized for searching textual information. Such a copy of data, though, will create new challenges in terms of keeping the indexed information up to date and accurate.

→ For more information on the algorithms and approaches used to overcome the challenges of indexing, **see** "Keeping the Index Up to Date," **p. 497**.

NOTE
> Since the index is a copy of data that still continues to exist elsewhere, it requires additional storage. Due to the dedicated common index format, this size can be reduced to about 30% of all searchable text, though.

The Coordinator can specify which documents need to be indexed. And of course there is no need to specify each individual document; instead, the Coordinator can benefit from typical document storage models—a hierarchical model (such as in a file system) or a linked model where references to other documents are made (such as in a Web site). The Coordinator simply specifies a content source, which is defined by the first (or top) document and the crawl depth.

CAUTION
> Multiple content sources can be specified. Some of them may overlap, however. This might cause some problems, such as multiple references to the same document, or missing documents if one of the overlapping content sources is removed.

As we discussed previously, one major design goal of SPS was to be self-serviceable. Allowing a Coordinator to specify the content sources crawled and updated by SharePoint Portal Server might be appropriate in some cases. However, the real work of identifying and updating the content of the index is often best left to *subject matter experts*, or SMEs. SharePoint Portal Server facilitates this well. Instead of requiring a pure administrator, the department leveraging SPS may now self-service its environment—within the boundaries set by the administrator.

→ For more details on the administrator's tasks, **see** "Index Housekeeping," **p. 488**.

5

A key benefit of the SharePoint Portal Server architecture is that a clear split between the content source and the document format is made. And that comes in handy, because now the component responsible for retrieving the searchable text can be reused. For example, Microsoft PowerPoint documents can reside in different places, but the logic to "crack" the document format always remains the same.

SEPARATING DOCUMENT LOCATION AND DOCUMENT CONTENT

So let's take a closer look under the hood. For every content source from which the documents are gathered, the Microsoft Search Service process—MSSearch, or the process that maintains the index—launches a dedicated task. These tasks are implemented as a Protocol Handler, which retrieves document content through the protocol (hence the name) required to access the repository in which the document resides. Such protocols include, for example, HTTP for Web sites or MAPI for Exchange 5.5 public folders. Note the difference between a Protocol Handler and a content source—the Protocol Handler is the method used to access the content source, which is really just the basis of the data that will eventually find itself indexed.

OUT-OF-THE-BOX CONTENT SOURCES

SharePoint Portal Server provides out-of-the-box support for the following types of content sources:

- SharePoint Portal Server workspaces
- Microsoft Exchange public folders (both Exchange 2000 and Exchange 5.5)
- File shares
- Web sites
- Lotus Notes
- FTP (File Transfer Protocol) sites (included in the Resource Kit for SharePoint Portal Server)
- SharePoint Team Services (added in Service Pack 1)

NOTE

You cannot crawl secured Web sites, i.e. sites that are only accessible through the HTTPS protocol.

Each of these content sources are covered in greater detail elsewhere in this book, from different perspectives like features and capabilities (Chapter 2), to accessing content (Chapter 8), to security considerations (Chapter 11), to crawling (Chapter 18).

OUT-OF-THE-BOX IFILTERS

Now that we understand the role of Protocol Handlers, we need to understand how the searchable information is obtained. This is the responsibility of filters (also known as

IFilters) that are loaded by the Protocol Handler. That is, data pulled from the Protocol Handler is passed to the various filters, which then extract the text data from the content sources and send it off to the index. This architecture allows filters, which are responsible for the actual retrieval of text within the document, to be reused by any Protocol Handler, while the Protocol Handler knows nothing about the content. The set of document formats that are supported out-of-the-box are

- Plain text files
- Microsoft Word
- Microsoft Excel
- Microsoft PowerPoint
- HTML
- MIME (Multipurpose Internet Mail Extensions) encoded Mail Messages, as for example stored in Exchange 2000
- TIFF (Tagged Image File Format) files using *Optical Character Recognition*, or OCR, technology to retrieve textual content, for example from facsimile messages
- RTF (Rich Text Format) (included in the SharePoint Portal Server Resource Kit)
- XML (included in the SharePoint Portal Server Resource Kit)
- Various third-party data formats, as developed and supported by those third parties

NOTE Optical character recognition will only work for Latin, Cyrillic, and Greek character sets. This covers European languages but excludes Thai, Japanese, Chinese, and others (often referred to as "double-byte" languages, given their complexity).

OPTICAL CHARACTER RECOGNITION OF TIFF FILES

As OCR is an extremely resource-intensive task, it is not enabled by default. Before enabling it, ensure that you understand the impact of doing so on your particular SharePoint Portal Server deployment. Hardware resources like CPU, RAM, Pagefile, and disk space will be impacted. Work with your hardware vendor and systems integrator, if necessary, to characterize, size for, and perhaps even perform a pilot to better understand this impact. Once the magnitude of the impact is understood and addressed, enable OCR recognition by double-clicking `tiff_ocr_on.reg` in the Support\Tools directory of the Microsoft SharePoint Portal Server CD. You may also enable OCR within TIFF files by performing the following:

- From the SPS server, click Start, Run.
- Type `regedit`, and then press Enter or click OK—the Registry Editor starts.
- Navigate to HKEY_LOCAL_MACHINE\SYSTEM\CurrentControlSet\Control\ MSPaper, and right-click it.

- Click New, then click DWORD Value—a new key appears.
- Give the key the name PerformOCR.
- Right-click PerformOCR, and click Modify—a dialog box named Edit DWORD Value is displayed.
- To actually enable OCR, enter a value of 1—note that to disable OCR, type 0.
- Click OK, and then close the Registry Editor.
- At this point, it is necessary to restart the MSSearch service via the Control Panel.

Now that OCR is enabled, you can enable *automatic file rotation*, where a TIFF is rotated in memory before being scanned. This greatly increases the scanning accuracy of files that are oriented sideways or even upside down (due to being initially scanned sideways or upside down). Of course, the trade-off is an even larger impact on the server's RAM and CPU resources. Be sure to test this impact prior to implementing automatic file rotation.

GATHERING ARCHITECTURE

This search engine and index is the successor to earlier Microsoft search products, such as the Index Server and Site Server. Based on this mature technology, the results of some advanced Microsoft-driven research projects have been integrated into this enhanced search engine, including auto categorization and an improved ranking algorithm. This origin is important to know, given that the search engine is a component that is also used by Microsoft SQL Server and Microsoft Exchange 2000.

NOTE SharePoint Portal Server upgrades MSSEARCH.EXE, the process or service that largely implements the search engine. Due to dependencies, some problems exist with the uninstallation of Microsoft SQL Server or Microsoft Exchange 2000, if they are installed on the same server. Such configuration, though, is discouraged for production use due to the resource requirements for each of these products.

The following figure summarizes the core components involved when content is gathered. Access protocols, which typically include some network components and processing documents that may contain some unexpected characters, may cause a Protocol Handler or an IFilter to malfunction. To avoid this bringing down the entire search engine, these components run in separate MSSDMN processes that are started by the MSSearch process as needed.

Let's illustrate this with an example of a content source which refers to a file share. This share is crawled using the Protocol Handler registered for the "file:" protocol. For each Office document found, the Office IFilter retrieves all information that is of interest or required to find the document in a later search: the text and Office properties.

Figure 5.4
A schematic overview
of the components
that are involved in
building and maintain-
ing the index.

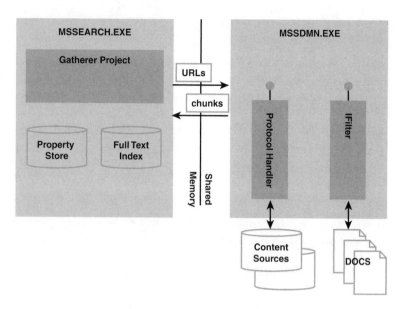

NOTE

> Protocol Handlers and filters can be written by anyone, though this is an advanced pro-
> gramming task. Filters have already been introduced with the Windows 2000 Index Server,
> and the required interfaces are documented in the Platform SDK. Third parties have suc-
> cessfully implemented filters, such as Adobe's filter for the PDF file format. The SharePoint
> Portal Server SDK includes documentation for creating a Protocol Handler. Unfortunately,
> the sample "Simple Protocol Handler" is not fully functional and is so "simple" that some
> of the important concepts such as property mapping and security are not covered at all.

SITE PATH RULES

The Coordinator can specify the *crawl depth* for content sources; for example, just the initial
or home page or all pages on that site. URLs that include a question mark are by default
excluded. You will encounter these kinds of URLs typically when you are indexing Active
Server Pages, as the portion following the question mark is passed as a query string to the
actual script that is executing. In other words, these parameterized Web pages will by
default not be indexed.

Using *Site Path Rules*, however, you can enable these types of complex links. They also
allow for a much finer granularity with respect to the Web pages that get indexed. And
finally, Site Path Rules allow defining a specific account to crawl a particular Web Site.

→ To read more about how Site Path Rules can be applied, **see** "Keeping the Index Up to Date," **p. 497**.

RESPECTING SECURITY AND OTHER CONVENTIONS

SharePoint Portal Server will typically crawl under an administrative account, so that as much information as possible can be gathered in the index. Consequently, the index may contain information that should not be visible to a specific user when the search is issued. Even though opening the real document through the URL would be prohibited through the access checks enforced by the underlying repository, the existence alone—and more so the value—of some properties would make the result set not accurate. Therefore the security information from the original source is also copied into the index. For any search result, the security information is applied and documents to which users do not have read access are filtered out.

Some Web site administrators prefer that their Web sites are not crawled. That is, they do not wish their site information to be stored in an index—and they may have good reasons for that, as their information may be highly volatile or confidential. To this end, SharePoint Portal Server will respect the conventions used in the robots.txt file on the top of the Web site (see `http://info.webcrawler.com/mak/projects/robots/norobots.html`) and the HTML META robots tag within a document (`<meta name="robots" content="no index">`).

→ For more discussion regarding the use of robots, **see** "Using Robots.txt and HTML Tags to Prevent Access," **p. 213**.

UPDATING THE INDEX

With the introduction of the index as a local copy of the real data, a new problem has been introduced: the fact that the copy may quickly become out of date. Users expect that a search is accurate, or at least as accurate as possible. This means that the chance for both missed matches as well as incorrect matches must be minimized.

Ideally, the content sources, or even better the underlying repository, would notify the index of changes. But this requires the existence of an event model that can be exploited, which is only available for the local SharePoint Portal Server content (as well as for any content on an NTFS file share). Unfortunately, most content sources will not notify the index of any changes. For this reason, SharePoint Portal Server was designed to leverage the following mechanisms:

- **Full updates**   When a full update is performed, first all information about documents that were found in this content source is removed. Then the process of gathering all content starts. For a file system, for example, the "directories" will get enumerated, while for a Web site the new URLs found in the Web pages will get added to the list of documents.

- **Incremental updates**   For an incremental update, SharePoint Portal Server will retrieve the last date of change from every document in the index. If that date is later than the last time of indexing, the information is out of date and the index will get updated. This method still is fairly resource intensive, as every indexed document is checked. But compared to the full update, clearly for large documents a substantial win is accomplished.

Obviously, the incremental update is preferred over a full update. The following exceptions should be noted, however: If you are indexing a Web site, the Incremental Update will not notice if there is no link made to a specific document. This document thus remains searchable, although references no longer exist. Only if the document is removed with the last link will the Incremental Update notice the removal, and then update its index accordingly. Another scenario where a Full Update is required is a change of some global configuration information that is applied to all documents of a particular content source. As this information doesn't originate from the original document, but is added while indexing, unchanged documents will have the old information until they get re-indexed.

- **Adaptive updates** This is the most advanced mechanism to update the index, using a heuristic approach to determine if a document is to be indexed. While incremental updates do not eliminate the need to inspect the last modified date for each document, adaptive crawling takes this one step further. The algorithm coming from Microsoft research work is based on the assumption that information that changed frequently in the past is likely to get changed again in the near future. Therefore, SharePoint Portal Server gathers statistics regarding the rate of change for each document. To ensure that the indexed information of documents that have not changed for a long while remains accurate, an incremental crawl is scheduled once in a while as well.

TIP

> Crawling for changed information is a resource-intensive operation—not only on the indexing side, but also on the remote server's side. Consider the usage of adaptive updates whenever possible. In Chapter 19, "Managing Indexing," more operational hints, such as the scheduling of updates, can be found.

USING PROPERTIES TO ENHANCE DOCUMENTS

5

Documents can be much more than just simple text files! That is, documents consist of more than just text that might be of interest to end-user searches. They also include properties such as "Creation Date" and "File Size." Moreover, Microsoft Office products have a set of predefined properties such as "Author" or "Last Saved At." Obviously, the index should understand the concept of properties, because they allow the user to formulate specific searches, such as "all documents written last week by Mr. Miles". The SharePoint Portal Server index indeed does support properties, not only of type string but also of other common basic types such as dates and integers.

How are properties being defined and how are their values specified? This is accomplished through Document Profiles, which allow you to associate existing properties or to define new properties. The actual value is specified whenever the Edit Profile dialog (see Figure 5.5) is invoked.

→ To drill down into Document Profiles, **see** "Introduction to the Workspace," **p. 220**.

Figure 5.5
In the Edit Profile dialog, properties such as "Author" or "Company" can be set.

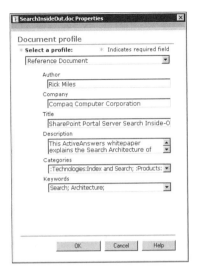

TIP

> In enhanced folders, the Edit Profile dialog is always invoked with the Check In command. The authors are therefore encouraged to provide the additional properties. On standard folders, authors need to invoke this dialog explicitly, something that is easy to forget.

The SharePoint Portal Server search will not rely just on the properties that are explicitly assigned through the Document Profile, but instead all properties that are found in a document will be placed into the index. The component that is responsible for this is the filter responsible for the particular document format. For documents of an unknown format, of course, only properties assigned in the Document Profile plus a couple of system properties, like the last modification date, are available.

So let's take one more look at the earlier example searching for "all documents written last week by Mr. Miles". It should be pointed out that in the current release of SPS, you cannot formulate the query exactly like this except through the Advanced Search Web Part (see Figure 5.6). Here, you can specify the appropriate properties and conditions.

The Advanced Search Web Part shows us that the "Author" property should contain "Miles". The exact match is not applied, as "Mr. Miles" may author information with his first name included. The "written last week" condition is now formulated as "Created in the last 7 days".

Figure 5.6
Notice the modified search condition in the Advanced Search Web Part.

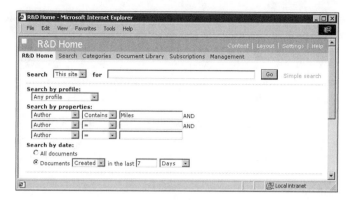

This little example also illustrates that properties may affect the relevance of a search result. If the user—being lazy—just enters "Miles" in the simple search dialog, any "Miles" in the index will be matched. This will not only include references made in other documents to Mr. Miles's work, but may also contain documents that refer, for example, to "five miles of cabling". Still, the simple search will return documents written by Mr. Miles early in the list. This is because SharePoint Portal Server is smart enough to know that a match with the Author property is more relevant than a match within the document. This ability of SPS is referred to as *rank coercion*. It is interesting to note that the rank of search results (based on specific document properties that likely contain useful information) can be changed. For detailed information on how to modify rank coercion, refer to the SharePoint Portal Server SDK.

Though a match with a string property often indicates a better match, this is not always true; in fact some properties should not be included at all. One such property is the type of a document (defined as content-class), which should become clear by the following example: When looking for the word "Calendar", clearly items of type "Calendar" should be excluded. This feature is called *property weighting*, or more often, *even attribute weighting*.

5

TIP

Property weighting only applies to text searches. Boolean or numeric conditions cannot be weighted; they are either true or false.

KEYWORDS

Keywords are a great mechanism that allow authors classifying their documents to add one or more keywords that characterize the content. For a Sales and Marketing department, the list of keywords could, for example, include all product names. This allows authors to select the appropriate keywords for documents that refer to one or more products.

As with any list type property, the Coordinator is responsible for defining the list of keywords. The Coordinator also can specify whether the list of keywords is fixed or whether the list is extensible. In the first case, the author can only choose from the list of defined keywords; in the latter case, new keywords can be defined. These new keywords, however, will not show up for other documents. This can cause similar keywords to be used for the same purpose. An example could be "Sales Report" and "Sales-Report".

If you don't know a good set of keywords, allow authors to add their own keywords. By monitoring the usage, you can populate the keyword dictionary with commonly used terms. In cases where almost identical keywords are used, you should change them all to one term. Consider restricting the usage to the list of defined keywords as soon as you feel comfortable. This will ensure consistent usage.

Obviously, a keyword match is of high relevance, as the author explicitly tagged the document with this information. Try to keep this list short and manageable so authors can select the correct keyword quickly.

CATEGORIES—A DIFFERENT VIEW ON INFORMATION

Users typically will search for documents if they know what they are looking for, but do not know where to find it. But there is also the case where users prefer to browse for information, or where the designer of the portal wants to direct users to the information they seek through an organized hierarchy of topics. For this, a mechanism is needed to structure the information in a different, intuitive manner. An important aspect here is that these users are typically not the authors of the information—otherwise, they would know where the information could be found in the first place. Rather, these users are typically readers.

This is where classification of information into categories can become very important, since categories allow consumers of content to browse for information rather than search. Categories are typically represented as a tree with main categories and subcategories. Setting up this tree requires knowledge of the type of content that is to be categorized, as well as knowledge of the target audience, the readers of information. This kind of knowledge is not typical for an administrator with a strong IT background, but rather for a librarian who understands both the content and the principles of categorization. This is a profession that existed well before any computer—any organization found in a library is built around the same principles of categorization.

SharePoint Portal Server provides support for such a category tree (see Figure 5.7), which can be browsed by the end user through the categories dashboard or through dedicated Web Folders.

Figure 5.7
The Categories dashboard shows the category tree of an IT Research and Development portal.

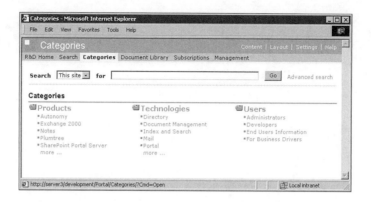

DEFINING A CATEGORY TREE

The setup of the category tree is done by the Coordinator of the workspace, not the administrator. To create categories, the Coordinator needs to do the following:

1. Open the Categories Web Folder of the workspace.
2. Right-click New and select Category.
3. It will now take a little while until a folder is created which will be named "New Category."
4. Rename that folder to reflect the desired category.

To create subcategories, navigate first to the correct parent folder before the new category is created.

> **CAUTION**
>
> Out of the box, SharePoint Portal Server installs a sample category tree with terms such as "Category 1." As this most certainly does not meet your categorization scheme, you may wish to delete these categories before you add any content, to avoid confusion.

The preceding steps will create a new category, but you should consider specifying a little more information to enhance the user experience. This can be done using the properties page of the category folder, as seen in Figure 5.8.

> **TIP**
>
> If you specify an image, make sure that it does not exceed 32 × 32 pixels. Otherwise it will overlap with the description on the Categories dashboard.

5

Figure 5.8
Fill in all details in the
Categories Properties
dialog to see a result
as in Figure 5.9.

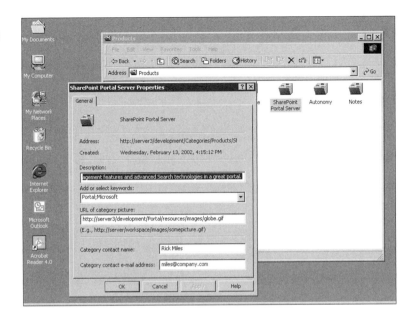

Figure 5.9
The category dash-
board with the details
as specified in Figure
5.8.

The description field will be shown as a tool tip in the portal whenever you hover over the category. But more importantly, if a category matches a specific query, the description will be included in the results pane. Users that are not familiar with the category can see in a quick glance if this is relevant to the category tree. Associating an image with a category will cause a user browsing through the category tree to see these images. Also, the ability to specify keywords for a category makes it possible for users to find a differently named category should a keyword match occur. Finally, entering a contact with an email address allows the reader to comment, for example, on the usage or value of a particular category.

TIP

> Start with a simple category tree. Keep the end user in mind when you design your categories; deeply nested categories, for example, are generally not appreciated. If you cannot resist implementing a complex tree, keep in mind that there is a limit of about 550 categories that can be defined for a given workspace.

Categories are stored in SharePoint Portal Server in the order that they are created. This may be confusing to the end user when he or she needs to select a category from this unsorted tree. Fortunately, the SharePoint Portal Server Resource Kit (`http://www.microsoft.com/sharepoint/techinfo/reskit/category_sort.asp`) includes a tool to sort categories alphabetically. One way of automating a solution to this problem includes scheduling a task to re-sort all categories on a daily or other regular basis.

ASSIGNING CATEGORIES

Once a category tree is defined, you can assign an individual document to zero, one, or more categories. This is done by the Author through the Web Folder's Properties dialog of the document. To assign a category to a document, do the following:

1. Ensure that the document is checked out. You can see if a document is checked out by looking for the little icon representing a pen. If the document is not checked out, right-click on the document and select the Check Out option.

2. Right-click on the document and select the Properties option.

3. Select the Search and Categories tab (see Figure 5.11).

4. Select the appropriate categories from the drop-down box.

Figure 5.10
When you click on the categories drop-down box, the selected and available categories will be shown.

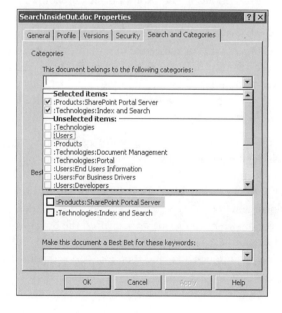

In the previous screenshot, you also see that SharePoint Portal Server can suggest categories. This comes into play once you have enabled auto categorization, which will be discussed next.

Categories are implemented as multi-valued properties, using the colon as a special separator such that a tree view can be built. In Figure 5.11, for example, you see ":Technologies:Index and Search", where "Index and Search" is a subcategory of "Technologies" as shown in Figure 5.8.

TIP

> If you are expecting frequent use of categories, place the category property on the Document Profile. This allows the author to define the categories during check in. This is also the only means by which you can specify categories through the browser.

AUTO CATEGORIZATION

For a useful implementation of categories, you need to be aware of two important aspects. First, as outlined above, the set of categories and subcategories must be defined. Once a categorization tree is defined, the second challenge arises—the actual categorization of content. Many years ago, this was done manually, by asking someone to read the information before applying the correct categories. This process is obviously easy to automate by simply defining a dedicated category property that gets filled in whenever necessary. But regardless of manual or automated processes, it is a tedious, time-consuming task to categorize a lot of information.

This is where auto categorization comes into play, another feature of SharePoint Portal Server originating from research out of Microsoft. This feature allows you to define a sample set of categorized documents that is used to train the auto categorization engine. After training, SharePoint Portal Server then automatically assigns categories to any documents that get indexed. For documents that are stored within the workspace, the Coordinator can choose to either propose categories or assign them automatically to documents that get published. But probably even more powerful is the ability to automatically assign categories to external documents. The proposal of categories is obviously no choice for external documents, because the publishing process is outside the control of SharePoint Portal Server.

The first step for auto categorization is the definition of a set of training documents, for which categories are assigned manually. Obviously, automatically assigned categories match best if as many examples as possible can be provided, taking into account that documents belong to multiple categories. Training categories will result ultimately in a list of words that best distinguish documents in one category versus documents in other categories. Consequently, the variety or sheer number of words within the document is important. Therefore, you should strive to use longer, primarily textual documents—spreadsheets, for example, typically don't contain much text, and therefore serve as poor training documents.

NOTE

> If you want to include external content in the training exercise, you can use Web Links, so that the document itself does not need to get imported to SharePoint Portal Server.

In practice, you will probably need to train iteratively, in particular for external content.

→ For more information on working with auto categorization, **see** "Managing Categories," **p. 319**.

CATEGORIES VERSUS KEYWORDS

Categories and keywords have some similar characteristics. Both are used for the classification of documents. Documents can be simultaneously assigned to several different categories and keywords, too.

One difference, though, is how both are presented to the end user. A user can browse through the category tree, both through the Web Folder interface and through the portal's dedicated categories dashboard. Categories thus allow presenting a folder structure for readers without changing the existing folder structure. Keywords are not shown that explicitly on the user interface. Moreover, they are not organized in a tree structure, even though one easily could define such a structure using conventions similar to the categories.

Categories are solely defined by the Coordinator. To create a new category, the Coordinator must be consulted. The list of keywords can be kept unrestricted, such that any author can add new keywords.

In larger deployment scenarios, categories will not be available on the enterprise dashboard if the content is propagated from dedicated indexing servers. Unlike keywords, categories will not be included in the propagated index. They are thus not available in an environment that almost exclusively consists of readers, an environment that is ideal for categories.

BEST BETS

Documents can be tagged by the author as a *Best Bet* for a particular keyword or category, such that if users search for this term they will see this document in a prevailing position on top of all other search results. This feature allows content organizers to determine what is important in their workspace. Taking the earlier example of keywords that represent the set of products that a company offers, one overview document per product could be marked as Best Bet. Thus, when searching for a particular product, this overview will attract the user's attention, while all other references will also remain available in the "Matching Documents" Web Part.

To assign a category, follow the steps previously outlined in the "Assigning Categories" section of this chapter.

Then select a category Best Bet. Note that this works differently for keywords; if you are selecting a Best Bet keyword you will not see it in the list of regular keywords.

→ For details on using and configuring Best Bets, **see** "Category Best Bets," **p. 318**.

LANGUAGE DEPENDENCIES

One important aspect of dealing with text and text processing is that text is language dependent. This means that text must be treated differently based on the language in which it is written. Differences include, for example, word separation, commonly used words, word expansion and replacement, and word stemming. SharePoint Portal Server provides this kind of linguistic support for the following languages:

- Chinese (both simplified and traditional)
- Dutch
- English
- French
- German
- Italian
- Japanese
- Korean
- Spanish
- Swedish
- Thai

The set of languages for which linguistic support is provided is larger than the set of languages for which a translated SharePoint Portal Server user interface is available. Currently the user interface is available in English, French, German, Japanese, Italian, and Spanish.

If linguistic support is missing, SharePoint Portal Server will fall back on some language-neutral default implementation. Unfortunately, the interfaces that are used to provide linguistic support are not documented. The list of languages therefore cannot be extended.

WORD BREAKING

In western languages, words are typically separated by spaces. But other characters such as the hyphen, semicolon, and the colon serve as separators. The separation, called word breaking, is less simple in some far eastern languages. For Japanese, a mapping to a common character set is implemented, such that the same words written in one document or the other remain the same. SharePoint Portal Server provides a number of word breaking modules. Interestingly, though, it is not possible to create custom word breakers.

For example, searching for the term "server-based" (without single or double quotes) will also include documents that contain either the word "server" or the word "based". Luckily, relevance ranking pops in—clearly the existence of both words next to each other is ranked higher.

TIP

> To exclude matching only with a single word, you need to indicate that this is a phrase. This is done by including double quotes around the search term.

WORD STEMMING

Word stemming regards looking at the roots of a word, to include variations of the word in search results. This is not a simple process when different languages are involved. The grammar of languages differs substantially; for example the rules to express past or future tense can be quite different. Other rules may involve the usage of prefixes or suffixes. To illustrate the complexity just for the English language, think about the following:

In English, the past tense is generally formed by adding the suffix "-ed", such as "jumped". But some verbs, such as "go" (with past tense forms "went" and "gone"), don't follow this simple rule. Other languages will require other rules, making word stemming the most complex linguistic capability that is provided in SharePoint Portal Server.

CAUTION

> SharePoint Portal Server only supports word stemming for verbs—plural forms of a noun will not be matched with a singular form (for example, babies will not match baby).

Many European languages embrace the idea of accents—which typically do not come into play when typing on a keyboard. Mapping accented characters to the common underlying character therefore will produce more hits.

NOISE WORDS

Some words are very common in a particular language and therefore will match with almost every document. These words would fill up the index with useless information and are therefore filtered. In other words, they are considered *noise*, and thus known as *noise words*. In an English document, you will frequently find the noise word "these". But if the document was in German, you should not exclude this word from the index—"these" means "thesis," a quite specific word when searching science-related information.

THESAURUS

Another linguistic feature built in to SharePoint Portal Server is a thesaurus. It allows the substitution or expansion (the usage of synonyms) of words at query time. This feature allows the user to use an acronym such as "MS", which will get replaced with "Microsoft"; or to use the term "IE" synonymously with the term "Internet Explorer".

NOTE

> If an acronym is commonly used, such as "MS" in a software engineering environment, you can use it as a synonym, because many documents will also use the acronym.

5

To bypass the thesaurus, the user can specify a phrase match, including the term or terms in double quotes.

The terms in the thesaurus should be specific to the terminology that is used within the organization; therefore the thesaurus is by default empty.

→ To learn more about customization of the thesaurus, **see** "Customizing the Thesaurus," **p. 492**.

INDEX PROPAGATION

By now you should understand that building up an index is a resource-intensive task—not only on the machine that gathers all the information, but also on the remote systems from which information is indexed. Wouldn't it be useful to combine different indices to set up an even bigger index, or to dedicate a machine to do just indexing?

That is exactly what SharePoint Portal Server provides. With the creation of a new workspace, you can specify that the workspace is just used to crawl data. Document management and portal functionality are disabled to free up resources for indexing. Though this is a per-workspace option, it will typically be applied to dedicated servers, as the idea is to split the load of indexing, document management, and the portal across different physical machines. Therefore, you will come across the term *Dedicated Content Indexing Servers*, or *Dedicated Index Servers*.

SEARCHING FOR DATA

At this point we have a decent understanding of how the index is built up and what kind of properties are available to support searching for data. So it's now time to dive a little more into the search architecture from a query perspective, as searching for data is the reason for building up the index in the first place.

As a Knowledge Discovery tool, SharePoint Portal Server has been designed around the idea of a Web portal. Not only the browser, but also the access through Web Folders and Office XP make use of the HTTP Web protocol and extensions such as WebDAV, which reside on top of it.

NOTE

> In its origin, the Web was designed to browse for information, not for authoring information or to facilitate search in a rich manner. For this reason, Microsoft has actively worked together with the Internet Engineering Task Force to extend the HTTP protocol, resulting in the WebDAV (Web Distributed Authoring and Versioning) protocol, documented in RFC 2518. WebDAV includes a standardized set of operations that are optimized for authoring documents on the Web, like copying and pasting files, moving files and creating directories, and working with document properties. WebDAV makes the Web aware of properties, but unfortunately does not provide for a structured query on these properties.

The SharePoint Portal Server–specific WebDAV protocol is implemented in a dedicated ISAPI extension, the extension mechanism used by Microsoft's Internet Information Server. If a search request is issued, the request will be passed to the search engine. The query will be analyzed, and if some full-text operations are included, word breakers will break down the words, noise words will be filtered out, word stemming will be applied, and finally a lookup in the thesaurus will be done before the index is questioned. This process is illustrated in Figure 5.11.

TIP

> The language dependencies apply both at index and at query time. If, for example, a German document is indexed, "these" is not filtered out, as it is not a noise word. But if you are querying from an English browser, you will never find the word "these", simply because it will be taken out, being an English noise word.

Figure 5.11
This figure shows the components that are involved with an SPS query. It complements the architecture displayed earlier in Figure 5.4.

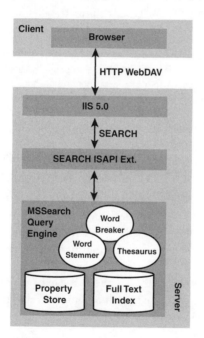

RANKING RESULTS

In response to a user query, it is important to return the relevant information first. This can become a challenge, as user queries tend to be fairly short. Typically only a few terms are specified, and therefore returning meaningful results is certainly a challenge. But again, the work of Microsoft's Research Labs comes to the rescue. They have developed an algorithm known as an *Okapi ranking* or *probabilistic ranking* that weights the frequency of words relative to document length and their overall occurrence in the system. For example, when searching for the words "Windows" and "Paint" on the Microsoft Developer Network,

"Paint" is more relevant than "Windows", while on a construction company site, "Windows" may be more relevant. Thus documents that frequently contain the word "Windows" will get ranked higher for a SharePoint Portal Server implementation of a construction department than for a software engineering department.

Another element in relevance ranking is that a complete phrase match is a much better result than just the appearance of all or even only some of the words. To specify a phrase, you enclose the phrase in double quotes. Leaving them off will still find all occurrences of the phrase, but also the individual words. As any phrase match is of higher relevance, you likely will not notice much of a difference other than that the number of returned results is much higher without quotes than with quotes. Just to illustrate that with an example, if you are looking for the term "Computer Industry", enclosing the phrase within quotes will ensure that you find just documents that contain that phrase. Leaving the quotes off, you also would find a document that discusses "How a Computer increases the productivity in any industry," but that document would show up later in the results due to the lower rank.

NOTE

If you are interested in some background on the advanced research work that Microsoft is doing, resulting in such valuable extensions as the probabilistic ranking algorithm, take a look at http://research.microsoft.com. More research information on the Okapi algorithm may also be found at http://research.microsoft.com/users/robertson/papers/trec_papers.htm.

SUBSCRIPTIONS—A WAY TO SEARCH INTO THE FUTURE

5

Searching for information is valuable, but wouldn't it be better if the system could find the information that you are interested in whenever that information becomes available in the future? Microsoft has implemented a Persisted Query System that allows you to register for such searches, which could consist of simple modifications of folders or documents, additions to a category, or even complex custom searches. In fact, the queries that can be registered with the PQS system are equivalent to the queries that can be expressed in a regular search. As discussed earlier in this chapter, the Search Summary Web Part provides the interface to subscribe to such a search.

If a new document matches the persisted search query in a subscription, the match will be shown in the subscription's Web Part. Further, if the user provides an email address with the subscription also, an email notification will be sent to the user.

The benefit of the Persisted Query System is that it searches every new or changed document only once for matching queries. This is far more efficient than discovering changes through a regularly scheduled search—in fact, most people will not do these regular searches and thus will certainly miss key updates to information. On the other hand, a very general query will cause the subscriptions to fire frequently. Therefore, the Coordinator can set some quotas on the number of subscriptions per workspace and per user, and the number of results per notification.

SUMMARY

SharePoint Portal Server offers a very powerful, mature search technology that makes it an effective Knowledge Discovery tool within any organization. The architecture allows searching for information in *any store*, indexing new content via protocol handlers in *many formats*, applying filters to retrieve the text from a variety of front-end and client access methods, and much more. Its feature set is robust, the result of years of research and experience with older Microsoft products. For additional detailed information on crawling content sources and managing indexing, refer to Chapters 18 and 19, respectively. If you would like to switch gears for a while, though, read on through the next few chapters as we cover SharePoint Portal Server from planning, design, and administration perspectives.

5

SharePoint Planning, Design, and Administration

CHAPTER 6

CAPACITY PLANNING WITHIN YOUR ENVIRONMENT

In this chapter

UNDERSTANDING THE REQUIREMENTS

When planning for maximum capacity, it is important to determine the business requirements for how SharePoint Portal Server will be used within your environment. SharePoint Portal Server administrators should not only plan for the current state requirements; future state requirements should also be considered. In previous chapters, we learned that SharePoint Portal Server is a flexible and efficient solution that can provide centralized portal services to thousands of users across your enterprise. Chapter 5 provided an overview of indexing and searching content. Once content sources are established, SharePoint Portal Server crawls, or reads through, content to create an index of the content.

After the indexes are created, you can then use SharePoint Portal Server to search for desired content across your enterprise. Decisions must be made as to whether a single SharePoint Portal Server will be sufficient to perform all tasks, including indexing and searching. While it is possible for one server to perform all tasks, the performance might not be acceptable, and you will likely consider distributing the tasks across multiple servers. Another consideration is to deploy SharePoint Portal Server across multiple sites to reduce the performance impact to the network. In this chapter, we will discuss some of the technical considerations for capacity planning within your SharePoint Portal Server environment.

CPU, network, and storage costs are closely linked to specific server-related tasks. It is important to plan the configuration that provides an optimal user experience, while understanding how to monitor key resources and add additional components as the demand of the server increases. There are many issues to consider, such as

- What is the total number of concurrent expected users for SharePoint Portal Server? What is the maximum user activity your server can support?
- What is the expected number of users that will be using document management features? How many documents do you expect to maintain?
- How many users will use SharePoint Portal Server primarily for searching?
- How many workspaces do you expect to maintain on a single server?

NOTE Having more than 15 workspaces per server is not recommended. Adding workspaces to a single server may cause unacceptable server load and user performance due to increased user activity.

- When is an index too large for efficient propagation? Excessive amounts of documents within an index will take longer for the index to propagate to a dedicated search server.
- How much storage will be required? If document versioning activity is high, hard disk space is consumed at a fairly rapid pace.
- Is it necessary to consider multiple servers, while dedicating individual servers to specific tasks? If multiple content sources will be enabled, you should consider dedicating one server for searching, while another server is dedicated to creating and updating indexes.

- What content will need to be crawled and included in the index? For example, you may want to crawl file servers, external Web sites, Exchange 5.5 and Exchange 2000 servers, Lotus Notes databases, and other SharePoint Portal Servers.

Reviewing the Number of Servers

The challenge is to determine how many servers are needed, whether services should be partitioned across multiple servers within the same site, and whether multiple servers should be distributed across various geographical locations.

It is always a good idea to start with a single site portal and then scale the solution to address specific departmental or business unit requirements.

You want to start considering multiple sites if your organization has large groups of users spread out across many sites, separated by a slow network link. Another factor that may impact your decision to consider multiple sites is if your solution requires separate functional goals. For example, some large sites may require their own search server to allow acceptable performance for enterprise searches. Furthermore, some departments or business units may require their own divisional workspace or team collaboration environment. While a single server can accommodate multiple workspaces on the same server, individual servers may be needed to accommodate acceptable performance. Lastly, some departments or business units may require their own server due to logical or political organizational requirements.

With SharePoint Portal Server, you could deploy a solution across many servers and many sites and link them together to provide one integrated enterprise portal solution. These multiple sites could be deployed across your distributed enterprise, and then one master search portal could be deployed to search internal portal sites, Web sites, file servers, and other resources that are capable of being crawled.

You should also consider multiple sites if single site boundaries are exceeded. In general, a single SharePoint Portal Server can store up to one million document versions. You should carefully plan your category hierarchy to make sure the one million document version limit is not exceeded. SharePoint Portal Server can crawl up to 3.5 million documents to be included in the index. It is recommended that you consider multiple servers dedicated for crawling content if the site is a large search-oriented site. Doing this will reduce the load on the search server and allow optimal performance for searches, without being impacted by a performance degradation of the crawling process in the background.

Server Deployment Recommendations

This section discusses various deployment recommendations, as they relate to minimums and maximums for SharePoint Portal Server. We learned earlier that most companies start their portal deployment with a single site workspace with a single dashboard view for end users. We then grow the portal based on the business requirements of your solution. As you plan your deployment, it is important to consider the following growth limitations.

SINGLE SERVER OR SMALL SITES

For a single site, you should consider that a single SharePoint Portal Server is limited to one million document versions. When planning your deployment, you should consider the number of levels in the category hierarchy to ensure this limitation is not exceeded.

In addition to the limitations of the document versions, a single SharePoint Portal Server is limited to crawling 3.5 million documents. For enterprise solutions that require crawling this number of documents, you would normally employ multiple servers dedicated to the crawling process. When multiple servers are used for crawling content, the server dedicated to searching is less consumed, and therefore better performance can be expected. Lastly, each server has a licensing limitation of 10,000 users per server. However, whether a single server can support 10,000 users simultaneously is a planning task that requires extensive due diligence and performance testing.

MULTIPLE SERVERS OR LARGE SITES

Once a single server solution is deployed and operational, you should continually monitor and manage the growth signals, which may indicate that additional sites are required. Reasons to consider additional sites are

- Enterprise or business unit goal differences.
- Users across many sites; link speeds between sites not adequate.

We learned earlier in this chapter how SharePoint Portal Server could be deployed across many individual sites and aggregated together logically through a single master portal site. The solution requires several servers, some of which are dedicated to crawling, some dedicated to document management, and others dedicated to searching. Indexes from the crawled content are propagated to the search server in order to minimize the impact on server resources for having to create the indexes.

6 EXAMPLE SERVER SCENARIOS

In this section, we will describe four real-world scenarios. The first is a small single-server site that uses SharePoint Portal Server primarily for document management. The second scenario is an example of another small single-server intranet site with limited document needs and a primary purpose of searching for desired content across the organization. In both these examples, a single server is being used. However, this does not necessarily represent best practices or a recommended strategy. Rather, it represents certain real-world scenarios that may exist, where small sites with limited budgets could accommodate both the document management and search functionality on the same server. The third and fourth examples discuss the use of SharePoint Portal Server across multiple sites. This third example discusses a need for a large portal search site, but does not have tremendous document management requirements. The fourth example discusses a scenario with requirements for enterprise search capability and integrated functionality of multiple document management servers.

SINGLE-SERVER DOCUMENT MANAGEMENT PORTAL

Within this example, we assume that a SharePoint Portal Server was deployed to address the business requirements of a single business unit. The primary focus of this business unit is to enable a single-server intranet site for document management. In addition to the document management, the server will be used to crawl a small amount of content from other content sources. As stated, the primary purpose of the site is to enable the integrated document management functionality, such as creating documents, managing multiple versions of documents, routing and approval, and so on. Our example assumes that we also enabled an external crawl for the Web sites of several of the business unit's competitors. The single server provides one workspace for all content and exposes the content as a dashboard customized for a particular business unit. This site could be expanded to accommodate other needs of the organization.

Figure 6.1
Single departmental solution with indexed content to file servers and Exchange public folders.

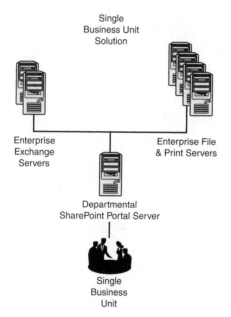

Single Business Unit Solution

Enterprise Exchange Servers

Enterprise File & Print Servers

Departmental SharePoint Portal Server

Single Business Unit

6

SINGLE-SERVER INTRANET SEARCH PORTAL

This scenario assumes that we have several business units that are accessing a single intranet search portal to search for desired content. The search content linked to the portal is not necessarily tied to a single business unit. In contrast to scenario #1, this scenario includes limited document management functionality, but has a heavy focus on being the single site for searching content across the enterprise as well as external to the intranet site.

End users from various departments can access the site to search for files stored on file servers, Lotus Notes databases, Exchange public folders, and database servers. The portal is also used to post essential enterprise-related communications, such as new customer account status, essential competitor news, new product announcements, and other key sales and customer satisfaction-related information. Like scenario #1 previously, scenario #2 could easily be hosted on a single server to store the content sources, while providing a dashboard site to expose the workspace for all end users. The site includes extensive indexed content from various internal servers within the enterprise. End users access the site to search for this content. The solution includes limited searching for content on Internet sites, as well as limited document management needs. If this solution also had requirements for managing a large amount of documents, we would likely need to include an additional server and dedicate one server to document management and the other to indexing and searching content.

Figure 6.2
Single Search Portal site with indexed content of file servers, Notes databases, and Exchange public folders.

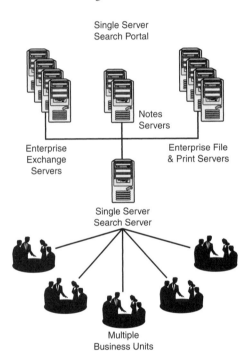

Single Server Search Portal

Notes Servers

Enterprise Exchange Servers

Enterprise File & Print Servers

Single Server Search Server

Multiple Business Units

MULTIPLE SERVER SEARCH PORTAL

Once your SharePoint Portal Server solution requirements outgrow a single server due to lack of acceptable performance during peak periods, you should consider partitioning services across multiple servers. You should also consider multiple servers if you have a very large number of users, or a large amount of documents that need to be managed. Scenario #3 assumes a set of requirements in which a SharePoint Portal Server solution is enabled as a single portal search for a large enterprise. For this particular multi-server solution, document management is being utilized, but is considered very limited, as the enterprise portal's main function is enterprise search.

Our solution will use one server dedicated to searching, and an additional server performing the role of creating and updating indexes. In our sample scenario, we have a need for searching content on several file servers, Exchange 2000 public folders, and several existing intranet sites. We have one server dedicated to indexing that creates an index of all required content. Once the index is created, the index server will propagate the index to the server dedicated to searching. This index can be propagated immediately after it is generated, or if network traffic is excessive, the index could be scheduled for propagation to occur during non-peak hours. Once the search server receives the propagated index, the search server provides the required dashboard site. The search server is the home of the workspace and is where content is stored. However, the server dedicated to indexing only includes indexes for content sources.

CAUTION

> The reason we want to consider two separate servers in our solution is due to the fact that creating an index of content stored outside the workspace is extremely CPU-intensive.

Figure 6.3
SharePoint Portal
Server solution with
dedicated search and
index servers.

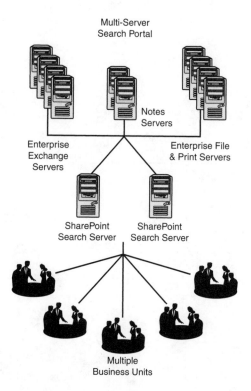

MULTIPLE SERVER MULTI-PURPOSE PORTAL

Out last example includes a best practice approach for a multi-server, multi-site situation in which a majority of SharePoint Portal Server's features and capabilities will be utilized. This enterprise solution assumes that a large number of documents will need to be managed and aggregated from many other SharePoint Portal Servers. In addition, the enterprise needs a single portal site for searching for content across the enterprise. We assume a large corporation, in which each department has their own document management servers. Our solution also assumes that we have multiple servers crawling the distributed document management servers, and propagating indexes to a single server dedicated to searching. To accommodate these requirements, we created a master portal site at our corporate office in Houston, Texas. At this site, we created three new SharePoint Portal Servers. The first server is a server dedicated to searching. We then created a second server dedicated to creating and updating indexes. The third server is a very large server dedicated to document management. This server has an amount of storage space carefully planned to be able to handle multiple versions of documents.

NOTE

The corporate office has more than ten thousand users, which is why we created a separate document management server. All remote sites also have their own document management server, and some sites have an additional server that crawls these remote site servers, propagating indexes to the centralized search server in Houston.

Figure 6.4
Multi-purpose portal solution with elements of search, index, and document management servers exposed through centralized master portal site.

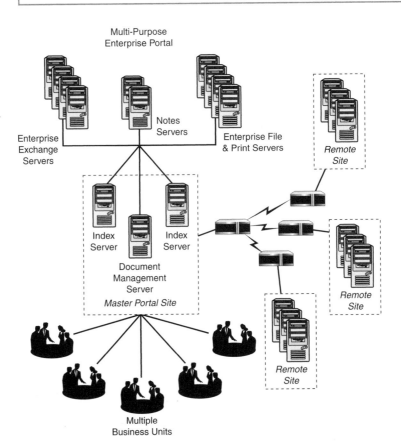

6

PLANNING REQUIRED SERVER HARDWARE

Planning the required hardware is an essential step in the pre-deployment process. The most important hardware components to plan for are the speed of the CPU, amount of RAM, and hard disk space. SharePoint Portal Server is a CPU-intensive application. Failure to provide sufficient CPU resources will result in unacceptable server response times, which will lead to a less than satisfied user experience. CPU planning should accommodate user loads during peak and non-peak periods without impacting the users' server response time. Another important hardware component is RAM. Failure to provide sufficient RAM will also result in unacceptable server response times. Lastly, you need sufficient hard disk space to accommodate multiple document versions. Failure to plan for sufficient disk space will result in an inability to search for or save documents to the portal.

Many organizations struggle to plan for performance and scalability requirements. The challenge is that it is difficult to forecast how the site will be adopted by your end user community. Once the initial site is deployed, it is important to monitor the resources of the site and how well the current hardware specifications are handling the load. The resources to monitor are addressed later in this chapter.

Table 6.1 discusses the important deployment metrics that are needed to effectively plan your hardware for your portal environment.

TABLE 6.1 PLANNING DEPLOYMENT METRICS

Deployment Metric	Description
Number of Users	Total number of potential users for a site.
Percent of active users per day	A percentage of the total users that may actually use the dashboard site during a given day. The range is 10–100%, but is often overestimated. The average is usually approximately 30%.
Number of operations per active user per day	The number of operations that a typical user performs on the dashboard site during a given day. The number usually ranges from 1 to 10.
Number of hours per day	The total number of hours in which portal activity occurs. The range is from 12 to 24 hours.
Peak factor	An approximate number that estimates the extent at which the peak dashboard site throughput exceeds the average throughput. The number range is from 1 to 4.

NOTE

One may be able to estimate the required number of active operations per user per day by analyzing the Web server log of another portal server within the environment.

NOTE

> When analyzing the Web server log, one should only review page views, not site hits. The reason is that site hits are often much higher than Web page views.

The preceding deployment metrics are used in the following formula to provide the peak throughput in operations per second:

(number of users × percent of active users per day × number of operations per active user per day × Peak factor) / (360,000 × number of hours per day)

NOTE

> Within the formula, the number 360,000 is determined by 100 (for percent conversion, so you don't have to convert the percentage to a decimal) × 60 (number of minutes in an hour) × 60 (number of seconds in a minute).

NOTE

> HTTP is the communication protocol between a client and the SharePoint Portal Server. HTTP is a connectionless protocol, and the number of concurrent users cannot be accurately measured. This is why Operations per second is an essential measurement component.

CALCULATING A SMALL SITE

Let's assume that a small business unit consists of 1,200 total users. Of the 1,200 users, one particular business unit consists of approximately 300 users who use the site on a daily basis. As a result, this particular business unit represents 25% of the active users of the site. We estimate that the active users average 10 operations per day with a peak factor of 4. The hours this site is active is estimated at 12 hours per day. In addition to the 300 active users, 800–900 users hit the site on an occasional basis. Table 6.2 below shows the deployment metrics that will be used in the calculation formula:

TABLE 6.2 SMALL SITE CALCULATION EXAMPLE

Deployment Metric	Quantity
Number of users	1,200
Percent of active users per day	25
Number of operations per active user per day	10
Number of hours per day	12
Peak factor	4

Assuming these metrics, the anticipated peak throughput is .28 operations per second.

$(1200 \times 25 \times 10 \times 4) / (360{,}000 \times 12) = 0.28$

The above site could be accommodated with a server such as a 500MHz Pentium III with 512 megabytes (MB) of RAM.

CALCULATING A MEDIUM-SIZED SITE

Another example is a medium-sized portal consisting of a total of 5,000 users, 1,000 of which are active users. The percent of active users per day is thus 20%. We estimate that the active users will average 6 operations per day with a peak factor of 3. The hours this site is active is estimated at 14 hours per day. Table 6.3 below shows the deployment metrics that will be used in the calculation formula:

TABLE 6.3 MEDIUM SIZE SITE CALCULATION EXAMPLE	
Deployment Metric	**Quantity**
Number of users	5000
Percent of active users per day	20
Number of operations per active user per day	6
Number of hours per day	14
Peak factor	3

Assuming these metrics, the anticipated peak throughput is .36 operations per second.

$(5000 \times 20 \times 6 \times 3) / (360{,}000 \times 14) = .3571431.1852$

The above site could be accommodated with a server such as a 500MHz Pentium III with 1 gigabyte (GB) of RAM.

CALCULATING A LARGE SEARCH SITE

The last example is a large search site portal, consisting of approximately 20,000 users. The portal site is used to search over content that was crawled from other sources across the organization. The site is not used to manage a large number of documents, and user loads are distributed throughout the day due to time zone differences. The 20,000 users are infrequent portal site users, considering this is not the main portal site they access. We will assume the number of active users is 15% that will average 4 operations per day with a peak factor of 2. However, we will assume this site gets activity approximately 20 hours out of a 24-hour day. Table 6.4 below shows the deployment metrics that will be used in the calculation formula:

6

TABLE 6.4   LARGE SITE CALCULATION EXAMPLE

Deployment Metric	Quantity
Number of users	20,000
Percent of active users per day	15
Number of operations per active user per day	4
Number of hours per day	20
Peak factor	2

Assuming these metrics, the anticipated peak throughput is .33 operations per second.

$$(20000 \times 15 \times 4 \times 2) / (360{,}000 \times 20) = .333333$$

The above site could be accommodated with a server such as a 700MHz Pentium III with 2 gigabytes (GB) of RAM.

NOTE

> It should also be noted that in order to enhance the performance of the server dedicated to searching content, it is recommended to consider a separate dedicated server for crawling content. Usually, a good time to consider a dedicated crawling server is when the search site reaches a threshold of 100,000 documents.

PLANNING THE CLIENT

Unlike the server, there is not an individual client application for SharePoint end users. The portal is exposed to end users as a dashboard site, and users access the site using a Web browser. End users can perform a majority of the portal search-related tasks using the Web browser. The client components are an extension of the Windows Explorer and Microsoft Office applications. We know that documents are stored within the workspace. Within the workspace, we have a collection of management folders, documents, content sources, and so on. Content that needs to be managed from the workspace using Windows Explorer requires installation of the client components on a computer running Windows 2000.

→ To learn more about installing client components, **see** "Installing the Client Components," **p. 167**.

Administrators can assign specific roles to end users, which specifies what functions the end users can perform within the workspace.

→ To learn more security roles, **see** "Permissions," **p. 281**.

Within the client based applications such as Office XP, end users can create documents and post them to the portal using integrated menu-based commands. Upon adding the client components, the next step is to add a Web folder as a pointer to the workspace. The Web pointer will be enabled as follows: `http://Name-of-Server/Name-of-Workspace`.

Depending on whether you have Windows 2000 Professional or Windows 98, the process for adding a Web folder will be slightly different. If you are using Windows 98, within Web folders, in My Computer, click on Add Web Folder to set up the Web folder to the desired location. If you are using Windows 2000, go to Web folders in My Computer, then launch the Add Network Place Wizard to set up the Web folder to point to the desired workspace location.

→ To learn more about installing client component functionality, **see** "Installing the Client Components," **p. 167**.

MONITORING AND MANAGING PERFORMANCE

Once the site is deployed and operational, it is critical to ensure your end users never have to complain about unacceptable performance of the portal site.

To ensure an optimal end user experience, the server must have sufficient resources. This section discusses the server resources that should be carefully managed during a deployment.

CPU

The first resource, and likely the most important, is the CPU. The most CPU resource-intensive task is adding documents to the index. To ensure optimal CPU performance, it is not recommended to have more than 100,000 documents on a single server. Exceeding the 100,000 limit requires consideration of adding a dedicated server to the crawling process.

DISK SPACE

If a large number of documents will be stored on a server and added to the index, it is also important to monitor hard disk space. Storage requirements can be calculated based on the total number of documents available for searching, as well as stored within the workspace. When SharePoint is installed, approximately 150MB of disk space is consumed by the initial installation. This 150MB is incremented by approximately 50MB when the first workspace is created. Each time a workspace is added, you will need to add approximately 20MB. To calculate how much space is consumed by each document, you should consider the following formulas, depending on whether you are working with standard or enhanced folders.

Assuming you are working with standard folders, using a document profile with 10 properties, you will consume approximately 12KB for metadata storage, and 30 percent of the size of the document for index storage, in addition to the actual size of the document. For this example, assuming the size of the document is 2MB, our formula to calculate storage requirements is 12KB + (1.3 × 2MB).

For enhanced folders, we will use the same document profile, with 10 properties consuming 12KB of metadata storage for each version, 30 percent of the document size for index storage once the document has been published, and 100 percent of the document size for each stored version of the document. For this example, assuming the document size is 4MB, the following formula would apply: 12KB + (1.3 × 4MB). This is the default formula, assuming that the document has been checked in and approved, but has never been checked out. If, for instance, the document has been checked out, the formula would be calculated as follows: (# of versions +1) × (document size + 12KB) + (0.3 × size of document).

INDEX GROWTH

Another key planning consideration to closely monitor is the index growth, as indexes can scale rapidly depending on the document types added to the index. Many index parameters can be configured that may have an impact on the size of the index. For example, Microsoft Word and Excel files have less of an impact on indexes than text and HTML files. The dedicated search server that houses a crawling server's index requires twice the amount of free space on the volume before the initial index propagation occurs. Once the initial propagation is complete, the total size of the index must be available as free space. Lastly, the number of searchable words in the document also has an impact on the index size.

LOG FILES

In addition to the index growth, log files should also be managed. As a matter of best practice, log files should be limited to 25MB of disk space. Log files use transaction logging as well as circular logging.

The last physical component that must be managed carefully is the RAM. Planning the required amount of RAM is essential to ensuring optimal performance. Similar to CPU, the amount of RAM must be planned to accommodate the total number of documents in the workspace, as well as documents included within the index. Best practice advise is to plan for a server with a base RAM of 256MB. For each 100,000 documents added to the workspace or index, you will need to add 100MB of RAM.

Calculating how long it takes to back up a server can be done by first determining the size of the backup file. This backup file can be determined by calculating the size of the wss.mdb and the full-text index. In case you are wondering how long it takes to write a backup, you will first need to determine the speed of the hard drive. Most modern servers today (such as a 500MHz Pentium III with a RAID 5 disk array) write data at a pace of approximately 5MB per second. At this pace, a backup of 25GB would take approximately an hour. Depending on the speed of your particular disk subsystem, your performance may vary. Specific procedures for backup, restore, and duplication can be found in Chapter 13.

6

MONITORING USING STANDARD PERFORMANCE COUNTERS

The previous section discussed what resources to manage; now we are going to learn how to manage the most important resources. We know that over time, the number of users adopting and accessing the portal site will increase. As this trend scales up, we need to make sure that our site will grow to accommodate additional users and additional content.

Furthermore, we also need to know how to physically look at resource consumption and be able to tell when thresholds are being exceeded.

TIP

> As a matter of best practice, it is important to perform regular health checks and establish a performance baseline prior to going live with your SharePoint Portal Server. This enables you to track degradation of performance over time.

The use of performance counters can be used to monitor the day-to-day performance of your servers. Figure 6.5 below provides the procedure for accessing performance counters.

To access performance counters , click Run, then Programs, Administrative Tools, and then Performance. Once the Performance Monitor launches, right-click on the right pane to add counters.

Figure 6.5
Performance counters are used to track trends in system performance.

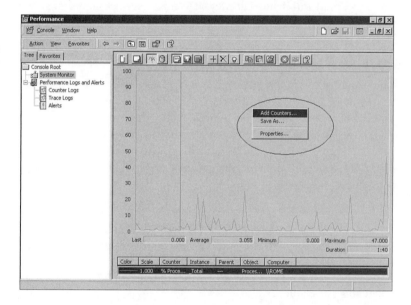

The types of counters you may find most useful are as follows:

- **% Processor Time**—A counter of the Processor performance object. This counter is used to manage the current state of activity on the server. It is highly recommended that this counter never exceed 80 percent, even during peak periods.

CAUTION

> Failure to maintain below 80 percent will likely result in unacceptable end user performance. If performance is consistently above 80%, you may need a larger server with more CPUs, or you may need to partition off the crawling process to a dedicated server.

6

■ **Available Mbytes** —A counter of the Memory performance object.

CAUTION

> This counter should never drop below 5MB, as end user performance will be severely impacted.

NOTE

> The disk volume that includes the workspace and indexes should never fall below 10MB of free available space without severe user performance degradation.

■ **Successful Check-in Latency** —Average time taken to check in documents to the portal.

■ **Successful Copies Latency**— Average time it takes to copy documents to the portal.

■ **Successful Publishes Latency**— Average time for publishing documents to the portal.

SEARCH AND INDEX RESOURCE TUNING

The two most commonly performed tuning processes are for searching and indexing. SharePoint Portal Server allows the administrator to assign each process a higher or lower priority, based on your business requirements. If the search and indexing features are both enabled on the same server, this tuning feature enables you to optimize the performance and balance the role across resources accordingly. In contrast, if you are using several dedicated servers for searching and indexing, you can use these control features to assign resources according to the distribution method.

Within the default settings for a fresh installation of SharePoint Portal Server, these controls are distributed evenly for search and indexing. The settings allow you several configuration options. Adjusting the tuning bar toward Background will give priority to other applications. Adjusting the tuning bar toward Dedicated will assign a majority of the system resources to creating or updating indexing. Figure 6.6 provides the procedure for accessing this tuning bar feature.

To configure resource usage on a SharePoint Portal Server, do the following:

1. Within the console tree of SharePoint Portal Server Administrator, right-click on the server that you want to adjust.

2. Click on properties and then click on the General tab (see Figure 6.6).

3. Slide the Search resource usage or Index resource usage to the preferred setting, and click Apply.

If additional applications are also loaded on this same server, it is recommended that you not adjust resource usage controls. Adjusting these controls on a SharePoint Portal Server that has other applications loaded on it can impact resources that are dedicated the other applications.

Figure 6.6
Specifying search and
index resource usage.

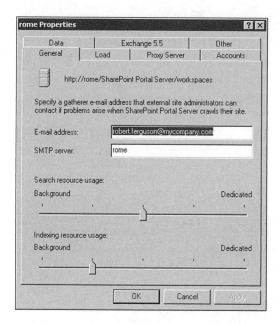

SETTING THE BAR ON ACCEPTABLE PERFORMANCE

If you are responsible for managing the SharePoint Portal Server site, the last thing you would want is an unhappy end user community. You have heard of the motto "no news is good news." Your goal should be to plan your deployment in such a way that you never hear complaints of unacceptable performance. To do this, you will need to be aware that when measuring the performance of a server, you will want to look at performance as it relates to the four categories in Table 6.5.

TABLE 6.5   COMMON PERFORMANCE MANAGEMENT INDICATORS

Function	Description
Common Operations	Viewing the home page on the dashboard site, browsing folders and categories, retrieving documents, and performing a simple search.
Uncommon Operations	Uncommon operations include all other operations, such as check-in, check-out, publish, approve, and so on.
Long-running operations	Long-running operations include moving, copying, or deleting folders; deleting or renaming categories; and changing inherited security.
Rare Operations	Rare operations include creating document profiles, creating categories, and creating content sources.

Extensive testing has been done by Microsoft and other key SharePoint Portal Server partners. The general recommendation for acceptable performance is that common operations should not exceed 3 seconds. Uncommon or rare operations should not exceed 5 seconds and no single operation should have latency beyond 10 seconds. The only exception is long-running operations, which may take longer due to your specific environment. Setting a logical threshold according to these three recommendations will help to ensure users experience acceptable performance.

NOTE

It should be noted that although some operations are more costly to servers, common operations such as viewing the home page, performing a simple search, or browsing folders have minimal impact on throughput requirements. Microsoft recommends that most standard SharePoint Portal Server environments will use a profile that consists of 95% common operations and 5% uncommon operations. It is also recommended that you plan for an occasional rare or long-running operation.

MAXIMUM THROUGHPUT RECOMMENDATIONS

This section will discuss general best practice *throughput* recommendations, which is defined as the process for measuring data transfer rate. It is very difficult to plan for optimal performance for your specific environment; many considerations must be considered, such as the characteristics that make up the profile of activity you expect from your end user community. This profile will have an impact on your recommendations on how you plan for maximum throughput and resource consumption. Ultimately, all these considerations will determine the server hardware and storage that will accommodate your particular portal infrastructure.

NOTE

Microsoft has already performed extensive testing and capacity planning for SharePoint, and they have published a detailed recommendations document. The document is called "Capacity Planning for SharePoint Portal Server" and is located at http://www.microsoft.com/sharepoint.

6

In general, best practice maximum throughput recommendations and important considerations are as follows in Table 6.6.

Function	Recommended Maximum	Description
Documents per server	500,000	The maximum number of documents per server has a dependency on the number of document versions. With the assumption of an average of two versions per document, the maximum documents per server is 500,000. If the average versions per document were four, the recommended maximum would be 250,000.
Document versions	1,000,000	Each document may have multiple document versions, with a maximum of 1,000,000.
Versions per document	1,000	The maximum recommended number of versions per document is 1,000. However, keep in mind that the total number of document versions is 1,000,000.
Document profiles	500	Even though document profiles have minimal impact on server performance, the maximum recommended number of document profiles is 500.
Categories	500	The maximum number of suggested categories per server is 500.
Number of documents per folder or category	200	While the maximum recommended number of documents per folder is 200, it is important to note that a folder could store up to 3,000 documents. However, the time it takes to render Web browser pages for more than 200 files is usually unacceptable.
Average number of role principals	150–600	The maximum number of role principals per folder can vary depending on the role. The maximum number of role principals is restricted by the maximum size of a security descriptor, which is 64KB. The maximum number of coordinators is 150, and the maximum number of readers is 600. Since role principals could consist of groups, a large number of users could be granted access to a document.

TABLE 6.6   BEST PRACTICE PERFORMANCE METRICS

6

continues

TABLE 6.6   CONTINUED

Function	Recommended Maximum	Description
Average file size	50MB	The maximum recommended document size is 50MB.
Number of subscriptions	100,000	Even with minimal impact on server performance, the maximum recommended number of subscriptions per workspace is 100,000.
Content Sources	100	The maximum recommended number of content sources is 100.
Documents included within the index	3,500,000	Due to memory constraints, the maximum recommended number of documents included in the index is 3.5 million per server. Memory is consumed due to database cache growth to support searches over both full-text and document metadata.

The number of documents per server, which is dependant on the average number of document versions, is the same regardless of the number of workspaces on the server. This means that if a server consisting of several workspaces requires storage for one million document versions, then this limitation applies to the aggregate of all workspaces combined, not just a single workspace.

SPECIAL CONSIDERATIONS

There are some tasks that require special consideration and careful planning. Some tasks are classified as long-running operations, such as such as moving, copying, or deleting folders; deleting or renaming categories; creating content sources; and changing inherited security.

Table 6.7 provides example calculations for certain tasks that require special consideration:

TABLE 6.7   PERFORMANCE EXPECTATIONS MATRIX

Function	Performance Expectation	Description
Changing role membership	~3 folders per/second	When copying a folder, all documents and sub-folders are copied at an approximate rate of two files per second. Copying 10,000 documents is estimated to take approximately 1.3 hours.

Function	Performance Expectation	Description
Renaming Categories	~5 documents per second	When categories are renamed, all categorization data for all documents belonging to the categories is updated. For example, if your category hierarchy consists of 50 categories and 20 documents within in each category, the entire category hierarchy can be modified in approximately 3 minutes 33 seconds.
Crawling	~12–18 documents per second	For the most common document types, a quad-processor can crawl 12–18 documents per second. If you are crawling 500,000 documents, the initial crawl process will take 12 hours. With the use of adaptive updates, you can decrease crawling time by 6×. In our example, you would be able to crawl the 500,000 documents within two hours using the Adaptive Update process.
Search	<5 seconds	The optimal throughput of searches from the dashboard site varies depending on the number of documents included in the index. It is important to ensure sufficient RAM for the database cache to achieve optimal throughput for searches. A quad-processor 500MHz server with 2GB of RAM and 3.5 million documents included in the index can respond to 95% of all searches in less than five seconds, with a maximum throughput of 20 searches per minute.
Index Propagation	60 seconds per 20K documents	The amount of time required to propagate an index to the dashboard server can vary depending on the kinds of documents included in the index, and the amount of metadata in the index. Typically, propagation takes one minute for every 20,000 documents in the index.

NOTE

The preceding recommendations were made assuming a multi-processor 500MHz Pentium III with 2GB of RAM being used.

Adaptive updates are discussed in detail in Chapter 19.

SUMMARY

In this chapter, we discussed the capacity planning requirements that need to be explored as we begin to plan your SharePoint Portal Server environment. We discussed how to determine the number of servers needed, and we compared and contrasted several scenarios, including single servers, multiple servers within the same site, and multiple servers distributed across multiple sites within the enterprise.

We discussed how to plan for required hardware, and we presented example calculations for small, medium, and large site installations. We provided a formula for determining your number of operations per second, and we discussed approximately how many users the various scenarios would accommodate. We talked about procedures for monitoring and managing performance using standard performance counters, and we provided a process for tuning servers according to the type of role the server will perform. Lastly, we provided sample metrics to help you understand what is considered acceptable performance, as well as discussed other special considerations that you should understand as you plan the capacity requirements for your organization.

6

CHAPTER 7

INSTALLATION AND CONFIGURATION

In this chapter

Preface

The purpose of this chapter is to provide granular processes and procedures for installing and configuring SharePoint Portal Server. You will not find a great deal of conceptual information as to why the processes and procedures are performed. This chapter should be used primarily as a reference for how to perform particular installation and configuration tasks.

Server Requirements

The following are the requirements for each server running Microsoft SharePoint Portal Server:

- Intel Pentium III–compatible processor minimum recommended.
- 256 megabytes (MB) of (RAM) minimum recommended.
- 550MB minimum of available disk space. The drive must be formatted as NTFS file system.
- Microsoft Windows 2000 Server or Windows 2000 Advanced Server operating system, and Windows 2000 Service Pack 1 (SP1) or later.

NOTE

> Best case scenario, you should install SharePoint Portal Server on a clean Win2000 Server. But if you upgraded from Win NT4, installing SharePoint Portal Server can cause install failures; to correct this, from a command prompt, **you must** manually register the oledb32.dll file before installation to avoid failure. You will find it here: Program Files\Common Files\System\Ole DB\oledb32.dll. Then type `regsvr32 oledb32.dll`.

Windows 2000 Required Updates

If you are installing on a Windows 2000 Server with Service Pack 1, install the following updates:

- Windows 2000 Patch: Token Handle Leak in LSASS Using Basic Authentication. See Q291340
- Windows 2000 Patch: GetEffectiveRightsFromAcl Causes ERROR_NO_SUCH_DOMAIN. See Q286360

NOTE

> Updates are obtained from Q articles, which are found at `http://support.microsoft.com`.

7

If you are installing on Windows 2000 Server with Service Pack 2, install the following update:

> Windows 2000 Patch: Token Handle Leak in LSASS Using Basic Authentication. See Q291340

NOTE

This new version of the hotfix replaces the previous hotfix (Q288861) release.

PREREQUISITES FOR INSTALLING SHAREPOINT PORTAL SERVER

The following prerequisites must be met before installing SharePoint Portal Server:

- Windows 2000 Hotfix (Pre-SP2) cannot be installed on the computer. If it is installed, remove it before installing SharePoint Portal Server. See Q269862.
- The Windows Remote Registry service must be running.
- Ensure that W3SVC/1 (Default Web Site in IIS) is started.
- SharePoint Portal Server setup performs a test to warn of invalid IIS settings. The TCP port in W3SVC/1 must be set to 80 with IP Address (All unassigned). If multiple entries have been configured in Advanced Settings, setup only checks the first entry. Other configurations may be acceptable, as long as localhost on port 80 is a valid way to connect to W3SVC/1 on the computer.

CAUTION

Do **not** change the port to an alternative HTTP port (such as 8000 or 8080) after installation. Ensure that port 80 is specified and remains as the primary port for the server.

- (IIS) 5.0 must be installed and the service must be running.
- Ensure SMTP Service is installed and running.

The latest fixes and patches can be located at the following Microsoft Web site:

http://www.microsoft.com/sharepoint/

In addition, Q articles can be found at http://support.microsoft.com.

CLIENT REQUIREMENTS

The following are requirements for the client components of SharePoint Portal Server:

- Intel Pentium-compatible 200 megahertz (MHz) or higher processor recommended.
- 64MB of RAM minimum recommended.

7

- 30MB of available disk space on Windows 2000 systems; 50MB of available disk space on all other systems.
- Microsoft Windows 98, Microsoft Windows NT version 4.0 with SP6A, or Windows 2000 Professional, Server, or Advanced Server. Coordinator functions require Windows 2000 Professional, Server, or Advanced Server.
- Microsoft Internet Explorer 5 or later.
- Microsoft Outlook Express 5 o later.

DASHBOARD SITE REQUIREMENTS

The client components are not required to access the dashboard. For the Windows OS, you can use the following browsers:

- Internet Explorer 4.01 or later
- Netscape Navigator 4.51 or later (for Italian and Spanish versions of SharePoint Portal Server)
- Netscape Navigator 4.75 or later (for English, French, German, and Japanese versions of SharePoint Portal Server)

> **NOTE** Netscape users must use Internet Services Manager to enable Basic authentication for the workspace node on the Default Web Site. Also enable Basic authentication for the MSOffice node for discussions to work.

- You must enable Microsoft JScript or Netscape JavaScript support in your browser for the dashboard site to function
- The Macintosh and Solaris operating systems are not supported

COEXISTENCE ISSUES

The following software does not coexist with SharePoint Portal Server:

- Microsoft Exchange 2000 Standard or Enterprise Server
- Microsoft SQL 2000 Server
- Microsoft Exchange Server version 5.5 and earlier
- Microsoft Site Server (any version)
- Microsoft Office Server Extensions

Setup fails if this software is already installed. If you install this software after installing SharePoint Portal Server, SharePoint Portal Server will stop functioning properly.

7

CAUTION

> A clustered environment is *not supported*. You *cannot install* and you *must not join* the server to a clustered environment.

SHAREPOINT PORTAL SERVER AND EXCHANGE 2000 SERVER

It is not recommended—nor will Microsoft support it—if you install SharePoint Portal Server and Exchange 2000 on the same computer. It can and probably will create certain known issues. However, we realize that your specific business requirements may justify the need to install SharePoint Portal Server and Exchange 2000 on the same server. To enable both applications on the same server, perform the following tasks:

TIP

> You *must* install Exchange *before* SharePoint Portal Server. The Windows 2000 and Exchange 2000 SP1 patches must be applied.

During installation, the Microsoft Search (MSSearch) service is upgraded and the (MSExchangeIS) service is stopped for a short period of time. The full-text index format of all existing indexes on that computer is upgraded the next time the MSSearch starts.

NOTE

> Upgrading the full-text index format can take several hours, depending on the number and size of the existing indexes. There must be enough disk space on the computer to accommodate 120% of the size of the largest full-text index on the drive.

SharePoint Portal Server upgrades MSSearch and full-text indexes; you should not install SharePoint Portal Server on a server that participates in an Exchange Server clustering environment or add a computer running SharePoint Portal Server to a clustered environment. SharePoint Portal Server will not install if four storage groups already exist on the Exchange server. Since some services are shared between SharePoint Portal Server and Exchange2000, removing either one can be trouble for the other: It will cease to operate properly. If this occurs, you must manually restart the following services:

- IIS Admin Service
- SharePoint Portal Server
- Exchange Information Store
- SMTP
- World Wide Web Publishing Service
- Network News Transport Protocol (NNTP)
- Exchange MTA Stacks
- Exchange POP3
- Exchange IMAP4
- Exchange Routing Engine

7

You can also create a standard batch file to automatically start these services.

NOTE

> If you remove SharePoint Portal Server from an Exchange 2000 server, Exchange will continue to work.

SHAREPOINT PORTAL SERVER AND MICROSOFT SQL SERVER

SharePoint Portal Server will upgrade the existing MSSearch and the full-text index format of all the existing indexes on a computer running Microsoft SQL Server 7.0 or Microsoft SQL Server 2000. The next time MSSearch starts, there must be enough disk space on the computer to accommodate 120% of the size of the largest full-text index on the drive or the upgrade will fail.

NOTE

> Upgrading the full-text index format can take several hours, depending on the number and size of the existing indexes. A message will inform you that the service will be upgraded.

CAUTION

> Because SharePoint Portal Server upgrades MSSearch and full-text indexes, do not install SharePoint Portal Server on a server that participates in a SQL Server clustering environment or add a computer running SharePoint Portal Server to a clustered environment.

You can install SQL Server on a computer already running SharePoint Portal Server. In this instance, SQL Server uses MSSearch installed by SharePoint Portal Server. If you remove SharePoint Portal Server from a computer that has SQL Server installed, SharePoint Portal Server will not remove the upgraded MSSearch because it is a shared service with SQL Server.

INSTALLING SHAREPOINT PORTAL SERVER ON A DOMAIN CONTROLLER

If you install SharePoint Portal Server on a domain controller:

- There is not a local Administrators group. If a Coordinator makes an error, there is no possibility for a local administrator to resolve security issues. Only users assigned to the Coordinator role can specify security on folders.
- You may need to restart the DC after installing SharePoint Portal Server.

RENAMING A SHAREPOINT PORTAL SERVER COMPUTER

You can rename a SharePoint Portal Server computer at any time. After renaming the server, you must restart it.

DEPLOYMENT PLANNING CONSIDERATIONS

Begin by assessing your existing content, identifying the needs and habits of your users, and outlining your deployment goals. This information can help you decide how to streamline your document management processes and create an effective dashboard site to deliver valuable information to your organization.

SERVER PLANNING

You can use SharePoint Portal Server to complete the following tasks:

- **Document management.** You can use SharePoint Portal Server to store and manage content in the workspace.

- **Creating or updating indexes.** SharePoint Portal Server *crawls*, or reads through, content to create an index of the content. You can use SharePoint Portal Server to crawl and create indexes for content such as Web sites and pages, file servers, Lotus Notes version 4.6a and R5 databases, computers running Microsoft Exchange Server 5.5 and Exchange 2000 Server, and other SharePoint Portal Server computers.

- **Searching.** After indexes are created, you can use SharePoint Portal Server to search for content.

TIP

> For optimal performance, distribute these tasks across multiple servers.

→ To learn more about load planning on single server vs. multiple servers, **see** "Server Deployment Recommendations," **p. 125**.

Before you determine how many servers you need, consider how your organization will use SharePoint Portal Server. When doing so, it is a good idea to plan for your current requirements as well as for your future needs.

→ To learn more about planning your deployment, **see** "Planning a Deployment for ABC Company," **p. 520**.

Your server configuration depends on how you intend to use SharePoint Portal Server. Before selecting a configuration, consider the following questions:

- How many users will use SharePoint Portal Server primarily for document management?

- How many users will use SharePoint Portal Server primarily for searching?

- How many documents do you expect to maintain?

- How many concurrent users do you expect on a server?

- How many workspaces do you expect to maintain on a single server? The recommendation is to have no more than 15 workspaces per server.

- What content do you want to crawl for the index, and where is it located? For example, do you want to crawl other SharePoint Portal Server computers, Exchange 5.5 or Exchange 2000 Server computers, Lotus Notes databases, file servers, or Web sites?

7

■ Do you expect the number of users for a specific workspace to increase significantly? If so, you may want to consider hosting that workspace on its own server.

■ Will you need to increase the number of servers to dedicate individual servers to specific tasks? If you expect to crawl large numbers of content sources, you may want to dedicate one server to creating and updating indexes and another server to searching.

→ For more details about planning a deployment, **see** "Planning a Deployment for ABC Company," **p. 520**.

CLIENT PLANNING

By design, there is not an individual client application. SharePoint Portal Server commands are extensions, integrated in the menus of Windows Explorer and Microsoft Office applications. Within those applications you cannot access SharePoint Portal Server commands from the menus, but you can use other applications to create documents.

Therefore, you must use Windows Explorer or a Web browser to perform SharePoint Portal Server document management tasks on documents created by using those applications.

Users must install the client components in order to meet the following conditions:

■ To provide complete workspace management functions. Including the ability to configure security, and create and manage content sources.

■ To access all other SharePoint Portal Server Help.

After you have installed the client components, you must add a Web folder that points to the workspace. The address of the workspace is http://server_name/workspace_name.

> **NOTE**
>
> The procedure for adding a Web folder varies depending on the operating system you are using. For detailed instructions, see your operating system Help.

■ On Windows 2000 Professional, go to My Network Places and use the Add Network Place Wizard to add a Web folder that points to http://server_name/workspace_name.

■ On Windows 98, go to Web Folders in My Computer, and then use Add Web Folder to add a Web folder that points to http://server_name/workspace_name.

NETWORK PLANNING

Prior to implementing SharePoint Portal Server, you should review and address any network concerns. The main concern is to ensure that TCP/IP is the protocol running on your network. Once TCP/IP is installed, you can install SharePoint Portal Server on Windows NT version 4.0, Windows 2000 Server, or Windows 2000 Advanced Server. Portal Server honors the trust relationships between domains. If you want to use a fully qualified domain name (FQDN) and index workspace propagation together, both the server dedicated to creating and updating indexes and the destination server must be in Windows 2000 domains. However, as stated earlier, do not install a server running clustering as this is not supported.

PROXY SERVER

If your organization uses proxy servers, you should plan where to place the proxy servers in relation to your servers. If you are using index propagation, ensure that there is not a proxy server between the server dedicated to creating and updating indexes and the server dedicated to searching, or ensure that any proxy server between the two servers allows Windows file share access. Refer to the readme file and Microsoft's Web site for more information on this section.

Your proxy server must be configured to pass the following verbs.

- SharePoint Portal Server Hypertext Transfer Protocol (HTTP) verbs.
- The Distributed Authoring and Versioning (DAV) set of HTTP extensions.
- A custom SharePoint Portal Server verb called INVOKE. By default, SharePoint Portal Server uses the proxy server settings of the default content access account, taken from the current proxy server settings in Microsoft Internet Explorer.

NOTE

> Changes to the proxy server settings do not affect other applications. For example, you can configure the server to use a specific proxy server without affecting Internet Explorer.

The proxy setting for Internet Explorer on the client can affect how the client and dashboard site communicate with the server, because the client components and the dashboard site communicate with the server by using HTTP.

TIP

> You must use a tool called **proxycfg.exe** located in the drive:\SharePoint Portal Server\Bin directory to configure proxy settings for the ServerXMLHTTP object, if the dashboard site is behind the proxy. The dashboard site uses ServerXMLHTTP to make HTTP requests. These requests are necessary to return the correct page to the client. The ServerXMLHTTP object has its own proxy settings. See "Advanced Topics" in *Administrator's Help* for more detail.

The client components and the server communicate by using the Distributed Component Object Model (DCOM). If you are using SharePoint Portal Server over the Internet and DCOM is not enabled between the client and the server computers, the Category Assistant feature of SharePoint Portal Server does not function on the client computer. In addition, the user is unable to manage updates or content sources.

FULLY QUALIFIED DOMAIN NAMES (FQDN)

Specify a FQDN for your server. Then you can access the server by using the FQDN either on your intranet or on the Internet.

7

On your intranet, you access the server by using `http://server_name/workspace_name`. If you want to use an FQDN, you access the server by using `http://server_name.domain/workspace_name`. For example, the FQDN of a server named Works on the adventure-works.com domain would be `Works.adventure-works.com`.

If you want to use SharePoint Portal Server with FQDNs, you must use the proxycfg.exe tool located under the SharePoint Portal Server\Bin directory to exclude access to the SharePoint Portal Server computer through the proxy server. The location of this directory depends on where you installed SharePoint Portal Server.

→ To learn more using the Proxycfg.exe tool, **see** "Using the Proxycfg.exe Tool," **p. 625**.

INSTALLATION OF SHAREPOINT PORTAL SERVER

1. Log on to the computer running Windows 2000 as a local or domain administrator. Note that if you are installing SharePoint Portal Server on a computer running Exchange Server, you must be a domain administrator.

2. Insert the SharePoint Portal Server CD into your CD-ROM drive. See Figure 7.1 below for visual of installation screen.

Figure 7.1
Default installation splash screen.

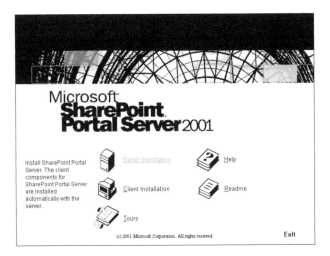

3. Click **Server Installation**. The SharePoint Portal Server setup wizard appears.

   You can also go to the Server folder on the CD, and then double-click **Setup.exe**.

4. Follow the instructions that appear in the setup wizard.

On the **Product Identification** page, type the CD Key in the spaces provided. The CD Key uniquely identifies your copy of SharePoint Portal Server and enables you to receive technical support. The CD Key is located on the back of your SharePoint Portal Server CD case. If the number you type is not accepted, check the following:

7

- If you are using the keypad to the right of your keyboard, ensure that NUM LOCK is on.

- Ensure that you are not using the letter *I* for the number one.

- Ensure that you are not using the letter *O* for the number zero.

On the SharePoint Portal Server Installation Folders page, specify the location on the server's disk where you want to install the SharePoint Portal Server program files and data files. If you want a different location, click Change Folder.

Figure 7.2
Default dialog box to determine where to store files associated with the installation.

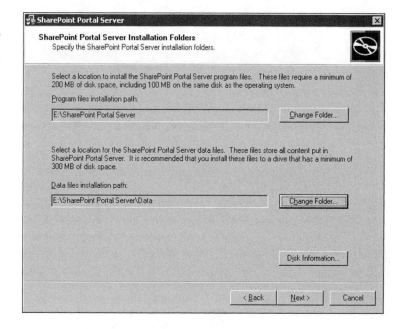

Click **Disk Information** for information about the amount of disk space required and the amount remaining. If there are existing files in the installation paths, setup removes these files. Note the following restrictions for the path:

- The path name can have a maximum length of 100 characters.

- The path name can contain only characters in the lower ASCII range. The lower ASCII code set includes the characters with codes 32–127. The workspace name cannot exceed 25 characters in length.

- The path cannot point to a root directory. For example, E:\ is not allowed, but E:\SharePoint Portal Server is allowed.

On the **SPS Indexing Settings** page, specify the default content Access account and the gatherer email address. An external site administrator can contact this address if problems occur when SPS crawls the external site. The default content access account is used to

7

crawl content sources. These settings are necessary for SPS to crawl content stored outside the workspace and include it in an index.

Figure 7.3
Default page for
Server Index Settings.

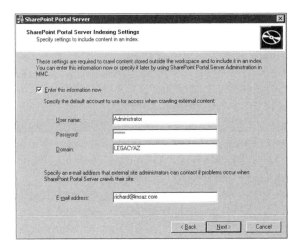

SharePoint Portal Server Administration in Microsoft Management Console (MMC) will allow you to manage the local server and workspace. However, you can only use the MMC to perform administration tasks on the local server. If you need to control or manage remote server, you will need to do this through a terminal server connection.

To open SharePoint Portal Server Administration:

1. Click **Start**.
2. Point to **Programs**.
3. Point to **Administrative Tools**.
4. Click **SharePoint Portal Server Administration**.

CREATING A WORKSPACE ON THE SERVER

After you run SharePoint Portal Server setup, the New Workspace Wizard appears. This wizard helps you create a default workspace. If you click Cancel, the New Workspace Wizard does not appear. However, you can create a workspace later by using SharePoint Portal Server Administration.

1. On the first page of the wizard, click **Next**.
2. Within the **Workspace Definition** dialog box, type a Workspace for the Workspace that you are creating.

7

NOTE

> Workspace names can consist of characters from lower ASCII except for the following: # :
> \ ? * < > % / | " { } ~ [ ] Space ! ( ) = ; . , @ & +. The lower
> ASCII code set includes the characters with codes 32–127. The workspace name cannot
> exceed 25 characters in length.

NOTE

> The wizard verifies that the workspace name is unique and does not conflict with any other
> workspace names or propagated index names on the server. If the name is already in use,
> the wizard prompts you to enter a unique name. You cannot edit a workspace name after
> you create the workspace. If you are creating an index workspace, the name of the work-
> space you are creating must be different from that of the destination workspace.

In the Workspace Definition dialog box, type a description for the workspace. Click
advanced if you want to distribute the task of searching and crawling content among several
servers.

Figure 7.4
The Advanced option
allows you specify a
server to be config-
ured as an indexed
workspace.

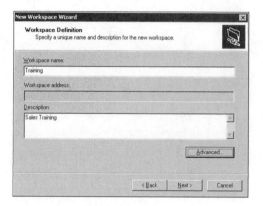

Within the Advanced Workspace Definition dialog box, you can click on the check box to
configure the server as an index workspace. Enabling this option will dedicate the available
resources of this server to crawling. Indexed workspaces are used to manage content
sources, not individual documents. The index can also be propagated to a workspace on
another server, which would allow the remote server to be dedicated to searching.

→ To learn more about indexing and dedicating servers to searching or crawling, **see** "Optimizing SPS
Architecture for Crawling," **p. 470**.

7

Figure 7.5
Enabling the check box will dedicate this server to crawling.

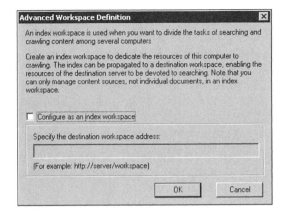

To configure the server as an index workspace, perform the following tasks:

1. Within the Advanced Workspace Definition dialog box, click the check box next to Configure as an Index Workspace.

2. In Specify the destination workspace address, type the destination workspace for the propagated index. The name of the destination workspace will use the following syntax: `http://server_name/workspace_name`.

3. Click OK to save the changes.

The wizard prompts you to provide the name of a propagation access account, which is required before you can propagate an index. This account must have local administrator permissions on the destination server.

The destination workspace must exist before you create the index workspace. The wizard ensures that a workspace with the same name as the index workspace does not already exist on the destination. You cannot change the destination workspace after you have created the index workspace. If the destination server is not a SharePoint Portal Server computer, the wizard logs an error in the Application Log in Windows 2000 Event Viewer.

You can create index workspaces with the same name (and propagating to the same destination) on multiple servers dedicated to creating and updating indexes. The last index to propagate has its index active on the destination. You can use this setup to continually update the destination by appropriately scheduling the crawls for each index workspace.

NOTE

It is a good idea to maintain a list of index workspace names, the servers on which they are stored, and the servers and workspaces to which they are propagated.

7

TIP

> To use FQDN and index workspace propagation together, both the server dedicated to indexing and the destination server must be in Windows 2000 domains.

The workspace contact page then is launched. Perform the following steps to complete the installation wizard process.

1. In **Workspace contact name**, type the name of the user or group that you are assigning as the workspace contact. The workspace contact is the individual user or group with overall responsibility for the workspace.

2. In **Workspace contact e-mail address**, type the email address for the workspace contact. The contact email address can be that of an individual user or a group.

3. Click Next (see Figure 7.6).

Figure 7.6
Populate the required fields and proceed to the next dialog box.

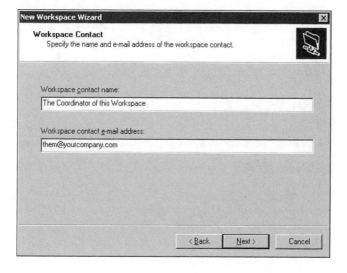

4. Click **Finish** to complete the wizard and create the new workspace. After SharePoint Portal Server creates the workspace, it displays a message stating that the wizard will open the workspace and create a link to it in **My Network Places**.

5. Click **OK**. The link is created, the **Configure Your Workspace** page opens, and the dashboard site opens. For index workspaces, an introduction page opens and the link points to the **Content Sources** folder within the workspace.

TIP

> After you create the workspace, you must configure security on the workspace node by using SharePoint Portal Server Administration or Web folders. The Windows 2000 local Administrators group has permission to read documents and configure security on any folder or document in a workspace.

7

WORKSPACE CREATION FAILURE

Workspace creation may fail for the following reasons:

- Are you trying to use a workspace name that is the same as another workspace name on the server, the same as another workspace name on the destination workspace (for an index workspace), or the same as an existing IIS virtual directory?

- Are you trying to use characters that are not allowed in the workspace name? Workspace names can consist of characters from lower ASCII except for the following:

  `# : \ ? * < > % / | " { } ~ [ ] Space ! ( ) = ; . , @ & +`

  The lower ASCII code set includes the characters with codes 32–127.

- Is there sufficient disk space?

- Are you creating an index workspace?

NOTE

> If you want to use FQDN and index workspace propagation together, both the server dedicated to creating and updating indexes and the destination server must be in Windows 2000 domains.

CREATING ADDITIONAL WORKSPACES

After the initial workspace is created during install, additional workspaces can only be created using the SharePoint Portal Server Administration. During installation, SharePoint Portal Server automatically adds the Administration snap-in to the MMC.

To start SharePoint Portal Server Administration

1. On the Start menu, point to Programs, point to Administrative Tools, and click SharePoint Portal Server Administration.

2. Double-click the SharePoint Portal Server icon in the console tree on the left pane to view SharePoint Portal Server computer.

3. Double-click the server to see any existing workspaces.

4. Right-click on the SharePoint Portal Server computer (for example, Sales).

5. Point to New, and click Workspace.

6. Follow the prompts. You can access your new workspace through `http://localhost/workspacename`.

DELETING A WORKSPACE

You can delete a workspace by using SharePoint Portal Server (MMC).

Workspace deletion can fail for the following reasons:

- Are you trying to delete an index workspace? If so, does the destination workspace exist?

- Is the destination server online?

If the destination workspace is unavailable at the time the index workspace is deleted, you are notified and prompted to continue. If you choose to continue, the index workspace deletion succeeds. To then delete the propagated index from the destination server, see ToolsHowTo.txt in the Support\Tools directory on the SharePoint Portal Server CD.

USING UNATTENDED INSTALLATION OPTIONS FOR THE SERVER

You can run SharePoint Portal Server setup in unattended mode, if you are installing a large number of servers or want to customize your installation. SharePoint Portal Server supports the following unattended options.

If you have Terminal Services, you can use it to install SharePoint Portal Server remotely on multiple computers in your organization.

Using an .ini file is an excellent choice if you need to install identical configurations of SharePoint Portal Server on multiple computers.

However, before running setup in this mode, you must create the .ini file that contains the default installation settings that you want to use. After you create the .ini file, you can edit it by using a text editor. By editing the .ini file, you can specify additional options and gain more control over your installation.

To create the .ini file used for unattended setup, you must run the SharePoint Portal Server setup wizard. The wizard stores the settings that you specify in the .ini file.

When installing SharePoint Portal Server by using an .ini file, dialog boxes or error messages that require user intervention are not displayed unless prerequisites are missing.

To install SharePoint Portal Server by using an .ini file, do the following steps:

1. Create an .ini file.

   - Click **Start**, and then click **Run**.

   - In **Open**, type *path_to_server_setup_file* `setup /Create Unattended` *path filename*`.ini`, where *filename* is the name of the .ini file that you want to create. For example, if the setup file is in the Setup directory on drive D and you want to create sample.ini on the E drive, type `D:\Setup\setup /Create Unattended E:\sample.ini`.

   - Click **OK**.

   - Follow the instructions that appear in the SharePoint Portal Server setup wizard. All settings that you choose are included in the .ini file that you create.

7

CAUTION

> If you enter the user name and password for the default content access account when creating the file, the password is *not* encrypted and appears in the file.

2. Edit the .ini file.

- In a text editor such as Microsoft WordPad, open *filename*.ini where *filename* is the name of the .ini file that you created.
- Modify parameters in the file for the settings that you want SharePoint Portal Server setup to use.

NOTE

> If you plan to use an unattended installation file on servers with varying storage configurations, ensure that hard-coded paths are valid for each server configuration before starting the installation. An example of a hard-coded path reference is "C:\". You can force the installer to automatically choose the correct default path by removing an entry line completely.

The default location of where to store files can be modified for certain installation elements during installation. Additional details are provided on which components can be modified.

InstallDirectory. You can specify the installation location for SharePoint Portal Server program files.

TIP

> Altering the default location for the Microsoft Document Store and the MSSearch is not recommended.
>
> The recommended option for the MSSearch and Document Store installation directories are as follows:
>
> InstallDirectory=*operating_system_drive*\Program Files\Common Files\Microsoft Shared\ Document Store
>
> InstallDirectory=*operating_system_drive*\Program Files\Common Files\Microsoft Shared\ MSSearch

Search Gatherer Log Directory. Each time SharePoint Portal Server creates a workspace index, it creates a log file for that workspace. This log file contains data about crawling content sources and records access errors. After installation, you can use SharePoint Portal Server Administration to change this path.

Search Index Directory. When creating a workspace, SharePoint Portal Server creates an index under this root node. SharePoint Portal Server also creates all indexes propagated to the server under this root node. After installation, you can use SharePoint Portal Server Administration to change this path. If you want to move existing indexes to a new location, see ToolsHowTo.txt in the Support\Tools directory on the SharePoint Portal Server CD.

Search Property Store Database Directory. After installation, you cannot modify the file location by using SharePoint Portal Server Administration. However, during setup you can specify the location of the property store file. To modify the file location, see ToolsHowTo.txt in the Support\Tools directory on the SharePoint Portal Server CD. This file contains the metadata from documents.

Search Property Store Log Directory. After installation, you cannot modify the location of these files by using SharePoint Portal Server Administration. During setup you can specify the location of the property store log files. To modify the file location, see ToolsHowTo.txt in the Support\Tools directory on the SharePoint Portal Server CD.

TIP

> For optimal performance, the property store and property store log files should be on dedicated physical volumes. SharePoint Portal Server shares this file across all workspaces.

Document Store Database Directory. You can specify the location of the Document Store Database file. Every SharePoint Portal Server computer contains one public store (wss.mdb). All workspaces hosted on the server reside on the Document Store. After installation, you can use SharePoint Portal Server Administration to change this path. If this location changes, the existing file moves to the new location.

Document Store Streaming Database Directory. You can specify the location of the Document Store-Streaming Database file. Used for streaming files, the Document Store-Streaming Database file (wss.stm) contains data and is a companion to the Document Store-Database file (wss.mdb). Together, these two files form the database. SharePoint Portal Server document streams make up a sizable part of the total amount of data. After installation, you can use SharePoint Portal Server Administration to change this path. If this location changes, the existing file moves to the new location. Move these files to a larger drive (ideally a dynamic disk that you can easily resize) because it can increase substantially over time.

Document Store Database Log Directory. You can specify the location of the Document Store-Database Log files. After installation, you can use SharePoint Portal Server Administration to change this path. If this location changes, the existing files move to the new location. For optimal performance, place the log files on a dedicated physical volume.

CAUTION

> **All other installation components should not be changed.**
>
> You can modify the parameter `apply indexing settings` in the .ini file to set the default content access account and gatherer email address during the unattended installation. The default content access account is the user name and password used when crawling content outside the workspace. SharePoint Portal Server provides the gatherer email address to each Web site it crawls when creating an index. If a problem occurs while crawling (for example, the crawler is hitting the site too much), the Web site's administrator can contact this address.

7

TIP

> If `apply indexing settings` equals 0, the default content access account and gatherer email address are not set when you run the unattended installation. You can set these options after installation by using SharePoint Portal Server Administration.

To specify the account and email address, do the following:

1. Set `apply indexing settings=1`
2. Set `Default Content Access Account=user_name,domain,password`
3. Set `gatherer e-mail address=you@yourcompany.com`
4. Run setup.
5. On the server you want to run setup, Click **Start**, and then click **Run**.
6. In **Open**, type *path_to_server_setup_file* **setup /UnattendFile** *path filename*.**ini** where filename is the name of the .ini file you created.
7. Click **OK**. You do not see the finish page or the **New Workspace Wizard** page.

GATHERING INFORMATION FROM THE SERVER INSTALLATION LOGS

You can examine the following logs for information about server installation:

- **Errorlog.txt file**. Located in \Program Files\Microsoft Integration\SharePoint Portal Server\Logs for successful installations. For failed installations, this file is located in the %temp% directory. The error "VAIFY Failed" tells you that the portion of setup that configures default SharePoint Portal Server settings in the Microsoft Document Store failed.

  If you experience a nonfatal error that documents an ordering problem, you might read lines like this in the log file:

  "[Date, Time] Dependency Manager: [2] Ordering problem: Microsoft SharePoint Portal Server Microsoft Search."

  The ordering problem could originate from Microsoft Search (MSSearch), SharePoint Portal Server, Exchange Server, or a combination of these. It is informing you that the order in which things are being installed is different from the order SharePoint Portal Server requested. It is safe to ignore this message.

- **Eventlog.txt file**. Located in \Program Files\Microsoft Integration\SharePoint Portal Server\Logs for successful installations. For failed installations, this file is located in the %temp% directory. This file contains a detailed list of the actions performed during the installation. Lines that contain errors are copied to Errorlog.txt.

- **Setup.log file**. Located in \Program Files\Microsoft Integration\SharePoint Portal Server\Logs.

- **SPSClient.Log file**. Located in \Program Files\Microsoft Integration\SharePoint Portal Server\Logs for successful server installations.

■ **Exchange Server Setup Progress.log file**. Located at the root of the operating system drive. Installing SharePoint Portal Server on Exchange 2000 Server results in multiple instances of this file. This log tells you whether the Document Store installed correctly, and can help you identify issues such as

A server name has an illegal character.

IIS 5.0 is not installed, so the Document Store cannot be installed.

SMTP service is not installed.

SHAREPOINT PORTAL SERVER DOES NOT INSTALL

If SharePoint Portal Server does not install, check the following:

■ An unsupported operating system. Only Windows 2000 Server and Advanced Server, Service Pack 1 (SP1) or later, are supported.

■ Exchange 2000 Enterprise Server. Only Exchange 2000 Server SP1 or later is supported.

■ Microsoft Exchange Server version 5.5 and earlier.

■ Microsoft Site Server (any version) .

■ Microsoft Office Server Extensions.

CAUTION

> SharePoint Portal Server is *not* supported in a clustered environment. You *cannot* install SharePoint Portal Server in a clustered environment, and *you must not join* the SharePoint Portal Server computer to a clustered environment.

SLOW SETUP

If setup is very slow or fails after long periods of inactivity, check the following:

■ Does your system meet the recommended processor and RAM requirements?

■ If you are installing over a network, is your network experiencing slow or impaired operations?

THE SERVER NO LONGER FUNCTIONS

Did you attempt to uninstall Exchange 2000 Server after you installed SharePoint Portal Server? Even if you canceled the removal of Exchange 2000 Server, SharePoint Portal Server may no longer function. To fix SharePoint Portal Server, you must manually start the following services:

■ IIS Administration Service (IISAdmin)

■ SharePoint Portal Server (Msdmserv)

■ MSExchangeIS

7

- SMTP
- W3SVC
- Network News Transfer Protocol (NNTP)
- Exchange message transfer agent (MTA) Stacks
- Exchange Post Office Protocol version 3 (POP3)
- Exchange Internet Message Access Protocol version 4 (IMAP4)
- Exchange Routing Engine

Did you uninstall any of the server prerequisites after installing SharePoint Portal Server? SharePoint Portal Server requires

- Windows 2000 Server or Advanced Server SP1 or later operating system.
- IIS 5.0.
- SMTP service. This is a Windows 2000 Server component.

For more information about server requirements, see the beginning of this chapter.

UNINSTALLING OR REPAIRING SHAREPOINT PORTAL SERVER

Before uninstalling SharePoint Portal Server, you must

- Verify that all command prompts are closed.
- Remove any additional virtual roots mapped to the Document Store drive. The Document Store is mapped to network drive M by default.

> **NOTE** If network drive M is already in use when you install SharePoint Portal Server, the Document Store is mapped to another network drive.

When you uninstall SharePoint Portal Server, all files and folders are removed, as well as any user-created or modified files, client components, and all workspaces.

If you repair SharePoint Portal Server, it automatically repairs the client components.

> **NOTE** If you remove SharePoint Portal Server from a computer that has Microsoft SQL Server or Exchange Server installed, the upgraded MSSearch service is not removed, because it is a shared service with Exchange Server and SQL Server.

7

SharePoint Portal Server requires access to the original installation point to uninstall the Microsoft Embedded Exchange files. If this has moved, insert the SharePoint Portal Server CD and continue uninstalling. You can also point to the \Server\Document Store directory at the installation point.

INSTALLING THE CLIENT COMPONENTS OF SHAREPOINT PORTAL SERVER

The following steps describe how to install the client components.

1. Log on to the client computer as a user with administrator privileges.

2. Connect to the server location where the client installation files are. These files must be shared or otherwise available. By default, these files are located at Program Files\SharePoint Portal Server\ClientDrop\Languages*Lang*, where *Lang* corresponds to the language of the client.

3. Double-click **Setup.exe**. The Client Components for SharePoint Portal Server setup wizard appears.

4. Follow the instructions that appear in the wizard.

Installing from the SharePoint Portal Server CD:

- Insert the SharePoint Portal Server CD into your CD-ROM drive, and then click **Client Installation**. The Client Components for SharePoint Portal Server setup wizard appears.

- You can also go to the Client folder on the CD, and then double-click **Setup.exe**.

NOTE
> The client components require Microsoft Data Access Components (MDAC) 2.5 or higher. If this is not already present on the computer, the client installation process installs MDAC 2.5 SP1. The client components are not required if you have Microsoft Office XP installed. XP includes integrated functionality enabled through menu based drop-down menus.

You must add a Web folder that points to the workspace after you have installed the client components; the address of the workspace is http://server_name/workspace_name.

The procedure for adding a Web folder varies depending on your operating system. See your operating system Help for detailed instructions.

- In Windows 2000 Professional, go to My Network Places and use the Add Network Place Wizard to add a Web folder that points to http://server_name/workspace_name.

- In Windows 98, go to Web Folders in My Computer, and use Add Web Folder to add a Web folder that points to http://server_name/workspace_name.

7

USING UNATTENDED INSTALLATION OPTIONS FOR THE CLIENT

As an administrator, you have several options to choose from when it comes to installing the client components on many systems throughout your enterprise. Some of the options are listed below::

- Using Client Components for SharePoint Portal Server setup wizard, which guides you through the installation process. This is a manual process and is normally used to install the client components on a small number of computers.

- Using Systems Management Server to automatically install a client remotely on multiple computers in your organization. Microsoft System Management Server is a separate tool and requires an installation script to be created. The tool is just the push mechanism to deploy the software installation script as a package.

- Windows Installer is another automated deployment tool. This is the tool that allows the installation process to be executed in an unattended manner by launching an executable. Windows Installer scripts can be deployed using SMS.

- Active Directory service to control and enable the SharePoint Portal Server client setup program available to your users automatically in Control Panel under Add/Remove Programs. This process allows the user or administrator to publish and expose applications to groups of users through traditional Windows 2000 security.

CLIENT INSTALLATION FAILURE

Ensure the client computer meets these installation requirements:

- Internet Explorer 5 or later is required.
- Outlook Express 5 or later is required.
- The client components do not install on Windows 95.
- Only Windows NT version 4.0, with SP6A or later, is acceptable.
- You must be the administrator.

RECURRING INSTALLATION ERRORS

If you experience recurring errors, a detailed log file can help you diagnose the problem.

To run setup with a detailed log file, perform these steps.

1. Go to the directory containing setup.exe for the client components.
2. On the taskbar, click **Start**, point to **Programs**, point to **Accessories**, and then click **Command Prompt**.
3. Type `setup /L*v "path_and_file_name_for_the_log_file"`.

   For example, if you want to store the log file named clientsetup.log in the Client Setup directory on drive C, type `setup /L*v "C:\Client Setup\clientsetup.log"`.

If you require assistance interpreting the information in the log file, you can call Microsoft Product Support Services.

Uninstalling or Repairing Client Components

You can uninstall or repair client components of SharePoint Portal Server by using Add/Remove Programs in the Control Panel, or the command line.

To remove or repair the client components by using the command line

1. On the taskbar, click **Start**, point to **Programs**, point to **Accessories**, and then click **Command Prompt**.

2. Type `"path\`**`setup`**`"` *`switch`* `"path\`**`SPSClient.msi`**`"` where *path* is the path to the setup.exe and SPSClient.msi files. Use the **/x** switch to uninstall the client components. Use the **/f** switch to repair the client components.

   For example, to remove the client components, where setup.exe and SPSClient.msi are in E:\Client Files, you would type

   ```
   "E:\Client Files\setup" /x "E:\Client Files\SPSClient.msi"
   ```

   To repair the components in the preceding example, you would type

   ```
   "E:\Client Files\setup" /f "E:\Client Files\SPSClient.msi"
   ```

The *User's Help* (webfoldr.chm) file remains when you uninstall the client components. It replaces the original Web folders Help file.

If you have removed one or more of the installation prerequisites, you cannot uninstall or repair the client components unless you disable the prerequisite check.

This can be accomplished by adding DISABLEPREREQ=1 to the command line. To disable the prerequisite check in the preceding examples

- When removing the client components, you would type

  ```
  "E:\Client Files\setup" /x "E:\Client Files\SPSClient.msi" DISABLEPREREQ=1
  ```

- When repairing the client components, you would type

  ```
  "E:\Client Files\setup" /f "E:\Client Files\SPSClient.msi" DISABLEPREREQ=1
  ```

Using Systems Management Server (SMS)

To install the client components on multiple computers, SharePoint Portal Server provides a .pdf file that can be used with SMS. This file is called SPSClient.pdf and is located in the Client directory on the SharePoint Portal Server CD, and in Program Files\SharePoint Portal Server\ClientDrop\Languages*Lang*, where *Lang* corresponds to the language of the client.

For more information, see the SMS product documentation.

7

After you have installed the client components, you must add a Web folder that points to the workspace. The address of the workspace is `http://server_name/workspace_name`.

USING WINDOWS INSTALLER

Windows installer uses industry standard .msi files. Once the .msi files are created, you can manually launch an installation script from the command prompt. For example, let's assume that the SharePoint Portal Server client installation script was created as an .msi SPScleint.msi. To use Windows Installer, perform the following steps:

1. Click **Start**, and then click **Run**.

2. In **Open**, type `msiexec /qn /I "path\SPSClient.msi"`.

The quotation marks are required only if the path contains spaces. For example, if SPSClient.msi is on a file share called ServerName\SharePoint Portal Server Client Setup, quotation marks are required because of the spaces in "SharePoint Portal Server Client Setup." You would type `msiexec /qn /I \\\\ServerName\\SharePoint Portal Server Client Setup\\SPSClient.msi`.

> **NOTE**
>
> If your operating system is Windows 98 and Windows Installer is present, include the path to msiexec.exe. For example, if msiexec.exe is located in C:\Windows\System, type `C:\Windows\System\msiexec /qn /I "C:\SharePoint Portal Server Client\SPSClient.msi"`.
>
> You can also add the directory that contains msiexec.exe to the system path. Adding the directory to the local path will avoid having to type out the entire directory.

3. Click **OK**. SharePoint Portal Server installs the client without displaying user interface messages. This is an unattended installation process.

4. After you have installed the client components, you must add a Web folder that points to the workspace. The address of the workspace is `http://server_name/workspace_name`.

For more information about Windows Installer, including options other than unattended installations, see Windows Help on any computer on which Windows Installer is present.

USING ACTIVE DIRECTORY

To use Active Directory, follow these steps:

1. On the domain controller computer, create a folder containing SPSClient.msi. *You must share this folder.*

    This file is called SPSClient.pdf and is located in the Client directory on the SharePoint Portal Server CD, and in Program Files\SharePoint Portal Server\ ClientDrop\Languages*Lang*, where *Lang* corresponds to the language of the client.

2. Add the Group Policy snap-in.

2.1 On the taskbar, click **Start**, and then click **Run.**

2.2 Type MMC and then click **OK**. The MMC console opens.

2.3 On the **Console** menu, click **Add/Remove Snap-in**. The **Add/Remove Snap-in** dialog box appears.

2.4 On the **Standalone** tab, click **Add**. The **Add Standalone Snap-in** dialog box appears.

2.5 In Available Standalone Snap-ins, click Group Policy, and then click Add. The Select Group Policy Object dialog box appears.

2.6 Click Browse. The Browse for a Group Policy Object dialog box appears.

2.7 Click **Default Domain Policy**, click **OK**, and then click **Finish**.

2.8 Click **Close**. The **Group Policy** snap-in now appears on the Standalone tab in the Add/Remove Snap-in dialog box.

2.9 Click **OK**.

3. Add the SharePoint Portal Server client package.

> **NOTE**
>
> Applying the package as stated will result in everyone within the domain receiving the package. You may want to add the package to a controlled group to limit who gets the package installed. If you are the SharePoint Portal Server Admin and do not have Domain Admin rights, you will need to work with the domain administrator to perform these tasks.

To complete the process for publication the package through Active Directory, perform the following tasks:

1. Expand the Default Domain Policy node.
2. Expand the User Configuration node.
3. Expand the **Software Settings** node.
4. Right-click **Software installation**, point to **New**, and then click **Package**.
5. Browse to the folder you created in step 1, and double-click **SPSClient.msi**. The Deploy Software dialog box appears.
6. Click **Published**, and then click **OK**.

At this point the package is enabled and the end user can simply install the client components through **Add/Remove Programs** in the **Control Panel**.

> **NOTE**
>
> Remember, after installing the client components, you must add a Web folder that points to the workspace. The address of the workspace is
> `http://server_name/workspace_name`.

7

OVERVIEW OF COMMON ADMINISTRATIVE TASKS

The objective of this section is to provide details for performing the most common administrative processes and procedures.

HOW TO CREATE A DOCUMENT PROFILE

Each document in the workspace is defined by a document profile, which contains a set of document properties.

→ To learn more about document profiles, **see** "Document Profiles," **p. 264**.

Open the workspace to access the management folder. See Figure 7.7.

Figure 7.7
Starting point for creating a document profile.

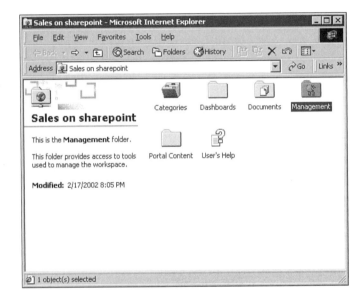

1. Within the workspace, click on Management to expose the document profile options by clicking on the Document Profiles icon.

2. Clicking on the Document Profiles option will expose the document profiles available (see Figure 7.8).

3. Double-click **Add Document Profile**.

4. Provide a descriptive name for the document profile, and then select an existing profile to use as a template. The **Base Document** profile is the default template. Click **Next.**

7

Figure 7.8
All document profile
options including the
option for adding a
new document profile.

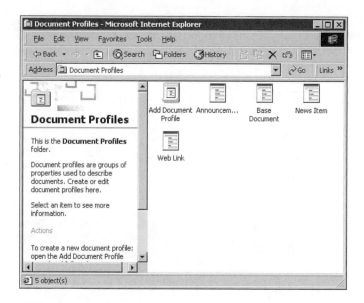

Figure 7.9
Default dialog box for
adding a name for
your profile and
assigning a document
profile template.

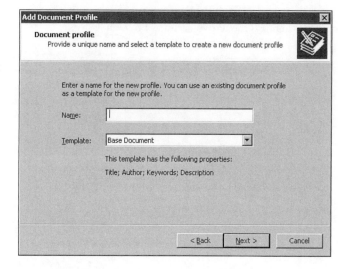

5. Define the properties that comprise the fields on the document profile.

   • To select or deselect a property to appear on the document profile, click the box next to the property name.

   • Click **New** to add a new property.

   • To edit the attributes of an existing property, select the property by highlighting the property name, and then click **Edit**.

7

Figure 7.10
You must choose the properties that need to be associated with this profile.

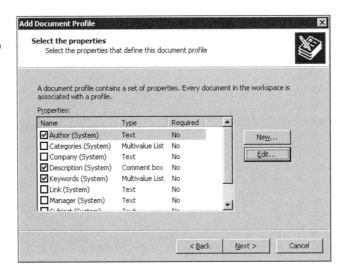

6. Click **Next.**

7. To choose the order in which the properties appear on the document profile, select a property, and then use the **Move** arrows. Then click **Next.**

Figure 7.11
You can easily change the order for how fields are displayed.

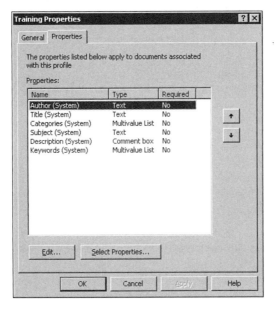

9. Click **Finish**.

7

The new document profile appears in the Document Profiles folder when the wizard is complete. The document profile is available for use on the Properties page for folders and the Properties page for documents.

HOW TO CRAWL A WEB SERVER

A Web server is just one of the available content sources SharePoint Portal Server can crawl. A content source represents a location, indicated by a URL where documents that are stored outside the workspace can be accessed for inclusion in an index. This content can be located outside of the workspace but on the same server, on another server on your intranet, or on the Internet. Examples of content sources include Web sites, file systems, databases, and other SharePoint Portal Server workspaces.

To create a Web page content source perform the following steps:

1. Open the **Management** folder, and then the **Content Sources** folder.
2. Double-click **Add Content Source** (see Figure 7.12).

Figure 7.12
Options available within Content Sources folder.

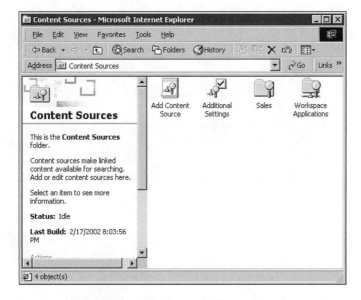

3. The Content Source Wizard opens. Click **Next**.
4. The content source type, Web site, should be highlighted. Click **Next** (see Figure 7.13).
5. Enter the URL for the Web site you would like to crawl (see Figure 7.14).

7

Figure 7.13
All available content sources to choose from.

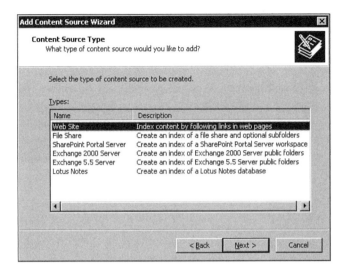

Figure 7.14
Default dialog box for configuring a content source. This box is where you provide a name and specify the index depth.

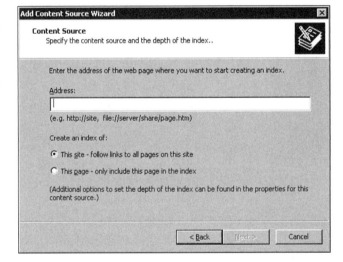

6. The next time the index is updated, SharePoint Portal Server makes information from this content source available for you to access. Now you can subscribe to search queries and categories that include documents from this content source. When information posts you are interested in, you are notified.

HOW TO CREATE CATEGORIES

You configure categories in the Categories folder in the workspace. You apply categories to documents by using the document profile form.

Categories provide a managed group of terms that help users characterize documents in the workspace.

Users can classify a document in one or more categories. For example, a document can be classified in categories such as Managing, Productivity, and Engineering to attract customers to a new product.

1. In the workspace, open the **Categories** folder (see Figure 7.15).

Figure 7.15
Default view of categories folder.

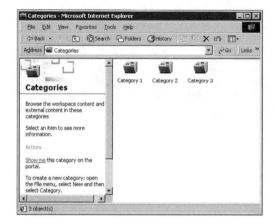

2. From the **File** menu, point to **New**, and then click **Category**.
3. Type a unique name for the new category.
4. Press **Enter**.

It is automatically available for searching on the dashboard site.

The index is updated to include the new category value. This enables others to use it when categorizing their documents using the document profile form.

How to Check in a Document

When you check in your document, a new version (your latest draft) becomes the working version in the workspace. You can check in the document from the workspace, the dashboard site, or a Microsoft Office application. When you have added a document to the workspace, or when you have completed work on a document that you have checked out, you must check it in to enable other folder users to view the latest version of the document.

→ There are a few ways to accomplish document check-in. For more details and to explore all the various check-in methods, **see** "Check-in/Check-out," **p. 25.**

To check in a document from the workspace, perform the following steps:

1. Drag desired file to Documents folder or locate the document in the workspace.
2. Right-click the document, and then click **Check In**.

3. The Version Comments dialog box appears. Simply complete the fields (see Figure 7.16), then click **OK.**

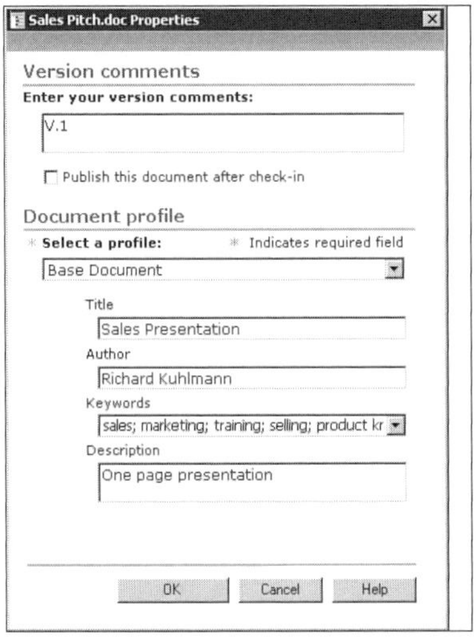

Figure 7.16

Enter meaningful version comments and populate all other required fields associated with the document profile.

NOTE

To publish your document, on the check-in form select the **Publish this document after check-in** box. If the folder in which the document is stored has an approval route, the document is published only after it is approved. If no approval route is associated, the document is automatically published and made available for searching and viewing on the dashboard site.

4. Click OK.

Checking in a document allows others to see your work in the workspace and review the changes you have made.

To check in a document from Office

1. On the **File** menu, click **Check In**.

2. A check-in form appears. Complete the Version Comments and make any necessary changes to the document profile form.

3. Click OK.

From the Dashboard, perform the following steps:

1. Click the **Document Library** tab (see Figure 7.17).

Figure 7.17
Default dashboard view and starting point for adding a document.

2. Click **Add Document**, which launches the Add a document dialog box (see Figure 7.18).

Figure 7.18
View of Add a Document dialog window.

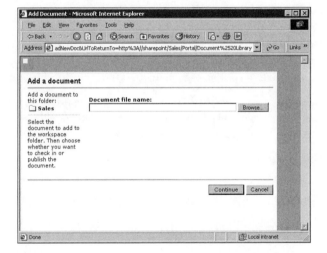

3. Click **Browse** and find your desired document; then click continue.
4. Again, populate the fields with the required data and click **Save**.

How to Specify an Approval Route

A new, public version is created automatically after a document is approved. Use this process as a system to review and approve workspace documents in enhanced folders before publishing them on the dashboard site.

To specify an approval route follow these steps:

1. Right-click on an enhanced folder.

→ Enhanced folders allow additional functionality such as approval routing. For additional information on Enhanced Folders, **see** "Enhanced Folders," **p. 287**.

2. Click **Properties** and click on the **Approval** tab.

3. From the **Approval** tab, click **Add** to create a list of approvers.

4. Click the up or down arrow to change the order for a serial approval route.

5. Add comments for the approvers in the **Comments for approval e-mail** text box.

Every document that is published within a folder with an approval route configured immediately begins the process as outlined from the approval tab.

CREATING YOUR FOLDER STRUCTURE

Decide what type of folder to use for each group of documents, and then create the folder hierarchy in the workspace. You have two choices of accomplishing this: Duplicate your existing folder structure or design a new one.

Obviously the quickest method is to duplicate your existing folder structure and make any modifications. Dragging a folder and its contents into the workspace can be done. However, the top-level Documents folder is an enhanced folder. Therefore, any folder you drag into the Documents folder inherits its settings from the parent folder. To break the folder setting inheritance, create a new folder in the workspace, enable or disable the folder setting inheritance as needed, and then move the documents into the new workspace folder.

To take the greatest advantage of SharePoint Portal Server features, you can redesign your structure. More planning is involved but can yield greater benefits by eliminating redundancy, clarifying processes, and improving document discovery.

■ Each user can have multiple roles in the workspace.

■ You can distribute management tasks among a number of Coordinators.

■ You can organize information in the dashboard site by using categories to group similar documents.

■ A document may appear in several different categories.

TIP

> If a document's content must be approved by one or more people, consider adding approval routing to the document publishing process. In approval routing, a document is sent to one or more people, and each person can approve or reject the document. Each step in the approval process is complete when the required people approve or reject the document. An approver receives an email notification when a document requires his review. Only enhanced folders have the option for approval routing.

7

CAUTION

> When you create subfolders, an approval process must be configured for each folder. They do not inherit approval process settings from their parent folders.

OPTIMIZING PERFORMANCE

An excellent way to monitor the performance of the SharePoint Portal Server computer is to use performance counters. This can assist you in troubleshooting and capacity planning.

Windows 2000 can track and log performance data that is generated. The data is described as a *performance object* and is typically named for the component generating the data. Every performance object provides *counters* that represent data on specific aspects of the object. For example, if you want to monitor the Microsoft Search (MSSearch) service, select the performance object called *Microsoft Gatherer*, and then select the counter called Heartbeats. For all performance objects, you can select either specific counters or track all counters.

→ For additional details about monitoring performance, **see** "Monitoring and Managing Performance," **p. 135**.

MONITORING A PERFORMANCE COUNTER

1. On the taskbar, click **Start**, point to **Programs**, point to **Administrative Tools**, and then click **Performance**.

2. In the console tree, click **System Monitor**, and then click **+** (Add) on the toolbar.

3. In **Add Counters**, click **Select counters from computer**, and then select the server you want to examine.

4. In **Performance object**, click the object name. You can monitor counters for the following objects:

   - SharePoint Portal Document Management Server
   - SharePoint Portal Server Subscriptions
   - Microsoft Gatherer
   - Microsoft Gatherer Projects
   - Microsoft Search
   - Microsoft Search Catalogs
   - Microsoft Search Indexer Catalogs
   - MSExchange Oledb Resource
   - MSExchange Oledb Events
   - MSExchange Web Mail

5. To monitor
   - All counters for the object, click **All counters**.
   - One or a few of the counters, click **Select counters from list**, select the counter you want to monitor, and then click **Add**.

7

6. If you want to see a description of the counters, click **Explain**.

7. When you finish selecting counters, click **Close**.

→ For additional details about using performance counters, **see** "Monitoring Using Standard Performance Counters," **p. 136**.

MONITORING INDEXING

The following objects can be used to monitor performance associated with indexes:

- **Microsoft Gatherer Project** object, Status Error counter, to see the number of documents that SharePoint Portal Server crawled but did not include in the index.

- **Microsoft Gatherer** object, Notifications Rate counter, to monitor the rate of notifications (from modified items in the file system or the Microsoft Document Store).

- **Microsoft Gatherer Projects** object, Crawls in progress counter, to see the number of crawls in progress.

- **Microsoft Gatherer Projects** object, Document Add Rate or Document Delete Rate counter, if performance slows while creating the index and you want to monitor the rate of document additions or deletions during the crawl process.

- **Microsoft Search Indexer Catalogs** object, Number of Documents counter, to see the number of documents in the index.

- **Microsoft Search Indexer Catalogs** object, Documents Filtered and Files To Be Filtered counters, to see if the crawl was successful. The Documents Filtered counter should be increasing, and the Files To Be Filtered counter should be decreasing.

- **Microsoft Gatherer Projects** object, Error Rate, Retries Rate, and Success Rate counters, to compare statistics for each crawl if you are performing the same crawl consistently.

INDEX PROPAGATION

The following object monitors performance for index propagation:

Microsoft Search Indexer Catalogs object, Number of Propagations counter. If you want to monitor index propagation and see the number of propagations in progress.

SEARCH

The following objects monitor performance for the search process:

- **Microsoft Gatherer** object, Heartbeats counter, to see if the search service is running

- **Microsoft Search** object, Failed Queries counter, to know if queries are failing.

- **Microsoft Search** object, Queries or Succeeded Queries counter, to know if queries are running.

7

The following objects monitor performance for document management:

- **SharePoint Portal Document Management Server** object, Successful Checkins Latency, Successful Copies Latency, and Successful Publishes Latency counters, to monitor the average time taken to perform a document management function such as check-in, copy, or publish.

- **SharePoint Portal Document Management Server** object, Failed Moves counter, to monitor failed move requests.

- **SharePoint Portal Document Management Server** object, Failed Copies counter, to monitor failed copy requests.

- **SharePoint Portal Document Management Server** object, Failed Deletes counter, to monitor failed delete requests.

ADJUST SYSTEM RESOURCE USAGE

To specify resource usage, follow these steps:

1. In the console tree, select the server for which you want to adjust the search or index resource usage.

2. Open the SharePoint Portal Server MMC

3. On the **Action** menu, click **Properties**.

   You can also right-click the server name, and then click **Properties** on the shortcut menu.

4. Click the **General** tab (see Figure 7.19).

Figure 7.19
Using the General tab allows adjusting Search and Indexing resource usage.

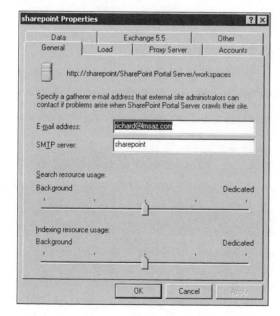

7

5. Change Search resource usage or Indexing resource usage to the desired setting.

6. Click **Apply**.

> **TIP**
>
> If you're running Exchange 2000 or SQL Server, avoid adjusting the controls to Dedicated or Near-Dedicated usage for either searching or index creation.

If you have multiple servers, balance resource usage by

- Distributing searching and index creation.
- Dedicating resources on each computer to the specific task it performs.
- If you use one server, performing both index building and searching.
- Balance resource usage evenly between the two processes.

ADJUST THE QUERY TIME-OUT

You can edit the waiting period for each index, limiting each query to a specific number of milliseconds. This releases server processes consumed by unsuccessful queries instead of waiting and keeping the server busy.

Adjust this setting on the Index tab of the Properties page for the workspace node.

> **TIP**
>
> If response time is a priority for your organization, configure the time-out to be 1,000 milliseconds. By default, the time-out is 10,000 milliseconds.

To specify the time-out, follow these steps:

1. Open the SharePoint Portal Server MMC.

2. In the console tree, select the server that contains the workspace for which you want to specify the query time-out.

3. Click to expand the server, and then select the workspace for which you want to specify the query time-out.

4. On the **Action** menu, click **Properties**.

   You can also right-click the workspace name, and then click **Properties** on the shortcut menu.

5. Click the **Index** tab (see Figure 7.20).

6. In **Number of milliseconds to limit each query to**, type the number of milliseconds for the duration of the query before it times out.

7. Click **Apply**.

7

Figure 7.20
The index tab exposes settings for limiting each query.

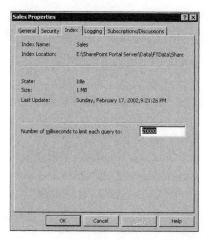

MOVE DATA STORE, LOG, AND PROPERTY STORE FILES

To increase performance or simplify file management, specify the location of the following data store and log files.

Search Indexes. Use SharePoint Portal Server Administration in the MMC to change this path.

> **NOTE**
>
> Subsequent indexes are created in the new location; if this path changes, the existing indexes do not move to the new index location.
>
> See ToolsHowTo.txt in the Support\Tools directory on the SharePoint Portal Server CD to move existing indexes to a new location.

Search Temporary Files. For best performance, the temporary files location should point to a disk other than the system drive or the drive containing any SharePoint Portal Server data files, including the index files.

> **TIP**
>
> For optimal performance, make sure the property store files, search indexes, system page files, and the Microsoft Document Store files are stored on a disk separate from the MSSearch temporary folder. There must be sufficient disk space for MSSearch to operate correctly.

Search Gatherer Logs. Each time an index is created, a log file for that workspace is created also, containing data about crawling content and access errors. Use SharePoint Portal Server MMC to change this path, if necessary.

This log file can be viewed from a user-friendly ASP page in the Content Sources folder, located in the Management folder in the workspace. You can specify the size and settings of these log files. By specifying log successes, you can approximate the size by allowing 100 bytes per URL.

7

To specify gatherer log settings for the workspace, follow these steps:

1. Open the SharePoint Portal Server MMC.

2. In the console tree, select the server that contains the workspace for which you want to specify gatherer log settings.

3. Click to expand the server, and then select the workspace for which you want to specify gatherer log settings.

4. On the **Action** menu, click **Properties**.

   You can also right-click the server name, and then click **Properties** on the shortcut menu.

5. Click the **Logging** tab (see Figure 7.21).

Figure 7.21
Tab for adjusting log successes and items excluded by site path rules.

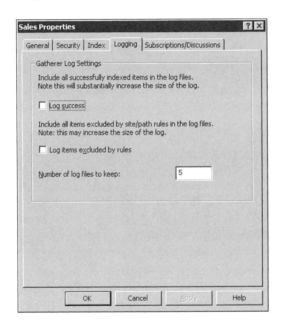

6. Type or select the gatherer log settings:

   • If you want to log successful accesses, select the **Log success** check box.

   • If you want to log accesses excluded by rules, select the **Log items excluded by rules** check box.

   • Type the number of log files to keep in **Number of log files to keep**.

7. Click **Apply**.

   Microsoft Document Store-Database. Every SharePoint Portal Server computer contains one public store (wss.mdb). All workspaces hosted on the server reside on the Document Store. Using the MMC, you can change this path. If this location changes, the existing file moves to the new location.

Document Store-Streaming Database.wss.stm is a companion to the Document Store Database file (wss.mdb). Together these two files form the database. Move this file to a larger drive (ideally a dynamic disk that you can easily resize) because the file can increase substantially over time. Use the MMC to change this path. If this location changes, the existing file moves to the new location.

Document Store-Database Log. For optimal performance, place the log files on a dedicated physical volume. These are the log files for the Document Store. Use the MMC to change this path. If this location changes, the existing files move to the new location.

Property Store. To modify the file location, see ToolsHowTo.txt in the Support\Tools directory on the SharePoint Portal Server CD. This file contains the metadata from documents. You cannot modify it using the MMC.

Property Store Log Files. To modify the file location, see ToolsHowTo.txt in the Support\Tools directory on the SharePoint Portal Server CD. These are the log files for the property store. You cannot modify it using the MMC.

TIP

> For optimal performance, the property store and property store log files should be on dedicated physical volumes. This file is shared across all workspaces. Do the same for the Document Store files and Document Store log files.

USING INCREMENTAL OR ADAPTIVE UPDATES

Performing an incremental or adaptive update of an index instead of a full update can improve server performance.

An incremental update is faster than performing a full update. However it only includes content that has changed. Unless there is some reason to perform a full update, this is a great periodic solution, without chewing up precious resources or time.

TIP

> Configure SharePoint Portal Server to perform an incremental update daily and a full update weekly if you are excluding document types in your incremental update. This allows you to have daily updates of changed content and periodic full updates of all content.

NOTE

> You can start an incremental update only if the index status is Idle. You can view the index status either on the Index tab of the Properties page of the workspace node or in the details pane of SharePoint Portal Server MMC.

7

To update an incremental index, perform these steps:

1. Open the SharePoint Portal Server MMC.
2. In the console tree, select the server that contains the index you want to update.

3. Click to expand the server, and then select the workspace that contains the index (see Figure 7.22).

Figure 7.22
View of Administrative snap-in, which is the default location for performing the incremental update.

4. In the **Action** menu, point to **All Tasks**, and then click **Start Incremental Update**. You can also right-click, point to **All Tasks** on the shortcut menu, and then click **Start Incremental Update**.

> **NOTE**
> If you have not previously performed a full update then the first time you run any kind of update will by default be your first full update. Subsequent incremental updates will be true incremental updates.

> **TIP**
> If power to the server is interrupted during an update, the update continues after power is restored. The crawl resumes after it finishes initializing.

An adaptive update is similar to the incremental update, by far the fastest of the three. However, some updated content might be missed. But, SharePoint Portal Server always crawls documents that have not been retrieved for two weeks, even if they have not been updated. After about a week of daily adaptive updates, the system becomes increasingly efficient. Once the system settles into a steady state, performance improves depending on the number of documents and the frequency of changes to the documents.

> **NOTE**
> If you're crawling fewer than 2,500 documents, this type of update is unlikely to give any performance improvement.

You can start an adaptive update only if the index status is Idle. You can view the index status either on the Index tab of the Properties page of the workspace node or in the details pane of SharePoint Portal Server MMC.

To update an adaptive index, perform these steps:

1. Open the SharePoint Portal Server MMC.

2. In the console tree, select the server that contains the index you want to update.

3. Click to expand the server, and then select the workspace that contains the index.

4. On the **Action** menu, point to **All Tasks**, and then click **Start Adaptive Update**.

   You can also right-click, point to **All Tasks** on the shortcut menu, and then click **Start Adaptive Update**.

NOTE | If you have not previously performed a full update then the first time you run any kind of update will by default be your first full update. The second update is an incremental update. The third time will be a true adaptive update.

UPDATING A FULL INDEX

A full update adds new content, modifies changed content, refreshes the index for existing unchanged content, and removes deleted content from the index.

You should perform a full update in the following situations:

- Whenever you change the rules specified for content sources. These rules control what content is included in the index. You can edit these rules from the Content Sources folder located in the Management folder in the workspace.

- If a category is renamed.

- When you have changed a noise word file. A noise word is a word such as "the" or "an" that is not useful in an index.

- After you have reset the index.

- If the system experiences a power failure. You should perform a full update after power is restored if you notice that documents are missing.

You can start a full update only if the index status is Idle. You can view the index status either on the Index tab of the Properties page of the workspace node or in the details pane of SharePoint Portal Server MMC.

To update a full index, perform the following steps:

1. Open the SharePoint Portal Server MMC.

2. In the console tree, select the server that contains the index you want to update.

3. Click to expand the server, and then select the workspace that contains the index.

4. On the **Action** menu, point to **All Tasks**, and then click **Start Full Update**.

   You can also right-click, point to **All Tasks** on the shortcut menu, and then click **Start Full Update**.

A full update includes notification content sources in the index.

7

SUMMARY

In this chapter, we discussed the requirements for a successful implementation of SharePoint Portal Server. We provided an overview of the prerequisites for the server and client prior to proceeding with the implementation. We discussed co-existence and what is supported by Microsoft. We talked about deployment planning considerations for server, client, and the network as well as proxy settings that should be planned for. Step-by-step installation instructions were provided for the server as well as the client, including information on unattended and scripted installations for both the server and client. Lastly, we discussed a series of the most common administrative tasks that are performed on a SharePoint Portal Server.

CHAPTER **8**

MANAGING THE SERVERS

In this chapter

8

INTRODUCTION

In this chapter, we will explore common administrative tasks specifically for managing a SharePoint Portal Server. Some of the tasks that we will discuss within this chapter are covered in more detail in other chapters. For example, Chapter 9 discusses managing the workspace, which is considered a more detailed granular administration task within the context of managing the server. Because of this, we have created a separate chapter specifically for all the tasks associated with managing the workspace. Chapter 10 discusses processes and procedures for managing folders and documents, and Chapter 19 discusses detailed tasks for managing indexing. As you can see, all of these tasks could be classified as activities that are applicable to the management of a server. However, due to the amount of detailed information on these sub-tasks, we decided that many of these tasks required their own chapter.

Chapter 8 will discuss server-specific management tasks available within the server properties page of the SharePoint Portal Server administrative tools. Examples of the types of administrative tasks we will discuss include how to access the General property page to adjust Index and Search resource usage, specifying the various methods of configuring SharePoint Portal Server with Microsoft Proxy Server, configuring load options and specifying site hit frequency rules, changing the location of data store log and property store files, configuring SharePoint Portal Server to integrate with Lotus Notes by configuring the protocol handler, and how to start and stop the SharePoint Portal Server services. In addition, we will discuss advanced topics such as using IFilters, editing the noise word file, editing the thesaurus, and more.

SERVER MANAGEMENT TASKS

Within the SharePoint Portal Server administrative tools interface, you will see the local/current server.

To modify the server settings of a specific SharePoint Portal Server, you can right-click on the server and select Properties, which will then display all the property pages for this particular server (see Figure 8.1).

→ To read more detail on each of these server settings and how they impact workspace management, **see** "Modifying and Managing Global Workspace Settings," **p. 252**.

The property pages that are displayed are

- General
- Load
- Proxy Server
- Accounts
- Data
- Exchange 5.5
- Other

These tabs will be discussed in more detail in the following sections.

Figure 8.1
View of all property
pages available when
you right-click on a
particular server
object within
SharePoint Portal
Server Administration.

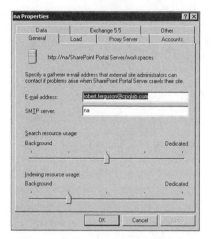

8

THE GENERAL SETTINGS PAGE

The General Settings page is used to specify an SMTP server and a gatherer email address
that administrators from external sites can contact if any issues arise when your SharePoint
Portal Server is configured to crawl their site. In addition, this is the page where you can
modify settings for Search and Index usage to balance the performance of SharePoint
Portal Server.

Figure 8.2
Settings within the
General page.

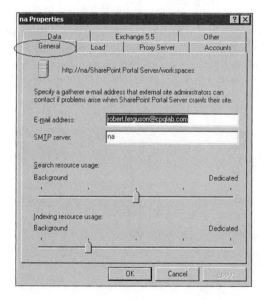

8

MODIFYING THE EMAIL ADDRESS

The email address you specify may need to be changed from time to time. To change the email address that external site administrators will use as their contact

1. Right-click on the server object within SharePoint Portal Server Administration and click Properties.
2. Click on the General tab.
3. Type in the email address and SMTP server, and click OK.

SPECIFYING SEARCH AND INDEX RESOURCE USAGE

In addition to setting the email address, you can also configure the Search and Index Usage on a server. Searching content and Index creation are two resource-intensive processes that are performed on your SharePoint Portal Server. By adjusting the resource usage settings, you are optimizing the performance of your server and assigning a higher or lower priority to one or the other (searching content or creating indexes). In small environments, it is recommended that you balance the search and index usage settings evenly. In larger environments, you will likely have a dedicated search server and a dedicated index server. In the larger environment, you should adjust the Search resource usage for the search server to Dedicated, and set the Index resource usage to Background. On the Index server, you should adjust the Search resource usage to Background and change the Index resource usage to Dedicated.

CAUTION

> In the unlikely and not-recommended event you happen to be running other applications such as Microsoft Exchange or Microsoft SQL Server on the same server as SharePoint Portal Server, you should not change the resource usage controls. Changing the resource usage settings on the server can impact these other applications, which may result in unacceptable performance.

To change the resource usage settings

1. Right-click on the server object within SharePoint Portal Server Administration and click Properties.
2. Select the General tab, and then click and drag the resource usage bar to the required setting.
3. When you are done, click Apply and then OK.

LOAD OPTION SETTINGS

The Load Page is used to modify settings associated with creating indexes. Many people do not realize that when you configure SharePoint Portal Server to crawl a remote site, you are impacting resources from the SharePoint Portal Server that creates the index as well as

8

resources for servers that provide the content that is being indexed. The load page is used to set site frequency rules and time-out options, so that the performance of the computers being crawled can be maintained. With site frequency rules, an administrator can specify how many documents can be requested at a given time. In addition, you can set a time interval between consecutive requests. Lastly, you can set time-out settings, which will enable you to configure how long a SharePoint Portal Server will wait for a response or connection from an external site. Figure 8.3 shows where you modify the number of seconds to wait for a connection or request acknowledgement.

Figure 8.3
Modifying the number of seconds for a connection or request acknowledgement.

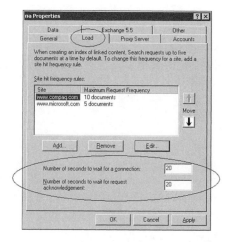

NOTE

All the settings within this Load page are important, and can help ensure that your SharePoint Portal Server does not attempt to request too many documents from external sites. Failure to configure these settings properly can result in other servers and users experiencing denial of access to those particular sites.

WEB SITE CONNECTION WAIT TIME

The number of seconds to wait for a connection setting should not be set to less than 10 seconds or greater than 120 seconds (2 minutes). If wait time is set for less than 10 seconds, SharePoint Portal Server skips over busy servers, which results in some content not getting indexed. If wait time is set too high (such as more than 2 minutes) SharePoint Portal Server spends a great deal of time trying to crawl nonexistent sites, bad links, or servers that are not available.

TIP

For crawling Exchange public folders, the recommended wait time is 60 seconds. Wait time must be greater than 10 seconds.

8

 If you have set your Exchange time-out to something over 10 seconds but find your SharePoint Portal Server unable to index a particular Exchange content source, see "Exchange Server Unavailable for Ten Minutes" in the "Troubleshooting" section at the end of the chapter.

REQUEST ACKNOWLEDGEMENT WAIT TIME

The number of seconds to wait for request acknowledgement is a setting that allows you to specify how long the server should wait for a Web page or file after connecting to a Web site. Similar to the minimum and maximum settings for waiting for a connection, a wait time of 10 seconds is too low, and 2 minutes is too high. The default wait time is 20 seconds.

ADDING A SITE HIT FREQUENCY RULE

Configuring site hit frequency rules enables you to better control the level of Web site activity that SPS generates while crawling. The rules allow you to specify the frequency for accessing documents from a Web site, as well as the number of documents that can be requested.

As specified previously, within the Load tab, you can configure the number of seconds to wait for a connection as well as the number of seconds to wait for a request acknowledgement. These settings are shown in Figure 8.3. Figure 8.4 shows how to add a site hit frequency rule.

Figure 8.4
Configuring a site hit frequency rule.

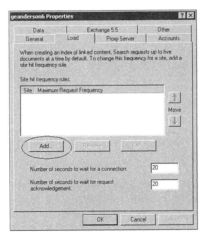

NOTE

Out of the box default functionality provides for a site hit frequency of five documents at the same time.

It is a best practice that you configure site hit frequency rules for external Web sites to a much lower setting than you would your own intranet sites. As stated previously, failure to restrict site hit frequency for external sites may result in denial of access. To add a site hit frequency rule

1. Right-click on the server object within SharePoint Portal Server Administration.
2. Click Properties and then click the Load tab.
3. Within the Load tab, click Add.
4. When the Add Site Hit Frequency Rule dialog box appears, type the name of the site in the Site name field. For example, you could type in http://www.microsoft.com.
5. Specify the frequency by selecting one of the three options.

Figure 8.5
Add Site Hit Frequency
Rule dialog box.

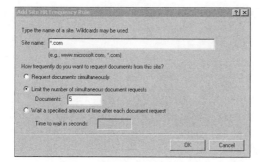

Once you specify the name of the server, you then need to specify the frequency for requesting documents from this site. Your options are outlined in Table 8.1:

TABLE 8.1   SITE HIT FREQUENCY OPTIONS

Option	Description
Request documents simultaneously	All available system resources are used by SharePoint Portal Server to request as many documents as possible. You can specify this setting on an internal intranet server, but it will likely be too intrusive to resources for external Internet sites.
Limit the number of simultaneous document requests	This setting allows you to limit the number of documents that can be requested from a specific site. The default is five document requests at one time.
Wait a specified amount of time for each document request	When enabled, SharePoint Portal Server will request documents one at a time and delay a specified amount of time prior to making the next request.

8

REMOVING OR EDITING A SITE HIT FREQUENCY RULE

Once site hit frequency rules are configured, you can modify these settings or delete rules as required. To edit or remove a site hit frequency rule

1. Right-click on the server object within SharePoint Portal Server Administration.

2. Click Properties and then click the Load tab.

3. Within the Site Hit Frequency Rule sub-window, select the rule that you want to remove or edit.

4. Once selected, click on Remove or Edit. If you select Remove, the rule will be removed. If you select Edit, the Site Hit Frequency Rule dialog box appears for this rule.

5. Click Apply and then OK.

PROXY SERVER OPTIONS

Microsoft Proxy Server reduces download time by caching recently accessed Web pages. In addition, the Proxy Server prevents unauthorized Internet access to your corporate intranet. The opportune time to configure the proxy server settings is when indexes for external Web sites are created. You have three settings related to configuring Proxy Server with SharePoint Portal Server. The three settings are specified in Figure 8.6.

Figure 8.6
Proxy Server page settings.

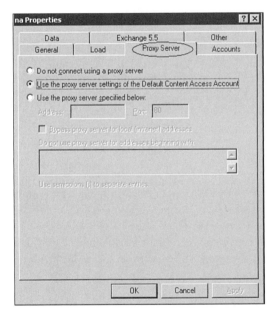

The three settings available are

- Do not connect using a proxy server
- Use the proxy settings of the Default Content Access Account
- Use the proxy server specified below

NOTE
> SharePoint Portal Server uses the proxy server setting of the default content access account, and the default content access account uses the current proxy server settings configured within Microsoft Internet Explorer.

→ To learn more about the role of Proxy servers and storage cards from a security perspective, **see** "Proxy Servers," **p. 291**.

Proxy Considerations

One of the configuration options when setting up indexing is to configure SharePoint Portal Server not to use a Proxy Server.

→ To read more about configuring SPS to not use a Proxy Server, **see** "Crawling Without a Proxy Server," **p. 465**.

On the other hand, you may also leverage Proxy settings of the default content access account. Selecting this option within the Proxy Server settings page will configure SharePoint Portal Server to use the Proxy Server settings installed on the server by Internet Explorer.

To use the Proxy Server settings of the default content access account

1. Right-click on the server object within SharePoint Portal Server Administration.
2. Click Properties and then click the Proxy Server tab.
3. Click Use the proxy server settings of the Default Content Access Account.
4. Click Apply and then OK.

Finally, SharePoint Portal Server can be configured to use a specific Proxy Server. Once configured, other applications on the server are not impacted if you change the Proxy Server settings for the SharePoint Portal Server.

To configure SharePoint Portal Server to use a specific Proxy Server

1. Right-click on the server object within SharePoint Portal Server Administration.
2. Click Properties and then click the Proxy Server tab.
3. Click Use the proxy server specified below.
4. Enter the proxy server Address and Port. Specify whether you want to use the proxy server when creating an index for local addresses. If you do, click on Bypass proxy server for local (intranet) addresses.

8

5. If you have specific addresses that you do not want to use the proxy server, enter the addresses within the window labeled Do not use proxy server for addresses beginning with.

6. Click Apply and then OK.

ACCESS ACCOUNT OPTIONS

When discussing the concept of Access Accounts within SharePoint Portal Server, there are two types of access accounts that can be discussed. They are the previously discussed default content access account and the propagation access account. As an index is created, SharePoint Portal Server will take advantage of the current security associated with Web sites and servers. SharePoint Portal Server must have an access account specified in the list view of the Account property page of the server. When indexes for content outside the workspace are created, SharePoint Portal Server uses this default content access account to access the remote server. In order for this to happen, the default account requires Read permissions for any Web site or server that will need to be crawled. When propagating indexes to remote SharePoint Portal Server computers, a propagation access account and password must be specified. This security requirement dictates that the propagation access account must have administrator rights on both servers. Figure 8.7 provides an illustration of the Access property page.

Figure 8.7
Access account settings page.

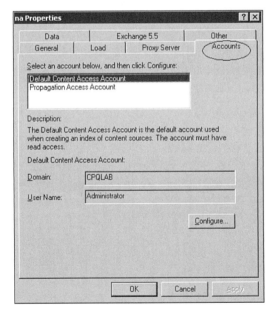

DEFAULT CONTENT ACCESS ACCOUNT

The default content access account is only used if a site access account is not configured (which is done via the SharePoint Portal Server Indexing Settings page). During the creation of an index for a remote Web site or server, the default content access account is utilized. If the account has not been configured, the anonymous account will be specified. You must have Read access to the remote site or else you will only be able to create an index of sites or servers within your intranet. The account you specify, normally during installation, will apply to all content sources unless site path rules are configured.

→ For a discussion on site path rules, **see** "Gathering Architecture," **p. 102**.

To configure the default content access account, perform the following tasks:

1. Right-click on the server object within SharePoint Portal Server Administration.
2. Click Properties and then click the Accounts property page.
3. Click on Default Content Access Account, and click Configure in the lower right corner.
4. When the Account Information dialog box appears, enter the domain, account name, and password. Re-enter the password in the last box to confirm the password.
5. Click OK and then Apply.

NOTE

> If using a Proxy Server, the account used to access the Internet requires the appropriate permissions on the proxy server in order to create indexes for sites outside the workspace or intranet.

PROPAGATION ACCESS ACCOUNT

Index Propagation allows administrators to *propagate* an index of a workspace from one SharePoint Portal Server to another, in an effort to minimize the impact on performance on the destination server. For example, let's assume that a single site has two servers, one dedicated to searching and managing documents, and the other dedicated to creating and managing indexes. In this scenario, you could generate an index on the server dedicated to indexing, and propagate the index to the server dedicated to searching and document management. This will limit the performance requirements on the server dedicated to searching and document management, as the resource-intensive index management tasks are performed exclusively on the dedicated server for indexing. To configure the propagation access account, perform the following tasks:

1. Right-click on the server object within SharePoint Portal Server Administration.
2. Click Properties and then click the Accounts property page.
3. Click on Propagation Access Account, and click Configure in the lower right corner.

8

4. When the Account Information dialog box appears, enter the domain, account name, and password. Re-enter the password in the last box to confirm the password.

5. Click OK and then Apply.

NOTE

> The propagation access account must have local administration security permissions on both the source and destination servers.

LOCATION OF DATA STORE AND LOG FILES

SharePoint Portal Server allows you to specify the location of Data store and log files. This ability to modify the default location can substantially increase the overall SPS server performance and reduce the complexity associated with managing these files. Figure 8.8 provides a visual representation of the data and log files settings page, which is the page for changing the default location.

Figure 8.8
Server data and log file settings page.

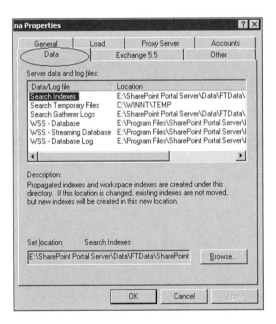

→ For detailed information regarding sizing and performance characterization of the SPS data store, log files, and more, **see** "Performance Requirements," **p. 586.**

MODIFYING DATA STORE, LOG, AND PROPERTY STORE FILE LOCATIONS

Once you access the server data and log file settings page, there exist six data or log files that may be changed. The six components include

- Search Indexes
- Search Temporary Files
- Search Gatherer Logs
- Web Storage System (WSS)—Database
- Web Storage System (WSS)—Streaming Database
- Web Storage System (WSS)—Database Log

These settings are described in more detail in Table 8.2:

TABLE 8.2   SEARCH AND WSS SETTINGS

Setting Type	Description
Search Indexes	This particular field is used to change the location of a search index. Workspace indexes as well as indexes that are propagated from other servers are stored in the directory specified within this field.
Search Temporary Files	During the crawl process, the Microsoft Search (MSSearch) component creates temporary files. The Search Temporary Files field is used to change the default location, which is normally WINNT\TEMP on the system drive. However, in the absence of a WINNT\TEMP folder, the folder indicated within the system TEMP variable is used. It is recommended that this location point to a disk separate from the disk that contains SharePoint Portal Server system data or index files.
Search Gatherer Logs	The Search Gatherer Logs field is used to change the default location of search gatherer logs. Gatherer log files contain important information regarding URLs that are accessed during the creation of an index for a content source. Examples of the types of data contained in these log files include access errors, successful accesses, and accesses that are denied using rules based index restrictions. These log files are generated for the workspace each time an index is created, and can be viewed by accessing the Content Sources folder, which is a subfolder of the Management Workspace.

continues

8

TABLE 8.2 CONTINUED	
Setting Type	**Description**
Web Storage System (WSS)— Database	This field is used to change the path of the Web Storage System database. This database, also known as the public store, contains all workspaces for this server, and every SharePoint Portal Server has only one. This Web Storage System Database file is called wss.mdb.
Web Storage System (WSS)— Streaming Database	This field is used to change the path for the Web Storage System Streaming Database. The Web Storage System (wss.mdb) and the Web Storage System Streaming Database (wss.stm) are two separate physical files that are combined to comprise the actual database. Quite often, the mss.stm file is larger than the wss.mdb file due to the type of data that resides within this file.
Web Storage System (WSS)— Database Log	This field is used to specify or change the location of Web storage system database logs. The file location can be changed to separate partitions. However, the log file should be located on the same computer as the Web Storage System.

CAUTION

It is extremely important to note that when you change the path to Search Indexes, Search Temporary Files, and Search Gatherer Logs, the files are not automatically redirected to the new location. Once the new location is specified, SharePoint Portal Server will begin to create indexes in the new location from this point forward. If you want to move existing indexes to the new location, please refer to the process as documented in the file called Toolshowto.txt, which is located on the \Support\Tools directory of the SharePoint Portal Server CD.

TIP

Only the WSS database, the WSS streaming database, and the WSS database logs are automatically redirected after file locations are modified. If you also happen to have Exchange 2000 loaded on the same computer, you should use the Exchange System Manager to modify the location of the files that comprise the Web Storage System.

If you do not have Exchange 2000 loaded on the same computer, you can perform the following steps to change the location of the data store and log files:

1. Right-click on the server object within SharePoint Portal Server Administration.
2. Click Properties and then click the Data property page.
3. Click on the file that you want to change the default location of, and click Browse.
4. Within the Browse for Folder dialog box, specify a location, and click on OK and then Apply.

TIP

> A root folder cannot be specified as the desired redirection location, and if you do not have enough available disk space for the file you are redirecting, you will get an error message.

→ Specifying settings and viewing gatherer log files are covered in more detail in "Viewing the Gatherer Log," **p. 480**.

Exchange Server 5.5 Options

SharePoint Portal Server provides the capability to also crawl content that resides within Exchange Server 5.5 servers. Crawling content sources will be covered extensively in Chapter 18, and crawling prerequisites such as installing Outlook, installing the CDO feature within Outlook, as well as other best practice recommendations are discussed as well. Our discussion within this section of the chapter will focus on covering specific administrative server-related functionality for enabling SharePoint Portal Server to crawl public folders on Exchange 5.5 Servers.

SharePoint Portal Server is limited to the specification of a single Exchange Server per SharePoint Portal Server. If public folders that need to be crawled reside on multiple Exchange Servers, you will likely need multiple SharePoint Portal Servers. The only other way around this requirement is if you have multiple Exchange Servers replicate to a single Exchange Server, and you point your SharePoint Portal Servers to the Exchange Server with all the replicated public folders.

To access the Exchange 5.5 settings page, perform the following tasks:

1. Right-click on the server object within SharePoint Portal Server Administration.
2. Click Properties and then click the Exchange 5.5 property page.

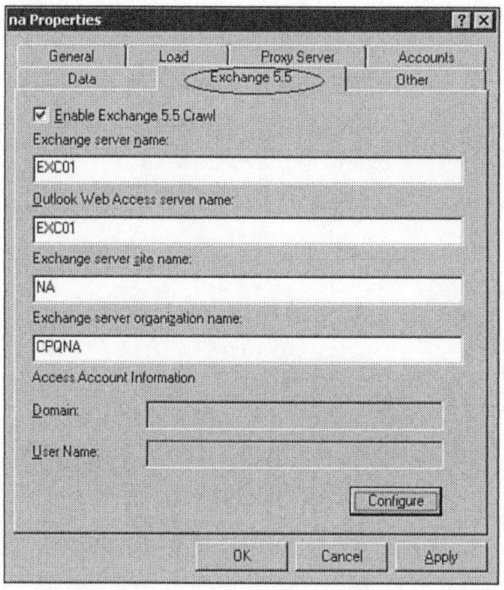

Figure 8.9
Exchange 5.5 settings page.

8

NOTE

> When public folders on Exchange 5.5 servers are crawled, only the data within public folder messages or attachments with the supported filters will be indexed. When we refer to filters, we are referring to IFilters, which are used to register file extensions so files can be recognized and indexed. SharePoint Portal Server includes filters for HTML, TIFF, text files, and Microsoft documents. Currently, .PST files or private mailboxes cannot be crawled.

EXCHANGE SERVER DETAILS

Within the Exchange 5.5 settings tab, you will find several fields that need to be populated before public folders on an Exchange 5.5 server can be crawled. The specific fields that need to be configured are

- Exchange Server Name
- Exchange Server Site Name
- Exchange Server Organization Name

For those of you that are new to crawling Exchange, Table 8.3 provides a high-level overview of the Exchange details that are needed.

TABLE 8.3 EXCHANGE 5.5 CRAWLING SETTINGS

Exchange Details	Description
Exchange Server Name	The name of the Exchange 5.5 server that SharePoint Portal Server will use to access public folders. While only one public folder server can be specified, you can replicate other public stores to this server to be crawled.
Exchange Server Site Name	Specify the site name within Exchange System Manager. A *site* is identified as Exchange Servers connected between a high-bandwidth network. For example, you may have a U.S. site that contains all servers within the USA. Another site might be AP, for all Exchange servers within Asia Pacific.
Exchange Server Organization Name	This field is used to specify the name of the Exchange Organization. This field is a top-level naming convention.
Exchange Outlook Web Access Server	When setting up crawling to Exchange 5.5 public folders, SharePoint Portal Server must be configured to access the public folders using Outlook Web Access (OWA). This enables end users to access data within public folders from their Web browser.

8

EXCHANGE SERVER SECURITY INFORMATION

In order for a SharePoint Portal Server to crawl public folders on Exchange 5.5 servers, the appropriate security must be enabled for access to the data. First of all, SharePoint Portal Server requires an account with administrator access to the site, as well as the site configuration containers of the Exchange Server. In addition, the crawling process adheres to Exchange security for crawled content. In other words, the user performing the search must have the appropriate public folder security access in order to get desired data returned from their Portal Server search.

SharePoint Portal Server uses the Administrator account to check security access to the public folder during the search. If the account is changed in Microsoft NT 4.0 or Windows 2000, you must change the account information within SharePoint Portal Server Administration. Failure to change the account information will result in a failed search when a user performs a query that requires interaction from the Exchange 5.5 server. This failed search query will also generate an error in the Application Log of the Event Viewer application.

NOTE
> If you have other applications such as Exchange 2000 or SQL Server loaded on this same server, you should schedule downtime to stop or restart this service in effort to avoid unnecessary downtime to these other key applications.

If you do change the account within SharePoint Portal Server Administration, in order for the change to take effect it is required to stop and restart MSSearch.

To modify the Exchange administrator account, perform the following:

1. Right-click on the server object within SharePoint Portal Server Administration.
2. Click Properties and then click the Exchange 5.5 property page.
3. Click Enable Exchange 5.5 Crawl and then click Configure.
4. After the Account Information dialog box appears, enter the appropriate account information:

Enter the domain.

Enter the user name.

Enter the password.

Type the password again in Confirm.

Click OK and then Apply.

NOTE
> The account details may need to be obtained from the Exchange Administrator of this 5.5 server where public folders reside. You will need the administrator account information with access to the site and site configuration containers of the Exchange server.

OTHER SETTINGS TAB

The last Settings tab that we will discuss here is the final property page of the Server object, labeled "Other." Upon accessing this Other settings page, note two options. The first option consists of a check box used for restricting Web discussions to items stored in the workspaces on this server. The second option is a Run Wizard button, which allows you to launch a wizard to configure a content source and build an index for it as you crawl a Lotus notes database. Figure 8.10 provides a visual representation of the Other settings options.

Figure 8.10
The Other settings page is illustrated here.

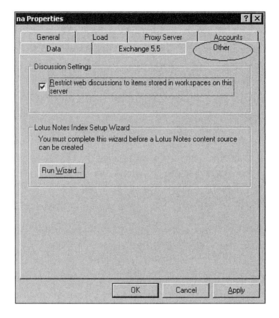

To access the Other settings page, perform the following tasks:

1. Right-click on the server object within SharePoint Portal Server Administration.
2. Click the Other property page tab.

DISCUSSION SETTINGS

If you do not make any changes to the default installation of SharePoint Portal Server, users are allowed to discuss documents that are outside the workspace. To prevent a potential breach in your organization's security policies and procedures, it is highly recommended that you restrict Web discussions to documents stored in the workspaces on the server. Figure 8.11 displays a visual representation of what to change to restrict this access.

Figure 8.11
Restricting Web discussions to workspaces on this server.

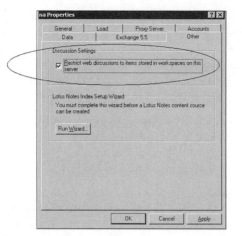

8

Once Web discussions are restricted and limited to the workspace, the Discuss action on the dashboard site is unavailable for any content that is outside the workspace.

→ We discuss how to set specific Web discussion settings for the Workspace in "Enabling Web Discussions," **p. 253**.

To change the settings associated with Web discussions on the server, perform the following tasks:

1. Right-click on the server object within SharePoint Portal Server Administration and click on Properties.
2. Click the Other property page tab.
3. To limit Web discussions to only documents stored in workspaces on the current server, select the check box called Restrict Web discussions to items stored in workspaces on this server. If you want to enable Web discussion outside the workspace, clear this check box.
4. Click Apply.

CONFIGURING LOTUS NOTES WITH SHAREPOINT PORTAL SERVER

Setting up crawling for Lotus Notes databases involves more than simply launching the Notes Setup Wizard. There are several steps that need to be considered prior to launching the wizard. Some of the considerations to be addressed first include

- Location of the notes.ini file.
- Location of the Notes installation folder.
- Notes user password associated with the default Notes account on the Notes client. This password is needed by the protocol handler to access the Notes server on behalf of the Notes user. If the end user does not need a password to access the Notes server, you do not need to enter a password in this field.

8

- Notes security disabled—You can only select to ignore Notes security if all the data stored on your company's Lotus Notes server is public or you are only indexing public Notes databases. In this case, it will take less time to configure because user names do not have to be mapped from Notes to Windows. In addition, creating and searching indexes are also faster than if Notes security were enabled.

- Notes security enabled—Most companies use Notes in a manner in which security is required. In this case, you will need to configure the protocol handler such that when SharePoint Portal Server crawls a Notes database and creates an index of the content, each user name must map to a Windows NT or Windows 2000 name in order to preserve the settings of the database on the Notes server.

- Notes custom View—In addition to simply enabling Notes security, you will also need to create a custom view on the Lotus Notes server that provides the Lotus Notes and Windows NT or Windows 2000 user names mapped to one another. The Notes administrator must mark the view as a Shared View so that it is available to all clients. The file is secured on the Notes server, and is exposed to the SharePoint environment through the SharePoint Portal Server administrator.

CAUTION

> Ignoring Notes security is not recommended unless you are absolutely sure that the Notes data is designated as public data with no security restrictions.

TIP

> To provide a sample scenario, if you are the Lotus Notes administrator, you create a database with a view named Domino2W2K that includes two columns, Domino and W2K. In the Domino column, you enter all the Domino user names. In the W2K column, you enter the user names for Windows 2000. You will need the View Name when the protocol handler is configured for your mapping scenario.

LOTUS NOTES INDEXING SETUP WIZARD

In order to configure SharePoint Portal Server to crawl a database on a Lotus Notes Server, you must configure the Lotus Notes protocol handler on the SharePoint Portal Server. This protocol handler is configured by launching the Lotus Notes Index Setup Wizard. To access the Lotus Notes Index Setup Wizard, perform the following:

1. Right-click on the server object within SharePoint Portal Server Administration.

2. Click the Other property page tab.

3. Click the Run Wizard button, and then click Next.

4. In the Lotus Notes Index Setup Wizard dialog box, enter the required information as follows:

    Location of notes.ini file: (such as C:\domino\notes\notes.ini)

    Location of Lotus Notes install directory: (such as C:\domino\source)

Enter password

Confirm password

If you do not want the security settings of the Notes database to be honored by SharePoint Portal Server, click Ignore Lotus Notes security while building an index.

If you decide you do want to enable security, you will be prompted with an additional dialog box that will allow you to enter the View Name for the view that contains the mapping for Notes and Windows NT or Windows 2000 username columns. You will also need to specify the names of columns in the views (for example, Domino and W2K).

Click Next and then Finish.

STARTING AND STOPPING SERVICES

From time to time, it may be necessary to start or stop services associated with SharePoint Portal Server. For example, as stated in the earlier section on Exchange Server, when you change the Exchange user account that SharePoint Portal Server uses to access an Exchange Server, you need to stop and restart the MSSearch service. To that end, we cautioned our readers, as simply stopping and restarting the services will have an impact on other applications or services if performed carelessly. We also noted that if you run SharePoint Portal Server along with Exchange Server on the same computer, stopping the MSSearch service during peak production hours will impact your Exchange operations, negatively impacting your end-user community.

The primary services commonly used by SharePoint Portal Server include

- Internet Information Services Admin Service (IISADMIN)
- Microsoft Search (MSSearch)
- SharePoint Portal Server (Msdmserv)
- Microsoft Exchange Information Store (MSExchangeIS)

NOTE

It is highly recommended that you clearly understand the impact of stopping and restarting services. Many services have dependencies on other services, and just when you think that you are simply stopping one service, you may be surprised to find out that other dependent services were also stopped, which may disrupt your production IT business operations. Be careful.

To stop and start a service on a SharePoint Portal Server, perform the following:

1. From your taskbar, click on Start, Programs, Administrative Tools, and then Services.
2. Right-click the service that you desire to stop and click OK.
3. To restart, click Start.

To view service dependencies, perform the following:

1. From your taskbar, click on Start, Programs, Administrative Tools, and then Services.
2. Right-click the service that you want to check for dependent services, and click on Properties.
3. Click on the Dependencies tab (see Figure 8.12).

It should be noted that it is possible to restart many services at once in Windows 2000. For example, restarting the IISAdmin service will also start other dependent services.

Figure 8.12
Dependencies properties page.

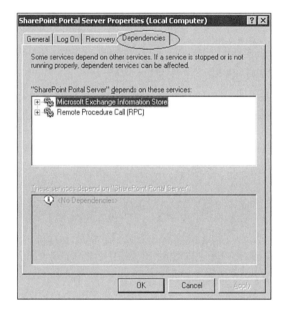

ADVANCED TOPICS

There are several advanced topics that do not necessarily fall under the classification of a particular server management function. For the sake of planning and server management, we decided to group these together here. In this section we will discuss the following:

- Configuring IFilters
- Using Robots.txt and HTML tags to prevent access
- Installing Outlook Web Access Help files
- Reclaiming disk space from the Web Storage System

CONFIGURING IFILTERS

Before we talk about how to configure IFilters, many of you may be asking questions such as "What is an IFilter and why are they useful?" IFilters enable you to register a particular file extension and begin crawling for documents and including these file types within the index. The actual procedure for configuring file types depends on the IFilter that you are registering. Third-party providers can be specified and registered, including Adobe .pdf files. There are also filters for HTML documents, Microsoft Office files, TIFF files, and text files. When content sources are configured, the workspace administrator specifies the file types that will be included within the index.

NOTE

> It is possible that some file types exist but no filters are registered for these files. When you include file types that do not have registered IFilters within your index, the index will only include the file properties and not the actual files.

→ To learn more about IFilters, **see** "Using and Configuring IFilters," **p. 467**, and "The Importance of IFilters," **p. 599**.

IFilters may also play a role in troubleshooting and diagnosis, as well as allowing for the reading of various content sources and data format types.

 If you need a tool that reports the time it takes to access a document stored in your SharePoint Portal Server, perhaps because access times seem extremely long, see "Access Time to a Document is Long" in the "Troubleshooting" section at the end of the chapter.

USING ROBOTS.TXT AND HTML TAGS TO PREVENT ACCESS

The robots.txt file is used to prevent other servers from crawling your workspace and impacting the performance of your end users' portal experience. The file indicates explicitly where Web crawlers are allowed to explore within a particular Web site. The SharePoint Portal Server crawl process looks for this file and follows the rules specified within the file. The file is not installed automatically, so you will need to manually create the file and store it in the home directory of the Default Web Site for the SharePoint Portal Server computer. To verify the proper path of the Default Web Site, perform the following tasks:

1. Launch the Administrative Tools application and click on Internet Services Manager.
2. Expand the SharePoint Portal Server, right-click the Default Web Site, and click Properties.
3. Click on the Home Directory Property page and note the location for Local Path.
4. Place the robots.txt file in the same directory as Local Path on the Home Directory property page.

Figure 8.13
Verifying the file location for robots.txt.

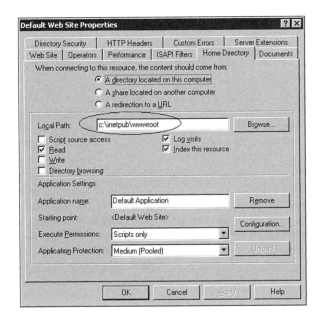

NOTE

> SharePoint Portal Server references this file one time per day. If you make changes to this file, you should start and stop the MSSearch service to ensure that your changes go into effect immediately.

→ The use of the Robots.txt file is covered in great depth in "Excluding and Restricting Crawling," **p. 469**.

INSTALLING OUTLOOK WEB ACCESS HELP FILES

Some organizations will need Outlook Web Access (OWA) Help files on the SharePoint Portal Server. You will need to install the language-specific Help Files if you have developers who are developing applications that will use OWA. To install the language-specific help files, perform the following tasks:

1. Within Windows Explorer, browse to Program Files\Common Files\Microsoft Shared\Web Storage System\Exchweb and create a folder named Help.

2. On the SharePoint Portal Server CD, browse to Server\Web Storage System\ Exchweb\Help. This directory contains the help files for the following languages:

   English

   Japanese

   Chinese (Simplified)

   Chinese (Traditional)

   Italian

Spanish

Korean

German

French

3. Once the appropriate folder is identified, you will need to copy the entire folder from the CD into the Help folder that you created in step 1.

WEB STORAGE SYSTEM DISK SPACE RECLAIM

By default, every evening at 12:00 midnight, a defrag process is launched on the Web Storage System (wss.mdb) of the SharePoint Portal Server. This process does a great job of freeing all deleted space, but the only way to physically reduce the size of the file is to run ESEUTIL.EXE. This utility runs several other checks and balances on the wss.mdb file, including performing integrity checks, defrag, physically reducing the size of the file, as well as repairing the file if necessary. To manually reclaim disk space, perform the following:

1. From the taskbar, click on Start, Programs, Accessories, and click on Command Prompt.

2. At the command prompt, enter `net stop MSExchangeIS` and hit the Enter key.

3. Select Yes to acknowledge other dependent services and to start the process.

4. Change directories to the \BIN directory where the ESEUTIL.EXE resides. Usually, the file location is \Program Files\Common Files\Microsoft Shared\Web Storage System\Bin.

5. Once you are in this subdirectory, type `ESEUTIL /d "path/wss.mdb"` where *path* points to the directory of wss.mdb. You can type `ESUETIL /?` If you need further assistance with this command.

6. Once the process is complete, at the DOS prompt, type `net start MSExhangeIS` and hit Enter. All appropriate services will be restarted.

⚠️ *If you find yourself with users complaining that they cannot access the system and the WSS reclaim process is executing, see "No SPS User Access While WSS Reclaim Is in Progress" in the "Troubleshooting" section at the end of the chapter.*

→ To obtain additional WSS performance-related information, **see** "WSS Optimization," **p. 471**.

TROUBLESHOOTING

EXCHANGE SERVER UNAVAILABLE FOR TEN MINUTES

I have set my Exchange time-out but I'm still unable to index.

If 32 time-outs are received from a specific Exchange server being crawled during Index creation, SharePoint Portal Server logically blocks out the server as unavailable for additional requests for 10 minutes. This may be caused by the Exchange server simply being unavailable or down for maintenance. On the other hand, though, it may simply speak to the need to increase the time-out value to a greater number. Microsoft recommends 120 seconds as an excellent starting point in this case.

No SPS User Access While WSS Reclaim Is in Progress

I need a tool that reports the time it takes to access a document stored in SharePoint Portal Server.

The amount of time that the WSS disk space reclaim process will take will vary depending on the size of the database. However, it should be noted that your SPS server is simply not available to your end-user community while this process is running. This is because the WSS file system must be locked to perform the reclaim. It is recommended therefore that the process be scheduled during a non-peak window, or within a scheduled downtime period, according to your planned maintenance processes and procedures.

Access Time to a Document Is Long

My users are telling me that they can't access the system and the WSS reclaim process is executing. What should I do?

In some cases, you may notice that the access time it takes to access a document stored in SPS is much longer than usual. To verify how the load of the server is affecting its overall performance, use the RTF IFilter tool. This tool provides for a simple test to verify that the SharePoint Portal Server computer is functioning normally, and the output created by the test is reported to assist in diagnosing the problem. You may obtain this tool under the \Tools\server_latency directory, on the SPS Resource Kit CD (or available at no charge on Microsoft's Web site) .

SUMMARY

To summarize this chapter, we discussed the common server management tasks, most of which are covered in great detail in other chapters. In this chapter we discussed various methods of configuring SharePoint Portal Server with Microsoft Proxy Server, and we discussed the overall benefits of a proxy server within our environment. We discussed the Load Tab and how to configure site hit frequency rules. We looked at how we can balance the Search and Index resource usage load across our SharePoint Portal Servers. And we described how to adjust the Search resource usage and Indexing research usage bars in a manner that dedicated resources to the process accordingly, or allowed a single server to balance these settings on the same server.

We also discussed the importance of specifying the gatherer email address, so other site administrators can contact an individual if they experience any problems with our crawling process as it impacts their site. Use of access and propagation accounts were covered, and details were provided for how to change the location of server data and log files. We provided a high-level overview around crawling public folders on Exchange 5.5 servers, plus the information required in order to set up the crawl process. And we looked at Exchange Server security concerns that need to be addressed. Additionally, we talked about enabling

Web discussions on the SPS server, and how this can limit discussions to within the workspace. We also provided a high-level overview regarding configuring the protocol handler and running the Lotus Notes Index Setup Wizard.

Lastly, we discussed several advanced processes and procedures, like starting and stopping services, configuring IFilters to allow custom files types to be recognized, using Robots.txt files to restrict Web crawlers to designated areas of a particular site, installing Help Files associated with Outlook Web Access, and using ESEUTIL.EXE to reclaim disk space associated with the defrag process.

In the next chapter, we address management of SharePoint Portal Server at a more granular level, and focus on managing the SPS workspace.

Managing the Workspace

In this chapter

9

INTRODUCTION TO THE WORKSPACE

In this chapter, we will look at what makes up a SharePoint Portal Server workspace, and how to manage the workspace both holistically and at a component level. As we cover this information, we will drill down into the areas that keep most Administrators and Coordinators on their toes—security considerations, managing internal and external content, workspace capacity planning, and more. We will also address the goal of simplifying workspace management by sharing various checklists, detailed procedures, and structured processes throughout this chapter.

To review, a default workspace is created after SharePoint Portal Server is installed. The workspace is actually a Web folder or a Network Place itself. However, the workspace can be thought of as an organized compilation of data, distributed and managed by Document, Management, Category, and Portal Content folders, including a Web page with links to Help files and configuration wizards. As such, the workspace affords access to data—views, content, and shortcuts to content—and includes organized data categories. This data, most of which is housed in the *Document Library*, may consist of any file types. The following are representative file types found in typical workspaces:

- Text and image-based documents
- Presentations
- Spreadsheets
- Graphics files and fax images
- Audio files
- Web pages
- Scripts
- Links to content stored elsewhere, such as on Microsoft Exchange Servers, file servers/shares, other Web sites, Lotus Notes databases, and other SharePoint Portal Server workspaces

The default dashboard site also facilitates access to the Document Library, along with Categories, other dashboard site content, Search, Subscriptions, Home, Help, and a Management folder (for users with this level of access). This last folder, the Management folder, makes possible management of all of the portal content or data in the form of management tools—the workspace node is managed by using this folder or SharePoint Portal Server Administration. Links to document profiles and discussions may also exist in the workplace/dashboard site.

→ For introductory and general information regarding the dashboard, **see** "Dashboard Overview," **p. 42**.

All of this data, or content, is accessed by users via Web folders, or through the associated digital dashboard site. The folders mentioned previously—Home, Search, Categories, Document Library, Subscriptions, Management, and so on—simply organize and assist in managing this data. Each one will be discussed in detail in the next few pages. What is important to understand first, though, is that the workspace is the vehicle leveraged by the dashboard to house and publish Portal data, or pointers to data, for the benefit of its users.

DOCUMENTS FOLDER

The Documents folder resides under the Document Library folder of the digital dashboard, and is where documents are stored and managed in SharePoint Portal Server. Much of the work associated with preparing the workspace for document management and group collaboration involves configuring the Documents folder. While this folder is visible to all users, regardless of roles or security considerations, not all data necessarily is. Other important considerations include

- Only data stored in the Documents folder or in the Portal Content folder in the workspace are added to an index.
- A hierarchy of Document folder subfolders is usually fashioned to create an organized workspace, and aid in managing the Portal's content.
- Different Coordinators may be assigned to each subfolder, thus allowing distributed management and configuration of the various workspace folders.
- All subfolders inherit enhanced folder settings unless otherwise specified—the Documents folder is an enhanced folder.

PORTAL CONTENT FOLDER

The Portal Content folder, like the Documents folder, resides underneath the Document Library. It contains default folders used to configure and manage the information displayed on the dashboard's default Web Parts. Some of these include Resources, Announcements, News, and Quick Links folders, which correspond to identically named Web Parts. These and other details are covered to a greater degree in the next section. What is important to remember is that the Portal Content folder is simply a folder that contains frequently reviewed content, accessed via the digital dashboard.

MANAGEMENT FOLDER

Tools and folders used by the Coordinators to manage the Portal's data—and to configure the workspace, document profiles, and content sources—reside in this folder. While other tools, Web Parts, and so on exist to manage data, this folder allows specifically for managing the following:

- Document Profiles
- Content sources
- Subscriptions
- Discussions

9

DOCUMENT PROFILES

Every document in the workspace is coupled to a document profile and its associated set of properties. In fact, the Document Profiles folder located in the Management folder allows you to create, organize, and store document profiles.

- All document profiles are based on a template, and contain some basic properties, like the title and any keywords that might apply. This further allows for rapid organization, and plays a key role in permitting data to be searchable.

- Users can use a profile form to add incremental data to a document's profile. To this end, document profiles may be leveraged to determine which documents are stored in a folder, or to limit the kinds of documents that may be housed in specific folders.

CONTENT SOURCES

Indicated by a URL, a content source represents a location used to access documents residing outside of the workspace. This content can be located outside of the workspace but on the same server (that is, another workspace on the server), on another server on your intranet, or on the Internet. Lots of types of information may be added to a workspace as content sources.

→ To read more about content sources in general, **see** "Content Source Types," **p. 30**.

> **NOTE**
> SharePoint must be configured to crawl Exchange 5.5 public folders and Lotus Notes databases.

> **NOTE**
> Before adding a Lotus Notes content source, the Lotus Notes client must first be installed and then the server must be configured with the NotesSetup utility.

A content source may be added to a workspace by following the steps in the Add Content Source Wizard. This is accessed in the Content Sources folder—you must have Microsoft Windows 2000 installed on your computer to view the Content Sources folder and to create and manage content sources. That is, computers running Microsoft Windows 98 or Microsoft Windows NT cannot access the Content Sources folder.

Additionally, after a content source is added to the workspace, SharePoint Portal Server regularly creates and updates an index of the content made available through that content source. And once the content source is included in the index, users with the appropriate level of security or role can search for and view its content on the dashboard site.

> **TIP**
> Unlike documents, users can neither check out nor edit content sources or the documents accessed through the content sources.

Subscriptions and discussions are discussed later in this chapter, in "Managing Subscription Settings," and "Enabling Web Discussions," respectively.

CATEGORIES FOLDER

This folder is complementary to the Documents folder, as the Categories folder aids in classifying, describing, and organizing documents into a hierarchy of topics and subtopics. This is accomplished via a series of special folders called Category folders. Categories are highly recommended across the board as a must for assisting portal users in finding content relevant to their needs.

Some of the more salient points regarding managing Categories include

- Coordinators at the workspace level can create and modify the category hierarchy.
- An optional category contact for each category may be identified, to allow for feedback on the category's content.
- The category contact may be different for each category, or it may be the same person for all categories.
- A single document may be associated with multiple categories (to better describe or categorize it than would otherwise be possible).
- Categories contain links to the documents regardless of their storage location.
- A document is added to a category by using the profile form. Any number of roles may accomplish this—the Coordinator at the workspace level, a category contact, or the Author of the document can add the document to a category.
- The Category Assistant may also be configured to categorize documents automatically.
- Categorization may also be accomplished by using the Search and Categories tab on the Properties page of a document.

Thus, categories assist SharePoint Portal Server users in locating and managing information. This is done by sorting documents into a hierarchy of groups—categories—under different headings according to subject matter. These categories provide a list of terms, too, that help users consistently characterize documents, thereby facilitating sound document management practices.

THE DASHBOARD

Before we drill down into managing the workspace, a quick dashboard review is in order. While the workspace may be viewed as the data repository, the digital dashboard, or Dashboard, serves as perhaps the simplest and most effective way of accessing this data. That is, users with appropriate roles can access the workspace via a couple different ways—Microsoft Windows Explorer or Microsoft Office 2000, for example. However, using the dashboard site from a Web browser is oftentimes the simplest, as no client components, nor a minimum version of Microsoft Office, are required for basic functionality.

9

The dashboard site is a specialized Web site automatically created by SharePoint Portal Server after the associated workspace is created. There is a one-to-one relationship between workspaces and dashboards, where up to 15 workspaces and associated dashboards may reside on a single server. The dashboard provides a Web view of the workspace, and enables users with the appropriate security roles to perform the following:

- Search for, view, and manage workspace documents
- Search for and view content from other sources

The dashboard site also allows users to perform document management tasks and search functions. In these cases, though, users must be running Office XP applications, or install the client components on a computer running Office 2000 to provide complete workspace management functions.

DASHBOARD COMPONENTS

The dashboard site consists of the following:

- A customizable site title.
- A search bar with a drop-down menu and text box, facilitating search scopes and search terms.
- A customizable logo for the dashboard site.
- A collection of site navigation buttons that link to other dashboards, such as Home, Documents, Categories, Subscriptions, Management, Help, and Feedback.

One or more Web Parts can appear on the dashboards that make up the site. To review, a Web Part is a customizable section of the dashboard site that contains a specific type of content or aids in accessing content. The default home page contains four default Web Parts:

- News
- Quick Links
- Announcements
- Subscriptions Summary

In many ways, managing the dashboard amounts to managing the various Web Parts. The first three of these default Web Parts corresponds to subfolders of the same name under the Portal Content folder in the workspace. These subfolders store the information that appears in the corresponding Web Parts. The fourth default Web Part, the Subscriptions Summary Web Part, contains information—subscription data—after end users have actually subscribed to something.

→ For an excellent overview of the SPS default Web Parts, **see** "Dashboard Overview," **p. 42**.

MANAGING THE SUBSCRIPTION AND OTHER WEB PARTS

Managing Web Parts is the job of the Administrator or Coordinator. The Coordinator at the workspace level, for example, can add, delete, and customize Web Parts. In addition, he can also add information to the News, Announcements, and Quick Links Web Parts. Fortunately, assembling and customizing Web Parts is an easy and flexible way to customize a SharePoint Portal Server Web site. And the Coordinator is further blessed by the fact that the dashboard site included with SharePoint Portal Server packages a lot of standard functionality into the various default and other Web Parts.

In terms of management, the Coordinator at the workspace level configures the links to the content that resides on all of the default Web Parts (with the exception of the Subscriptions Web Part) by simply adding documents to the related subfolder in the workspace. End users manage their own subscriptions, however. Since SharePoint Portal Server notifies users automatically that content which has been subscribed to has been updated, no Coordinator involvement from this perspective is required. That is, Coordinators do not need to determine the content of the Subscriptions Web Part—selection of the content is left to the discretion of the end users, and updates are performed automatically by SPS.

Additional Subscription Web Part management details include

- A user can quickly view his two most current subscription notifications, along with links to any relevant documents.
- If the user has no active subscriptions, the associated folder in the workspace is empty.
- Both Coordinators and end users have the power to delete user subscriptions from the dashboard site. End users are of course restricted by default to their own subscriptions.

Other Web Parts may be built and customized as well. The Coordinator at the workspace level can configure and customize these additional Web Parts for the dashboard site pages. Some of the more commonly created Web Parts involve those that display business information such as news headlines and stock tickers, or facilitate collaboration using tools like Microsoft NetMeeting. Other Web Parts might be configured to display information specific to an certain subsets of users, such as a customized "Search" Web Part for the site. Regardless, management of these Web Parts is performed by the Coordinator at the workspace level.

 If you subscribe to content, but do not receive a subscription notification, you might have a simple Windows 2000 authentication issue. See "Windows 2000 Authentication and Subscription Notification" in the "Troubleshooting" section at the end of the chapter.

HOLISTIC WORKSPACE MANAGEMENT

While managing the workspace consists of managing, configuring, and updating perhaps multiple workspaces and dashboards, the initial goal of workspace management is simply creating the workspace itself. The next few pages address creating and deleting workspaces, followed by holistic, or end-to-end, workspace administration considerations. Finally, we conclude this section with a discussion on managing multiple workspaces.

The bulk of time initially spent managing workspaces really amounts to administrative and similar tasks. Later, as the SharePoint Portal Server evolves and workspaces morph into, or are replaced by, newer instances, or are split to support new organizational requirements and boundaries, it becomes necessary to one day delete little-used workspaces and reclaim/reorganize SharePoint Portal Server resources.

CREATING A WORKSPACE

After SharePoint Portal Server setup is complete, the New Workspace Wizard appears. This wizard assists us in creating the default workspace. Note that even if Cancel is selected, and the New Workspace Wizard does not appear, a new workspace may be created at any time by using SharePoint Portal Server Administration. To do so, perform the following:

1. In the console tree, select your SPS server.

2. On the Action menu, point to New, and click Workspace. You may also right-click the server name, point to New on the shortcut menu, and then click Workspace. At this point, the New Workspace Wizard appears. Click Next.

3. On the Workspace Definition page, in the Workspace name field, type the name of the new workspace to be created. It is also recommended that a description be included in the Description field. See Figure 9.1 for an example.

Figure 9.1
Creating a new work-space in SharePoint Portal Server for the Marketing group.

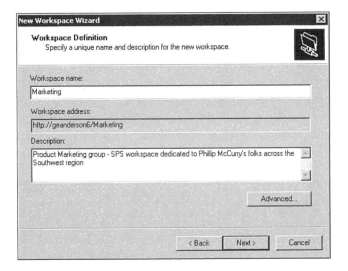

NOTE

Note that workspace names can consist of characters from lower ASCII, and cannot exceed 25 characters in length. The following characters are *not* supported:

```
#  :  \  ?  *  <  >  %  /  |  "  {  }  ~  [  ]  Space  !  (  )  =  ;  .  ,  @  &  +
```

The wizard verifies that the workspace name is indeed unique, confirming that the name does not conflict with any other workspace names or propagated index names on the SharePoint Portal Server. If the workspace name does already exist, SharePoint Portal Server prompts you to enter a unique name.

CAUTION

A workspace name cannot be changed after it is created. And if you are creating an index workspace, the name of the workspace that you are creating must be different from that of the destination workspace. Fortunately, the New Workspace Wizard ensures that a workspace with the same name as the index workspace does not already exist on the destination.

4. If a dedicated index workspace is being created, click Advanced. Select the Configure as an index workspace check box. In Specify the destination workspace address, type the destination workspace for the propagated index. The name of the destination workspace is in the form of `http://server/workspace/`. Click OK.

5. If creating an index workspace, SharePoint Portal Server prompts you for a propagation access account, which is required before you can propagate an index. Note that this account must have local Administrator permissions on the destination server.

CAUTION

You may create index workspaces with the same name (and propagating to the same destination) on multiple servers dedicated to creating and updating indexes. If fully qualified domain names and index workspace propagation are desired together, though, both the server dedicated to indexing and the destination server must be in Windows 2000 domains.

Once the workspace installation is completed, the following New Workspace Wizard "administrative" tasks must be addressed:

6. On the Workspace Contact page, for the workspace contact name, enter a name of a user or group.

7. In the Workspace contact email address field, type the email address for the workspace contact previously entered. Refer to Figure 9.2 for an example.

8. Click Next, and the Completing the New Workspace Wizard screen is displayed (see Figure 9.3). Review all information provided on this screen, and then click Finish to complete the wizard. Once all wizard options are addressed, another screen is displayed, for anywhere from a few minutes to 20 minutes or more, indicating that the creation of the workspace will take some time.

The workspace is now created, and a message is displayed stating that the wizard will open the workspace and create a shortcut for it in My Network Places.

Figure 9.2
A Workspace contact name and email address are important in terms of identifying the responsible Coordinator of a workspace, especially when multiple workspaces reside on a single SPS server.

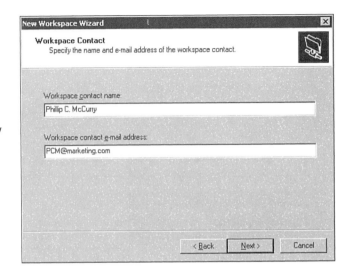

Figure 9.3
Review all information provided on this screen for accuracy, and then click Finish to actually complete the New Workspace Wizard.

9. Click OK. The shortcut is now created. The Configure Your Workspace page opens, and the dashboard site opens, too. For index workspaces, an introduction page opens as well, and the shortcut points to the Content Sources folder within the workspace.

Once the new workspace is created, a Security Warning screen related to installing the Microsoft Digital Dashboard Service Component may be displayed, as Figure 9.4 illustrates. Click Yes to continue with the installation. Note that this screen typically is displayed during the installation of the first workspace on a particular SPS server. Subsequent installations will not display this screen if the box entitled Always trust content from Microsoft Corporation is checked the first time this screen is displayed.

Figure 9.4
The Digital Dashboard is automatically installed once you click Yes on the Security Warning screen.

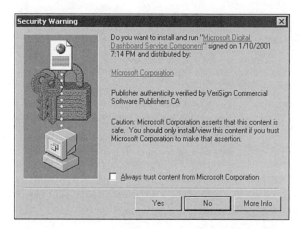

Finally, security on the workspace node may then be configured by using SharePoint Portal Server Administration or Web folders. Note that the Windows 2000 local Administrators group has permission to read documents and configure security on any folder or document in a workspace. Security considerations are addressed in greater detail later in this chapter.

EXPORTING AND DELETING A WORKSPACE

Eventually, when the need arises to delete a workspace, SharePoint Portal Server Administration must again be leveraged. When a workspace is deleted, the information stored in that workspace is no longer available to users. SharePoint Portal Server deletes the files associated with that workspace and the virtual root reference—the virtual root setting of that workspace (which maps the URL of the workspace to the physical storage location). In addition, the following occurs:

- All index processes, such as creating, updating, or propagating an index, are stopped.
- Scheduled tasks for crawling content sources and processing subscriptions are deleted.
- Index workspaces are unregistered with their destination workspaces.
- Propagated indexes are deleted from their destination workspaces.
- All of the documents stored in the workspace are deleted.

CAUTION

> If a destination workspace is deleted before deleting an index workspace, the index workspace deletion succeeds as expected. However, if the destination workspace is unavailable at the time the index workspace is deleted, you are notified and prompted to continue. Selecting the continue option forces the index workspace deletion to succeed.

A workspace can only be deleted by using SharePoint Portal Server Administration. Given the unrecoverable nature of this operation, it is recommended that before a workspace is deleted, the Coordinator should consider exporting the contents of the workspace to another location on the server, or backing up the files and configuration settings. To export the contents of a workspace, you can use the Software Development Kit that ships with SPS to write your own export/import tool. You may also use the Application Deployment Wizard in the Microsoft Web Storage System Software Development Kit to package and deploy your entire dashboard. In the latter method, the wizard packages the Web Storage System data and application logic into a *cabinet file*, the .cab file format popular with Microsoft. The .cab file may then be exported to another server by using the Deploy Application component of the same wizard. To perform this method of export/import, do the following:

1. Install the Web Storage System Developer Tools, by downloading them from `http://msdn.microsoft.com/downloads/default.asp?URL=/code/sample.asp?URL=/MSDN-FILES/027/001/557/msdncompositedoc.xml`.

2. Begin the process of packaging the Digital Dashboard you would like to export into a single .cab file by clicking the Start menu, Programs, Web Storage System SDK, Web Storage System Tools, Application Deployment Wizard.

3. At the Wizard's Welcome screen, click the option titled Package Application, and then click Next.

4. At the Instruction page, click Next.

5. Enter the URL of the digital dashboard, including the dashboard folder name; for example, `http://server/public/folder_name`.

6. Select the check box labeled Include all sub-folders (which ensures that all sub-dashboards and related Web Parts are included in the packaging process), and then click Next.

7. Enter the logon information for the server, in the format domain/user_name (to ensure communication between servers in different domains).

8. Select the option titled Package to single CAB file. Type a location and name for the .cab file, like C:\temp\dashboard1.cab, and then click Next.

9. Enter SampleFilter.xml for the default schema filter file, and then click Next. At this point, the package begins to be assembled and therefore the export is performed. Once this process is completed, continue with the steps below to deploy it to another server.

10. Launch the Application Deployment Wizard again, as outlined previously in step 2.

11. At the Welcome screen, select the Deploy Application option, and then click Next.

12. Type the URL of the production server, including the dashboard folder name to be used, like `http://server/public/folder_name`, and then click Next.

13. Enter the logon information for the server, again leveraging the format domain/user_name.

14. Finally, click the Deploy from single CAB file option, type the location and name of the source .cab file (for example, C:\temp\dashboard1.cab), and then click Next. Deployment, or the actual import, of the dashboard application begins.

15. Once the import is complete, a Finish button is displayed. Click it.

As we can see, the Application Deployment Wizard is a straightforward method for exporting and importing dashboard applications from one server to another. It should be noted that this functionality is quite flexible, too. That is, we can copy a dashboard from a computer running Exchange 2000 Server onto a computer running SPS, or vice versa.

Once we have safeguarded our data and application logic by exporting it from, and importing it to, another server, we are in a position to actually delete the workspace. Perform the following steps:

■ In the console tree, select the server that contains the workspace that will be deleted.

■ Click to expand the server, and then select the workspace to be deleted.

■ From the Action menu, select All Tasks, and then click Delete Workspace. Alternatively, right-click the server name, select All Tasks on the shortcut menu, and then click Delete Workspace.

■ Click Yes to confirm the deletion of the workspace (refer to Figure 9.5). A Delete Workspace Confirmation box is displayed. Clicking the Yes button irrevocably removes the selected workspace.

Figure 9.5
Deleting a workspace is easily accomplished through SharePoint Portal Server Administration, by clicking the workspace to be deleted, then clicking All Tasks, and then selecting Delete Workspace.

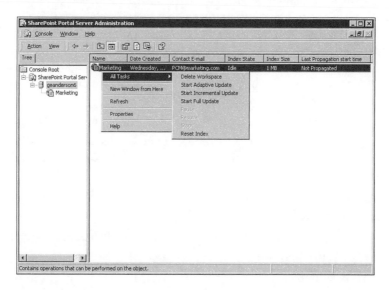

Remember, deleting a workspace is final. However, with the protection that our export process provides us, we should be confident in deleting workspaces that become obsolete or otherwise of no immediate or foreseeable value.

HIGH-LEVEL ROLE OF THE WORKSPACE COORDINATOR

The development of a *technical support organization*, or TSO, is one of the many high-level deployment tasks that should be addressed prior to completing any installation of SharePoint Portal Server. While this deployment consideration is covered in depth elsewhere in this book, administration and maintenance tasks will change as the portal grows and changes over time. Therefore, it is likely that the team tasked with supporting the portal will also require training or changes in team members, structure, and so on. The central figure in addressing workspace administration is the *Workspace Coordinator*, covered in detail next.

→ To read more about the general role of the Workspace Coordinator, **see** "Workspace Coordinator Role," **p. 49**.

The key role from a workspace management perspective is the Workspace Coordinator. In smaller SharePoint Portal Server deployments, or in small organizations, one person typically acts as both the server Administrator and the Coordinator on the top level of the workspace. That is, one "Administrator" performs all of the tasks associated with managing both SharePoint Portal Server and Microsoft Windows 2000 Server, for example. In larger organizations or more complex deployments, this role may consist of multiple Coordinators, and perhaps even multiple server Administrators.

The Coordinator role exemplifies a role packed with responsibilities. Workspace Coordinators manage content sources, document profiles, categories, and subscriptions, and usually drive customization of the related dashboard site. They hold permission to configure user roles on folders, and are authorized to perform Author-related tasks. In terms of managing enhanced folders, Coordinators do even more—they define and configure approval processes, undo the check-out of a document, and have the ability to even end the publishing process. Plus, as we have read previously, they can also view and delete other users' subscriptions. This comes in handy as end users move in and out of roles within an organization, or leave the organization completely.

The Workspace Coordinator utilizes SharePoint Portal Server Administration in MMC to manage the SharePoint Portal Server environment. His goals initially lie in understanding user requirements and correctly configuring the portal. Tasks like the following are critical:

- The Workspace Coordinator attaches the server(s) to an organization-wide security infrastructure and directory.
- Works with the user community, deployment team, and hardware/software/integration partners to ensure that the portal is installed, configured, and optimized.
- Creates the initial workspaces on the server.
- Works with the customer community to create new and modify existing Web Parts for the workspace.
- Monitors overall disk space available, CPU statistics, and other resources so as to ensure a baseline level of performance, and determines when additional servers or workspaces might be required.

- Configures security on the top level of the workspace, via SharePoint Portal Server Administration or by using Workspace Settings in the Management folder of the workspace.

- Maintains a list of index workspace names, the server on which each workspace is stored, and the server and workspace to which each is propagated.

- Pays particular attention to the two resource-intensive processes that nearly all SharePoint Portal Server computers perform—searching and index creation.

- Responsible for performing full, incremental, or adaptive updates to an index, if required.

- Backs up, tests, and restores the server(s), including mastering the duplication process for disaster recovery purposes.

- Installs and registers IFilters.

- Modifies the noise word and thesaurus files and creates custom search queries.

- Configures the servers to crawl Microsoft Exchange Server 2000, 5.5, and Lotus Notes content sources.

ADMINISTERING MULTIPLE WORKSPACES

The Workspace Coordinator works with the users responsible for content to determine the number and type of SharePoint Portal Server computers required and the number of workspaces required on each server. As a limit to the number of supported workspaces per server exists, this task grows in importance as the number of workspaces increases. This task also grows in complexity as the types of workspaces expand to include dedicated index and crawl servers, and so on.

For example, in a SharePoint Portal Server deployment primarily aimed at document management, a single server may be all that is required from a technology perspective, but many workspaces may be required to meet the various business and organizational needs. And depending upon how many users may be active in each workspace, and the raw number of documents that might be stored per workspace, this could grow to include multiple servers as well.

Perhaps the most effective practice to use to address managing multiple workspaces involves editing the workspace description. A workspace description is optional, but it provides a simple way of differentiating between workspaces. This is especially important when more than one Workspace Coordinator or Administrator creates multiple workspaces on the same server. It benefits new Workspace Coordinators as well.

MODIFYING OR ADDING A WORKSPACE DESCRIPTION

The workspace/dashboard description may be viewed by using Web views in Web folders. Additionally, the General tab on the Properties page of the workspace (in the MMC) may be used to view this description.

1. In the relevant workspace, open the Management folder, and then select the Settings hyperlink or folder.

2. On the Properties page, click the General tab.

3. In the Description field (refer to Figure 9.6), type a description for this workspace.

4. Click OK.

Figure 9.6
Adding a description to a workspace/dashboard.

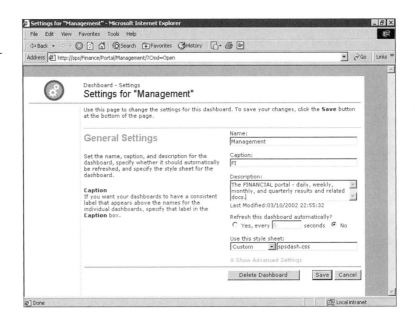

Forcing the use of the description helps push baseline data out to the technical support organization tasked with supporting the workspaces. Adding a detailed description and technical support contact data for each workspace should be a required practice.

ADDING NEW WEB PARTS TO THE WORKSPACE

The Workspace Coordinator also works with the customer community to determine when to modify or add new Web Parts to a particular workspace. While much of this type of activity is performed shortly after the workspace is created, a certain amount of Web Part development tends to take place throughout the life cycle of a workspace.

To add a new Web Part to a workspace, perform the following from the workspace dashboard:

- From the Home folder, click on the Content hyperlink.
- Select the option to Create a New Web Part (see Figure 9.7).

Figure 9.7
This screen shot displays the currently installed Web Parts, as well as provides access to some of the wizards commonly used when managing the workspace, like the Create a New Web Part link.

WORKSPACE MANAGEMENT CONSIDERATIONS

Once they are in place, successfully managing a Microsoft SharePoint Portal Server workspace or multiple workspaces consumes time and resources. Many different people, areas, disciplines, and SharePoint components are involved, not to mention the impact that business requirements and technology constraints play in an evolving portal solution. In the next few pages, we will drill down into managing the workspace from a number of different perspectives, including the following:

- General workspace utilization considerations, such as server configurations, server "sizing," number and characterization of users, number of documents or content sources, methods of organizing this portal data, and so on.

- Managing workspace security, such as how the Administrator, Coordinator, and other roles impact workspace management, and how portal data is otherwise protected or secured.

- Managing and securing content, for example, internal and external workspace content.

- Managing critical workspace components, such as approaches to managing and tuning indexes, building taxonomies, using categories and the Category Assistant, and more.

- Managing workspace capacity planning, such as growing vertically versus growing horizontally, and single versus multiple server configurations.

- Other workspace management considerations, such as how to manage and modify workspace settings, enable subscriptions, manage Web discussions, and more.

MANAGING GENERAL WORKSPACE UTILIZATION

Managing general workspace utilization starts with planning the initial SharePoint Portal Server deployment, and continues through the life of the portal. For our purposes here, we will examine the following:

- Planning exercises that drive the configuration of the Portal, and therefore the workspace(s) themselves
- Workspace configuration drivers, including the number and types of users, documents, and other content sources, and how all of this determines the role that each workspace may play in the overall portal solution
- Portal data organization, and how this evolves over time
- Portal user characteristics, and how this evolves as well

→ To read more on planning for SPS, **see** "Deployment Planning Considerations," **p. 151**.

Before a software package or a server is ever purchased, the business community determines the need for an enterprise portal product to meet some kind of critical or value-added business requirement. Perhaps the need is identified as a simple data sharing or document management system, or perhaps a collaboration solution is identified as paramount to improving productivity. Regardless, the following considerations and questions come into play in terms of the baseline generic portal solution:

- How do we manage content today?
- Where do we maintain that data?
- How much raw data are we actually talking about?
- What kind of data or file types do we maintain?
- Who actually uses the data?
- How is the data organized?
- What are the retention period requirements?

Once a general understanding of the data is determined, characterizing the users of that data—users of the proposed SharePoint Portal Server solution who will actually leverage the data or portal capabilities to perform their jobs effectively—must be performed. This includes determining who they are, when they need their data, how they currently get to the data they need today, and how they ultimately would like to find and access this data. One popular method of gathering this type of user-based information is through the use of questionnaires. Check with your hardware vendor or systems integrator to determine if they already have developed an SPS sizing questionnaire.

→ To read more about the kinds of questions that are posed in a sizing questionnaire, and other SPS sizing-related tools and approaches, **see** "Planning Required Server Hardware," **p. 131**.

After these needs are analyzed and documented, specific details may be uncovered that allow us to even better characterize the future SharePoint Portal Server end users, and provide us a baseline for hardware sizing of the development and production solutions, including the number and distribution of workspaces:

- Who can view documents? Edit them? Publish?
- What steps should be taken prior to publishing documents? Then, how should it actually be published?
- How important is tracking the history of a document?
- Are check-in or check-out of documents a concern?
- Are enhanced folders otherwise required, or are standard folders adequate?
- How are index updates scheduled?
- How are search scopes defined and created?

For example, this last set of questions may drive creating dedicated index workspaces on one or more SharePoint Portal Servers, and some number of user/data workspaces on another server or servers. Some of these servers may be distributed due to geographical considerations, and some may require high-performance disk subsystems to store frequently accessed or updated company-wide documents. Still other workspaces may need to be configured to crawl external data sources, or be configured to cascade up to a corporate Portal. The variations are nearly endless, and speak to the diverse requirements of businesses and other organizations today. A key point to remember is that the practice of "sizing" and characterizing users does not end with the deployment of the Production SharePoint Portal Server solution. Rather, this practice carries on through the life of the portal in the name of capacity planning, previously addressed in Chapter 6.

MANAGING WORKSPACE SECURITY

While security concerns are interwoven throughout a SharePoint Portal Server implementation, from development through testing through the deployment of productive solutions, special attention is given here to managing workspace security for the following reasons:

- Folder layout security risks
- Role-based security risks
- Approval routes security risks
- Document Profiles security risks
- Document publishing and version control security risks

FOLDER LAYOUT SECURITY RISKS

How documents are actually organized in the workspace is impacted by security—this determines whether combining folders or separating a folder's documents into different folders is required. Security is a fundamental reason to divide documents into multiple groups. That is, some documents should not be seen by some users. In this case, the design of the folder layout is therefore impacted. By storing content in separate folders, access to each folder and therefore the content under each folder is better controlled.

→ To learn more about folder security and how to hide a folder, **see** "Using Hidden Subfolders," **p. 288**.

9

ROLE-BASED SECURITY RISKS

Coordinators control security for documents and other content stored within each SharePoint Portal Server workspace by assigning users to the appropriate roles on a folder or a document. Coordinators manage roles by using either the Properties page for the specific folder, or via the Properties page for a workspace document. Note that roles may be assigned both at the individual folder level and at the top level of the workspace. Users may also be denied access to a specific document, for example if restricting an entire folder is too restrictive. This flexible role-based security model thus allows for customized access to content.

A set of three security roles is offered by SharePoint Portal Server, providing not only a flexible but also a secure method for managing user access to content. SharePoint Portal Server uses role-based security to control access to portal content regardless of whether the content is being accessed via a Web browser, Web folders, or Microsoft Office. The actual permissions associated with each specific role cannot be changed, though, underscoring the importance of accurately assigning users to roles.

SharePoint Portal Server includes the following roles—Reader, Author, and Coordinator—each of which has been discussed previously. However, in the context of workspace security and management, the following are important:

- The Author role must be respected in terms of the inherent security risks posed via publishing, not to mention the impact that an Author may have due to the role's ability to create, rename, and delete folders.

- Authors cannot change the roles or the approval policy on folders created by the Author or anyone else.

- The Coordinator creates indexes of updated content when necessary, or schedules this to occur automatically.

→ To learn about SPS roles and overall role security, **see** "Roles," **p. 281**.

As we covered previously, SharePoint Portal Server automatically assigns the Administrator who creates the workspace to the Coordinator role on the top level of the workspace, and on each folder. What is of importance here, though, is that this role may be assigned at a folder level. Thus, distributed permissions are supported—if you assign a user to the Coordinator role at the folder level, that user is a Coordinator for that folder only.

It should also be noted at this time that SharePoint Portal Server allows for a Deny Access security option, too, though on documents only. This setting supersedes all other access permissions except those associated with the local Administrators group. Specific users or groups may be denied access to view a particular document. In this way, the document is no longer visible to the denied user or group, not even in search results.

SECURITY RISKS ASSOCIATED WITH APPROVAL ROUTES

As a Coordinator, creating approval routes is a wonderful way of ensuring that a document is reviewed before publishing. When an Author chooses to publish a document, a route can be created to automatically push the document to one or more persons for review prior to publishing. Each of these individuals on the approval route has the option of approving or rejecting the document. However, these approval routes should be carefully managed, and they should be protected from unauthorized access as well. Indifferent management of approval routes can result in documents being routed to unauthorized Authors. Another result might include publishing a document without the benefit of adequate Q&A or review, potentially exposing or embarrassing an organization.

SharePoint Portal Server offers two routing options for reviewing a document before publishing it:

9

- Serial approval routing (one approver after another, sequentially)
- Parallel approval routing (all approvers at once)

Both types of approval routing consist of a series of steps that ultimately lead to publication. The Serial Approval routing process requires that each person approve the document prior to it moving to the next person. The last person's approval actually results in publishing the document. In Parallel Approval routing, any of the approvers may reject the document at any time.

→ For more information on approval routing, **see** "Approval Process Types," **p. 51,** and "Bypassing and Canceling the Approval Process," **p. 56**.

Regardless of the routing method, managing the approval routes—keeping the names and associated email addresses up-to-date—will not only reduce security risks, but also increase the overall quality of the documents residing on the SharePoint Portal Server production system.

DOCUMENT PROFILES SECURITY RISKS

While document profiles offer a way to add searchable information, called metadata, to a document, this metadata is not protected from a security perspective. That is, an unwary Coordinator might add a custom property like an Account Number to a document. The Account Number could make it easier to organize and find similar documents throughout the organization. But the Account Number is "wide open" to all eyes, for security settings in SharePoint Portal Server only restrict access to document contents, not metadata. Members of the Windows 2000 Everyone group can view all metadata associated with any document, including these custom properties. So while this extra information might help identify the document or allow for better searchability, if the metadata is sensitive in itself, the risk of abuse exists. Therefore, it is recommended that potential metadata be carefully reviewed prior to including it as a document property.

DOCUMENT PUBLISHING VERSION CONTROL SECURITY RISKS

While SharePoint Portal Server supports both private and public versions of any document, either of these presents a security risk. For example, published documents might be made available to users without a need for access to the document. Worse, private or previous versions of documents may "float" and eventually be compromised due to a lazy Coordinator

9

assigning Author roles too liberally. As an Author or Coordinator, a document may be published automatically each time it is saved to the server—or multiple private document drafts may instead be maintained, with publishing only occurring once the document is complete. So even though SharePoint Portal Server records a document's history to help track changes and eliminate the possibility of people overwriting another user's modifications, the draft versions of each document represent a security risk that must be addressed.

SECURING INTERNAL WORKSPACE CONTENT

Special attention to managing internal content is paramount to maintaining a secure SharePoint Portal Server production environment. Of course, "too much security" works to the detriment of an organization in achieving its goals. Internal content stored in the workspace includes documents in both standard and enhanced folders. A Coordinator can easily add or remove users from either type of folder, or deny access to a particular document. In this way, securing internal content—content within the local workspace—is relatively straightforward. To do this, the Coordinator uses any of the following:

- The Security tab of Workspace Settings in the Management folder (for the workspace level)
- The folder Properties page (for the folder level)
- The document Properties page (for the document level)

The next few pages detail the special considerations and gotchas that apply to managing workspaces housing content internally.

LOCAL ADMINISTRATORS GROUP SECURITY CONSIDERATIONS

SharePoint Portal Server assigns the Windows 2000 local Administrators group to the Coordinator role. What does this mean? All members of this local Administrators group can add themselves or others to the workspace as Coordinators. Then, each has the ability to configure security on any document in any folder. It is this ability to configure security that helps to safeguard data, should the data be accidentally or purposely made unavailable to those who should have access to it. That is, the local Administrators group can be used to restore roles on individual folders.

Of course, distributing the ability to configure security can work against the better good of the organization supporting the portal. Pay particular attention to minimizing the number of folks in the local Administrators group to only those who require it. And note that disallowing access to a document does not affect the local Administrators group's access to that document.

W2K DOMAIN CONTROLLER CONSIDERATIONS

Another interesting security consideration regards SharePoint Portal Server when it is installed on a domain controller. Domain controllers have no local Administrators group. Thus, only users explicitly assigned to the Coordinator role can specify security on folders.

If the Coordinator inadvertently makes a mistake, therefore, no local Administrator is able to come to the rescue!

Best practices for installing and deploying applications, whether SharePoint Portal Server or another departmental or enterprise application, dictate that dedicated infrastructure servers are preferred over combination application/infrastructure servers. That is, the services and function associated with Domain Controllers, DNS servers, WINS servers, or file/print servers, and so on are better left on a server platform dedicated to providing those functions. The increase in managing the number of servers is offset by the decrease in managing the day-to-day operations, not to mention future upgrades, associated with both the applications and the infrastructure services.

NTFS AND WORKSPACE SECURITY CONSIDERATIONS

Internal content must be secured across all information sources—SharePoint Portal Server exposes all information to the appropriate users according to Windows security settings. Therefore, a lack of a clearly defined NTFS security policy can pose a dramatic security risk. So, identify possible security risks and revise the security policy for each potential hazard to ensure accurate and sufficient permissions for the appropriate groups of people.

CONSIDERATIONS IN SECURING AND MANAGING FOLDERS

Securing internal content also requires managing the following set of folders and their subfolders, all of which support workspace management functions:

- Management
- Portal
- System
- Shadow
- Categories

Note that only Coordinators on the top level of the workspace can manage these folders. Fortunately, except for the Management folder, these folders are not actually visible to typical workspace users. Also, it should be mentioned that security can not be directly configured on these folders.

Workspace management functions, such as creating document profiles, are also available through the Web folders interface only. Other interesting security considerations exist—some of these are discussed in the following sections—all within the realm of securing and managing internal content in the workspace.

INHERITING SECURITY SETTINGS

When a new subfolder is created, it inherits security settings such as role settings from its parent folder by default. This may be overridden if not desired by customizing the role settings on the subfolder. If the parent folder's settings are changed, new subfolders may be specified to use the new settings.

Folders inherit *only* the role settings, however. For enhanced folders, SharePoint Portal Server copies the approvers and the approval route to the subfolder when it is created; however, subsequent changes to this setting on the parent folder are not passed to the subfolders.

USING ROLES TO HIDE FOLDER HIERARCHIES

In addition to general user-based security considerations, roles can be used to hide folder hierarchies as well, such that users may search for and find documents in subfolders but not actually have access to the parent folders. For example, a parent folder may contain subfolders with data that should not be viewed by certain organizations. Users in those organizations may be granted access to the other subfolders, but denied access to the parent folder and sensitive subfolders. In this case, the users can view the subfolders and content they need to see by using the subfolder's URL. Windows Explorer effectively hides the parent folder—to the point where it is not even visible.

MANAGING COMPOUND DOCUMENTS

A compound document is a document that actually consists of multiple files and perhaps different file types, for example a Web page (which usually consists of HTML and various GIFs, JPEGs, and so on—refer to Figure 9.8). What is important to note from a management perspective is that SharePoint Portal Server supports compound documents only in standard folders. Further, only Coordinators can configure security on a subfolder of a compound document.

Figure 9.8
A sample illustration of a compound document in the form of a typical Web page, complete with JPEGs and GIFs.

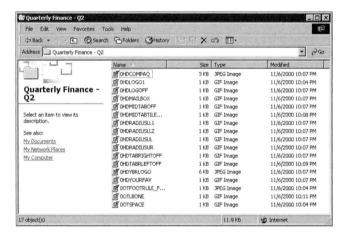

IFS AND IIS ACCESS CONSIDERATIONS

The Installable File System (IFS) and Internet Information Services (IIS) can fully access workspace folders. SharePoint Portal Server workspaces have an associated virtual directory created in IIS under the Default Web Site. Here, security may be managed for the dashboard site.

Note that users can access the IFS by using Windows Explorer on the SharePoint Portal Server computer, and this access is read-only. SharePoint Portal Server maps IFS to network drive M:, unless a mapping previously existed. It is not recommended to use IFS (network drive M:) to create SharePoint Portal Server folders or documents, assign security to folders or documents, and so forth, as misuse of M: may result in data loss.

SECURING EXTERNAL WORKSPACE CONTENT

Like content that is housed internally, content housed externally to the local workspace also poses certain risks to an organization. Managing external content, in large part, amounts to addressing those risks associated with actually managing Categories that contain documents and information from external content sources. Remember, "external" does not necessarily mean external to a company's data. The term "external" simply applies to any data housed outside of the local workspace.

In a nutshell, managing external content boils down to the following rules of thumb or best practices:

- Separate external content from internal content when this makes sense from a business perspective—store the content in separate folders to maintain excellent security.

- Do not count on share-level security, as it is not supported by SharePoint Portal Server. Only user-level security policies already associated with file shares and databases are supported.

- Pay particular attention to content sources that reside on other than NTFS file systems.

In addition, SharePoint Portal Server security is impacted by the following SharePoint Portal Server limitations and constraints:

- File shares or Web sites employing Secure Socket Layer (SSL) for encryption cannot be crawled.

- Encrypted documents are not crawled.

- SharePoint Portal Server may not recognize local group accounts on servers being crawled if they exist in another domain. If you plan to crawl content located on a server in another domain, do not try to secure content by using local group accounts—the users will not be able to view the crawled content. Instead, use universal group accounts, global group accounts, or domain local group accounts.

- SharePoint Portal Server does not enforce security on Web sites at query time. It specifies what Microsoft describes as a "per-path logon for crawling," but unfortunately, everyone has access to the results.

- Microsoft Exchange 2000 or 5.5 servers hosting encrypted messages are not crawled.

- While SharePoint Portal Server can access Unix systems or Novell NetWare systems via NFS, the corresponding client for the Unix or NetWare file system on the SharePoint Portal Server computer must be installed. And it must be noted that per-file security on non-NTFS file systems is lost—SharePoint Portal Server maintains per-share security.

- When crawling non-NTFS file systems without the benefit of security mapping, SharePoint Portal Server logs on as anonymous (or guest), and does not have access to any content that is not accessible to any anonymous user. Thus, all crawled documents are searchable by any user. Administrators should be aware of this to avoid compromising content that is secured in a manner not compatible with NTFS.

- Generally speaking, all documents included in the index from a non-NTFS file system are searchable by all Readers on the SharePoint Portal workspace. SharePoint Portal Server does not have built-in support for any other network file system protocols, so security on the file share is enforced only as well as it is exposed by whatever NTFS emulation software is employed.

9

MANAGING CRITICAL WORKSPACE COMPONENTS

While we have already looked at many discrete workspace components with an eye toward security and holistic management, management of some of the really critical SharePoint Portal Server components or resources like the following are detailed below:

- Managing and tuning indexes
- Index workspaces
- User access
- Taxonomies
- Categories and the Category Assistant

MANAGING AND TUNING INDEXES

Microsoft SharePoint Portal Server can create indexes for published content stored on Web sites and pages, file systems, Lotus Notes databases, Microsoft Exchange Server 5.5/2000 servers, and other SharePoint Portal Servers. Managing indexes represents a special challenge to the Workspace Coordinator. Every workspace includes indexes that allow users to search for documents available from that workspace. These documents can be located in a different workspace on the same server, on another server on your intranet, or on the Internet.

Before we proceed, it should again be noted that SharePoint Portal Server automatically creates an index for a workspace during the installation process. And when documents are added to the workspace, or existing documents are modified, the portal modifies the index to include the changes. Also, when new content is added or their settings are changed, the content source must be crawled to update the index. An index may be manually updated as well by using SharePoint Portal Server Administration, or by using Web folders. Finally, you can schedule SharePoint Portal Server to update indexes automatically.

Creating and updating an index can incur heavy processor and disk utilization. The indexing process can also consume quite a bit of time, depending upon the amount of text in the content being crawled. These factors are impacted by the methods employed by SharePoint Portal Server to break down a document and add its contents to an index, and consist of the following:

- Filtering the document—A filter removes formatting and extracts the text of the document and any properties defined in the file itself. SharePoint Portal Server has a limit of 16 megabytes (MB) of text data (graphics data is not included in this 16MB limit) that it filters from a single document. Should this limit be exceeded, SharePoint Portal Server enters a warning in the gatherer log and the document is considered successfully indexed. Note that filters are available for text files, Microsoft Office documents, HTML files, and Tagged Image File Format (TIFF) files.

- Word-breaking the document—A word-breaker is a component that determines where the word boundaries are in the stream of characters in the query or in the document being crawled. When SharePoint Portal Server crawls documents that are in multiple languages, the customized word-breaker for each language enables the resulting terms to be more accurate for that language. If no word-breaker is available for a particular language, the neutral word-breaker is used. Words are broken at neutral characters such as spaces and punctuation marks.

→ To drill down into more details on word breaking, **see** "Word Breaking," **p. 114**.

As for tuning indexes, the Workspace Coordinator should specify the Query Time-Out value, which represents the wait period for querying an index. In this way, the risks of long-running, complex, or poorly running queries is minimized, freeing valuable computing resources for other users and processes. Of course, if this value is set too low, queries will actually time-out before they complete.

TIP

> For fastest average response times, a good rule of thumb for initially setting query time-outs is 1,000 milliseconds, or one second—use this as your starting point to create a baseline. By default, this time-out is 10,000 milliseconds.

To specify the Query Time-Out, perform the following:

1. In the console tree, select the appropriate server which houses the workspace for which you want to specify the query time-out.
2. Expand the server, and select the workspace.
3. From the Action menu, click Properties. Or, right-click the workspace name and click Properties.
4. Select the Index tab.
5. Type in the number of milliseconds representing the period of time a query may execute before timing out.
6. Click Apply.

If the Query Time-Out value appears to be too low, it may be increased by following the previous process, to the point where the specific workspace's typical "large" query completes successfully. One nice thing about search results in SharePoint Portal Server is that partial results may be presented. In this case, a message box is displayed indicating that not all results are being displayed.

THE INDEX WORKSPACE

For workspaces with multiple indexes or heavy index activity, a dedicated *index workspace*, or index dedicated to managing content sources by building and updating indexes, may be created. This workspace usually resides on a dedicated server, as well, one dedicated to indexing. Special considerations include

- Unlike other workspaces, there exists no dashboard site for index workspaces.
- Propagation allows for distributing index resources. Indexes can only be propagated from index workspaces and only to a single destination workspace on another server, typically one dedicated to searching.
- A destination workspace can only accept indexes from up to four index workspaces.

As mentioned previously, creating a dedicated index workspace is simply a matter of running through the New Workspace Wizard, clicking the Advanced button, and selecting the option to Configure as an index workspace, as displayed in Figure 9.9:

Figure 9.9
Creating a dedicated index workspace.

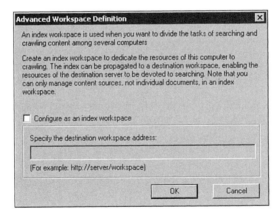

As an aid to workspace management, Microsoft recommends that the Workspace Coordinator maintain a list of the index workspace names, the server(s) on which they are stored, and the server(s) and workspace(s) to which they are propagated.

USING SERVER ADMINISTRATION TO MANAGE INDEXES

Much of the work of managing SharePoint Portal Server indexes involves using Server Administration or Web folders, and includes performing tasks like

- Pausing, resuming, or stopping an index from updating
- Starting a full, incremental, or adaptive update of an index
- Starting or stopping the propagating of an index
- Resetting an index
- Viewing index properties, such as the period of time to wait when querying an index

→ To read more about creating and managing indexes and index workspaces, **see** "Infrastructure and Security Considerations," **p. 512,** and "Setting Up a Dedicated Indexing Server," **p. 513**.

MANAGING USER ACCESS TO A WORKSPACE

Before a user can do more than simply read selected content in a workspace, the user must be assigned a role. This gives the user permission to perform specific tasks in the workspace. Like many other management tasks, this is accomplished via Server Administration, and applies to the highest level of the workspace (called the *workspace node*) and to any folders that inherit security from the node. However, to provide access to a subset of folders in a workspace, Web folders must be used.

When a user is added to a workspace, SharePoint Portal Server automatically assigns the role of Reader to that user. In this way, the new user is instantly granted read permissions on all published documents in the workspace. To change or augment these permissions, a new role must be assigned to the user.

LEVERAGING TAXONOMIES TO CATEGORIZE

Another significant challenge for Workspace Coordinators is how to effectively and efficiently categorize the vast array of documents—internal and external content—found in many workspaces. Doing so involves organizing folders into a hierarchy or structure that makes sense to the user community. This organization of folders is also termed a *taxonomy*— a good taxonomy will help to produce a workspace that is both functional and familiar to end users.

The creation of an effective taxonomy is especially challenging due to the randomness of much of the data, though. There is often no inherent structure to the data residing in the portal, for instance, making organization difficult. So, one of the Workspace Coordinator's most important management tasks involves working with the business units to co-develop a folder and category hierarchy for organizing portal content.

In this section, some of the tools available in Microsoft SharePoint Portal Server for organizing information—for delegated coordination, collaboration, and browsing—are discussed. We also briefly cover a method of importing an existing folder hierarchy into a workspace.

9

Microsoft believes that one of the best ways to get started building taxonomies is to simply jump in and learn as you go, working in a pilot or technical sandbox environment prior to the future development and production environments. Certainly, experimentation goes a long way toward fully understanding the impact that different taxonomy approaches have on workspace configuration and ultimate folder layout. Regardless of how you start, though, it is nearly guaranteed that the first cut at building a taxonomy will quickly evolve into something new. Some of the reasons for this include

- The folder creation rate never ceases, though it may be slower than in traditional file systems.
- Business needs may drive adding additional document profiles.
- Properties add dictionary values.
- Actually using a taxonomy forces expansion of the number of categories.

One method that may be employed to create taxonomies for a workspace follows, and came out of Microsoft's own project management group tasked with deploying SharePoint Portal Server. A complex folder hierarchy already existed, but it was quickly determined that simply dragging and dropping this existing folder hierarchy into the workspace would not achieve goals around optimization and organization of the portal's data.

THE GOAL OF DEVELOPING A TAXONOMY

One of the initial goals in building a taxonomy is to adapt the current folder structure into a set of folders, document profiles, properties, and more. By doing so, we seek to not only capture the original folder hierarchy details, but also add to it "richer" data. The result should include

- Fewer folders than the original hierarchy.
- Creating a set of workspace document profiles, properties, and dictionaries.
- Illuminating and capturing metadata as explicit document properties.

It will quickly become apparent that building taxonomies requires "knowing" the content— engaging the business units and their functional experts is therefore key to successfully developing a useful taxonomy. See the SharePoint Portal Server Software Development Kit (SDK), available at http://msdn.microsoft.com/, for more information in regard to creating scripts to build a workspace taxonomy.

MANAGING CATEGORIES AND THE CATEGORY ASSISTANT

Once the taxonomy—category hierarchy or structure—is established, the next step is to actually categorize the content in the workspace. This may be accomplished by manually assigning categories (by editing the document properties), or by automatically assigning categories using the Category Assistant. SharePoint Portal Server possesses the ability to automatically categorize published and crawled documents in the workspace. This seemingly complex task is actually pretty straightforward—SharePoint's Category Assistant assigns categories from your category structure to existing documents. How does this work? Based on an adaptive algorithm, the Category Assistant actually learns how to organize by being "taught" to do so via examples. This requires manually applying categories to a representative collection of documents for the Category Assistant to use as training examples. The Category Assistant compares the representative documents assigned to one category with documents from other categories, and in this way identifies the most characteristic words. Eventually, each category is distinguished from others in terms of the list of words that best describes its content. Not surprisingly, the more distinguishing words like those found in a document's title are given greater weight in the category definitions.

 Since SharePoint Portal Server associates documents with categories when it updates the index, there may be a delay before a document appears in an assigned category. The length of the delay depends on the index method utilized, and the amount of content that is included in the index. See "Index Method Causes Differing Delays" in the "Troubleshooting" section at the end of the chapter.

ACCESSING AND CONFIGURING THE CATEGORY ASSISTANT

The Category Assistant may be accessed from the Properties page of the top-level category folder. SharePoint Portal Server enables the feature by default, but the Category Assistant does not perform any categorization until it is trained. A Web Part called *Category Management* also exists, allowing a Workspace Coordinator to create, edit, and delete categories from the dashboard without the benefit of SharePoint Portal Server's client components. To learn more about this Web Part, refer to Microsoft's SharePoint Portal Server Resource Kit.

Regardless of how the Category Assistant is invoked, it makes a lot of sense from a management perspective to spend the time necessary to train well the Category Assistant. Adhere to the following management best practices for best results:

- Provide as many examples as possible. These examples should encompass as many facets of the category as possible.
- Consider applying multiple categories to a document. This is done as a matter of course, and should not be disabled.
- If working manually, assign a document to multiple/any categories that a user might search or access.

THE IMPORTANCE OF TRAINING THE CATEGORY ASSISTANT

Training the Category Assistant is the most important step in categorizing documents automatically—it requires training examples for each category. Without good training examples, the accuracy of the Category Assistant is limited, as already discussed. The following are management rules of thumb regarding training the Category Assistant:

- It is recommended that you use a minimum of 10 documents per category for training purposes.
- Ideal training documents are related to the same category topic.

- Training documents should also be mainly text-based. Word processing documents are excellent training examples. Documents such as spreadsheets do not offer as much text for the Category Assistant to use for categorization.

- Good training documents are also lengthy enough to include enough text for the Category Assistant to analyze the documents and identify the keywords that define a category.

→ To read more about actually configuring and training the Category Assistant, **see** "Auto Categorizing Documents," **p. 308**.

The task of managing or actually performing the training of the Category Assistant usually falls into the hands of the Workspace Coordinator. A couple training options exist, however. In the first, Authors are allowed to categorize documents. This distributes training responsibilities quite nicely, and allows for a large pool of documents. In the second option, training responsibilities may instead be assigned to an individual.

Documents may be manually categorized as well, by editing the Search and Categories tab on the Properties page of the document. By using Windows Explorer, an Author or Coordinator can select one or more values from the checklist of workspace categories. If the document is stored in an enhanced folder, it must be checked out prior to changing the document's category assignments. For a small number of documents, you can use this method of categorization exclusively.

A document may also be categorized by using document profiles. If the Coordinator has configured the document profile to display categories, the Author will be able to select categories when they check in the document. Adding the Categories property to document profiles provides a way to enforce category assignment when Authors check in a document. It also nicely distributes the task of document categorization among multiple Authors.

If a lot of content is crawled outside of the workspace, it may be preferable to apply categories automatically. Finally, should it become necessary, note that the Category Assistant may be disabled by clearing the Enable Category Assistant check box.

MANAGING THE WORKSPACE CAPACITY PLANNING PROCESS

Other workspace management tasks must be addressed as well, though the urgency or frequency may vary. These include tasks like addressing workspace capacity planning, modifying workspace settings, managing Web discussions, managing subscriptions, setting version maximums, and more.

While many issues exist relevant to managing capacity, or *capacity planning*, the assumption here is that capacity planning is performed once a productive SharePoint Portal Server is in place—it is an ongoing process. Prior to this go-live point in time, capacity planning is usually termed "sizing," and includes all of the work and planning around characterizing the users and content of a Portal deployment.

Good capacity planning includes continually monitoring the use of each server to ensure that the overall user experience—such as response time—is acceptable. In the next few chapters, we address capacity planning in terms of growing vertically (adding more data/content to workspaces, for example), and growing horizontally (adding more and perhaps diverse workspaces). Many considerations surround capacity planning, including

- Adding local content increases SharePoint Portal Server disk space requirements, as does enabling document management features such as support for document versioning.

- Adding content increases the time required to propagate indexes. At some point in this process, it must be determined at what size an index becomes too large to propagate efficiently.

- Adding workspaces to a single server increases the server work load, due primarily to increased user activity. Thus, it becomes critical to characterize typical user activity so as to extrapolate the number of active users that a particular server configuration may support.

- Depending upon the role that the SharePoint Portal Server fulfills for a particular organization, future local delta requirements for hardware resources like disk space, network, and CPU must be accounted for.

- Again, depending upon the role or activity, incremental SharePoint Portal Server machines may need to be added to the production solution. This could include servers dedicated to index workspaces, crawling, and so on.

SINGLE SERVER CAPACITY PLANNING

Many companies deploy their entire production SharePoint Portal server environment using a single server. While this is a fine approach in many cases, consider the following limitations and constraints and subsequent impact to managing the associated workspaces:

- A single server can track and store one million document versions. Thus, choices such as category hierarchy, versioning, and so on must be managed well so as not to exceed this number.

- A single server can host 3.5 million documents in an index. That is, a single-server SharePoint Portal Server deployment can crawl 3.5 million documents. The activity associated with searching indexes or crawling content may therefore preclude using the server for much of anything else.

- Each server supports a maximum of 10,000 licensed users. In some cases, this number might actually be reached in a single server deployment, though in most cases additional servers are added before this license number becomes an issue.

- Geographic requirements may dictate a distributed approach rather than a single-server "central" approach.

9

MULTIPLE SERVER CAPACITY PLANNING

Most companies benefit from multiple production SharePoint Portal Server machines for reasons like the following:

- Users distributed geographically may suffer unacceptable network latency times in single-server configurations.

- Different organizations within the same company may have different portal business needs or goals, such as enterprise search, document sharing, document management, team collaboration, the need for an enterprise-wide "master" portal tied in to other "departmental" portals within the company, and so on.

- Different organizations within the same company will certainly have different functional goals—that is, the needs of the marketing organization will differ greatly from the needs of the product support organization or the sales group.

MONITORING PERFORMANCE COUNTERS

Much in the way of performance monitoring tools is available to technical support organizations tasked with supporting Microsoft SharePoint Portal Server. A key tool, however, is Microsoft's own Performance Monitor, or PerfMon.

→ To find out more about the precise PerfMon counters that may be used for monitoring SharePoint Portal Server, **see** "Monitoring Using Standard Performance Counters," **p. 136**., and "Performance Counters," **p. 508**.

MODIFYING AND MANAGING GLOBAL WORKSPACE SETTINGS

In terms of workspace management, there are some global settings that need to be configured initially and then reviewed over time. This is easily accomplished by changing the properties of the workspace. From the workspace Settings folder in the Management folder, the Properties page of the workspace may be accessed to reconfigure the following settings for the entire workspace:

- General settings, including specifying a workspace description/contact, an email address for the workspace contact (which could likely change over time), and the number of major versions of each document to be stored on the server.

- Security settings, such as adding users to and removing users from the workspace, and denoting roles at the workspace level.

- Index settings, including viewing the index status and specifying the query time limit for content source updates.

- Logging settings, such as specifying which items to include in or exclude from the log files, and how many log files to keep on the server.

ENABLING WEB DISCUSSIONS

By default, Web discussions for a workspace are enabled. Users can be prevented from using Web discussions for documents in a particular workspace on the server, however. From a security management perspective, determining whether to enable searching and indexing of Web discussion items is important—this feature is disabled by default because discussion items are not secured.

SharePoint Portal Server does not include Web discussions in the index when crawling other SharePoint Portal Server computers or other workspaces on the same server. Although SharePoint Portal Server returns documents from those servers or workspaces in search results, the discussion items are not included in the search results.

MANAGING SUBSCRIPTION SETTINGS

Subscription settings include specifying subscription limits per user and per workspace, and specifying subscription result limits. This also includes enabling and disabling Web discussions in the workspace, and enabling and disabling the inclusion of Web discussions in search scopes and in the index. You can specify subscription settings for the workspace. Note the following limitations:

- Subscriptions per workspace—By default, the workspace subscription setting is 5,000 (does not apply to index workspaces).
- Subscriptions per user—By default, the user subscription setting is 20 (does not apply to index workspaces).

SPECIFYING DOCUMENT RETENTION MAJOR VERSION MAXIMUMS

For each workspace, the number of previous major versions to retain of a document may be set (this does not affect the number of minor versions retained).

To specify the number of major versions retained per document, perform the following:

1. In the console tree, select the server that contains the workspace to be managed from a Major Versions perspective.
2. Click to expand the server, and then select the workspace that contains the document version setting.
3. From the Action menu, click Properties. Or right-click the workspace name, and then click Properties on the shortcut menu.
4. Click the General tab.
5. Type the Number of major versions retained per document check box, and then type the number of document versions to retain.
6. Click Apply.

It should be noted that "999" is the maximum value that may be configured for this setting.

TROUBLESHOOTING

INDEX METHOD CAUSES DIFFERING DELAYS

How long are the delays before a document appears in the assigned category?

Based on the type of indexing selected, the delay period between when a content source is updated and when this change is actually reflected back in the workspace index may vary significantly. The notification update is the most efficient and direct, whereas the full update is the most time-consuming and therefore the slowest. An incremental update falls somewhere between.

WINDOWS 2000 AUTHENTICATION AND SUBSCRIPTION NOTIFICATIONS

I subscribe to content, but have not received a subscription notification.

When a user creates a subscription, the user does not receive a subscription notification if the right to read the document is assigned through a Windows 2000 Authenticated User or other special SID, including

- Anonymous Logon
- Batch
- Dialup
- Interactive
- Network
- Terminal Server User

CHAPTER SUMMARY

In conclusion, managing the workspace amounts to much more than simply monitoring the number of users, amount of content, and a few performance counters. Workspace management involves examining the SharePoint Portal Server solution end-to-end or holistically, as well as drilling down into specific workspace and dashboard components. Sizing the initial production environment, followed up by comprehensive capacity planning, helps to ensure an excellent user experience, while attention to security considerations ensures that confidential data is not compromised. Special attention to managing and securing internal and external content, managing indexes, planning an effective taxonomy, using categories and the Category Assistant, enabling subscriptions, managing Web discussions, and more round out the Workspace Coordinator's tactical roles, helping to ensure a well-performing and highly useful SharePoint Portal.

CHAPTER 10

MANAGING FOLDERS AND DOCUMENTS

In this chapter   *By Jared Walker*

MANAGING FOLDERS WITHIN THE WORKSPACE

As the most fundamental element of the document library, folders are the foundation of document management. You can help to ensure the greatest benefit from the workspace by carefully evaluating which folder features are needed and populating the workspace with the appropriate combination of folder types.

→ To refresh your familiarity with the various folder features, see Chapter 4, "Overview of Document Management."

FOLDER TYPES

As discussed in Chapter 3, there are two different types of folders available within the workspace: standard and enhanced.

Enhanced folders provide support for all content management features. These include check-in and check-out functions, public and private (draft) views, document profiles, version history, and publishing approval processes. By default, all folders created in the document library have enhanced folder settings enabled. If you disable enhanced folder features, you change the folder to a standard folder.

The following table shows a comparison of the SharePoint Portal Server features supported by each folder type.

TABLE 10.1   COMPARISON OF FOLDER FEATURE SUPPORT

Feature	Enhanced	Standard
Categories	✓	✓
Indexed documents	✓	✓
Profile metadata	✓	✓
Roles	✓	✓
Approval Routing	✓	X
Check-in/check-out	✓	X
Version History	✓	X
Private Views	✓	X

All folders within the document library support the categories, indexed documents, profile metadata, and roles features of SharePoint Portal Server. If you wish to enable or disable the enhanced features of a folder, you must first empty the folder. Enhanced folder settings can only be changed on an empty folder. You enable/disable enhanced folder settings on the General tab of the folder properties. If an enhanced folder is moved into a standard folder, it retains its enhanced features. A standard folder moved to an enhanced folder remains standard.

Standard folders have some unique behaviors that are important to know. Multi-part or compound documents (documents with relative links to external documents, and so on) are only supported in standard folders. Also, any documents added to a standard folder are immediately published.

 Compound or multi-part documents are only supported in standard folders; see "Managing Compound Documents" in the "Troubleshooting" section at the end of the chapter.

FOLDER PROPERTIES AND SETTINGS

All of the features available for a folder are visible in that folder's properties page. Folder properties are broken down onto four tabs: General, Security, Profiles, and Approval.

GENERAL TAB

The General tab (see Figure 10.1) displays basic bookkeeping information for the folder—folder name, address, size and contents, and the date and time the folder was created and last modified. Also, the selection box to enable or disable enhanced folder features can be found here.

Figure 10.1
General folder information is composed of system generated metadata.

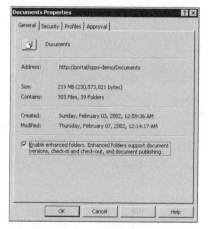

SECURITY TAB AND ROLES

The ability to restrict access to certain folders and the documents they may contain is important for document management. The Security Tab, see Figure 10.2, displays information pertaining to inheritance and access control for the contents of the folder. Two separate inheritance controls are available. The first, Use parent folder's security settings, is located toward the top of the window and blocks or allows setting inheritance for folders and documents within the folder. The second control, called Reset all subfolders to use these security settings, located at the bottom of the window, can be used to reset all the subfolders to the same settings as the current (parent) folder or as specified according to role-based settings.

CAUTION

Please note that applying this option will immediately change all of the folder's subfolders' settings! If any of the subfolders require special feature settings, you should avoid using this option, or you should document the subfolders' settings so that you can reapply them afterward.

Figure 10.2
The default configuration of a folder's security settings. Note the Reset settings check box at the bottom of the properties window.

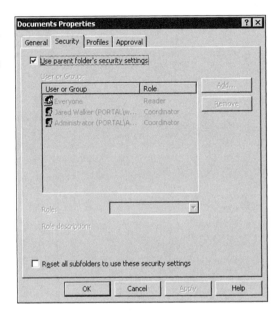

If the folder is configured not to use its parent's security settings then you can configure security permissions by selecting either local or domain users or groups and assigning them a role.

Users and groups can have multiple roles in the workspace, but only a single role in any given folder. In instances where users of a group are also specified independently in the security listing, the most permissive role assignment is enforced.

There are three security roles:

■ Reader—A reader can read documents that have been published in the folder.

CAUTION

By default, the Everyone group is configured as a reader. If you wish to restrict universal access to published documents, be sure to remove the Everyone group from the security list.

■ Author—An author can both create new documents and read and edit all documents in the folder.

■ Coordinator—A coordinator can assign roles to users and groups, select document profiles, and create and edit documents in the folder.

Figure 10.3
Role assignments are accessed on the Security tab of the folder's properties.

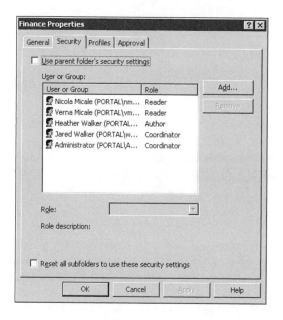

TIP

> Don't be confused by roles. The role-based security model is merely a simplified representation of the traditional Windows security model. NT Groups are added to SharePoint Security roles to grant permissions. By combining normal access controls into easy to understand "roles," users who would not ordinarily be capable of administering security may be entrusted with administering access to their own folders.

PROFILES TAB

The Profiles tab (see Figure 10.4) displays the available list of document profiles and indicates which of the profiles can currently be applied to documents within the folder. You can enable a document profile for use in the folder by clicking the check box next to its name. By clicking on the name of an available document profile, you display its profile description in the Profile description area of the window. You may also change the default document profile for the folder by selecting your choice from the pull-down list at the bottom of the window.

Once the document profiles are selected, the selected list could then be applied to documents within the folder.

Figure 10.4
Selection of available document profiles and the default profile from the Profiles tab.

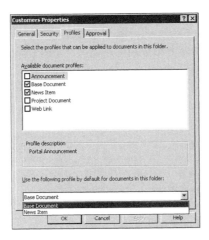

APPROVAL TAB

Often within document management, one or more people must review a document's content for accuracy or completeness before it can be approved for release or publication. SharePoint Portal Server's document approval routing feature provides a mechanism to enable and enforce that process. From the Approval tab, you can enable or disable document approval routing. If approval routing is enabled, documents must be approved by one or more people designated as approvers before they can be published and made available to readers.

Both local and domain user accounts can be selected as approvers. Once selected, you have the option of including the approver's email address. If an email address is present, the user will receive an automatic email notification when a document is awaiting their approval. There is also a comments field at the bottom of the window, where you can enter text to be included in the notification email.

One of two possible approval routes must also be chosen if approval is enabled: One after another or All at once.

With One after another routing, also called *serial approval routing*, each person in the approvers list for that folder must approve the document in turn. Each person must approve the document before the next person in the list will receive an approval request notification. You can set the order of approval by using the up and down arrow buttons to the right of the Approvers section. If all of the approvers approve the document, SharePoint Portal Server publishes it. If any of the approvers reject the document, the approval process ends and the document returns to checked-in status.

All at once, also called *parallel approval routing*, sends a notification to all listed approvers at the same time, indicating that the document is awaiting review. At any time, any approver can approve or reject the document.

Figure 10.5
Serial approvers are ordered by number as shown in the Approvers box. That order can be changed by using the arrow buttons to the left of the box.

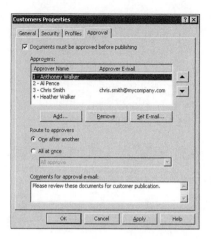

One of two approval scenarios must also be chosen. The first scenario, All approve, requires that all of the approvers approve the document before SharePoint Portal Server will publish it. If any of the approvers reject the document then the approval process ends and the document is returned to checked-in status, unpublished. The second approval scenario, "Only one approval required," sends a notification to each person on the approvers list. Once somebody on the list approves the document, it is published.

Figure 10.6
Parallel approval notifies all selected approvers at the same time, requiring either one or all to approve or reject as selected.

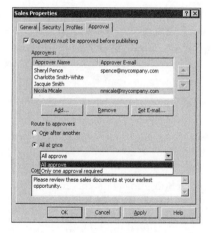

As you can see, the approval routing process allows you to plan and implement your approval strategy according to your business requirements.

FOLDER INHERITANCE

By default, all subfolders inherit folder settings from their parent folder. Since the Documents folder in the workspace is enhanced by default, any folders created or dragged into the Documents folder inherit its enhanced folder settings. Folders from outside the workspace that are dragged into any enhanced folder automatically become enhanced folders. Likewise, folders dragged into a standard folder in the workspace become standard folders. If you wish to break the folder inheritance setting before moving documents into the folder, simply create a new folder in the workspace and enable or disable inheritance on the Security tab within folder properties. Figure 10.7 provides an example of what happens when you try to change the enhanced settings of a folder that is populated with documents.

Figure 10.7
Example of the error message that is generated when you attempt to change enhanced features of a folder.

It is always best practice to plan your folder inheritance strategy prior to creating your folder hierarchy.

CREATING AND CONFIGURING YOUR FOLDER HIERARCHY

Configuring the Documents folder is a large part of preparing for document management and collaboration within the workspace. The Documents folder is the folder that contains all of the folders and documents within the workspace. This folder is an enhanced folder and, by default, is configured with the Everyone group assigned the Reader role and the user account that created the workspace as Coordinator.

THE DOCUMENT LIBRARY

Within the Documents folder, you begin constructing your folder hierarchy by identifying which types of folders you will need to use for the various collections of documents within your document library. You will need to create a folder structure within the workspace that reflects the organizational method you choose for your documents. There are four essential ways to organize your documents.

The quickest and perhaps simplest organizational method is to reproduce existing folder structures, making any needed modifications to accommodate desired document management features as you go. Since you can drag a folder and its contents into the workspace, where it inherits the settings from its parent folder, minimal administrative intervention would be required. This folder structure is also the most intuitive for users since it re-creates a familiar environment.

The second option centers on creating folder structures for documents with like security and management requirements. Since the only security setting at the document level is Deny Access, collecting documents with similar security characteristics set at the folder level provides significant administrative advantages. For example, if documents can be grouped generally by department and then more granularly by the workgroups within each department, folders could be created for each department and workgroup in turn.

The third option focuses on the document publishing process. Using this method, folders are created in a structure that reflects delineations in approval requirements. Again, using inheritance, all documents within a series of folders whose parent folder was configured with a given approval route would all acquire that approval route requirement. This greatly simplifies locating and browsing documents for both authors and approvers.

The forth option involves creating folders based on similarities in document content to enhance the results of search queries. There are situations when searches on large numbers of documents traditionally yield poor results, because words commonly used in the search criteria do not actually occur within the documents themselves. To overcome this problem, you can use document profiles to apply metadata to documents. As previously discussed, *metadata* is additional descriptive information for the document that is not inherently part of the document's content.

For example, you may have a wealth of documents detailing information about various types of chairs, tables, couches, and so on, but they might not all necessarily contain the word "furniture." By adding "furniture" to the keywords field of a file's document profile, it would be identified correctly in future searches.

TIP

> Simplicity is important. When planning, resist the urge to employ features or capabilities that are not specifically needed to meet your operational requirements. While leveraging advanced features is appealing, it adds additional complexity that can greatly affect overall administrative demands and introduce possible difficulties without necessarily providing a justifiable level of utility in return.

MANAGING DOCUMENTS WITHIN THE WORKSPACE

Document management within the workspace is primarily focused on collaboration, version control, publication, and searching. Each document consists not only of its content, but also of a variety of configuration settings and metadata attributes that help to determine how it is utilized by the organization.

DOCUMENT ACTIONS

In addition to the usual open, save, and copy capabilities presented by Windows Explorer, you can also access most document management features by right-clicking on a document within the workspace.

CHECK-IN/CHECK-OUT

If you have the proper security role for the folder in which a document resides, you can choose to check-in or check-out a document by right-clicking and selecting the corresponding action. It is possible to use the Undo Check Out feature to abandon any changes you have made to an existing document and restore it to a checked-in state without restoring a subsequent version.

PUBLISH

As a document author or coordinator, you can initiate the document publishing process by right-clicking on the document and selecting Publish from the menu. If the document is not configured to require approval, it will be immediately published within the workspace. If the document does require approval, the appropriate notification is sent to the approver(s) and the file awaits review and approval or rejection.

APPROVAL

If you are selected as an approver for a document, you can approve or reject the document by right-clicking on the document in the workspace and selecting Approve or Reject. If you are a member of the local administrator group, you can bypass the approval process and publish the document directly.

EDIT PROFILE

If you have checked out a document from the workspace, you can also access its document profile from Windows Explorer. Right-click on the document and select Edit Profile. This will take you to the Document Profile editor and allow you review and edit the metadata property values.

DOCUMENT PROFILES

As discussed earlier in the chapter, document profiles provide a way to apply additional metadata attributes to documents, in order to enhance search and indexing capabilities. While certain system-generated metadata like the file size and modification date is already included in the document profile, metadata provides additional descriptive information for the document, especially keywords that are not part of the text of the document. Existing document profiles and the Add Document Profile Wizard can be found in the Management/Document Profiles folder in the workspace.

SharePoint Portal Server comes preconfigured with four document profiles: Announcement, Base Document, News Item, and Web Link. Each profile contains a different list of properties, corresponding to typical metadata properties useful for managing the corresponding document type. A workspace can contain multiple document profiles, and individual folders can be configured to make any combination of available document profiles applicable to documents they contain. By default, the Documents folder is configured to apply the Base Document profile to its documents.

CUSTOM DOCUMENT PROFILES

If, upon evaluation of the contents of your documents, you determine that the existing document profiles do not contain the metadata attributes you feel would best fit documents in your workspace, you can create custom document profiles. There are several planning steps that should be considered in choosing to create and deploy custom document profiles:

1. Examine the properties of the Base Document profile. Determine what additional attributes would be logical and useful additions to the document's metadata.

2. From the workspace, navigate to the Management/Document Profiles folder, run the Add Document Profile Wizard, and follow the prompts.

3. Choose a meaningful word or phrase to name your document profile. Select an existing document profile that most closely matches the profile you are creating to use a template in the creation of your new profile.

4. Select only the properties that you require, and decide which should have single or multiple values. If you do not find an existing property element in the list that is appropriate to the metadata information you wish to capture, you can create a new property by defining its name and the type of value it should contain, and specifying whether the value is to be required by the author before the document can be successfully checked-in.

5. Configure the order in which you would like the properties to be displayed within the document profile dialog. Select a property from the list, and use the up and down arrow buttons to change its order within the list.

6. Confirm your choices and complete the wizard to make your new document profile available within folders in your workspace.

While creating new document profiles, you can also create new document profile fields to allow additional levels of customization. Figure 10.8 provides an example of creating a new property called Department.

Figure 10.8
Custom metadata properties can be created and configured to meet unique needs.

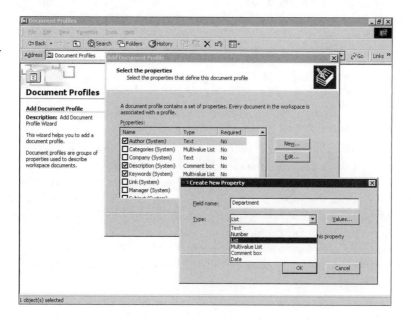

Once your document profile is created, you can choose to make your custom document profile available as the default folder for any folder within the workspace. To use the document profile, simply select it from the available document profiles list on the Profiles tab of the folder properties window.

DOCUMENT PROPERTIES AND SETTINGS

To modify the properties of a document, you will be required to access a series of tabs or properties of the document. The properties of the document you will work with are as follows:

- General
- Profile
- Version
- Security
- Search and Categories

The properties are discussed in more detail in the following sections.

GENERAL TAB

This tab displays the system-generated metadata information for the file, including the file's address, size, date created and modified, applied document profile, public status, and document status.

The published status describes the document in relationship to its status as a published or unpublished document. Once the document has been published, this field displays the version of the most recent published version of the document.

The Status field lists the current document status: checked-in or checked-out. If the document is checked out to a user, the version of the document and the user to whom the file is checked out are displayed. If the document is checked in, the current version of the document is displayed.

PROFILE TAB

This tab displays the list of properties from the document profile applied to the document, as well as the values for each metadata element currently stored within the profile. If the document is checked in or checked out to another user, this information is read-only. In order to edit the profile information, you must first check out the document from the workspace. If you elect to edit the profile, click the Edit Profile button at the bottom of the window. The Document Profile window will appear (see Figure 10.9) allowing you to select any of the available document profiles for that folder and add or change the value for any of the metadata properties contained by the applied document profile. Fields with an asterisk (*) are required fields.

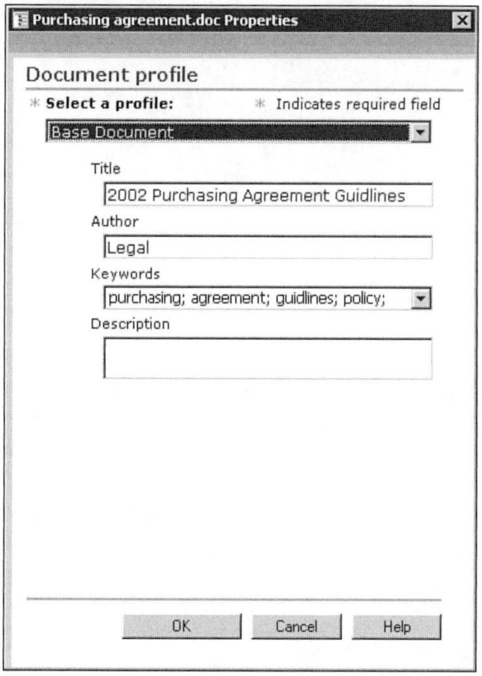

Figure 10.9
From the Profile tab, metadata values can be viewed and edited, or an alternative document profile can be selected.

Carefully evaluate the value of metadata information for your organization, and configure your document profiles accordingly. Using metadata to enhance the accuracy of searches can bring valuable information into the hands of your organization. However, adding additional document properties and requiring specific property information for any group of files puts additional demands on document authors and can slow the migration process when first populating your document library.

VERSIONS TAB

Here you can see the version history for each document and select to view previous versions of the document, as well as view previous document profile metadata information. Any version comments stored with the document are also visible from here.

Each time a file is stored in an enhanced folder, SharePoint Portal Server records a history record for that file. This history record, maintained through the check-in/check-out and version features, prevents multiple authors from editing the same version of a document and overwriting another user's changes. Each time a file is checked in or published, it receives a new version number and the previous version is archived. If you check out a document, you are retrieving the most recent version, unless you expressly select a previous version. You can review version history information in the document's properties.

Figure 10.10
Each version of the document is tracked and retained by the server. Retention time is also an adjustable setting within the MMC.

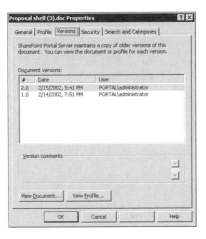

Versions are incremented in the standard major.minor fashion. Once published, a document is set to version 1.0. Any subsequent changes made to the document increment the minor revision to 1.1, 1.2, and so on. When the document is re-published, the major revision is incremented to 2.0.

SECURITY TAB

While most of the security controls are at the folder level, the document does have one important access control setting. From this tab, you can deny access to the document by selecting local or domain user or group accounts. Users who are denied access to a document will not see the document when browsing through folders or in search results.

Figure 10.11
The Deny Access list can contain both users and groups.

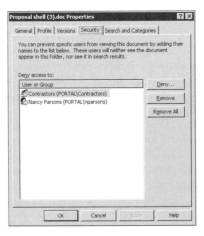

The Deny Access setting is an extremely powerful setting. It is best practice to use this feature only where absolutely necessary. Failure to use this setting carefully could result in increased administrative effort to manage.

SEARCH AND CATEGORIES TAB

A valuable tool in enhancing search results is the use of categories. Categories are a way that SharePoint Portal Server collects together similar documents through category assignment. You can select to include the document in any of the available categories and/or include the document in automatic categorization by the Category Assistant.

Additionally, you can choose which of the applied categories and keywords best represent the content of the document through use of the Best Bet options. When you select preferred categories and specific keywords, the document is more likely to appear in related search results.

→ To learn more about categorizing documents, **see** "Categorizing Documents," **p. 307**.

USING FOLDERS AND DOCUMENTS THROUGH THE DASHBOARD SITE

Many document management tasks and a handful of folder management tasks can be performed using a Web browser and the dashboard site. Direct access to folders and documents can be obtained by clicking on Document Library, located in the dashboard's menu bar. This will provide you with a link to the workspace's Document folder and present you with clearly defined navigational and management options.

Figure 10.12
Users can browse
through the document
library using normal
Web site navigation.

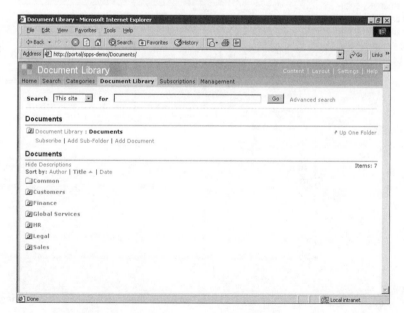

Remember that the dashboard site is more focused on presenting information and facilitating searching than on enabling Web-based administration of the workspace.

FOLDERS THROUGH THE DASHBOARD SITE

There are a handful of folder management options available while using the dashboard site. If you have security permissions that will permit the manipulation of a folder, you will typically be able to rename it, delete it, or add subfolders do it. While standard and enhanced folders are represented by different folder icons on the dashboard site, they both have the same management characteristics.

DOCUMENTS THROUGH THE DASHBOARD SITE

In addition to the dashboard's extensive focus on search capabilities, many of the document management features of SharePoint Portal Server are available from a Web view.

 In order for Web view to be viewable within the workspace, you must install Microsoft Active Desktop, which requires Internet Explorer 5. See "Web Views and Active Desktop" in the "Troubleshooting" section at the end of the chapter.

Given the proper security permissions, you can delete or rename documents, review and navigate a document's version history in an enhanced folder, replace a document with an updated version in a standard folder, perform standard check-in/check-out functions, and publish a document.

Figure 10.13
From the folder view you can access document and folder management features and browse available documents.

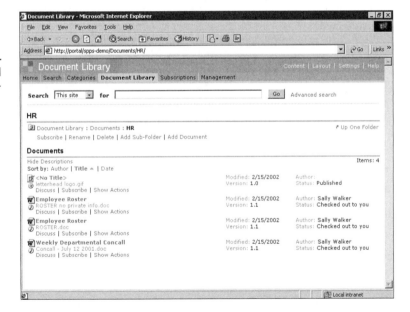

SharePoint Portal Server allows three ways to check in and check out documents, including

- Web folders
- Dashboard site
- Integrated within Office

To check in a document using the Web folder view

1. Click on My Network Places.
2. Click on the Portal icon that was specified during installation.
3. Double-click on Documents and then on one of your data folders.
4. Copy the file to the directory you want to work with.
5. Right-click the document and click Check In.
6. Complete the document profile and click OK.

To check in a document using the dashboard site

1. Click Document Library from the main menu.
2. Under the document library heading, display the folders and documents available.
3. Click on the folder for where you want to place the document.
4. Click Add Document and under document file name, click Browse to locate the document you want to add from your computer.
5. You can either check in or publish the document and then click Continue.
6. Populate the document profile information and click OK.

To check in a document using Office

1. Create your document using Microsoft Word.
2. Click on Save from the File menu.
3. Within the save dialog box, click on the Web folders option and then double-click a Web folder linked to a workspace.
4. Double-click a subfolder in the workspace to select it as the destination document folder.
5. Click on Save to end the process.

NOTE

> If you check in the document, it is available for other authors and editors for review. However, this document will not be available in the search results or categories until the document is published. In contrast, if you select to publish the document, your audience can view it immediately unless you specified an approval route process. If an approval route is specified, the document must be in an approved state before readers can view the document.

PLANNING FOR FOLDER AND DOCUMENT MANAGEMENT

One of the most crucial components of document management is preparing the overall structure of folders and documents within the document library. With an understanding of the characteristics of folders and documents within a workspace, you can choose a document management strategy suited to the needs of your users. The strategy you choose will have an immediate impact both on the way information is used and the administrative requirements of its ongoing maintenance.

ASSESSING YOUR ENVIRONMENT

Before you can choose the best ways to manage documents for your organization, you must clearly define what your users' requirements are. The way that you organize the information within your workspace, and the SharePoint Portal Server features you employ, will define the way your users will interact with their documents and each other.

You should perform a user survey to collect information about the group you are designing for, to ensure that they will have the tools and capabilities they require to fulfill their work objectives. Here are several questions you should ask to build a clear picture of your users' needs and reveal process elements important in choosing how you will organize and manage documents:

- What sort of documents and materials will be used, and where are they stored?
- How do users currently search for or locate documents and other information resources?
- What is the volume of information targeted for inclusion in your workspace?
- Are there other information sources, aside from those currently targeted for the workspace, that would be useful to the users?
- What is the current document management process like? What types of authorship roles currently exist? (sole, collaborative, and so on)
- Who are the intended users of the workspace? How do they currently use and manage their documents? What changes in the process would be useful or have been requested?
- What is the general skill level of the user population? Are they proficient in the navigation and use of Windows, Office applications, and Internet Explorer?
- What approval and publication process exists, if any? Where are the control points in the process?
- Is this part of a larger document management system?
- What is the overall lifespan of documents? What happens to old or outdated materials?
- How will your SharePoint portal be used in the future?
- What other people or groups might use documents stored within the workspace? (other groups within the organization, customers, general public access, and so forth)

By analyzing the answers to these questions, you can build a management strategy that best suits your environment. Through careful configuration of your documents, utilizing the tools and techniques that will maximize your users' productivity and meet business objectives, you will realize the benefits of SharePoint Portal Server.

If you are already familiar with the organization and its needs, this survey can be an informal one. If you are unfamiliar with the organization, perhaps serving in a consulting capacity, take the time to more formally meet with members of the organization and discuss their current document management processes. Identify their goals and requirements, discuss the strengths and weaknesses they observe in the way they currently manage their information, and use their feedback to plan and design your document management strategy.

TIP

> An often overlooked component of a document management strategy is the application of an overall naming convention for folders and documents. The names of files and folders can be used to convey clear, intuitive information about their informational contents or business purpose. If you have the opportunity to introduce a naming standard as part of your document management strategy, do it—you'll be glad you did!

UNDERSTANDING MANAGEMENT STRATEGIES

The key to your document management strategy is understanding the way in which users will need to use and/or collaborate on documents within their workspace, and then to identify which folder and document features will best meet those needs. There are many management techniques available to tailor the environment to match your goals—your strategy is a combination of document control processes and information organization.

The responses in your survey should illustrate the need for specific features within SharePoint Portal Server, as well as suggest the overall structure for folders within your workspace and the document management process best suited for your organization.

TROUBLESHOOTING

MANAGING COMPOUND DOCUMENTS

Which types of folders support compound or multi-part documents?

Compound or multi-part documents are only supported in standard folders. Compound documents are documents such as a Word document with a linked Excel file, a master document created in Word, or HTML files with relative links.

WEB VIEWS AND ACTIVE DESKTOP

What are the limitations between Internet Explorer versions 4 and 5 with respect to Web views and Active Desktop?

Active Desktop is available with Internet Explorer 5. If you previously had Internet Explorer 4, and were using Active Desktop with this version, you should consider upgrading to version 5. Lastly, if the Windows Explorer pane is being used to view Search, Favorites, History, or Folders, the descriptions of the Web view are not visible unless the Explorer pane is closed. If you have Internet Explorer 5 and are unable to view Active Desktop, uninstall Internet Explorer 5. Install Internet Explorer 4 with Active Desktop and then upgrade to Internet Explorer 5.

REAL WORLD EXAMPLE: CHOOSING A DOCUMENT MANAGEMENT STRATEGY

You can most easily define your management strategy by detailing your management goals. The following two examples describe business situations requiring changes in the way information is managed within an organization. In each, select information collected from the user survey is extracted, document management goals are described, and the corresponding server features and management techniques they require are listed. Additional considerations, focusing on folder and document management, are then explained, highlighting feature dependencies and notable configuration requirements.

COMPLIANCE REPORTS

The situation...

Users within the Quality and Compliance department of a large organization use a handful of document templates to create large numbers of weekly report documents for delivery to departmental managers and executives throughout the organization. These reports are compiled from documents from a variety of information sources, and are the combination of several individuals' contributions. Each report must be reviewed and approved by one of the department's three assistant managers prior to release. Reports are time-sensitive and do not change once released. All reports are permanently archived for future analysis and review. Additionally, there are numerous executive reports produced upon request, and periodic informational documents are created on an ongoing basis.

Source materials are acceptable for general departmental access. Reports, current and archival, are considered confidential and should only be visible to a handful of department members, select managers, and executives throughout the organization.

Users complain that it is difficult to locate files. Source documents, current report documents, and archival reports all reside in a single location. Naming of files is inconsistent and there is no current method to search document contents to easily locate specific information.

Management would like to implement stricter controls on the release of reports and the disposition of source and archival information, to ensure that confidentiality and accuracy are maintained. It would be useful for the organization if managers and executives outside the department had the ability to retrieve reports at-will rather than requesting documents via email, sometimes resulting in several exchanges before the appropriate report document is located and delivered.

The following table illustrates the management goals sought by the Compliance department and the features and management techniques that would best deliver them:

TABLE 10.2 COMPLIANCE DEPARTMENT GOALS AND MANAGEMENT TECHNIQUES

Document Management Goals	SharePoint Portal Server Features and Management Techniques
Organize documents by separating source materials, current reports, and archival documents.	Create separate folders for source materials, current reports, and archival reports. Add sub-folders to organize information by source and audience as needed. Sort existing documents and populate them into their corresponding folders.
Limit access to report documents.	Select a document publication process that ensures that reports are only visible to their authors, select managers, and executives through the use of roles and security access controls. Use enhanced folders.
Streamline the process for creating reports.	Use discussions to facilitate collaboration on reports. Use check-in/out to reduce duplication of effort. Use subscriptions to notify authors when changes in draft documents occur.
Approve all documents before their release.	Enable document approval in enhanced folders to route documents to assistant managers prior to publication. Once published, documents will be visible to users with the appropriate file security privileges.
Locate information and search documents rapidly.	Organize documents into folders. Use more Categories, Best Bets, and keywords to more easily locate relevant documents through searches or browsing.
Enable managers and executives to locate and retrieve current and archival reports.	Grant managers and executives reader access to report folders. Use a customized digital dashboard to organize current reports and simplify their delivery. Use subscriptions to indicate when new reports are published, and notify the appropriate group of managers or executives both on the digital dashboard and through email.

Since the department will need to utilize approval routing and check-in/check-out features for report documents, all of the reports should be placed in nested enhanced folders. Reports should be organized by type and then week of the year. Roles and file security properties should be configured at the parent folder to provide consistency through inheritance as new folders are created each week. Selected author roles should be assigned for each folder to enable controls on authorship and to enable private drafts. By topping it all off with the use of search and indexing capabilities, the department will fully realize the benefits SharePoint Portal Server has to offer.

SALES DEPARTMENT

A small manufacturing company has only recently begun integrating structured information technologies into its business. Given the traditional small business culture, the only controls on access to company documents have been used for accounting information, as secured by a password-protected file share. All other shared documents currently reside on a network share consisting of numerous well-organized folders. Any information that a user did not wish accessible to the company in general has traditionally been stored on that user's local hard drive or various types of removable media at the desktop. Each segment of the company creates and maintains detailed documents for every stage of product design, manufacturing, and shipping.

The company has been growing rapidly in recent years, and the sales group has determined that they need a document management solution to meet their growing needs. They want a way to manage documents and materials used in the sales process. Since they not only bring in new business, but maintain and develop existing customer relationships, they often monitor the progress of orders for their various accounts and want to be able to quickly locate and retrieve information from any document in the company that might be relevant in their efforts.

The sales group is very competitive. Individual sales people closely guard their pursuit of new accounts and do not want certain documents pertaining to potential sales wins to be visible by other sales people. All successful sales proposals are collected for general use, but, since they often contain confidential customer account information, access should be limited to sales and management.

All general sales materials (brochures, sample sheets, and so on) should be readily available to internal and external readers for promotional use. Company management wants access to all sales materials for general oversight, and to ensure business continuity in case of emergency or staffing change.

The following table shows the stated needs of the sales group and company management. For each, the features and management techniques are listed that are best suited to make them a reality:

TABLE 10.3 SALES GROUP GOALS AND MANAGEMENT TECHNIQUES

Document Management Goals	SharePoint Portal Server Features and Management Techniques
Segregate sales information by sales person.	Create folders for each sales person, and configure that person as its Coordinator. Ensure that the Everyone group is removed.

Document Management Goals	SharePoint Portal Server Features and Management Techniques
Collect and organize finalized documents, especially for reference and reuse purposes.	Create a high-level folder for sales docu ments, and configure it to allow departmental access. Use enhanced folders to enable version history. Create parent folders for managing individual salesperson documents, published customer documents, confidential customer documents, and general sales documents.
Ensure that confidential customer information is not disclosed.	Create a confidential customer documents folder and remove the Everyone group from the access list.
Search file share.	Configure SharePoint Portal Server to crawl the single company file share.
Provide select documents to customers.	Configure a dashboard site for customer access. Create an account for each customer company and assign it as a Reader for its own published document folder.
Ensure managerial access to documents.	Create a management group and assign it a Coordinator role for the parent sales folder.
Provide company-wide access to general sales materials.	Create a standard folder for general sales documents leaving the Everyone group assigned as a Reader.

Using folders as access boundaries provides both the ability to secure the sensitive sales information requested by the sales people and the ability to organize the remaining sales documents according to who will be permitted to use them. Since most of the information is not intended for use by the company as a whole, the Everyone group should only be included at the general sales documents folder. In the confidential customer documents folder, subfolders for each customer can be used to collect together customer documents and to allow for easy assignment of security roles, to ensure that only the salespeople and the given customer have access to those materials.

Also note that since access permissions are observed both in the Web folders view and the dashboard view, the sales people would have a powerful tool to retrieve or manage any of their documents from remote locations—a potential boon if they need additional information while meeting with customers. The dashboard site can also be easily reconfigured to serve as a communication and information delivery tool for enhancing communication with the customers.

FINAL THOUGHTS ON CHOOSING YOUR MANAGEMENT STRATEGY

As illustrated by the preceding examples, finding the correlation between user needs and the various features within SharePoint Portal Server is the key in providing the document management capabilities required by your users. Your specific management strategy will likely vary from these examples in many ways, but the underlying process is the same: assess, analyze, and deliver.

Here are a few additional suggestions to ensure your success:

- Try to solicit information from a wide sampling of users.
- Take time to validate your observations by asking the group of users you are planning for if you have successfully identified their document management needs.
- Ensure that users are prepared for the changes required in the transition to SharePoint Portal Server. Provide training and special support assistance if needed to make the change a smooth and comfortable one.

TIP

It is best practice to plan and pilot your document management strategy ahead of time.

SUMMARY

In this chapter, we drilled into detail on the document management process. We discussed the process of managing folders within the workspace, and provided an overview of each property tab when managing folders. We discussed the folder hierarchy and then drilled down into managing documents from within the workspace as well as from the dashboard site. We provided details on the document property tabs and we discussed folder inheritance. We ended the chapter with a couple of real-world scenarios on choosing a document management strategy.

CHAPTER **11**

PLANNING AND MANAGING SECURITY

In this chapter

By Jared Walker

SHAREPOINT SECURITY CONCEPTS

With SharePoint Portal Server, security is crucial for both document management and providing effective searching. The foundation of document management security is the ability to selectively restrict access to confidential or sensitive information while controlling the change, approval, and publication processes.

This chapter discusses planning and managing SharePoint Portal Server security.

Information security is typically used to provide three types of protection:

- Protection against user error
- Protection against unauthorized access to information
- Protection against malicious attacks and behavior

Within SharePoint Portal Server, most security configuration and management functions are performed at the folder-level through the manipulation of folder properties. At the folder-level, you can assign security roles, configure approval routes, and reset security to child folders and documents. While security settings are managed primarily through folder-level settings, security is enforced at the file-level, not the share-level.

SharePoint Portal Server also recognizes security policies or settings that are currently in use within your organization's environment. Information found on messaging servers, databases, and file shares are all subject to whatever existing security configurations exist on those systems. When search results are provided for documents located on these information sources, the security policies applicable for each document are enforced by SharePoint Portal Server. In SPS, if a user has filesystem level permissions to view a document, but not share level permissions, the document will still be indexed and displayed in a search, but the user will receive an error and will not be able to view the document if selected.

File-level security is controlled through the use of three fixed security roles. These roles offer a flexible and manageable method for controlling user access to documents in the workspace. Roles can be assigned to both local and domain users and groups in your Windows NT or Windows 2000 environments. Additionally, users and groups can be explicitly denied access to individual files through the use of the Deny Access feature.

You can only create subfolders within the Documents and Portal Contents folders in the workspace. By default, subfolders inherit security settings from their parent folders. You can override this default behavior by disabling the inheritance in the parent folder's security settings. Once a subfolder has been created, changes to a parent folder's security settings are only propagated if inheritance is enabled or if they are explicitly reset from the Security tab in the parent folder's properties dialog box (see Figure 11.1).

Figure 11.1
Security inheritance and subfolder propagation are both configured in the Security tab.

It is important to note that only the role settings are inherited by subfolders. Approver and approval route information is copied to the subfolder when it is created, but subsequent changes in approval settings for a folder are not propagated to subfolders. If you need to change these settings, they must be made on a folder-by-folder basis.

PERMISSIONS

SharePoint Portal Server understands and enforces normal Windows NT and Windows 2000 security policies. The server uses both local and domain groups and accounts to set security permissions within the workspace; and, when the server accesses information sources outside the workspace, the normal NT security model still applies.

USERS AND GROUPS

The standard entities for assigning security controls are the user and group accounts within Windows NT or Windows 2000. It is recommended that you use domain, rather than local, users and groups when assigning roles within the workspace, to facilitate the use of content sources on another server. When the SharePoint Portal Server crawls other servers, it cannot recognize local user server accounts on the target servers.

ROLES

There are three security roles accessible from the Security tab of a folder properties dialog box: Reader, Author, and Coordinator. More than one user can be configured with these roles in any given folder (See Figure 11.2). This is useful in distributing management responsibilities, allowing general access to documents, and enabling collaboration.

Figure 11.2
This folder has two users assigned as Coordinators, two as Authors, and multiple Readers.

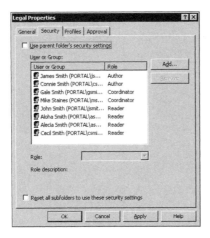

READER

A Reader can read documents that have been published in the workspace, but cannot change them. This role also allows a user to search the workspace. In standard folders, all documents are automatically published by SharePoint Portal Server and are visible to all Readers. In enhanced folders, Readers can only view published documents and the folders they reside in. Documents pending approval or that have not yet been published are not visible to Readers. When performing a search, only published documents for which the user has sufficient permissions to read will be listed in the search results.

AUTHOR

An Author can read all documents, create new documents, edit all documents, and delete any documents in the folder. In enhanced folders, Authors can publish documents. Authors can also create, rename, and delete folders and subfolders. When a subfolder is created, it inherits the roles and folder policies from the parent folder, and cannot be changed by an Author.

COORDINATOR

A Coordinator can assign roles to users and groups, select and modify document profiles, create and edit documents in the folder, delete documents, and create and configure sub-folders. A Coordinator can also read and/or delete documents that have been created but not yet checked in, as well as undo the check-out of a document. For enhanced folders, Coordinators can select approvers and approval routes, cancel publishing, or bypass the approval of a document if needed.

TIP

For those who are already familiar with Windows NT and Windows 2000 security, don't be confused by the use of roles. The role-based security model is merely a simplified representation of the traditional Windows NT security model. By combining multiple access permissions into easy to understand "roles," users who would not ordinarily be capable of administering security may be entrusted with administering access to their own folders within the workspace.

WORKSPACE SECURITY

There are two default role assignments made with the creation of the workspace that deserve special attention. The administrative account that creates the workspace is automatically assigned the Coordinator role for the workspace and each folder within the workspace. This role is called the node Coordinator. In addition, the Windows 2000 Everyone group is assigned the Reader role for all folders in the workspace when it is created by SharePoint Portal Server. This means that all published documents within the workspace are visible unless the default security settings of folders are changed.

Workspace management functions are supported in the Categories, Management, Portal, Shadow, and System folders and are managed by the node Coordinator. These are top-level folders within the workspace; security cannot be directly configured on these folders and they are not generally visible to workspace users.

TIP

If you do not have a specific need to make published documents universally visible, you should remove the Windows 2000 Everyone group from the security list of applicable folders within the workspace. To avoid needing to modify large numbers of folders, consider making this change immediately following installation.

Users and groups can be assigned multiple roles throughout the workspace, but only a single role in any given folder. For example, a user could be assigned the Coordinator role in one folder and the Reader role in another. In instances where more than one role has been assigned to a user, for example through differing role assignments to different groups, the most permissive role assignment possessed by a user is enforced by SharePoint Portal Server. The only instance that supersedes this rule is the use of the Deny Access feature. With this feature, it is possible for a user to have a role within a folder and yet not have access to a specific document within that same folder; the file would not be displayed to that user in the results of a search. Deny Access does not affect the local Administrators group's ability to access the document.

 To perform a permissions audit on the folder to determine where the problem lies, see "Correcting Inappropriate Folder Permissions" in the "Troubleshooting" section at the end of the chapter.

11

In addition to the node Coordinator and various folder Coordinator role assignments, members of the Windows 2000 local Administrators group have the ability to read documents and configure security on any folder or document residing in the workspace. This is important in maintaining the security of the workspace because it provides a mechanism to restore proper security settings or make changes in the event that normal access through assigned Coordinator roles is unavailable. The local Administrators group can reset permissions on individual folders or propagate them throughout the workspace. The document-level Deny Access does not affect the local Administrators group's ability to access the document. From the workspace properties dialog box, a local administrator can access user roles, and additional server information, within the SharePoint Portal Server Administration tool (see Figure 11.3) .

Figure 11.3
A number of node Coordinators are assigned to the workspace, along with the Everyone group Reader assignment.

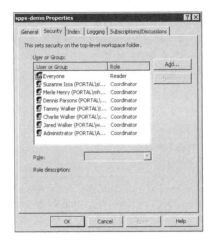

11

CAUTION

It is important to note that domain controllers do not have local Administrators groups. If you install SharePoint Portal Server on a domain controller, there is no local administrator to resolve security issues if a Coordinator makes an error or the system is the victim of a malicious attack.

➜ For more information on configuring individual document and folder settings, see Chapter 4, "Overview of Document Management," or Chapter 10, "Managing Folders and Documents."

MANAGING ROLES

across the workspace are managed by users with either node Coordinator assignments or local administrative privileges. The node Coordinator can assign user roles at the workspace node and at any individual folder that inherits its security settings from the node itself. A user must be assigned to the workspace node to administer folders supporting management functions.

CAUTION

> It is possible to exclude the node Coordinator from a subfolder within the workspace by disabling inheritance and removing the node Coordinator from the user list for a folder. Once removed, only a local administrator can intervene in the event that a configuration error or malicious attack prevents a folder Coordinator from successfully administering the folder.

If a Coordinator has the client components installed on a computer running Windows 2000, the user can manage security at the folder and document level using the Properties page of documents and folders within the workspace. Users cannot manage SharePoint Portal Server roles if they are using computers running Windows 98, Windows NT 4.0, or Windows Me.

PLANNING AND IMPLEMENTING SECURITY

The essential goals of workspace security are to restrict access to sensitive information, define and enforce document approval and publishing processes, and ensure that search results only reveal information about documents that the user should be made aware of and allowed to access.

The planning process begins by surveying your documents and the various content sources you wish to include in your index. It is also important to identify the users who will need access to documents, any process controls that may be required, and the intended mechanisms for providing access to your documents using SharePoint Portal Server and Web folders or a dashboard site. Security and document management go hand-in-hand, so include this as part of your overall user survey if possible. The following information from your survey most directly pertains to setting up security within the workspace:

Who will manage the workspace node on a day-to-day basis?

Who, if anyone, will manage subfolders within the workspace?

How will folders be configured to provide logical organization to documents and enable the use of selected SharePoint Portal Server features?

What sort of document control processes, if any, need to be enforced, and who should administer them?

What, if any, documents contain sensitive information and should only be visible or accessible by select users or groups of users? Will all documents be published for unrestricted access?

What security considerations need to be made for external content sources?

→ For more information on the user survey see Chapter 10, "Managing Folders and Documents."

Once your folder structure and document management processes have been identified, the process of applying the appropriate security controls is pretty straightforward. In general, any folder that contains information requiring selective access control or enhanced folder features such as version control, approval routing, or check-in/check-out will require specific security configuration. If a folder does not contain documents requiring restricted access or document management features, its security configuration will likely be very simple. In addition, content sources outside the workspace that contain documents requiring any access control restrictions will also require special consideration when configuring SharePoint Portal Server to crawl the sources.

To ensure that your documents are secure, see "Identify Documents Accessible by Unintended Users" in the "Troubleshooting" section at the end of the chapter.

As a general rule, it's a good idea to configure basic access permissions through the use of domain or local groups and assign more specific access permissions through individual user accounts. This method reduces the administrative complexity of managing security, and simplifies troubleshooting in the event a user is found to have inappropriate access rights.

Within the workspace, the use of groups to assign roles is encouraged. The Reader role—the most basic level within SharePoint Portal Server—is often best assigned to a group of users as a single group assignment. Author or Coordinator roles, which both have the ability to make changes to contents of the workspace, should be assigned to small groups or individual user accounts, depending on the number of users applicable for each role.

The granularity of assigning roles is somewhat subjective. A small organization's workspace will likely be used by a limited number of users and will typically require comparatively little administrative intervention once configured and deployed. A large organization may employ SharePoint Portal Server to service a large number of employees or groups, and may have a correspondingly complicated set of security requirements as a result. In either scenario, industry best practice has shown that managing security through the use of groups diminishes the likelihood of misconfiguration and greatly reduces the administrative demands of the environment. This is particularly relevant when sweeping changes are required to reflect the reassignment of security permissions or to make large-scale changes to the security configuration of the workspace, since configuring or changing a role assignment to a group requires the same administrative effort as that required for a single user.

SECURITY FOR CONTENT IN THE WORKSPACE

Within the workspace, security is configured at the folder and file level by users assigned the Coordinator role, or by a local administrator. The type of administration required for a given folder is determined by a combination of folder type, features used at the folder, and the process controls being employed.

USING YOUR FOLDER HIERARCHY

The assignment of roles determines the "who," "how," and "where" of document security within the workspace—all of which should be reflected in the workspace's folder structure and the SharePoint Portal Server features being used. Examine your folder structure and identify any logical boundaries that distinguish groups of users and the role assignments they require. Identify logical groupings of documents by type, use, audience. In most instances, your folder hierarchy will separate documents into groupings that require similar security configurations.

Apply the required role assignments to a parent folder and propagate them throughout the folder tree. If any exceptions are required within that tree, drill down to that folder and change its configuration. When version controls or approval routing is needed, enable those features at a parent folder and nest subfolders with similar characteristics within it.

TIP

> If you make changes to the security settings in a parent folder that need to be enforced in subfolders, be sure to select Reset All Subfolders and apply the changes to the folder hierarchy. Unless changes are propagated throughout the folder tree, only the parent folder will be affected.

Remember that all folders use the Reader, Author, and Coordinator roles to assign access permissions to documents and subfolders. Individual user or group access to a single document can be blocked with the Deny Access feature. Documents blocked for a user will not be visible in the folder, nor will they be listed in the results of a search. Any published document for which a user has at least Reader permissions and which is not blocked for that user will be visible when browsing the folder and will be displayed in search results.

STANDARD FOLDERS

Standard folders are folders where enhanced folder features have been disabled. The most important distinction of a standard folder, from a security vantage, is that any document placed into the folder is automatically published within SharePoint Portal Server. If a user has been assigned at least a Reader role for the folder where a document resides, it will be visible to that user when browsing the folder, and will be displayed in any encompassing search results.

Since the only security setting available for a standard folder is role assignment, these folders are best used when document management requirements are at a minimum.

ENHANCED FOLDERS

Enhanced folders provide document management features for version control, document check-in/check-out, and approval routing. When configuring security for an enhanced folder, remember that only security settings are inherited by subfolders unless inheritance has been disabled. While approvers and approval routes are copied to subfolders when they are created, changes in approval configuration at a parent folder are not inherited by subfolders. In order to change the approval configuration for subfolders, you must manually reconfigure each folder individually.

→ For more information on configuring folder settings, see Chapter 10, "Managing Folders and Documents."

Using "Hidden" Subfolders

Sometimes it is useful to create folders that are not visible to users browsing the workspace, but which contain documents that the user can access, given the specific folder location. This might be advantageous if users are needlessly browsing the workspace without cause, or if the folder structure implies information about the materials within the workspace that the Coordinator does not want to reveal. Recall that a folder is only visible to a user if that user has a role assigned to the folder, so if a user does not have a role assignment for the parent folder, the contents of the folder cannot be seen by browsing.

To "hide" a folder within the workspace

1. Create a parent folder and ensure that the user is not included in the roles for the folder.

2. Create a subfolder that you wish the user to have access to.

3. Assign the user a role on the folder.

While the user will be unable to navigate to the subfolder through Windows Explorer, the subfolder can be accessed directly using its URL. Additionally, documents in the subfolder will be included in search results.

This *security through obscurity* method does not actually prevent access to obscured information; rather it reduces the ease of locating documents, and limits the ways in which users can find content within the workspace. When utilizing this configuration, take special care to ensure that subfolder role settings are reconfigured if any parent folder propagates any configuration changes.

11

Security for Content Outside the Workspace

SharePoint Portal Server is capable of crawling a variety of outside content sources and including them in its content index for use in search queries. Any security settings currently assigned to servers, file shares, and databases within your organization are recognized by SharePoint Portal Server. Note, however, that only file-level security settings are enforced, not share-level.

When crawling an outside content source within the same domain as the SharePoint Portal Server, the security scheme for the content source is mapped to Windows 2000 security, and is applied when a user searches the index for documents. Users only see documents if they have sufficient security permissions to access them.

If the content source is in another domain, do use domain local groups on the target server to secure its content. Users will not be able to view crawled content if the SharePoint Portal Server cannot recognize the local group account used on the target server and the corresponding *SIDs*—unique alphanumeric identifiers for each computer, user, and group in a Windows domain. SharePoint Portal server handles security for different types of content sources in a variety of ways.

FILE SHARES

For file servers, file-level security is enforced at query time by SharePoint Portal Server. Encrypted documents are not crawled. If the file system used on the file share does not have file-level security attributes for SharePoint Portal Server to map security to, share-level security is not enforced in its place. While share-level security is not enforced, a per-path login is assigned for crawling, allowing the server access to content through share-level security.

WEB SITES

No security is enforced at query time for Web site content. While SharePoint Portal Server does specify a per-path login for crawling Web sites, this does not limit the access to information collected from the site in query results. Web sites or Web shares using Secure Socket Layer (SSL) encryption cannot be crawled.

OTHER SHAREPOINT PORTAL SERVERS

SharePoint Portal Server can crawl the workspaces on other SharePoint Portal Servers. When this occurs, file-level security is enforced at query time.

EXCHANGE 5.5 AND 2000 SERVERS

SharePoint Portal Server enforces message-level security at query time for information within these servers. Encrypted messages cannot be examined and are excluded from the crawl. The SharePoint Portal Server administrator must configure the server to crawl Exchange Server content sources before a Coordinator can create Exchange Server content sources for crawling.

11

LOTUS NOTES SERVERS

Record-level security is enforced at query time by mapping the Lotus Notes user ID to the Windows NT user ID. The SharePoint Portal Server administrator must configure the server to crawl Lotus Notes content sources before a Coordinator can create Lotus Notes content sources for crawling.

NFS AND NETWARE SERVERS

Content on Unix NFS and Novell NetWare can be accessed using the corresponding network client, which must be installed on the SharePoint Portal Server. The server does not understand the security descriptors used by NFS and NetWare—both non-NTFS file systems. While this means that per-file security is lost, per-share security is maintained by the server. Without security mappings, SharePoint Portal Server logs on to the share as anonymous or guest and cannot access any content that is not accessible to these accounts. The server crawls the accessible documents and stamps them with read access for the Windows 2000 Everyone group. This means that documents crawled from these content sources are searchable by any user. Administrators must take special care to ensure that information regarding documents residing on these content sources that have been secured in way that is not compatible with Windows NT security is not revealed in search results. Also, the server can send specified security credentials while accessing these foreign file systems by specifying that the account and password requires Basic authentication in the site path rules for the remote file system.

TIP

> A common source of complication is the synchronization of credentials between SharePoint Portal Server and outside content sources, since changes made are not automatically updated in the server's configuration settings. If you begin to experience sudden difficulties accessing an outside content source, first check to ensure that the user ID and password being used to access the content source have not changed.

CONFIGURING INDEXING ACCESS ACCOUNTS

There are two index access accounts that can be configured with the SharePoint Portal Server Administration tool—both on the Accounts tab of the server properties dialog box. The first is the Default Content Access Account. This account, which must have read access, is the default account used by SharePoint Portal Server when it creates an index of content sources. The second is the Propagation Access Account (see Figure 11.4). This account must have administrative access on the targeted computer, and is used by the server when propagating workspace indexes to other SharePoint Portal Servers.

Figure 11.4

The Propagation Access Account must be configured to facilitate the propagation of indexes to other SharePoint Portal Server computers.

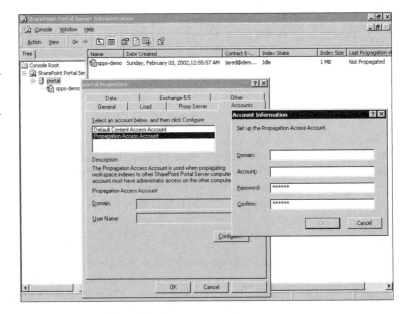

INTERNET/INTRANET SECURITY

Because SPS can be configured to crawl Web content sources within and outside of its given environment, as well as provide file management services through the Web-based Digital Dashboard, securing your SPS server from unauthorized Internet/intranet entities is vital. It is important to carefully evaluate your server's exposure to Web users, to ensure both the ongoing integrity of your documents and the confidentiality of information they contain.

PROXY SERVERS

Securing your SharePoint Portal Server from unauthorized Internet and intranet Web users is greatly enhanced through the use of a proxy server. Proxy servers prevent unauthorized access by authenticating incoming requests and allowing or denying access to the server based on defined security guidelines. Proxy servers are also useful in enhancing the performance of outgoing Web queries by caching recently accessed Web pages, often resulting in a reduction in page load times.

By default, SharePoint Portal Server uses the proxy server settings taken from Microsoft Internet Explorer for the default content access account, and can be changed at any time. Changes made to the server's proxy settings do not affect other applications, such as Internet Explorer. Since both the client components and the dashboard site communicate with the server by using HTTP, proxy settings can affect how both interact with the server.

If you use a proxy server, you must configure the server to pass the HTTP verbs, the Distributed Authoring and Versioning (DAV) HTTP extensions, and INVOKE—a custom SharePoint Portal Server verb.

PROVIDING CONTENT TO THE INTERNET

In order to use SharePoint Portal Server to provide content and searching capabilities to users located on the Internet, you must do the following:

Enable the use of fully qualified domain names (FQDN) within SharePoint Portal Server.

Create a Domain Name System (DNS) entry for the server name.

Create a virtual Web site and point it to the SharePoint Portal Server computer.

Change the security settings on the Directory Security tab of the virtual Web site's properties dialog box. SharePoint Portal Server uses NTLM authentication by default. To enable access by Internet users, you must change the security settings to either Basic authentication or Anonymous (See Figure 11.5). Note that if Anonymous authentication is chosen for the virtual Web site, users cannot create subscriptions from the dashboard.

11

Figure 11.5
Authentication methods are configured in the IIS tool.

Ensure that proper firewall and routing configurations have been made to allow communication with the Internet.

There are many considerations when configuring and deploying a Web server. If you are not familiar with these technologies and the ramifications of their use, consult your local Webmaster or system administrator for more information on how to configure your server and virtual Web site to operate safely and securely on your organization's network.

TIP

> Before and after making your SharePoint Portal Server available to Internet access, you should regularly review indexed content, to ensure against revealing information from unguarded or misconfigured file shares to users outside your organization.

FIREWALLS

If you plan to use SharePoint Portal Server index propagation in an environment with firewalls, you must ensure that proper communication can occur between the servers. If there is a firewall between the servers configured to search content sources and the servers configured to create and update indexes, it must be configured to permit index propagation to take place. Since index propagation uses the standard Windows file sharing protocol, ensure that any firewall between the servers allows standard Windows file share access.

If you have a firewall and want to use SharePoint Portal server to provide content to the Internet, you must map the server's IP address to an external name.

IIS AND IFS SECURITY

There is an associated vroot or virtual directory created in IIS, under the default Web site that is associated with SharePoint Portal Server workspaces. Dashboard site security can be managed there. While you can navigate the SharePoint Portal Server IFS using Windows

Explorer, the access is read-only. Also, refrain from manipulating the IFS security attributes, as it may result in data loss through corruption of the SharePoint Portal Server security role information. Any management function of the workspace should only be performed through the Web folders interface.

DASHBOARD SECURITY

Dashboard security is configured through the IIS administrative tool at the vroot directory for the SharePoint Portal Server virtual Web site. By drilling down to the folders or documents that comprise the site, you can manipulate authentication requirements, general IP address and domain name access restrictions, or any other parameter allowed by IIS.

SUBSCRIPTION NOTIFICATIONS AND DISCUSSIONS

A user does not receive a subscription notification if they are assigned the right to see a document through a Windows 2000 Authenticated User or other special SID. Examples of special SIDs include Anonymous Logon, Batch, Dialup, Interactive, Network, and Terminal Server User. If a user is assigned access rights through a group containing both special SIDs and a non-special SID, the user receives notifications.

Discussions rely on NTLM authentication and are not available for use if the workspace has been configured to use Basic authentication only. If your site has been configured this way, you can correct this problem by turning NTLM authentication on for the SharePoint Portal Server vroot in the Internet Information Services Manager (ISM), located in the Administrative Tools folder in the Start Menu.

Load the ISM and select the properties for SharePoint Portal Server by right-clicking on it and selecting it from the menu. Click the Directory Security tab, click Edit in the Anonymous access and authentication control box, and select the Integrated Windows Authentication check box at the bottom of the window. Click OK and close properties.

Note that discussion items are not secure, and are visible to a user even if that user does not have access permissions for the document the discussion pertains to. Since actual document content may be part of the discussion itself, this could potentially reveal sensitive or confidential information from the document. Because of this, Web discussions are not included in the index by default, and you can restrict Web discussions to items stored on a server from the server properties dialog box's Other tab, using the SharePoint Portal Server Administration tool (see Figure 11.6). Also note that Web discussions are not included in the index by SharePoint Portal Server when it crawls other SharePoint Portal Servers, even if the documents contain discussion items.

If you do not have Web discussions restricted to items stored in their own workspaces, the Internet browsing activity and username are logged in IIS for each user who connects to the server and leaves the Online Collaboration toolbar open in Internet Explorer. To prevent logging this information, instruct your users to close the collaboration toolbar when they are finished with their document discussion, both in Office and Internet Explorer.

11

Figure 11.6
Stored discussion items can be restricted to those stored in the workspaces of the SharePoint Portal Server.

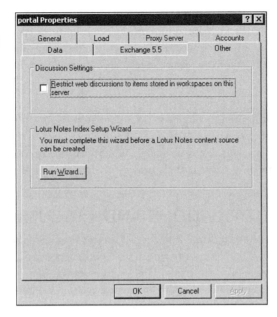

MANAGING SECURITY

The process of managing security is a combination of ongoing monitoring and mainte-nance of security settings and system logs, combined with periodic review of overall securi-ty configuration. This helps to ensure that all security needs are being properly fulfilled and no abhorrent system activity is occurring. The processes you use to monitor and main-tain security within your environment are vital in maintaining overall security integrity.

ONGOING MAINTENANCE

There are a number of security practices which you should use to maintain the security of your SharePoint Portal Server on an ongoing basis. Since security is configured largely at the file-level, there are a few basic things to check on a regular basis to ensure that security is being properly maintained.

Node Coordinators should periodically examine the security settings of the folders within the workspace. Ensure that high-level folders are accurately configured to reflect the intended security role assignments you have delegated to them. If node Coordinators also actively maintain subfolders within the workspace, examine them as well to ensure they are also properly configured.

Folder Coordinators should closely monitor the role assignments for the folders they maintain on a regular basis, to ensure that no erroneous or inappropriate role assign-ments are made.

Local server administrators should periodically examine server configuration settings, to ensure no unauthorized changes have been made and to update access credentials for outside content sources as needed. Server logs should be reviewed on a regular basis to identify any server errors or security warnings logged by the system.

Test searches should be conducted on a regular basis to ensure that outside content is being successfully crawled, and that access credentials to those servers are still valid.

TIP

> If the workspace will be primarily maintained by someone outside of the organization's traditional IT infrastructure, consider creating an administrative group assigned the Coordinator role at the workspace level. This group would allow easy monitoring and troubleshooting in the event that problems occur, and would more easily aid the people who administer the larger corporate environment in ensuring not only proper system configuration, but security settings as well. If more than one SharePoint Portal Server will be deployed within the organization, consider including this group at all servers.

TESTING WITH LABS AND TEST USERS

Before implementing major changes to security settings within SharePoint Portal Server, it is often useful to validate those changes on test servers, or by using specifically created test accounts and groups to model the changes and ensure they will yield only the intended results.

If lab testing is possible, configure your test servers to match your production system as closely as possible, and duplicate the workspace(s) from the production server. Once ready, apply your intended changes and monitor the system for any deviation from expected results. If lab testing is not an option, consider using collections of sample documents and specially created test user accounts that mimic those of actual users to simulate the informational elements of your production workspace.

If your testing indicates behavior or results that were not deliberately sought by your changes, investigate the deviations and devise an alternative.

INDEXING PROBLEMS

Document indexing occurs frequently within SharePoint Portal Server. With the workspace and any number of external content sources available for searching, it is important to perform test searches, using test accounts, to ensure that results do not return sensitive information.

If users report problems in the index, or are being given search results including materials they should not be made aware of, use the following process to resolve the problem:

Identify and correct the security configuration error resulting in the erroneous indexing.

Reset the index and allow SharePoint Portal Server to completely re-index all of its content sources.

Perform test searches to verify that the index has been fixed, and that no additional problems have been introduced by these changes.

Perform a follow-up review of all external content sources crawled by the SharePoint Portal Server, and ensure that additional similar security configuration errors do not exist.

TROUBLESHOOTING

CORRECTING INAPPROPRIATE FOLDER PERMISSIONS

My folder's access permissions have changed, how should I correct it?

If you discover that a folder's access permissions have changed, or simply no longer accurately provide the access controls you require, perform a permissions audit on the folder to determine where the problem lies. Begin by identifying all of the users and groups granted access permissions at the folder level, and compare them to the user population you intend to access documents within that folder hierarchy. Where differences exist, add or remove users and groups to create the desired access group. If there are no indefinable discrepancies at the folder level, move your audit to the parent folder(s), working your way back to the root of the workspace as necessary.

IDENTIFY DOCUMENTS ACCESSIBLE BY UNINTENDED USERS

How can I ensure that my documents are secure?

To ensure that your documents are secure, establish a regiment of access testing to verify the security configuration of your SharePoint Portal Server. Create test accounts, modeled on real users and groups in your environment, and include them in your access control lists for folders you wish to examine. Using your test account's credentials, try to access documents throughout your workspace through both the Web folder and digital dashboard. Test not only documents you know the test account should be able to access, but target documents in folders outside the test users' intended access permissions as well. Perform search queries for documents your test account should not be able to see, to further ensure that your information is as secure, and sometimes obscure, as was designed.

REAL WORLD EXAMPLE: ADDITIONAL SECURITY CONSIDERATIONS

The following are some additional security measures that can be taken to further ensure the integrity of your information.

CONTROLLING WEB/SEARCH ENGINE INDEXING

If you are providing Internet access to your SharePoint Portal Server, your site will probably be located and crawled by Internet portal sites and search engine WebCrawler bots. These so-called *Web Robots* perform a function similar to the content crawling function of

SharePoint Portal Server—they locate a Web site and follow all available links on the site, indexing what they find as they go. Managing this external search activity is important if you wish to restrict access to your site's pages, or to control what information on your Web site is recorded by search engines for inclusion in their indexes.

Most search engines and Web portals observe a set of standard methods for telling their Web Robots what your preferences are when they reach your site. If no specific directives are given to the contrary, most Web Robots will consider themselves welcome and will interrogate your site according to their design and objectives. To prevent this, you must instruct Web Robots to limit the scope of their crawling or prevent it altogether.

The most common method of controlling Web Robots involves the use of a file in the site's root directory called ROBOTS.TXT. This file can include restrictions on directories, exclusions for certain file types, or other limitations you wish observed when crawling your site. Web Robots should request this file when they first contact the server and process whatever directives you have in it. The following is a sample file instructing bots not to index the site http://www.mydomain.com/:

```
# robots.txt file for http://www.mydomain.com/
# directive that no robots should visit this site
User-agent: *
Disallow: /
```

If you are unable to use a ROBOTS.TXT file, for example if you do not have administrative access to the Web site root directory, there are alternative methods that are generally effective. The most common alternative is the use of META tags in the header of the site's HTML documents. The following example is the equivalent of the ROBOTS.TXT example file above:

```
<META NAME="ROBOTS" CONTENT="NOINDEX, NOFOLLOW">
```

HTML pages that include this tag should be neither indexed nor analyzed for links by Web Robots.

PHYSICAL SECURITY

An often overlooked security measure is to limit physical access to server systems by locating them in a controlled environment. While network and logical security precautions may deter attempts at circumventing the access restrictions placed on your information, a knowledgeable person who can lay their hands on your server is often capable of gaining access to any information they choose.

The two most critical methods of physical tampering are from the system console and the floppy/boot drive. It is not uncommon for system administrators to leave servers unattended while logged in to the console with administrative privileges. A savvy passerby could easily load the administrative tools and create new administrative accounts, change access permissions, or destroy valuable data. Locking server consoles when administrative users are not present and limiting access to those consoles greatly reduce the likelihood of this type of security incursion. Additionally, if a savvy user can insert a bootable floppy into a server and power cycle it, it is possible to load Trojan software or run security hacking tools before the server operating system can be loaded and its security features enabled.

PATCHES AND UPDATES

It is important for server administrators to keep their systems up to date with the most current available security patches and bug fixes. There are a number of open security forums and notification services available on the Internet, and software vendors often regularly post update information to their support Web sites when new bugs have been identified. Since SPS runs on Microsoft IIS, it is particularly important to apply system published updates when available (`http://windowsupdate.microsoft.com/`). Microsoft Security (`http://www.microsoft.com/security/`) also posts security bulletins and strategy information that is invaluable for any server administrator.

SUMMARY

The successful planning and management of SPS security requires a measure of both forethought and administrative attentiveness. Whether you're concerned with maintaining an entire workspace or a single folder, the features you employ to control access to your documents in large part defines the interaction between users and their information. Use user and group assignments to grant permissions to documents, and roles to determine how your documents are managed in the workspace. Remember that content sources outside the workspace are valuable resources, but be sure and consider the accessibility implications of each system's inherent control mechanisms. Finally, take time to secure your SharePoint Portal Servers from unintended Internet access through the use of firewalls and proper IIS configuration. When properly configured, SPS will enable you to restrict access to your information, control the document publication process, and maintain the confidentiality and integrity of your valuable documents.

CHAPTER 12

CREATING CATEGORIES

In this chapter

OVERVIEW OF CATEGORIES

SharePoint Portal Server provides the ability to organize documents with a feature called categories. *Categories* are helpful when users do not know where specific documents are stored, giving them the ability to search by a specific topic.

The association of documents and subjects provides a logical structure of the information through the dashboard site. It is imperative that the category structure strategy is in place and caters to the requirements of its users. This chapter will explain how to plan, create, and manage a category structure.

Categories are an optional feature in SharePoint Portal Server, but are often or best used when documents relate to a specific subject. A sound category structure increases the ability to search for documents by providing a simple directory-like organizational structure. For example, you can organize information in your SPS workspace by using categories to group similar documents. This allows end users to browse through information by topic, rather than by relying on a directory structure that might only make sense to a few content experts. For end users who are new to a particular workspace, categories are a big time-saver. That is, categories accommodate end-users not necessarily comfortable with the layout and make-up of your portal data, without changing the existing folder structure and processes that are in use already. And on a final note, similar to server directories and subdirectories, categories can be designed to include subcategories.

With SharePoint Portal Server, documents associated with a category are only links to the physical documents that lie in the workspace. This powerful feature provides the ability to link a single document with multiple categories. SharePoint Portal Server can also categorize documents from the workspace document library and from crawled content sites. Because you can associate a single document with several categories, you can also remove a document from a category without affecting it or its association with other documents and categories.

The categories hierarchy associated with a workspace can be viewed in two distinct places, the dashboard site (see Figure 12.1) and the Web folder view (see Figure 12.2).

Categories displayed from the dashboard site are displayed in a Web Part on the home page. By clicking the category link (for example, Category 1), a new detailed view of the category and its subcategories is displayed.

As you can see, categories work something like folders: You can expand them to see subcategories and documents just like folders can be expanded to view subfolders and data. They also allow the user to view and search for documents logically and easily.

12

Figure 12.1
View of a category hierarchy from the dashboard site.

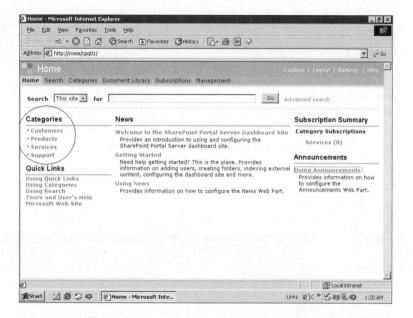

Figure 12.2
View of a category hierarchy from a Web folder view.

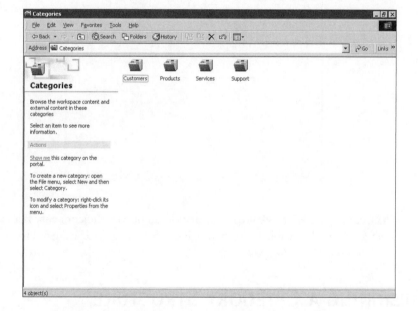

THE CATEGORY DICTIONARY

Like most applications, SharePoint Portal Server utilizes common database functions—such as a schema, data dictionary, and metadata—to provide searching capability. The schema references the tables and fields of the database. The data dictionary, referred to as the category dictionary, is a list of files in its database. *Metadata*, or data about your data, describes how, when, and by whom a particular set of data was collected, and how the data is formatted.

Categories in SharePoint Portal Server appear to be folders in the workspace, yet they are actually an extension of the schema. The hierarchical category dictionary is kept in sync with the categories in the workspace. Therefore, when you create a new category, a corresponding value is created in the category dictionary. SharePoint Portal Server's use of categories allows you to group documents into folders based on shared metadata.

So when a user is searching for a document through Windows Explorer or the dashboard site, a query is being performed and the documents associated with a particular category value are displayed.

Figure 12.3
View of the Categories folder in the workspace.

SharePoint Portal Server's use of categories can provide functionality that normal content storage has not been able to easily provide. This feature is considered to be one the biggest added values.

DESIGNING A CATEGORY STRUCTURE

After you have determined that utilizing categories will be an added value to your organization's use of SharePoint Portal Server, you will need to begin designing a logical and feasible hierarchy. Designing a category structure involves planning and collaborating with your users and content owners.

The target audiences for the category feature are content authors, readers, and visitors. You should consider these users stakeholders in your category design. Content authors will be very familiar with the workspace; therefore, readers and visitors should be the primary focus for your category structure design. They require logical guidance to the information for which they are searching. Ultimately, you want to design a category tree that would be easy to use for a visitor who has never used the workspace before to be able to quickly locate a document.

Developing a stakeholder forum or steering committee is suggested to help you throughout the development of your workspace and its features. This will help ensure that your final product is acceptable and utilized by the target audience. SharePoint Portal Server will be successful if the end product provides added value to the resources that will use it and provide them with information that is readily and easily available.

In order to create a successful category structure, an assessment of the current document organization is necessary. Understanding whether the current content organization is working well or whether it is difficult to use will help you achieve the following design goals:

> **Design Goal #1**: Create a simple to use structure that end users will both understand and be somewhat familiar with.
>
> **Design Goal #2**: Create your category hierarchy to facilitate expansion and growth.

After interviewing your users and content owners, you can begin to develop your category structure. Determining the number of categories to create depends on the size of your organization and the nature of your business. You will need to determine the following:

- Determine how to organize content.

  Depending on the requirements you received from your users and content owners (through the interviewing process) you will need to choose how you will organize your content. There are a variety of ways to do this. You may choose to do it by department, project, geographic location, or subject matter.

- Determine the top level categories.

  For example, if you are responsible for a large company spread out across many locations, you might want to use geographic categories. Therefore, you may require hundreds of categories, each duplicated underneath every geography, to effectively support efficient user browsing. However, if you are part of a small firm, you may want to use department names as your top-level category structure, and therefore may only have a few.

- Determine the number of subcategory levels.

  It is important that you do not have an extensive number of subcategories which would eventually become difficult for users to navigate through. We suggest that you begin with a simple category structure consisting of one to three levels. Later you can modify the category structure as needed.

12

→ For more ideas regarding planning a category structure, **see** "Developing the Workspace," **p. 533**. and "Workspace and Dashboard Considerations," **p. 561**

⚠ *While modifying your category structure is fairly easy to do, timing is critical. See "Poor Performance During Category Maintenance" in the "Troubleshooting" section at the end of the chapter for ideas regarding both the process and the approach.*

From our experience, categories defined in the first draft will most likely change. With time, your category structure will evolve based on the response from your users and their feedback and suggestions. You should also monitor the most frequent searches and possibly turn those search terms into categories. One method of tracking the most frequently performed searches is by perusing the end-user subscriptions.

We suggest plotting out your proposed category structure in Microsoft Word (see Figure 12.4) before implementation. This will help you explain to users and content owners how you propose to set up the document organization. Obtaining their approval will help to eliminate changes after implementation.

Figure 12.4
View of category structure preliminary design.

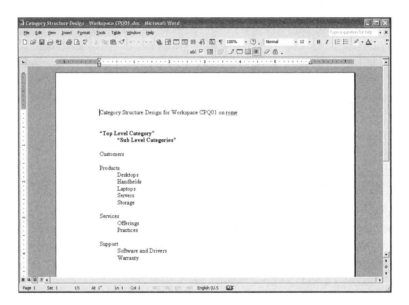

TIP

It is suggested to include no more than 500 categories in a single workspace.

By building a quality category structure that includes a solid design and as few subcategories as really needed, future rework will be minimized. That is, sound end-user and content owner participation, plus efficient planning, will help to create a valuable category structure. It will also provide the immediate ability for the users to quickly understand how to access the information they need.

CREATING TOP LEVEL CATEGORIES

After you have determined a sound category structure and confirmed the design with your end-users and other stakeholders, you may begin to create the top-level categories. Only the Coordinator role in the SharePoint Portal Server workspace can create new categories.

All top-level categories will be associated with a top-level category folder in the Categories folder in the workspace directory. Subcategories will also have a folder associated to them under the appropriate category.

The Coordinator will use Windows Explorer to create the categories in the workspace. To create new top-level categories in the workspace, do the following:

1. Open the Windows Explorer.

2. Navigate to the appropriate workspace.

3. Open the Categories folder in the workspace.

4. Go to File, New, Category (see Figure 12.5).

5. Name the category as noted in your design, ensuring that it is unique.

6. Continue with the process, creating top-level categories as required by your design (see Figure 12.6).

Figure 12.5
View of creating a new top-level category.

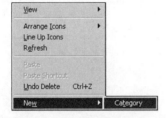

Figure 12.6
View of top-level category folders.

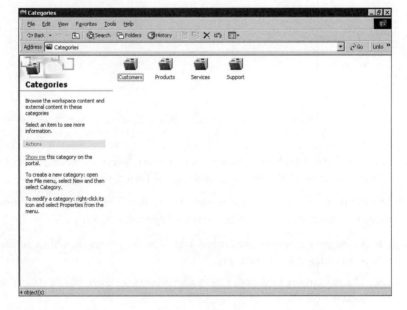

When you have implemented your top-level category structure, you should begin to create your subcategories for each top level category (see Figure 12.7).

To create new subcategories, do the following:

1. Open the Windows Explorer.
2. Open the Categories folder in the workspace.
3. Open the top-level category.
4. Go to File, New, Category.
5. Name the category.
6. Repeat steps 3 and 4 above until the category structure reflects your design. See Figure 12.7 for a sample structure.

Figure 12.7
View of subcategory folders.

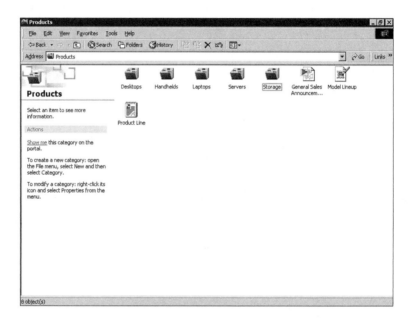

After you have completed creating your category hierarchy as defined in your design, it will appear in the dashboard site, as shown in Figure 12.8.

In addition to creating a new category folder, SharePoint Portal server automatically executes a number of activities when a new category is created.

- **A category query is generated**, which enables users the ability to search for documents related to the category.
- **The schema is updated**, which allows users to assign the new category value to their documents.

- **A path is identified** for the category which uniquely identifies the category in the workspace. For example, the URL for the category named Desktops in the top-level category named Products, as seen in Figure 12.8, would be
  `http://rome/CPQ01/Portal/Categories/Products/Desktops`.

Figure 12.8
View of category hierarchy on dashboard site.

> **NOTE**
>
> The following generic URL defines the naming convention for a categories path:
>
> `http://server_name/SharePointPortalServer/workspace_name/`
> `Categories/top-levelcategory/category`

It is important to create your categories by following your design as closely as possible. If there is a need to change the categories and their arrangement, you must first obtain approval from your stakeholders and then update the design.

CATEGORIZING DOCUMENTS

After you have completed creating your category hierarchy as documented in the design, and adding documents for your users in the workspace, you can begin assigning categories to the content in your workspace.

→ For detailed directions on adding documents to your workspace, **see** "Managing Folders and Documents," **p. 255**.

Of course, categorizing your existing workspace documents is not absolutely necessary. That is, your end users will be able to start categorizing new content as it is developed and dropped into the workspace. However, we suggest taking the initiative to categorize the documents already assigned to your workspace, so that your users will immediately be able to utilize the functionality that SharePoint Portal provides across all documents in the workspace. Microsoft realized the amount of work potentially required in categorizing existing documents, and gave us two methods of doing so. You must choose the most efficient way to accomplish this objective, choosing between the following:

- Automatically: Using the Category Assistant
- Manually: Editing a document's properties (metadata)

These two methods, including pros and cons or each, are discussed next.

AUTO CATEGORIZING DOCUMENTS

Without a bit of assistance, categorizing documents can prove to be extremely difficult and challenging, not to mention tedious, to even the most content-knowledgeable of Coordinators. To decrease the amount of effort required to categorize documents, SharePoint Portal Server provides an administrative tool called the Category Assistant. The Category Assistant can automatically categorize published documents as well as crawled documents in the workspace. This feature is extremely helpful when you plan to automatically assign categories (leveraging your category structure) to a large number of files that already exist in your workspace, or to documents as they are created.

The Category Assistant is a tool that requires a certain amount of configuration and training to optimize all of the functionality it can provide. By comparing documents assigned to a specific category with other categorized documents, the Category Assistant identifies the most common characteristics (words) and can then automatically assign an existing or new document to a category based on this information. This process of teaching the Category Assistant about your content is referred to as *training*.

An algorithm is used to learn the meaning of a topic after the Category Assistant has been trained. Before you can use the Category Assistant, a series of activities has to occur which includes manually applying categories to a selection of documents so that they may be used as examples for training.

Before we explain how to start or actually use the Category Assistant, an explanation of how this tool actually works is in order. When the Category Assistant attempts to automatically assign a new document to a category or multiple categories, the following process is being performed:

1. The Category Assistant compares the list of categories and their definition to a list of words in each new document it reads.
2. The words in each document are weighed in terms of importance. The comparison of category definitions to each document yields a *confidence number* that corresponds to the confidence with which the Category Assistant would place a document in a given category.
3. The confidence number is then compared to a *precision number* set by the workspace Coordinator. The precision number allows the Coordinator to control to what degree each document is measured for its fit in a particular category.

4. SPS tags each document with a category only if the confidence number is above the precision level set by the Coordinator. The document is automatically tagged with a single category or multiple categories in the "property" value of the document.

⚠️ *Should you run into problems with how documents are categorized, see "Documents Not Categorized as Expected" in the "Troubleshooting" section at the end of the chapter.*

More explicitly, metadata is used to stamp a document to categorize it. Each document has a hidden property or attribute called *Autocategories* (urn:attributes:autocategories). This document metadata is populated with the categories that describe the document during auto categorization. The resulting *property* is different from the properties used by a user to manually categorize a document. There are two reasons why SharePoint Portal Server distinguishes between these two different types of properties:

- To provide the ability to overwrite an automatic categorization of a document without affecting the manual categories already assigned.
- To distinguish between a manual and automatically assigned category.

These events occur after the index has been updated in SharePoint Portal Server. Therefore, there may be a delay before you see a document appear in the assigned category. The length of the delay depends on two things: the amount of content that is in the index and the index method you used.

→ To learn more about the various indexing methods employed by SPS, **see** "Updating the Index," **p. 104**.

To create views for the Web Folders and dashboard site, SharePoint Portal Server performs queries on both types of properties except when the Category Assistant is disabled (see Figure 12.9). If the Category Assistant is disabled, the query for the attribute Autocategories is eliminated. This feature also allows the Coordinator to restrict the view of automatically categorized documents when the Category Assistant is not performing properly and troubleshooting is necessary. We will discuss how to configure the Category Assistant in the next section.

12

Figure 12.9
View of the Category Assistant.

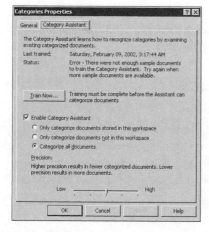

CONFIGURING THE CATEGORY ASSISTANT

You must take a planned approach to optimize the use of SharePoint Portal Server's Category Assistant. To access the Category Assistant, simply click the Properties page of the top-level category folder.

To configure the Category Assistant in SharePoint Portal Server, there are a number of ways to ensure efficiency and success.

This feature is available by default, but does not begin to provide any real value until it is trained. Therefore, you should create a plan that encompasses the amount and different types of examples (categorized documents) that you will provide the Category Assistant to utilize as training documents. When developing this plan, there are a number of objectives you should seek to accomplish.

- Determine the number of category examples you will provide. Remember, the more references that the Category Assistant is able to utilize for the comparison activity, the more detailed and precise the automatic categorization of your documents will be. It would be beneficial to create one or more examples for category.

- For each category, determine the different examples you want to provide. For example, the subcategory about Laptops might include training examples for each type of Laptop that may relate to this category.

- Determine the different categories that each of your training documents may apply to. You will want to apply multiple categories to a document if they are applicable. This will increase the efficiency of your Category Assistant.

You may want to collaborate with your content owners and stakeholder committee to review the examples with them. They can help obtain the previous objectives quickly and with ease. This may possibly decrease the amount of time you will need to prepare before beginning to train the Category Assistant.

With the above in mind, you can now begin to configure and train the Category Assistant. Perform the following:

1. From the Category Assistant property page, select the documents you wish to automatically categorize. You have three choices:

   All documents (default)

   Documents stored in the workspace

   Documents outside of the workspace

2. Set the parameter for the precision level. Remember, the precision level measures the exactness of categorization. If you set a high precision level, you might have fewer documents that will be auto categorized. A high level will require a more exact match between the comparison of a document's characteristics (words) and the definition of the category.

3. Finally, click the Train Now button (see Figure 12.10). When you click this button, the category definitions can be created. After the training process occurs, all additional documents that are indexed will go through this automatic categorization process as well.

Figure 12.10
Category Assistant
properties page.

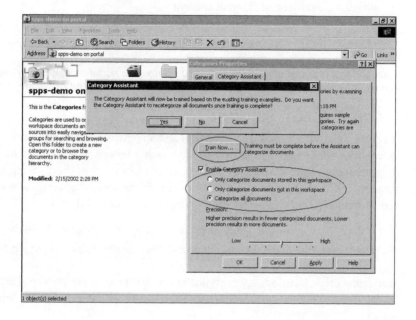

> You can disable the Category Assistant by clearing the Enable Category Assistant check box.

It is very important for the Coordinator to develop and follow a plan regarding how the Category Assistant will be used. By determining an approach to use and configure this feature, you will decrease the amount of manual categorization that is required and increase the quality of functionality that is provided to the users of the workspace. Some of the best approaches include

- Explain how the Category Assistant works to the people supplying the training documents or otherwise managing the content.
- Title documents descriptively. This is important because words in the title of a document are given greater weight in the category definitions.
- Use the Precision setting consistently, so that the weighting applied to each document is uniform.
- Develop a standard "suite" of test-dense sample documents to use as ideal examples of good training documents. Share these examples with the community responsible for training the Category Assistant for their particular workspaces. Details on training the Category Assistant are covered in the next section, and apply to things like minimum words per document, types of documents, and so on.

- Leverage the authors in your workspace to continually refine and add training examples to the Category Assistant (also covered next).

- Use training documents that represent a broad range of subject category examples, including internal and external content.

- Finally, test all new categories, as well as the changes or impact that new training examples have on the Category Assistant, in your Technical Sandbox or test environment.

> ⚠ *If you find that your authors are not able to categorize your portal content, see "Authors Complain They Cannot Categorize Documents" in the "Troubleshooting" section at the end of the chapter.*

TRAINING THE CATEGORY ASSISTANT

It is very important to properly train the Category Assistant, which equates to providing excellent text-based example documents for each category. The accuracy of automatically categorizing documents depends on the quality and variety of these examples. That is, to properly utilize the Category Assistant and begin the process of auto categorizing, you must provide a base foundation of training examples. To accomplish this

1. Determine who will be responsible for training the Category Assistant.
2. Determine the most efficient types of document examples with which to begin.

Like many other features in SharePoint Portal Server, training the Category Assistant can be delegated to one or more resources. There are two different ways you can delegate this activity.

- Author Categorization

   If you would like to maximize the number of examples you provide, this feature should be utilized, as it allows the workload of categorizing to be distributed across the content experts. This in turn increases the number and quality of training documents provided to the Category Assistant. In order to accomplish this, the Coordinator will distribute the training responsibilities to a group of authors by adding the Categories property to the document profiles. It is important to make sure that the authors understand the category structure. Why? Because as they check in and categorize their documents, they ultimately will add training examples to be used by the Category Assistant.

- Single Resource Categorization

   You can control the Category Assistant process by removing the Categories property from your document profile. If this is the method you choose, you will then assign categories by editing the Search and Categories tab of the Properties page of a specific document.

To remove the Categories property from a document profile (for example, from the Add Document Profile Wizard), perform the following:

1. Select the document profile to use as a template (note that the Base Document Profile is the default template).

2. Click Next.

3. Clear the check box next to the Categories property.

Figure 12.11
Categories property in
document profile.

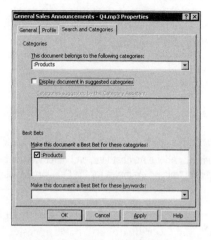

Figure 12.12
Search and
Categories tab of
document Properties
page.

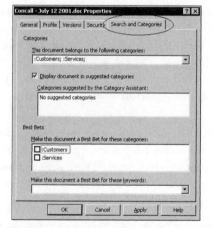

Note that SharePoint Portal Server acknowledges any document that is manually categorized as a training example. As documents are checked in and categorized, this activity
therefore contributes to training your Category Assistant. With this functionality, and the
approach described previously, the Coordinator is no longer solely responsible for managing
all of the training documents for the Category Assistant.

NOTE

> We suggest at least a minimum of 10 to 15 examples for each category, each with perhaps
> 2,000 words.

Because SharePoint Portal Server uses training examples to determine the definition of a specific category, it is important to provide examples with enough information to accomplish this. If there are not enough quality training documents then the Category Assistant will be limited in terms of its ability to categorize a document. To make certain that you are providing good training documents, ensure that the documents you utilize while creating your first examples have the following characteristics.

- Common category topic
- Primarily text based
- Contain a sufficient amount of text—2,000 words is a good starting point

TIP

> Microsoft Word documents, Adobe Acrobat files, and other word processing or text-based documents make excellent training examples for the Category Assistant.

Training the Category Assistant can be a relatively easy task if well thought out and defined. By executing this activity efficiently, the Coordinator will have an easier job of managing the performance of auto categorizing documents in the workspace with the Category Assistant. After the Category Assistant has been run against a set of documents, determining the proposed category structure for a particular document is quite easy. In Web folders, simply right-click the document you wish to view, and then click Properties. Note that the Search and Categories tab is available at this point. The categories are listed under the **Categories Suggested by the Category Assistant** heading. We can disable or override these suggested categories from here as well. Details to this end are covered next.

OVERRIDING THE CATEGORY ASSISTANT

12

SharePoint Portal Server provides the ability for you to override the Category Assistant for individual or all documents when you deem necessary. There may be times when the category does not properly assign a document to the correct category or categories. This may be due to a conflict in the training examples provided.

When overriding the Category Assistant for an individual document, the Coordinator can correct the Category Assignment by editing the properties by doing the following:

1. Go to the documents Properties page.
2. Go to the Search and Categories tab.
3. Clear the check box Display document in suggested categories.
4. Manually assign the appropriate categories.

There may be an occasion when you want to override the Category Assistant for all documents. For example, you may find that there comes a time when the Category Assistant is not assigning categories properly to the documents in your workspace. Therefore you may wish to halt auto categorizing. You can disable the Category Assistant by doing the following:

1. Go to the Properties Page of the top-level category folder.

2. Clear the Enable Category Assistant check box (see Figure 12.13).

Figure 12.13
Disabling the
Category Assistant.

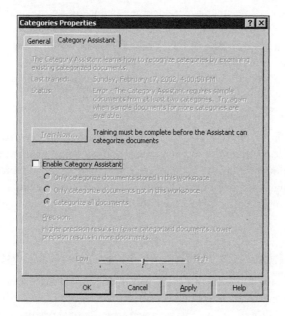

CAUTION

> Disabling the Category Assistant is a difficult decision and should be intensely reviewed before executing this action. It is very difficult to return to an automatic categorization system after you override the Category Assistant for all documents, simply because there is not an automated way to do this. That is, you will need to manually update the Search and Categories tab on the Properties page of each document. Your changes will take effect after the next index update.

MANUAL CATEGORIZATION

SharePoint Portal Server recognizes the need to be flexible and provide different methods of categorizing documents. You may have a situation when you need to manually categorize a document for any number of reasons; the document may be abstract but still associated to a certain category, or you may want to ensure that a specific document is properly categorized. For example, if your Microsoft Word document on handheld computing devices was only categorized under your Wireless category, you might also want to add it to your Desktop Computing Platforms category (as handhelds represent a new paradigm in desktop computing, but do not necessarily find themselves characterized in that way).

There are two ways to manually assign categories to an individual document:

- Editing the Search and Categories tab of the document's Properties page.

  An easy way to manually categorize a document is by editing the Search and Categories tab on the Properties page of the document. Then an author or Coordinator can select one or multiple values from the checklist of workspace categories by using Windows Explorer. Although the documents must be checked out in order to change the document's category assignments, if they are stored in an enhanced folder. If your workspace contains a small number of documents, this is a good method to use.

- Adding the Categories property to the documents profile.

  If the Coordinator has configured the document profile to display categories then the author will be able to select the categories that apply when checking in the document. When the Coordinator adds the Categories property to the document profile, it forces the author to assign categories to it. This method is efficient to use when the workspace is going to contain a large number of documents.

CATEGORIZING LINKS OUTSIDE THE WORKSPACE

There are times when the users of your workspace may want to share and comment on information residing on a Web site which is outside of your workspace. SharePoint Portal Server gives you the ability to link to this data with the use of shortcuts and metadata. See Chapter 18, "Configuring SharePoint Portal Server to Crawl Other Content Sources" to learn more about adding links (shortcuts) to your workspace.

With this feature you can treat the links, or *stubs* (when you add a shortcut to the workspace, the object created is referred to as a stub—see Figure 12.14) like the other content in your workspace. You can manually assign categories to this information so that it is also filed properly under the correct category and is as easy to find as the local documents.

If your workspace will contain a large amount of content outside of the workspace, you can also apply categories automatically, as described earlier in this chapter.

To enable this ability to categorize documents outside of the workspace, SharePoint Portal Server provides another special document profile called the Web Link that includes a property called Link. The property determines the target of the shortcut when an .URL file is added to the workspace folder, and the Web Link profile is applied. The Link property is automatically updated, but the .LNK file is not.

To update the .LNK file with this property requires manual intervention for each shortcut. To update this property, use the following steps:

1. Right-click the shortcut to open the profile form.
2. Select Edit Profile. The link will be populated by SharePoint Portal Server.
3. Click OK to close the form.

Figure 12.14
View of a Web Link in the workspace.

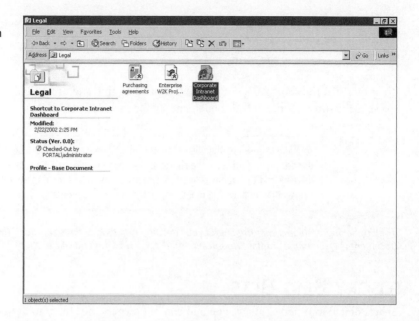

With this feature you can categorize multiple shortcuts just as you would for documents. The only additional task that has to be performed on each individual shortcut is to update the .LNK property as described above.

Again, a shortcut that is added to the workspace in SharePoint Portal Server is referred to as a stub. The following three things occur when the *Link* property is set on a stub.

1. A one-page crawl of the link target is performed.

2. Any properties on the stub are automatically applied to the link target.

3. The dashboard site displays a hyperlink to the target of the Link property (which is a link to the shortcut in the workspace).

For example, if you create a shortcut to `http://www.awardwinninglaptops.com` and then set the Categories property to Laptops, the Web site will be included in the content links of that Laptops category.

However, the dashboard site will display a link to `http://awardwinninglaptops.com`.

If you want to create a shortcut to content outside of the workspace in a folder associated to the Web Link document profile, you should do the following:

1. Add a shortcut to the content that you want to categorize.

2. Right-click the shortcut to open the profile form.

3. Select Edit Profile.

4. Apply the Web Link document profile to the shortcut.

12

5. Apply the appropriate categories.

6. Fill in the Link property.

7. Click OK to close the form.

To ensure that the shortcut is not changed while dragging and dropping it into the workspace, make sure that the default document profile includes the Link property.

CAUTION

> To avoid overwriting the title of the document retrieved by a shortcut, you must ensure that the document profile for the shortcuts does not include the Title property, but *does* include the Link and Categories properties. Otherwise, the title, even if there is not one, will be overwritten by the value that is populated in the Title property.

 If you're having problems with the title of your document getting overwritten, see "The Title of Your Document Is Overwritten" in the "Troubleshooting" section at the end of the chapter.

CATEGORY BEST BETS

SharePoint Portal Server allows you and content owners the ability to designate documents that are particularly relevant to a category as Category Best Bets. Documents assigned as Category Best Bets are visually promoted in the category listings within your dashboard site.

→ To read more about Best Bets, **see** "Searching Based on Best Bets," **p. 23**.

To enable Category Best Bets you must do the following:

1. Go to the base document profile.

2. Add the Category Best Bets property to this base document profile.

3. Click OK.

When the dashboard site displays a category, it will check this Category Best Bets property to determine whether to note the document as a Best Bet.

Figure 12.15
View of Adding Category Best Bets to the base document profile.

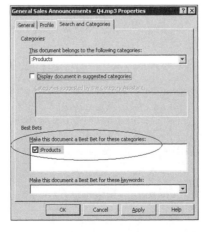

To configure Category Best Bets on a particular document, the following actions must occur:

1. Using Windows Explorer, navigate to the document you wish to work with.
2. Right-click the document and select Properties
3. Go to the Search and Categories property page of the document.
4. Note that the document currently belongs to a number of categories (look underneath the heading "This document belongs to the following categories:").
5. Note further that below this is a section for enabling Best Bets. Here, you may click on the various categories to either enable them (with a check mark) or disable them (no check mark) as a category Best Bet.
6. When finished selecting the Best Bets, click OK.

Shortcuts to content outside of the workspace can also be selected as Category Best Bets.

The proper use of Category Best Bets can help bring an appropriate amount of attention to information and content that a user should review when using a particular category, regardless of whether the document resides in the local workspace.

MANAGING CATEGORIES

Managing categories can be a fairly simple task if the appropriate management processes are put in place. You should establish standards and requirements around adding and removing categories, similar in approach to the change control/change management processes discussed in Chapter 20.

→ To read about change management as it applies to SharePoint Portal Server deployments, **see** "Addressing Change Management," **p. 536**.

It is a good idea to create a change management procedure with your users and content owners as they request to add, delete, or make changes to the category structure and its attributes. SharePoint Portal Server only allows the Coordinator role to perform management functions on the category structure. All other roles have read-only access. Therefore, if a large number of changes are required throughout the life of your workspace, this could become a very tedious responsibility.

Because categories inherit their security settings from the workspace *Categories* folder, security can only be managed from the workspace. Categories are different from regular directory folders. Remember, as we have previously discussed, you cannot move a category inside the category hierarchy that you have created.

DELETING CATEGORIES

When you delete a category, the documents associated with it are not removed. However, the category itself and its subcategories are removed. All of the documents associated to a category that is deleted are changed by the removal of the category value from the Categories property.

Deleting a category, depending on the number of documents associated with it, should be a very well-thought-out decision. The reason? You will not have a record of these documents and their association to the category once it is deleted. Therefore, you may want to consider reassigning the documents to other categories or simply renaming the category until you determine how or if you will re-categorize those documents.

To delete a category named "computers," perform the following:

1. In the workspace housing the "computers" category, open the Categories folder.
2. Right-click the category to be deleted, in our case "computers."
3. Click Delete.
4. Click Yes.

Deleting categories is often performed as part of regular SPS workspace maintenance, as you cannot move categories in the same way that folders might be moved. The only way to effectively move a category is to delete it and then create a new one elsewhere.

 To better understand the entire process involved with moving a category, refer to "Not Possible to Move Categories" in the "Troubleshooting" section at the end of the chapter.

RENAMING CATEGORIES

There may be an instance where your workspace community suggests that you rename a category. When you rename a category, the new category will have the same documents associated to it as the original category, and the end users will receive updates in the category property with the new category name. To rename a category named "computers" to "platforms," do the following:

1. In the workspace housing the "computers" category, open the Categories folder.
2. Right-click the category to be renamed, in our case "computers."
3. Click Rename.
4. Type the new name for the category, "platforms."
5. Press Enter.

Remember, like the ability to delete a category, only Coordinators at the workspace level may rename a category.

It is suggested that the Coordinator perform management and maintenance functions on categories during maintenance windows or when usage of the workspace is low.

To help Coordinators manage categories in the workspace, SharePoint Portal Server provides a Web Part (administrative tool) to create, edit, and delete categories without using the SharePoint Portal Server client. The Web Part is called Category.exe and can be found at http://www.microsoft.com/Sharepoint/techinfo/reskit/category_management.asp. Additionally, the Category Sort Order tool may also be leveraged to manage categories. This tool, found on the SPS Resource Kit CD, sorts the values for the Categories property in a workspace into alphabetical order. The order of these values determines the order in which the category list displays when an end-user categorizes a document. See the \Tools\category_sort folder on the resource kit to obtain this tool.

USING CATEGORIES

While most end-users will simply drill down into the category structure to find the documents in which they are interested, the method in which this takes place is largely misunderstood. In this section, we discuss two behind-the-scenes operations that are taking place while your end users navigate through folders or assign new categories.

 Limitations exist in assigning categories to a document. One in particular relates to being limited to assigning only a single category to a document. For details, see "Only One Category May Be Assigned to a Document" in the "Troubleshooting" section at the end of this chapter.

We noted previously that a category query is generated when a category is first created. This category query allows end users the ability to search for documents related to the category. You use this query any time you drill down into a category. Remember, any time a user opens a category folder in Windows Explorer or browses to a category on the dashboard site, SPS is actually running this search query. The category query merely filters for and then displays all of the documents that are associated with the category you are viewing.

In addition, when a category is created, the schema is also updated. This allows users to assign the new category value to their own documents. That is, the new category becomes available as yet another category that can be assigned either manually to a document, or by using the Category Assistant.

TROUBLESHOOTING

ONLY ONE CATEGORY MAY BE ASSIGNED TO A DOCUMENT

What are the limitations in assigning categories to documents?

When mapping from HTML meta tags, you may only map a single value to a document. Since SharePoint Portal Server assigns only a single value to the Categories property, SPS therefore only supports a single category in this way.

THE TITLE OF YOUR DOCUMENT IS OVERWRITTEN

I'm having problems with the title of my document getting overwritten.

If the document profile for a shortcut includes the Title property, regardless of other property settings, the title of your document will be overwritten. To avoid overwriting the title of the document retrieved by a shortcut, you must ensure that the document profile for the shortcut does *not* include the Title property.

NOT POSSIBLE TO MOVE CATEGORIES

I'm deleting and renaming categories but I can't move them within the category hierarchy. What should I do?

While you can delete and rename categories, SPS does not allow you to move them within the category hierarchy. Even if the name of the category is changed, the new category will contain the same documents it contained previously. This is because the rename operation simply updates all the documents with the new category name. To effectively move a category named SERVERS, therefore, requires the following:

1. A new temporary category (for example, TEMP) must be created in the new proper location within the category hierarchy.

2. Associate the documents in the old SERVERS category with this new TEMP category.

3. Delete the old SERVERS category.

4. Rename the TEMP category to SERVERS.

POOR PERFORMANCE DURING CATEGORY MAINTENANCE

When is the best time to update the system?

While there is rarely ever an ideal time to make changes or updates to a system, it is important that changes to the category structure be performed off-hours, or when as few users as possible are on the system. This is because category maintenance is very CPU- and disk-intensive. To gauge the impact and overall timeline required for a category maintenance window, clock and measure the performance hit in your Technical Sandbox or test environment before applying changes to the Production SPS system. Besides representing a sound change management approach to implementing updates, it also helps you to ensure that the process can be completed within the timeframe you expect. Note that many SPS shops implement big changes on a regular monthly or quarterly schedule—this not only prepares your workspace community for regular maintenance windows, but also gives you a target downtime window to shoot for.

AUTHORS COMPLAIN THEY CANNOT CATEGORIZE DOCUMENTS

My authors are complaining about not being able to categorize portal content.

In order for authors to have the ability to categorize documents, the Coordinator of the workspace must first add the Categories property to the document profiles of the documents being authored.

DOCUMENTS NOT CATEGORIZED AS EXPECTED

I'm categorizing documents but some won't fit like I thought they would.

While this is a generic issue, one common mistake made by novices regards use of the precision number (normally set by the workspace Coordinator). Remember, the precision number allows the Coordinator to control to what degree each document is measured for its fit in a particular category. If the precision number for a particular category is set too high, very few documents (if any) will be categorized. We recommend establishing a standard precision number from which to start all new categorizing activities, and testing the impact of changes to this number in your Technical Sandbox or test system prior to implementing changes in Production.

SUMMARY

In conclusion, categories can be a very efficient method of organizing your portal's content to facilitate searches and allow quick access to documents, content, and links to a particular set of subjects. By providing this functionality to the end users of your workspace, you will enable them to retrieve the information they need easily, and therefore address the real "work" of their jobs rather than spending time searching for information. If you plan on introducing categories in your workspace, though, you will need to plan, implement, and manage this feature effectively to be successful. That is, continued maintenance of your category structure is essential to providing the potential value that categories promise.

CHAPTER **13**

BACKUP, RESTORE, AND DUPLICATION

In this chapter

DESIGNING A BACKUP AND RESTORE STRATEGY

SharePoint Portal Server enables you to recover the entire server through its backup, restore, and duplication features.

It is important to develop a solid backup and restore solution so that in the event of a failure or disastrous event, you can recover your workspace efficiently with minimal downtime. The Backup and Restore processes are a key component of the overall system planning and administration of SharePoint Portal Server. In this chapter, we will explain how to develop a quality strategy and explain the procedures for backup and restoration of your SharePoint Portal Server system.

SharePoint Portal Server provides a very flexible backup and restore process that can be easily automated. As with other backup and restore solutions, scripts can be executed to automate the backup, restore, and duplication processes. The backup and restore scripts are automatically installed by SharePoint Portal Server.

Designing a backup and restore strategy for SharePoint Portal server is very simple, but requires a certain amount of planning. This component of SharePoint Portal Server provides an important safeguard for protecting critical data stored on your server, and especially your workspace.

With proper planning techniques you can recover from many failures, including

- User error
- Media failure
- Permanent loss of your server
- Disastrous event at location of server

It is very important to document your processes and procedures surrounding the backup and restore solution. There may be an event in which other resources would need to understand these processes and how they were accomplished.

The following activities should be included in your backup and restore strategy planning.

- Determine data availability requirements
- Assess and create backup procedures
- Assess and create recovery procedures
- Determine support operations
- Develop a complete backup and restore model

After these activities are complete, you can make the necessary technical and financial trade-offs, and determine the most effective backup and restore procedures for your SharePoint Portal Server system.

DATA AVAILABILITY REQUIREMENTS

One of the first steps you need to take before choosing the appropriate backup and restore strategy is defining the availability requirements of your data. You need to understand when your data needs to be accessible for the users, content owners, and administrators of SharePoint Portal Server. Also, analyzing the potential impact of data loss to your business is imperative.

The following questions will help you determine the availability requirements for your SharePoint Portal workspace:

- At what time of each day is the workspace heavily utilized by users, content owners, and administrators?
- What are the availability requirements?
- What is the acceptable downtime?
- How easy would it be to re-create the data and configuration of the SharePoint Portal Server system?
- What are the financial downtime costs to the business?

During the backup process, SharePoint Portal Server does not allow certain functions to be performed; we will explain this in this chapter, and it should be taken into consideration. Keep in mind that it is always a good idea to run your backup procedures during minimal usage periods to eliminate the possibility of errors. The overall backup strategy should define time and frequency of your backups.

NOTE

> It is a best practice to review these requirements with your stakeholders before creating your backup and restore procedures.

BACKUP PROCESS

After you clearly understand the requirements surrounding data accessibility, you can begin to assess how SharePoint Portal Server's backup features will best suit your environment, and develop your procedures accordingly.

The backup process is separate from that of the traditional Windows Backup Utility, and alone is not a viable solution. Although the utility will perform a backup, it does not back up all of the required data for your SharePoint Portal Server. When trying to restore your data with this utility, you will experience failure. Copying files or using the Windows Backup Utility through the Installable File System (IFS) is not supported. However, you can use IFS to view the contents of the read-only Microsoft Web Storage System that is used by SharePoint Portal Server.

13

SharePoint Portal Server's backup process has to be executed at the server and cannot be performed at a client computer unless the Administrator is accessing the server using Windows Terminal Server. Therefore, you must back up the server by running a script at the command prompt. This activity requires you to have local administrator permissions.

During the backup process, an image is created of the server which can be used to create an identical and complete instance of the server when the backup was executed. The server remains online, but crawls are eliminated during the backup. However, throughout the execution of the backup, users can add new documents, but they will not be included in the backup image that is in process. These newly published documents are also not available to be searched until after the backup is complete.

The following activities cannot occur during the backup image process:

- Create new content sources
- Edit or modify existing sources

> **NOTE**
>
> If the creation or deletion of a workspace is in progress when the backup executes, the backup will fail and the activity for the workspace will supersede it. However, if the backup was in progress before a modification or addition of a workspace begins, the backup process will complete successfully.

This backup process (image) can be directed to a share on a remote disk or to another hard disk on the same server. The image created as part of the backup process contains the following data:

- Microsoft Search (MS Search) service system resources which includes
  - Property store
  - Subscription store
  - Full text index files
  - Propagated indexes
- Web Storage System files including
  - Database files
  - Log files
  - Backup patch files
- Server configuration information including
  - Web Storage System information configuration
  - Content source information
  - Server properties
  - Access accounts

- Applications folder
  - Subfolders for each workspace
  - Applications designed for Web Storage System
  - Application specific data stored in Web Storage System
- Shortcuts or content sources

NOTE

All application-specific data stored outside of the Web Storage System is not included in the image.

CAUTION

During the restore, if the reference content does not exist on the computer in which the restore is performed, the shortcuts and content source will not work. You must also manually restore shortcuts to workspaces in My Network Places.

This image does not contain the following:

- Content source crawls.

NOTE

Consult user online help documentation for more information on how to restore source crawls

- Scheduled processing subscription tasks.

NOTE

Subscription tasks can be found in the C:\WINNT\TASKS directory.

- Gatherer logs. These log files are created each time SharePoint Portal Server updates the index. These also contain information about URLs that are accessed while creating an index.

SharePoint Portal Server does not encrypt the backup image, including the metadata and documents. For security purposes, it does encrypt and store only the password for the content sources account in the backup image.

13

CAUTION

If the password used to create the backup image is lost, the restoration will be successful but the passwords for the content source account will be invalid. Therefore, crawls of the content source may be subject to authentication failure.

BEFORE BACKING UP THE SERVER

All backup solutions require a certain amount of pre-check activities to occur. Before the backup process begins, you must check that you have sufficient disk space on the target backup source. By calculating the size of the full-text indexes, you can calculate the amount of disk space your backup will consume. Ninety percent of the disk space required for the backup will consist of the Web Storage Space and the indexes.

The SharePoint Portal Server Administration in the Microsoft Management Console provided with Windows 2000 Server provides a view of the full-text index size when you click on the server node. The details pane will provide a list of the workspaces and their index size (see Figure 13.1).

Figure 13.1
View of index size in
Windows 2000 MMC.

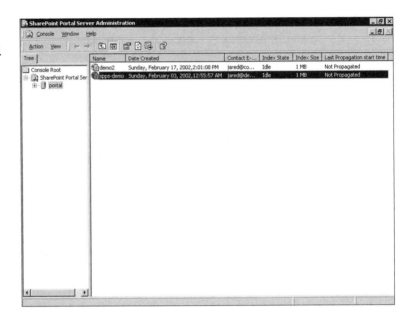

The size of the Web Storage System can be viewed in the directory at the path SharePoint Portal Server\Data\Web Storage System.

If you cannot locate this file, you can access its location information on the SharePoint Portal Server Administration properties page on the Data tab.

It is important that you verify that the following tasks have occurred before executing a backup activity:

- Valid path for the backup file. The directory must exist, but the file must not because the script will create it. Therefore, you must have a valid path to the location where you want to store this image file.

13

CAUTION

> If you choose to automate your backups with a script, you must either rename the old file or create a new name for each time a new backup is run.

■ Remote Disk Access. When backing up to a remote location, you must have a sufficient network access account that includes local administrator rights on that server and write access on that remote disk.

NOTE

> If you are using the Task Scheduler, the user account that the job has been created with must have the proper permissions.

BACKUP PROCEDURES

SharePoint Portal Server supports both manual and automated backup procedures. Although automated scripts are not provided within the software, the proper command lines to be included in a script are included. You can create scripts to automate the server backup process and to create scheduled jobs for backup creation and management.

 If you experience trouble with your server backup, see "Troubleshooting the Server Backup" in the "Troubleshooting" section at the end of the chapter.

LOCAL DISK BACKUP PROCEDURES

To execute the backup procedures, follow these steps:

1. Go to the Taskbar and click Start.
2. Point to Programs, then Accessories.
3. Click on Command Prompt.
4. Go to the SharePoint Portal Server\Bin directory (this depends on where the installation directory is located; see Figure 13.2).
5. Type MSDM/b "path to backup file name" [password].

NOTE

> In most circumstances this path is C:\program files.

6. Press Enter.

NOTE

> During the backup process, the MSDM utility will display a status window. The backup can be canceled by clicking Abort in this dialog box.

13

Figure 13.2
View of Bin directory
in Command Prompt
screen.

REMOTE DISK BACKUP PROCEDURES

To execute the backup procedures, take the following steps:

1. Go to the Taskbar and click Start.
2. Point to Programs, then Accessories.
3. Click on Command Prompt.
4. Go to the SharePoint Portal Server\Bin directory. (This depends on where the installation directory is located.)
5. Specify network access account.
6. Type MSDMBack /a domain\user password (this account only needs to be utilized once).
7. Press Enter.

The /b switch indicates that this is a backup procedure.

During the backup process, the MSDM utility will display a status window. The backup can be canceled by clicking Abort in this dialog box (see Figure 13.3).

Figure 13.3
View of the MSDM
utility's Abort option.

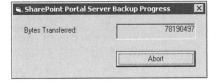

Once the SharePoint Portal Server MSDMBack script has completed, you can then use the Windows 2000 Backup and Recovery Tools, or a third-party tool of your choice, to move the image to tape. You can also drag and drop the image to another disk.

If any errors should occur, they will appear in the Windows 2000 Event Viewer Application Log, which is referred to as the Event log.

NOTE

> Other application backup processes can be running simultaneously with the SharePoint Portal Server backup process.

VERIFYING BACKUPS

Although it is not required, verifying that your backups are successful and useful is very important.

When validating your backups, complete the following:

- Check the backup to ensure that files have been written
- Check that the files are readable

MANAGING BACKUPS

Managing your backups is a key component to the overall backup process. If they are not efficiently stored or not well taken care of, they may not be in good working order in the event that you might need to use them.

You may already have a tape backup storage and management system in place in your organization. It would be wise to utilize your backup management procedures if they exist. If not, when maintaining backups make sure you do the following:

- Store in a secure place, preferably a different location than the server.
- Keep older backups in case your recent backup is damaged, destroyed, lost, or was not successful without your knowledge.
- Create a system for overwriting old backup tapes.
- Utilize an expiration date to prevent overwriting prematurely.
- Label backup media with date and SharePoint Portal Server name.

Now that you are knowledgeable about the ways in which SharePoint Portal Server handles backups, and you understand standard backup troubleshooting and management processes, you can begin to develop a backup strategy that best suits your infrastructure and environment.

TIP

> It is important to document this information in your SharePoint Portal Server documentation.

13

RESTORE PROCESS

After defining your backup strategy, you will naturally be able to determine how you will restore this data when needed. The restoration process will heavily rely on the success of the backup strategy. Therefore, it is important to understand exactly how it is managed.

It is important to understand that an individual workspace or document cannot be restored.

The restore process can be executed from a remote disk or a disk on the same server. When restoring a SharePoint Portal Server, you must take into account that the server is required to be offline. Therefore, your acceptable server downtime and business operations should be considered before you execute this procedure.

During the restoration process, all of the SharePoint Portal Server data is eliminated. This data is also inaccessible, and there is a chance the server may not be accessed if the process fails.

CAUTION

> If the password used to create the backup image is lost, the restoration will be successful but the passwords for the content source account will be invalid. Therefore, crawls of the content source may be subject to authentication failure.

BEFORE RESTORING THE SERVER

All backup solutions require a certain amount of pre-check activities to occur. Before the backup process begins, you must check the following:

- Sufficient disk space on target restore source.
- Ensure that disk space is on an NTFS (file system) partition.
- Validate that SharePoint Portal Server is installed.
- Validate Web Storage version. You must ensure that the Web Storage versions are the same on the target server and the backup image.

NOTE

> There may be an instance where the Web Storage System was installed by another application, like Exchange 2000. In this case, the target server for the restore must be on an Exchange 2000 server with the same version.

CAUTION

> The Restore will fail if the Web Storage Versions are different.

- Local Administrative Permissions. Ensure that you have local administrative rights on the target restore server.
- Restore data from tape. If the image was saved to tape, use the same utility to restore it before running the SharePoint Portal Server restore procedure.
- Remote Disk Access. When backing up to a remote location, you must have a sufficient network access account that includes local administrator rights on that server and write access on that remote disk.

13

CAUTION

> Be sure that you maintain consistency with service Packs on your SPS when using the SPS restore feature. The restore will fail if you are restoring data from a server with different SPS Service Pack versions.

RESTORE PROCEDURES

SharePoint Portal Server supports a manual restore procedure, due to the high sensitivity to data loss on the target server when the restore occurs.

LOCAL DISK RESTORE PROCEDURES

To execute the restore procedures, take the following steps:

1. Go to the Taskbar and click Start.
2. Point to Programs, then Accessories.
3. Click on Command Prompt.
4. Go to the SharePoint Portal Server\Bin directory (this depends on where the installation directory is located).
5. Type MSDM /r "path to backup file name" [password] [/o].

Figure 13.4
View of Bin directory in Command Prompt screen.

Figure 13.5
View of local disk restore command line.

13

REMOTE DISK RESTORE PROCEDURES

To execute the restore procedures, take the flowing steps:

1. Go to the Taskbar and click Start.

2. Point to Programs, then Accessories.

3. Click on Command Prompt.

4. Go to the SharePoint Portal Server\Bin directory (this depends on where the installation directory is located).

5. Type MSDMBack /a domain\user password.

6. Press Enter.

7. Type MSDM /r "path to backup file name" [password] [/o].

Figure 13.6
View of domain password entry for remote disk restores.

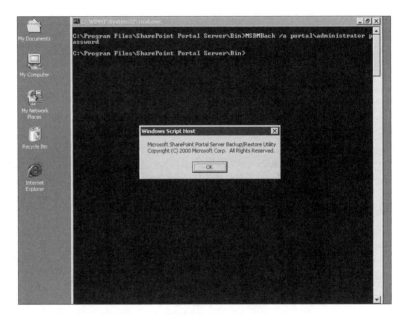

NOTE

The /r switch indicates that this is a restore procedure. The /o switch directs the restoration to place the full-text index in its original location and not in the default location.

During the backup process, the MSDM utility will display a status window. The backup can be canceled by clicking Abort in this dialog box.

Once the restore is complete, the SharePoint Portal Server will include all of the role assignments at the source server at the time the image was created. This may include SIDs, *security identifiers* that cannot be resolved as users or groups. SharePoint Portal Server will also process subscriptions based on default schedules upon restore.

Figure 13.7
View of remote disk restore command line.

If you experience trouble with SID resolution, see "Troubleshooting the Restore" in the "Troubleshooting" section at the end of the chapter.

You will then re-create the scheduled content source updates, as described in Chapter 18. As described in this chapter, the backup image does not include any scheduled content source crawls and should be re-created on the server that is restored. You must also restore the shortcuts that you created in My Network Places.

> **NOTE**
>
> For directions on how to re-create source updates, consult your online help documentation.

> **TIP**
>
> If you have a large number of workspaces, you can re-create the source updates by retrieving them from the C:\WINNT\TASKS directory.

After the restore and tasks defined above are complete, an incremental crawl of the local content of every workspace will execute. This crawl will ensure that the Web Storage System and the index are in sync.

Once all of the restore procedures are complete, it is imperative that you validate that the workspaces are accessible and completely operational before bringing the server back into production mode.

13

DUPLICATING SERVER

SharePoint Portal Server enables you to deploy multiple copies of your master dashboard site across your organization's network. The benefit to your organization is that users in the local site can access the site content without having to traverse the network. To accomplish this, you will use the backup and restore procedures in the preceding paragraphs to make these copies and restore these images to other remote servers in the same domain.

NOTE

You can compress drives to decrease the amount of network traffic that could occur.

To duplicate a server, do the following:

1. Use the backup procedures, as described earlier in this chapter in the section "Backup Procedures."

2. Use the restore process on the backup image to a remote server.

This process can also be automated using scripts with scheduled jobs, scheduling the duplication process to restore the image on the remote server.

DEVELOP SUPPORT OPERATIONS

After you have assessed SharePoint Portal Server's backup and restore processes and procedures, it is then necessary to determine who in your infrastructure support environment will take ownership of executing, monitoring, and managing these processes.

The following questions will help you determine the support requirements for your SharePoint Portal Server backup and restore processes:

- What support team should be responsible for performing the backup and restore operations?
- Will this support be centralized or decentralized?
- How will training be provided for these resources?

By thoroughly assessing the support requirements and clearly defining the support team's responsibilities, you will have a successful production environment in any event that may occur.

DEVELOPING A COMPLETE BACKUP AND RESTORE MODEL

When developing a complete backup and restore solution, you need to keep the following objectives in mind:

- Understand the business requirements surrounding the SharePoint Portal Server instance.
- Understand data loss risk.
- Assess downtime tolerance and performance.
- Develop procedures to minimize the effects of data.
- Keep your plan simple.
- After you have developed a solid backup and restore plan, it is important to validate its effectiveness with proper testing in a development/testing environment.

As with any process development activity, it is imperative that you document your decisions and procedures, and maintain the version control on your documentation.

TROUBLESHOOTING

TROUBLESHOOTING THE SERVER BACKUP

If you believe that your backup was not successful, you can review the Windows 2000 Event Log. You should also review the following conditions that could have occurred:

- Inadequate disk space for backup image
- Insufficient permissions on backup folder (directory)
- Backup process already in progress
- Required services are not running

    IISAdmin

    MSSearch

    Msdmserv

    MSExchangeIS

If you cannot resolve your issue with the backup process, contact your Microsoft Support resource.

TROUBLESHOOTING THE SERVER RESTORE

If you believe that your restore was not successful, you can review the Windows 2000 Event Log. You should also review the following conditions that could have occurred:

- Inadequate disk space for backup image
- Insufficient permissions on backup folder (directory)
- Restore process already in progress

- Required services are not running

  IISAdmin

  MSSearch

  Msdmserv

  MSExchangeIS

- Web Storage System versions are different between the backup image and target restore server

- The Windows Backup Utility was used for backup

- Restore server is in a different domain than source server, and domain groups and users that were once role members are not present

- Users or groups were deleted and re-created

- Users and groups that were used as role members were local accounts on the server, and the target restore server is different from the backup image source server

If you cannot resolve your issue with the restore process, contact your Microsoft Support resource.

SUMMARY

In summary, the backup and restore process allows you to recover an entire server. The server duplication process allows you to create a copy of a master dashboard site on multiple servers distributed across your enterprise. The backup and restore process cannot be done from a client computer unless you are using a terminal server client to access the server. In addition, you cannot back up individual workspaces or documents. Scripts can be created to automate the backup, restore, or duplication process. The backup process creates an image of the server. You can use this image to create a fully functioning instance of the server that is identical to the server at the time the backup image was created.

As a matter of best practice, if your portal is critical to your business, you should always test restores and perform offsite disaster recovery at least once per month. Lastly, in addition to having sound processes and procedures, part of your planning should account for how to plan for other potential single points of failure. Examples of single points of failure are motherboard, network cards, I/O subsystem, and so on. Make sure you have adequate service level agreements to get back to an operational state as fast as possible. Lastly, you can download a free utility from PKWARE.COM called PKIPC. With this tool, you can compress a zip file that is 750MB and reduce it to 450MB.

CUSTOMIZING SHAREPOINT

CUSTOMIZING DASHBOARDS

DASHBOARD AND WEB PARTS

This chapter will discuss how a dashboard consisting of a series of Web Parts can be customized so that it represents the information your users desire in a single, integrated view. Therefore we will take a look how the actual Web page shown by the browser is being generated, and which properties are available to influence this generation process. Finally, we will discuss various options to create new Web Parts. You can create and customize your own dashboards or Web Parts without writing a single line of code using the SharePoint Portal Server User Interface. For more advanced tasks, you can customize and extend Web Parts using tools such as Office XP Developer.

The SharePoint Portal Server Dashboard architecture allows building customized solutions that can consolidate personal, team, corporate, and external information, presenting it to the user in a single integrated view. For example, a Research and Development department can show information on the various ongoing projects, as well as important industry news. Corporate information, such as the current stock price, as well as personal information, such as the user's calendar, can be added, providing the user with relevant information from a variety of sources—all in one place using a common technology, the Digital Dashboard.

This Digital Dashboard technology is based on reusable User Interface components which are called Web Parts. Web Parts are the core building blocks of the dashboard, generating Hypertext Markup Language (HTML) that the browser can render. This HTML may get generated through technologies, such as Extensible Markup Language (XML) and scripts in Active Server Pages (ASPs).

Dashboards can be nested. A navigation bar on top enables users to select a sub-dashboard, to make use of other functionality. The Document Library, for example, will allow navigating through documents and folders stored in SharePoint Portal Server.

Figure 14.1 shows the out-of-the-box home dashboard for a new "Development" dashboard. Throughout this chapter, you will see how this dashboard gets customized to the needs of a Research & Development department.

Figure 14.1
The out-of-the-box home page for a new development workspace.

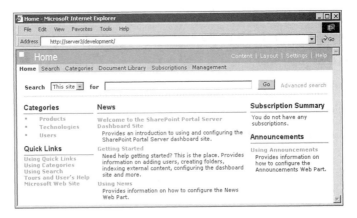

STORING DASHBOARDS AND WEB PARTS

SharePoint Portal Server not only includes the Digital Dashboard technology to provide a single integrated view on information; it also ships with a Document Store to store information, as di lscussed in earlier chapters. In fact, this Document Store is an ideal place to store dashboards and Web Parts, as it provides a means of access control, and allows for a rich set of properties that determine the characteristics of a dashboard or Web Part. Such properties include for example the Title, which heads a dashboard or Web Part, but also properties that determine the caching behavior, to optimize the dashboard performance.

As the dashboards and Web Parts are stored within SharePoint Portal Server, you can apply specific security settings using the SharePoint Portal Server roles discussed in Chapter 2. Dashboards or Web Parts that a user has no read permission for are excluded in the rendered Web page, unless you activate some of the advanced caching functions discussed later in this chapter.

Figure 14.2 shows the default security settings of the document library dashboard through the Web Folder interface. The default dashboard is stored in a hidden folder called `http://<server>/<workspace>/Portal`. Therefore you need to configure your Windows Explorer to show hidden files using Tools, Folder Options, View and selecting the "Show hidden files and folders" option.

Figure 14.2
By default, only the installing user is assigned Coordinator privileges; everyone else is reader.

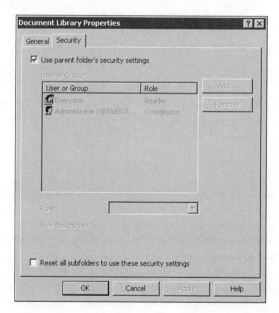

14

CAUTION

> Do not remove the "everyone reader" security setting for the document library, search, or categories dashboard. These dashboards are referenced from other dashboards. As you see in Figure 14.2, by default everyone is a reader, which means that everyone will have access to the dashboard, which is visible for everyone to add content, even though there may be only a small group of authors. Disabling access to the document library dashboard, though, means that any folder found in a category match or search result cannot be viewed through the portal.

Taking a look at Web Parts through the Installable File System, you will notice that they all have a size of 0. This is nothing to worry about—all content is stored in properties, and the default content associated with the file size is empty. To look through the Web Parts, do the following:

1. Click **Start**, select **Programs**, select **Accessories**, and then click **Command Prompt**.

2. Type `Subst M: \\.\backofficestore` and press Enter.

3. Type M:

4. To see the default dashboard's Web Parts, navigate using `CD \\localhost\SharePoint Portal Server\workspaces\<workspace>\Portal`.

5. Type `Dir`, and you will see files representing Web Parts, such as "Search.vbs", with a file size of zero.

RENDERING A DASHBOARD

To get a better understanding of dashboards and Web Parts, let's take a look under the hood to see how the dashboard is being generated. When a user requests a URL, for example `http://<server>/<workspace>`, the server calls the dashboard factory to generate the dashboard. As discussed previously, the dashboard itself is implemented as a dedicated folder within SharePoint Portal Server. In this dashboard, folders reside as dedicated items, the Web Parts that make up the dashboard.

NOTE

> The dashboard factory is implemented in a file called dashboard.asp. It resides, together with a lot of other support files, in the hidden `http://<server>/<workspace>/Portal/resources` folder. Many of these files cannot be opened in the Web Folder, as their extensions are not recognized. If you wish to take a closer look, you need to drag a copy first onto your desktop.
>
> If you consider modifying any of the out-of-the-box dashboard files, Microsoft may not support your installation anymore. In any case, make a backup of your portal folder and subfolders. To preserve the properties, you must use the Web Folder interface, not the regular Explorer through the Installable File System.

14

To render the dashboard, the dashboard factory will

1. Retrieve the list of Web Parts for the current dashboard, taking the user's access permissions into account.

2. Retrieve the list of sub-dashboards nested for the current folder, taking the user's access permissions into account.

3. Generate the HTML content for each Web Part, executing script code on the server or required Extensible Stylesheet Language (XSL) transformations if necessary.

4. Perform an XSL transformation using all Web Part HTML fragments, such that the entire dashboard Web page is created. The transformation creates the navigation bar and uses the HTML fragments from each Web Part to build the resulting Web page.

5. Return the result to the client browser, such that the user sees the dashboard.

The retrieval of Web Parts and sub-dashboards is done using a WebDAV query. The dashboard factory is a client using the WebDAV extensions of the HTTP protocol. In contrast to regular clients such as browsers, the dashboard factory must deal with multiple requests and security contexts at the same time. For this reason, a different, server-safe implementation of the HTTP protocol is used with its own proxy settings that are configured using the proxycfg tool.

→ For additional details about the proxycfg tool, **see** "Network Planning," **p. 152**.

You may wonder how the dashboard factory implemented in a single file called dashboard.asp can render different dashboards. And even more so, how is it possible that the dashboard factory renders the document library dashboard for any URL pointing to a folder within the Document Store, such as http://<server>/<workspace>/Documents?

This all is accomplished using some advanced capabilities of the Document Store, known as the Web Storage System Forms Registry. This Forms Registry is an extension of the Document Store schema, associating User Interface elements with content classes. The Forms Registry will, for example, redirect a user requesting a folder URL in the Document Store to the dashboard factory, passing the original URL as a query parameter such that the correct dashboard can be rendered.

CUSTOMIZING DASHBOARDS THROUGH THE PORTAL

If you are logged on to the dashboard as a Coordinator, you will see options to customize the dashboard in the top right region of the title bar (see Figure 14.3), as well as a link for help. Regular users will just see the help link. If you have applied some of the advanced caching options that ship with Service Pack 1, you will see four little squares, which you need to click first to get access to the customization pages.

14

Figure 14.3
The top right area of the dashboard, also known as the command area, as seen by the Coordinator, providing access to the customization pages.

The links will provide a Coordinator access to

- **Content Page**—To manage the Web Parts and sub-dashboard of the current dashboard. Through this page, you can define not only which Web Parts are to be included, but also the individual content which should appear in those Web Parts.

- **Layout Page**—To change the individual locations of the Web Parts by dragging individual Web Parts to their new location. The dashboard is arranged in five zones (top, left, center, right, and bottom) in which Web Parts can be placed. In addition, it is possible to change the order within a zone.

- **Settings Page**—To customize the settings of the dashboard, such as its name or the color scheme that is used.

CHANGING DASHBOARD SETTINGS

The Dashboard Settings page allows you to change information that is related to the dashboard itself, such as the name, the caption, the logo, the color scheme, and the order in which this dashboard will appear compared to other sibling dashboards.

The customizations are intuitive; therefore we'll focus on some common customization requirements, such as the correct labeling of the dashboard, together with a custom logo or the usage of a custom, company-defined color scheme.

To edit the dashboard name, caption, or description, do the following:

1. Log in as Workspace Coordinator, and open the dashboard that you want to customize in your browser.
2. Click the Settings link at the top right of the dashboard page.
3. Under General Settings, change the fields as desired:
4. In the Name field, type a unique name for the dashboard.
5. In the Caption field, type the text to appear below the dashboard name.
6. In the Description field, type a brief description of the dashboard.
7. Click Save.

14

TIP

> It is a good idea to change the name of the home dashboard to reflect the purpose of the workspace, as this name will be the default for users who bookmark this page. If users access different workspaces, the default name Home does not help to distinguish between the workspaces. The name will also appear as a tab on all sub-dashboards, such as the Search dashboard. With different names, users can place their current sub-dashboard into the correct context.

To change the logo image, do the following:

1. Log in as Workspace Coordinator, and open the dashboard that you want to customize in your browser.
2. Click the Settings link at the top of the dashboard page.
3. Under General Settings, click Show Advanced Settings.
4. Under Advanced Settings, select the Use the following image in the header check box.
5. In the space provided, enter the URL where the header image resides. It is a good practice to store your custom logo where all other SharePoint Portal Server Resources reside, the hidden `http://<server>/<workspace>/Portal/resources` folder. To store your logo there, open a Web Folder to this location and drag your logo into the folder. You now can use a relative URL, for example `./deplogo.gif`.
6. Click Save.

TIP

> Do not use logos that have a height much larger than 30 pixels, the height that is approximately used by the dashboard name and caption. With larger logos, you take more of your precious dashboard space, and the user needs to scroll more frequently.

To change the color scheme, do the following:

1. Log in as Workspace Coordinator and open the dashboard that you want to customize in your browser.
2. Click the Settings link at the top of the dashboard page.
3. Under Use this stylesheet, select either one of the 11 color schemes or a custom stylesheet.
4. Enter the style sheet to be used in the dashboard.
5. Click Save.

CAUTION

> From the Settings page, you also have the ability to delete the current dashboard (if it is not the home dashboard). When you delete a dashboard, you are effectively deleting the dashboard folder and all its contents. This means that any Web Parts or resource files that are part of the dashboard will also be deleted.

14

Figure 14.4

This screenshot shows the dashboard settings page for the customizations necessary to render Figure 14.5.

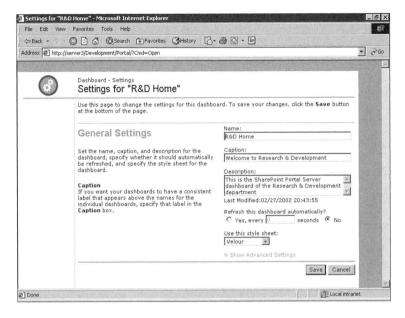

Figure 14.5

The screenshot shows the dashboard from Figure 14.1, now customized with the settings specified in Figure 14.4 to reflect the Research and Development department.

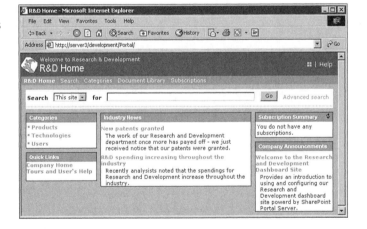

Typically you will need to apply the logo and color scheme customizations for all sub-dashboards as well. There is no inheritance of these settings from the home dashboard. At the end of this chapter, we'll discuss the usage of Microsoft Office XP Developer to allow these kinds of customizations in a more convenient fashion.

CUSTOMIZING QUICK LINKS, NEWS, AND ANNOUNCEMENTS OUT-OF-THE-BOX WEB PARTS

These three out-of-the-box Web Parts reside on the default home dashboard. They all share the same Web Part code—they just retrieve the content they display from a different location. This content is stored for each Web Part in a dedicated subfolder of the Portal Content Folder. This concept allows the Coordinator to assign dedicated people to author the information presented in the Web Parts. These people need to have the author role on the dedicated folder; they can modify the content shown in the Web Part without being a Coordinator.

To author new announcements do the following:

1. Log in as an author for announcements. That is a user that has the author role for the Portal Content\Announcements folder.

2. From your browser, open `http://server/workspace/`, and select the Document Library sub-dashboard.

3. Click on the Portal Content folder, and then on the Announcements folder.

4. Click the Add Document link to open the Add Document dialog.

5. Type the path to the document (or click the Browse button).

6. Click Continue to open the Document Profile.

7. Fill in the Title and the Description fields, as they will be shown by the Web Part.

8. Click Save.

Another, probably more convenient way is to use the Web Folder interface. Do the following:

1. Log in as an author for announcements. That is, a user who has the author role for the Portal Content\Announcements folder.

2. Open the Web Folder pointing to your workspace.

3. Open the Portal Content folder, and then the Announcements folder.

4. Drag your document into the folder.

5. Right-click the new document icon, and then click Edit Profile. The Announcement document profile appears.

6. Fill in the Title and the Description fields, as they will be shown by the Web Part.

7. Click OK to leave the document profile dialog.

NOTE

To remove an Announcement, delete the document associated with the item in the Announcements folder.

14

The Web Parts for News and Quick Links work similarly. You only need to select a different Portal Content subfolder.

You can easily create Quick Links if you first use Internet Explorer to find the URL. In your browser, right-click and select Create Shortcut, which will save a new file with the .url extension on your desktop. Drag this file into the Quick Links folder. When you now invoke the Document Profile to provide more details, you will see that the Web Link property is already been populated with the URL that is associated with the shortcut.

To ease the authoring of Announcements, Microsoft provides an updated version of the Announcement Web Part as part of the downloadable SharePoint Portal Server Resource Kit (`http://www.microsoft.com/sharepoint/techinfo/reskit/announcements.asp`). This new version enables authors to create content for the Announcements Web Part without the need for special authoring tools such as Microsoft FrontPage or Microsoft Word.

CREATING SUB-DASHBOARDS

You will have noticed that the dashboard page provides a top navigation bar that allows you to select other dashboards. These dashboards are sub-dashboards of the Home dashboard. The out-of-the-box dashboards—Categories, Search, Document Library, Subscriptions, and Management—are implemented as sub-dashboards of the Home dashboard. If you take a look under the covers you will notice that they are subfolders of the Portal folder.

Most commonly, you will create a sub-dashboard of the Home dashboard, such that another tab will be added to the top navigation bar. The sub-dashboard appears as a peer of the Home dashboard. If you create a sub-dashboard of any other dashboard, you will see the true hierarchy, showing the new dashboard on a child navigation bar of their parent dashboard. To create a new sub-dashboard, do the following:

1. Log in as Workspace Coordinator and open the dashboard that you want to customize in your browser.
2. Click the Content link at the top of the dashboard page to open the Contents page.
3. Under Import or Create, click Create a subdashboard.
4. The Settings page for a New Dashboard opens.
5. Change the name from "New Dashboard" such that it reflects the purpose of the dashboard. Other settings, such as logo or color scheme, can be set as well. This has been discussed earlier in this chapter.
6. Click Save to leave the Settings page, and you will be presented with a new, empty dashboard
7. To navigate to the parent dashboard, click the folder icon link in the child navigation bar.

ADD EXISTING WEB PARTS

Web Parts can present content from existing *back-end systems*, such as Exchange, Siebel, or SAP, and extract and present customized views of data stored therein.

As Web Parts can be made available for reuse, they can be found by many companies to augment their solutions. Microsoft, for example, itself provides Web Parts to provide integration with Microsoft Outlook and MSN.

Reusable Web Parts are made available by two means:

- Through a Web Part Gallery
- Persisted in a XML file with the .DWP extension

NOTE

If a Web Part is saved outside SharePoint Portal Server, it will be stored as a file with the .DWP extension. The actual encoding of this file is XML that fully describes the Web Part with all its properties and—if present—the code.

SharePoint Portal Server will recognize the Microsoft Web Part Gallery out-of-the-box. But you can modify the list of Web Part Catalogs, for example to provide your own company Web Part Gallery with validated and approved Web Parts instead. The setup of your own Web Part Catalog will be discussed later in this chapter.

To add, for example, a Web Part from the Microsoft Web Part Gallery that allows querying MSN Encarta's encyclopedia or dictionary, do the following:

1. Log in as Workspace Coordinator and open the dashboard that you want to customize in your browser.
2. Click the Content link at the top of the dashboard page to open the Contents page.
3. Under Web Part Catalogs, click Microsoft Web Part Gallery.
4. You now will see the Web Part Catalog page. Here you can select from a number of different Web Parts. Scroll through the list and select the Web Parts of your choice. In our example we select the MSN Encarta Reference.
5. Click Import at the bottom of the page.
6. You will be shown an End User License. To accept, click Accept at the bottom of the page.
7. You will see the Content page again, with the new Web Parts included.
8. Click Save to leave the Content page.

Another source for Web Parts is the SharePoint Portal Server Resource Kit (`http://www.microsoft.com/sharepoint/techinfo/reskit/default.asp`). In here, you will find Web Parts that ease managing and deploying SharePoint Portal Server. On the SharePoint Code Web site (`http://www.sharepointcode.com/`), which is not controlled by

14

Microsoft, you will find even more generic Web Parts. All these Web Parts are persisted as XML-encoded files with the extension .DWP. To import such a Web Part, do the following:

1. Log in as Workspace Coordinator and open the dashboard that you want to customize in your browser.

2. Click the Content link at the top of the dashboard page to open the Contents page.

3. Under Import or Create, click Import a Web Part File.

4. Navigate in the Select Web Part File to Import dialog to your .DWP file and click Open.

5. You will see the Content page again, with the new Web Parts included.

6. Click Save to leave the Content page (see Figure 14.6 and Figure 14.7) .

Figure 14.6
This figure shows a new sub-dashboard called "Web Research" with two Web Parts–the MSN Encarta Reference Web Part imported from the Microsoft Web Part Gallery, and a custom Web Part imported as an .DWP file.

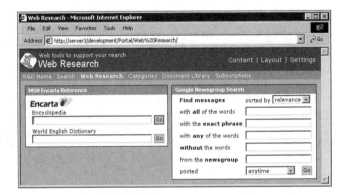

Figure 14.7
This screenshot shows the content customization page of the new sub-dashboard shown in Figure 14.6.

CUSTOMIZING WEB PARTS

Web Parts are, as discussed earlier, items in the SharePoint Portal Server Document Store with a defined set of properties. This set of properties includes

- **Basic** properties that are available with every item in the document store, such as title, description, and date the Web Part was last modified. When the dashboard gets rendered, the values of the Title and Description properties will be used appropriately.

- **Appearance** properties, such as height and width of the Web Part.

- **Behavior** properties, such as whether or not users have the ability to remove the Web Part from the dashboard, or whether they can minimize the Web Part.

- **Content** properties, such as the type of content the Web Part contains and the source from which the Web Part gets its content. For example, you can use the content properties to specify whether the content is embedded in the Web Part itself, or if it is located on another server.

There are more than 30 different properties that make up a Web Part. For a complete list, take a look at the Web Part Development Kit that can be downloaded from Microsoft (http://www.microsoft.com/Sharepoint/downloads/WPDK.asp). After installation, take a look in the documentation/ddrk30.chm help file.

> **NOTE**
>
> The Digital Dashboard technology is also implemented using Microsoft SQL Server as a repository in which Web Parts and dashboards are stored. This technology is only available as a download (http://msdn.microsoft.com/downloads/default.asp?URL=/code/sample.asp?url=/MSDN-FILES/027/001/620/msdncompositedoc.xml). SharePoint Portal Server and the Microsoft SQL Server Digital Dashboard implement the same version 3.0, and the information documented in the ddrk30.chm help applies largely to both.

You don't have to be an expert in these properties to start customizing or even building Web Parts. SharePoint Portal Server provides a very easy to use interface for building Web Parts through the dashboard. Later in this chapter, we will discuss other means of creating Web Parts targeted to the more professional developers, using tools such as Office XP Developer.

Similar to the Dashboard Settings page, there is a Web Part Settings page that allows you to change the settings of the currently selected Web Part. Changing a setting will change the appropriate property of the item representing the Web Part. The meaning of the General Settings section should be obvious. To do so do the following:

1. Log in as Workspace Coordinator and open the dashboard that you want to customize in your browser.

2. Click the Content link at the top of the dashboard page to open the Contents page.

3. Click on the name of the Web Part you want to customize to open the Settings page for this Web Part.

14

4. Change the settings as desired.

5. Click Save to leave the Web Part Settings page.

6. Click Save to leave the dashboard Contents page.

Figure 14.8
This figure illustrates how to tailor the name and description of the default News Web Part to reflect our company's business, as in Figure 14.5.

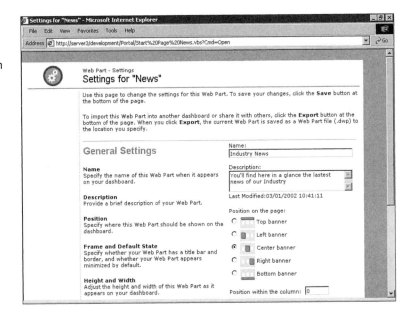

USING ADVANCED SETTINGS TO RENDER A WEB PART

The Advanced Settings section opens up a world of customization options to you. Some of the advanced Web Part settings influence the way a Web Part is being initialized and rendered. These settings are particularly important once you start to develop Web Parts yourself.

Once a Web Part is retrieved by the dashboard factory, the first thing the dashboard factory looks at is the "Check for master versions of the web parts" setting on the advanced dashboard. If that setting is checked, the dashboard factory checks if the advanced Web Part setting "The properties and content above are automatically matched to the properties of this master Web Part" is set and a link is specified. If the text box contains a value, the dashboard factory will check whether any updated versions of that Web Part are available, and if necessary update the Web Part in the dashboard. This algorithm allows for example for centralized updates of Web Parts.

After this initialization phase, the dashboard factory gets content to render the dashboard. The dashboard factory checks the "Isolate this Web Part's content from the other Web Parts" setting. If set, no further processing will occur; the dashboard factory will insert an iFrame with the URL specified in "Get Content from the following link" in the HTML that is returned to the browser. More information on Isolated Web Parts can be found in the section "Isolated Web Parts," later in this chapter.

For non-isolated Web Parts, the dashboard factory checks the type of content to determine whether the content runs on the server. If in the drop-down box, VBScript, JavaScript, or XML is specified, processing occurs on the server, based on the embedded content information.

For content of type HTML, the Get Content from the Following Link setting is optional. If set, the dashboard factory will try to retrieve the content through an HTTP request. If no Content Link is defined or an error occurs, the dashboard factory gets the embedded content.

TIP

> If you are working with Content Links, specify embedded content also, which could be as simple as a Cannot Retrieve the Content Link to provide user feedback in case some network problems prevent the dashboard factory from obtaining the desired information.

Next, the dashboard factory will check the "XSL to transform the content" setting. Like for the processing of the content, it is possible to specify a link and a fallback to embedded content. If any XSL is available, the dashboard factory will transform the earlier obtained results through the XSL Stylesheet to HTML.

Finally, the dashboard factory replaces token strings that allow for portable Web Parts, and inserts the HTML stream into the response that is sent back to the browser (See Figure 14.9).

Figure 14.9
This diagram shows the flow that is executed by the dashboard factory to render a Web Part.

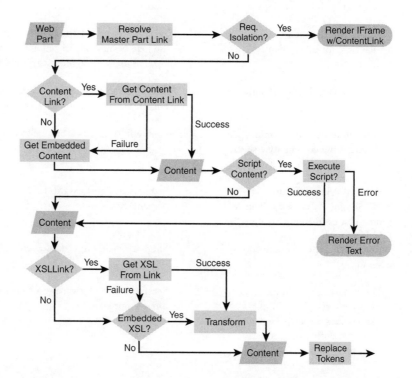

NOTE

> All the settings refer to individual properties, which you can see in the Microsoft Office XP Developer, discussed later in this chapter. The property names are often slightly different, but remain intuitive once you understand the rendering process.

ISOLATED WEB PARTS

If a Web Part is isolated, the content of that Web Part is placed in an isolated container within the browser using the IFRAME HTML element. If a Web Part is not isolated, the content is streamed together with all other non-isolated Web Parts in the dashboard page. Isolation of Web Parts thus impacts how Web Parts get rendered, which has already been briefly discussed earlier.

Isolated Web Parts behave quite different than non-isolated Web Parts. The differences are discussed in Table 14.1:

TABLE 14.1   DIFFERENCE IN BEHAVIOR OF ISOLATED AND NON-ISOLATED WEB PARTS

Isolated Web Parts	Non-isolated Web Parts
Content is retrieved by each client individually.	Content can be cached, and is eventually shared between users.
Can be placed on cached dashboards. users, all Web Parts must	To be able to cache the dashboard for multiple be shareable between users.
Rendering causes CPU load each time for every client.	Rendering causes CPU load on server, using caching; the load occurs only once for a particular user or even all users throughout the cache timeout period.
No inter-Web Part communication.	Inter-Web Part communication possible through the Digital Dashboard Service Component (DDSC).
Difficult to handle common style sheets, as the current style sheet settings are not passed by default.	Common style sheets are enforced.
Relative sizing difficult. SharePoint Portal Server will do a best estimate for sizing.	Sizing is straightforward. It is possible to use percentages.
Additional network connections set up.	Single connection to the server.
Direct authentication from client to target server. This implies that cookies can be passed, and that basic authentication prompting can occur.	Server needs to forward security credentials, which often is not possible.

14

Isolated Web Parts	Non-isolated Web Parts
Function names or HTML IDs never conflict with other parts. Script functions can assume they are the only script in the page, and that IDs uniquely identify elements in the Web Part content.	You should use the _WPQ_ token to make HTML IDs and function names unique within the dashboard.
Content is requested asynchronously from the rest of the page, which provides immediate feedback for Web Parts that take a long time to return content.	The content of all (non-isolated) Web Parts is streamed together after all information is retrieved on the server side.
Relative URLs are executed against the Frame source—the Content Link Setting.	Relative URLs are executed against the dashboard URL, which may cause unexpected results.

The out-of-the-box Web Parts of SharePoint Portal Server are non isolated, and you should also choose non-isolated Web Parts, unless your Web Parts contain data that

- is highly volatile
- needs application-specific security credentials
- takes long to obtain
- refers to a regular Web Page with some advanced settings, such as images or navigation

OTHER ADVANCED WEB PART SETTINGS

We have already discussed the upper part of the advanced Web Part Settings. They are primarily useful for the development of new Web Parts. We now will take a brief look at some other options.

For Web Parts that are shown through SharePoint Portal Server, you will typically not check the "Allow users to remove this Web Part from their dashboard" and "Allow users to minimize this Web Part on their dashboard" settings. These setting apply within SharePoint Portal Server only to Coordinators; users cannot modify the appearance of the dashboard through personal settings. To provide some personalization, it is possible to create Personal Dashboards, which will be discussed in "Personal Dashboards" later in this chapter. These options are present for future versions of SharePoint Portal Server, which may provide personalization features. If there is a need to provide content that can be minimized, consider using the DHTML object model. The Search Web Part with its Simple and Advanced searches is an example of where this technology is applied.

Next, on the Settings Web page you will find a set of text boxes that allow for some additional mini icons on the Web Part title bar. The usage is quite self-explanatory.

14

Next, there is a Web Part Storage option, which allows the Web Part itself to contain customization data. Finally, you can set some caching options, which will be discussed later in this chapter.

Web Part Storage

To allow Web Parts to be very flexible, it is possible to store some configuration data with the Web Part. In fact, this allows you to reuse the Web Part code for different Web Parts, such as for the Quick Links, News, and Announcements Web Parts.

You will notice that these Web Parts will show the latest five items (based on their modification date) by default. You can change this, allowing for more or less items, or use different selection criteria. To do so, do the following:

1. Log in as Workspace Coordinator and open the dashboard that you want to customize in your browser.
2. Click the Content link at the top of the dashboard page.
3. Select the name of the Web Part that you want to modify.
4. Under General Settings, click Show Advanced Settings.
5. Under Store the following data for this Web Part, at the bottom of the page, you will find three lines.
6. The first line refers to the folder where the actual items are kept—for the out-of-the-box Web Parts, you will find placeholders.
7. The second line is the sort criteria. By default, it is sorted by the modification date in descending order, which means that the last entries are first.
8. The last line, and probably the most interesting line, is the maximum number of items to be shown in the Web Part.
9. Change the information as you like, and click Save to leave the Web Part Settings page.
10. Click Save to leave the Content page.

Web Part developers will find more information in the Digital Dashboard documentation.

Personal Dashboards

The default dashboard is shared by all users. There is only a very limited amount of personalization possible, as the list and layout of Web Parts is determined by the Workspace Coordinator. To provide a more flexible place where users can maintain their own dashboard, SharePoint Portal Server provides Personal Dashboards.

To ensure that personal dashboards are not intermingled with the default dashboard, they are stored in a separate place, the Dashboards folder. A consequence of this is that personal dashboards will not appear as a tab in the out-of-the-box dashboards, because the tabs represent child or parent folders, as explained earlier in the "Creating Sub-dashboards" section. So the problem is that users need to know the URL to their personal dashboards.

14

In order to create personal dashboards, you must have at least author permissions for that folder. Personal Dashboards are created through the Personal Dashboards Web Part, which you will find by default on the Management dashboard. All users who have read access to that Web Part and have the necessary privileges for the Dashboards folder can create their own dashboards.

CAUTION

> With personal dashboards, you allow users to create their own Web Parts. These can run scripts on the server, a shared resource for all your users. The Web Part code thus can affect the server (though only to the extent of the user's security limitations).

To create a personal dashboard, do the following:

1. Open the Management dashboard of your workspace in your browser.
2. Click Create a new personal dashboard. The Dashboard—Settings page is displayed.
3. Provide a name for your digital dashboard.
4. Provide other settings if desired, such as captions and descriptions of your personal digital dashboard, in the text boxes.
5. Click Save.
6. To open your new personal dashboard, open the default dashboard and click on Document Library in the navigation bar.
7. Click Dashboards, and then click the link to your new dashboard.
8. You can reconfigure your personal dashboard settings by using the Content and Settings links at the top of the page. As your personal dashboard is initially empty, there will be no Layout link available.

The security context of the newly created dashboard is inherited from the Dashboards folder. In addition, users who create a personal dashboard are automatically granted Coordinator permissions. As a Coordinator, you will be able to access the Contents, Layout, and Settings customization pages for the new dashboard, as well as be able to change the security settings through the Web Folder. And you may wish to do so, simply because all users who are allowed to create Personal Dashboards can view your dashboard, due to their inherited author privilege.

CREATE WEB PART GALLERY

With the deployment of multiple departmental SharePoint Portal Servers or with the introduction of personal dashboards, a new question arises within an organization: How can Coordinators easily find Web Parts that are suitable to their business? Web Parts—externally or internally developed—can originate from multiple sources, and you may wish to ensure a proper licensing or quality.

14

This is where Web Part Galleries come in, as they enable an organization to publish its own list of approved Web Parts. To create a Web Part Gallery, do the following:

1. Log in as Workspace Coordinator and open the dashboard that you want to customize in your browser.
2. In the **Personal Dashboards** section, click **Create a new personal dashboard**.
3. Give the dashboard a descriptive name, typing it in the name field—for example "Web Part Gallery".
4. Click Save.
5. Open a Web Folder to your workspace (`http://<server>/<workspace>`).
6. Navigate to the hidden Portal\resources folder.
7. Select the file "catalogs.xml" and copy it to the desktop.
8. Make a backup of your original "catalogs.xml" file before you make any modifications, such that you can restore the original configuration.
9. Open the copy of catalogs.xml in Notepad.
10. You will see that in the `<DDF:WebPartCatalog>` XML node, the Microsoft Web Part Gallery is defined. You can either copy this node (if you want your Coordinators to continue using the Microsoft Web Part Gallery) or replace this node with your own content. The node names are descriptive:
    - `<DDF:CatalogName _locID="L_WebPartGallery_Text">` contains the text that is used in the Settings page
    - `<DDF:href _cID="L_CatalogHREF_Text">` refers to the URL of the catalog. Use the URL of the Personal Dashboard that you just created, appended with the querystring `?cmd=catalog`. In our example where the Personal Dashboard was called "Web Part Gallery", use `http://<server>/<workspace> http://<server>/<workspace>Web Part Gallery?cmd=catalog`.
    - `<DDF:Description _locID="L_GalleryDesc_Text">` contains a descriptive text shown in the Settings page.
11. Save catalogs.xml.
12. Copy catalogs.xml from the desktop back to the resources folder (See Figure 14.10).
13. As soon as you add Web Parts to the "Web Part Gallery" dashboard, these Web Parts are displayed in your gallery.

14

Figure 14.10
The figure shows part of the XML file and the appearance on the dashboard settings page.

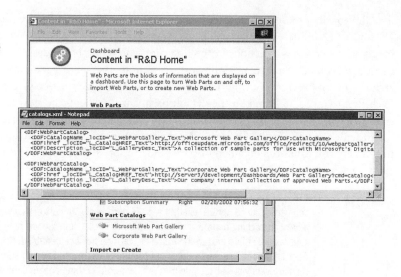

OPTIMIZING DASHBOARD PERFORMANCE

To optimize the dashboard performance, caching of Web Parts or even the whole dashboard page can be enabled. For Web Parts, three caching modes are available:

- **No caching**—This default option will ensure that the information presented in the Web Part is as accurate as possible, because the content is generated each time the page is requested.

- **Per user caching**— In this mode, the Web Part is cached on a per-user basis, such that, for example, the Web Part can take the user's context into account. Any request made to display the dashboard within the cache timeout period will contain the same data. This setting can be useful for personalized, not highly volatile information, such as the list of subscriptions.

- **For All Users caching** —Web Parts that are configured for caching across all users will generate their content for all users upon the first request within the timeout period. Any personalization must be avoided, only general information, such as News or Announcements, should be generated by Web Parts configured with this setting.

With Service Pack 1, significant enhancements of the dashboard performance have been accomplished, mainly due to two new caching algorithms that you can use. It is now possible not only to cache Web Part information, but in addition you can cache recently-used dashboard information or even the whole dashboard content itself.

14

The drawback of these enhancements is the loss of some personalization features. Applying Dashboard Definition Caching will cause the list of all Web Parts and sub-dashboards to be based on the access permissions of the first user who requests the dashboard page. Full-page caching goes much further, and will cache the whole dashboard page with all its content relative to the first user requesting that page. Take for example the out-of-the-box Subscription Web Part that can be found on the default dashboard; it shows the subscriptions of the currently logged-in user. If this Web Part would be included in a full-page cache, all users will see the subscriptions of the first user. Thus with full-page caching enabled, such per-user personalization cannot be handled in server-side script. To bypass this, you can consider client-side scripts or use Web Parts that run in Isolated mode.

> **NOTE**
>
> You can easily recognize whether a dashboard has been customized with some of the advanced caching options available in Service Pack 1. If in the top right corner, four little squares are visible next to the Help link, caching has been enabled. Otherwise, Coordinators will see individual links to modify "Content | Layout | Settings | Help", and regular users will just see "Help". With advanced caching enabled, this personalization is hidden by the four little squares, and you will notice that clicking the squares will generate a URL with a `?showadminlinks=1` query parameter, causing the caching to be temporarily disabled such that the appropriate customization and help links can be generated.

CONFIGURE WEB PART CACHING

To improve the performance of the dashboard, it is recommended that you consider using of Web Part caching. To view or change the Web Part cache settings, do the following:

1. Log in as a Workspace Coordinator.
2. Open Internet Explorer and type the URL of the dashboard whose Web Parts you want to configure in the address bar.
3. If any of the Service Pack 1 dashboard performance optimizations have been applied, click on the icon with the four little squares next to the Help link in the top right corner.
4. Click the Content link in the top of the dashboard.
5. In Web Parts, select the Web Part that you want to view or configure.
6. On the General Settings page for the Web Part, click Show Advanced Settings.
7. At the very bottom of the page you will find the caching settings, following the question "Should the content of this Web Part be cached?". For example, to enable caching across all users, click "Yes", select "All Users" in the list, and specify an appropriate time-out in seconds.
8. Click Save to close the Web Part Settings page.
9. Click Save to close the Content page.

14

DASHBOARD DEFINITION CACHING

Dashboard Definition Caching is a new feature that became available in Service Pack 1. It enables you to cache the list of all Web Parts and all sub-dashboards. If caching is enabled, the information, once gathered, will be applied to all users for requests made within the next two hours. When the cache time-out has been exceeded, the dashboard retrieves the list of Web Parts and sub-dashboards and caches the results for another two-hour period. The advantage is that any requests within the two-hour period can be resolved from cached results, which will drastically improve the performance.

This performance improvement does come with a couple of limitations, though, as the list of sub-dashboards and Web Parts is the same for all users:

- All sub-dashboards and Web Parts are executed in the security context of the user who built the cache. Therefore, the security context should be the same for all sub-dashboards and Web Parts, because otherwise the dashboard may produce unexpected results. A consequence of this is that before you can enable the caching algorithms on the default dashboards, you must move the Management Dashboard to a Personal Dashboard. The Management Dashboard is only visible to Coordinators, and thus the link is only visible in their particular security context. More information on how to move a dashboard can be found in the next section.

- The Minimize and Close buttons may appear on Web Parts, but these buttons will not function as expected. To avoid this, clear the following two check boxes for all Web Parts on your caching-enabled dashboard:

  "Allow users to remove this Web Part from their dashboard"

  "Allow users to minimize this Web Part on their dashboard"

- None of the Web Parts should return an empty string or empty. The first will cause the Web Part's code to be displayed; the latter will cause the dashboard framework to disable caching.

MOVE THE MANAGEMENT SUB-DASHBOARD

As discussed in the previous paragraph, the Management sub-dashboard must be moved before you can enable dashboard definition caching on the default dashboard or one of its sub-dashboards. The Management sub-dashboard uses a different security configuration from the other sub-dashboards to allow only Coordinators to access it. Dashboard definition cashing requires the usage of the same security settings for all of the sub-dashboards, though, because the cache used by all users is built by the first user who accesses the dashboard.

The white paper that ships with Service Pack 1 in the Support\Documentation directory illustrates how the Management dashboard can be moved to a "Standalone" dashboard. This approach does require you to remember the URL of the Management dashboard, though. Personal dashboards, however, can be found through the Document Library. You may prefer this approach, even if it takes a little more effort to make the dashboard visible and to apply

14

the correct security context. To move the Management sub-dashboard to a personal dashboard called Management, do the following:

1. Log in as Workspace Coordinator on the server that hosts the workspace.
2. Click **Start**, select **Programs**, select **Accessories**, and then click **Command Prompt**.
3. Navigate to the SharePoint Portal Server\Bin directory, which by default is C:\Program Files\SharePoint Portal Server\Bin.
4. Type cscript movedashboard.vbs "**http://**_server_/_workspace_/**Portal**/**Management**" "**http://**_server_/_workspace_/**Dashboards**/**Management**" and then press Enter.
5. The Management dashboard is hidden; therefore you will not see it in the Dashboards folder of the Document Library. Using the following script, you can toggle the visibility:

```
Const adModeReadWrite = 3
Const adFailIfNotExists = -1

If wscript.Arguments.Count < 1 or len(wscript.Arguments(0)) = 0 Then
    wscript.Echo "ToggleHide <URL>" & vblf & " to toggle the visibility of
➥<URL>"
    wscript.Quit
End If

strURL = wscript.Arguments(0)
Set conn = CreateObject("ADODB.Connection")
Set record = CreateObject("ADODB.Record")

'open a connection & record
conn.Open "Provider=MSDAIPP.DSO; Data Source=" & strURL
record.open "", conn, adModeReadWrite, adFailIfNotExists

'Toggle the current value to set two properties that determine if the
'dashboard is shown in the portal
ishidden = Not record.Fields("DAV:ishidden")
➥record.Fields("DAV:ishidden") = ishidden
record.Fields("urn:schemas-microsoft-com:publishing:IsHiddenInPortal") =
ishidden
record.Fields.Update

'close and release the objects
record.close : set record = nothing
conn.close: set conn = nothing

If isHidden = true Then
    wscript.Echo "URL " & strURL & " is now hidden"
Else
    wscript.Echo "URL " & strURL & " is now visible"
End If
```

6. By default, the moved Management dashboard inherits the security settings of the dashboard folder, which will cause the dashboard to be visible to everyone. To change this, open the workspace Web Folder and navigate to the Dashboards folder.
7. Right-click the Management folder and select Properties.

8. Select the Security Tab.

9. Uncheck Use parent folder's security settings.

10. Select the Everyone—Reader row in the selection box.

11. Click Remove.

12. Click OK to close the Properties dialog.

13. From your browser, open `http://<server>/<workspace>/Dashboards/Management`, and then click Flush application level cache.

ENABLE DASHBOARD DEFINITION CACHING

The digital dashboard definition caching is controlled via a property set on the digital dashboard folder. To enable or disable the dashboard caching, do the following:

1. Log in as Workspace Coordinator to the server hosting the workspace.

2. Click **Start**, select **Programs**, select **Accessories**, and then click **Command Prompt**.

3. Navigate to the SharePoint Portal Server\Bin directory, which by default is C:\Program Files\SharePoint Portal Server\Bin.

4. To Enable caching for the root digital dashboard, type

```
cscript portalperf.vbs http://<server >/<workspace >/portal dashboarddef enable
```

To enable caching for a sub-dashboard type

```
cscript portalperf.vbs http://<server >/<workspace >/portal/<sub-dashboard>
➥dashboarddef enable
```

To disable the dashboard definition caching, replace the word `enable` with `disable` in the previous command line.

5. From your browser, open `http://<server>/<workspace>/Dashboards/Management`, and then click Flush application level cache.

FULL-PAGE CACHING

The caching of the Dashboard Definitions Catalog is a first step in optimizing your portal's performance that was introduced with Service Pack 1. All Web Parts of a dashboard with this caching enabled will still be executed, while this often may not be necessary. Instead, the HTML output generated from the assembly of all Web Parts of a dashboard can be cached for all users. This is known as *full-page caching*, a new feature added in Service Pack 1.

Full-page caching will look at the caching options for each Web Part of the dashboard. If "All User" caching is not enabled for all Web Parts (except for the Search Web Part), full-page caching does not work.

14

Under the Hood: The Search Web Part

Let's examine that "except for the Search Web Part" a little further for those of you who are already familiar with Web Part development. The Search Web Part illustrates well how Web Part developers can determine the caching behavior of their Web Part at runtime.

The Search Web Part is implemented in a Visual Basic Script function called getContent, which is called by the dashboard factory to retrieve the XML or HTML output. The getContent function takes a single parameter, which is an XML Node object that contains all the Web Part property information, including the caching behavior properties. If just the simple search dialog is shown, full-page caching is allowed regardless of the actual cache settings.

If the advanced search dialog is shown, caching is not applied, such that the more frequently used simple version remains cached. To override the full-page cache, which typically would occur if a request with the same dashboard URL is made, a `NoFullPageCache=1` flag will be passed with the request to render the dashboard. This allows Web Part developers to bypass the cache under certain circumstances, while the benefit of caching in common circumstances remains.

When the cache time-out has not been exceeded, SharePoint Portal Server will use the cached version generated from an earlier request. The cache "expires" based on the cache settings of the individual Web Parts in that folder. As one would expect, the time-out is set to the minimum value of all the cache time-outs of the individual Web Parts. So, for example, if there are four Web Parts that are configured with time-out values of 300, 500, 800, and 1000 seconds, the page will be cached for 300 seconds.

The use of full-page caching prevents some Web Parts from functioning according to their design, because any server-side script is only called once, on the first request, during the caching period. Content that is based on user credentials will not get updated accordingly; the content remains static.

For a portal home page, such static pages may be desirable, but in many cases you will require more flexible content. This can be accomplished using

- **Isolated Web Parts**, which instantiate an iFrame, an embedded instance of the browser within the current browser window. The iFrame's src property determines which content is to be shown. Pointing to an Active Server Pages (ASP) page, this page can then generate dynamic content. The Web Part itself is now static HTML, basically just an iFrame that can be cached across all users. An example of this method of dynamic content is the new Subscription Summary (iFrame) Web Part.

- **Dynamic HTML** (DHTML), which allows returning static content that will be interpreted by the client to generate a dynamic user interface. For example, DHTML allows you to return a list of information that gets formatted according to client settings, through the browser's built-in Document Object Model.

ENABLE FULL-PAGE CACHING

To enable full-page caching, one must set a property on the digital dashboard folder. In addition to this property, all Web Parts on the dashboard must allow for caching across all users to let full-page caching actually occur. Typically, this means that all the Web Parts have set their caching behavior property to All Users, as discussed earlier in this chapter. The Search Web Part is an exception to that rule.

CAUTION

> If you change the Search Web Part's caching behavior property, clicking the Advanced Search link will not show the advanced search dialog. Keep the default setting of no caching.

To enable or disable the dashboard caching, do the following:

1. Log in as Workspace Coordinator on the server hosting the workspace.

2. Click **Start**, select **Programs**, select **Accessories**, and then click **Command Prompt**.

3. Navigate to the SharePoint Portal Server\Bin directory, which by default is C:\Program Files\SharePoint Portal Server\Bin.

4. To Enable caching for the root digital dashboard, type

   ```
   cscript portalperf.vbs http://<server >/<workspace >/portal dashboarddef
   ➥fullpage
   ```

   To enable caching for a sub-dashboard, type

   ```
   cscript portalperf.vbs http://<server >/<workspace >/portal/<sub-dashboard>
   ➥fullpage enable
   ```

   To disable dashboard definition caching, replace the word `enable` with `disable` in the previous command line.

5. In your browser, open `http://<server>/<workspace>/Dashboards/Management`, and then click Flush application level cache.

A NEW SUBSCRIPTION SUMMARY WEB PART

Subscriptions are user specific, and therefore it is not possible to cache the default Subscription Summary Web Part that you will find on the main dashboard across all users. For this reason, Microsoft has provided an updated version of this Web Part called *"Subscription Summary (iFrame)"* with Service Pack 1. This Web Part is available from the Support\Tools directory on the SharePoint Portal Server 2001 SP 1 CD, or by download. This Web Part is designed to replace the existing Subscription Summary Web Part that you find on the home page of the dashboard. The new version can be used regardless of the cache settings applied to the page.

To replace the Web Part, do the following:

1. Log in as Workspace Coordinator.

2. Open Internet Explorer and type the URL `http://<server>/<workspace>` in the address bar.

14

3. If any of the Service Pack 1 dashboard performance optimizations have been applied, click on the icon with the four little squares next to the Help link in the top right corner.

4. Click the Content link in the top of the dashboard.

5. In Web Parts, select the Subscription Summary Web Part.

6. On the General Settings page for the Web Part, click Delete.

7. Click OK to confirm the deletion.

8. Back on the Content page, click Import a Web Part File, in the Import or Create section.

9. Navigate to the location of *IFSubSum.dwp* in the support\tools directory.

10. Select IFSubSum.dwp, and then click Open.

11. We need to edit this Web Part slightly; therefore, select the new Subscription Summary (iFrame) Web Part.

12. On the Settings for "Subscription Summary (iFrame)" page, click Show Advanced Settings.

13. Under Get content from the following link, replace "workspacename" with the name of your workspace.

14. Click Save to leave the Settings page.

15. Click Save to leave the Content page.

Because this Web Part is running as an isolated Web Part, it will not know if you have selected another style sheet file name to reflect your company's look and feel. This problem is common to all isolated Web Parts. The Subscription Summary (iFrame) Web Part illustrates how this problem can be addressed: In the URL that is defined under Get content from the following link, the `css=spsdash.css` query parameter refers to the actual style sheet used. Change this if necessary to the appropriate style sheet file name.

CREATING WEB PARTS

In the advanced Web Part Settings page, you already may have seen the text boxes that refer to the actual code of the Web Part. For this introductory chapter, we will only touch on writing code through the Web interface. There are more ways to create Web Parts, even without writing a single line of code. We will explore this option using Word 2002 and Excel 2002 out of the Microsoft Office XP suite. And to finish, the tool for a more professional manner of developing Web Parts will be introduced—Microsoft Office XP Developer.

14

USING THE PORTAL

On the advanced Web Part Settings page, you will find all the options to create a Web Part, including the ability to use VBScript or JavaScript that gets executed on the server side. For this introductory chapter on dashboard customizations, we will just mention two basic means to create a Web Part.

The easiest way to create a Web Part is to refer to an HTML page that resides elsewhere. If your company, for example, has a common Web page where corporate announcements are stored, you may just use the URL to that page. You should note, though, that Web pages are typically not designed for usage as Web Parts. Often too much white space and different color schemes are included, or full-screen sizing is assumed, both affecting the look of your portal when multiple Web Parts are present in your dashboard. Therefore, you should consider using the relevant information of that page as embedded content. To create a Web Part with a link to external content or embedded content, do the following:

1. Log in as a Workspace Coordinator.
2. Open Internet Explorer and type the URL of the dashboard whose Web Parts you want to configure in the address bar.
3. If any of the Service Pack 1 dashboard performance optimizations have been applied, click on the icon with the four little squares next to the Help link in the top right corner.
4. Click the Content link in the top of the dashboard.
5. Under Import or Create, click Create a New Web Part.
6. On the General Web Part Settings page, change the Name to reflect the purpose of the Web Part.
7. If you want to refer to an external link, in the Advanced Settings section, check Get content from the following link, and type the URL in the text box. If you want to provide embedded content, type (or paste) the content into the Embedded Content text area below.
8. Typically you will uncheck the "Allow users to remove this Web Part from their dashboard" and "Allow users to minimize this Web Part on their dashboard" settings, as discussed earlier in this chapter.
9. Click Save to close the Web Part Settings page.
10. Click Save to close the Content page (See Figure 14.11) .

14

Figure 14.11
This figure shows two Web Parts, one using a Content Link referring directly to the Babel Fish translation Web site (http://babelfish.altavista.com), and another that uses embedded content, in this case the form providing the translation services that you can find on the content link.

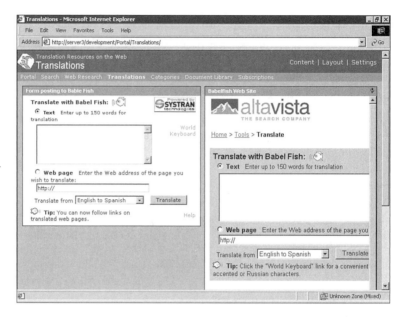

USING OFFICE XP

SharePoint Portal Server is, as you have seen already, deeply integrated with Office XP. Not only can you easily author information that is stored within the workspace, you can even save Office XP documents as Web Parts, such that the information becomes directly available to other users.

To create Web Parts, you need to have Coordinator privileges for the Dashboard folder. This permission is likely not granted to most users on the default dashboard. But Personal Dashboards allow for the instant creation of a portal that is shared, for example, among a team. Therefore, the Office XP Save as Web Part feature in particular is of great value for these adhoc dashboards, where more people can be granted the necessary Coordinator privilege. To save an Excel 2002, Word 2002, or PowerPoint 2002 document as a Web Part, do the following:

1. After you have finished entering content into your document, select File, Save As.

2. In the Save as type drop-down box, select Web Page (*.htm, *.html).

3. Enter in the HTTP address of the dashboard on which your document should appear as a Web Part, and give the Web Part a name. For example, for a Web Part called Statistics on a Personal dashboard called "Project Gamma", you would use
   `http://<Server>/<workspace>/Dashboards/Project Gamma/Statistics.htm`.

4. Click Save.

5. In the Web File Properties form, enter in a name and a description. You also can set the zone in which you want your Web Part to be displayed.

6. Click OK.

If you now open the dashboard you will find the new Web Part (see Figures 14.12 and 14.13).

Figure 14.12
This figure shows an Excel 2002 spreadsheet that is about to be saved as a Web Part.

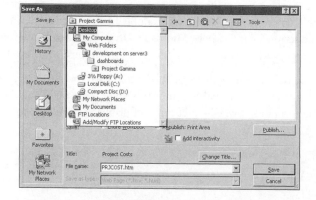

Figure 14.13
This figure shows the dashboard with the new Web Part, as result of saving the spreadsheet in Figure 14.12 as a Web Part.

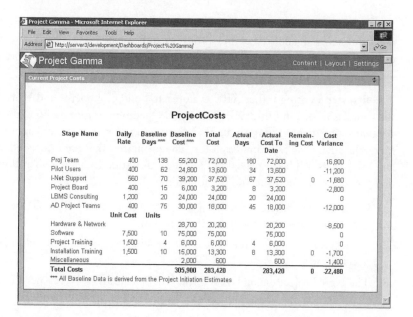

ProjectCosts

Stage Name	Daily Rate	Baseline Days ***	Baseline Cost ***	Total Cost	Actual Days	Actual Cost To Date	Remain- ing Cost	Cost Variance
Proj Team	400	138	55,200	72,000	180	72,000		16,800
Pilot Users	400	62	24,800	13,600	34	13,600		-11,200
I-Net Support	560	70	39,200	37,520	67	37,520	0	-1,680
Project Board	400	15	6,000	3,200	8	3,200		-2,800
LBMS Consulting	1,200	20	24,000	24,000	20	24,000		0
AD Project Teams	400	75	30,000	18,000	45	18,000		-12,000
	Unit Cost	**Units**						
Hardware & Network			28,700	20,200		20,200		-8,500
Software	7,500	10	75,000	75,000		75,000		0
Project Training	1,500	4	6,000	6,000	4	6,000		0
Installation Training	1,500	10	15,000	13,300	8	13,300	0	-1,700
Miscellaneous			2,000	600		600		-1,400
Total Costs			**305,900**	**283,420**		**283,420**	**0**	**-22,480**

*** All Baseline Data is derived from the Project Initiation Estimates

TIP

> Using Excel 2002, you can take advantage of the Office Web Components, which enable your users to sort the spreadsheet or change pivot tables through the browser, without actually changing the underlying data. To do so, save the Web Part with "interactivity", an option in the Excel Save As dialog.

14

USING MICROSOFT OFFICE XP DEVELOPER

The methods described earlier are very helpful for some incidental customizations of SharePoint Portal Server's portal, but for a professional developer, too many steps are needed in an unsuitable environment. Think for example of the creation of a Web Part that uses some Visual Basic script. This is where Microsoft Office XP Developer comes in, a tool for professional developers who want to create collaborative Office solutions beyond VBA.

As a developer, you will feel immediately comfortable with the environment, simply because Office XP Developer uses the Visual Studio .NET shell that you should be already familiar with. The product supports three distinct types of projects, all related to collaborative solutions.

- Exchange 2000 Workflow
- SQL Server Workflow
- Digital Dashboard

For this chapter and book, we will only use the Digital Dashboard project, but let me point out that Exchange 2000 Workflow projects can be hosted in a SharePoint Portal Server environment, using a subdirectory in `http://<server>/SharePoint Portal Server/applications/<workspace>`.

The first step in using Office XP Developer to build dashboards and Web Parts is to open the root dashboard in Office XP Developer. Opening the root dashboard will display the contents—the dashboard itself, its Web Parts and any resources, and any sub-dashboards—hierarchically in the Solution Explorer. The properties that are associated with dashboards and Web Parts will be displayed in the Properties grid. To open a SharePoint Portal Server dashboard for the first time, do the following:

1. From the Start menu, select Programs, then Microsoft Office XP Developer, and then select Microsoft Development Environment.
2. From the File menu of the Office XP Developer environment, select New, and then select Project.
3. The New Project dialog box is displayed. Select Office Developer Projects.
4. In the Templates window, select the Dashboard Project icon.
5. In the Location text box, enter the parent folder of your dashboard. The default home dashboard, for example, would be `http://<Server>/<workspace>`, while for any Personal Dashboard you would use `http://<Server>/<workspace>/Dashboards`.
6. Change the project name from "Dashboard" to "Portal" if you are opening the home dashboard; otherwise use the name of the Personal Dashboard.
7. Click OK.

8. The wizard will tell you that the project will be created as desired at `http://<server>/<workspace>/portal`. You don't have to worry about the term "creation"—if a Digital Dashboard is present at that location, it will be imported. As the SharePoint Portal Server Dashboards consist of quite a few files, Office XP Developer appears unresponsive, but the import will complete in a couple of minutes.

This will add a Portal.ddp project file to the Portal folder, which can subsequently be opened directly through the Web Folder interface. In addition, it will add a solution file to your client machine in My Documents\Office Developer Projects\PortalX\Portal.sln, which allows you to open the project again through the File, Open, Project menu entry of Office XP Developer (see Figure 14.14).

TIP

> Rename your Dashboard Solution, particularly if you have multiple workspaces on your server, as otherwise all solutions begin with "Portal" and can only be distinguished through a number. Renaming can easily be done in the properties pane.

Figure 14.14
This figure shows the Announcements Web Part in the Microsoft Office XP Developer environment. Notice the customization of the Title to "Company Announcements", to reflect better the usage of this out-of-the-box Web Part.

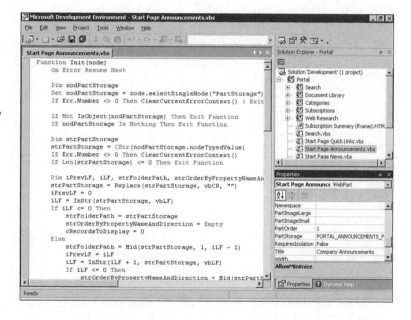

Working with Digital Dashboards and Web Parts becomes much easier with the Office XP Developer Dashboard project, as it allows you to set dashboard and Web Part properties through a properties pane within the Visual Studio .NET shell. Moreover, it becomes much easier to edit Web Parts, as for all the types supported by the Digital Dashboard project, a rich code pane with auto coloring and auto tag completion can be used.

14

TIP

> There are a couple of things you should know when working with Office XP Developer. In the Solution Explorer, unfortunately the files are randomly sorted, and more importantly, not all file types can be viewed within Office XP Developer. Most inconvenient is the missing support for Active Server Pages (.asp or .aspx), while many Web Parts will refer to functions defined in files such as Portal/resources/tahoeutils.asp.

SUMMARY

SharePoint Portal Server delivers a great, out-of-the-box starting point for building a portal that can easy be extended without the need to code. Instead, the customization pages provided through the portal interface enable you to tune your dashboard to your requirements, such that your portal becomes effective for your users. Web Parts, one of the core components of the Digital Dashboard architecture, are reusable and can be made available from your own IT department, your supplier of collaborative solutions, or from Microsoft. Check the Microsoft Web Part Gallery and the SharePoint Portal Server Resource Kit. Additionally, you can create Web Parts yourself—directly from Office XP applications if you like. And on the other side of the spectrum, there is Microsoft Office XP Developer—a tool to create and maintain dashboards and Web Parts for professional developers.

14

CREATE WEB PARTS USING YOUR EXISTING CODE

by Reza Dianat

In this chapter

15

INTEGRATING WITH SHAREPOINT PORTAL SERVER

SharePoint provides a wide range of possibilities for integration. It offers a platform for integration with other products such as Office XP and Exchange server, and support for the development of a variety of Web Parts using almost any type of programming language. Business people and knowledge experts can easily participate in creating Web Parts by just using Office XP. They can use the regular Office XP Word to create documents and save them as a Web Part, or create Excel spreadsheets or PowerPoint presentations as they used to and publish them on the Web, without having extensive knowledge about Web development. On the other hand, developers can use their existing skills such as HTML, Dynamic HTML, VBScript, JavaScript, XML, and XSL to create a more polished and advanced Web Part. In the following sections, we are going to show how you can use your existing skills to create Web Parts.

"DATE" WEB PART

The purpose of the Date Web Part is to show the current date in our Home dashboard. This is an easy few lines of code that shows the current date in your dashboard. To create the Date Web Part, you basically need a few lines of VBScript code, as shown in Listing 15.1.

LISTING 15.1 VBSCRIPT CODE FOR DATE WEB PART

```
Function getContent(xml)
  Dim strContent
  strContent = "<DIV style=""font-size: 100%"">"
  strContent = strContent & FormatDateTime(Now(), 1)
  strContent = strContent & "</DIV>"
  strContent = strContent & "<HR>"
  getContent = strContent
End Function
```

The getContent function shows the current date and returns in the format of Weekday, Month Name Day, Year.

Notice that we have used the Now() built-in date function to get the current date and pass it as a parameter to another VBScript function FormatDateTime(), with argument 1 as the second parameter that generates the current date in the desired format (for example, Sunday, November 18, 2001).

NOTE

> All the Web Parts are processed and rendered by the dashboard factory (dashboard.asp). The dashboard factory allows Web Parts to get their content from WSS, or run queries and scripts through the GetContent() function. For more information about Dashboard Architecture, see
>
> ```
> http://msdn.microsoft.com/library/default.asp?url=/library/
> en-us/spssdk/html/_dashboard_architecture.asp
> ```

15

To make a Web Part from these couple lines of VBScript code, we need to

1. From the main menu bar at the upper right corner of the SharePoint dashboard, click **Content**. Then, from the Content dashboard, click on **Create New Web Part**, located at the bottom of the screen under the Import or Create section (see Figure 15.1).

Figure 15.1
The content of the "Home" Web Part.

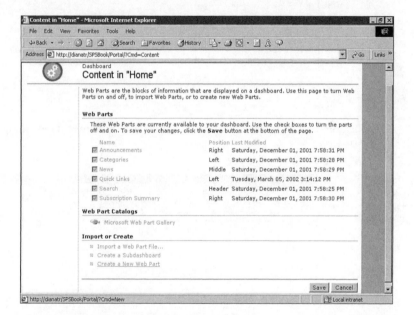

2. In the **General Settings** of the **Web Part – Settings** dashboard, enter Date Header for the **Name** of the Web Part, and for the **Description** of the Web Part, enter The Date Header Web Part displays the current date at the top of your digital dashboard. Since the output is a small message, we do not want to show it in a frame, so make sure the check box for **Display this Web Part in a frame** is not checked.

3. Select **Top banner** for the position of the Web Part.

4. For the rest of the settings in the **General Settings** section, accept the defaults.

5. In the **Advanced Settings** section, select **VBScript** from the drop-down menu as the type of content.

Figure 15.2
The General Settings for the "Date" Web Part.

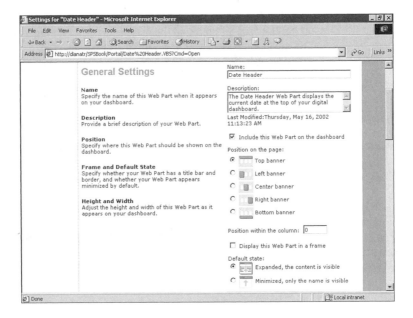

6. Click on the **Embedded content** text area box, and enter the code shown in Listing 15.1.

Figure 15.3
The Advanced Settings for the "Date" Web Part.

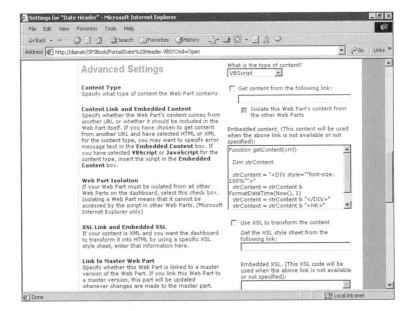

7. Accept the default settings for the rest of the options in the **Advanced Settings** section. Click on **Save** in the **Settings** dashboard, and click on **Save** again in the **Content** dashboard. In the Home dashboard, you can see the date on the left banner. You may use the Layout dashboard and move the Date Web Part to the upper-right banner of the Home dashboard. Figure 15.4 shows the final view of the Date Web Part.

Figure 15.4
Using VBScript to create a simple Date Web Part.

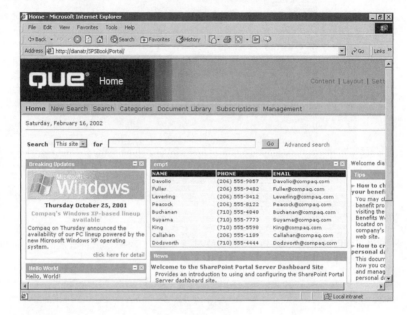

"WELCOME USER" WEB PART

The purpose of this Web Part is to display the name of the user who has logged in to the SharePoint Portal Server.

This is another line of code, and an easily developed Web Part.

To use this Web Part, your SharePoint must require user authentication, and obviously if SharePoint is configured for public access without any authentication, this Web Part cannot be used. The one line of code is

```
getContent = "Welcome " & mid(GetServerVariable("AUTH_USER"),
➥instr(GetServerVariable("AUTH_USER"), "\")+1)
```

When you set Basic Authentication as a mechanism for controlling access to your Web Part, the users' credentials are stored as server variables—AUTH_USER—and if the domain name is used as part of the username (for example, domain\username) the part after "\" will be the username. Using Mid and GetServerVariable functions, we can extract the username. This way we can get the username and concatenate it with the word "Welcome", so we can show "Welcome User" at the Home dashboard. To make this code into a Web Part requires the same steps as those for the Date Web Part. The final view of this Web Part is shown in Figure 15.5.

Figure 15.5

The "Welcome User" Web Part displays the name of user who has logged in to the SharePoint Portal Server.

15

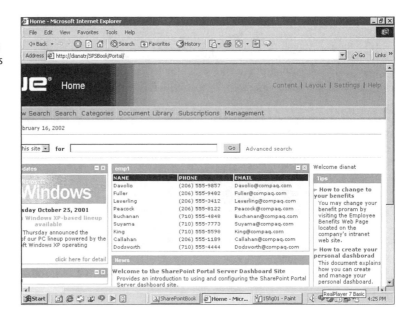

You can apply your desired font size or color to the Welcome User string by using an HTML DIV tag, as seen in the code for the Date Web Part.

GetServerVariable is a function in dbUtil.vbs. It uses request.servervariable to get the value "AUTH_USER". Listing 15.2 shows the GetServerVariable source code.

> **NOTE**
>
> dbUtil.vbs is a VBScript file located in the Portal/Resources Web folder. It has many functions and utilities that are used in different places in the SharePoint code. You can use Web Folder view to access this file and copy it to a different folder to take a look at it. The Portal folder is a hidden folder; to see the hidden files and folders make sure that you have enabled viewing of hidden files.

LISTING 15.2   THE GETSERVERVARIABLE IS A REUSABLE FUNCTION LOCATED IN DBUTIL.VBS FILE IN RESOURCES SUBDIRECTORY OF SHAREPOINT PORTAL SERVER

```
Function GetServerVariable(strVariable)
    On Error Resume Next

    Dim strTmp
    Dim nCodePage

    nCodePage = Session.CodePage
    Session.CodePage = 0     ' CP_ACP

    strTmp = Request.ServerVariables(strVariable)
```

```
        Session.CodePage = nCodePage

        GetServerVariable = strTmp

End Function
```

UNSTRUCTURED AND SEMI-STRUCTURED DATA

After reading through the previous chapters, you should have a good foundation of SharePoint Portal Server. It is based on the Web Storage System, which was introduced in Exchange 2000 Server. It is a storage mechanism for storing unstructured data such as word documents and PDF files, and storing semi-structured data like email. By now, you have also learned about the capabilities of SharePoint and how it provides solutions based on the Web Storage System.

Email is considered semi-structured because it has some fields that will always appear in any email, such as FROM, TO, CC, and SUBJECT, which represent structured fields, and a BODY that mainly is in free format without any specific structure. The structured data allows for better sorting or searching of emails based on those fields.

For example, in Outlook you can view email arranged in order by From, To, or Subject. In fact you might have noticed that there are more fields, such as Date, that you do not specify; rather, the system automatically takes care of the date field by stamping your email. These fields are another form of structured data, which enable you to search for emails in chronological order.

Then how about the Body of an email? Ordering email based on their Body (text) does not make sense, and searching the Body of emails is not precise, and would be based on keywords. This shows that having some sort of structure will help us in locating data quickly and accurately. If these types of structured data help us, why don't we use them for unstructured data? In fact, in SharePoint the idea of profiles serves the same purpose. However, the concept of profiles has existed in the Office products for a while; they were optional and not widely used. Now in SharePoint, you can mandate that each document must have a profile, and also mandate which fields must be filled. The profiles allow for more accurate searches and retrieval of data.

STRUCTURED DATA

Yet there is another form of data that is highly structured like relational databases. For more than two decades, companies have invested in databases and products such as SQL Server, Oracle, DB2, Informix, and Sybase. Payroll, personnel, finance, and all sorts of business data is stored in a highly structured format. A huge number of skill sets are developed around these products, and billions of lines of code are written to build applications around these products as well. Or how about directories and object-oriented databases, which represent yet another type and category of data structure?

15

NOTE

> It would be ideal to have a universal type of data storage that could store any type of unstructured, semi-structured, and structured data such as email, documents, voice, and movies, along with other structured types of data, which could all be searched and retrieved in a similar manner. As long as there is a demand for this, I am sure technology will have an answer for it.

Throughout this chapter I will show real-life scenarios and solutions built around SQL Server, using VB components and ASP pages, and I also will show how you can easily build Web Parts and use them through the SharePoint interface (dashboards).

Most likely, each organization has many different data structures, and the question is how we can use existing structured data and directory-based data with SharePoint Server, which is mainly intended for unstructured and semi-structured types of data. How can we use our existing skill sets to develop solutions around SQL Server and Active Directory, and then be able to integrate those solutions in the dashboards of the SharePoint Server?

If you have any type of relational database or Active Directory in your organization such as ASP, VB, COM, ADO, or ADSI, and are interested in developing solutions and Web Parts for the SharePoint Server, you should continue reading the rest of this chapter.

Also, I will introduce two Web Parts. One is an Employee Locator Web Part, which is presented in three versions; in each version we try to make it more robust and explain different paths that you can take for the design and development of Web Parts. The second Web Part is an Active Directory Lookup Web Part. These two Web Parts show how you can use your data that is stored in the relational databases and Active Directory, and represent it as useful Web Parts in the SharePoint interface. The whole idea of this chapter is to use your current skills with ASP, VB components, ADSI, SQL server, or other relational databases to develop Web Parts, or just plug your existing code into Web Parts.

EMPLOYEE LOCATOR WEB PART (VERSION 1)

The first Web Part is called the Employee Locator Web Part; it browses through a list of employees in the SharePoint dashboard.

Employee information might be stored in Oracle, SQL Server, or other relational databases. For the purpose of this Web Part, we will assume that it is stored in SQL Server 2000, but it really does not matter which backend database is used. The code will mainly stay the same.

CREATING EMPLOYEES TABLE

To simplify the process, I have used the employees table from a sample SQL Server database that is shipped with SQL 7 and SQL 2000 (the Northwind database), and added a field to the table for an email address. Figure 15.6 shows the data structure of the Employees table used for this example.

Figure 15.6
This figure displays the Employees table data structure after adding an email field.

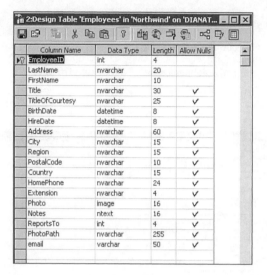

CREATING AN XML FILE FROM EMPLOYEES INFORMATION

In the first version of the Employee Locator, we will create an XML file from the employees table, so we need to

- Connect to the SQL Server database
- Create a recordset
- Save the recordset as an XML file

Listing 15.3 shows the VBScript code required to create an XML file from employees table. Figure 15.7 shows the result.

LISTING 15.3   THE FOLLOWING VBSCRIPT CODE GENERATES AN XML FILE FROM EMPLOYEES TABLE.

```
Option Explicit
Const adPersistXML = 1
Const adUseClient = 3
Const adOpenKeyset = 1
Const adLockOptimistic = 3

Dim strConnection
Dim rs
Dim strSQL

strConnection = "Provider=SQLOLEDB;Data Source=dianatr;Initial
➥ Catalog=NorthWind;User Id=sa;Password=;Connect Timeout=30;"
strSQL = " select EmployeeID, LastName, FirstName, HomePhone, email from
➥ Employees "
```

continues

LISTING 15.3   CONTINUED

```
set rs = CreateObject ("ADODB.RECORDSET")
rs.CursorLocation = adUseClient
rs.Open strSQL, strConnection, adOpenKeyset, adLockOptimistic
rs.Save "employee1.xml", adPersistXML
rs.close
```

Figure 15.7
Displays the content of the employee1.xml file generated through code in Listing 15.3 when it is opened with IE version 5 or higher.

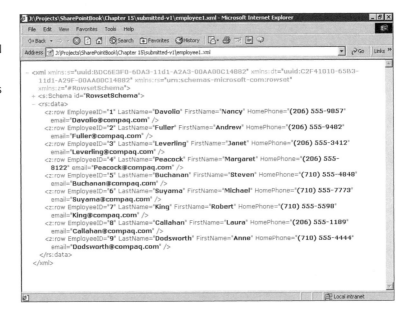

CREATING AN XSL FILE FOR DATA TRANSFORMATION

The next step is to transform the XML file into an HTML file, so we can show it in the Web Part. For this purpose, we created an XSL file that extracts the attributes (LastName, HomePhone, and email) of each row element (z:row) from the rs:data node. Then the address of each row, with respect to the root (xml), will be xml/rs:data/z:row.

LIST 15.4   THE XSL CODE THAT HAS BEEN USED FOR FORMATTING THE XML FILE

```
<?xml version="1.0"?>
<xsl:stylesheet xmlns:xsl="http://www.w3.org/TR/WD-xsl">
  <xsl:template match="/">
    <HTML>
      <BODY>
        <TABLE width="420">
          <TR bgcolor="Black">
```

```
            <TD width="130"><font face="Verdana" size="1" color="white">
➡<b>NAME</b></font></TD>
            <TD width="110"><font face="Verdana" size="1" color="white">
➡<b>PHONE</b></font></TD>
            <TD width="150"><font face="Verdana" size="1" color="white">
➡<b>EMAIL</b></font></TD>
          </TR>
    <xsl:for-each select="xml/rs:data/z:row">
     <TR bgcolor="#ffdead">
      <TD><font face="Verdana" size="1" color="black"><xsl:value-of
➡select="@LastName"/></font></TD>
      <TD><font face="Verdana" size="1" color="black"><xsl:value-of
➡select="@HomePhone"/></font></TD>
      <TD><font face="Verdana" size="1" color="black"><xsl:value-of
➡select="@email"/></font></TD>
     </TR>
    </xsl:for-each>
    </TABLE>         </BODY>
    </HTML>
  </xsl:template>
</xsl:stylesheet>
```

NOTE

If you are new to XML and XSL you may want to take a look at the following resources for a quick start.

`http://www.xml101.com/`

`http://msdn.microsoft.com/library/default.asp?url=/library/`
`en-us/xmlsdk30/htm/xmtutxmltutorial.asp`

`http://msdn.microsoft.com/library/default.asp?url=/library/`
`en-us/xmlsdk30/htm/xmtutxmltutorial.asp`

CREATING THE WEB PART

To create the Employee Web Part, we need to apply the XSL file (employee1.xsl) to the XML file (employee1.xml). We follow the steps mentioned in the "Date Web Part" section for creating a new Web Part, up until the advanced settings. At this point there are three options to integrate XML and XSL files for the Web Part.

USING XML AS CONTENT TYPE

- In the Advanced Settings, we select XML as the Content Type, and copy and paste the XML file into the **Embedded content** text area. We also copy and paste the XSL file into the **Embedded XSL** text area section (Figure 15.8).

- Save the settings. We are now done with the Employee Locator Web Part (Figure 15.9).

Figure 15.8
This figure shows how the **Advanced Settings** screen will look after having copied the code into the embedded text areas.

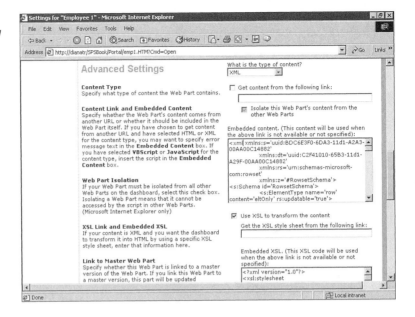

Figure 15.9
This figure shows the final form of the Employee Web Part in the Home dashboard.

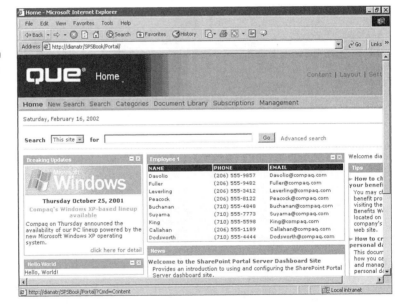

USING HTML AS CONTENT TYPE

In this case, we will use HTML as the content type for the Employee Web Part. For this purpose, we need to create a virtual directory in the Internet Information Server (IIS) that points to the employee1 subdirectory. Follow these steps to create the employee1 virtual directory:

1. Use Windows Explorer to create a new folder under **c:\inetpub\wwwroot** (if you are using other drives, use that drive letter instead of C) and name it **employee1**.

2. Copy the employee1.xml and employee1.xsl files to the employee1 folder.

3. Use the Internet System Manager to create a new virtual directory and call it employee1 (select the employee1 folder as the physical location).

4. In the Advanced Settings for the Web Part, select HTML as the content type.

5. Check the **Get content from the following link** check box, and type `http://`
   `servername`/employee1/employee1.xml in the text box for the link.

6. Check the **Use XSL to transform the content** check box, and in the text box **Get the XSL style sheet from the following link,** type `http://servername/`*employee1*/
   employee1.xsl for the link.

Figure 15.10 shows the Advanced Settings for the HTML Content Type option.

Figure 15.10
Employee Web Part
using HTML and
External Link.

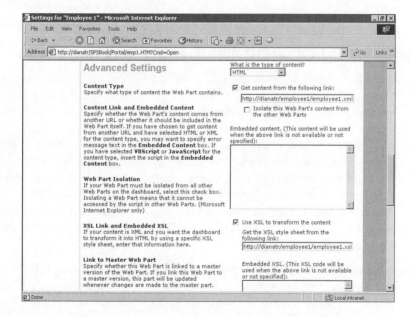

SAVING XML AND XSL FILES IN THE WEB STORAGE SYSTEM (WSS)

You might bypass creating a separate virtual directory in IIS, as we showed in the second option, and copy the XML and XSL files in a folder in the SharePoint Web Storage System (WSS).

1. In the Web folder interface of the SharePoint Portal Server, create a new folder under the **Portal Content** Web folder and name it **employee1**.

2. Copy the employee1.xml and employee1.xsl files to the employee1 folder.

3. In the Advanced Settings of the Web Part, select HTML as the content type.

4. Check the **Get content from the following link** check box, and type `http://`
`servername/workspacename/Portal Content/employee1/employee1.xml` in the text box
for the link.

5. Check the **Use XSL to transform the content** check box, and in the text box **Get the
XSL style sheet from the following link**, type `http://servername/employee1/`
`employee1.xml` for the link.

As you can see here, we accessed XML and XSL in the Web storage system the same way
(using HTTP) that we accessed them in the second option. In this example we showed that
all the items stored in the Web Storage System are URL addressable and can be viewed
using HTTP.

NOTE
In fact, the SharePoint Web Storage System is in compliance with the WebDAV protocol,
which is an extension to the HTTP 1.1 protocol.

EMPLOYEE LOCATOR WEB PART (VERSION 2)

In the first version of the Employee Locator, the employee information was generated in
two separate steps. First we retrieved data from SQL Server and saved it as an XML file,
and then we used an XSL file (employee1.xsl) to transform it into an HTML file. This
approach can be used in many different scenarios, as long as the frequency of changes to the
data is not high. In such cases, the XML file can be generated through a scheduled task that
generates the XML file on a daily or weekly basis, depending on the frequency of changes to
data. Although this can be a valid and reasonable solution, it might not work well for cases
when the data changes frequently. Probably a better approach for this scenario is to gain
access directly to the SQL Server, and reflect all the updates as users view the data in the
Web Part. Employee Locator version 2 will demonstrate how your Web Part can connect to
the database to show the data in real-time.

By changing just a few lines of code, we will be able to retrieve and present employee data
in real-time. In this version, we will use ActiveX Data Objects to store XML in a stream
instead of a physical XML file. Lets look at the differences between two versions of
Employee Locator Web Parts:

NOTE
For more information about ActiveX Data Objects (ADO), you may want to look at
`http://msdn.microsoft.com/library/default.asp?url=/library/`
`en-us/ado270/htm/mdmscsection1_ado.asp`

The first difference is the way that employee data was stored.

In version 1 of the Web Part, the data was stored in employee1.xml:

```
rs.Save "employee1.xml", adPersistXML
```

In version 2, the data was stored in a stream object and converted to a string:

```
set oStream = CreateObject ("ADODB.STREAM")
rs.Save oStream, adPersistXML
strRst = oStream.ReadText(adReadAll)
```

The second difference between the two Web Parts is the way that the XSL file is used for the transformation of the XML code. In both Web Parts, we have used the same XSL file, because the XML data is the same. This reveals another advantage of separation of data and user interface, which is, as you might have guessed, reusability. In the first version, we let the SharePoint dashboard factory take care of loading the XML file and applying the XSL. But in the second version, we have used the msxml DOM object for this purpose.

```
' Load the strRst string which has XML data into xmlBody DOM object
Set xmlBody = CreateObject("MSXML2.domdocument")
xmlBody.async = False
xmlBody.LoadXML strRst

' Load the xsl file into xmlBody DOM object
Set displayWeb = CreateObject("MSXML2.domdocument")
displayWeb.async = False
displayWeb.Load "e:\projects\SPSbook\employee1.xsl"

' Transform the XML into an HTML string
strBody = xmlBody.transformNode(displayWeb)
```

In the previous code, strBody has the final HTML form of employee data that must be presented in the Web Part.(Listing 15.5).

LISTING 15.5   THE COMPLETE VBSCRIPT CODE FOR RETRIEVING EMPLOYEE DATA FROM SQL SERVER IN XML FORMAT INTO A STRING

```
Const adPersistXML = 1
Const adUseClient = 3
Const adOpenKeyset = 1
Const adLockOptimistic = 3
Const adReadAll = -1

Dim strConnection
Dim rs
Dim strSQL
Dim oStream
Dim strRst
Dim xmlBody
Dim displayWeb
Dim strBody

strConnection = "Provider=SQLOLEDB;Data Source=dianatr;Initial
➥Catalog=NorthWind;User Id=sa;Password=;Connect Timeout=30;"
strSQL = " select EmployeeID, LastName, FirstName, HomePhone, email from
➥Employees "
set rs = CreateObject ("ADODB.RECORDSET")
rs.CursorLocation = adUseClient
```

continues

LISTING 15.5   CONTINUED

```
rs.Open strSQL, strConnection, adOpenKeyset, adLockOptimistic
set oStream = CreateObject ("ADODB.STREAM")
rs.Save oStream, adPersistXML
strRst = oStream.ReadText(adReadAll)

Set xmlBody = CreateObject("MSXML2.domdocument")
xmlBody.async = False
xmlBody.LoadXML strRst
Set displayWeb = CreateObject("MSXML2.domdocument")
displayWeb.async = False
displayWeb.Load "e:\projects\SPSbook\employee1.xsl"
strBody = xmlBody.transformNode(displayWeb)
rs.close
```

To create the second version of the Employee Locator Web Part, we follow the same steps mentioned in the "Date Web Part" section for creating a new Web Part. In the **Advanced Settings** section of **Web Part - Settings**, we select VBScript for the type of content, and then we create a function in the Embedded Content text area with three lines.

```
Function getContent() 'Line 1
<< Insert the code segment of Listing 15.5 here>>
getContent = strBody ' Line 2
End Function  'Line 3
```

Finally, we copy the VBScript code shown in Listing 15.5 and paste it in between lines 1 and 2. Then we save the settings, and we are done with the second version of the Employee Locator Web Part.

EMPLOYEE LOCATOR WEB PART (VERSION 3)

In the first version of the Employee Locator Web Part, you saw how we can retrieve data from a SQL Server database, save it in an offline form in an XML file, and transform it into an HTML format using an XSL file.

In the second version, we used the same approach for representing employee information, but with real-time access to the SQL Server database using an ADO stream object.

Both versions showed how the data is separated from the interface, which makes the code much easier to follow and more reusable. As you saw in the second version, we changed the logic of data retrieval without changing the XSL file that is responsible for reformatting XML into HTML. In spite of the separation of data and the interface, both versions use a two-tier model. However perfect this approach might be for these examples, it would be difficult to manage if we had a more complex set of business rules. Business rules are usually dynamic. For example, we may want to show only employee information based on specific criteria.

In the third version, we extend the concept of code reusability by applying a three-tiered model and use of components. In this version, we add a middle tier that can host business rules.

Now let's look at a logical diagram of a three-tier model.

Figure 15.11
A logical diagram of a three-tier model.

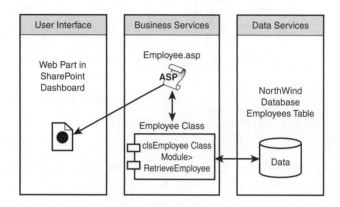

As you can see in Figure 15.11, there are three tiers, layers, or services. The first layer is the user interface that will be shown in the Web Part as HTML. The second tier is where business logic resides, and is called the business layer; in this layer, the Employee3.vbs file communicates with the VB component (clsEmployee class) by passing required parameters. The VB component connects to the database and retrieves data from the employee database, located in the third tier, the data tier.

In Employee Locator Web Part 3, we move the logic of data retrieval into a data component and we call it clsEmployee.

LISTING 15.6   A CODE SEGMENT THAT WILL BE MOVED TO THE EMPLOYEE CLASS

```
strSQL = " select EmployeeID, LastName, FirstName, HomePhone, email from
➥Employees "
set rs = CreateObject ("ADODB.RECORDSET")
rs.CursorLocation = adUseClient
rs.Open strSQL, strConnection, adOpenKeyset, adLockOptimistic
set oStream = CreateObject ("ADODB.STREAM")
rs.Save oStream, adPersistXML
strRst = oStream.ReadText(adReadAll)
```

Let's go through each step in detail and look at the code. I will explain what happens in each part.

CREATING THE VB COMPONENT

To create the VB component, we use Visual Basic 6 to create a new ActiveX DLL project. Then we create a new class (clsEmployee) with a public method (RetrieveEmployee) .

LISTING 15.7   THE RETRIEVEEMPLOYEE FUNCTION THAT CAPTURES EMPLOYEE TABLE DATA INTO A STREAM OBJECT

```
Public Function RetrieveEmployee(ByVal strConnection As String) As String
    Dim strSQL As String
    Dim oConn As New ADODB.Connection
    Dim rs As New ADODB.Recordset
    Dim oStream As New ADODB.Stream

    strSQL = " select EmployeeID, LastName, FirstName, HomePhone, email from
➥Employees "
    rs.CursorLocation = adUseClient
    rs.Open strSQL, strConnection, adOpenKeyset, adLockOptimistic
    rs.Save oStream, adPersistXML
    RetrieveEmployee = oStream.ReadText(adReadAll)
End Function
```

Finally, we create the employee.dll file by selecting **File** from the top menu bar and then clicking on **Make employee.dll**. We have finished the VB component.

Now we can create an Active Server page or a VBScript file to call the VB component. In this example, we modify the VBScript code that we used for Employee Locator 2, and replace the code segment for data retrieval with the Employee component. The final code is shown in Listing 15.8.

LISTING 15.8   THE VBSCRIPT CODE THAT GENERATES EMPLOYEE TABLE DATA INTO AN XML DOMDOCUMENT OBJECT AND APPLIES XSL FOR TRANSFORMATION INTO HTML

```
Option Explicit

Dim strConnection
Dim oEmployee
Dim strRst
Dim xmlBody
Dim displayweb
Dim strBody

strConnection = "Provider=SQLOLEDB;Data Source=dianatr;Initial
➥Catalog=NorthWind;User Id=sa;Password=;Connect Timeout=30;"
Set oEmployee = CreateObject("Employee.clsEmployee")
strRst = oEmployee.RetrieveEmployee (strConnection)

Set xmlBody = CreateObject("MSXML2.domdocument")
xmlBody.async = False
xmlBody.LoadXML strRst
Set displayWeb = CreateObject("MSXML2.domdocument")
displayWeb.async = False
displayWeb.Load "e:\projects\SPSbook\employee1.xsl"
strBody = xmlBody.transformNode(displayWeb)
```

To make the third version of the Employee Locator Web Part, we follow the same steps for creating the Employee Locator 2 Web Part. We select VBScript for **Content Type**, and insert the previous code in the **Embedded Content** text area box, in the **Advanced Settings** section of **New Part – Settings**.

ACTIVE DIRECTORY LOOKUP WEB PART

The purpose of this Web Part is to present users' information from Active Directory through your SharePoint dashboard. This example demonstrates how you can connect and retrieve data stored in an active directory. Figure 15.12 shows the final form of the Active Directory Lookup Web Part in the SharePoint Server interface.

Figure 15.12
Active Directory
Lookup Web Part.

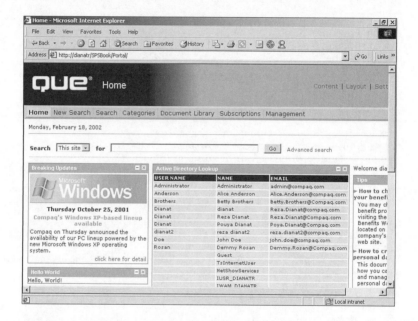

This Web Part basically follows the same concepts that I described for creating the Employee Locator Web Part. The only difference is that we are getting users' data from the Active Directory.

ACTIVE DIRECTORY CONNECTION

In the Employee Locator Web Part, we used the strConnection variable to connect to the SQL Server database. This variable provided required information such as OLEDB provider, name of the SQL Server, database name, and user credentials for accessing the database. To connect to the Windows 2000 Active Directory, we need similar information. In this case, the name of the Active Directory domain is required so we can connect to the Active Directory. The name of the domain controller is a variable that can be changed for different environments, so I pass the Active Directory connection information as a parameter. In this example, my domain controller is `dianatr.cop.cpqcorp.net` and I pass this as `strConnection` to a VB component.

```
strConnection = "dianatr.cop.cpqcorp.net"
```

CREATING VB COMPONENTS

For the Active Directory Lookup Web Part, I can use the same VBScript code used for the third version of Employee Locator, and just change the `strConnection` information (Listing 15.9).

LISTING 15.9   THE VBSCRIPT CODE FOR THE ACTIVE DIRECTORY LOOKUP WEB PART

```
Option Explicit
Dim strConnection
Dim oEmployee
Dim strRst
Dim xmlBody
Dim displayweb
Dim strBody

strConnection = "dianatr.cop.cpqcorp.net"
Set oEmployee = CreateObject("EmployeeAD.clsEmployeeAD")
strRst = oEmployee.RetrieveEmployeeAD(strConnection)

Set xmlBody = CreateObject("MSXML2.domdocument")
xmlBody.async = False
xmlBody.LoadXML strRst
Set displayWeb = CreateObject("MSXML2.domdocument")
displayWeb.async = False
displayWeb.Load
➥"E:\Projects\SharePointBook\Chapter 15\submitted-v1\employeeAD.xsl"
strBody = xmlBody.transformNode(displayWeb)
```

As shown in the previous listing, I have used the `EmployeeAD` component, which has a `RetrieveEmployeeAD` method for collecting the user information and returning it as an XML string. Listing 15.10 shows the `RetrieveEmployeeAD` public function.

LISTING 15.10   THE CODE FOR RETRIEVEEMPLOYEEAD, USING ACTIVE DIRECTORY PROVIDER TO CONNECT TO ACTIVE DIRECTORY

```
Public Function RetrieveEmployeeAD (ByVal strConnection As String) As String
    Dim strSQL As String
    Dim oConn As New ADODB.Connection
    Dim rs As New ADODB.Recordset
    Dim oStream As New ADODB.Stream
    Dim mdsPath As String

    'this is the ADSI-OLEDB provider name
    oConn.Provider = "ADsDSOObject"
```

```
    oConn.Open "Active Directory Provider"

    mdsPath = "'LDAP://" & strConnection & "'"
    strSQL = "select  mail, name, givenName, sn from " & mdsPath & " where
➥objectCategory='person' AND objectClass='user' order by sn asc "

    With rs
        .ActiveConnection = oConn
        .CursorLocation = adUseClient
        .CursorType = adOpenStatic
        .LockType = adLockBatchOptimistic
        .Source = strSQL
        .Open
        .ActiveConnection = Nothing
    End With

    rs.Save oStream, adPersistXML
    RetrieveEmployeeAD = oStream.ReadText(adReadAll)
    Set rs = Nothing
    Set oConn = Nothing
End Function
```

To create this component, we need to follow the same steps that were mentioned for creating the Employee component in the third version of the Employee Locator; the final product would be EmployeeAD.dll.

ACTIVE DIRECTORY LOOKUP XSL FILE

The XML data string returned from the EmployeeAD component has the same structure as the one used in the Employee Locator. The only difference is the name of data attributes, so we need to make some minor changes in the XSL file used for the Employee Locator. For this example, we have retrieved the UserID that is used for logging in to the domain, as well as the user's name and email address. Listing 15.11 shows the XSL file used for the Active Directory Lookup Web Part.

LISTING 15.11   THE XSL CODE FOR TRANSFORMING EMPLOYEE DATA FROM XML TO HTML
FORMAT

```
<?xml version="1.0"?>
<xsl:stylesheet xmlns:xsl="http://www.w3.org/TR/WD-xsl">
  <xsl:template match="/">
    <HTML>
      <BODY>
        <TABLE width="420">
          <tr bgcolor="Black">
            <td width="130"><font face="Verdana" size="1" color="white">
➥<b>USER NAME</b></font></td>
            <td width="110"><font face="Verdana" size="1" color="white">
➥<b>NAME</b></font></td>
            <td width="150"><font face="Verdana" size="1" color="white">
```

continues

LISTING 15.11   CONTINUED

```
➥<b>EMAIL</b></font></td>
        </tr>
    <xsl:for-each select="xml/rs:data/z:row">
    <TR bgcolor="#ffdead">
     <TD><font face="Verdana" size="1" color="black"><xsl:value-of
➥select="@sn"/></font></TD>
        <TD><font face="Verdana" size="1" color="black"><xsl:value-of
➥select="@name"/></font></TD>
        <TD><font face="Verdana" size="1" color="black"><xsl:value-of
➥select="@mail"/></font></TD>
    </TR>
    </xsl:for-each>
        </TABLE>
       </BODY>
      </HTML>
   </xsl:template>
</xsl:stylesheet>
```

To make the Active Directory Lookup Web Part, we follow the same steps used for creating the Employee Locator 2 and 3 Web Parts. We select VBScript for **Content Type**, and insert the code shown in Listing 15.10 in the **Embedded Content** text area box, located in the **Advanced Settings** section of **New Part – Settings**.

SUMMARY

SharePoint Portal Server provides a flexible environment for integration. In this chapter, we used HTML, ASP, VBScript, ADO, COM, XML, and XSL to access different storage systems. We showed how you can access relational databases and Active Directory hierarchical object-oriented databases to retrieve information. You might already have developed similar code and programs. Or maybe you have already invested in a mentioned skill set that you can now easily upgrade, and create your own Web Parts without starting from scratch and having to learn a totally new development tool.

CHAPTER 16

USING WEBDAV PROTOCOL TO CREATE WEB PARTS

In this chapter *by Reza Dianat*

16

WEB STORAGE SYSTEM

In Chapter 15, we saw how to access different storage systems, such as relational databases and Active Directory. We were able to query and retrieve information from SQL Server and Windows 2000 Active Directory in XML format. In this chapter, we want to explore the Web Storage System (WSS), which is the underlying storage mechanism in SharePoint Portal Server and Exchange 2000.

WSS is a hierarchical database that stores objects and has a schema that can be extended for different types of objects. Each item has a default schema that represents the properties and values of stored items. In the next section, we will introduce a tool that can be used for exploring these items. One of the most important benefits of WSS is that all items stored in the WSS are URL addressable. In the traditional Web systems, an end user or a subject matter expert with no knowledge of Web development had to go through many hurdles to publish a document on the Web. Using SharePoint eliminates these hurdles, and people who don't know about Web development can publish documents to the Web as easily as saving a file in a file system. WSS also is one of the few products that is implemented based on the WebDAV protocol, and takes advantages of HTTP 1.1 extensions, which will be discussed in more detail later in this chapter.

EXCHANGE EXPLORER

For different types of storage systems, there is a tool that allows you to visually explore their content. For example, you use Windows Explorer to view the content of the file system; you can use relational database management system tools to explore the tables and rows in the database. For exploring the content of WSS, there is a tool called Exchange Explorer, which previously was called Web Storage System Explorer. Exchange Explorer is one of the tools in Exchange SDK that you can download from the Microsoft Web site.

> **NOTE**
>
> For download and instructions for installation of the Exchange SDK, go to `http://www.msdn.microsoft.com/` and search for the "ExchangeSDKTools"; then follow the online instructions for the installation. The Web Storage System SDK comes with tools that can be used for both Exchange 2000 Server and SharePoint Portal Server Web storage systems, or you can download the Exchange SDK using the following URL:
>
> `http://msdn.microsoft.com/downloads/default.asp?url=/downloads/`
> `sample.asp?url=/msdn-files/027/001/833/msdncompositedoc.xml`

After the Exchange SDK is installed, you can access it through Start, Programs, Exchange SDK, Exchange SDK Development Tools, Exchange Explorer. Selecting Exchange Explorer will bring up an Authorization dialog box, as shown in Figure 16.1.

To access the WSS, we need to provide our credentials and the URL of the WSS public folder (such as `http://<ServerName>/public`).

Figure 16.1
To access the Web Storage System, you need to enter your credentials.

Figure 16.2 shows the Exchange/WSS Explorer with two panes. In the left pane there is a tree view of the WSS system, which shows the WSS hierarchy; each of these nodes is represented in the form of a folder in the Web folder interface. In the left pane tree view, there are two top-level folders called Applications and Workspaces. Under the Applications folder, we can define our own custom applications and their schemas. The Workspaces folder is kind of a system-managed folder, but we can explore and further customize its items, either through the Exchange (WSS) Explorer or programmatically using the ADO, OLE DB, and PKMCDO components.

The right pane shows the detail view, divided into upper and lower windows, and provides different views of selected items from the tree view in the left pane.

Figure 16.2
The content of the Web Storage System.

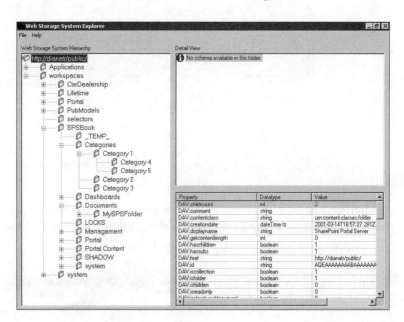

CAUTION

When working with items in the Workspaces folder, you should be very cautious and know exactly what you are doing; incorrect manipulation of items can corrupt and damage your SharePoint Portal interface. Before working with this tool, make sure you have a reliable WSS backup.

To see an item, click on a folder in the left pane, and the right pane of the WSS Explorer will show a list of items in that folder. Figure 16.3 shows that under the SPSBook workspace/Documents/MySPSFolder/, there are two items called CapacityPlanning.doc and Clustering Strategy.doc.

If you double-click on one of these documents, you can see the properties and values assigned to the document in the lower right pane of WSS Explorer window.

Figure 16.3
Shows the properties and values assigned to Clustering Strategy.doc.

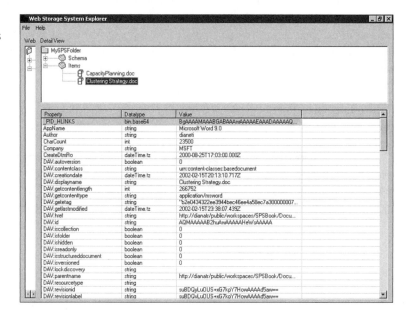

Clustering Strategy.doc is considered to be one object that has many properties, and each property has a data type and value that further identify the item. Table 16.2 shows some of the properties, data types, and values of this item.

TABLE 16.1   SOME OF THE PROPERTIES OF CLUSTERING STRATEGY WORD DOCUMENT

Property	Datatype	Value
AppName	string	Microsoft Word 9.0
Author	string	Dianeti
CharCount	int	23500

Property	Datatype	Value
Company	string	MSFT
DAV:autoversion	Boolean	0
DAV:contentclass	string	urn:content-Classes:basedocument
DAV:creationdate	dateTime.tz	2002-02-15T20:13:10.717Z
DAV:displayname	string	Clustering Strategy.doc
DAV:getlastmodified	dateTime.tz	2002-02-15T23:38:07.439Z

This is just a sample of properties, and there are more properties defined for this item. Although this document is considered an unstructured type, WSS provides some structure for it through this schema and definition of properties and values. These properties and values would help us to identify, search, locate, and sort documents more easily.

WEBDAV PROTOCOL

In the previous two sections, we introduced the basics of the WSS and a tool that we can use to visually browse, navigate, create, and modify the properties of the items stored in WSS. However, for this purpose we're required to install a client application—WSS Explorer—to access the WSS. In this section, we are going to introduce a powerful and robust protocol called Web Distributed Authoring and Versioning (WebDAV) that allows us to modify the contents and their properties over the Web.

WebDAV is an extension to the HTTP1.1 protocol that is accepted as W3C standard and is developed by the Internet Engineering Task Force (IETF), Microsoft, IBM, Novell, Netscape, and other parties to allow authoring and collaboration on the Web. The same way that HTTP changed the face of Internet, WebDAV will create a new milestone on improving the way that we use the Internet. Right now, IIS 5.0, Netscape, Apache, and most major Web servers support WebDAV, and companies are introducing more products that are WebDAV-compliant.

NOTE

In February 1998, IETF's Network Working Group introduced "Requirements for a Distributed Authoring and Versioning Protocol for the World Wide Web" in RFC 2291. After one year of hard work, the committee published "HTTP Extensions for Distributed Authoring—WEBDAV" in RFC 2518. For more information, you may refer to these RFCs.
```
http://ietf.org/rfc/rfc2291.txt?number=2291
http://ietf.org/rfc/rfc2291.txt?number=2518
```

The WebDAV protocol enhanced some of the HTTP1.1 methods and introduced some new methods (Verbs) that allow distributed authoring, collaboration, and search on Web content. Some of the major enhancements have been possible through the following features of WebDAV protocol.

Managing Name Spaces

Like the Universal Resource Locators (URL) that uniquely identify resources on the Web, the concept of Universal Resource Identifier (URI) and Universal Resource Name (URN) provides a mechanism that we can use to uniquely define, identify, and address a specific resource or content on the Web and not have to worry about the collision or conflict of names. For example, a property or field named Name can refer to the name of a person, location, movie, or product. To identify which Name we are referring to requires a context or a Name Space. The name spaces usually look like a URL, such as http://www.compaq.com/product, and the reason behind this widely used syntax is because the URLs are already guaranteed and managed to be unique, or in some cases you will see a Universal Unique Identifier (UUID) as an identifier for name spaces. The following are example of URNs:

```
xmlns:a="DAV:"
xmlns:b="urn:uuid:c2f41010-65b3-11d1-a29f-00aa00c14882/"
xmlns:c="xml:"
xmlns:d="urn:schemas-microsoft-com:office:office"
```

Notice that each name space starts with the xmlns prefix and a prefix such as a, b, c, or d. This a shorthand for expressing the long name spaces, to make them more readable and easier to type, and also reduces that amount of data that needs to be transmitted over wire. The following are examples of addressing each property in a specific name space:

```
<a:response>
<a:href>
<a:displayname>
<a:getlastmodified b:dt="dateTime.tz">
<d:author>
<d:title>
```

New Methods

WebDAV also extends the HTTP1.1 protocol by introducing new methods such as

- *PropFind*, which can be used for retrieval of content based on the properties of the content.

- *PropPatch*, which can be used for setting or removing properties of the content.

- *Mkcol*, which can be used to create collections such as Web folders.

- *Copy / Move*, which can be used for copying and moving a single unit of content or a collection from a source to a destination.

- *Lock / Unlock*, which can be used to protect "lost updates" and provide a mechanism for collaboration.

Later in this chapter, we will see sample code to show how these methods can be used.

WebDAV and XML

In HTTP, the main mechanism for passing parameters and data to a server was through query strings, or using POST with the form data. Using XML extends this capability by allowing the requests to be sent in XML format, and also increases the capability of the server for sending responses using XML. XML is a flexible and extensible markup language that empowers WebDAV for multi-processing, managing collections, representing hierarchical data, and addressing the properties within name spaces, features that were not possible in HTTP1.1. Built-in support for multiple character set encodings in XML extends and simplifies the internationalization capabilities of HTTP. XML also is known and accepted as an industry standard for interoperability and communication with different platforms, which makes XML an excellent fit for WebDAV, which was primarily designed for authoring in a distributed environment.

16

New HTTP Headers

Another of WebDAV's enhancements to HTTP1.1 is the introduction of new keywords in the request header, and some of them are as follows:

- *DAV Header*, which indicates that the head resource supports WebDAV protocol. If the request header has a DAV header, it means that the resource supports the WebDAV schema and protocol.

- *Depth Header*, which indicates the level of hierarchy through one of three parameters:

  "0" mean the resource itself.

  "1" means the resource and its immediate children.

  "infinity" means the entire tree, which is also the default if we don't use the depth header keyword.

- *Destination Header*, which must be indicated whenever we are using methods that require a destination, such as move or copy.

- *Overwrite Header*, which can take the value "F" to prevent overwriting the destination if it has the same name as the resource in a COPY or MOVE method, or "T" for overwriting, which is default value if it is not included in the header.

New Status Code

HTTP has five general status code categories that are returned by the server in response to the client's request. The first digit of the status code defines the class of response. The last two digits do not have any categorization role. These five categories are as follows (see RFC 2616):

Informational 1xx—The request is received and processing.

Successful 2xx —The action is received, understood, and accepted.

Redirection 3xx —To complete the request, further action is required.

Client Error 4xx —The request has bad syntax or cannot be fulfilled.

Server Error 5xx —Server has failed to respond to the request.

WebDAV protocol has introduced some new status codes, such as

- *102 Processing*—indicates that the server has received the request and is processing it.
- *207 Multi-Status* —unlike HTTP1.1, which could only return one status code, WebDAV can have multiple statuses for a request returned in a single XML format.
- *423 Locked* —indicates that the source or destination is locked.
- *424 Failed Dependency* —in a series of actions on a resource, one action failed because of its dependency on a prior action that previously failed.

This is WebDAV in a nutshell, and by now we should have a big picture of the capabilities of this protocol. In the next sections, we will present sample code that shows some of these methods, and what you need to take advantage of this powerful protocol.

MKCOL SAMPLE CODE

Now we are going to recapture some of the WebDAV protocol through examples. Through the Mkcol sample code, we are going to see how WebDAV provides capabilities for

- Creating collections
- Allowing multi-processing
- Benefitting from XML
- Returning multiple statuses in a response

NOTE | Please spend time reading this sample carefully, because it will save you time in understanding the other sample programs, which are very similar to this.

In this example, we use VBScript to

- Create a Web folder called SPSBOOK as a subfolder of the Documents folder of SPS.
- Use XML to send additional requests for setting the COMMENT property of the newly created SPSBOOK folder to "This is my SPSBOOK folder created by the mkcol method".
- Get the response back in XML format and save it to file.

Listing 16.1 shows the request header and the request body that will be sent to the host named dianatr. MKCOL is a WebDAV method for creating collections (in our example, SPSBOOK) and after SPSBOOK is created, we want additional processes from the server for setting the comment property of the folder to "This is my SPSBOOK folder".

LISTING 16.1   HOW TO USE MKCOL WEBDAV METHOD AS PART OF THE REQUEST HEADER AND SET ADDITIONAL PROPERTIES THROUGH THE BODY SECTION

```
MKCOL /spsbook/documents/SPSBOOK/ HTTP/1.1
Host: dianatr
Content-Type: text/xml
Content-Length: XXX

<?xml version="1.0"?>
<D:propertyupdate xmlns:D="DAV:" >
    <D:set>
        <D:prop>
            <D:comment>This is my SPSBOOK folder</D:comment>
        </D:prop>
    </D:set>
</D:propertyupdate>
```

We create an xmlhttp COM object and define MKCOL in the request, as shown here:

```
Set DAVRequest = CreateObject("MSXML2.xmlhttp")
DAVRequest.open "MKCOL", strURL, False, strUser, strPassword
```

Then we create a string that has XML as part of the request body. This XML sets the comment property of the SPSBOOK folder:

```
strXMLRequest = "" + _
 "<?xml version='1.0'?>" + _
 "<D:propertyupdate xmlns:D='DAV:'>" + _
    "<D:set>" + _
        "<D:prop>" + _
            "<D:comment>This is my SPSBOOK folder</D:comment>" + _
        "</D:prop>" + _
    "</D:set>" + _
 "</D:propertyupdate>"
```

We also need to indicate the content type as text/xml, which can be set up through the setRequestHeader method:

```
DAVRequest.setRequestHeader "Content-Type", "text/xml"
```

Finally we send the request along with the XML string

```
DAVRequest.send strXMLRequest
```

We get the response in XML format. I have created a DOMDOCUMENT object to load the XML response into, and save it to the mkcol.xml file for the purpose of the presentation.

```
Set xmlResponse = CreateObject("MSXML2.domdocument")
xmlResponse.async = False
xmlResponse.load DAVRequest.responseXML
xmlResponse.save "mkcol.xml"
```

The content of the response in the mkcol.xml file is shown in Listing 16.2.

16

LISTING 16.2 THE RESPONSE SENT IN XML FORMAT FROM THE WEB SERVER FOR THE MKCOL REQUEST

```
<?xml version="1.0"?>
<a:multistatus mlns:a="DAV:">
<a:response>
<a:href>http://dianatr/spsbook/Documents/SPSBOOK</a:href>
<a:status>HTTP/1.1 201 Created</a:status>
<a:propstat>
<a:status>HTTP/1.1 200 OK</a:status>
<a:prop>
<a:comment/>
</a:prop>
</a:propstat>
</a:response>
```

For this request, you will receive status code 207, which indicates that the response carries status codes for multiple processes. The first action was creating the SPSBOOK folder, and the status code for this action is 201, which means the SPSBOOK folder was created successfully. The second process was setting the comment property of the folder, and the status code of this process is 200, which means the property was set correctly.

Listing 16.3 shows the complete VBScript code. You can execute this code from the command line by running this command:

```
CSCRIPT mkcol.vbs
```

The output file mkcol.xml will be created in the same folder where you ran the cscript command.

LISTING 16.3 THE COMPLETE VBSCRIPT CODE FOR CREATING A COLLECTION USING MKCOL METHOD, AND AT THE SAME TIME SET SOME PROPERTIES FOR THE COLLECTION

```
Dim strServer
Dim strWorkspace
Dim strFolder
Dim strURL
Dim strUser
Dim strPassword
Dim DAVRequest
Dim strXMLRequest

strServer = "dianatr"
strWorkspace = "spsbook"
strFolder = "SPSBOOK"
strUser = "dianatr0\spsuser"
strPassword = "spspw"


strURL = "http://" + strServer + "/" + strWorkspace + "/DOCUMENTS/SPSBOOK"
strURL = Replace(strURL, " ", "%20")

strXMLRequest = "" + _
  "<?xml version='1.0'?>" + _
```

```
    "<D:propertyupdate xmlns:D='DAV:'>" + _
        "<D:set>" + _
            "<D:prop>" + _
                "<D:comment>This is my SPSBOOK folder</D:comment>" + _
            "</D:prop>" + _
        "</D:set>" + _
    "</D:propertyupdate>"

Set DAVRequest = CreateObject("MSXML2.xmlhttp")
DAVRequest.open "MKCOL", strURL, False, strUser, strPassword
DAVRequest.setRequestHeader "Content-Type", "text/xml"
DAVRequest.send strXMLRequest

Set xmlResponse = CreateObject("MSXML2.domdocument")
xmlResponse.async = False
xmlResponse.load DAVRequest.responseXML
xmlResponse.save "mkcol.xml"
```

16

PROPPATCH SAMPLE CODE

In this example, we will see how we can create and set the properties of a Word document using the PROPPATCH method.

The name of the document is promotoc4.doc, and it is located in the /DOCUMENT/MARKETING/APRIL/ folder.

We want to change the DAV:owner property and create new properties such as Author, Company, and Title. The last three properties are the properties of an MS Word document, so we should refer to the URN as `xmlns:o='urn:schemas-microsoft-com:office:office'` and use the o: prefix in front of these properties to identify them correctly.

The strURL variable needs to point to the resource as

```
strURL = "http://" + strServer + "/" + strWorkspace +
➥"/DOCUMENTS/MARKETING/APRIL/promotoc4.doc"
```

The XML string needs to be modified to

```
strXMLRequest = "" + _
"<?xml version='1.0'?>" + _
 "<D:propertyupdate xmlns:D='DAV:' xmlns:o='urn:schemas-microsoft-
➥com:office:office'>" + _
    "<D:set>" + _
        "<D:prop>" + _
            "<D:owner>Reza Dianat</D:owner>" + _
            "<o:Author>Reza Dianat</o:Author>" + _
            "<o:company>COMPAQ</o:company>" + _
            "<o:title>Promotion</o:title>" + _
        "</D:prop>" + _
    "</D:set>" + _
 "</D:propertyupdate>"
```

We also need to identify the PROPPATCH method in the request header:

```
DAVRequest.open "PROPPATCH", strURL, False, strUser, strPassword
```

LISTING 16.4   THE PROPPATCH REQUEST

```
PROPPATCH /spsbook/documents/marketing/april/promotco4.doc HTTP/1.1
Host: dianatr
Content-Type: text/xml
Content-Length: XXX

<?xml version='1.0'?>
 <D:propertyupdate xmlns:D='DAV:' xmlns:o='urn:schemas-microsoft-
➥com:office:office'>
     <D:set>
      <D:prop>
             <D:owner>Reza Dianat</D:owner>
             <o:Author>Reza Dianat</o:Author>
             <o:company>COMPAQ</o:company>
             <o:title>Promotion</o:title>
          </D:prop>
     </D:set>
 </D:propertyupdate>
```

Listing 16.5 shows the XML response that is saved in the proppatch.xml file. Status code 200 means all the properties were updated successfully.

LISTING 16.5   THE WEB SERVER RESPONSE TO THE PROPPATCH REQUEST

```
<?xml version="1.0" ?>
<a:multistatus xmlns:b="urn:schemas-microsoft-com:office:office" xmlns:a="DAV:">
<a:response>
<a:href>http://dianatr/spsbook/Documents/Marketing/April/promotoc4.doc</a:href>
<a:propstat>
<a:status>HTTP/1.1 200 OK</a:status>
<a:prop>
<a:owner />
<b:Author />
<b:company />
<b:title />
</a:prop>
</a:propstat>
</a:response>
</a:multistatus>
```

LISTING 16.6   THE COMPLETE VBSCRIPT CODE FOR THE PROPPTACH METHOD

```
Dim strPassword
Dim DAVRequest
Dim strXMLRequest

strServer = "dianatr"
strWorkspace = "spsbook"
strUser = "dianatr0\spsuser"
strPassword = "spspw"

strURL = "http://" + strServer + "/" + strWorkspace +
➥"/DOCUMENTS/MARKETING/APRIL/promotoc4.doc"
```

```
strURL = Replace(strURL, " ", "%20")

strXMLRequest = "" + _
"<?xml version='1.0'?>" + _
"<D:propertyupdate xmlns:D='DAV:' xmlns:o='urn:schemas-microsoft-
➥com:office:office'>" + _
    "<D:set>" + _
     "<D:prop>" + _
            "<D:owner>Reza Dianat</D:owner>" + _
            "<o:Author>Reza Dianat</o:Author>" + _
            "<o:company>COMPAQ</o:company>" + _
            "<o:title>Promotion</o:title>" + _
        "</D:prop>" + _
    "</D:set>" + _
"</D:propertyupdate>"

Set DAVRequest = CreateObject("MSXML2.xmlhttp")
DAVRequest.open "PROPPATCH", strURL, False, strUser, strPassword
DAVRequest.setRequestHeader "Content-Type", "text/xml"
DAVRequest.send strXMLRequest

Set xmlBody = CreateObject("MSXML2.domdocument")
xmlBody.async = False
xmlBody.load DAVRequest.responseXML
xmlBody.save "proppatch.xml"
```

PROPFIND Sample Code

In this example, we will use the PROPFIND WebDAV method to retrieve the properties of the promotoc4.doc MS Word document, located in the /DOCUMENTS/MARKETING/APRIL/ folder. We set these properties (owner, author, company, and title) in the previous example by using the PROPPATCH method.

In this example, the source identified by strURL will be the same as the source defined in the PROPPATCH sample as

```
strURL = "http://" + strServer + "/" + strWorkspace +
➥"/DOCUMENTS/MARKETING/APRIL/promotoc4.doc"
```

The XML string will change as follows:

```
strXMLRequest = "" + _
"<?xml version='1.0'?>" + _
 "<D:propfind xmlns:D='DAV:' xmlns:o='urn:schemas-microsoft-
➥com:office:office'>" + _
    "<D:prop>" + _
            "<D:owner/>" + _
            "<o:Author/>" + _
            "<o:company/>" + _
            "<o:title/>" + _
        "</D:prop>" + _
 "</D:propfind>"
```

The method in the request header needs to be changed to PROPFIND:

```
DAVRequest.open "PROPFIND", strURL, False, strUser, strPassword
```

16

LISTING 16.7   THE PROPFIND REQUEST

```
PROPFIND /spsbook/documents/marketing/april/promotco4.doc HTTP/1.1
Host: dianatr
Content-Type: text/xml
Content-Length: XXX


<?xml version='1.0'?>
 <D:propfind xmlns:D='DAV:' xmlns:o='urn:schemas-microsoft-
➥com:office:office'>
      <D:prop>
            <D:owner/>
            <o:Author/>
            <o:company/>
            <o:title/>
      </D:prop>
</D:propfind>
```

The XML response is shown in Listing 16.8.

LISTING 16.8   THE WEB SERVER RESPONSE TO THE PROPFIND METHOD AND THE LIST OF
PROPERTIES REQUESTED IN OUR XML REQUEST BODY

```
<?xml version="1.0" ?>
<a:multistatus xmlns:b="urn:uuid:c2f41010-65b3-11d1-a29f-00aa00c14882/"
➥xmlns:c="xml:" xmlns:d="urn:schemas-microsoft-com:office:office" xmlns:a="DAV:">

<a:response>
<a:href>http://dianatr/spsbook/Documents/Marketing/April/promotoc4.doc</a:href>
<a:propstat>
<a:status>HTTP/1.1 200 OK</a:status>
<a:prop>
<a:owner>Reza Dianat</a:owner>
<d:Author>Reza Dianat</d:Author>
<d:company>COMPAQ</d:company>
<d:title>Promotion</d:title>
</a:prop>
</a:propstat>
</a:response>
</a:multistatus>
```

MOVE AND COPY SAMPLE CODE

In this sample, we will introduce two more settings in the request header, Destination and
Overwrite. We need the destination and source to be able to copy or move resources.

We also need to define what should be done if we have a resource with the same name. The
default action will be overwrite, and we can change the default by indicating "F" for the
overwrite value.

Listing 16.9 shows the sample code for copying the SPSLOCK.doc document from the /documents/marketing/ folder to /portal Content/resources/:

LISTING 16.9   THE SAMPLE VBSCRIPT CODE FOR THE COPY METHOD OF WEBDAV PROTOCOL

```
Dim strServer
Dim strWorkspace
Dim strFolder
Dim strURL
Dim strUser
Dim strPassword
Dim DAVRequest

strServer = "dianatr"
strWorkspace = "spsbook"
strUser = "dianatr0\spsuser"
strPassword = "spspw"

strURL = "http://" + strServer + "/" + strWorkspace +
➥"/DOCUMENTS/MARKETING/SPSLOCK.doc"
strURL = Replace(strURL, " ", "%20")

strURLDest = "http://" + strServer + "/" + strWorkspace + "/portal
➥content/resources/SPSLOCK.doc "
strURLDest = Replace(strURLDest, " ", "%20")

Set DAVRequest = CreateObject("MSXML2.xmlhttp")

DAVRequest.open "COPY", strURL, False, strUser, strPassword
DAVRequest.setRequestHeader "Content-Type", "text/xml"
DAVRequest.setRequestHeader "Destination:", StrURLDest
DAVRequest.setRequestHeader "Overwrite", "T"

DAVRequest.send
```

The MOVE method provides a combination of deleting the source resources and copying the resource to a destination, and returns status code 201, which means the collection was successfully created or the resource was successfully moved.

LOCK SAMPLE CODE

As mentioned earlier, the WebDAV LOCK method provides a mechanism for avoiding *lost updates*. Right now, only basic exclusive lock is supported, which means that updates to resources will be serialized. When a person issues a lock on a resource, he will be able to access and update the locked resource. With the LOCK method specified in the request header, we need to provide more information about the lock in the body of the request in XML form. Sample code provided in Listing 16.10 shows complete VBScript code for issuing a lock, and Listing 16.11 shows the response returned from the server.

16

LISTING 16.10 THE SAMPLE CODE FOR LOCK METHOD OF WEBDAV PROTOCOL

```
Dim strServer
Dim strWorkspace
Dim strFolder
Dim strURL
Dim strUser
Dim strPassword
Dim DAVRequest
Dim strXMLRequest

strServer = "dianatr"
strWorkspace = "spsbook"
strUser = "dianatr0\spsuser"
strPassword = "spspw"


strURL = "http://" + strServer + "/" + strWorkspace + "/Portal
➥Content/tips/SPSLOCK.doc"
strURL = Replace(strURL, " ", "%20")

strXMLRequest = "" + _
"<?xml version='1.0' ?>" + _
 "<a:lockinfo xmlns:a='DAV:'>" + _
     "<a:lockscope><a:exclusive /></a:lockscope>" + _
     "<a:locktype><a:write /></a:locktype>" + _
     "<a:owner>" + _
         "<a:href>http://dianatr</a:href>" + _
     "</a:owner>" + _
 "</a:lockinfo>"

set DAVRequest = CreateObject("MSXML2.xmlhttp")
DAVRequest.open "LOCK", strURL, False, strUser, strPassword
DAVRequest.setRequestHeader "Content-Type", "text/xml"
DAVRequest.send strXMLRequest

Set xmlBody = CreateObject("MSXML2.domdocument")
xmlBody.async = False
xmlBody.load DAVRequest.responseXML
xmlBody.save "lock.xml"
```

As you see in Listing 16.10, we have identified the lock type as write, and we have defined the owner property. When the source is locked, the DAV:lockdiscovery property of the resource will be updated to a string, with its value being a concatenation of the owner value with a system-generated lock token value. There are still problems with the locking standards on WebDAV, so IETF has decided to make it an optional feature, and WebDAV-compliant products might choose not to support the LOCK method at all. Some of these problems are

- How long we want to lock a resource for.
- What mechanism is in place for avoiding monopolization of a resource.

Right now, to refresh a lock or unlock a resource we should know the Lock-token value, such as 91939B1E-1C14-47D3-91F8-511C4BBBAB08:2228155915641552899, which is not very user friendly.

TIP

> A lock token is a universally unique identifier that the system will generate whenever it issues a LOCK successfully. This token will be returned as part of the response body, as shown in Listing 16.11.

16

LISTING 16.11   THE RESPONSE RETURNED FROM THE WEB SERVER FOR THE LOCK METHOD

```
<?xml version="1.0" ?>
<a:prop xmlns:a="DAV:">
<a:lockdiscovery>
<a:activelock>
<a:locktype>
<a:write />
</a:locktype>
<a:lockscope>
<a:exclusive />
</a:lockscope>
<a:owner xmlns:a="DAV:">
<a:href>http://dianatr</a:href>
</a:owner>
<a:locktoken>
<a:href>opaquelocktoken:
➥91939B1E-1C14-47D3-91F8-511C4BBBAB08:2228155915641552899</a:href>
</a:locktoken>
<a:depth>infinity</a:depth>
<a:timeout>Second-180</a:timeout>
</a:activelock>
</a:lockdiscovery>
</a:prop>
```

As you see in Listing 16.11, we can identify the time period when a resource needs to be locked. To manage this, we can assign a timeout value as part of the request header; otherwise the system will assign 180 seconds as the default value.

NOTE

> As a prefix to the token value, you also see opaquelocktoken, which uses the Universal Unique Identifier (UUID) mechanism, to guarantee uniqueness of the token all the time.

REFRESH THE LOCK

We can use if with the lock token value to refresh the lock.

```
DAVRequest.setRequestHeader "if",
➥"<http://dianatr/spsbook/Portal%20COntent/tips/SPSLOCK.doc>(<opaquelocktoken:
➥91939B1E-1C14-47D3-91F8-511C4BBBAB08:2372271103717408771>)"
```

UNLOCK A RESOURCE

To unlock a resource, we just need to know the Lock-Token value that the server generates when it issues a lock.

```
DAVRequest.setRequestHeader "Lock-Token",
➥"<opaquelocktoken:91939B1E-1C14-47D3-91F8-511C4BBBAB08:2444328697755336707>"
```

CUSTOMIZED DOCUMENTS FOLDER WEB PART

In this section, we are going to use the WebDAV PROPFIND method to create a Web Part from the content of the Documents folder in the Document Library dashboard. Figure 16.4 shows the final form of the Web Part.

Figure 16.4
Documents Folder
Web Part.

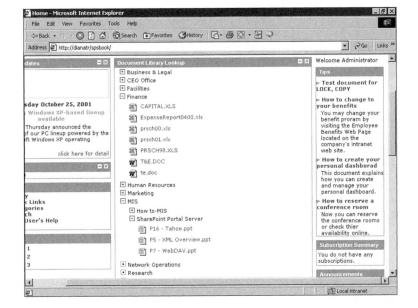

This Web Part retrieves all the subfolders and some properties of documents in the Documents folder of the SPSBook workspace, and applies different XSLT files to present them in a tree view format, as you see in Figure 16.4.

This Web part uses three small images, with +, -, or square icons in front of each item. You can click on + to expand or – to collapse a node in the tree, and a square sign represents nodes without children. At the leaves of the tree, you will see the display name of documents, which are in the form of hyperlinks. To see the document in your dashboard, you can click on the name of the document.

Using this Web Part, users will be able to navigate through lists of folders to locate and view the content without leaving the home dashboard.

Let's walk through the code and see what the major building blocks of this Web Part are.

USING PROPFIND TO QUERY THE /DOCUMENTS/ FOLDER

Along with the PROFIND that is identified in the request header is following line:

```
DAVRequest.open "PROPFIND", strURL, False, strUser, strPassword
```

We send the list of properties that we want to retrieve in the form of XML, as shown in Listing 16.12.

> **LISTING 16.12 THE BODY OF THE REQUEST THAT IS SENT TO THE WEB SERVER IN XML FORMAT**

```
<?xml version='1.0'?>
<D:propfind xmlns:D='DAV:' xmlns:o='urn:schemas-microsoft-com:office:office'>
    <D:prop>
        <D:displayname/>
        <D:href/>
        <D:getlastmodified/>
        <D:isfolder/>
        <D:iscollection/>
        <D:haschildren/>
        <D:uid/>
        <D:parentname/>
        <o:author/>
        <o:title/>
    </D:prop>
</D:propfind>
```

To retrieve all subfolders and documents up to the last leaf of the Document folder, we use the infinity value for the depth in the request header, and send the request.

```
DAVRequest.setRequestHeader "Depth", "infinity"
DAVRequest.send strXMLRequest
```

Then we create a DOMDOCUMENT object to store the response in the xmlBody object, as shown here:

```
Set xmlBody = CreateObject("MSXML2.domdocument")
xmlBody.async = False
xmlBody.load DAVRequest.responseXML
```

Now we have all the contents, and we just need to reformat them and present them.

USING XSLT TO TRANSFORM THE RESPONSE TO XML

For the purpose of simplification, I have used two different XSL files. The first XSL file does some cleaning, ordering, and adds some required elements for tracking parent/child relationships. The second XSL file uses these additional elements and converts the new XML document to an HTML format that is represented in the Web Part.

Let's look at some of the main elements of this XSL file (xslt41.xsl).

We create a new root for the new XML file as <content>, apply a template for all elements with status code 200 (OK), and sort all the elements based on their URL as defined in the href property. Listing 16.13 shows the code:

LISTING 16.13   THE CODE SEGMENT OF XSL TO FILTER ONLY THE RESPONSES THAT HAVE STATUS CODE 200 (OK)

```
<content>
<xsl:apply-templates
➥select="a:multistatus/a:response/a:propstat[a:status='HTTP/1.1 200 OK']">
<xsl:sort select="a:prop/a:href"/>
</xsl:apply-templates>
</content>
```

First of all, because we are trying to retrieve a wide range of properties, we will see `<a:status>HTTP/1.1 404 Resource Not Found</a:status>` in the returned initial XML document. The reason for 404 error codes arises from the fact that folders and documents in the WSS have different schemas and properties, so when we try to retrieve properties that are defined in the request body (Listing 16.12), those properties will not be found in WSS. Then through XSL, we can filter out those elements by the following code line in the XSL file:

```
select="a:multistatus/a:response/a:propstat[a:status='HTTP/1.1 200 OK']">
```

One additional element that we have included is `<filetype>`, which represents the type of document, based on their extensions (such as DOC, HTM, XLS).

```
<filetype>
  <xsl:variable name="filetype">
  <xsl:value-of select="a:displayname"/>
  </xsl:variable>
  <xsl:value-of select="substring-after ($filetype, '.')"/>
</filetype>
```

The other element that we added is the position of each element in the XML document, and this is accomplished through

```
<posit>
  <xsl:value-of select="user:folderh()"/>
</posit>
```

where `folderh()` is a user-defined function shown in the following code, and returns a sequential number for each element.

```
var ii = 0;
function folderh() {
    ii += 1;
    return (ii);
}
```

The other task of this XSL file is assigning a value for each element in the hierarchical XML document, so we can create the appropriate tree. This element is called `<level>`. For calculating the level of each element, I have used the `flevel` function, which accepts the parent name of the element, and determines the level of the specific folder or document based on number of "/" occurrences in the URL.

```
<level>
  <xsl:value-of select="user:flevel(concat(a:parentname,' '))"/>
```

```
    </level>

    function flevel(a) {
        var cnt = 0;
        var StrIndex = a.match(/\//g);
        cnt = StrIndex.length-4;
      return (cnt);
    }
```

REFORMATTING XML DOCUMENTS TO HTML FORMAT

The second XSL file has two main client-side JavaScript functions:

The addheading() function adds a dynamic HTML function to the client for managing expand and collapse of the nodes in the tree view. The second function is indentCategory(), which provides the appropriate indentation for each element in the tree. The amount of the indentation is determined based on the level and type of the element (folder or document).

> **NOTE**
>
> Based on the file type of documents, I have assigned an image file that represents the file type. For example, if a file is MS Word with the DOC extension, a Word icon will be shown. In each SPS workspace, there is a subfolder called DocTypeIcons, which is located in the hidden portal/resources folder. This subfolder has most images that are used for the presentation of different document types. The paths for the images used in the Documents Web Part are relative paths that point to the DocTypeIcons subfolder.

You can find the complete source code of this Web Part and related XSL files at the end of this chapter.

LISTING 16.14   XSLT41.XSL FILE

```
'-------------------------------------------------------------
<?xml version="1.0"?>
<xsl:stylesheet xmlns:xsl = "http://www.w3.org/1999/XSL/Transform"
➥xmlns:msxsl="urn:schemas-microsoft-com:xslt" xmlns:a="DAV:"
➥xmlns:d='urn:schemas-microsoft-com:office:office'
➥xmlns:user="http://www.compaq.com/userfunctions" version = "1.0">
  <msxsl:script language="JavaScript" implements-prefix="user">
    var ii = 0;

    function folderh() {
        ii += 1;
        return (ii);
    }
    function flevel(a) {
        var cnt = 0;
        var StrIndex = a.match(/\//g);
        cnt = StrIndex.length-4;
      return (cnt);
```

continues

Listing 16.14 Continued

```
    }

  </msxsl:script>

<xsl:output method="xml" omit-xml-declaration="yes" indent="no" />
<xsl:template match="/">


<content>
<xsl:apply-templates
➥select="a:multistatus/a:response/a:propstat[a:status='HTTP/1.1 200 OK']">

<xsl:sort select="a:prop/a:href"/>

</xsl:apply-templates>
</content>

</xsl:template>

<xsl:template match="a:propstat">
   <xsl:for-each select="a:prop">
      <xsl:variable name="status">
      <xsl:value-of select="a:status"/>
      </xsl:variable>

      <xsl:element name="folder">
      <xsl:attribute name="id">
      <xsl:value-of select="a:uid"/>
      </xsl:attribute>

    <foldername>
      <xsl:variable name="target">
      <xsl:value-of select="a:href"/>
      </xsl:variable>
      <xsl:value-of select="substring-after ($target, 'Content/')" />
    </foldername>

    <posit>
     <xsl:value-of select="user:folderh()"/>
    </posit>

    <filetype>
      <xsl:variable name="filetype">
      <xsl:value-of select="a:displayname"/>
      </xsl:variable>
      <xsl:value-of select="substring-after ($filetype, '.')"/>
    </filetype>

    <displayname><xsl:value-of select="a:displayname"/></displayname>
    <href><xsl:value-of select="a:href"/></href>
    <isfolder><xsl:value-of select="a:isfolder"/></isfolder>
    <iscollection><xsl:value-of select="a:iscollection"/></iscollection>
    <haschildren><xsl:value-of select="a:haschildren"/></haschildren>
    <level>
       <xsl:value-of select="user:flevel(concat(a:parentname,' '))"/>
```

```
    </level>
    <title><xsl:value-of select="d:title"/></title>
    <author><xsl:value-of select="d:author"/></author>
    <parentname><xsl:value-of select="a:parentname"/></parentname>
    <getlastmodified><xsl:value-of select="a:getlastmodified"/></getlastmodified>
    </xsl:element>
</xsl:for-each>
</xsl:template>
<xsl:template match="a:href">

</xsl:template>
</xsl:stylesheet>
```

LISTING 16.15   XSLT42.XSL FILE

```
<?xml version="1.0"?>
<xsl:stylesheet xmlns:xsl="uri:xsl">

    <xsl:script><![CDATA[
function addheading() {
var heading = "";
heading +="        function makedisplayed(a, b, c) \n";
heading +="        { \n";
heading +="            if (a.style.display=='none'){\n";
heading +="                a.style.display='';\n";
heading +="                b.style.display='';\n";
heading +="                c.style.display='none';\n";
heading +="            }\n";
heading +="            else {\n";
heading +="                a.style.display='none';\n";
heading +="                b.style.display='none';\n";
heading +="                c.style.display='';\n";
heading +="            }\n";
heading +="        }\n";
return heading;
}

    ]]></xsl:script>
<xsl:template match="/">
    <HEAD>
    <SCRIPT LANGUAGE='JavaScript'>
    <xsl:eval>addheading()</xsl:eval>
    </SCRIPT>
    </HEAD>
        <TABLE>
            <xsl:for-each select="content">
                <xsl:apply-templates match="folder" />
            </xsl:for-each>
        </TABLE>

</xsl:template>
    <xsl:template match="folder">
        <xsl:eval no-entities="true">indentCategory(this)</xsl:eval>
```

continues

16

LISTING 16.15 CONTINUED

```
    </xsl:template>

<xsl:script><![CDATA[
var IndexOffset = 0;
function indentCategory(e)     {
if (e){
    var href = e.selectSingleNode("href");
    var dname = e.selectSingleNode("displayname");
    var dfolder = e.selectSingleNode("isfolder");

    var fileicon = e.selectSingleNode("filetype").text;
    var currLevel = e.selectSingleNode("level").text;
    var hasChildren = e.selectSingleNode("haschildren").text;
    var hrefText = "";
    var dnameText = "";
    var dfolderText = "";
    var dfolderText = dfolder.text;

    var id = e.selectSingleNode("@id").text;
    if (fileicon.length > 1) {
      fileicon ="DocTypeIcons\\" + fileicon + "16.gif";
    }
    else {
      fileicon ="DocTypeIcons\\DET16.gif";
    }

    var pos = e.selectSingleNode("posit").text;
    pos = Math.abs(pos)+1;
    var m = e.parentNode.childNodes.length
    if (pos <= m){
        eval('var g = e.parentNode.selectSingleNode(\"/content/folder[posit=" +
➥pos +"]\");');
        var isFolder = g.childNodes.item(5).text;
        var nexthasChildren = g.childNodes.item(7).text;
        var nextLevel = g.childNodes.item(8).text;
    }
    else {
        var isFolder = 1;
        var hasChildren = 0;
    }

    if (href){
        hrefText = "href=\"" + href.text + "\" ";
    }
    if (dname){
        dnameText = dname.text;
    }

    var cat = e.selectSingleNode("displayname");
    if (cat){
    } else {
        return hrefText + " " + dnameText;
    }
    var catTxt = cat.text;
    var spaces = "";
```

```
        var retStr2 = "";
        var cnt = currLevel;
        var ahref = "";

        for (var i=0; i<currLevel-1; i++) {
            spaces += "  ";
        }

        for (var j=1; j<cnt+1; j++){
            var test = ""; //"  haschildren="+hasChildren+"  isFolder"+isFolder;

            if (cnt == j) {
                if (1 == dfolderText) {
                    if (1 == hasChildren) {
                        ahref = "JavaScript:makedisplayed(document.all.item(\"tr"+id+
"\"), document.all.item(\"m"+id+"\"), document.all.item(\"p"+id+"\"))";
                        retStr2 += "<TR><TD> </TD>\n" +
                        "<TD width=\"100%\" valign=\"top\" align=\"left\">" +  spaces +
                        "<A href='"+ ahref +"'><IMG border=0 src=\"blueplus.jpg\"
id='p"+id+"'></IMG><IMG border=0 src=\"blueminus.jpg\" style=display:'none'
id='m"+id+"'></IMG></A>" + " " + dnameText +test+"</TD></TR>";
                        retStr2 += "<TR  style=display:'none' id='tr"+ id +"'>
<TD> </TD><TD><TABLE>";
                    }
                    else {
                        retStr2 += "<TR><TD> </TD>\n" +
                        "<TD width=\"100%\" valign=\"top\" align=\"left\">" +  spaces +
"<IMG border=0 src=\"empty.gif\" id='p"+id+"'></IMG>" +
                        " " + dnameText +test+"</TD></TR>";


                    }
                }
                else {
                    retStr2 += "<TR><TD> </TD>\n" +
                    "<TD width=\"100%\" valign=\"top\" align=\"left\">" +
                    spaces  + "<IMG align = 'center' border=0 src='" + fileicon +"'/>"
                    + "  " +"<A " + hrefText + ">"+ dnameText+test+"</A>
</TD></TR>";

                    if (1==isFolder && currLevel > 0 && 0==dfolderText){
                        retStr2 += "</TD></TABLE></TR>";
                    }
                    if ((cnt>2) && (1==isFolder) && (currLevel-1>nextLevel)){
                        retStr2 += "</TD></TABLE></TR>";
                    }                       if ((cnt>2) && (0==isFolder) &&
(currLevel>nextLevel)){
                        retStr2 += "</TD></TABLE></TR>";
                    }
                }
            }
             }

            if ((1==isFolder) && (1==dfolderText) && (cnt>1) && (currLevel >
nextLevel)){
```

continues

16

LISTING 16.15 CONTINUED

```
                retStr2 += "</TD></TABLE></TR>";
                }

        return retStr2;

        } else {
            return "";
        }
    }
]]></xsl:script>

</xsl:stylesheet>
```

LISTING 16.16 FUNCTION GETCONTENT()

```
Function getContent(XML)
Dim strServer
Dim strWorkspace
Dim strFolder
Dim strURL
Dim strUser
Dim strPassword
Dim DAVRequest
Dim strXMLRequest

strServer = "dianatr"
strWorkspace = "spsbook"
strFolder = "Documents"
strUser = "dianatr0\spsuser"
strPassword = "spspw"

strURL = "http://" + strServer + "/" + strWorkspace + "/" + strFolder
strURL = Replace(strURL, " ", "%20")

strXMLRequest = "" + _
 "<?xml version='1.0'?>" + _
 "<D:propfind xmlns:D='DAV:' xmlns:o='urn:schemas-microsoft-com:office:office'>"
➡+ _
 "<D:prop>" + _
 "<D:displayname/>" + _
 "<D:href/>" + _
 "<D:getlastmodified/>" + _
 "<D:isfolder/>" + _
 "<D:iscollection/>" + _
 "<D:haschildren/>" + _
 "<D:uid/>" + _
 "<D:parentname/>" + _
 "<o:author/>" + _
 "<o:title/>" + _
 "</D:prop>" + _
 "</D:propfind>"

Set DAVRequest = CreateObject("MSXML2.xmlhttp")
DAVRequest.open "PROPFIND", strURL, False, strUser, strPassword
```

```
DAVRequest.setRequestHeader "Content-Type", "text/xml; charset=""UTF-16"""
DAVRequest.setRequestHeader "Depth", "infinity"
DAVRequest.send strXMLRequest

Set xmlBody = CreateObject("MSXML2.domdocument")
xmlBody.async = False
xmlBody.load DAVRequest.responseXML

Set displayss4 = CreateObject("MSXML2.domdocument")
displayss4.async = False
displayss4.Load "E:\Projects\SharePointBook\Chapter 16\xslt41.xsl"
strBody = xmlBody.transformNode(displayss4)

Set xmlBody42 = CreateObject("MSXML2.domdocument")
xmlBody42.async = False
xmlBody42.loadxml strBody
Set displayss42 = CreateObject("MSXML2.domdocument")
displayss42.async = False
displayss42.Load "E:\Projects\SharePointBook\Chapter 16\xslt42.xsl"
strBody = xmlBody42.transformNode(displayss42)
getContent = strBody
End Function
```

16

FURTHER READINGS

There is plenty of resources on the WebDAV protocol that you can refer to for more information. There is a site (http://www.webdav.org) that posts and updates activities regarding the WebDAV protocol, and for those who are new to this protocol, I suggest you start with http://www.webdav.org/other/faq.html, which provides you with "DAV Frequently Asked Questions."

SUMMARY

Throughout this chapter, we introduced the Web Storage System and how you can explore, modify, or add properties and values of the Web Storage System by using the Exchange Explorer tool. Then we introduced the WebDAV protocol and explained what major extensions are added to HTTP1.1. Through simple sample code, we showed how you can create collections on remote servers over HTTP, how you can set or get the properties of documents and search for specific properties of documents, how you can control access to a document by locking or unlocking a document, and how you can copy or move content on remote servers. Finally, we showed in detail how you can use WebDAV new methods to create useful Web Parts.

CHAPTER 17

CUSTOMIZING SHAREPOINT USING XML AND XSL

In this chapter

XML AND XSL

The intent of this chapter is not to teach eXtensible Markup Language (XML) or eXtensible Stylesheet Language (XSL), and the assumption is that you are already familiar with XML. Although for some of you who did not have the time to explore these powerful markup languages, this chapter can still help you gain insight into features that are available through these languages. If you are new to XML and XSL, you may want to get started by reading resources available on

http://www.xml101.com/

http://msdn.microsoft.com/library/default.asp?url=/library/en-us/xmlsdk30/htm/ xmtutxmltutorial.asp

Throughout this chapter you will find how to create useful Web Parts and customize the dashboard interface of SharePoint Portal Server.

17

"HELLO WORLD" WEB PART

As a developer, the best way to learn about a product is hands-on experience. By looking at available pieces of code or examples, you can later build upon them, thereby going on to more complex tasks, which is why developers like to hear the revised technical Jerry Maguirism "Show me the code." I start with very simple examples and later explain more sophisticated code for creating Web Parts using XML and XSL. Every programming book that I have read to this point starts with the simple example of "Hello World". In this section, I will use this basic sample code and build a Web Part for it.

This is the easiest three lines of code that you can put in the SharePoint dashboard as a Web Part. The purpose of this code is to show you how and where you can define and integrate your code into SharePoint Portal Server. To create the "Hello World" Web Part, follow these steps:

NOTE | You must have Author or Coordinator privileges to do the following actions.

1. From the main menu bar at the upper right corner of the SharePoint dashboard, click **Content**. Then, from the Content dashboard, click on the **Create New Web Part** at the bottom of the screen under the **Import or Create** section.

2. Now you are in the **Web Part—Settings** dashboard. This dashboard has two parts. The first part is called **General Settings**, and the next part is **Advanced Settings**. In **General Settings** you can define the overall settings of the Web Part, such as the Name, Description, Size, and Position of the Web Part in one of the five banners (Top, Left, Center, Right, or Bottom) of the dashboard, and you can select your Web Part to be shown in a frame or without a frame.

TIP

Frames make your Web Part more visible and distinguished in the dashboard, but they take up more space, and if you are worried about the real state of your dashboard, you may uncheck the **Display Web Part in a frame** box.

3. For the "Hello World" Web Part, enter Hello World in the **Name** text box .

4. Enter Hello World Web Part in the description box. The description of the Web Part is optional, but using it is a good habit, to provide as much information as possible about your Web Part. You may also add the name of author and version number of the Web Part in the description section.

5. To make the "Hello World" Web Part visible on the dashboard, the **Include this Web Part on the dashboard** check box must be checked. This box is checked by default.

6. Select **Left banner** for the position of the Web Part.

7. For the rest of the settings in the **General Settings** section, accept the defaults.

   Figure 17.1 shows the Hello World Web Part General settings after you have finished step 7.

Figure 17.1
The General Settings for the "Hello World" Web Part.

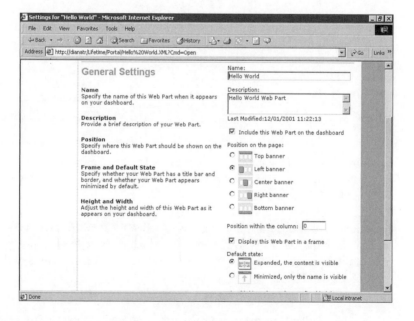

8. In the **Advanced Settings** section, select **XML** from the drop-down menu as the type of content.

9. Click on the **Embedded content** text area box and enter the following three lines of code:

```
<message>
   Hello, world!
</message>
```

TIP

> XML is case sensitive, and the opening and closing tags must match. (For example, you cannot have `<Message>` and `</message>` as matching tags.)

10. Accept the default settings for the rest of the options in the **Advanced Settings** section. Figure 17.2 shows the Advanced settings that are completed by step 10.

Figure 17.2
The settings in the Advanced Settings of the Hello World Web Part.

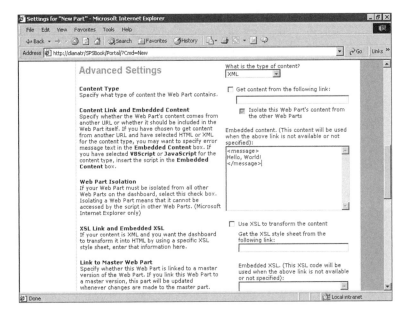

11. Now click the **Save** button, and choose **Save** once again on the next screen (Content dashboard). Figure 17.3 shows the "Hello World" Web Part in the SharePoint dashboard.

You might have noticed that nothing was specified for the XSL part in **Advanced Settings**. In the case of the "Hello World" Web Part, which is just a one-line message, the form and style of the message will inherit the settings of the Web Part specified in the cascading style sheet of the dashboard.

TIP

> Don't use the text area boxes in the **Advanced Settings** for developing code. You should use Visual Studio or other tools that allow you to debug and view the output of your code.
>
> Especially in the case of XML and XSL, any typo or incorrect syntax will result in an ambiguous error message in the dashboard. For XML and XSL code, make sure the code is well formed and valid. If your XML and XSL are well formed and valid, you should be able to view it in Internet Explorer 5.5 or higher. You may also use XML parser, which is available at `http://msdn.microsoft.com/xml/default.asp`.

Figure 17.3
The final form of the "Hello World" Web Part.

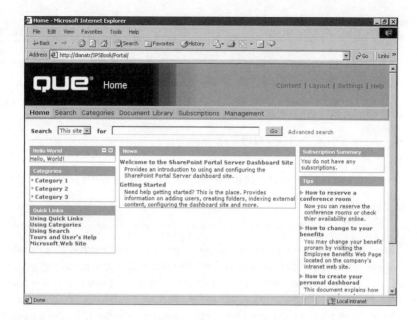

"BREAKING UPDATES" WEB PART

The "Hello World" Web Part was not exciting and you will not find it useful, but at least you have an idea of what needs to be done to create and integrate your code within the SharePoint environment. Now, I want to introduce a very useful Web Part. I have called this the "Breaking Updates" Web Part. This Web Part can be used to disseminate daily news, alerts, or any other news that is important to communicate with employees. This Web Part also keeps your site alive, and you will find more employees accessing the SharePoint portal to get the latest update. This Web Part should be of specific interest for companies that are using the SharePoint portal as their intranet.

Lets look at the structure of this Web Part in detail. Listing 17.1 shows the XML code for this Web Part.

LISTING 17.1   THE XML FOR THE BREAKING UPDATES WEB PART

```
<?xml version="1.0"?>
<BreakingUpdates>
  <message priority="high">
      <title>
          Security Alert
      </title>
      <date>
         Monday November 12, 2001
      </date>
```

continues

17

LISTING 17.1 CONTINUED

```
    <topimage>
      http://dianatr/SPSbook/portal content/Resources/images/form-globe36.gif
    </topimage>
    <content>
        The Code Red Virus has infected some of the computers in the company.
➡ To avoid spreading the virus further and for the clean up procedure, please
check
➡ instructions in the following link:
    </content>
    <url>
        http://dianatr/SPSbook/BreakingUpdates/code-red-instructions.htm
    </url>
  </message>
</BreakingUpdates>
```

This Web Part can have one or multiple messages that are all embedded inside the root tag, `<BreakingUpdates>`, and are closed with its matching tag, `</BreakingUpdates>`. Each message also has a priority attribute that determines the importance of the message. For example, if there is a virus alert, I want it to be displayed in a different color, or placed at the top of the list due to its urgency. The general structure of the XML document is as follows:

```
<BreakingUpdates>
  <message>
      :::::
  </message>
  <message>
      :::::
  </message>
  <message>
      :::::
  </message>
  ::::::::::
</BreakingUpdates>
```

Each message has five elements:

- `<title>` displays the title of the news item.
- `<date>` displays the date of the news or alert.
- `<topimage>` is an optional image that can be shown at the top of the news.
- `<content>` has a summary of the news.
- `<url>` is a link to the details of the news.

TIP

> Try to keep the resources used by Web Parts in one location, or think of organizing them as you proceed with your SharePoint development. For example, in the case of the Breaking Update Web Part, you will have images and HTML or other types of documents about the details of the news, which can easily get out of control if you have not thought about it ahead of time. I recommend creating a subfolder under the **Content Portal** folder for each Web Part, to store all the resources used by that specific Web Part.

For this Web Part we need to create an XSL file too. The XSL code used for this Web Part is shown in Listing 17.2.

LISTING 17.2   XSL CODE FOR THE BREAKING UPDATES WEB PART

```
<?xml version="1.0"?>
<xsl:stylesheet xmlns:xsl="http://www.w3.org/TR/WD-xsl">
<xsl:template match="/">
  <html>
    <head>
    </head>
    <body>
      <table>
          <xsl:apply-templates select="BreakingUpdates"/>
      </table>
    </body>
  </html>
</xsl:template>

<xsl:template match="BreakingUpdates">
  <xsl:for-each select="message">
  <tr>
    <td align="center">
      <IMG>
          <xsl:attribute name="src">
          <xsl:value-of select="topimage"/>
          </xsl:attribute>
      </IMG>
    </td>
  </tr>
  <tr>
     <xsl:element name="td">
<xsl:attribute name="align">center</xsl:attribute>
     <strong><xsl:value-of select="date"/></strong>
</xsl:element>
  </tr>
  <tr>
     <xsl:element name="td">
<xsl:attribute name="align">center</xsl:attribute>
    <font>
        <xsl:attribute name="color">
          <xsl:if test=".[@priority='high']">red</xsl:if>
          <xsl:if test=".[@priority='low']">black</xsl:if>
        </xsl:attribute>
        <strong><xsl:value-of select="title"/></strong>
    </font>
</xsl:element>
  </tr>

  <tr>
    <xsl:element name="td">
        <xsl:attribute name="align">left</xsl:attribute>
        <xsl:value-of select="content"/>
```

continues

17

LISTING 17.2 CONTINUED

```
    </xsl:element>
  </tr>
  <tr>
    <td align="right"><a>
    <xsl:attribute name="href">
      <xsl:value-of select="url"/>
    </xsl:attribute>
    click here for details</a></td>
  </tr>
```

Since this is the first mention of XSL code, let's walk through the different sections of the code and explain the purpose of each segment.

One of the most important things in XML and XSL is the *Name Spaces*, which must be unique because you are defining the tags—which can refer to different things—by their content. For example, when we define a <name> tag, that might be the name of an employee, a movie, or a street, so to be able to uniquely identify it, we need to define a name space. Name spaces are usually defined in a format similar to the URL because the URLs are already unique, but by no means do name spaces represent a site, and they should not be confused with the URLs. In our example, the following line of code represents a unique *name space*.

```
<xsl:stylesheet xmlns:xsl="http://www.w3.org/TR/WD-xsl">
```

The next segment of code looks for everything from the root of a XML document, applies the BreakingUpdate template, returns the formatted result, and embeds it inside <table>...</table> tags.

```
<xsl:template match="/">
  <html>
    <head>
    </head>
    <body>
      <table>
        <xsl:apply-templates select="BreakingUpdate"/>
      </table>
    </body>
  </html>
</xsl:template>
```

TIP

Some HTML parsers ignore incorrect or missing ending tags, but in XML this is very different. In XML, every opening tag must have a matching closing tag.

The next two lines of code are as follows:

```
<xsl:template match="BreakingUpdate">
  <xsl:for-each select="message">
```

They will look within the `<BreakingUpdates>...</BreakingUpdates>` tags for all `<message>` tags, and apply the template to the content between each `<message>...</message>`.

The rest of the XSL code explains the formatting requirements for each of the XML elements, such as `<topimage>`, `<date>`, `<title>`, `<content>`, and `<url>`. As you can see, each element will be placed in a table row, which has only one cell:

```
<tr>
  <td align="center">
      ::::::::::::
  </td>
</tr>
```

N O T E

> You might have noticed that the `<td>` element is represented in different forms, just to show the possibilities of expressing the tags within XSL. My personal preference is using and expressing everything in the form of `<xsl:element name="td">` and then defining different attributes for the `"td"` element; however, this form requires more typing, yet it is more readable and easier to debug.

The rest of the code is straightforward, and just defines alignments and font selections, but there is a segment that represents another capability of XSL. These lines are

```
<xsl:attribute name="color">
    <xsl:if test=".[@priority='high']">red</xsl:if>
    <xsl:if test=".[@priority='low']">black</xsl:if>
</xsl:attribute>
```

As I explained earlier, an attribute is added to each *message* that describes the *priority* of the message, which enables it to distinguish between high- and low-priority messages. So if I want to show the title of high-priority messages in red and low-priority messages in black, I can use the previous code segment to check the values of the `priority` attribute and apply the required color based on its value.

Testing the XML and XSL to make sure that they are valid is very important. We can test the XML and XSL parts of code separately by just opening each of them in IE version 5.0 or higher. Figures 17.4 and 17.5 show XML and XSL code, and the way they look in the IE browser.

17

Figure 17.4
The XML document is valid and well formed.

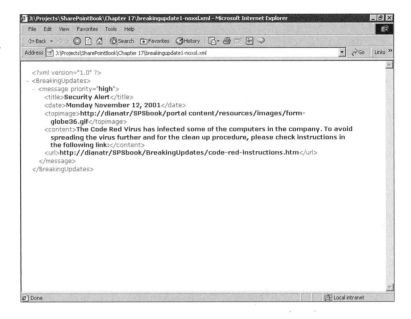

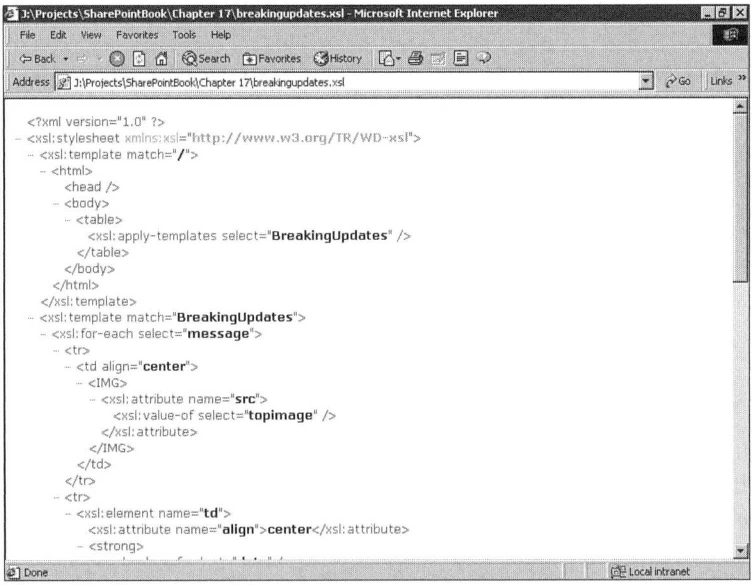

Figure 17.5
If the XSL code is well formed, this is what you should see in the IE browser.

17

One more test is required to make sure that the XML and XSL operate correctly together. For this purpose, we can add a line to the XML file that points to its related XSL file. If the name of the XSL file is breakingupdates.xsl, the XML file's second line will be like the following segment.

```
<?xml version="1.0"?>
<?xml-stylesheet type="text/xsl" href="breakingupdates.xsl"?>
<BreakingUpdates>
    ::::::::::::
</BreakingUpdates>
```

Now we can open the XML file in the browser, and we should be able to see the Breaking Updates screen shown in Figure 17.6.

Figure 17.6
The finished version of the Breaking Updates Web Part.

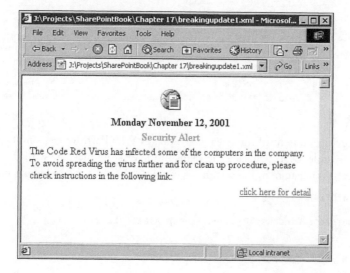

After we've completed testing, we can start putting the XML and XSL code in the assigned boxes in the SharePoint dashboard. The steps for creating the Breaking Updates Web Part are the same as the Hello World Web Part, with one difference: the XSL. To demonstrate this in the **Web Part—Settings** dashboard, click **Use XSL to transform the content**, and then copy and paste the XSL code to the text area box titled **Embedded XSL**. (This XSL code will be used when the previous link is not available or not specified.)

Then save the settings, and the Breaking Updates Web Part will be shown on the main SharePoint dashboard (see Figure 17.7).

Figure 17.7
The Breaking Updates
Web Part in the Home
Dashboard.

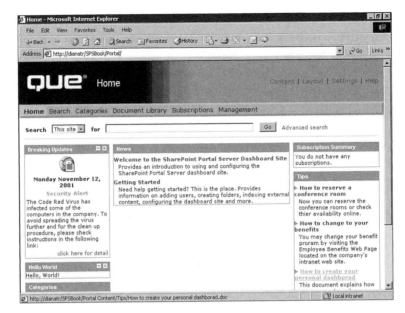

To change the content of the Breaking Updates Web Part, we can simply add another
<message> node, or just replace the items of the existing message with the new message, and
we are set—no change in the settings is required. Look at the following message:

```
<message priority="high">
   <title>
      Compaq's Windows XP-based lineup available
   </title>
   <date>
      Thursday October 25, 2001
   </date>
   <topimage>
      http://dianatr/SPSbook/portal content/resources/images/windowsXP.gif
   </topimage>
   <content>
         Compaq on Thursday announced the availability of our PC lineup powered
by the new Microsoft Windows XP operating system.
   </content>
   <url>
      http://dianatr/SPSbook/BreakingUpdates/windowsxp.htm
   </url>
</message>
```

We just changed the elements of the message node, and that's it; the new Breaking Update
will be shown as in Figure 17.8.

Figure 17.8
The new message is shown in the "Breaking Updates" Web Part.

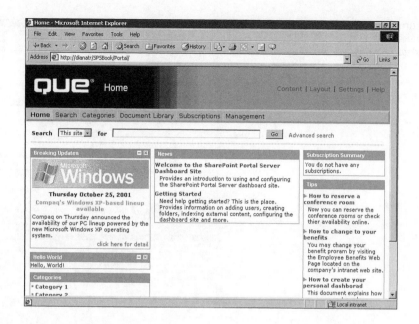

WEB STORAGE SYSTEM SDK

As explained before, the Web Storage System is the underlying storage mechanism for the SharePoint Portal Server, and all items that are shown on the dashboard as well as all objects that are used for building the SharePoint Server portal are stored in the Web Storage System (WSS). Through SharePoint dashboards and Web folders, we can work and interact with items that are stored in the WSS, but for developers, who want to create applications for SharePoint Server, there is a *tool in Exchange* Software Development Kit (SDK), available for free at the Microsoft Web site.

→ To learn more about Exchange Explorer and how to get and use this tool, **see** "Exchange Explorer," **p. 400**.

The Web Storage System Explorer is a critical tool that every SharePoint developer should spend some time with. It gives a better understanding of the underlying design of the Web Storage System and how to develop customized applications for SharePoint Server.

Figure 17.9 shows the SPSBOOK workspace content in Exchange Explorer.

CAUTION

> When working with items in the Workspaces folder, you should be very cautious and know exactly what you are doing; incorrect manipulation of items can corrupt and damage your SharePoint Portal interface. Before working with this tool, make sure you have a reliable WSS backup.

Figure 17.9
The SPSBOOK Workspace schema in Exchange Explorer.

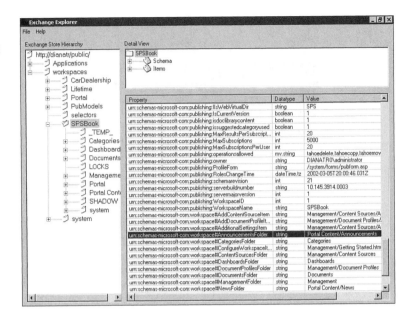

For each workspace that you create in the SharePoint Server, a folder will be created under the Workspaces folder, and if you expand one of these folders you will find a list of sub-folders that you may have already seen through the Web folder interface or the SharePoint dashboard interface, such as Dashboards, Document, and Portal content. If you have enabled Show Hidden Files, some of them—such as Management, System, Lock, Portal, an so on—would be visible in dim color in the Web Folder interface.

A folder's visibility is a property of that folder, with a Boolean value of 1 representing hidden folders, and 0 representing visible folders. In fact, you can check these values by double-clicking on a folder in the left pane and checking the value of DAV:ishidden in the lower-right pane of the WSS Explorer.

Also, there is a schema definition for each workspace. We can see the schema of our sample workspace **SPSbook** by double-clicking on the SPSbook folder, and view work in the lower window. There is a list of properties. Skim through these properties; you will see the properties for the Announcements and News folder, which are

urn:schemas-microsoft-com:workspace#AnnouncementsFolder has type string, and its value is portal content/Announcements, which is the physical location of the Announcements folder relative to the SPSBook workspace.

urn:schemas-microsoft-com:workspace#NewsFolder has type string, and its value is portal content/News, which is the physical location of the News folder relative to the SPSBook workspace.

This is how Announcements and News Web Parts are identified in the SharePoint Portal Server. You will use this information to create the next Web Part, which is the "Tips" Web Part.

"Tips" Web Part

When you install SharePoint Portal Server, it automatically creates a workspace for you with a default dashboard. This dashboard is basic, and you can take it as a starting point and customize it based on your needs. For example, SharePoint provides two Web Parts for News and Announcements out-of-the-box; by default these Web Parts show the five most recent News or Announcements that you define in the Portal Content under the News and Announcements folders. In this example, I want to create a Web Part similar to the functionality of those two Web Parts that has a list of the five most recent Tips. Using this Web Part you can provide "How to" information such as how to reserve the conference room, install specific applications, request an email account, or many other frequently asked questions. Based on my experience with different SharePoint projects, I have found lots of interest and demand for such a Web Part. The other piece of good news is you don't need to do that much coding. You can create this Web Part by just following a few simple steps.

First, let's briefly explain the functionality of those Web Parts. Since these two Web Parts (News and Announcements) have the same structure and functionality, I will just explain the Announcements Web Part.

The content of the Announcements Web Part comes from the Announcements Web folder, which is located under Portal Content. When you create a new announcement and store it in the Announcement folder, the title and description of that announcement appear on the Announcements Web Part in the main dashboard of SharePoint, and you can get the details of a specific announcement by just clicking the title of the announcement, which is in the form of hyperlink.

To see how this Web Part is created, you can click on the **Content** option in the upper menu bar of the dashboard. Then, from the Content dashboard, which lists all your Web Parts, click on the Announcements Web Part; this puts you on the **Web part—Settings** dashboard. Next, click on **Advanced Settings**. There are three code segments that are located in three text areas. The first part is the Function Init(node), in the Embedded content text area. The second part is the XSL, located in the Embedded XSL text area. The third part is at the bottom of the dashboard under **Store the following data for this Web Part**, for which you will see three lines of code:

```
PORTAL_ANNOUNCEMENTS_FOLDER_PATH_HOLDER
"DAV:getlastmodified" DESC
5
```

The first line—PORTAL_ANNOUNCEMENTS_FOLDER_PATH_HOLDER—is a variable that defines the path of the Announcements folder. The second line defines the order of the announcements that will be shown in the Announcement folder. The third line is a variable that specifies how many announcements are to be shown in the Announcements Web Part. To show more than five announcements, you can increase this number, but be aware that there are some drawbacks to setting this number too high; first, performance will be degraded because more items need to be rendered and more bytes need to be returned, and second, if you limit the height of the Web Part or the real state area on your dashboard screen, lots of scrolling will be necessary to see all the announcements. First, let's see what is required to create such a Web Part. We can just copy the code, make some minor changes, and put it to work.

The Function Init(node) in the Embedded content box is VBScript code that basically gets the three previously mentioned parameters, and queries the Web Storage System to retrieve them from the Announcements folder in XML form. Then the XSL code in the Embedded XSL box displays the content in the desired style so that it appears in the Announcements Web Part. The only place where we see the announcement-related variable is in the following segment of code in the Init(node) function.

```
strFolderPath = Replace "PORTAL_ANNOUNCEMENTS_FOLDER_PATH_HOLDER", "/" &
GetWorkspacePropertyByUri(g_cdostrURI_AnnouncementsFolder))
```

There is one more piece of the puzzle, and that's the `RefreshWorkspacePropertyCache()` subroutine in the TahoeUtils.asp program. This ASP program is in the portal/resources folder and has some functions and utilities that are used by SharePoint. Now that we have tracked all the components involved in creation of the Announcements Web Part, let's see how we can create the Tips Web Part. There are six steps that we need to follow:

1. Create a subfolder in the SPSBook Web folder for the Tips Web Part. When you create a workspace in SharePoint Portal Server, SharePoint creates a Web folder in Network Places with the same name as the workspace. In our case, the name shown on My Network Places is SPSBook on dianatr, where SPSBook is the name of the workspace and dianatr is the name of my server.

   Figure 17.10 shows a list of Web folders that I have on My Network Places. I have created three workspaces—Cardealership, Lifetime, and SPSBook—and a Web folder is created for each of them.

Figure 17.10
A list of Web folders in My Network Places.

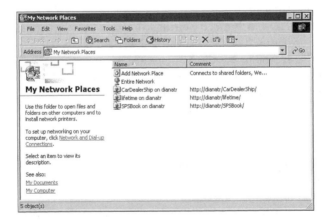

Then double-click SPSBook; you will find a list of all folders for SPSBook, and one of them is Portal Content. Figure 17.11 shows the list of folders for SPSBook. Double-clicking on Portal Content shows the list of folders within Portal Content, and as you can see in Figure 17.12, Announcements and News are two folders that reside here. Right-click and select **New** and then **Folder** from the menu, and enter `Tips` for the name of the new folder (see Figure 17.12).

Figure 17.11
A list of folders for SPSBook Web folder.

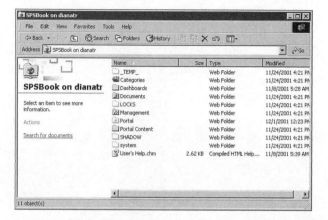

Figure 17.12
How to create a new folder/subfolder.

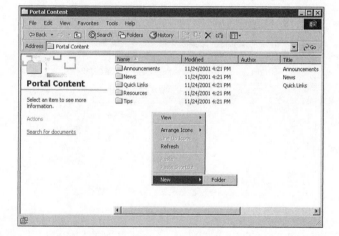

2. Now we need to define a property and value for the Tips folder in the SPSBook workspace. To add this property, you need to use the Web Storage System Explorer that was explained in the previous section. For this purpose, right-click on the lower-right pane of the WSS Explorer and select **Add property** from the menu (see Figure 17.13).

When **Add property** is selected from the menu, a new Add Property dialog box comes up (Figure 17.14). Enter `urn:schemas-microsoft-com:workspace#TipsFolder` in the Name text box and accept the default data type as `string`. In the value text area, enter `Portal Content/Tips`, the physical location of the folder that we created in step 1, and select **OK**.

Figure 17.13
You can use Web Storage System Explorer to add or modify properties of the items stored in the WSS.

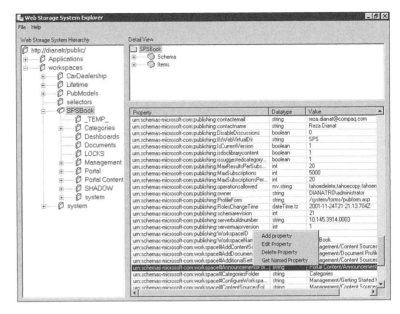

Figure 17.14
To add a new item to the SharePoint Portal Server through WSS Explorer, enter the name of the new property, the Data type, and the value of the property in the Add Property dialog box.

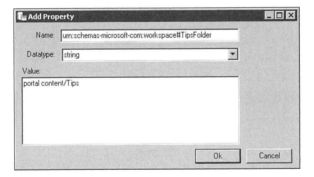

3. Export the Announcements Web Part. To do so, select Content from the top bar menu of the main dashboard (Home dashboard) and click on the Announcements Web Part, which puts you in the Announcement Settings dashboard. At the bottom of the dashboard, click **Export**, and in the **Export web part to file** dialog box, **save** the file to announcements.dwp on your local drive (C:\).

4. Make changes in the TahoeUtils.ASP program. Copy the TahoeUtils.asp from the portal/resources folder to your local drive (c:\). Open this file with Visual Studio or Notepad, and search for the word "Announcements" in the TahoeUtils.asp file.

CAUTION

> To keep the support of Microsoft on your SharePoint Portal Server, you are allowed to change DashboardExtenstions.VBS and Catalog.XML files. Changing TahoeUtils.VBS or other files is not supported by Microsoft, and the new installation of SharePoint or the upgrade will override your changes. But working and practicing with the "Tips" Web Part gives you an under-the-hood view of the News and Announcements and Quick Links Web Parts of the SharePoint Portal Server.

Duplicate every line that you find with the Announcement keyword and replace the "Announcements" with "Tips". There are six instances of "Announcements" in five lines of code that all must be replaced with "Tips". Listing 17.3 shows the line of codes that have changed.

LISTING 17.3   CODE SEGMENTS FROM TAHOEUTILS.VBS THAT NEED TO BE DUPLICATED AND CHANGED FOR THE "TIPS" WEB PART

```
1) Const g_cdostrURI_TipsFolder =
➥"urn:schemas-microsoft-com:workspace#TipsFolder"

2) strTemp = CStr(wksp.fields(g_cdostrURI_TipsFolder).value)

3) If (Err.Number <> 0) Or (Len(strTemp) <= 0) Then SaveCurrentErrorContext
➥    "RefreshWorkspacePropertyCache() - Error getting the tipfolder name from
➥workspace root." : Exit Sub

4) SetCachedItem g_clCacheAllUsers, g_strWorkspacePropsCachePrefix &
➥g_cdostrURI_TipsFolder, strTemp, g_csecWorkspacePropsCache

5) If Err.Number <> 0 Then SaveCurrentErrorContext
➥"RefreshWorkspacePropertyCache() - Error saving the tipfolder name from workspace
➥root." : Exit Sub
```

Listing 17.3 shows five lines of the code from TahoeUtils.asp that need to be modified for the Tips Web Part.

NOTE

> Make sure to keep a clean copy of TahoeUtils.asp someplace; in case of any problems, you can reverse your changes. Now save your changes, and copy the TahoeUtils.asp file back to the portal/resources folder in the SPSBook Web folder.

5. Import the Announcement Web Part. Now select Content from the top bar menu of the Home dashboard, and from the bottom of the Content dashboard under **Import or Create**, select **Import a web part file**. In the **Select web part file to import** dialog box, locate the announcements.dwp file that you exported to your local drive (C:\) in step 3 and click **Open**. This puts you back in the Content dashboard, and you will see two Announcements Web Parts listed in the Content dashboard. Click on the Announcements Web Part with the more recent Last Modified date. Now you are in the Announcement Settings dashboard.

6. Change the Name of the Web Part to Tips. Click **Advanced Settings**. Next, in the Embedded content text area box, search for the following line of code.

```
strFolderPath = Replace(strFolderPath,
"PORTAL_Announcements_FOLDER_PATH_HOLDER",
"/" & GetWorkspacePropertyByUri(g_cdostrURI_ AnnouncementsFolder))
```

and change Announcements to Tips as follows:

```
    strFolderPath = Replace(strFolderPath, "PORTAL_TIPS_FOLDER_PATH_HOLDER",
➡"/" &
GetWorkspacePropertyByUri(g_cdostrURI_TipsFolder))
```

In the **Store the following data for this Web Part** text area box, change the PORTAL_ANNOUNCEMENTS_FOLDER_PATH_HOLDER variable to PORTAL_TIPS_FOLDER_PATH_HOLDER, **save** your changes, and click on the Save button again in the Content dashboard. Figure 17.15 shows the final Tip Web Part in the Home dashboard.

Figure 17.15
Tips Web Part without any Tips.

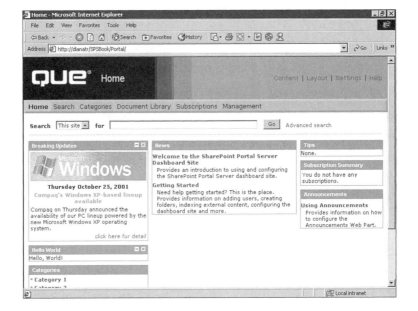

As you see, this Web Part is initially empty and does not have any Tips. I created three documents in Microsoft Word, copied them to the Tips folder under the Portal Content folder, and added a description to the profile of these documents. Now if I go to the SharePoint Home dashboard, I will see a list of titles and descriptions of the Tips in the Tips Web Part (see Figure 17.16).

Figure 17.16
A Tips Web Part that shows the title and a summary description of three tips.

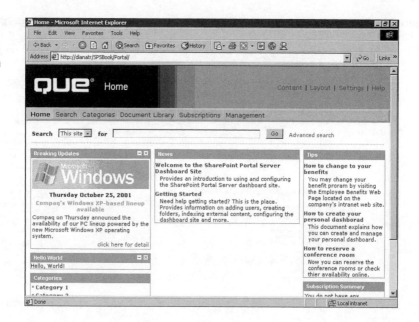

Now that we have finished with the Tips Web Part, we want to go ahead and add a little bit of flavor to it and make the title of each Tip more distinguished in the Web Part. This can be easily done in a few steps.

I have picked a very small size image (58 bytes), a red bullet on white background, to show in front of each title in the Tips Web Part. I copy this image (called bullet_red_onwhite.gif) to the Portal/Resources folder. Then I go to the Embedded XSL area box of the Tips Web Part in Advanced Settings, and insert the line that is shown in bold in the following code segment:

```
<xsl:template match="a:response">
    <TR><TD><IMG height="6" border="0" src="pixel.gif"/></TD></TR>
    <TR>
        <TD valign="top" align="left" colspan="2">
<IMG height="12" width="8" border="0" src= "bullet_red_onwhite.gif"/>
            <A>
                <xsl:choose>
```

Now Click on the **Save** button to save the changes in the XSL code, and click **Save** again on the next screen (Content dashboard). Figure 17.17 shows the difference the changes that this one line code has made to the Tips Web Part.

TIP

> When using images and graphics, always consider the number of bytes that will be sent to your home dashboard. Using too many graphics or large size images can slow down the response time on your home dashboard.

Figure 17.17
The Tips Web Part
with a red bullet in
front of each title.

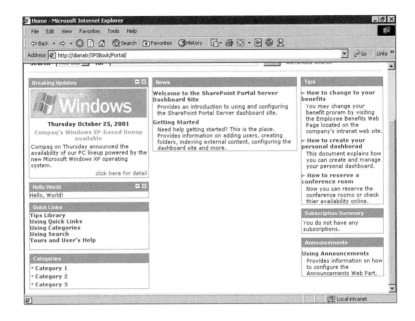

VIEW LIST OF ALL THE TIPS

As mentioned earlier, you can define how many items will be shown in your Web Part in
Advanced Settings, under the **Store the following data for this Web Part** text area box.
The default value of this number is five, and it means only five items—News,
Announcements, or Tips in our Tips Web Part—will be shown in the Web Part. You can
change this number if you would like to show more items, but you must be cautious.
Increasing this number will cause the Web Part to occupy more space in the dashboard,
and it will also slow down the performance of your home page because more items need to
be rendered and returned to the dashboard. So you might ask how we can see a list of all
Tips or News. One way is just going though a series of clicks.

First you should select the **Document Library**, then select the **Portal Content** folder
from the Document Library dashboard, and finally click on the **Tips** folder to look at the
list of documents that are posted to the Tips Web Part. But there is an easier way, which
does not require this many clicks and navigation delays to get to the list of all the tips. You
can add a link in the Quick Links Web Part that points directly to the Tips folder.

The Quick Links Web Part is very similar to the News and Announcements Web Parts. To create a new link, we can just copy and paste one of the existing links in the Quick Links Web folder, rename it with the title that you want to be shown in the Quick Links Web Part, and edit the profile. In this case, I opened the Quick Links Web folder, copied and pasted **Microsoft SPS Web Site.url**, and renamed it **Tips Library.url**. Then I changed the property values of the link in the Web Link Profile.

From the **Select a profile** drop-down menu, select Web Link as the type of profile, and for the value of the **Link** text box, enter `http://<Server Name>/<Workspace Name> /Portal Content/Tips.`

In the **Title** text box, enter `Tips Library`, and for the **Description** enter "This is a quick link to a list of all the tips that are posted in the Tips Web Part" and select **OK**.

Figure 17.18 shows the Document Profile for the Tips Library Quick Link.

Figure 17.18
Tips Library quick link properties.

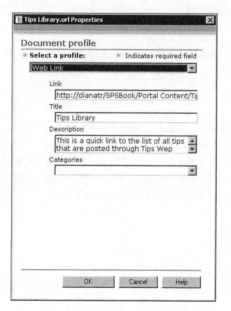

Now if we return to the Home dashboard of the SharePoint Server, we can see that **Tips Library** has been added as a link in the **Quick Links** Web Part. To reach the list of Tips posted to the Tips Web Part, we can just click on the Tips Library link.

Figure 17.19
Tips Library link in the
Quick Links Web Part.

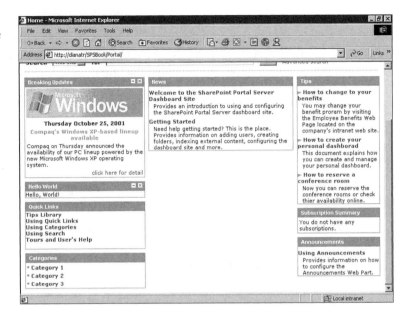

SUMMARY

Throughout this chapter, you became familiar with how to create simple and useful Web Parts using XML and XSL. We also introduced the concept of the Web Storage System and exploring the Web Storage System using the Exchange Explorer tool. By introducing the "Tips" Web Part, we walked through steps required for creating Web Parts that have the same functionality as Announcements and News Web Parts.

PART IV

PLANNING AND MANAGING INDEXING

CHAPTER 18

CONFIGURING SPS TO CRAWL OTHER CONTENT SOURCES

In this chapter

GENERAL OVERVIEW

One way that portals like SharePoint provide great value to their users is by facilitating search capabilities. Sometimes the documents being searched reside locally on the portal, and sometimes they reside external to the portal. Given that it is impractical to physically copy every potential document that may be leveraged by an organization to the "local" portal disk subsystem, the concept of *crawling* evolved. Crawling allows for content that is stored both locally and on remote systems to be indexed locally, such that a search for a particular word, phrase, or metadata field can be addressed by simply searching one or more indexes maintained on the local SharePoint server.

Regardless of how "wide" or "deep" a portal crawls, the data indexed is only as valuable as the *taxonomy*, or structure, applied to that data. That is, the less detailed the taxonomy, the less valuable the results from a search become. Real world examples abound. For example, anyone who has performed a search on one of the large Internet portals knows the frustration of getting 100,000 hits on even relatively detailed searches. The taxonomy supporting the search often fails to meet our needs, even though the crawled data and resulting indexes are quite detailed.

→ To read more about the role and importance of taxonomies, **see** "The Goal of Developing a Taxonomy," **p. 248**.

The importance of taxonomies is covered in greater detail in Chapter 9. Here, though, we will focus on how to configure and crawl various content sources. We will also address SPS functional considerations, performance considerations, troubleshooting, and more, from a crawling perspective. Thus, before we go further, it's important to note the following general crawl objectives:

- To crawl specific sites to compile a full-text index of site content, and thus improve the searchability of the data

- To tag content pages with metadata, and then index this data, to help further refine the results from a search

In the next few pages, we drill down into the process employed by Microsoft SharePoint Server to crawl.

→ For a basic review on crawling, **see** "How to Crawl a Web Server," **p. 175**.

HOW MICROSOFT SPS CRAWLS

Different portal products emphasize various features, such as document management, personalization, threaded discussions, and so on. But the most pervasive feature in any Portal product is the ability to facilitate searching by crawling, indexing, analyzing, and sorting large quantities of data. In this way, the portal becomes a capable machine for turning raw data into real information, whether the data resides on a corporate intranet or across the globe.

To crawl simply means to search through content for inclusion in an index. Once indexed, the data may then be sorted into various categories or classifications according to a set of rules—the taxonomy. The taxonomy organizes the data around business-oriented customer-driven concepts that are meaningful to the end-user community. At this point, the raw data becomes useful, as it is made available to users through two primary vehicles:

- Search capabilities
- Customizable "views" of the data

It is Microsoft's *search engine*, which runs as a service, that facilitates such robust crawling capabilities. SharePoint utilizes a highly refined search engine resulting from years of research and development. This search engine—also known as MSSearch—employs crawling search algorithms that utilize probability rankings, inverse queries, and vector machine categorization. In simplest terms, though, the search engine compares the query (search criteria) to the documents that have been indexed, and then chooses the documents that are most relevant to the query.

THE CRAWLING PROCESS

SharePoint Portal Server crawls or reads through content to create an index of the content. In this way, searches for content requested by the portal's end-user community yield results outside of the content physically residing on the portal. The crawling process includes or touches upon the following SharePoint Portal Server resources or capabilities:

18

- Content sources
- Crawling
- Building an index
- Searching

Each of these is covered in greater detail in the following sections. As you read through these next few sections, keep in mind the goal of crawling—to facilitate searching.

CONTENT AND CONTENT SOURCES

Content is the phenomenal collection of data that organizations struggle to manage and publish. Microsoft has developed a number of products over the years that address content management—SharePoint Portal Server and Content Management Server are just two examples. In SPS's case, content may include any information stored in almost any file share, Web share, Exchange 5.5 or Exchange 2000 public folder, Lotus Notes databases, or other SPS workspace. It is indexed, stored, and made accessible via a Web browser, Microsoft Office 2000/XP, or the Windows Explorer.

Content also refers to information that is of value to a particular audience or end-user community, whether a department in an organization or an entire corporation. This content that the corporate portal crawls and indexes is created and maintained by subject-matter experts within the organization, folks with the goal of sharing their content with other folks who presumably require access to the content for any number of business and other reasons.

A *content source*, on the other hand, is a starting point that SharePoint Portal Server leverages to build an index of documents stored in a precise location outside the workspace. These documents are then available for users to search for and view via the dashboard site. Content sources are added to the workspace, and include Web links, file shares, Exchange Server 5.5 public folders, Exchange 2000 public folders, Lotus Notes databases, and other SPS workspace Web folders. The next few pages detail how to generically add or crawl content sources, and then specifically how to configure SPS to crawl each of the content sources listed previously.

ADDING A CONTENT SOURCE

The first steps to enabling crawling are to define and then add content sources to be crawled by SharePoint Portal Server. This is accomplished by using the Add Content Source Wizard:

1. Determine the content source to be added.

2. Select the content type to be included in the index (such as one of the content sources described previously).

3. Open the Management folder, and then open the Content Sources folder.

4. Double-click Add Content Source.

5. The Add Content Source Wizard opens. Follow the on-screen instructions to complete the wizard. First, provide a path—an address or URL—that guides SharePoint Portal Server to the content to be crawled. Then, address any other details like scheduling index updates, creating search scopes for use with content sources, and creating rules for the content to be included in the index.

6. At this point, SharePoint Portal Server places the new content source in the Content Sources folder, thereby making the source available for users to search for and view on the dashboard site.

⚠ *If you experience general problems with crawling content sources, see "Troubleshooting Crawling a Content Source" in the "Troubleshooting" section at the end of the chapter.*

CONFIGURING SPS TO CRAWL WEB LINKS

Configuring SharePoint Portal Server to crawl Web links is perhaps the simplest crawling to compose. To do this is simply a matter of adding a content source that points to a Web site or Web page, by providing an address or URL for the site or page to be accessed. For example, enter the path `http://www.hp.com`.

TIP

To crawl Web links, note that no specific configuration is required in SharePoint Server Administration (this is very different from the work required to set up crawling Exchange 5.5 or Lotus Notes content sources, described later).

 If you have problems crawling a Web site that has successfully been crawled in the past, see "Failure in Crawling a Web Site" in the "Troubleshooting" section at the end of the chapter.

CONFIGURING SPS TO CRAWL FILE SHARES

Like configuring SPS to crawl Web links, crawling file shares is also a straightforward process. To add a content source for a file system or folder, simply provide the path to the location of the file or folder to be accessed, such as `//server/share/page.htm` or `\\server\share\folder`.

CAUTION

When creating a file share content source, do not specify a local or a mapped address, like `C:\My Documents\mydoc.doc`. Content sources that point to a file share must specify a path that follows universal naming convention (UNC), such as `\\server\share` or `http://server/share`. If you specify a local address, SharePoint Portal Server looks on that user's local drive C: for the document, rather than the drive C: from which the content source was created.

USING SHAREPOINT PORTAL SERVER ADMINISTRATION

Unlike crawling Web sites or file shares, SharePoint Portal Server must be specifically configured to crawl Exchange Server 5.5 public folders or Lotus Notes content sources. This configuration is performed via SharePoint Portal Server Administration. To access this utility from a SharePoint Portal Server machine

1. Click the Start button.
2. Click Programs.
3. Click Administrative Tools.
4. Click SharePoint Portal Server Administration.
5. At this point, the utility starts and displays the Console Root. Find the SPS server icon to be configured for crawling an Exchange 5.5 or Lotus Notes content source, and highlight it by clicking it once.
6. Finally, right-click this icon, and click Properties—from here, a number of tabs and options are presented. See Figure 18.1. We will discuss these tabs, and the configuration options that are presented, throughout this chapter.

18

Figure 18.1
SharePoint Portal Server properties—in this case, we are drilling down into the SharePoint Portal Server named "SPS."

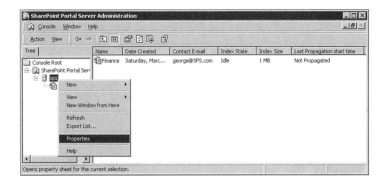

CRAWLING EXCHANGE SERVER 5.5 PUBLIC FOLDERS

To add a content source for an Exchange Server 5.5 public folder, the location of the public folder must be provided. An example of an Exchange 5.5 public folder address is `http://server/Public/Public_Folders`.

To specify the Exchange 5.5 server to crawl, open up SharePoint Server Administration, and

1. In the console tree, select the server from which you want to crawl Exchange public folders.

2. On the Action menu, click Properties (or right-click the server name, and then select Properties on the shortcut menu).

3. Click the Exchange 5.5 tab.

4. Ensure that the Enable Exchange 5.5 Crawl check box is selected.

5. In the Exchange server name field, type the name of the Exchange server that contains the public folder which you want SharePoint Portal Server to crawl.

6. In the Exchange server site name field, type the name of the Exchange server site that contains the public folder which you want SharePoint Portal Server to crawl.

7. In the Exchange server organization name field, type the name of the Exchange server organization that contains the public folder which you want SharePoint Portal Server to crawl.

8. Click Apply.

SPS only crawls public folder messages and contents of any attachments with supported filters. SharePoint Portal Server includes filters for Microsoft Office documents, HTML files, Tagged Image File Format (TIFF) files, and text files.

CAUTION

Private Exchange mailboxes, personal folders, and public favorites folders are not crawled.

To enable users to access information in Exchange 5.5 public folders, the *Outlook Web Access Server (OWA)* must be specified. OWA enables users to access Exchange server information from any Web browser.

The OWA server can be a dedicated server, or it can be an Exchange server with OWA enabled. The OWA server does not need to be the same server specified in the Exchange server name box. To specify the OWA server, refer to the following figure and steps:

1. In the console tree, select the server from which you want to crawl Exchange 5.5 public folders.

2. On the Action menu, click Properties (or right-click the server name, and then select Properties on the shortcut menu).

3. Click the Exchange 5.5 tab.

4. Verify that the Enable Exchange 5.5 Crawl check box is selected.

5. In the Outlook Web Access server name field, type the name of the OWA server/name of the OWA-enabled Exchange server.

6. Click Apply.

Figure 18.2
SharePoint Portal
Server properties,
completing the
Exchange 5.5 tab's
Outlook Web Access
server name field.

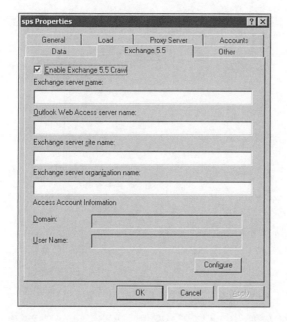

If you run into issues crawling Exchange 5.5, see "Exchange 5.5 Content Source Crawling Issues" in the "Troubleshooting" section at the end of the chapter.

CRAWLING EXCHANGE 2000 PUBLIC FOLDERS

Given the use of the *Web Storage System*, or WSS, in Exchange 2000, crawling Exchange 2000 public folders is nearly as simple as crawling Web sites. For example, assume that you want to crawl a folder named `http://server/Public/Public Folders/Some Folder`. To add a content source for an Exchange 2000 public folder, simply provide the location of the public folder.

CAUTION

The default Number of seconds to wait for request acknowledgement under the Load tab is 20 seconds, which may not be enough time for SPS to effectively crawl Exchange and other large content sources. Microsoft recommends that this wait time setting be modified to 60 seconds in such cases, allowing enough time for SPS to index the public folders of Exchange servers that might be quite busy during certain times of the day. See Figure 18.3 for clarification.

Figure 18.3

From the SharePoint Portal Server properties, modify the Load tab parameter indicating the number of seconds to wait for request acknowledgement here.

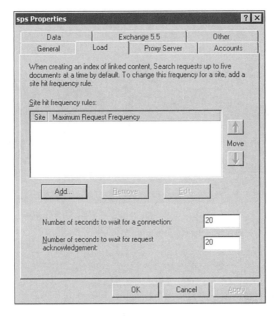

CONFIGURING SPS TO CRAWL LOTUS NOTES DATABASES

Both Lotus Domino 4.6a and R5 may be crawled. SharePoint does not differentiate between .NSF file types, regardless of the type of database, email or otherwise. However, the process to crawl these content sources is a bit more complex than other content sources.

- First, the Lotus Notes client must be installed on the SharePoint Portal Server.
- The server must be configured with the NotesSetup utility before content sources based on Lotus Notes databases may be added.

- To actually add a content source for a Lotus Notes database, the name of the database and the address of the database server to be accessed must be provided. An example of such a database might be data1.nsf, and an address might look like //lotusnoteserver.

- SharePoint Portal Server cannot crawl the database until the Lotus Notes *protocol handler* is finally configured. The protocol handler is simply a tool used to map property types between SPS and Lotus Notes. The protocol handler supports both number and text property types, and resolves numeric and string types to these two types. When a content source for SPS is mapped to Lotus Notes, the property type for each Notes property is displayed, whereas the property type for each SharePoint Portal Server property is not.

Before the Lotus Notes protocol handler may be configured, though, the following must be addressed:

- SharePoint Portal Server must be installed on the computer.
- A Lotus Notes server, version 4.6a or R5, must be available on the network.

TIP
> Ensure that the Lotus Notes server computer name does not contain a space. SharePoint Portal Server cannot crawl a Lotus Notes server that contains a space in its name.

18

- A Lotus Notes client must be installed (and tested for connectivity to the Lotus Notes server) on the same server as SharePoint Portal Server—this must occur prior to configuring the protocol handler.

Once the protocol handler is configured, Web folders may be edited to create a content source for the Lotus Notes database. At that time, an index could also be created to include the database.

Again, note that once the content source for Lotus Notes is created, and SharePoint Portal Server properties are mapped to Notes properties, only the property type for each Notes property is subsequently displayed—the property type for each SharePoint Portal Server property is not displayed.

CAUTION
> If the user maps a number to a string (or a string to a number), no error message displays.

THE LOTUS NOTES SECURITY MODEL

When SharePoint Portal Server creates an index of content stored on a Lotus Notes server, it uses the security settings for each Notes object to re-create security settings for that object in SharePoint Portal Server. This is done by using the Windows 2000 security model, not Notes' security.

The Lotus Notes security model differs significantly from Windows 2000. To maintain a secure content source while maintaining the security settings of the Notes database, user names must be set up to map one-for-one every Notes user name to a Windows 2000 user name. If this level of security is not required of the content residing in the Notes database, the protocol handler may be configured differently. That is, the security settings of the Notes database may be ignored if everyone who has access to the index created by SharePoint Portal Server also has access to the content stored in the Notes database.

➜ For details on planning and managing security in an SPS environment, including that related to Lotus Notes, **see** "Lotus Notes Servers," **p. 289**.

TIP

> If Lotus Notes security is "ignored," SharePoint Portal Server will actually perform a bit faster than otherwise during index creation and searching. In this case, SharePoint Portal Server also requires less time to configure because there is no need to map user names between Notes and Windows 2000, too.

CAUTION

> The extra bit of performance gained in lieu of ignoring Lotus Notes security is asinine if the result compromises data that should otherwise be secured. Understand the security requirements of your data before determining security configurations!

CREATING A LOTUS NOTES VIEW

If security is a consideration, and therefore Lotus Notes user names must be mapped to Windows 2000 user names, a shared view is essential. This is a job of the Lotus Notes administrator, who not only creates the user names, but also formats the Notes user names and ensures that the view is sorted on the Notes user name column.

CAUTION

> The view must be registered as a Shared View so that all clients can access it. Similarly, the database upon which this view is built contains the security mappings and should be protected accordingly. However, it must be accessible to the SharePoint Portal Server administrator.

CONFIGURING THE LOTUS NOTES PROTOCOL HANDLER

Determine the following *before* the protocol handler is configured:

- Location of the notes.ini file on SharePoint Portal Server. The full path name is required, for example. `E:\lotus\domino\notes.ini`.

- Location of the Lotus Notes installation directory on the SharePoint Portal Server computer, plus the full path name again (for example, `E:\lotus\domino\notes`).

- Notes user password (used by the default Notes account on the Notes client), and the protocol handler, to access the Notes server by impersonating the Notes user. Parenthetically, no password is required if the Notes user does not need a password to access the Notes server from the Notes client.

- To honor the security settings of the Notes database, SharePoint Portal Server must also contend with the following:

  Name of the Notes server with the view mapping the Notes user names to Windows user names.

  Name of the Notes database file that contains the view.

  Name of the view itself.

  Name of the columns in the view that map Notes to Windows user names.

At this point, now that Lotus Notes has been prepared for use with SPS, the protocol handler needs to be configured:

1. Execute the Lotus Notes Index Setup Wizard—in the console tree, select the server for which you want to install the Notes Protocol Handler.

2. In the Action menu, click Properties (or right-click the server name, and then select Properties on the shortcut menu).

3. Click the Other tab.

4. Click the Run Wizard button, as displayed in Figure 18.4—the Lotus Notes Index Setup Wizard is displayed.

Figure 18.4
The importance of running the Lotus Notes Index Setup Wizard prior to creating Notes content sources is clearly illustrated here.

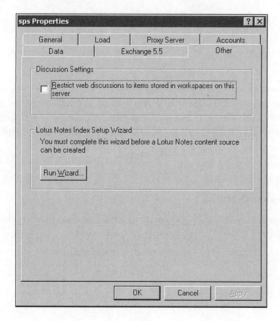

18

5. Click Next.

6. On the Register Lotus Notes For Use With Microsoft SharePoint Portal Server page, verify the following:

   Location of the notes.ini file (if necessary, type it in, such as
   `E:\lotus\domino\notes.ini`).

   Location of the Notes installation (if necessary, type it in, such as
   `E:\lotus\domino\notes`).

7. Type the Notes user password in the Password box, and then confirm it via Confirm Password.

8. If you wish to ignore the security settings of the Notes database, select the option to Ignore Lotus Notes security.

9. Click Next.

10. On the Specify Lotus Notes Owner Field to Windows User Name Mapping page:

    Enter the name of the Notes server in the Lotus Notes server name box. This represents the Notes server hosting the Notes-to-Windows NT mapping.

    Enter the Notes database file name—note that the database file ends in .nsf.

    Enter the name of the view in View name. This is the name of the view that contains the Notes and Windows NT ID columns.

    Enter the name of the Notes ID column in Lotus Notes field name column title. This is the title of the column in the view.

    Enter the name of the Windows user name column in the Windows user name column title.

    Click Next.

    Finally, at the Completing the Lotus Notes Index Setup Wizard page, click Finish.

CAUTION

If the wizard fails, the MSSearch Service must be stopped and started again prior to rerunning the wizard. Also note that troubleshooting issues may be complicated by the fact that the wizard will display only one error message, regardless of the number of actual errors generated.

CRAWLING OTHER SPS WORKSPACES

SharePoint Portal Server may crawl workspaces external to the local workspace. To add a content source for a Web folder that is external to your workspace, simply provide the location of the Web folder, such as `http://server/workspace/folder`.

CAUTION

You may only add content sources that point to Web folders which are external to the workspace in which you are currently working. That is, you cannot add a content source to crawl the same workspace that contains the content source, and by the same token, you cannot add a content source in the current workspace that points to the same workspace.

CRAWLING WITHOUT A PROXY SERVER

As we have seen, SharePoint Portal Server can be configured to crawl a variety of content sources. In some cases, it might be advantageous to set up an external Web site crawl so that a proxy server is not required. SharePoint Portal Server can create indexes of external sites if another means of access to these sites is available, such as remote Winsock.

To configure SPS to *not* use a proxy server

- In the console tree, select the server to be configured to not use a proxy server.
- In the Action menu, click Properties (or right-click the server name, and then select Properties on the shortcut menu).
- Click the Proxy Server tab.
- Click Do not connect using a proxy server.
- Click Apply. It's that easy!

Figure 18.5
Click the Proxy Server tab in Server Properties to change, configure, or disable the use of a proxy server.

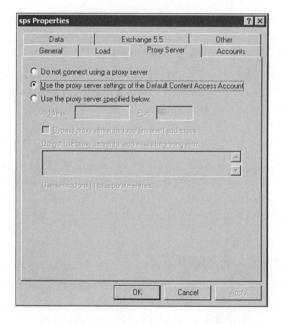

 For those of you running into problems configuring crawling with a proxy server in place, see "Proxy Server Issues" in the "Troubleshooting" section at the end of the chapter.

BUILDING AN INDEX VIA CRAWLED CONTENT

Now that we have seen how to crawl various content sources, we are back on track looking at the end-to-end process. At this point, we will assume that all of the crawls we have performed have created or updated one or more of our workplace indexes.

Back when we initially created our SPS workspace, SharePoint Portal Server automatically created an index for that workspace. When we added documents to the workspace or modified existing documents, SharePoint Portal Server modified the index to include the changes. When we added content sources or changed their settings, we then crawled the content sources to update the index.

> **TIP**
>
> Indexes may also be updated manually by using SharePoint Portal Server Administration via the Microsoft Management Console (MMC), or by using Web folders. Indexes may also be updated automatically by sending notifications (available only for file shares located on an NTFS partition of a server running Windows NT 4.0 or 2000) .

The actual process employed by SharePoint Portal Server to add a document in an index is accomplished by

- Filtering the document.
- Word breaking the document.

→ For additional information regarding word breaking, **see** "Word Breaking", **p. 114**.

LEVERAGING THE WORK OF CRAWLING BY SEARCHING

After indexes are created, SharePoint Portal Server may then be used to search for content. Ultimately, this is what crawling is all about—facilitating end-user searching. To do so, the dashboard site (like the initial workspace index, also created automatically upon installing SPS) is most often employed. The content being searched may reside in the current workspace, or it may reside outside of the workspace and linked to it by a content source.

The culmination of the search provides us with "search results". As end users become more knowledgeable regarding the content that they are searching, their searches will naturally become more pointed and narrow. In this way, users will enjoy faster response times as they specify better search criteria that ultimately thins the search results.

FUNCTIONAL CONSIDERATIONS

In the next few sections, we will look into functional considerations that must be addressed to enable crawling the content sources detailed in the previous pages.

AFTER ADDING CONTENT

When you add content sources to a workspace or change their settings, the content sources must be crawled so as to update the index. Regularly scheduled updates can make a lot of sense in this regard, to ensure that all of the content that appears on the dashboard site for search and viewing is recent.

CAUTION

> Keep in mind that crawling and creating/updating indexes is quite processor- and disk-intensive, as well as potentially network-intensive. Therefore, schedule crawls accordingly.

USING AND CONFIGURING IFILTERS

To crawl documents that have proprietary file extensions, you must register the IFilter for that file type. When configuring content sources, specify the file types to include in the index. For example, a coordinator may want to include files with .gwa extensions in the index.

Each file type has an IFilter associated with it. The IFilter for a particular file type must be registered on the SPS computer crawling that file type. Once the IFilter is registered, documents of that file type can be crawled and included in the index. Note that if a file type is added to an index but no filter is registered, only the file properties are included in the index.

Refer to the documentation accompanying each IFilter in regard to the procedure to register it—each is potentially quite unique. Fortunately, SharePoint Portal Server includes filters for Microsoft Office documents, HTML files, Tagged Image File Format (TIFF) files, and text files.

 Should you experience difficulties in working with a particular TIFF file type, see "TIFF Issues" in the "Troubleshooting" section at the end of the chapter.

FILE EXTENSION TYPE RULES

You can use file extension type rules to specify file types (indicated by file extensions) to include or exclude when crawling an index of all content sources. The file type inclusion/exclusion rules apply only to content that is stored outside the workspace but included in the index through content sources. Content stored in the workplace does not apply. SharePoint Portal Server updates the index to include content from document shortcuts in the same way as other content sources, though.

To add a file extension type

1. In the workspace, open the Management folder, and then open the Content Sources folder.
2. Double-click Additional Settings.
3. Click the Rules tab.
4. Click File Types.
5. Select the file type inclusion/exclusion method.
6. Type the file extension type that you want to include/exclude.

7. Click Add.

8. Click OK.

To remove a file extension type

1. Select the Rules tab.

2. Click File Types.

3. In the list that appears, select a file extension type, and then click Remove.

4. Click Yes.

5. Click OK.

CRAWLING TO MAP CUSTOM METADATA TO PROPERTIES

In the process of crawling, SharePoint Portal Server gathers full-text information from documents and includes it in the index. However, the ability to natively map *metadata*, or data about the data, to properties of SharePoint Portal Server is restricted to only the contents of Lotus Notes databases. Mapping metadata from other sources (that is, from file share and Web site content sources) is possible, though not natively. That is, no user interface exists for this mapping. Instead, this is accomplished by writing custom code.

 If you need additional assistance troubleshooting Lotus Notes content source crawling, see "Troubles Crawling a Lotus Notes Content Source" in the "Troubleshooting" section at the end of the chapter.

Examples of metadata for various sources include the following:

■ Properties for HTML files are often maintained in <META> tags.

■ Properties for Microsoft Office documents are usually maintained in OLE structured storage (this metadata may be displayed by clicking on Properties from the File menu within the specific Office applications, such as Excel or Word) .

There are a number of steps required to configure a SharePoint Portal Server workspace to crawl external content, while allowing the properties and meta tags in that external content to be promoted as properties in SharePoint Portal Server. To promote properties from external content into SharePoint Portal Server properties

1. Create a document profile that includes the list of profile properties to be made available through SharePoint Portal Server. This profile may include custom properties.

2. Create a content source that points to the external data. When saving it, do not create an index.

3. Modify and apply the property mapping code to map the external content meta tags and property tags to the SharePoint Portal Server document profile properties. See Microsoft's SharePoint Portal Server Resource Kit for more details and sample code to accomplish this.

4. Flush any cached schema by stopping and starting the SharePoint Portal Server services (via Control Panel, Services).

5. Start the full update for the content source.

EXCLUDING AND RESTRICTING CRAWLING

SharePoint Portal Server complies with the rules of robots exclusion. Web servers use these rules to control access to their sites by preventing *robots*, a generic term for Web crawlers or spiders, from accessing certain areas of their Web sites. SPS always searches for the Robots.txt file when crawling, and conforms to the restrictions in it. A Robots.txt file indicates specifically where robots are permitted on the site, and also allows for specific crawlers to be blocked from crawling the site. For example, to prevent a specific robot known for frequently tying up valuable CPU and disk resources from accessing your portal, update the Robots.txt file. You can also simply limit access to specific workspaces on the server in this manner.

The Robots.txt file is not actually installed with SharePoint Portal Server, but it can be manually created or copied from another server and placed in the root of the server. Keep in mind that the Robots.txt file is only "read" by SPS once a day. If you copy a new Robots.txt file to the root node of the workspace or even change the existing Robots.txt file, the changes will not go into effect at once. If the changes need to be implemented immediately, the SPS service needs to be restarted.

In lieu of blocking crawling altogether, access to certain documents and subsequent links may be blocked by using HTML *meta tags*. A meta tag tells a crawler whether indexing a document or following its links is permitted. This is done by using INDEX/NOINDEX and FOLLOW/NOFOLLOW attributes in the tag. Use NOINDEX and NOFOLLOW, for example, to completely prevent a document from being crawled and its embedded links from being followed.

PERFORMANCE CONSIDERATIONS

The crawling and indexing process can consume a significant amount of both wall-clock time and hardware resources if there is a large amount of text in the content being crawled. Fortunately, to optimize these processes, a number of SPS-related architecture considerations, parameters, or components may be addressed or "tuned," including the overall architecture, optimizing the server configuration, and configuring/tuning the crawling process itself.

 If you find yourself in the unenviable position of trying to troubleshoot crawling issues arising after a power failure, or trying to resume crawling after restoring your crawling server from a tape backup, see "Troubleshooting the Impact of Power Failures During Crawling" and "Crawl Issues After Performing an SPS Restore," respectively, in the "Troubleshooting" section at the end of the chapter.

OPTIMIZING SPS ARCHITECTURE FOR CRAWLING

While SharePoint Portal Server may be installed on a single machine, for anything but the smallest of implementations this is simply not a realistic solution. Even a portal installation for 200 users should be spread across no less than two or three servers: one server dedicated to crawling and indexing, one to document management and other content-related services, and perhaps even another to searching.

→ For two real-world sample scenarios where specifying a dedicated crawl server is appropriate, **see** "Installing the Crawling Servers," **p. 560** in Chapter 21, and "Configuring Crawling," **p. 598** in Chapter 22.

This is true in most implementations—SharePoint Portal Server services should be distributed across multiple servers for optimum performance. The next few pages drill down into methods of optimizing crawling.

SHARED VERSUS DEDICATED WORKSPACES OR SERVERS

Rather than maintaining a single server for both crawling/indexing and supporting user searches, an excellent practice is to split these functions out.

For example, one or more servers may be configured to create and update indexes. These servers are dedicated to crawling content sources—they are not used for document management or searching. Each index is then propagated to the workspace on another server or servers dedicated to searching, called a destination workspace. Typically, this amounts to what is known as an index workspace.

The servers dedicated to crawling/indexing create an index of this content and then propagate or copy the indexes to the index workspace(s) on the servers dedicated to searching.

Note that the server or servers dedicated to searching contain one workspace for every four indexes to be propagated. These, like the crawling/indexing servers above, are dedicated in terms of "single function" too. They provide the dashboard site, and store documents displayed on the dashboard site too, such as announcements, holiday schedules, and organization information.

SYNCHRONIZING CRAWL/INDEX AND SEARCH SERVERS

SharePoint Portal Server supports synchronizing servers dedicated to crawling with servers dedicated to searching. During the synchronization process, the servers compare metadata about the index content, category hierarchy information, subscriptions, and auto-categorization rules.

However, synchronization becomes a problem if your organization uses firewalls. Placement and configuration of these firewalls must be methodically planned. That is, index propagation requires the standard Windows file sharing protocol—if you are using index propagation, most firewalls simply cannot exist between the server dedicated to creating and updating indexes and the server dedicated to searching. Best case: If a firewall must exist between these servers, it must allow Windows file share access.

Optimizing the Data Store

To increase performance or simplify file management, the location of the following data store and log files associated with the SharePoint Portal Server computer must be carefully addressed:

Search Indexes—By default, the index resides under the root node. SharePoint Portal Server Administration may be used to change this path, for example if a fast pair of dedicated hardware-mirrored RAID 1 disks is later needed to maximize write performance and availability. Note that if this path changes, the existing indexes do not automatically move to the new index location—only new indexes are automatically created in the new location.

> **TIP**
>
> To move existing indexes to a new location, see ToolsHowTo.txt in the Support\Tools directory on the SharePoint Portal Server CD.

Search Temporary Files—SharePoint Portal Server may need to create temporary files for documents being crawled. Again, use SharePoint Portal Server Administration to move the files to a different drive on the same computer. For best performance and availability, the temporary files location should point to a dedicated fast pair of hardware-mirrored disks.

In both of the preceding cases—indexes and temporary files—a fast pair of dedicated hardware-mirrored drives speaks to the need to keep other files—including data, property store files, indexes, WSS system files, operating system, pagefile, and so on—off of these dedicated drive pairs. That is, these other files and resources should reside on their own set or sets of disk drives.

Optimizing MSSearch

By default, the Microsoft Search (MSSearch) service temporary files are kept in the folder specified by the system TMP variable (typically WINNT\TEMP on the C: drive). If the C:\WINNT\TEMP directory does not exist, the temporary files are stored in the folder specified by the system TEMP variable (sometimes C:\TEMP, depending on IT standards and customs). To optimize performance, reset the TMP variable to point to a dedicated fast pair of hardware-mirrored drives.

> **CAUTION**
>
> It is imperative that enough space exists on this drive to store the MSSearch temporary files. Otherwise, MSSearch will fail to operate correctly.

WSS Optimization

Every SharePoint Portal Server computer contains one public store (wss.mdb), and all workspaces hosted on the server sit on this Web Storage System—the Microsoft Web Storage System Database file. Use SharePoint Portal Server Administration to change this path, for example to a fast and comfortably sized high-performance RAID set. Upon doing so, the existing file moves to the new location.

Figure 18.6
Click the Data tab in Server Properties to quickly identify the location of various SPS data and log files.

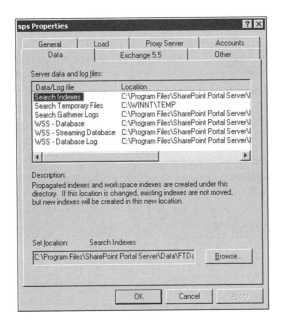

The Web Storage System-Streaming Database (wss.stm) is used for streaming files, and as such contains data and is a companion to the Web Storage System Database file mentioned above. Together, these two files form the SharePoint database. Like wss.mdb, this file should also be moved to a comfortably sized high-performance RAID set. Over time, these two files will tend to grow quickly.

The log files for the Web Storage System Database should also be placed on a separate pair of fast hardware-mirrored drives for optimum performance and availability. Given the "write" nature of logs in general, an array controller supporting battery-backed cached writes is most desirable. Use SharePoint Portal Server Administration to change this path, noting that when the location changes, the existing files will move to the new location.

OPTIMIZING THE PROPERTY STORE

The placement of the Property Store and Property Store Log files, which contain the metadata from documents, should also be addressed. Unlike the other files above, the file location *cannot* be modified by using SharePoint Portal Server Administration. To modify these file locations, refer to the ToolsHowTo.txt document in the Support\Tools directory on the SharePoint Portal Server CD.

TIP

> For optimal performance, the Property Store and Property Store Log files should be split out onto dedicated physical drives. These files are accessed and shared across all work-spaces on the local SharePoint Portal Server.

As a general rule of thumb, assuming budget approval, if you crawl a large quantity of documents (multimillion documents) or simply need the fastest portal implementation available, optimize performance by placing the indexes, property store, log files, Web Storage System files, and Web Storage System log files each on dedicated drives. Hardware-based RAID 1 or 0+1 implementations are best for both logs and data files, though data files (given their less stringent write requirements) can often be successfully housed on RAID 5 volumes, thereby reducing overall cost.

→ For a more thorough discussion of the various RAID types and the benefits of each, **see** "RAID 1 Versus RAID 5," **p. 589**.

LOAD OPTIONS OPTIMIZATION

As creating an index requires resources both from the server that creates the index and from the server that stores the content included in the index, Microsoft determined early on that a method of specifying Load options or settings would be helpful in tuning SharePoint. Using these settings helps to ensure that the load on the computers being crawled is manageable.

Load options consist of site hit frequency rules and time-out settings. These are detailed in the following sections.

SITE HIT FREQUENCY

A site hit frequency rule determines how often SharePoint Portal Server requests documents from a Web site, and how many documents are requested. By default, the site hit frequency is limited to five simultaneous document requests—refer to Figure 18.7. You can use the site hit frequency rule to modify demand on specific sites. Though you may want a higher document request frequency for creating or updating an index on your own intranet, it is recommended that you specify a lower frequency for external Web sites, so that you do not overload the sites with document requests. Web sites can identify you from the email address provided when creating an index. If you overload a site with requests, you could be denied access to that site in the future.

18

Figure 18.7
Default Site Hit
Frequency Rule set-
tings.

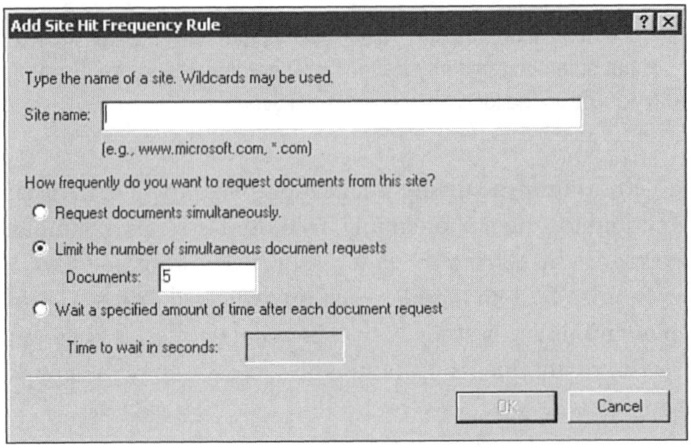

To add a site hit frequency rule

1. In the console tree, select the server for which you want to add a site hit frequency rule.

2. On the Action menu, click Properties (or right-click the server name, and then select Properties on the shortcut menu).

3. Click the Load tab.

4. Click Add.

5. The Add Site Hit Frequency Rule dialog box appears.

6. In Site name, type the site name, such as http://example.microsoft.com. Multiple site name expressions may be entered, and these are evaluated in order (therefore, "*" should always be the last expression).

7. Select one of the following frequency options:

   • Request documents simultaneously. SharePoint Portal Server uses all potential/allocated system resources to request as many documents as possible, with no delay between document requests. This setting is usually too resource-intensive for Internet sites, but may be acceptable for some intranet sites.

   • Limit the number of simultaneous document requests, thereby specifying the maximum number of documents that SharePoint Portal Server can request at one time from the site. The default setting for all sites is five simultaneous document requests.

   • Wait a specified amount of time after each document request, that is, delay a certain period of time between document requests. SharePoint Portal Server requests one document per site at one time, and then waits for the specified amount of time to elapse before requesting the next document.

8. If the frequency is too high, SharePoint Portal Server can easily overload Web sites with requests. Consider specifying lower frequency rates for Internet sites over which you may have no control, and increasing the frequency for intranet sites over which you do have control. Otherwise, an astute Web server administrator will simply block you from crawling their site by updating his own Robots.txt file.

9. Click OK.

TIME-OUT SETTINGS

Time-out settings determine how long SharePoint Portal Server waits for either a connection to a particular site or a response from a site. Use these settings to minimize time waiting for connections to servers that are down, too busy to respond, or otherwise unavailable.

OPTIMIZING INDEX RESOURCE USAGE

The General tab of the server properties allows for index resource usage to be tuned. In fact, it is here that a "dedicated" index server is created—by moving the slider control all the way over to the right, the server becomes a dedicated index server. This slider also allows for granular control of the amount of memory and other resources that the server allocates to updating indexes.

Figure 18.8
The Indexing resource usage slide bar enables you to configure how the SharePoint Portal Server's resources are used, varying from dedicated to background.

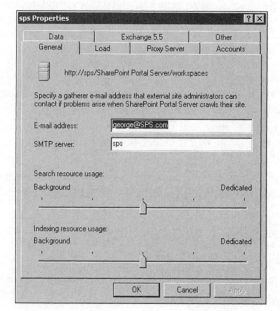

To tune indexing resource usage

1. In the console tree, select the server for which you want to add a site hit frequency rule.

2. On the Action menu, click Properties (or right-click the server name, and then select Properties on the shortcut menu).

3. Click the General tab, if necessary.

4. Adjust the slide bar for Indexing resource usage, as required.

5. Click Apply.

6. Click OK.

→ For detailed indexing and search usage data, **see** "Indexing and Search Resource Usage", **p. 494** in Chapter 19.

THE CRAWLING PROCESS—AN OPTIMIZATION OVERVIEW

In regard to optimizing the actual crawling process to increase performance, the crawl method employed to update indexes is of paramount importance. In this section, we look closely at three methods of tuning the crawl process—Adaptive vs. Incremental vs. Notification Updates.

Regardless of the tuning method, we must use the Scheduled Updates tab on the Additional Settings Properties page to schedule incremental and adaptive updates for the content sources in the index.

ADAPTIVE UPDATES

An *adaptive build* is an incremental build with an added statistical formula that allows SharePoint Portal Server to maintain a record of how often content changes. With this data, SPS will then crawl only the content that is statistically most likely to have changed. All content sources that do not support notification updates (see the next section) participate in adaptive updates by default. Note that if no updates have ever been done, the first time an adaptive update is performed is the same as performing a full update. Similarly, the second time an adaptive update is performed is the same as performing an incremental update. Only by the third time the adaptive update is performed is a real improvement in performance apparent.

To configure an adaptive update

1. Select the Adaptive updates check box.

2. On the Schedule tab of the Adaptive Updates Properties page, select the appropriate time and days for the index updates.

3. Click OK twice.

An adaptive update does not provide a significant performance improvement on small corpuses (those fewer than approximately 2,500 documents). But it is faster than an incremental or full update, at the expense of occasionally missing some updated content. To compensate for this, Microsoft ensures that documents that have not been touched by SPS for two weeks will always be included, even if they have not been updated. Thus, worst case, the index has two-week-old data.

Performance improvement between an adaptive update and an incremental update (discussed more in the next section) depends on the number of documents and the frequency of changes to the documents. The higher the percentage of documents that change infrequently, the better the performance is.

INCREMENTAL UPDATES

An incremental update of an index contains only changed content—deleted content is removed from the index, and unchanged content remains as is. Therefore, performing an incremental update will always be faster than performing a full update. If an incremental update is the first update that you create—that is, if you have not previously performed a full update—that incremental update is actually a full update. This occurs only if the incremental update is the first update you do. Subsequent incremental updates are true incremental updates.

To configure an incremental update

1. Select the Incremental updates check box.
2. On the Schedule tab of the Incremental Updates Properties page, select the appropriate time and days for the index updates.
3. Click OK twice.

18

NOTIFICATION UPDATES

A notification update is the most efficient of all types of index updates. SharePoint Portal Server uses this method by default when possible. If a content source supports notification updates, it automatically sends a notification of any changes made to the index. This notification triggers an update of the individual content source in the index. Notifications are available only for crawling file shares located on an NTFS partition on a computer running Windows NT 4.0 or Windows 2000.

> **NOTE**
>
> SharePoint Portal Server also updates notification-based content sources when the index is reset.

LIMITATIONS OF SPS CRAWLING

While SharePoint Portal Server is a powerful search tool, featuring strong search and portal core functionality, it does have certain limitations. For example, general mapping capabilities like those found in products from Orbital Software or Tacit do not exist. In SharePoint, then, such mapping is accomplished simply through writing custom code.

SharePoint Portal Server also does not include Web discussions in the index when crawling sister SPS machines or workspaces. Thus, while it finds and indexes other documents from those servers and workspaces, discussion items are sorely lacking in search results.

Filtering limitations also present a challenge in Microsoft SharePoint Portal Server. Filters remove formatting and extract both the text of the document and any properties defined in the file itself. SharePoint Portal Server has a limit of 16 megabytes (MB) of text data that it filters from a single document. After this limit is reached, SPS enters a warning in the *gatherer log* (a log file created by SPS after an index is updated) and SharePoint Portal Server considers the document successfully indexed.

TIP

> The 16MB limit applies only to the text in the document, not to figures or graphs or other non-text material. The file size of the document as a whole does not matter.

If you find yourself without a clear place to start in troubleshooting general index–related issues, see "Viewing the Gatherer Log" in the "Troubleshooting" section at the end of the chapter.

Finally, as we have read previously, destination workspaces can only accept up to four propagated indexes. If you create more than four index workspaces on a server dedicated to crawling, you must create additional workspaces on the destination server to propagate the additional indexes.

TIP

> One workaround involves using multiple index workspaces. One index workspace, for example, might be dedicated to crawling your intranet site and other internal content sources, while a second index workspace might be dedicated to crawling Internet-based content.

SECURITY CONSIDERATIONS

In the next few sections, we will look at security from a crawling perspective. Security is obviously essential in regard to document management tasks and the search function in particular. It is critical to restrict access to sensitive information, whether this involves restricting the viewing of a document to only those who may edit or approve it, or "hiding" documents from those with no reason to even know that they exist. In this latter case, when viewing the results of searches, a user will not even be aware of the fact that documents to which they have no access are not displayed—they simply do not exist for this user.

CONFIGURING SECURITY

SharePoint Portal Server recognizes any security policies currently assigned to an organization's servers, file shares, and databases. Additionally, SPS maps the security scheme for each content source to Windows 2000 security and applies it both when the content is crawled and when a user performs a search on the content.

If SharePoint Portal Server is configured to crawl content located on a server in a different domain, do not use domain local group accounts to secure the content on the server being crawled. This is because SPS may not be able to recognize domain local group accounts, resulting in content not being crawled as expected.

MANAGING ACCESS ACCOUNTS

Access to content stored outside of the workspace is managed from SharePoint Portal Server Administration. Access accounts are used to specify user names and passwords in order to provide the required permissions to access Web sites, servers, and network resources. These accounts are configured on the Accounts tab of the Properties page for the server node. See Figure 18.9.

Figure 18.9
Configuring accounts for creating indexes for content sources is a simple task in SharePoint Portal Server.

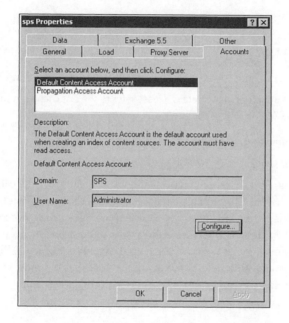

The default content access account provides the default user name and password for SharePoint Portal Server to supply when crawling content outside of the current workspace. The account must have Read permission, and the user name and password must resolve to an existing Windows NT or Windows 2000 account. Changing the details of this account is quite straightforward. Simply click the Configure button identified in the previous figure (18.9), and the following screen is displayed, allowing for easily updating account data.

Figure 18.10
Changing/updating account information is a straightforward task—simply update the boxes for domain, account, password, and password confirmation, and then ensure that the account is updated from an NT/Windows 2000 perspective as well. And don't forget to stop and start the MSSearch service!

TROUBLESHOOTING

Troubleshooting crawling and index-creation-related issues is covered in this section.

→ Note that for additional troubleshooting details, please refer to the last chapter in this book, "Troubleshooting," beginning **p. 615**, Chapter 23.

VIEWING THE GATHERER LOG

I need to view the Gatherer Log after SPS updates an index.

Each time SharePoint Portal Server updates an index, it creates what is called a *gatherer log file* for the workspace. This file contains data about URLs that SharePoint Portal Server accesses while creating an index. The file records successful accesses, access errors, and accesses disallowed by rules (should the administrator or coordinator need to debug the index restrictions). This log may be viewed for up to five days from an ASP page in the workspace. After five days, SPS deletes the log. Take note that the most recent log can be determined by observing the file name—the name with the largest number is the most recent. Thus, workspacename.2.gthr is newer than workspacename.1.gthr.

To actually view the gatherer log

1. In the workspace, open the Management folder, and then open the Content Sources folder.

2. To view the gatherer log for a specific content source or several specific content sources, click once to select the content source or sources. To view the log for the entire folder, do not select any content sources—simply go to the next step below.

3. In the Web view of the Content Sources folder, click the link named Click here for Detailed Log. The Web view is in the lower left corner of the folder view.

4. The Gatherer Log Viewer page now opens in a browser window, and the following three sections are expanded—overview/statistics, detailed log entries, and filter criteria. Under Filter criteria, the following may be viewed:

Content Source—This allows filtering by specific content sources. By default, All in Range is selected.

Documents Added, Removed, or Updated—Note that the All the above option is selected by default.

5. If you do not supply any additional filtering criteria, SharePoint Portal Server builds a log by default. According to Microsoft's SPS Resource Kit, this log loads from the most recent log entry to the least recent log entry, from the beginning of the log file, starting with information from the most recent crawl, or from the maximum number of entries allowed; whichever is fastest.

6. Click Submit to include your new filter criteria, or click Reset to reload complete information from the logs and to recalculate all statistics.

7. Wait for the gatherer log to compile a summary of scanned file statistics and information.

Fortunately, to assist us in tuning and configuring SPS, Microsoft has included a number of Performance Monitor counters that we can leverage. One counter in particular regarding the Microsoft Gatherer performance object includes Documents Delayed Retry, which is the number of documents that are retried after a time-out. When this number is greater than zero, the Web Storage System on the local server being crawled is actually shut down.

Another important crawling counter tracked by the Microsoft Gatherer performance object is Threads Accessing Network, which is the number of threads waiting for a response from the filter process. If no activity is occurring and this number equals the number of filtering threads, this may indicate a network problem or unavailability of the server being crawled.

A host of crawl-based counters are tracked in another object as well, the Microsoft Gatherer Projects performance object. These are identified and described in Table 18.1:

TABLE 18.1   MICROSOFT GATHERER COUNTERS

Counter Name	Counter Description
Adaptive Crawl Accepts	Documents accepted by adaptive update.
Adaptive Crawl Error Samples	Documents accessed for error sampling.
Adaptive Crawl Errors	Documents that adaptive update incorrectly rejects.
Adaptive Crawl Excludes	Documents that adaptive update excludes.
Adaptive Crawl False Positives	Number of false positives that occur when the adaptive update has predicted that a document has changed when it has not. If this number is high, the adaptive update algorithm is not modeling the changes in the documents correctly.

continues

TABLE 18.1   CONTINUED

Counter Name	Counter Description
Adaptive Crawl Total	Documents to which adaptive update logic was applied.
Changed Documents	Documents that have changed since the last crawl.
Crawls in progress	Number of crawls in progress.
Incremental Crawls	Number of incremental crawls in progress.
Not Modified	Number of documents that were not filtered because no modification was detected since the last crawl.
Started Documents	Number of documents initiated into the Gatherer service. This includes the number of documents on hold, in the active queue, and currently filtered. When this number goes to zero during a crawl, the crawl will be completed.
URLs in History	Number of files (URLs) in the history list. This indicates the total number of URLs covered by the crawl, either successfully indexed or failed.

TIFF ISSUES

I'm having problems dealing with TIFF files. How can I correct this?

As previously discussed, SharePoint Portal Server Setup automatically installs an IFilter for TIFF files. This filter handles both .tif and .tiff file extensions. When crawling TIFF files, SPS only looks at file properties—this process is quite clean. If optical character recognition (OCR) is enabled, though, SharePoint Portal Server scans the TIFF document and attempts to recognize words and characters such that additional data may be gleaned and included in the index. This process is less than perfect, but quite valuable in many cases.

Should issues arise with TIFF files, a registry key may be updated to specify writing TIFF-based error messages in the Application Log (one of three logs accessible via the Microsoft Windows 2000 Event Viewer, also referred to as the Windows 2000 event log). By default, the SPS Server logs TIFF error messages in the gatherer log.

CAUTION

> After editing any of the TIFF filter registry keys, the Microsoft Search (MSSearch) service must be restarted. If the SharePoint Portal Server being restarted also serves as an Exchange or SQL Server, keep in mind that restarting the MSSearch service will impact these applications as well.

TROUBLESHOOTING CRAWLING A CONTENT SOURCE

I'm having problems crawling content sources.

If crawling a content source fails, verify the following:

- Is access denied? If so, has the default content access account expired? If another content access account is being used, is this account still valid? If the account is valid and access is still denied, a permissions issue may exist in terms of accessing or reading the content.

- Is the "file not found"? If this is the case, check the URL for the content source. Try accessing the URL from a standard Web browser while logged on as the specified access account, thus verifying at some level whether the URL is valid and the account information is good.

Also, be sure to review the gatherer log as previously discussed. In this way, detailed information on the search may be of assistance in troubleshooting.

FAILURE OF CRAWLING A WEB SITE

I'm having problems crawling a Web site but I have done it in the past. What gives?

If crawling simply fails to work on a Web site on the Internet, and it has worked previously, the time-out settings or the proxy settings may simply need to be reconfigured. Review these areas, and verify entries.

TROUBLES CRAWLING A LOTUS NOTES CONTENT SOURCE

If crawling a Lotus Notes content source fails, start troubleshooting by confirming the following possibilities:

- Has the Lotus Notes protocol handler been configured correctly? If running the Lotus Notes Index Setup Wizard fails for any reason, don't forget to restart MSSearch before running the wizard again!

- Does the protocol handler need to be reconfigured? Reconfiguration of the protocol handler is required in the event that the Lotus Notes installation has changed. Reconfiguration is also required if Lotus Notes security changes (which may be likely, for example if users are added, changed, or removed in regard to the access ID).

- If the security mapping has changed, the MSSearch service must be stopped and restarted for the changes to take effect.

- Has the Lotus Notes administrator changed the port number that the Lotus Notes server uses? If this is the case, any content sources must be fully updated.

- Does the Lotus Notes server name contain a space? This is a no-no, as SharePoint Portal Server cannot crawl a Lotus Notes server that contains a space in the computer name.

EXCHANGE 5.5 CONTENT SOURCE CRAWLING ISSUES

My search results aren't what I expected when crawling Exchange 5.5.

If crawling an Exchange Server 5.5 content source fails or search results are not as expected, explore the following possibilities:

- Is Outlook installed on the SharePoint Portal Server computer? If so, is the optional Collaboration Data Objects (CDO) feature—included with Outlook—installed on the server, too? Not only must CDO be installed on the SharePoint Portal Server computer, but it is also recommended that Outlook be the only installed mail client.

- Does the administrator account specified on the Exchange 5.5 tab of the Properties page of the server node have permissions on the site of the server running Exchange? Ditto for the site configuration containers, too—the administrator account must have permissions on both the site and site configuration containers. SharePoint Portal Server uses the administrator account to verify access when a user searches from the dashboard site.

- Has the administrator account changed? If this account or password is changed in Windows NT 4.0 or Windows 2000, the account in SharePoint Portal Server Administration must also be updated immediately. Otherwise, if a user executes a search query from the dashboard site that contains one or more Exchange Server 5.5 items in the results, the entire query fails. SPS then simply logs an error in the event log.

- Do queries continue to fail after the account in SharePoint Portal Server Administration has been changed? Ensure that the MSSearch service has been stopped and restarted—this is required for the change to take effect, and the queries to actually have a shot at completing correctly.

PROXY SERVER ISSUES

I have a proxy server in place and it is causing me problems configuring crawling.

When using a proxy server and crawling Internet sites, issues may arise that are described in the following scenarios:

- Does the account being used for the crawl have privileges on the proxy server? The account used to crawl Internet sites must have privileges on the proxy server, else crawling Internet sites is impossible.

> **TIP**
>
> If the default content access account is being used, try to access the URL with Internet Explorer while simply logged on as the default content access account.

- Does crawling content on an Internet site fail? When crawling Internet sites, SharePoint Portal Server first tries to use the default content access account. If that account is not configured, SharePoint Portal Server tries to use Anonymous. In either case, crawling fails unless the site allows access.

TROUBLESHOOTING THE IMPACT OF POWER FAILURES DURING CRAWLING

We had a major power failure. Now I have to resume crawling and I'm having a lot of problems. What should I do?

If power to the server is interrupted during a crawl or update, the crawl or update continues after power is restored. First, though, the index is displayed as in the "initializing" state for a certain period of time (the period of time ranges from seconds to perhaps hours, depending on the size of the crawl). The crawl resumes after it finishes initializing. Meanwhile, the index is available for queries during this time.

Specifically, the following status messages may be displayed for the update once power is restored to the server:

TABLE 18.2   INDEX STATUS MESSAGES

Status	Definition
Compiling	MSSearch is assembling the index.
Flushing	MSSearch is assembling the index at the end of a search/run.
Idle	No update of the index is in progress.
Indexing	An update of the index is in progress. MSSearch searches content to update the index by following links contained in documents, or by following directory trees in a file system or other hierarchical storage systems such as Lotus Notes databases, Exchange servers, and other SharePoint Portal Server computers.
Initializing	The server is loading the index.
Paused	The update is paused.
Processing notifications	MSSearch has received one or more notifications. MSSearch receives one notification per document. When processing notifications, the server extracts the properties and contents of each document and adds them to the index. Processing notifications occurs when the notifications queue is not empty and no crawls are in progress.
Propagating	MSSearch is propagating the index to the server dedicated to searching.
Retrying propagation	MSSearch is trying to propagate the index after a failed attempt.
Shutdown	The index is being deleted, or there is a critical error that is preventing access to the index.

CRAWL ISSUES AFTER PERFORMING AN SPS RESTORE

I've restored my server from backup. Will I have to re-create scheduled content source crawls from Windows 2000 Scheduled Tasks?

Most SPS implementations leverage scheduled content source updates. However, if a server has been restored from backup, the SPS backup image does not include any scheduled content source crawls from Windows 2000 Scheduled Tasks. Thus, these must be re-created on the restored server.

In addition, any shortcuts to workspaces in My Network Places must also be restored.

→ For complete information on backup and restore of SPS workspaces, **see** "Restore Process", **p. 333**.

As the final step in this process, the SharePoint Portal Server restore process initiates an incremental crawl of the internal content of every workspace. By doing so, consistency between the Web Storage System and the index is guaranteed. Incremental crawls are also initiated when notifications of changes to content sources on file systems occur. This, too, guarantees consistency between the Web Storage System and the index.

SUMMARY

We have looked into detail at how to configure SharePoint Portal Server to crawl a host of different content sources, including the following:

- File systems/shares
- Exchange Server 5.5 and Exchange 2000
- Web stores
- Intranet and extranet sites
- Lotus Notes/Domino databases
- Workspaces on other SharePoint Portal Servers

We also addressed functional and performance considerations in regard to the preceding, and capped off these topics with a discussion on troubleshooting. In the next chapter, we will take these discussions to the next level, focusing on the results of crawling—the creation, maintenance, and use of indexes by SharePoint Portal Server.

CHAPTER 19

MANAGING INDEXING

In this chapter

INDEX HOUSEKEEPING

In this chapter we will discuss a variety of topics that are of interest if you are using SharePoint Portal Server to search for data. This includes tasks such as index housekeeping, extending the list of searchable document formats, or setting up an enterprise environment with multiple SharePoint Portal Servers where dedicated content index servers will propagate the index.

Remember, the index is a kind of local database optimized for searching textual information. The actual information resides not only in SharePoint Portal Server, but also in external, remote repositories. This data originates from different document formats, such as HTML, Microsoft Word, or Microsoft PowerPoint—and for each of these formats a filter is required to extract the textual information.

→ To learn more about the core elements of the index architecture, **see** "Building the Index," **p. 99**.

To execute the tasks that are discussed in this chapter, it is assumed that you are workspace Coordinator. The tasks for which you need to have administrative privileges will be called out separately.

After the installation, SharePoint Portal Server and its index is ready for use. But as with any fairly complex environment, you can improve the system's usability and performance by good housekeeping. This involves the selection of the appropriate disks for timely access, the scheduling of index updates to ensure that the information is accurate, and customizations that influence the search results.

NOTE

> Remember that the index is just one important piece of SharePoint Portal Server. Another element, the Document Store, stores documents which are maintained through the document management features. This storage system is a separate component with its own housekeeping facilities.

19

SPECIFYING LOCATION OF THE INDEX

To increase performance or to ensure that the necessary disk space is present, the Administrator can specify the location of the index and the associated files. These files can be classified as

■ **Search Property Store** The indexed properties are kept for all workspaces together in a file called SPS.EDB. Because the property store contains properties from each indexed document, the SPS.EDB file will become fairly large. To ensure optimal performance, it is loaded into main memory. As it may be too large to cache it entirely, it may get paged into memory on demand. Associated with this file are related transaction log files. These files are created by default in the C:\Program Files\SharePoint Portal Server\Data\FTData directory.

- **Search Index Catalogs**   Individual full text search data is stored next to the property store, which spans across all workspaces. These files are also referred to as "catalog". SharePoint Portal Server stores all these files in directories that are named after the workspace. The default file location under which a subdirectory is created for each workspace is C:\Program Files\SharePoint Portal Server\Data\FTData\ SharePointPortalServer\Projects.

> **NOTE**
> If you take a look at this directory, you will notice that for each regular workspace, two sub-directories are created. One is named after the workspace, whereas the other contains of the workspace name appended with _train$$$. This latter directory is used to train the auto categorization tool. If an index is propagated to the server, you will also find a directory with the originating workspace name, but of course not one with the _train$$$ suffix.

- **Search Temporary Files**   During crawling, SharePoint Portal Server may create temporary files. By default these files are stored in the folder specified by the system TMP variable (typically C:\WINNT\TEMP).
- **Search Gatherer Logs**   Each time SharePoint Portal Server updates the index, it creates a log, for example to record access errors, about the URLs that have been crawled.

> **NOTE**
> These log files are not related to the transaction log files. Both files are in a binary format. However, the gatherer log files can be viewed by the Coordinator from a user-friendly Active Server Pages (ASP) page as you will see later in this chapter.

The location of any of these files can be changed. Through the existing SharePoint Portal Server Management Console it is only possible to change the file locations used for newly created workspaces. For already existing workspaces, the location can only be changed using some script-based support tools that can be found on the SharePoint Portal Server media kit in the support/tools directory. These tools are not installed on your server.

19

> **TIP**
> Plan where you want to locate the files! You can define the locations during the installation of SharePoint Portal Server. You should consider disk space capacity and whether or not you should allocate the data over different disks in order to improve the performance. For example, the temporary files location should point to a disk other than the system drive and other than the drive containing the index files.

DISK SPACE REQUIREMENTS

There are three disk space components: the catalogs, the property store, and the gatherer logs.

The size of the catalog is largely determined by the textual information (the *corpus*) that gets indexed per workspace. This corpus includes not only the content stored within SharePoint

Portal Server, but also all external information, such as Web sites, that gets indexed through content sources. The catalog itself needs about 15% of the corpus size.

The property store is a single file that is shared by all workspaces. It also contains information that is derived from the indexed documents. Consequently the size of this single file is the sum of all catalog sizes plus some extra space for the non-text properties. To be on the safe side reserve 10MB per workspace for these properties.

The size of the gatherer log largely depends on the settings that can be specified in the SharePoint Portal Server Administration. If you specified log successes, you can approximate the size of the log by allowing 100 bytes per URL. If items excluded by rules are logged as well, the log can be substantially larger (as much as 10 times). For example, in Web crawls each .GIF file found will generate a 100-byte exclusion message. This size needs to be multiplied by the number of gatherer log files that should be kept. You can set the number of kept log files as well as the other logging options by using the Administration settings as outlined later in this chapter.

CHANGING THE FILE LOCATIONS

To change the location of indices and gatherer logs of workspaces, do the following:

1. Log in as Administrator on the server running SharePoint Portal Server.

2. Open Programs, Administrative Tools, SharePoint Portal Server Administration.

3. In the Microsoft Management Console (MMC) interface, select the Data tab (see Figure 19.1) .

4. Click the browse button to change the appropriate setting.

5. Click OK.

Figure 19.1
The default locations of all SharePoint Portal Server files can be changed through the Microsoft Management Console.

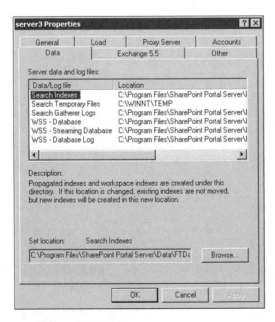

TIP

Although you can change the path, the existing indexes or gatherer logs will not be moved to the new location. To do this, you must use the unsupported CATUTIL tool, which you can find in the Support\Tools directory on the SharePoint Portal Server CD. With this tool you can also move the property store to a different directory.

OPTIMIZING SEARCH RESULTS

SharePoint Portal Server ranks text search results based on a very advanced algorithm, also known as probabilistic ranking. The result is dependent on the frequency of words not only within a particular document, but also in the overall corpus. For this reason, it is possible to filter frequently occurring words, so-called noise words. Another feature is the thesaurus, which gives you the ability to substitute or expand words so that more matching documents are found.

CAUTION

Noise words and the thesaurus are applied for all workspaces on a single server. If the index gets propagated to another system, you should apply the same settings not only on the target server, but also on all the other servers that propagate their indices to that same target server. Otherwise you may notice inconsistencies in ranking.

CUSTOMIZING NOISE WORDS

Noise words, words that are very common, are filtered out of the query and index as they will match with many documents. The list of words clearly is language dependent, but certainly also subject dependent. On a Microsoft Technologies portal, for example, the word "Windows" is likely present in almost any document. Therefore it is possible to edit the list of noise words to either add or remove words. Initially, the thesaurus is empty, and that is quite understandable, as the substitution or expansion of words is highly dependent on the subject. On our technologies portal, MS would get expanded to Microsoft, whereas on a medical portal it probably would refer to the chronic disease multiple sclerosis.

To modify the list of noise words do the following:

1. Log in as Administrator on the server running SharePoint Portal Server.
2. Go to the directory where the SharePoint Portal Server Property Store is located. By default this is in C:\Program Files\SharePoint Portal Server\Data\FTData\ SharePointPortalServer\.
3. Go to the Config subdirectory.
4. Select the appropriate noise text file depending on your language. All files begin with "noise" and have a three-letter language postfix. For any language that is not supported out-of-the-box by SharePoint Portal Server, the neutral noise word file noiseneu.txt will be used.

19

5. Make a backup copy of your selected noise file before you make any modifications.

6. Open the file—by default Notepad will be opened as the noise word files have the extension .txt.

7. Make your changes, keeping each word on a single line.

8. When you are done you need to re-index each workspace on the server. To do so, open Programs, Administrative Tools, SharePoint Portal Server Administration.

9. Select each workspace node and click Action, All Tasks, Start Full Update.

> **NOTE**
>
> When you start a full index, all users that have subscribed to any changes will get notified. Even though nothing in the real content changed, the notifications will be generated, as in the case of a full index. All index information will be removed to ensure that only properly linked information is stored. By changing some settings in your Windows registry, you can disable notifications while a full index is taking place. See later in this chapter for more information.

CUSTOMIZING THE THESAURUS

The thesaurus is another language-dependent feature available in SharePoint Portal Server. The thesaurus allows the substitution or expansion of words. This feature allows you, for example, to substitute the term "IE" with the term "Internet Explorer".

To modify the list of noise words, do the following:

1. Log in as Administrator on the server running SharePoint Portal Server.

2. Go to the directory where the SharePoint Portal Server Property Store is located. By default this is in C:\Program Files\SharePoint Portal Server\Data\FTData\SharePointPortalServer\.

3. Go to the Config subdirectory.

4. Select the appropriate thesaurus XML file depending on your language. All files begin with "ts" and have a three-letter language postfix. For any language that is not supported out-of-the-box by SharePoint Portal Server, the neutral thesaurus file tsneu.xml will be used.

5. Open the file with your favorite XML editing tool, for example Notepad (see Figure 19.2).

6. Make your changes. You will see a commented example (XML comments begin with <!-- and end with -->) of the expected XML syntax in the opened XML file.

7. Verify that you have written valid XML. Open the thesaurus file in Internet Explorer. An invalidly encoded XML file will cause an error message in the Windows Application log once the thesaurus is loaded with the first query request.

8. Restart the Microsoft Search Service.

Figure 19.2
The figure shows an opened example thesaurus file.

```
tsenu.xml - Notepad
File  Edit  Format  Help
<XML ID="Microsoft Search Thesaurus">
        <thesaurus xmlns="x-schema:tsSchema.xml">
                <expansion>
                        <sub>SharePoint Portal Server</sub>
                        <sub>SPS</sub>
                </expansion>
                <replacement>
                        <pat>SPPS</pat>
                        <sub>SharePoint Portal Server</sub>
                        <sub>SPS</sub>
                </replacement>
        </thesaurus>
</XML>
```

Figure 19.2 shows the US English thesaurus file (tsenu.xml), where the terms "SPS" and "SharePoint Portal Server" can be used synonymously. Some people also refer to SharePoint Portal Server as "SPPS", a usage that is discouraged by Microsoft. Documents should not contain SPPS; if they do, then they will not be found unless the user encloses them in double quotes.

> **NOTE**
>
> Thesaurus (and noise word entries) are case-sensitive and accent-sensitive, whereas words in the index are not stored with case or accent variations. For example, if you add the word SharePoint to the thesaurus, and someone searches for Sharepoint (lowercase p!), the thesaurus will not be applied. To get the expected results, add thesaurus (and noise word) list entries for all common case variations of a word.

> **TIP**
>
> To know which thesaurus files are used, you can check the Windows Application Event log. To find the log entry, restart the Microsoft Search service first. Issue a search request from a browser where the language is set to your choice. Look for informational entries from the MssCi source with the id 4155.

MAXIMUM NUMBER OF SEARCH RESULTS

SharePoint Portal Server returns at most the 200 most relevant documents that match a user's query out-of-the-box. To improve the query performance, you may wish to limit the results, while in some other deployment scenarios you might need to return even more. The maximum number is maintained in the registry.

If you feel comfortable with registry updates, you may modify the value. Check the key HKLM\Software\Microsoft\Search\1.0\Applications\SharePoint Portal Server\Catalogs\<workspace name>, where you will find a DWORD value MaxResultRows. The value is set by default to 0xc8, which equals 200.

> **NOTE**
>
> Generally this kind of update is only of interest if you write your own solution. If you want to retrieve more than 200 results in the portal, you need to increase some global variables used by the out-of-the-box Web Parts.

19

ADJUSTING THE QUERY TIME-OUT

For each workspace, you can edit the time that a query will take. Such a limit releases server processes consumed by unsuccessful queries, instead of waiting and keeping the server busy.

To adjust these settings, do the following:

1. Log in as Workspace Coordinator.
2. Open the Management Web Folder of your workspace.
3. Select Workspace Settings.
4. Select the Index tab.
5. Specify the query time-out in milliseconds. The default value is 20,000 milliseconds.

INDEXING AND SEARCH RESOURCE USAGE

Indexing, responding to user queries, and rendering the dashboard are resource-intensive tasks. System resources are needed to crawl and retrieve the textual information, and also on the remote system whose content gets indexed and the network in-between. Therefore it is possible to tune the resource usage in such a manner that the available resources are used at their best.

ADJUSTING LOCAL RESOURCE USAGE

The resources used for searching and indexing will affect the users' perceived performance. In larger deployments, which will be discussed in more detail later in this chapter, you may wish to change the default settings. Especially if you have divided the SharePoint Portal Server tasks over multiple servers.

For example, on a server that primarily renders the dashboard, you should adjust both the Search resource usage and Index resource usage of the server to "background." To change the settings do the following:

1. Log in as Administrator on the server running SharePoint Portal Server.
2. Open the SharePoint Portal Server Microsoft Management Console by clicking Programs, Administrative Tools, SharePoint Portal Server Administration.
3. Right-click the SharePoint Portal Server computer name, select Properties, and then click the "General" tab.
4. Adjust the Search resource usage and Indexing resource usage settings to the desired values.

LIMITING REMOTE RESOURCE USAGE

The Administrator can specify rules and settings that determine the network load and the remote servers' load. They consist of site hit frequency rules and time-out settings. These rules are not workspace-specific; they are global to the server. Also these rules make it possible for the Administrator to enforce best practices from an infrastructure point of view, while a content knowledgeable Coordinator defines the individual Web sites that need to be crawled.

You can specify site hit frequency rules to limit the concurrent number and interval between requests to a remote Web site made by the crawler. You should use these rules to avoid overloading an external site. If the frequency is too high, you may receive a denial of access to that site in the future.

NOTE
> The site frequency rules will not only be used for Web site crawls. They also apply if a remote SharePoint Portal Server workspace is crawled.

To add or modify a site frequency rule, do the following:

1. Log in as Administrator on the server running SharePoint Portal Server.
2. Open the SharePoint Portal Server Microsoft Management Console by clicking Programs, Administrative Tools, SharePoint Portal Server Administration.
3. Right-click the SharePoint Portal Server computer name, select Properties, and then click the Load tab.
4. Click Add for a new rule, or select a rule and click Edit to modify a rule.
5. The Add Site Hit Frequency Rule dialog opens (see Figure 19.3).
6. In Site name, type the site name, for example, `http://www.microsoft.com`. The reference to the protocol (`http://`) is optional. You can use "`*`" as a wildcard; for example, `*.microsoft.com` will apply the rule to all Microsoft Web sites.
7. Select one of the following frequency options:
   - **Request documents simultaneously** If this setting is specified, SharePoint Portal Server will request as many documents in parallel as possible. For Internet sites, this setting is usually resource intensive.
   - **Limit the number of simultaneous document requests** You can specify the maximum number of documents that SharePoint Portal Server crawler can request at one time from the site. The default setting for all sites is five simultaneous document requests.

19

- **Wait a specified amount of time after each document request** You can specify a delay between document requests. SharePoint Portal Server crawler requests one document per site at one time, and then waits for the specified amount of time before making additional requests.

8. Click OK

Figure 19.3
This figure shows a site frequency rule that will ensure that any Microsoft Web site is hit only once a second. All other Web sites but those residing on the "qwic" server will only be hit once every 10 seconds.

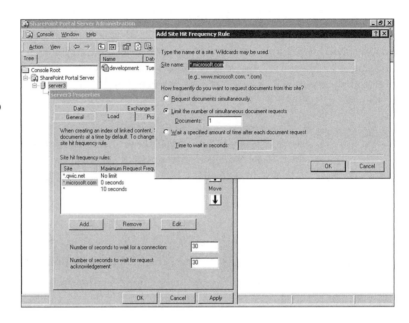

If you have defined generic and more specific site frequency rules, you must make sure that they are ordered correctly. Place the most specific rule first. You cannot exclude crawling the Internet, but you can make that indexing process extremely slow by defining a rule for * with a very long wait time for each document request. Place that rule last, and make sure to include a rule for your own intranet. If your domain is, for example, qwic.net, include a rule for *.qwic.net with simultaneous access.

Time-out settings determine how long SharePoint Portal Server waits for either a connection to or a response from a site. For unresponsive Web sites, you may need to increase the time-out value, but keep in mind that this can impact the time it takes to complete an index update due to wasted connection time.

To specify the time-out values, do the following:

1. Log in as Administrator on the server running SharePoint Portal Server.

2. Open the SharePoint Portal Server Microsoft Management Console by clicking Programs, Administrative Tools, SharePoint Portal Server Administration.

3. Right-click the SharePoint Portal Server computer name, select Properties, and then click the Load tab.

4. In the Number of Seconds to Wait for a Connection field, type the number of seconds that you want SharePoint Portal Server to wait for a connection time-out.

5. In the Number of Seconds to Wait for Request Acknowledgment field, type the number of seconds you want SharePoint Portal Server to wait for a requested Web page or document before timing out.

6. Click OK.

If the crawler encounters 32 consecutive time-outs for one server, the server will be designated as unavailable. No requests to that server will be done for the next 10 minutes.

KEEPING THE INDEX UP-TO-DATE

Let's share the good news first—if you are using SharePoint Portal Server out-of-the-box, the index will be kept up to date. The Web Storage System, the place where all documents are maintained by SharePoint Portal Server, sends notifications to the index engine.

The same notification mechanism is available for content sources pointing to a file share. The notification mechanism does not work, however, when indexing other workspaces, Web sites, Exchange Public Folders, and Lotus Notes databases. To keep the index accurate, you must fall back to mechanisms that actively crawl for changes.

→ To learn more about incremental updates, **see** "Building the Index," **p. 99**.

The incremental update ensures that all changes in content (not necessarily in links to that content) are detected. This mechanism, however, requires that each URL will get checked for changes, while most of them may not.

Microsoft has added the *adaptive update* capability to overcome the load that is generated with checking every URL. An adaptive update will only check those URLs that—based on the history of changes—are likely out of date. Each URL will be checked at least every two weeks to ensure that changes on documents that remained unchanged for a long while are detected. Whenever possible, you should use adaptive overnight crawling to optimize the resource usage. Incremental updates, which will take much longer, should be scheduled for the weekend. For both types of updates, a scheduled task must be configured.

19

CAUTION

> Adaptive updates are set by default for content sources other than the local Web Storage System and the file system. But the adaptive update will only be performed if a schedule is defined. No schedule is defined with SharePoint Portal Server out-of-the-box.

SCHEDULING AND CONFIGURING ADAPTIVE UPDATES

Adaptive updates can either be scheduled or executed manually. In a production environment, the scheduled operation is to be preferred, in particular because the additional network and other load can occur in off-peak hours, such as late at night.

If you have not run any other updates, the first time you run an adaptive update is equal to running a full update, and the second time you run an adaptive update is equal to running an incremental update. You see the first improvement the third time you run an adaptive update. The efficiency increases over time and over multiple updates because more history is available for the algorithm to work with. Perform the following steps for updating:

1. Log in as Administrator.

2. Open the Management / Content Sources Web Folder of your workspace.

3. Click Additional Settings.

4. Select the Scheduled Updates tab.

5. Check, if necessary, Adaptive Updates; otherwise click Schedule.

6. The Adaptive Update Properties dialog opens (see Figure 19.4).

7. Fill in the details of your schedule on the Schedule tab. You can fine-tune the task on the Settings tab. Do not modify the settings on the Task tab.

8. Click OK.

9. If you are creating a new task, the Account Information dialog will open. Specify the password and confirm the password; then click OK.

10. Click OK

Figure 19.4
The figure shows an adaptive update schedule that is run every working day at 10:00 p.m.

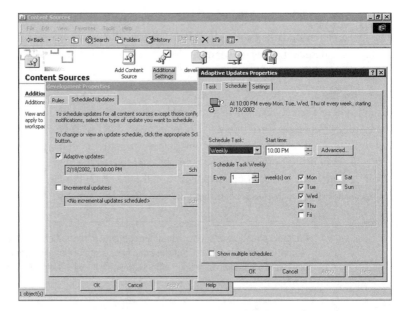

The schedule is implemented as Windows tasks. You can see these tasks if you take a look in the C:\WINNT\Tasks directory.

> **TIP**
> The scheduled update tasks are not part of the backup procedure of SharePoint Portal Server; back them up separately for a complete restore of your system.

A Coordinator can access the Additional Setting tab to create schedules, but for a new schedule you need to supply an account with administrative privileges. If the schedule already exists, and thus is created with administrative privileges, you may find that you cannot open the existing schedule. Therefore always maintain schedules through a single account with local administration privileges.

FULL UPDATES

Some operations affect the accuracy of the index. These operations include

- Installation of a new filter
- Completion of new Auto Categorization Training
- Removal of a content source (reclaiming disk space)
- Change of site rules that affect existing content sources
- Definition or rename of a Search Scope for an existing content source
- Detection of unreferenced Web pages

Therefore, you should consider starting a full index in off-time hours if such a situation occurs. Indexing can take a considerable amount of time—even more than 24 hours. Use your past experience to determine a moment with the least impact to the users.

There are several ways to start an index update. If you want to update all content sources, do the following:

1. Log in as Coordinator.
2. Open the Management Web Folder and right-click the Content Sources folder.
3. Select the update method you want to perform.

> **TIP**
> This operation, unlike the operation for an individual content source as outlined below, can also be started from the SharePoint Portal Server Microsoft Management Console by right-clicking the workspace node.

If you know that the changes apply only for some content sources, for example, if you changed the site path rule that is specific to that content source, you should use the following procedure:

1. Log in as Coordinator.
2. Open the Management, Content Sources Web Folder.

19

3. Right-click the appropriate content source icon.

4. Select the update method you want to perform.

When starting a full index, you will notice that the document will be reported as changed and consequently matching subscriptions will fire. This can be very annoying, aside from the fact that if many users requested email notifications, the mail server could become extremely busy when you perform a full update.

Before performing a full update, you can disable notifications by adding a property to the workspace, which will disable *all* notifications. Make sure that after the full update completes, you re-enable notifications again.

You can add and toggle the property urn:schemas-microsoft-com:publishing:DisableSubscriptionNotifications, which allows you to disable the notifications on the workspace folder by using the Visual Basic Script below.

LISTING 19.1   TOGGLE SUBSCRIPTION NOTIFICATIONS SCRIPT

```
const adModeReadWrite = 3
Set wshArguments = wscript.Arguments

If wshArguments.Count < 2 Then
    wscript.Echo "This little tool will toggle the subscription notifications"
    wscript.Echo "Usage  subnot <server> <workspace>"
End If

' We need to open the Exchange OLEDB provider directly on the server.
strURL = "http://" & wshArguments.Item(0) & _
         "/SharePoint Portal Server/workspaces/" & wshArguments.Item(1)

Set adoCon = CreateObject("ADODB.Connection")
adoCon.ConnectionString = strURL
adoCon.Provider = "Exoledb.datasource"
adoCon.Open

' Open the workspace directory read/write to set a property on that folder
Set adoRec = CreateObject("ADODB.Record")
adoRec.Open strURL, adoCon, adModeReadWrite
bDisableNotifications = _
adoRec.Fields
("urn:schemas-microsoft-com:publishing:DisableSubscriptionNotifications")

' The property may not be present, which means that the default behavior
' to send notifications is active
If bDisableNotifications = "" Then
    bDisableNotifications = false
End If

' Toggle the property or create if necessary the property with a not default value
adoRec.Fields
("urn:schemas-microsoft-com:publishing:DisableSubscriptionNotifications") = _
   not bDisableNotifications
adoRec.Fields.Update
```

Restart the Microsoft Search service such that the changes take affect immediately.

Which Account is used to crawl for data?

SharePoint Portal Server will crawl all data using a dedicated account, the default access account, unless a specific account is defined for a specific URL. These specific accounts can be set through Site Paths, which are described in general in Chapter 18.

DEFAULT CONTENT ACCESS ACCOUNT

If no site access account is specified, the default content access account will be used for index updates. If this account has not been configured, SharePoint Portal Server will use the anonymous account. If the account used has no Read permission for the data that gets crawled, the content is not indexed and an access error is reported in the gatherer log.

The default content access account is typically set with the installation of SharePoint Portal Server. To change the account at a later moment, do the following:

1. Log in as Administrator on the server running SharePoint Portal Server.
2. Open the SharePoint Portal Server Microsoft Management Console by clicking Programs, Administrative Tools, SharePoint Portal Server Administration.
3. Right-click the SharePoint Portal Server computer name, select Properties, and then click the Accounts tab.
4. Select Default Content Access Account. The description and account properties for this account appear.
5. Click Configure. The Account Information dialog box appears.
6. Specify the account information: Type the domain, account (user name), and password, and then confirm the password typing it again.
7. Click OK.
8. Click Apply.

19

DEFINING SITE ACCESS ACCOUNT

If you want to configure an account for a specific content source, you can define a site path rule for that content source and associate an account with it by performing the following steps:

1. Log in as Coordinator.
2. Open the Management / Content Sources Web Folder of your workspace.
3. Click Additional Settings.
4. Select the Rules tab.
5. Click Site Path to open the Site Paths dialog.
6. Click New.

7. Enter the path that resembles the content source. To apply the site path to all items of that content source, the path should end with the * wildcard. If your content source pointed to a document, substitute the document name with *. For example, for a content source `http://www.microsoft.com/sharepoint/portalserver.asp`, use `http://www.microsoft.com/sharepoint/*`.

8. Select Include this path; the Options button will be enabled.

9. Click Options to open the Options dialog.

10. Click Account.

11. Specify the account information: Type the domain, account (user name), and password, and confirm the password by typing it again.

12. Select the appropriate authentication method. For remote Web sites, you likely need to select Basic Authentication.

13. Click OK to leave the Options dialog.

14. Click OK to leave the Site Paths dialog.

15. Click No in the Index Update Required dialog, as you do not know which specific content source needs to be updated.

16. Click OK to leave the Additional Settings dialog.

17. Right-click in the Web folder on the content source for which you created the site access account.

18. Select Start Full Update.

NOTE

Site Paths Accounts allow you to index information that resides in a different, untrusted domain. By default the credentials of the default content access account are used and passed using the secure integrated Windows authentication method. For information in an untrusted account, however, you need to use basic authentication unless you can use an identical username and password in each domain.

EXCLUDING CONTENT

When you initially add a content source, you can specify whether you want to include just this page or the whole site in the index. The dialog also informs you that you can use the Configuration tab of the Properties dialog for a finer granularity. These options have been discussed in Chapter 18. SharePoint Portal Server provides another mechanism called Site Path rules. This allows independent content sources to fine-tune the access to Web sites.

TIP

When your search results do not show some documents that you would expect to get indexed, check if some Site Path rules apply. The options on an individual content source allow only for some basic settings, whereas Site Path rules provide a much richer set of options that apply for all content sources.

EXCLUDING SOME AREAS OF A WEB SITE

The options that you can specify with a particular content source will always contain a whole site, whereas you may wish to index only some portions of it. For example, how could one set up a content source which indexes just the SharePoint-specific information on the general Microsoft Web site? The URL of the content source would be `http://www.microsoft.com/sharepoint/portalserver.asp`, but due to the banner's All Products option you will start indexing the whole `www.microsoft.com` site.

The answer can be found in Site Path rules (see Figure 19.5). Not only do they provide the option to define a dedicated account for a particular content source, they also allow the exclusion of specific URLs.

Figure 19.5
This figure shows the Site Path rules for the example of Microsoft's SharePoint Portal Server Web Site discussed previously.

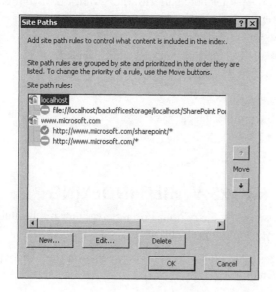

Site Path rules are evaluated in order; this means that you need to enable the specific path first and then disable the more generic path. If you don't see the content being indexed as you expected, enable logging of excluded URLs and check the gatherer logs as discussed later in this chapter. Entries such as "URL is excluded because of restrictions defined in site path rules" may indicate that, for example, the ordering is incorrect.

ENABLING COMPLEX LINKS

Active Server Pages that, for example, reveal content of a SQL database can use parameters to show specific content. Such a URL may look like `http://myserver/Northwind/orders.asp?OrderID=12029`. In this example, OrderID is the parameter which is appended to the actual URL with a question mark. It is a generic principle to add parameters with a question mark, which is also known as query string. SharePoint Portal Server will not index these parameterized Web pages by default. Using

Site Path rules, it is possible to enable support for this type of *complex links*. To do so, do the following:

1. Log in as Coordinator.

2. Open the Management / Content Sources Web Folder of your workspace.

3. Click Additional Settings.

4. Select the Rules tab.

5. Click Site Path to open the Site Paths dialog.

6. Click New.

7. Enter the path that resembles the content source. To apply the site path to all items of that content source, the path should end with the * wildcard. If your content source pointed to a document, substitute the document name with *. In our example you would use `http://myserver/Northwind/*`.

8. Select Include this path; the Options button will be enabled.

9. Click Options to open the Options dialog.

10. Check Enable Complex Links.

11. Click OK to leave the options dialog.

12. Click OK to leave the Site Paths dialog.

CHECKING FOR ERRORS WHILE INDEXING

There are numerous reasons why SharePoint Portal Server may not be able to index a certain document. The most common problems are

- Insufficient privileges to access a page. This may occur on sites where particular URLs are password-protected.

- Network or remote server problems that make it impossible to access the site.

- "Broken" links included on a Web page.

- SharePoint Portal Server Site Path rules that exclude a particular URL.

- The file type that is associated with the URL is not supported by SharePoint Portal Server.

- URLs that include query parameters. Query parameters are appended to the URL following a question mark (?). Each parameter is separated by an ampersand (&). You will see these constructs typically with Active Server Pages.

A first indication whether a content source is indexed successfully is the "health" indicator that shows up in the left pane of your Content Sources Web Folder after selecting that content source (see Figure 19.6).

Health Indicator

Figure 19.6
This figure shows the Content Sources Web Folder with the Discussions content source selected. In the left pane you see details, such as the health, of that content source.

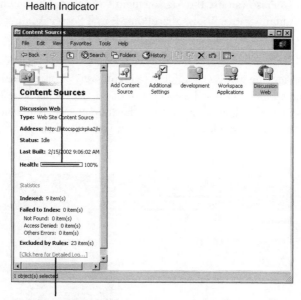

Click here for detailed log

The best place to check for errors is the gatherer log, which is created for each crawl. Within the log file, successful accesses, access errors, and accesses prohibited by rules can be reported. Tracking successful accesses and accesses prohibited by rules need to be explicitly enabled. These options come in handy if index restrictions, such as Site Path rules, need to be verified or debugged. To enable these options, do the following:

1. Log in as Workspace Coordinator.
2. Open the Management Web Folder of your workspace.
3. Select Workspace Settings.
4. Select the Logging tab.
5. Select Log success or Log items excluded by rules as appropriate.
6. Click OK.

NOTE

Enabling these options will produce significantly larger log files. They are global to the workspace and thus will affect crawls for other content sources. Turn these options off as soon as the crawl behaves as expected.

19

As Administrator, you also can use the Management Console to change the logging settings. Open Programs, Administrative Tools, SharePoint Portal Server Administration and select the workspace node in the tree on the left. Right-click or select the Properties option from the Actions menu to see the same dialog that is shown with step 3 above.

Coordinators can view the gatherer log file (see Figure 19.7) from an Active Server Page that includes some options to filter the events. To do so, click Click here for detailed log in the left pane of your Web folder after selecting the content source in which you are interested. This option is located in the lower-right corner, under the health indicator mentioned earlier.

Figure 19.7
This figure shows the gatherer log rendered as a Web page. The details show that .gif files will not be indexed.

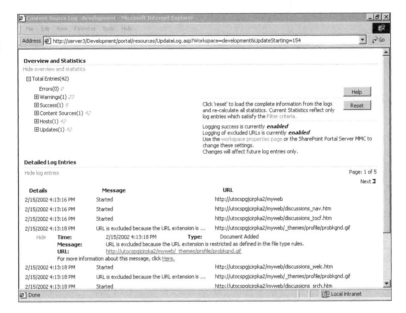

The gatherer log is written in a binary format. There is an undocumented object model to retrieve the information in a readable format. Administrators, for example, can view the gatherer log by using a Visual Basic script file that is included on the SharePoint Portal Server CD. You can find the gthrlog.vbs script in the Support\Tools directory.

AUTO CATEGORIZATION

SharePoint Portal Server provides the ability to auto categorize content. To do so, it needs a small training sample to characterize the categories. If auto categorization is enabled, these characteristics will be matched against index updates. Similar documents will than be placed in the same category.

The training will be done using all documents that are currently categorized within the workspace. With 100 characteristic documents, you typically will get good results. The length and the variety of documents clearly have an impact, so make sure that the training set spans the whole spectrum of content and that the documents contain at least two pages of text. Working with auto categorization, you have the option to apply these categories on external documents, on documents stored within the SharePoint Portal Server workspace, or both. To enable auto categorization and to run the training, do the following:

1. Log in as Workspace Coordinator.
2. Open the Management Web Folder of your workspace.
3. Select the Categories folder.
4. Right-click the Categories folder and select Properties.
5. Select the Category Assistant tab.
6. Click Train Now.
7. If you have already run a training session earlier, you will be asked if the existing automatically assigned categories should be revised. Re-categorization is fairly resource intensive.
8. Select Enable Category Assistant.
9. Make your choice which documents are to be auto categorized.
10. Set the precision.
11. Click OK.

If you have decided to auto categorize external content, then the appropriate categories will be applied to all index updates. You cannot exclude particular content sources or override the automatically assigned category. If you find that an external document does not match the automatically assigned category, it can only be assigned to another category (or no category at all) through the following procedure:

1. Place a Web Link to that document into the SharePoint Portal Server workspace.
2. Categorize that Web Link.

NOTE

> In subsequent auto categorization training, this Web Link will be another training document. SharePoint Portal Server will learn from its previous mistake. If you select re-categorization, incorrectly categorized documents that are similar to the training document will get the new categories assigned.

For documents within the SharePoint Portal Server workspace, the categories will be suggested, and unless you tick off the Display document in suggested categories check box, the user will see the document in the suggested categories. You can, however, override the suggested categories. Explicitly selecting the same categories as suggested (see Figure 19.8) will ensure that the training document's characteristics will be included for auto categorization.

Figure 19.8
The properties dialog shows suggested categories.

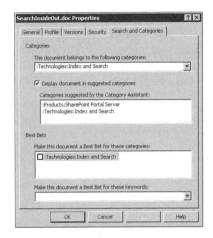

PERFORMANCE COUNTERS

Now that we have introduced some of the underlying components of the indexing process, the performance counters that are available to monitor the health of the index become easier to understand. The following performance objects may be of interest to you:

- **Microsoft Gatherer**   server-wide counters of indexing activities
- **Microsoft Gatherer Projects**   workspace-specific counters of indexing activities
- **Microsoft Search**   server-wide counters about query activities
- **Microsoft Search Catalogs**   workspace-specific counters about query activities
- **Microsoft Search Indexer Catalog**   workspace-specific counters about the index
- **SharePoint Portal Server Subscriptions**   workspace-specific counters about the subscription service

A number of counters are present for each of the performance objects. The Administrator help gives a couple examples to trace down some problems. Alternatively you can use the Explain button for each of the counters (see Figure 19.9) to get more information for the selected counter.

The counters of the Indexing Service do not apply for SharePoint Portal Server.

Figure 19.9
This figure shows some performance data gathered during a crawl. The Waiting Documents counter is of interest to see how many URLs are already found, for example as links, but still need to get indexed. If this number is 0, the crawl is completed.

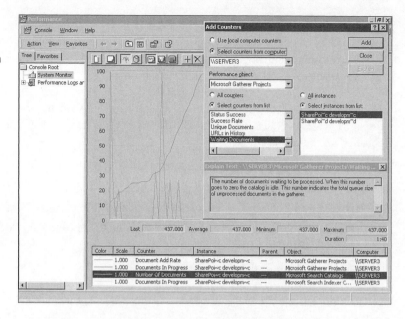

SEARCHING OTHER DOCUMENT FORMATS

SharePoint Portal Server provides, as discussed in Chapter 5, filters used to retrieve text and properties for most common document formats. But the list may not include your favorite document formats, such as PDF, a common format for archived information. In such cases, you need to check if an IFilter is available. If you cannot find a suitable IFilter, you can consider the usage of the plain text filter, or just index the system properties such as name, creation date, and last modification date.

> **TIP**
>
> You can download an IFilter for PDF from Adobe. Check
> `http://www.adobe.com/support/downloads/detail.jsp?ftpID=1276`.
>
> For PDFs that are saved as images, you will be limited to searching the metadata only, and not the text. To determine if the PDF is an image or contains indexable text, you can open the PDF and use the Select/Find text option from the menu. If you can do this, then the content should be indexable.

Document formats are typically determined from the filename extension. Therefore, to enable searching of new document formats, we need to make SharePoint Portal Server aware of the new document extension.

1. Open the Management/Content Sources Web folder.
2. Select the Additional Settings icon.

3. Select File Types.

4. Add your new extension.

5. When closing the dialog, you will be prompted whether the index needs to be updated. If you want to install a filter for this format, select No.

After you have added your file type, you should not see subsequent index updates with the message "URL is excluded because the URL extension is restricted as defined in the file type rules" in the gatherer log.

The next step is to improve user feedback by adding icons that the user associates with the new format. Therefore you need a 16×16 pixel gif file. Perform the following steps:

1. Name the gif file <ext>16.gif. So, for example, for PDF files name it pdf16.gif.

2. Open a Web folder to your workspace and enable to view hidden folders and items.

3. Open the hidden Portal/Resources/DocTypeIcons folder.

4. Drag the gif file into this folder.

The last (optional) step is to install a filter for this document format. Therefore, you need to install the filter according to the guidelines of the supplier. A filter is implemented as a Dynamic Link Library (DLL) that is loaded once specific registry entries are set. Typically the procedure is as follows:

1. Stop the Microsoft Search service.

2. Install the filter. If no instructions are given, you may just register the DLL using the regsvr32 command.

3. Start the Microsoft Search service.

4. If you know specific content sources that do contain documents with that extension, for example a particular Web site, perform a full update just for this content source. Otherwise, start a full update of all content sources.

TIP

> Depending on the document format, you may be able to reuse an existing filter, such as the "plain text" IFilter. To do so, open the registry editor and go to the key HKR\.<your extension> (HKR is used as an abbreviation for HKEY_CLASSES_ROOT) and create a new key with the name PersistentHandler. Set the default entry to {c1243ca0-bf96-11cd-b579-08002b30bfeb}, the Class ID of the Text IFilter.
>
> Similar steps are necessary to index mht files, single-file Web Archives encoded in MIME. While there is a MIME IFilter, Microsoft has excluded it from the release. To include support for these files, open the registry editor and go to the key HKR\CLSID\{3050F3D9-98B5-11CF-BB82-00AA00BDCE0B} and create a new key with the name PersistentHandler. Set the default entry to {5645C8C1-E277-11CF-8FDA-00AA00A14F93}, the Class ID of the MIME IFilter.

LARGER DEPLOYMENTS

A key concept within SharePoint Portal Server is the decentralized management and storage of information. The documents can be maintained within the owning departments by those who know best how to answer the new challenges.

But despite the decentralized management, it is possible to provide a common view of all information that is available within a company. Obviously, this is a resource-intensive task that does not go well together with generating the end-user view of that information. Using indexing workspaces, it is possible to dedicate servers (see Figure 19.10) to this resource-intensive task of crawling for document changes. These consolidated changes will be propagated to a target system where these indices will get merged to a common index that serves the user's search requests.

Figure 19.10
This figure illustrates a larger deployment of SharePoint Portal Server.

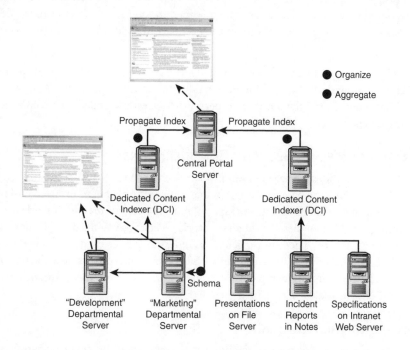

SETTING UP THE INFORMATION INFRASTRUCTURE

If multiple workspaces on various servers administered by different Coordinators come into play, you need to address the common information infrastructure. Everyone in the organization should use the same words for the same thing—an amount field should, for example, always be used in the same currency. A company with offices in the U.S. and Japan should make a choice for either Japanese Yen or US Dollar as currency. Otherwise, you cannot interpret a search result—an expense claim, for example, of 12.300 could be a 100 US$ bill.

To overcome the problem that decentralized information remains locked up with the department, you should centrally manage the document profiles (and thus the definition of the custom properties) that are essential for the enterprise. Ideally the category tree would be shared throughout the enterprise. But the current release of SharePoint Portal Server will not maintain categories in a propagated index. Once you have laid out the document profiles, keywords, and categories, you can roll out departmental SharePoint Portal Servers. Rolling up the metadata will ensure that all information remains available for the whole enterprise. This roll-up is done through dedicated indexing machines propagating their index to the enterprise search portal.

The architecture with a departmental document management server, indexing servers, and a single common portal does not resolve two potential bottlenecks.

First it needs the central common portal not only to render the Digital Dashboard, but it also needs to respond timely to user queries. This problem can be solved if the content is propagated to a server that only executes searches. The Search Web Parts on the central common portal can fairly easily be modified to redirect the queries to the dedicated search server. You can even decide to let the departmental workspaces use this central search facility.

The second problem is more profound—the common portal is a single point of failure and may not be ideally located for all users due to network limitations. With this first version of SharePoint Portal Server, there is currently no recommended architecture to solve this problem.

INFRASTRUCTURE AND SECURITY CONSIDERATIONS

Up to four index workspaces can propagate their index to a common server. It is not possible to "chain" the propagation of indices, nor is it possible to propagate to multiple servers. The names of the indexing workspaces and the name of the target workspace must all be different. This implies that in an enterprise scenario, you need to plan for the location of these index workspaces in particular, as indexing may cause quite some network load. You therefore likely want to place your dedicated indexing servers near the network hubs: In a worldwide operating company, for example, place one in North America, one in Europe, and one in Asia.

SCHEDULING THE PROPAGATION

You also need to plan when the index gets propagated. By default, SharePoint Portal Server automatically propagates its index after creating or updating it. This can be unfortunate, as, for example, with two content sources scheduled to be updated at different times, the index propagates twice.

You can also schedule a task to run a script to propagate on a regular basis. To do so, take a look at the srchadm.vbs script that is in the SharePoint Portal Server CD's support/tools directory. The following command

```
cscript srchadm.vbs build /c:<workspacename> /o:prop
```

will propagate the index of the indexing workspace with the name <workspacename>.

WINDOWS SECURITY DOMAINS

The security credentials must be shared across all servers, for example by using single domain. Alternatively you can establish trust relationships. This is required due to the Propagation Access Account which must be defined in the indexing workspace as a valid account with local administration privileges on the destination server.

But there is an even more profound reason to have the security credentials shared across all servers. As discussed in Chapter 5, the index stores security information to ensure that only documents that are readable by the user who issued the search request are returned. This security information is built on the server with the workspace index and used on the destination server. For this reason, do not use local accounts in SharePoint Portal Server roles used by the document management system.

TARGETING SERVER DISK SPACE REQUIREMENTS

Before a catalog can be propagated from the indexing workspace to the target workspace, you must ensure that there is enough disk space available on the destination server. Not only must the destination server have free space that equals the size of the catalog, also additional working space is required to bring the catalog online after the catalog is copied. Typically, the recommended minimum additional working space is 50 megabytes (MB) of disk space.

TIP

> In case of failures, check the Application event log on both servers. Insufficient working space, for example, can only be detected on the destination server. On success, an informational entry will be written in each Application event log.

SharePoint Portal Server uses the propagation access account when propagating indexes from one SharePoint Portal Server computer to another. This account must have local Administrator permissions on the destination server.

Index propagation uses the standard Windows SMB file sharing protocol. Firewalls between the two servers might not allow the SMB packages to pass.

SETTING UP A DEDICATED INDEXING SERVER

Crawling and indexing can be a very resource-intensive task, in particular if multiple Web sites or large Exchange Public folder trees are referenced as content sources. In that situation, you should consider the usage of a dedicated server that is not used as a document repository or as a portal. SharePoint Portal Server can be configured to be responsible just for the indexing task, however, on the workspace level. In real-life deployment scenarios, though, you would not mix the same server indexing workspaces with regular workspace. Not only would you lose all benefits of the dedicated indexing workspace, additional overhead for the index propagation would slow down the system.

Because indexing workspaces typically run on a dedicated server, you will come across the term *Dedicated Content Indexing (DCI) Servers*.

To create an indexing workspace, you must be an Administrator with access (either physical or through Terminal Services) to the server:

1. Open the SharePoint Portal Server MMC Snap-In by clicking Start, Administrative Tools, SharePoint Portal Server.

2. Select the SharePoint Portal Server/<your server> node.

3. Choose the Action, New command to start the workspace wizard.

4. Skip the welcome screen and enter your workspace name and description.

5. Click the Advanced button. This is (almost) your only chance. If you click Finish after the next step without filling in the details in the Advanced dialog, a regular workspace will be created.

6. In the Advanced dialog, check Configure as Index Workspace and type the URL to the workspace to which the index will be propagated. This workspace must reside on a different server and have a different name.

7. If you have not yet set a propagation account, you will be prompted now to supply an account and password.

8. Click Next and fill in the workspace contact details.

9. You will be presented the information that you have provided. If Propagation Target is defined in the summary screen, slightly hidden in the amount of information, you are going to create an Indexing workspace. If everything is filled in correctly, click Finish.

After having set up an index workspace, a shortcut to the Management/Content Sources Web Folder will be automatically created in your My Network Places. If the Coordinator is a different user, this shortcut must be created manually.

CAUTION

Do not create shortcuts to other Web folders, such as the workspace root, even though this is possible. You created an indexing workspace, where the document management features are not supposed to work.

In the Content Sources Web Folder you will notice by default one content source called "Portal Shortcuts". If you inspect the properties, you'll see that it is dedicated to crawling any shortcuts on the destination server. These shortcuts on the target server might point to content that is located outside the workspace. This feature is provided to allow for configurations such that the target server does not need to crawl at all.

Only the first index workspace that propagates to the target workspace actually crawls the shortcuts. For any other index workspaces that propagate to the target workspace, an error will be reported in the gatherer log. You can use the Catutil.exe utility, which can be found on the SharePoint Portal Server CD under Support/Tools, to specify which server propagates the shortcuts to the target server. The "Portal Content" content source on all other indexing server can be deleted.

Summary

SharePoint Portal Server's indexing capabilities allow for powerful search solutions with fine granular control over the content that gets indexed. Due to the flexible architecture, it is possible to scale the solution using dedicated indexing servers that propagate their gathered information to a central site. The Coordinator remains the final control and enforcement of the company best practices with the Administrator.

19

PART V

REAL WORLD SCENARIOS

CHAPTER 20

EXAMPLE SCENARIO 1—PLANNING A DEPLOYMENT

In this chapter

PLANNING A DEPLOYMENT FOR ABC COMPANY

Planning a SharePoint Portal Server implementation involves much more than simply setting up a production-ready server and clicking your way through File-Run-Setup. Before a server is ever pulled out of a shipping box, before any software is ever removed from its plastic wrapper, a comprehensive project plan must be crafted. The solutions architecture must be laid out. Additionally, a systemwide approach to managing change must be developed and followed. In this chapter, we cover laying a foundation for a secure and well-performing SharePoint implementation in terms of the following:

- Business goals and requirements
- Building the technical support organization
- Hardware vendor selection
- Solutions architecture
- Security plan development
- Developing the workspace(s)
- Preparing the dashboard site(s)
- Addressing change management
- Preparing for go-live
- Planning for post go-live support

To make the application of the following more meaningful, we have approached this chapter in such a way as to walk the Finance Department of ABC Company (the "company," or "ABC," a fictional entity) through planning their own SharePoint Portal Server deployment.

BUSINESS GOALS AND REQUIREMENTS

Understanding what each business unit needs in terms of a document and content management solution is critical to a successful implementation. Goals and needs should drive everything from budget to implementation timelines, high-availability requirements, service level agreements, post go-live support, and more. Questions like the following must be posed:

- How do we manage content today (server-based file/print, Exchange public folders, miscellaneous internal and external Web sites, and so on)?
- Where do we maintain that data (server file shares, local client hard drives, databases, intranet Web servers, and so forth)?
- What kind of data do we keep (Word docs, Exchange folders, Excel Spreadsheets, PowerPoint presentations, Lotus Notes, MS Access databases, flat files, data residing in SQL 2000 databases, and so on)?

20

- Who actually uses the data, and what are the retention period requirements (different business units may need the same data but have different format requirements, need it for a longer period of time than other groups, or need it exported into another application for further analysis)?

Once a general understanding of the preceding is achieved, a more detailed understanding is typically required to determine what the end users of the proposed SharePoint Portal Server solution actually require to perform their jobs effectively. Even then, a further determination as to how they will access and use the content within the Portal is required. One popular method of gathering this data is through the use of simple end-user–based questionnaires designed to uncover the following user characteristics and behaviors:

- What is your job/task role?
- What do you use the current system of content and document management for?
- What kind of data would you like to see that is not a part of the current solution?
- When do you need access to the content management system?
  - Standard 9 a.m.–5 p.m.
  - "After hours"
  - Occasional weekends to support month-end close
  - Other requirements driven by the business
- How do you actually find/access the data?
  - By performing keyword searches
  - Navigating through various shares and folders
  - Browsing through data organized into categories

In the case of ABC Company, they were like many other mid-market companies that did not have a dedicated content or document management solution in place. Rather, the financial group relied on a number of file shares named after functional roles (such as "logistics", "AR", "AP", "Benefits", "HR", and nearly 20 more), spread out across multiple file/print Microsoft NT and Windows 2000 servers. The bulk of the data consisted of Microsoft Word and Excel documents, though there had been a need for access to high-level month-end and quarter-end roll-up PowerPoint slideshows presented to upper management. Additionally, data was often maintained in private Exchange 2000 mailboxes and only shared as requested by colleagues. Other data was sitting out on a Web server just deployed in the previous year, but a recent security breach compromising employee payroll records had made many of the financial folks uneasy. And more recently, an in-house custom application–based attempt to roll up all of this enterprise-wide data had failed during the pilot phase—the pilot users found the interface cumbersome to use, and access to the data was slow due to poor search capabilities.

20

Finally, the general availability of a few of ABC's servers had been extremely poor, the result of what seemed to be less-than-stringent *change control* processes more than faulty hardware or OS stability issues. For example, the company suffered two days of unplanned downtime on six different servers when the NT/W2K Administrator decided it was time to update to the latest system management agents, and corrupted the local registry on each machine with a botched upgrade.

> **NOTE** *Change control* refers to the practice of first testing a suggested or potential change to a production system in a technical sandbox or other SPS environment.

While the end-user population (primarily financial analysts and controllers) was happy with 7 a.m.–7 p.m. access at this point in time, it should be noted that weekend access was required the week before and the week after each month-end close. And with Asian and European financial groups soon to come online in the next six months, mandatory real-time 24×7 access to all portal resources would become a reality shortly.

With this end-user–driven data, and the higher-level business group data requirements outlined previously, an organization structure could now be put into place to begin the implementation/deployment planning process.

Building the Technical Support Organization

A number of forces drive the size and scope of the organization tasked with designing, building, and supporting the SharePoint Portal Server solution. Indeed, a support organization will likely revise itself after a SharePoint Portal project goes "live" (go-live), but for purposes here, we will focus on the following "pre–go-live" requirements that drive staffing the portal support organization:

- Functional or "capability" requirements
- Accessibility requirements
- Availability/High-Availability requirements
- Performance requirements
- Scalability requirements
- Security requirements
- Administration requirements
- Other requirements

We have seen each of the requirements listed previously mentioned in different chapters throughout this book. Astute readers will also note that these requirements also map to different technology and functional areas covered in Microsoft-provided or hardware-vendor-provided SPS sizing questionnaires. In the next few pages, we'll take a closer look at each of these.

→ To see the SharePoint Portal Server sizing questionnaire in action, **see** "The Sizing Questionnaire," **p. 586**.

FUNCTIONAL REQUIREMENTS

Functional requirements drive the configuration of the dashboard, and therefore typically involve technical specialists focused on designing effective layouts, as well as technical specialists experienced in configuring the dashboard (developers, also generically referred to as programmers). For our purposes here, defining the functional requirements in terms of the following will provide enough information to drive the development of our technical support organization:

- Number of organizations
- Types of organizations (almost exclusively financial in the case of ABC Company, although limited manufacturing, warehousing, and other folks would eventually benefit from sharing some of the data)
- Sensitivity of data which will reside in the portal

ACCESSIBILITY REQUIREMENTS

Accessibility refers to the ability to actually acquire or get to the data. Some users may be limited in terms of the connection speed they will enjoy with the portal (such as 28.8 modems or slow WAN links). Others may be wired for 100 megabit switched LAN connections, but run slower desktop technology, have limited memory resources, or be saddled with older OSs. Yet others may have no native Internet or intranet browser capability. Therefore, early in the deployment planning process, it becomes essential to estimate and characterize the total number of end users, determining which of these will be accessing the portal via dial-up, WAN, or LAN-based links, and whether this drives changes to the desktop, the network links, or even the SharePoint Portal Server implementation itself. ABC Company simplified and documented this exercise by developing the straightforward "End User Client Matrix" illustrated here:

Figure 20.1
Sample illustration of an End-User Client Matrix. This particular example displays four connections types (<56kb, 56-128kb, WAN, LAN) and five client machine attributes (OS, CPU speed, RAM, Browser Version, and Outlook Express Version).

	Network Connections				Client Machine Attributes				
	56 kb	56-128 kb	WAN	LAN	OS/SP	CPU MHz	RAM (MB)	Browser Version	Outlook Version
Business Group 1 - NA					NT4 WS/SP6a	20 @ <300	64	5	5.00x+
	5	10	0	55	W2K Pro/SP1	50 @ >400	128+	5.5	5.01+
Business Group 2 - EMEA			20		NT4 WS/SP5	20 @ >400	128+	5.5	5.00x+
Business Group 3 - ASIA			30		NT4 WS/SP3	20 @ 200	32	4.0x+	5.00x+
HQ and Other - NA	4	1	15	25	NT4 WS/SP6a	5 @ <300	64	5	5.00x+
					W2K Pro/SP1	37 @ >400	128+	5.5	5.01+
					W2K Pro/SP2	2 @ >900	256+	6	5.01+

Another area of accessibility involves addressing the special needs of people who are deaf, hard of hearing, or otherwise challenged in terms of getting to the portal data. Microsoft is committed to making its products—from OSs through applications—available for everyone, as evidenced in the following:

- Features and hints for customizing Windows 2000
- Online and audio-based Microsoft software documentation (plus cassette, floppy disk, and compact disc [CD] formats)
- Third-party utilities that enhance accessibility
- Special Microsoft services for the deaf and hard-of-hearing

AVAILABILITY REQUIREMENTS

Like functional requirements, availability requirements are also driven by user needs, though they are most often addressed by traditional IT organizations staffed with providing operations, maintenance, and specialized high-availability support. Often termed *high availability* requirements, or *HA* for short, these requirements refer to the need of the solution to actually be up and available for a certain percentage of total "wall-clock" time. This is where the infamous "3 nines," "4 nines," and "5 nines" of availability originate, equating to 99.9%, 99.99%, and 99.999% availability, respectively.

In reality, 99.9%, or 3 nines, is actually quite high for the majority of enterprise solutions deployed today. An implementation expected to be up 99.9% of the time (assuming 24×7 availability and a 365 day year, which equates to 31,536,000 target seconds of availability per year) can only be down 31,536 seconds (525 minutes, or just under 9 hours per year). In other words, a 99.9% HA solution will be expected to be up/available 31,504,464 seconds of the year. Ask most IT shops out there if they can withstand 9 hours of unplanned downtime per year, and the answer is usually "Sure, sounds great; where do I sign up?"

Of course, some enterprise applications require even less downtime. There are companies today that can only withstand five minutes of unplanned downtime per year—otherwise, lives might be put in danger (as in refineries, power plants, and so on), or millions of dollars might be at risk. Availability is all about money, in fact—ABC Company hired a third-party systems integrator to assist them in determining their HA requirements. Their consultant started their HA conversation with "I can give you any level of availability that you'd like—higher availability simply costs more money." The next step then became an exercise in calculating ROI, or return on investment. They quickly estimated the hardware, software, and resource costs to implement a SharePoint Portal Server solution capable of providing 3 nines of availability, and next determined that to "give back" an incremental hour of unplanned downtime ran up another $500,000. The question then became "Will you suffer more than $500,000 in lost revenue or productivity if you are down an incremental hour?" As the answer was "no!" they determined that three 9s was *good enough*.

Ah, "good enough." A mantra at some companies, an anathema at others—"good enough" scares the QPM folks to death! But good enough is all about getting 95% of what you need at only 20% of the cost of a solution that satisfies 100% of your needs. Confused?

Unfortunately, many companies fail to do the "5 nines of availability" math, and simply request the highest levels of availability from their hardware partners. Their need for this level of availability is simply a perceived requirement. Once the budget and ROI numbers are worked out, this perceived requirement usually works its way back down to something that less than three 9s can address—something closer to "good enough" (got it now?). But this practice certainly helps explain the abuse and over-use of the term "5 nines of availability" in today's information technology world.

PERFORMANCE REQUIREMENTS

Though availability is important, a minimum level of overall portal performance is critical as well. For our purposes here, performance requirements tend to drive the makeup of the technical support organization in one primary way—the need for specialized technical resources becomes mandatory if "niche" performance-improvement products or techniques are employed. Some of the products and techniques include

- Caching servers
- Load balancing routers or servers
- Software or OS-based load balancing

At ABC Company, the initial thoughts were that their performance goals could be achieved without the need for specialized performance options.

SCALABILITY REQUIREMENTS

Scalability requirements speak to how quickly the current solution can scale or grow to meet planned or unplanned increases in the number of users accessing the portal. For example, with the increase in users that ABC Company will realize after bringing Asia and Europe online, the solution to be implemented must be capable of growing without "trashing everything and starting over." This is where sound architecture planning becomes critical.

SECURITY REQUIREMENTS

Security requirements are perhaps more important than any of the preceding. As ABC Company has already discovered, once a security breach has occurred, things are never the same. That is, you just can't squeeze the toothpaste back into the tube—it doesn't work that way! But an organization *can* learn from their mistakes, and ensure that both the design and implementation of the new SharePoint Portal Server addresses security as a primary consideration, not as an afterthought.

The process of introducing and managing change within the SPS environment also serves to maintain the security of the system. Change management (used interchangeably with the term *change control*) is addressed later in this chapter.

Paramount to the discussion of security is a discussion on the nature and sensitivity of the data that will reside in the portal. Payroll data, data related to benefits, data regarding customers or new product roadmaps, and so on are prime examples of "sensitive" data—the kind of information that only hurts the organization or entire company when it is compromised. ABC understands this more than ever.

ADMINISTRATION REQUIREMENTS

Administration requirements drive the composition of the technical support organization from a day-to-day operations perspective. It makes no sense at all to invest time and energy into a portal solution only to leave it un-maintained—better to continue using your unorganized file shares and private mailboxes, and save your money! Many organizations fail to realize this fact, though, until they have already deployed an application into production. Then, the challenge becomes trying to retrofit and retool an existing operations team to meet the needs of the new application.

A question central to how existing resources would be leveraged to support the new portal project at ABC Company was "Who actually manages the data we have today?" That is, does a centralized IT organization or departmental-based IT organization manage the various forms of data and content? Or, rather, is data management the responsibility of local business group super users, distributed administrators, or another entity? Answering this question yields two great truths:

1. The location, size, and breadth of data becomes apparent.
2. Individuals with skillsets (or at minimum, a vested interest) in managing data come to the surface, representing potential technical support organization team members, or perhaps even barriers to the success of the project.

In the case of ABC Company, however, we were fortunate. ABC's Data Center Computer Systems/Operations Team consisted of long-time company-badged computer operators, specialized in maintaining a multitude of servers and systems running various flavors of Microsoft enterprise operating systems (NT Enterprise Edition, Windows 2000 Advanced Server, and an XP pilot project currently in progress), as well as a number of Unix variants. ABC's 24×7 operations team welcomed the challenge of learning how to best support a new application, and were positioned well to do so in staggered stages or phases, as three individuals worked 12-hour shifts, and all workers were divided into two teams (Sunday-Tuesday, Thursday-Saturday, and split Wednesdays).

OTHER REQUIREMENTS

Other requirements that might drive the size and scope of the technical team include

- Problems uncovered via the completed questionnaires, in terms of content provided, timeframes provided, and data formats provided, will drive business needs
- Security concerns regarding ability of one group to view another group's documents will drive security needs

- Inability to manage or track revisions of documents will drive traditional content-management needs across the business organizations

ABC Company quickly realized that they had no real content management expertise. They knew over time that they would develop this expertise; however, the need to get up to speed quickly became a driving factor. In the end, they elicited the assistance of a third-party consultant specializing in content management, with deep experience in Microsoft's platforms and products. The arrangement was such that the quality and speed of knowledge transfer provided to ABC's own technical support organization drove the billable hourly rate of the consulting contract—within three weeks, ABC was not only well on their way to self-sufficiency, but also was in a financial position to take advantage of the consultant again, should the need arise.

ABC measured the value gained through introducing the consultant in a number of ways, including feedback from each team member tasked with eventually supporting SharePoint Portal Server, plus the ability of each team member to manage the portal from an operations perspective. Of course, other milestones could have come into play, like the ability to install and configure a particular feature or component of SPS. Each case would differ, underscoring the importance of identifying measurable success criteria at the beginning of each consulting engagement.

MAKEUP OF A TYPICAL TECHNICAL SUPPORT ORGANIZATION

At the end of the day, a typical technical support organization for supporting a productive Microsoft SharePoint Portal Server implementation might include the following specialists, or *Subject Matter Experts (SMEs)*:

- Server hardware
- Disk subsystem/Storage Area Network (SAN)
- Network infrastructure
- Windows 2000 administration
- Exchange Server administration
- SharePoint Portal Server infrastructure
- SharePoint Portal Server configuration
- Database administration
- Computer/Systems operations
- Access to third-party Systems Integrators (SIs) with deep experience in the previous areas as well

20

NOTE

> The above does not necessitate full-time dedicated resources to the SharePoint project. Rather, individuals currently tasked with similar functions managing other enterprise resources are often asked to perform those functions here as well.

An excellent example included the Backup/Restore Operator at ABC Company (a member of the Computer/Systems Operations, or CSO, staff)—given that this function is addressed for every server in the data center, it only made good business sense to incrementally add the SharePoint server systems to the B/R Operator's responsibilities.

→ To learn more about developing the technical support organization for a fictional enterprise SPS deployment, **see** "Staffing Challenges," **p. 582**.

But we are getting ahead of ourselves. In the next section, we will step back to the first few weeks of the SharePoint deployment planning process, and dive into the hardware vendor selection approach.

HARDWARE VENDOR SELECTION

As high performance, highly available Intel and AMD-based Microsoft Windows 2000 and .NET servers become the norm in the Enterprise Data Center, the question of which hardware vendor to choose for your SharePoint Portal Server implementation seems to become somewhat moot. Nearly every top tier server manufacturer provides a sound product at a reasonable price-point, offering comparable performance metrics with similar post-sales support options. Nearly all of them offer specialized high-availability features like hot plug hard disk drives, RAID Array hard disk drive controllers capable of supporting configurations where it is possible to lose multiple drives while still protecting valuable data, hot plug fans and power supplies, redundant ECC-protected RAM, redundant processors and processor power modules, fault-tolerant network configuration options, hot plug PCI slots supporting redundant or hot-replace controllers, and more.

However, a number of differentiators still exist between the different server hardware vendors today:

- Price-Performance—the ratio of the two is sometimes overlooked. True, nearly every vendor can provide a certain level of performance, but at what price per transaction or gigabyte?

- Service & Support—some vendors maintain their own highly trained professional services organizations. Others rely on third parties to provide support. Additionally, not all vendors offer the ability to respond to issues in two or four hours. Finally, minimizing third parties usually benefits the customer from a total cost of ownership perspective.

- One-stop shopping—not all vendors offer the breadth or depth of products and services that are required in a typical portal implementation (or any enterprise application implementation, for that matter). To minimize post-support finger-pointing, stick with a single vendor that can address at a minimum your enterprise server, disk subsystem, and systems management requirements.

20

Additionally, a company's internal computing standards might dictate the preference of one server or disk subsystem platform over another simply for the sake of server standardization. For example, if a company has standardized on the Widget model XYZ server platform, the following is true:

- The company's IT organization has experience with this XYZ platform—they know it, they know how the OS behaves on it, they know how to install and maintain it, back it up effectively, and so forth

- IT has spares (network cards, disk drives, and so on) on hand that are likely interchangeable or at minimum compatible with newer, similar Widget-based technology

- IT and IT Management have a relationship in place with their Widget account team, including a single point of contact capable of leveraging multiple product and services organizations inside Widget when the need arises

Once the hardware vendor has been selected, the process of sizing the SharePoint Portal Server solution landscape begins. In the next section, we will address this, as well as different approaches towards architecting the SPS solution landscape and sizing particular components of the landscape.

SOLUTIONS ARCHITECTURE

The same tenets that drive the makeup of the technical support organization also, not coincidentally, drive the overall solutions architecture. To reiterate, these are

- Functional or "capability" requirements
- Availability/high-availability requirements
- Performance requirements
- Scalability requirements
- Security requirements
- Administration requirements
- Other requirements

Each of these becomes critical to the design and implementation of the individual server-based components within the overall SharePoint Portal Server solution. However, it makes good sense to step back a bit and analyze the portal solution from a holistic perspective prior to drilling down further.

OVERVIEW—THE PORTAL SYSTEM LANDSCAPE

During the life of the SharePoint Portal Server implementation, a number of systems (sometimes referred to as *instances* or *environments*) will be used to ensure the quality and availability of the Production Portal system. For example, the following four environments are quite common in large SPS deployments:

- **Technical Sandbox**—a server system or environment where the technical folks can install, configure, integrate, back up, restore, and uninstall components of the portal solution. This is nearly always deployed first.

- **Development system** —an environment used to develop and test changes to the dashboard.

- **Test system** —may be deployed to test the impact that a certain load (referred to as *load testing*) places on the overall solution, for example to determine the impact that different loads have on end-user search response times.

- **Production system** —the system that end users leverage for the productive use and good of the company. This is the last system typically deployed.

The sum total of all of these environments is typically referred to as the Portal System Landscape. Other environments exist as well, and provide different services or play different roles within the SPS landscape. We will go into more specifics of these systems in the next section, including when they might become a critical component of the landscape.

In smaller deployments, a two- or possibly three-system landscape is architected and deployed, usually consisting of a combined Technical Sandbox/Development system and a Production system. Larger four- or five-system landscapes are not uncommon, however, in massive implementations, or implementations where the highest levels of availability are desired. Note the relationship between the number of systems in the landscape and the availability requirements of the solution—more systems equates to higher availability. Why? Because more systems equate to incrementally greater quality assurance testing, testing that better guarantees improved availability of the ultimate production portal.

Each of the systems in a system landscape actually consists of the following:

- A SharePoint Portal Server

- One or more representative SharePoint clients (for example, if the end-user population uses both Windows NT 4/SP6 Workstation with Internet Explorer 5.0, as well as W2K Pro with Internet Explorer 6, each of these clients should be maintained as a component of the "system")

- Any Integration-Points or server components that will play a role in the Production system (such as an Exchange server, dedicated Search and Crawl servers, SQL Server 2000, distributed IIS 5.0 servers, and so on)—thus, additional servers or products may be installed as a component of each system.

It's important to note that it makes little sense to save a few dollars by not including any of the above system landscape components. For example, if both Office 2000 and Office XP are deployed on different client platforms, then both must be included, as the integration functionality is slightly different between the two products.

THE SPS SYSTEM LANDSCAPE

Maintaining a number of discrete portal systems to support a single and perhaps small production portal implementation may seem like a lot of hardware, software, and resources to manage. Before justifying these expenses, though, let us drill down into the specific purpose or roles that each of these systems support, noting again that all of these systems ultimately support and help to maintain a well-performing production system.

As we alluded to earlier, each of these systems is actually a *mini-environment* used for specific tasks related to the productive portal deployment:

1. Technical Sandbox System—This system is reserved for use by the technical implementation teams to practice and perfect Microsoft SharePoint Portal Server, IIS, W2K, and other software component installations, upgrades, integration with other solution components, setup/testing of data replication, backup and restore processes, server duplications processes, and so on.

2. Development System— This system is created and maintained for continued portal configuration and/or customization, maintenance, Microsoft SharePoint Portal Server upgrades, and bug fixes. This instance also serves as the originator of configurations and customizations that will eventually be "promoted" into production (although a Test/QA system, if it is in place, may be leveraged first).

3. Training System— Usually reserved for very large implementations, this system is maintained for ongoing internal training of end-user personnel ("How to use the SharePoint Finance Portal," Portal 101 classes, and so on).

4. Test/QA System (a.k.a. Quality Assurance) —Another optional system typically seen in the largest implementations, this system is maintained for integration and testing of configuration changes, customizations across multiple dashboards, and so on prior to promoting these changes into the Production Instance.

5. Staging System —Usually identical to Production, this system is used as the last stop for changes in a system. The Staging system is often subjected to stress/load tests so as to determine the expected impact of a change on the actual production system *before* this change is promoted to Production.

6. Production System —This system supports the business groups and supports the business needs addressed by Microsoft SharePoint Portal Server, and is the system the end users leverage for information sharing, content and document management, and so on.

7. Disaster Recovery System —This system is implemented when the cost of unplanned downtime exceeds the cost of implementing, maintaining, and supporting the Production system. DR systems, as they are generically referred to, are almost always located in different physical locations.

→ To read more about leveraging the concept of promoting changes within your SPS system to assist you in troubleshooting SPS-related issues, **see** "General Troubleshooting Approach," **p. 618**.

20

In the case of ABC Company, it was determined by the technical support organization that a three-system landscape—dedicated Technical Sandbox, Development, and Production systems—made the most sense from an availability and financial perspective. They liked the idea of maintaining a Technical Sandbox system completely separate from all other systems, as it would allow them freedom to test new features, fixes, and updates up and down the solutions stack, without ever impacting the development or production systems. Additionally, they justified the incremental cost of a third portal landscape system under the umbrella of "disaster recovery," establishing the Development system at a location miles away from the Production and Technical Sandbox systems.

Many companies are adopting strategies similar to that employed by ABC—note also that the Technical Sandbox system is often referred to as the "best-kept secret" to maintaining a *highly available* production operating environment. That is, changes are introduced in the Production environment only after testing them in an identical (or as near identical as practical) technical sandbox environment, and then further ratified via the development system. Further, the promotion of configuration changes can also be tested in this manner, therefore ensuring that the promotion of changes from Development to Production is smooth. It is no wonder that a Technical Sandbox system was identified as a key element in ABC's Microsoft SharePoint Portal Server deployment and implementation strategy.

FUTURE GROWTH VERSUS MAXIMIZING APPROACH

Two schools of thought exist in regard to configuring servers, server components, and computing appliances. In the first case, sometimes called *Future Growth Strategy* or *In the Box Growth*, CPU, memory, disk, and peripheral I/O slot system configurations are designed to meet a minimal supported level of fault tolerance while allowing for future growth of the systems. That is, in configurations where the memory needed to meet the user requirements would require *all* disk drive bays, or all memory slots, or all CPU sockets of the computing platform expected to be used, a larger disk drive, higher density DIMM kit, and so on is actually used instead. In this way, the larger kit provides open slots/bays/and so forth to provide for future hardware upgrades. Such an approach to configuring allows for "built-in capacity growth" of the individual servers and appliances within a given solution—an open/available drive bay/etc exists up front.

A second school of thought for configuring individual servers and appliances within a solution suggests that a *Maximizing* strategy allows for lower total cost of ownership. Rather than leaving memory slots, CPU sockets, drive bays, and so on available—and risking the ability to actually procure one of these components in the years to come—defenders of the *Maximizing* strategy seek to provide maximum capability in (hopefully!) a fewer number of servers/appliances. In addition, proponents of this school of thought believe that the typical costs associated with "opening a box"—planning for and taking down a server for hardware upgrades—exceed the delta in cost between configuring it for future growth and "maxing it out."

Note that neither school of thought seeks to sacrifice availability, though. Availability through redundancy—maintaining "2x" or "1+x" servers when only "x" is required to address a given load—still applies to both schools of thought. In the first case, though, three lightly configured servers may be specified, whereas in the latter, two heavily configured servers are preferred.

ABC Company had subscribed to both schools of thought in the past. Through experience, though, they came to believe that it was more trouble than it was worth to find a new supported CPU, or additional supported RAM. Experience also told them that the downtime associated with bringing a server offline for a hardware upgrade was also not worth their effort. Therefore, they quickly decided that a "max out the box" approach would be their best bet for the SharePoint Portal Server implementation.

SECURITY PLAN DEVELOPMENT

Developing a security plan is critical in two areas—for document management tasks as well as in support of searching. Access to sensitive information must be restricted, and in document approval scenarios, only those with discrete edit or approve rights may be able to view a document until it is ready to be pushed out to a more general audience.

In search scenarios, it is important that documents that are not to be made available for select user communities must not be compromised. That is, the results of a search must not yield documents to which a particular user should have no access.

Microsoft SharePoint Portal Server security leverages standard Windows-based encrypted authentication to ensure password security. Additionally, access to documents may be controlled by using a fixed set of three roles—assigning a specific role to a user gives that user permission to perform specific tasks in the workspace. Note that you must configure each workspace folder to include a set of users or groups assigned to specific roles.

NOTE

When SharePoint Portal Server crawls documents stored on an organization's servers, the security policy on each document is enforced when SharePoint Portal Server provides search results—SharePoint Portal Server recognizes any security policies that are currently assigned to the organization's servers, databases, or file shares. This is good news for a company like ABC, where many documents spread out across multiple servers, shares, and networks will be ultimately crawled. As SharePoint Portal Server enforces file-level security, not share-level security, all documents maintain a tight level of inherent security.

20

DEVELOPING THE WORKSPACE

One of the most basic functions of preparing the workspace for document management and group collaboration involves configuring the Documents folder. Designing the folder structure takes us back to some of the original questions we faced when drilling down into the business goals of the project.

- How are documents organized? By type? iFilter? Group?
- Who can view them? Edit them? Add more?

- What steps should be taken prior to publishing documents? Then, how should it actually be published?
- How important is tracking the history of a document?
- Are check-in or check-out of documents a concern?
- Are enhanced folders otherwise required, or are standard folder adequate?
- How are index updates scheduled?
- How are search scopes defined and created?

Figure 20.2
This table illustrates each folder type, and features supported.

Feature	Standard folder	Enhanced folder
Roles	Yes	Yes
Document version history	No	Yes
Check-in/check-out	No	Yes
Private draft versions	No	Yes
Approval routing	No	Yes
Profile metadata	Yes	Yes
Indexed documents	Yes	Yes
Categories	Yes	Yes

BEST PRACTICES APPROACH TO DEVELOPING THE WORKSPACE

While the preceding points and many others must be addressed, ABC Company took a "best practices" approach to developing their workspace. For example, they were able to leverage the Base Document profile (a template) for the bulk of their documents, as they had created a simple folder layout. ABC also brought in a number of functional specialists familiar with their content, so as to find data patterns that aided in organizing this content. Then they locked down document profiles and metadata properties to ensure that consistency was maintained (which, therefore, improved search results).

ABC Company also determined that Web Discussions would provide a superior mechanism for collaboration than had previously been enjoyed. Just the fact that SharePoint Portal Server would consolidate comments on a document in one location would save ABC countless man-hours, while simultaneously forcing a single discussion rather than the many multi-threaded discussions they tended to have when reviewing documents via email.

Finally, ABC migrated their two remaining Lotus Notes databases to Microsoft-based solutions, and benefited in a number of ways—note that while this was not required from a SharePoint Portal Server perspective, it helped push an otherwise stalled IT migration and ultimately reduced the number/diversity of supported IT crawl sources and integration points, thereby reducing their total cost of ownership (TCO) over the long run on many different fronts.

PREPARING THE DASHBOARD SITE

Once the workspace is created, an associated Web site and dashboard is also created. Any browser-enabled user can leverage the power of your SharePoint Portal nearly immediately. However, an important first step for portal dashboard development is updating the home page, which should highlight information for the end users that is especially useful. Web Parts may also be added to display additional information. A typical dashboard site for a business group, or our Finance department at ABC Company, would include information relevant to the group's work and perhaps a Web Part or section dedicated to project status. If the entire ABC Company were going to use the portal, a dashboard site that featured an overall approach relevant to all business groups or departments would make sense (with perhaps section of the dashboard dedicated to critical or high-use organizations).

At ABC, the financial liaison sub-group to ABC's Human Resources department determined that searches for information about employee benefits would be extremely useful, as well as quite common. Therefore, they decided to post information about employee benefits on the home page under a Web Part called HR Benefits. To keep all financial group employees informed about new tax laws, another Web Part called Tax Updates was created as well, providing the latest feeds from a common subscription services.

ABC added additional value to their dashboard site by including Web Parts that displayed business information regarding company financial earnings, historical versus current analyses, and access to Microsoft NetMeeting (as another collaboration tool). Custom Web Parts were also planned early in the deployment process, to provide access to Excel spreadsheets with quarterly sales and margin figures for each of the discrete product groups.

LEVERAGING THE CATEGORY ASSISTANT

To facilitate excellent search capabilities, ABC spent the time up front determining categories in which to group similar documents and document types. Special attention was paid to hierarchies, especially the name and size of subcategories—no subcategory was allowed to contain more than 1,000 documents, for example. This was enforced through regular management/operations exception reporting performed by the technical support organization.

The Category Assistant was also leveraged to automatically assign categories to ABC's existing documents. It categorized new documents as well, by comparing the list of words for each category to the list of words contained in each new document. And to ABC's pleasant surprise, they found that SharePoint Portal Server actually automatically categorized most of their new documents into multiple categories, thereby enhancing and improving upon their typical search results. ABC ensured a high success rate in categorizing by using a relatively high precision number. The trade-off was, of course, that not all documents were categorized. But those that did get categorized mapped very nicely back to the category structure.

→ To learn more about category structures and the Category Assistant, **see** "Managing Categories and the Category Assistant," **p. 248**.

20

LEVERAGING BEST BETS

Finally, ABC Company took advantage of SharePoint Portal Server's "Best Bets" to further improve search efficiency. The Best Bets in a search consist of documents considered especially relevant to the search, and therefore aid the end user in ultimately finding the "best" result or answer to a given set of search criteria. And since SharePoint Portal Sever posts these Best Bets at the top of a search list, end users naturally gravitate towards pulling these documents first. Satisfied with their search results sooner than otherwise would occur, these end users need no longer search the portal. The result? Fewer searches/scans, and therefore improved search responses for every user.

> **NOTE**
>
> Two types of Best Bets exist:
>
> **Keyword Best Bet**—results that are relevant to a keyword.
>
> **Category Best Bet**—a document relevant to a particular category.

ABC found it particularly easy to identify a document as a Best Bet. By updating the Search and Categories tab on the Properties page of each document, they were able to enter metadata regarding both Keyword and Category Best Bets.

→ To read more about Best Bets and their role in the SPS production environment, **see** "Category Best Bets," **p. 318**.

ADDRESSING CHANGE MANAGEMENT

While the process of managing change merits complete volumes in and of itself, we would be amiss if change management was not covered at least briefly from a deployment planning perspective. Once a workspace and dashboard are close to being completed, thought must be given to how future changes will be promoted into the eventual productive implementation.

ABC Company believed that they had an adequate "change management" approach integrated into how they planned and deployed IT solutions for business problems. In reality, though, as we uncovered previously, a number of issues spoke to major change management shortcomings. For example

- Changes to production resources previously resulted in many hours of unplanned downtime
- A lack of "test" or "technical sandbox" resources previously necessitated implementing changes directly into production environments

A quick review of change management, outlining its value and importance in terms of maintaining a highly available portal solution, is in order.

20

CHANGE MANAGEMENT OVERVIEW

A productive SharePoint Portal Server environment is not expected to remain static. That is, as business requirements, software upgrades, OS and hardware updates, and more changes are requested/required, the environment will evolve over time. While this evolution is good in terms of keeping a customer's employees productive and informed, an enormous opportunity to introduce instability into the production environment exists. Therefore, if these changes are not managed well, and managed consistently, the result over time will be not unlike the state of many currently deployed enterprise portals—somewhat unreliable, prone to unscheduled downtime, and more difficult to manage than required. Traditionally, change management in PC server-based environments has been poor, the result of few mission-critical systems in these types of environments until perhaps four or five years ago. The successful PC server-based enterprise application projects have embraced what can only be described as a "Mainframe mentality" to change control—these folks have taken change control seriously, and it shows in their high system uptimes and low unplanned outages. The following has been written in an attempt to provide initial change management/change-control procedures—if this is adhered to and updated as required, the result will likely be a more available SharePoint Portal Server system, and ultimately happier, more productive end users.

IMPLEMENTATION OVERVIEW—PHASES OF IMPLEMENTATION

To understand the role that change management plays in an enterprise solution, it is important to understand the evolution of that solution in terms of phases of systems development—these phases tie nicely into our "system landscape" approach previously discussed.

The solution phases below are based on a typical implementation of an enterprise portal solution, the timeline of which might typically consume four weeks to perhaps many months or more:

1. Pilot Phase—This phase allows the customer to examine, test, evaluate, and explore the proposed Microsoft SharePoint Portal Server solution. This phase is necessary to "prove" that indeed the portal will solve the business problems at hand. It is also important in terms of ensuring that accurate training, development, and deployment plans can be made, and the enterprise portal project effectively estimated from a cost and time perspective. This phase may last from a week or more to perhaps a month in large enterprise-wide pilots. A preliminary hardware sizing may be beneficial at this point, to ensure that the pilot solution is configured adequately from the beginning, so as to best set the stage for the next phase.

2. Development Phase —Building upon the hardware/software solution prepared in support of the Pilot Phase, this phase consists of customer and/or consulting personnel configuring and customizing the system for use in the target business area(s). This phase occupies the bulk of the project plan, and typically continues throughout the life of a solution (though perhaps less intensely on initial business areas, to focus on new business areas/opportunities). Initial maintenance upgrades and bug fixes are performed

20

here as well, resulting in a fairly stable environment for continued development and the next phase. During this phase, it is also critical to begin planning for the expected configuration testing and pre-productive deployments—changes in business assumptions, implementation plans, and server/software technology roadmaps must be visited.

3. Training Phase —Like the Development Phase, this phase also begins when the Pilot Phase ends. Training of development and technical support organization personnel occurs first. Training of end user and other personnel begins once a preliminary level of configuration and/or customization has been completed. This phase is ongoing in some capacity throughout the life cycle of the solution.

4. Pre-production Test/QA Phase —This ongoing phase begins when the first configuration, integration, and quality assurance testing is performed on development results fed from the Development Phase. It continues, as required, to test the necessary changes and provide for change management throughout the Production Phase. Note that the final end-to-end Production SharePoint Portal Server hardware sizing is typically completed during this phase.

5. Production or Production Roll-out Phase —This phase begins when company organizations and business processes become dependent on the data being hosted or managed by the Portal.

SYSTEM STANDARDIZING—MINIMIZING CHANGE MANAGEMENT

For most companies, including ABC Company, maintaining a fewer number of specific items—whether they be a certain model of server, or type of disk drive, or manufacturer of network card—will cost less in the long run and prove easier to manage than maintaining a mix of products that might better fit each variance and niche-requirement within a computing environment. For example, at ABC, they selected Microsoft Windows 2000 Advanced Server as the standard OS, even though plain ol' Server would have been adequate in quite a few instances. Similarly, they standardized on a single model of server, even though it provided additional processing headroom in some instances, and therefore cost a bit more up front than other models—in the long run, the TCO would prove to be lower.

Additional reasons to standardize:

- Fewer hardware spares to maintain (less costly than maintaining one of each component)

- Take advantage of bulk-buying (quantity discounts, rather than "one of these" and "six of those" and "two of that")

- Less training required for support staff (no requirement to spend budget money training the Operations staff in supporting different variations of the OS, for example, or tracking issues specific to a certain version of an OS)

- The staff becomes very familiar and comfortable supporting fewer hardware platforms/components (no requirement to spend budget money training staff in supporting multiple server models, for example)

- Less unplanned downtime, as components are interchangeable (less risk of having to wait on a hard-to-find or out-of-stock part in the event of a critical server component failure)

SYSTEM GUIDELINES—"WHAT NOT TO DO"

While configuration guidelines and best-practices provide a foundation for building an enterprise portal solution, change management is also all about avoiding common pitfalls. That is, the goal of change management processes is also to avoid making common mistakes or engaging in poor practices that often compromise the integrity of the SharePoint Portal Server deployment. ABC Company decided early on in their portal deployment planning to follow change management best practices as outlined below:

- Do *not* make firmware, hardware, OS, driver, or application software changes—including updates/upgrades or applying service packs/patches—without *first* testing these changes in the Technical Sandbox environment for an appropriate period of time (ranging from one business day to more than a calendar month, depending on the scope of the change), and *second* getting sign-off from the appropriate responsible vendor (typically the vendor's organization for supporting SharePoint makes the most sense, though Microsoft itself and third parties may play a role here as well) .

- Do *not* fail to adhere to the flow or "promotion" of changes or data from the Technical Sandbox (where infrastructure changes are first tested) to Development (where data originates) to Test/QA (if it exists) to Training (if it exists) to the final Production solution. Failure to do so compromises the integrity of the Production platform, and therefore negates the presence of both the Technical Sandbox and/or the Development and Test/QA environments. The ability to maintain the history of data objects and configuration changes as they are moved through the Microsoft SharePoint Portal Server landscape is critical.

- Configuration changes to the dashboard, the workspace, or any integration point may *only* be modified on the original Development system—*never* perform these "development" tasks elsewhere! This is of significant importance regarding the Production system—absolutely *no changes* must ever be initiated here, as this would imply a complete lack of adequate and appropriate testing.

- Do *not* run additional enterprise applications on the same hardware platform responsible for providing Microsoft SharePoint Portal Server support, unless the system has been specifically sized and configured for both. For example, other business applications including email, database, or audio/streaming video applications typically reside on completely separate hardware platforms.

- Do *not* run network-intensive applications within the private networks dedicated for the Microsoft SharePoint Portal Server and related back-end database, Exchange, IIS, or other "core portal infrastructure" servers. To ensure a better level of consistency in terms of end-user response times, the network requirements of the Microsoft SharePoint Portal Server environment should not be compromised.

20

LEVERAGING THE SYSTEM LANDSCAPE

One of the most basic tenets of sound change management or change control includes leveraging the system landscape to test changes to the environment. One method often used is a *Change Control Checklist*. A sample checklist developed with the help of an outside consultant for the benefit of ABC Company, used to promote changes into production, follows:

Figure 20.3
ABC's Change Control Checklist used by the technical support organization for promoting changes to Production.

Thus, in summary, sound IT change management practices are essential for maintaining a highly available and well-performing SharePoint Portal deployment. Doing otherwise risks the success of the project and the integrity of the overall solution, as well as impacts the entire end-user community, technical support organization, and more. Be safe, and practice conservative and consistent change management.

PREPARING FOR GO-LIVE

The SharePoint Portal Server project leader or administrator must eventually address a host of issues related to readying the implementation for "go-live." Working with the technical support organization and ABC's consulting partner, some of the administrative and other tasks outlined for the benefit of ABC Company included the following:

- Documenting the end-to-end system landscape
- Integrating the system landscape
- Administration tasks
- Production operations
- Disaster recovery

DOCUMENTING THE SYSTEM LANDSCAPE

Perhaps one of the most procrastinated tasks in the world of information technology is the creation and maintenance of the "Standard Installation and Operating Procedures," or the SIOP (or SOP, depending). Given the potential complexity of a Microsoft SharePoint Portal Server deployment, as well as the visibility such a solution garners, development of the SIOP is crucial to long-term success.

THE SIOP

Detailed current-state documentation *must* be maintained and updated to ensure that a re-buildable and manageable solution is maintained. To this end, a master Standard Installation and Operating Procedures manual is mandatory, detailing the overall architecture of the solution, each component of the solution, current related configuration parameters, installation steps for each component, and "how-to's" regarding the specific configuration of each component.

KEEPING THE SIOP UP TO DATE

As the Microsoft SharePoint Portal Server environment evolves, the SIOP must be updated to reflect changes in the operating environment. For example, if a particular configuration change is required down the road, and is not documented, what will happen if a portion of the system landscape succumbs to fire or a natural disaster, or even something as simple as a corrupted disk? Without appropriate and current documentation, precious hours will be lost recovering the system. The next section discusses best practices in regard to maintaining system-specific documentation via the SIOP.

DOCUMENTATION BEST PRACTICES

Every IT organization tends to have at least some rudimentary rules of thumb or best practices surrounding documentation. Many IT organizations simply take screenshots of all product installations or configurations. Others copy and paste read-me files and similar such documents into a book of procedures. Still others simply collect all printed material that came with a piece of gear or a package of software, and place it in a common folder. The following consists of generally agreed-upon best practices:

- Document why any change is ever made to the system landscape—This is critical should the change ever be called into question. It is important to include *who* authorized the change as well as the *problem* or *issue* that was resolved by the change. Note this information on the page being updated, whether the page is a physical piece of paper or a soft/electronic-copy.

- Document the change—Using the existing page (whether printed, Microsoft Word, or Web-based) of the SIOP related to the change, make both an electronic and paper *copy* of the existing page, and then *update* the page electronically and print a copy of it in preparation for the next step.

20

■ Test the change using only the documentation as your guide—Using a printed copy of the now-updated page in the SIOP, follow your procedure to ensure that it is accurate. Make changes as necessary, and fine-tune the processes for complete accuracy and understanding. Screenshots of the appropriate interface allow even the most difficult of configuration steps to be documented easily and clearly.

■ File the pages(s) to be replaced in the SIOP in a safe place—Never be tempted to throw away any printed pages of the SIOP for at least two years! These can become critical documents should a change cause (or be thought to be the cause of) future issues—at 2:00 a.m. after a catastrophic failure, it is always preferable to be able to turn to step-by-step documentation (even "old" versions of documentation), rather than an incorrectly updated procedure. At those times of what usually amounts to unplanned downtime, it is a wonderful thing to remove as much error-prone "2:00 a.m. clouded thinking" as possible. In addition, by retaining the old pages, historical changes can be tracked—should a change ever be questioned, or should a change need to be rolled back, written documentation exists to do so in a cookie-cutter manner, thus removing any doubt that the change was indeed implemented correctly.

So remember, test each change to each installation, upgrade, or how-to procedure in the SIOP, save everything, and enjoy the fruits of your clear and updated documentation!

INTEGRATING THE SYSTEM LANDSCAPE

A SharePoint Portal Server solution does not exist in a vacuum. Rather, it operates typically as a cog in the much larger machine called Information Technology. Integrating the portal landscape into the overall IT landscape is performed at a number of levels, then, such as

■ Inclusion into the systems management approach (products and practices) employed by the organization

■ Domain model/Active Directory integration

■ Systemwide security model

■ Systemwide backup/restore model

ADMINISTRATION TASKS

Addressing product-specific tasks—those related specifically to SharePoint Portal Server (and not systemwide operations tasks, which are covered next)—includes the following:

■ Index management, such as propagating indexes to other servers from index workspaces, or performing full, incremental, or adaptive updates

■ Modifying the noise word file to exclude words like "the", "a", and "an", so as to make searches more valuable

■ Modifying the thesaurus, such that searching for a particular word yields hits on words with similar meanings

- Configuring the server to crawl

- Installing Web Parts, and installing/registering iFilters when using proprietary file extensions

Production Operations Tasks

A number of administrative tasks fall under the category of "Production Operations," and therefore are not specific to SharePoint Portal Server as a product. That is, all enterprise applications require that a number of systems-related tasks be addressed, including

Systems Management

All servers and resources within the SharePoint Portal Server landscape must be "added" to the toolset or utility responsible for managing the servers. Such utilities might include HP Openview, Microsoft SMS, Compaq Insight Manager, CA Unicenter, and so on.

Systems Maintenance

All servers must be monitored from a performance perspective, leveraging the systems management tools as well as utilities like Performance Monitor, or PerfMon. PerfMon may also be used for basic capacity planning and frontline problem troubleshooting.

Backup/Restore

All servers must be backed up regularly, and these backups need to be tested to ensure that a restore is actually possible. Note that the amount of traffic on your network resulting from the backup and restore process may be reduced substantially by backing up to and restoring from compressed drives.

Managing by Exception

The Operations team should be taught how to manage events that occur across the system landscape. For example, issues with Production should be addressed in one manner, while issues with a Technical Sandbox should be addressed in a different manner. As the portal solution matures, fewer and fewer issues should require the attention of Operations—rather, as issues and conditions are identified and sorted out over time, automatic methods of dealing with them should be implemented. In the end, only severe issues should have the attention of the Operations staff.

Escalating Issues

Once issues have been raised to the attention of the Operations staff, appropriate escalation procedures must be leveraged in all cases. Even cases where the issue is "known" merit escalation—it is not appropriate to see a "severe" error message, for example, and do nothing. Additionally, escalation processes normally reflect time-of-day or other similar time-critical properties, where escalation actions might differ for a particular issue if it occurs at 3 a.m. Saturday morning or 2 p.m. Thursday afternoon during month-end closing week.

20

Continuous Improvement/Feedback

The Operations team should continuously feed a knowledge base of issues and problems and their resolutions. In this way, less time is ultimately spent troubleshooting and more time is spent proactively managing the SPS landscape.

DISASTER RECOVERY

In this section, we address disaster recovery of the Microsoft SharePoint Portal Server Production system. It should be noted, however, that disaster recovery, or DR, may be important to system environments other than just Production. A multi-portal enterprise-wide Development system, for example, may be nearly as important to safeguard, especially just before go-live. An exercise in *ROI (return on investment)*—the cost of safeguarding the system versus the cost of recovering your system without benefit of a DR system—must be performed. Only then does the benefit of maintaining a DR system—whether for a Production system, Development system, or other component of the system landscape—become apparent.

Disaster recovery is much more than simply having backup and restore capabilities. Rather, DR seeks to provide production-level coverage in the absence of the production system landscape. This could mean many things, depending upon the configuration of the system. Generally, though, DR assumes that the entire system is unavailable, or that a critical single component, such as a dedicated search server, is down.

Central to good DR is duplicating the server(s) running SharePoint Portal Server. Duplication is a special term for Microsoft SharePoint Portal Server—while a typical back-up/restore process allows recovery of a server, Microsoft's server duplication process leverages SharePoint Portal Server's unique script-based backup and restore procedures. The restore script, for instance, allows for a copy of a master dashboard site to be created on multiple computers, even to the point of creating the master dashboard over multiple computers distributed across a network.

To provide this level of disaster tolerance, the SharePoint Portal Server backup and restore process is used to create multiple copies of the master server. This is performed by remotely restoring backup images of a server to other servers in the same domain. A server can also be duplicated by leveraging the backup/restore process in the following manner:

- Back up each SharePoint Portal Server to a remote or local hard drive.
- Restore from the backup image to this drive.

NOTE

> These scripts can easily be automated, such that jobs may be created and scheduled to create a backup image of the master server for duplication. You may also set up a scheduled duplication process to perform the restore on the remote drive.

For ABC Company, a Disaster Recovery Plan will only initially address the productive system, including the portal and dedicated search server resources. As mentioned previously, the ABC technical support organization selected a three-system landscape partly for reasons of disaster recovery. The Development Portal environment was established at a location miles away from the Production and Technical Sandbox systems, and a duplication backup/restore process was scripted to allow for recovery of the Production system on the Development system. Eventually, as the portal grows to encompass additional business groups and functionality, ABC will again need to address the scope and breadth of DR protection required. For the first six months after go-live, however, this approach will more than adequately serve their needs for disaster tolerance.

PLANNING FOR SUPPORT AFTER GO-LIVE

Eventually, ABC Company will go live on (hence the term "go-live") or productively use the SharePoint Portal Server solution and enjoy all of the benefits inherent to managing and sharing information in a business-efficient, cost-efficient manner. Given the careful and thorough planning surrounding the deployment, it is expected that the actual go-live day will amount to a "non-event"! However, without proper attention to post–go-live continuing operations/maintenance, the system will eventually fall prey to downtime. Thus, ABC plans to leverage its Data Center Operations team to continually provide value in terms of performing daily routine systems management, maintenance, and exception reporting tasks.

In addition, it is anticipated that the Operations Team Leader will meet regularly with the ABC organization leaders responsible for Server/SAN hardware, W2K administration, network administration, change management, and SharePoint development, as well as with SharePoint business group leaders representing financial matters in North America, Europe, and Asia. At every meeting, exception events from the previous week will be reviewed and analyzed, and new business requirements will be put on the table. New and emerging technical and business standards will be outlined, new initiatives (like server consolidation, network upgrades, and the inevitable inclusion of the new global business groups) will be discussed, and both the processes in place to promote changes to Production, as well as the status of various changes within the system landscape, will be reviewed. In short, everything pertaining to the system landscape from an operations and change management perspective will be continually examined and addressed. Doing so will allow for continuous improvement within ABC's SharePoint Portal Server deployment.

20

SUMMARY

In summary, the deployment planning process leveraged by ABC Company, though quite detailed in many respects, served the company well—sound planning and implementation ensured that all aspects of the deployment, from identifying business goals and requirements, to building the support organization, to designing an architecture capable of supporting the business, were addressed. Moreover, by initially including security, workspace development, and dashboard site preparation into the planning process, under the umbrella of sound change and systems management, the deployment process illustrated a complete end-to-end Microsoft SharePoint Portal deployment. And the result was both impressive and uneventful—the deployment of their SPS portal solution quietly and effectively ushered in a new age of information sharing and management at ABC Company.

CHAPTER **21**

EXAMPLE SCENARIO 2—SINGLE BUSINESS UNIT SOLUTION

In this chapter

DEPLOYING SHAREPOINT FOR A SINGLE BUSINESS UNIT—OVERVIEW

Regardless of whether SharePoint Portal Server is deployed for the benefit of a specific business unit or across an entire organization, it serves to assist an organization in getting the most out of its existing content, while effectively capturing information in new ways that add value and help an organization make better use of its data. In the previous chapter, we saw that planning a SharePoint Portal Server deployment involves a host of activities. Here, we will drill down into those activities and see what it takes to deploy SharePoint Portal Server for the benefit of a single business unit, or SBU.

A portal solution designed for the benefit of an SBU differs from an enterprise-wide solution in a multitude of ways—the fewer and usually very specific business requirements that the portal will fulfill, the breadth and scope of data residing under the umbrella of the portal, the physical location of typical users hoping to leverage this data, and so on. In the next few pages, we will explore deploying SharePoint Portal Server in support of different SBUs at a single company.

Whether an SBU or enterprise implementation, supporting 10 users in a single business unit or an entire company across the globe, deploying Microsoft SharePoint Server requires addressing the previously identified deployment activities:

- Business goals and requirements
- Building the technical support organization
- Hardware vendor selection
- Solutions architecture
- Security plan development
- Developing the workspace
- Preparing the dashboard site
- Addressing change management
- Preparing for go-live
- Planning for post–go-live support

It is merely the scope and application of these activities that differ. For example, developing a single workspace and dashboard facilitating collaboration for a department differs dramatically from deploying fifteen workspaces on Portal Servers installed across multiple sites. Much of the same "project plan" may be applied regardless, of course, but departmental or single business unit SharePoint Portal Server applications will tend to be much smaller in scope and size.

→ To jump right into deploying SPS across a complex enterprise environment, please **see** "Deploying SharePoint Portal Server Enterprise-Wide," **p. 578**.

21

In this chapter, we cover laying a foundation for a secure and well-performing SBU SharePoint implementation in terms of the following sample deployments:

- Leveraging team services in support of a small project
- Sharing content across a product engineering group
- Providing search services for a product support group
- Creating a document management system for a training department
- Providing collaboration capabilities in support of a marketing organization

To make the application of these SharePoint services and capabilities meaningful, we will follow SmallTime, LLP (or simply "SmallTime," a fictional entity) through planning and deploying SharePoint Portal Server to meet specific business needs satisfied by the services and capabilities outlined previously.

LEVERAGING TEAM SERVICES AT SMALLTIME

To reiterate from earlier chapters, SharePoint Team Services is a solution that allows teams to work together effectively, through sharing and collaborating in a limited capacity via a Web site. At SmallTime, a special-projects team has been established to support the company's participation at an industry conference. It is envisioned that the team would need to work together on group deliverables, share marketing and staffing-related documents, and communicate status with one another.

BUSINESS PROBLEM TO BE SOLVED

In the past, it was nearly impossible to track all of the discrete activities and "players" from different product support, engineering, technical support, marketing, and other groups involved with successfully participating at a conference. Booth setup and tear-down was often delayed, marketing and messaging materials were not cohesive, special events were planned last minute, and more. Experience gained staffing other shows and conferences had proven a nightmare when schedules and other things changed last minute. In the end, everyone agreed that they needed an approach to keep them all on the same page—SharePoint Team Services appeared the fastest and easiest way to allow this, as illustrated in Figure 21.1.

SmallTime's project team's primary goal is simply to put on a good show, within budget. The team believes that the ability to share data, organize information, manage documents, and enable collaboration—all via a familiar, easily accessible set of tools—will make them successful. The fact that SharePoint Team Services requires no special license is a nice added plus as well!

SUPPORT ORGANIZATION

The project team leader requested that IT, the Information Technology group, create a project Web site using SharePoint Team Services. In turn, IT made the project team leader the "site owner" and requested that each project member responsible for further developing the

21

site upgrade to either FrontPage 2002 or the release of Office XP that includes FrontPage. The team liked the idea of moving to XP best, which natively supports SharePoint Team Services. By doing so, each project team end user immediately had the ability to create and contribute to the new team Web site.

It should be noted that any one of the team members could have created the team Web site, which has also been characterized as a "three-click installation." Also, while the team elected to perform an Office XP upgrade, presumably on their local desktops/laptops, only Web browser access is actually required to use the site (Internet Explorer version 4.01 or later).

SOLUTIONS ARCHITECTURE

SharePoint Team Services provides a solution for workgroup information sharing that requires very little IT architecture support (refer to Figure 21.1). For the team's purposes, the browser-based, Microsoft FrontPage 2002 "development" environment is more than enough—there's no need for understanding or implementing Web Parts. Any team members with the appropriate permissions can create documents directly on their new Web site, using only Internet Explorer if desired.

Figure 21.1
SmallTime users find SharePoint Team Services a snap to use, even for managing complex projects where a host of activities, tasks, and people must be coordinated.

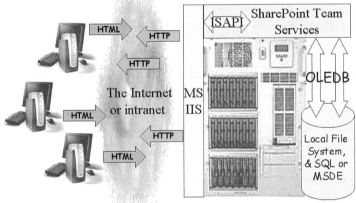

Team Services General Architecture

SECURITY CONSIDERATIONS

Unlike its more robust sister product, SharePoint Team Services actually offers more choices in terms of its role-based security options. The site owner can choose from a number of customizable roles, and different levels of permissions may be assigned to team members. In this case, though, given the temporary nature of the project and limited number of "core" team members, the project team leader assigned the core team the administrator role, and assigned everyone else author privileges. Sure, more granular roles could be assigned. But that wouldn't be in keeping with SmallTime's philosophy to keep things simple.

WEB SITE DEVELOPMENT CONSIDERATIONS

While dashboard and workspace considerations do not exist per se, development of the Web site is still a real requirement. SharePoint Team Services makes this quite straightforward, using either Microsoft FrontPage 2002 or the SharePoint Team Services *Software Development Kit*, or SDK.

The core team looked over the different Team Services features and functions they could employ, and in support of their original business-driven goals, decided to take advantage of the following to help them all stay on the same page:

- Web Discussions, to conduct "conversations" on documents or Web pages regarding their marketing and messaging materials to be displayed and distributed at the conference

- Preformatted team lists, to enable sharing team information like booth staffing lists, schedules for setup and tear-down of the booth, and more

- Team surveys, to facilitate democratic decision-making, the sharing of ideas like which special events to promote, and teamwide status updates where feedback would be beneficial or required

- Local search capabilities (within the team's Web site only), to allow searching for marketing phrases and special key words across the site

GO-LIVE CONSIDERATIONS

Like any really good Go-Live, getting the SharePoint Team Services Web site up and productive should be a "non-event" more than anything. In SmallTime's case, the core team was using the site in a productive manner within a few days, and other team members realized the benefits of information sharing, surveys, intrateam communication, and more shortly thereafter.

As IT still "owned" the actual server upon which the Team Services site was created, nightly backups and other operations and systems management/administration tasks were already taken care of behind the scenes. The project team took special care to maintain good version control, and were otherwise quite well protected from data loss.

Meanwhile, the team managed their project activities effectively, leveraging the features they needed in a portal product at virtually no extra cost to the organization. And more importantly, the conference came and went without a hitch!

SharePoint Team Services got the job done well for this project team. In the next few sections, we will take a look at other single business unit SharePoint implementations, leveraging SharePoint Portal Server and its inherently more robust feature set.

21

SHARING CONTENT AND FACILITATING SEARCHING AT SMALLTIME

In this case, the Product Engineering (PE) group at SmallTime is creating a SharePoint Portal to share information with a broad audience of engineers, as well as to provide these users with a certain amount of data search capabilities. A legacy portal is in place today, but has proven difficult to use and even more difficult to update and maintain.

BUSINESS PROBLEM TO BE SOLVED

The current portal has a number of significant problems. First, there exists no structure to the data residing in the portal. Second, the engineers are limited in terms of search capabilities—only text searches are supported, and the portal only allows searching in the body of the documents that it hosts. In addition, very few types and formats of documents are supported at all.

It should be noted that the Product Engineering group produces and posts a large amount of content to the portal in place today. Still, the engineers have a hard time finding what they need. And when they get lucky and happen upon the right document or set of search results, the process required to get to that point has in most cases been extremely time-consuming.

BUSINESS GOALS AND REQUIREMENTS

Product Engineering requires a dashboard site that not only offers a number of effective methods that may be employed to find the data for which they are searching, they also need improved search capabilities. And, of course, they need to share this data with their colleagues.

The PE group finally approaches the IT organization about using SharePoint Portal Server to improve their Product Engineering portal, with two goals in mind:

- All Product Engineering departments should have access to up-to-date product-related resources
- Engineers should be able to perform fast searches across all content maintained by the group

Overall, they simply want a more effective tool to help them find what they need when they need it.

21

SOLUTIONS ARCHITECTURE

While SharePoint Portal Server offers easy access to multiple information sources in an organization so that users can find the information they need efficiently, it is the search features that will be valued most. For example

- A huge number of indexed and searchable content sources may be added to the portal.

- By using metadata to categorize content throughout Product Engineering, the Category Assistant allows for users to browse through content organized by topic.

- To improve server performance and save disk space, indexes compiled from searchable content are created, and a schedule is selected to automatically update the index at regular intervals.

SUPPORT CONSIDERATIONS

Creating a good dashboard "search" site involves several steps. Once the server architecture requirements are nailed down via the help of SmallTime's hardware partner, SharePoint Portal Server can then be installed, the workspace set up, and the dashboard finally customized to meet the sharing and search needs of the Product Engineering group.

→ To learn more about SPS minimum installation requirements, **see** "Installation of SharePoint Portal Server," **p. 154**.

SIZING THE SPS SOLUTION

Product Engineering's portal lead worked directly with SmallTime's hardware partner to share important sizing-related information like

- What is the peak number of search users expected?
- How many of these users will be concurrent?
- How is the content geographically distributed?
- How much content does the group search on an average day, in terms of number of documents and gigabytes of data?
- How often does this content change?

Given the comprehensive nature of their hardware partner's SPS Sizing Questionnaire (see Figure 21.2), covering things like high availability requirements, disaster recovery considerations, and more, Product Engineering was well positioned to start this new portal project off on the right foot. The PE folks were also fortunate in that they could easily pull historical data from the current limited portal implementation, thus answering many of the business–oriented questions.

21

Figure 21.2
By partnering with their hardware vendor, the Product Engineering group quickly identified both business and technology-oriented matters that would impact the success of their new SPS deployment.

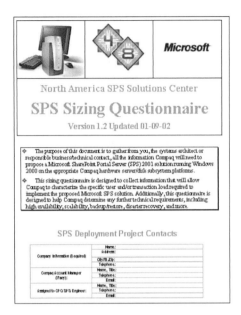

PERFORMING THE SHAREPOINT PORTAL SERVER INSTALLATION

Next, the IT group procured hardware and software resources consistent with the requirements outlined by their hardware partner. Then they installed everything, including the SharePoint Portal Server product, and next created a workspace devoted to search services. The workspace contained an organized collection of views, content, management folders, shortcuts, and so on.

Of course, creating the workspace then automatically generated the associated dashboard site. They were now ready to assign roles to users and begin customizing the dashboard.

SECURITY CONSIDERATIONS

To ensure that the dashboard site is secure, roles are used to control access to content. Everyone is assigned the reader role in the Product Engineering group. In addition, team leaders and others responsible for creating content are assigned the author role. The author role is also assigned to a number of folks who will be responsible for updating announcements on the dashboard's home page. Finally, the IT liaison with the Product Engineering group and another individual tasked with developing and updating the site are assigned Coordinator privileges for the workspace.

21

TIP

It is a good idea to assign more than one Coordinator to a workspace. Although this lessens security a bit, it nearly eliminates the problem of needing to get into the site when the only Coordinator is on vacation or home sick.

DASHBOARD CONSIDERATIONS

The bulk of "development" time is spent customizing the dashboard to allow for the robust search capabilities requested by Product Engineering. This development activity includes things like customizing and organizing the home page and dashboard site, identifying and organizing content, categorizing this content, and more.

CUSTOMIZING THE DASHBOARD SITE

After consulting with their IT liaison, the PE team leader will begin development by approaching the design of the dashboard first. Content will then be added to the home page, as well as moved from the existing portal. This will also facilitate making content available from various Product Engineering databases, Web servers, file servers, and other data repositories.

The PE team leader likes the idea of placing the company logo and "Product Engineering" title on the home page, as well as keeping the News and Subscription Summary Web Parts included by default. He performs additional customization as well. For example, in response to Product Engineering's repeated requests that rapid access to content like the latest "Most Frequently Asked Questions," "Top 20 Engineering Issues," and "New Product Roadmaps" be included, the PE team leader creates links to these resources right off of the home page. He also copies some of the look and feel of their legacy portal site to give the new site a familiar feel. Next, content displayed on the old portal home page is also moved to a Web Part on the dashboard site.

Finally, the PE team leader organizes the site with categories to guide the engineers in their searches. Searching content on the dashboard site is enabled specifically via

- Creating a category hierarchy
- Categorizing existing documents
- Designating documents as Best Bets

ADDING AND ORGANIZING CONTENT SOURCES

A list of content locations is also compiled from across the company to aid searching through the dashboard site. This is accomplished by using the Add Content Source Wizard, where site rules are specified to designate how much content and what types of content should be indexed at that site.

With that, the dashboard site now offers the ability to search for information more efficiently than its predecessor. The PE group looks at how features like categories and Best Bets will help the team of engineers access information company-wide. It is determined that they need to design a search strategy that leverages both categories and Best Bets by first creating a category structure. Then, they can begin organizing all of their content in a much more structured and logical approach than would otherwise be available.

21

CRAFTING THE CATEGORY STRUCTURE

Before crafting the category structure that will provide the basic framework for searching, the engineers are polled with questions like

- How do you categorize data today?
- What additional categories would be useful?
- What content would you like to see on the actual dashboard itself?
- What are the common words and terms used to identify the data, or for searching?

The common words and terms, in particular, will drive setting up Best Bets, while the categories will allow drilling down into the data in an organized manner.

Adding categories turned out to be a much simpler task than expected—after opening Explorer and clicking the Categories folder in the workspace, it was then just a matter of creating a category by clicking File, New, Category and typing in the name of the new category and pressing Enter. And repeat! Over and over…!

CATEGORIZING PRODUCT ENGINEERING'S CONTENT

Once the category structure is created, Product Engineering's content is ready to be distributed across these categories. One handy way of completing this otherwise tedious task is through the use of the Category Assistant.

Before this can occur, the Category Assistant must first be "trained," which really amounts to helping the tool recognize documents belonging to particular categories by checking in documents to the workspace. During check-in, you must specify at least one category. After check-in, you then publish the documents before they can be included in an index. Conveniently, though not a requirement yet for Product Engineering, you may also include external documents in the set of training documents by creating Web links to those documents in the workspace.

→ For more details on using the Category Assistant, **see** "Managing Categories and the Category Assistant," **p.248**.

After this is all accomplished, SharePoint Portal Server is set up to crawl documents for inclusion in an index. During this process, documents are associated with categories based on information from the training documents. Once the training is complete, Category Assistant will automatically assign categories to any uncategorized documents the next time the index is updated. It is important to understand how this process works, the kinds of documents that make good training documents, and so on. The project team found the following points quite useful for selecting training documents:

- Ensure that the folks in Product Engineering supplying the training documents understand how the Category Assistant actually works. Train them.
- Create a minimum number of perhaps ten categories for the Category Assistant to learn.

21

- Use training documents that contain a minimum of 2,000 words each. This rules out a number of file types like Excel and PowerPoint files, as they tend to have very few words overall. Word documents and Adobe PDFs tend to work out great, though.

- Test the Category Assistant process in a Technical Sandbox or similar SPS landscape system before attempting to do so in the Production system.

The team initially set the Category Assistant to "High Precision" while training it. Reducing the precision, however, increases the number of documents suggested by the Category Assistant. The downside is that the accuracy of the Category Assistant in placing files diminished a bit. Of course, this can be rectified by overriding the suggested categories, by clearing the Show Suggested Categories check box on the Search and Categories tab of the document properties.

SELECTING BEST BETS

SharePoint Portal Server supports two types of Best Bets—Category Best Bet and Keyword Best Bet. Based on feedback by the Product Engineering group, both types are useful and therefore created.

For Category Best Bets in particular, updating the Properties page for each recommended file to identify it a Best Bet for the appropriate category meets a key requirement—to allow search access for these directly from the home page.

GO-LIVE! USING THE PORTAL

Now that a portal actually capable of powerful searching has finally been installed and configured, the next step is testing it across a broader range of users. A subset of Product Engineering's engineers—termed "sample users"—provide feedback, allowing for tweaks here and there until the portal formatting and layout meet the approval of the majority. Capabilities are tested, and the original goals are re-examined to ensure that they have been indeed met. At this point, the SharePoint Portal solution is ready to use.

TRYING OUT THE NEW SPS SOLUTION

Bradley, a relatively new engineer at SmallTime, needs to look up specifics on one of the new product lines his customer is asking about. He launches Internet Explorer as usual, and is directed to the Product Engineering home page, again as usual. This time, though, he notices wonderful changes. After a few moments getting accustomed to the improved layout, he spots the New Product Roadmap Web Part, and within another few seconds locates the exact kind of data he needs. Bradley then notices a Sort By option at the top of the search results list. He clicks Date, and the most recently modified Product Roadmap PowerPoint moves to the top of the list. So far so good.

After passing on to his customer the information requested, Bradley returns to the site, interested in checking out the search capabilities he has heard so much about in the last few weeks. In the search box located at the top of every page, he types the code word for a product that came out last fall. The search results come up quickly, and he further notices that

21

results are sorted by Best Match. Impressive! He then drops back to the home page and pulls up the Most Frequently Asked Questions Web Part—the questions customers ask most frequently reside in what has become a very large database. Nearly half of his day is spent querying this data, in fact, and he is pleased to note that as he drills down into categories (ones that actually make sense, no less), the data he needs access to most often seems right at his fingertips.

Bradley returns to the Search box used to locate the New Product Roadmap data. He needs access to updates here on a regular basis, and is pleased to be able to "subscribe" to this search. Three days later, he receives an email notification that an updated Roadmap with new timelines and highly valuable product-positioning data is now available.

PROVIDING ROBUST SEARCH SERVICES FOR SMALLTIME

SharePoint Portal Server is really starting to catch on at SmallTime! This latest project, to provide superior search capabilities for the Product Support organization, hopes to capitalize on the flexibility of the Portal's dashboard site to create a central point of access. By doing so, Product Support will not just tweak their existing search services. Instead, they will actually consolidate search services throughout the Product Support department, and provide a robust department-wide utility for working smarter (see Figure 21.3).

Figure 21.3
Note the multiple GUI interfaces and various standalone "search service" systems employed prior to the SharePoint Portal Server implementation. Afterward, access to SmallTime's various product support tools requires only Internet Explorer.

Before SPS ...cutover... **After SPS**

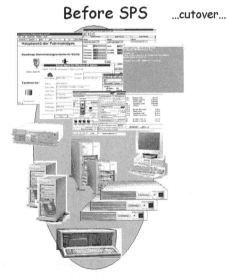

BUSINESS PROBLEM TO BE SOLVED

Product Support is responsible for providing pre-sales telephone support to new prospects and existing customers, as well as limited telephone post-sales support. As such, they require access to the latest SmallTime product specifications, engineering manuals, quick reference guides, technical support database, and more. They currently maintain a slew of client GUI interfaces and have trouble with version control of these sometimes proprietary client/server-based toolsets. As a result, the Product Support engineers spend too much time getting to the data they need, and therefore less time supporting their customers. They believe that a Web browser–based powerful search tool may be the solution to many of their problems.

SmallTime Product Support wants to limit the number of search tools and access methods they currently support. Searching needs to be comprehensive, covering both internal and external data source requirements (intra-SmallTime as well as across the Internet).

The Product Support group's search services are expected to grow in use—they exploit their albeit currently restrictive search capabilities in a big way today. It is also noted that very few people actually create or manage content.

SUPPORT ORGANIZATION

In what looks to be a SharePoint Portal Server Search Services deployment, IT is both concerned about proper sizing, and excited that they may be able to retire two of their legacy in-house search utilities/applications. With their hardware partner's assistance, and a quick sanity-check phone call to Microsoft, it was verified that the volume of traffic and number of hits, I/Os, and content sources would drive a four-server SPS design, consisting of two dedicated search servers and two dedicated crawl servers.

SOLUTIONS ARCHITECTURE

As noted earlier, this SharePoint Portal Server deployment requires dedicated server resources to crawl and categorize data, and additional server resources dedicated to searching. The crawl servers will be used to create and update indexes. These servers will be dedicated to crawling content sources. They will not be used for document management or searching.

The servers dedicated to searching will contain one workspace each for every two indexes to be propagated. Each index is propagated to the workspace on the particular server dedicated to searching. Some SharePoint Portal Server document management features may be leveraged for a small number of documents, but overall this functionality will not be a focus of the project.

From a solutions architecture perspective, it was important to provide maximum headroom to the search and crawl servers—neither one of these types of servers were installed on an existing Exchange 2000 or other server, for example. This design tenet also removed the complexity inherent to such an architecture.

PLANNING TASKS

To prepare for this SBU search services deployment, the following high-level planning-related tasks must be addressed:

- Determine skill-sets and then identify team leaders for the various SPS functions that are detailed below.

21

- Procure and prepare the servers, and install the prerequisite software required by SharePoint Portal Server.

- Connect the servers to the corporate IT network backbone, and the public net.

- Determine the number, type, and location of content sources, how often they will be crawled, and how the indexes will be updated.

- Plan for the layout and other required customization of the workspaces.

- Determine the level of operations and enterprise management support required after deployment.

As the Product Support organization grows larger, the search services may be beefed up by adding additional dedicated search servers to meet new search and indexing requirements. The size of your organization, the number of workspaces/indexes, and the number of end-users will drive the decision to include additional server search resources.

INSTALLING THE SEARCH SERVERS

SmallTime will address the following tasks during installation:

- Install SharePoint Portal Server on the servers procured and dedicated to searching.

- Create one workspace, via the New Workspace Wizard at the end of the installation.

- Skip creating index workspaces on these dedicated search servers.

- Specify the SMTP server for each search server by using SharePoint Portal Server Administration. Configure the SMTP server to receive approval email, and to receive subscription notification email.

- For the workspace on each server, use SharePoint Portal Server Administration to configure the workspace contact as a Coordinator on the workspace node. This enables the workspace contact the ability to customize the dashboard site.

- To dedicate each server as a search server, employ SharePoint Portal Server Administration to adjust the resource usage controls.

INSTALLING THE CRAWLING SERVERS

For each of the crawl servers, the following tasks will be addressed during installation:

- Install SharePoint Portal Server on each server procured and dedicated to crawling.

- Create four index workspaces per server.

- Maintain the previous list of index workspace names, noting the server on which they are stored, and the destination server and workspace where they are propagated.

- For each index workspace, identify and configure the Coordinator

- Similar to the search servers, use SharePoint Portal Server Administration to adjust the resource usage controls to dedicate the server resources for crawling.

■ Note that it was determined that both Microsoft Exchange Server 5.5 and Lotus Notes content sources would need to be crawled—each crawl server was configured for this capability as well. Of course, the team discussed dedicating one server to Exchange 5.5 and one to Lotus Notes. In the end, though, it was decided that it made more sense to cover all bases redundantly, such that if one server was unavailable, the other would be capable of accessing all content sources.

→ For detailed Exchange Server 5.5 and Lotus Notes crawling procedures, as well as procedures geared toward crawling other content sources, **see** "How Microsoft SPS Crawls," **p. 454**.

SECURITY CONSIDERATIONS

One key holdup in the project was determining who would be the workspace contact—each workspace needs such a contact, someone who acts as the point of contact for workspace-related issues. It had been incorrectly assumed that the server administrator would act as the workspace contact. Eventually, a security team leader was identified, who also acted as the security liaison to IT and assisted in assigning and modifying roles and rights.

WORKSPACE AND DASHBOARD CONSIDERATIONS

It is important to note that destination workspaces can only accept up to four propagated indexes. If SmallTime ever wishes to create more than four index workspaces on a server dedicated to crawling, they will need to create additional workspaces on the destination server to propagate the additional indexes. Further, they may simply use multiple index workspaces to better focus content sources. For example, one index workspace might be dedicated to crawling the internal organization and a second index workspace could be dedicated to crawling content out on the Internet.

SmallTime had to decide how many workspaces to store on the servers dedicated to crawling, noting the four index limit.

CLIENT ACCESS CONSIDERATIONS

Now that the servers dedicated to crawling and searching are installed and ready to go, and workspaces are created and customized, the client components of SharePoint Portal Server may need to be installed. Note that any user can use the dashboard site for document management features and for searching without having to install the client components on his computer. This is accomplished via Internet Explorer version 4.01 or later. However, to perform Coordinator functions—such as configuring security, adding content sources, or even creating document profiles—the client components will be required on each end user's computer within Product Support. In our project here, this requirement will primarily impact Product Support's IT liaison and the various SPS team leaders. Some of these individuals are already running Microsoft Office XP, and are therefore covered. Others will need to actually load the client components that ship with SPS.

21

ACCESSING THE WORKSPACE

Once these client components are installed on the appropriate users' computers, as required, each user must then add a Web folder that points to the workspace. The format of the workspace address is `http://server_name/workspace_name`. SmallTime decides that scripting this final piece of the puzzle might make sense, so as to automate the process and therefore minimize support calls from new users wishing to leverage these search services. But they also document the process, and disseminate this throughout the Product Support team, noting that the procedure for adding a Web folder varies depending upon the operating system installed on the client machine. For example, in Windows 2000 Professional, click on My Network Places and then use the Add Network Place Wizard to add a Web folder that points to `http://server_name/workspace_name`. In Windows 98, click on Web Folders in My Computer, and then use the Add Web Folder to add a Web folder.

OPERATIONS AND OTHER GO-LIVE CONSIDERATIONS

Product Support's IT liaison also needs to work with IT and the Product Support business/team leaders to determine how often each of the search and crawling servers must be backed up, decide whether or not this backup process should occur automatically, and determine whether to store the backup image on another computer. In addition, it must be determined whether a duplicate of one or more of the servers dedicated to searching or crawling should be created at a remote office for disaster tolerance—there is no need to duplicate one locally, they decide, as each crawling and searching server already is redundant.

→ For approaches and ideas on backing up and restoring SPS, **see** "Designing a Backup and Restore Strategy," **p. 326**.

CREATING A SIMPLE DOCUMENT MANAGEMENT SYSTEM FOR SMALLTIME

The Training department at SmallTime has grown over the last year, from offering a few limited classes and other periods of instruction to now providing nearly daily training across more than 50 of SmallTime's future, current, and older product lines. Managing the curriculum in terms of updates and revisions has simply gotten out of hand. Their enormous folder structure approach to managing documents has quite plainly become an inefficient document management solution. The current conglomeration and patch quilt of content does not lend itself to organizing documents, publishing new classroom materials, or collaborating on new training projects.

BUSINESS GOALS AND REQUIREMENTS

The department head of Training has seen and heard how other organizations at SmallTime have leveraged SharePoint Team Services or Portal Server to better share and manage documents. He believes that SharePoint will solve his own document management system, or DMS, challenges. After talking it over with his IT liaison, they immediately create a small task force aimed at implementing the cost effective SharePoint solution. They believe that maintaining a central "library" of training materials and better organizing this library's document folder structure will facilitate

- Automated publication processes
- Standardized methods of identifying and classifying information
- Controlled access to documents
- Distribution of content management throughout the department

SUPPORT ORGANIZATION AND SOLUTIONS ARCHITECTURE

The IT liaison works up quick sizing guidelines via Microsoft's SharePoint Planning and Installation Guide, and procures from the central IT group a single SmallTime-standard four-CPU server, with 2GB of RAM, enough drives for nearly 400GB of data, and all required software resources. He also procures three additional servers earmarked for crawling and searching (see Figure 21.4). Within a day, he has the hardware installed and configured, the OS and service packs loaded, all prerequisites installed, and SharePoint Portal Server itself installed.

Figure 21.4
SmallTime's Training department benefits from a highly scalable Document Management server and an architecture that moves processor- and disk-intensive searching and crawling to incremental dedicated SPS servers.

SmallTime's Training department will benefit from the headroom that a distributed architecture provides to its Document Management System.

Distributed and dedicated crawl and search servers

Highly scalable DMS Server and Disk Subsystem

No doubt, the solution from a capacity-planning perspective is "super-sized," but everyone is comfortable that no upgrades or other infrastructure-related changes will need to occur for a year or more. Additionally, this will nicely address the seasonal peaks in activity throughout the year, especially at quarter-end, that strain SmallTime's computing environment today.

DMS WORKSPACE CONSIDERATIONS

After performing the install, the IT liaison then created the initial workspace, called it "Training", and selected the Training team lead as the workspace contact.

21

When the document management system's workspace was created, a number of automatic events occurred, including

- SharePoint Portal Server created a dashboard site associated with the new Training workspace.

- SharePoint Portal Server automatically assigned the IT liaison the Coordinator role on the workspace node.

- The team leader's email address became the address to which SharePoint Portal Server would send replies from subscription notifications.

REVIEWING THE CURRENT FOLDER STRUCTURE

After the workspace was created, the IT liaison began planning a redesign of his Training department's current folder structure to take maximum advantage of these new document management capabilities. He wanted to fully leverage SharePoint Portal Server's document access control, versioning capabilities, and support for approval routing to assist the Training group in publishing new materials. He also discovered that document profiles would allow the team to apply searchable metadata to documents, thereby making them easier to access.

The IT liaison leveraged the assistance of his colleague in Product Support to discuss ways of moving content from the current folders and other sources into the new SharePoint Portal Server workspace. Together, they determined that the quickest way to move their existing content into the workspace would be to drag and drop the existing folder hierarchy right into the workspace. However, that would not solve the problems with the existing folder structure—it would still remain a cumbersome and difficult folder hierarchy if used in this way.

BUILDING THE FOLDER STRUCTURE TEAM

Starting from the beginning and reorganizing the folders was the best way to go. The IT liaison knew he could not do this on his own, though. Sure, it would be easy to come up with a folder structure that made sense to *him*, but not being an actual trainer himself put him at a severe disadvantage in terms of knowing what made sense for the *trainers* and other folks tasked with actually using the DMS. The current folder structure had obviously evolved over time into the cumbersome mess that existed today. Different teams had sought to organize and classify documents as they saw fit over the last few years, and many inconsistencies, redundancies, and strange hierarchies existed as a result. Some of the folder names no longer even reflected their content, and other folders were long abandoned and simply remained empty today.

The SharePoint Portal Server deployment seemed a good opportunity to re-evaluate the Training group's document management practices and overall method of organizing content. The IT liaison's colleague in Product Support pointed out that he could use the capabilities of SharePoint Portal Server to make this task easier, too. The IT liaison went back to his Training department head, and asked that a special project team consisting of training

21

content experts and senior instructors be created. The "FixIt" team, as they came to be known, wound up consisting of just enough folks to provide sound DMS ideas, approaches, and background data, but not so many as to get in the way of quick decision making—five. After convening for the first time the next day, they determined that they would need to immerse themselves in the data for a few days, to get a feel for their real document management needs and challenges.

METADATA AND THE EXISTING FOLDER STRUCTURE

Once the FixIt team had a sense of document types, categories, and profiles, they needed to nail down profiles such that a set of properties could be created to describe a document within the profile. The group converted many of the valid and useful folder names that currently existed into properties for use on document profiles. They also deleted empty and obsolete folders. They did not, however, address the need to remove or archive old documents—that would be outside the scope of their team mission, and would only serve to slow them down and put the real project at hand on hold. Perhaps later, another team would be assembled to address archiving.

For each new document profile, the team worked to create a list of properties that identified the associated documents. Specifically, they used the Add Document Profile Wizard to create the newly defined document profiles. This was time-consuming at first, but eventually they settled on a smaller number of document profiles than originally envisioned. As all document profiles were ultimately stored in the Management folder in the workspace, each of the designated folder Coordinators could then easily select from among the existing document profiles to associate them with a folder.

REDUCING THE DOCUMENT PROFILE LIST

As the FixIt team waded through all of their documents to get a feel for their own document management requirements, they felt a need to be very thorough when identifying the different types of documents. However, the identification of 50 different "configuring product" document profiles for 50 different product lines quickly got out of hand. So the team revisited their list, and consolidated many of the document profiles simply to reduce the list size. As a bonus, they also found redundancies that could be eliminated, and observed trends that further allowed them to reduce the list.

TIP

In effect, they discovered the hard way that it is critical to find a balance between the number of document profiles to choose from, and the raw number of choices in document profiles. Too many profiles only serve to confuse authors, and they prove difficult for Coordinators to manage as well. On the flip side, though, too few document profiles equate to more properties on the profile.

21

To allow for rapid document check-ins, the team also decided to limit required properties to only five per document profile.

In summary, FixIt wound up reducing the number of folders, minimizing the number of document profiles, and adding custom properties to the remaining document profiles. They also discussed later adding incremental properties so as to capture information that was not previously associated with each document.

BUILDING THE FOLDER STRUCTURE

Finally, the time has come to create the new folder structure that has been developed based on team consensus. This is completed within a few hours, and the next step becomes apparent—they must move all of their documents into the new workspace, ensuring that each document is appropriately inserted into the new folder structure. But it is not a simple matter of dragging documents from one folder structure to the new. That is just not feasible, and the team becomes concerned that the time required to manually move each document will keep them busy for weeks. And of course there is the matter of completing the document profiles as well.

After again consulting with his Product Support colleague, the Training team's IT liaison takes it upon himself to customize the script that the Product Support folks used to accomplish the same task. It is a custom script, but straightforward in that its goal is to import documents into a SharePoint workspace from an existing folder hierarchy. He carefully analyzes the script, and reads over the SharePoint Portal Server Software Development Kit (SDK) as required for clarification. A new script is developed and tested. Within a few hours, he has successfully copied all of the files from the legacy folder structure into the new workspace, both mapping them into the proper new folders and updating the document profiles for each document.

→ To read in detail about folder hierarchies, **see** "Creating and Configuring Your Folder Hierarchy," **p. 262**.

The FixIt team reviews the work and verifies that the script indeed worked as planned. The script is saved for future use (in the event that additional documents that must be added to the workspace come to light in the future), and the FixIt team is dissolved. Mission accomplished.

SECURITY CONSIDERATIONS

Before the folder structure sub-project kicked off, the IT liaison manually assigned the team leader's user account to the Coordinator role on the workspace node, using SharePoint Portal Server Administration. The team leader was now able to assign roles to folders that inherit security from the workspace node in the workspace.

The team leader also needed his backup to have Coordinator permissions on the workspace node, too. So he assigned his user name to the Coordinator role as well, using SharePoint Portal Server Administration just as the IT liaison had shown him.

At this point, the backup had Coordinator permissions and could perform the same actions on the workspace that his team leader could perform. This offloaded quite a burden from the team leader, and allowed for security considerations to be addressed in either member's absence.

Note that the backup is automatically a Coordinator on every SharePoint folder that inherits its security from the workspace node. The only difference is that the team leader also happens to be the workspace contact, and as such receives subscription-related emails, while his backup does not.

To simplify the process of securing access to the folders, additional group team leaders responsible for authoring and publishing were also assigned the Coordinator role. This allowed them to further assign roles to more of the individual trainers within their own teams, such as senior instructors and so on. By delegating the task of managing security to the folks that understood the day-to-day security needs of the team, the overall burden of security management was both distributed and reduced throughout the Training department. And everyone benefited from the faster security turnaround when the need arose to modify access, properties, and roles.

GO-LIVE CONSIDERATIONS

At this point, the SharePoint Portal Server DMS solution is ready to begin accepting and managing documents. The IT liaison coordinates some basic "Introduction to SharePoint DMS" training for his colleagues, and ensures that all operations tasks are addressed by central IT.

He also reviews the approval process put in place by the team leaders and senior instructors, by taking a look at the Approval tab on the Properties page of each the folder. While he did not know all of the business processes involved in approval routing, he figured that as long as the appropriate team leader had at least modified these settings from the defaults, the process would be set up and capable of being modified later.

Thus, with all of the above tasks completed, the Training department is ready to leverage the following:

- The new folder structure is both simplified and reorganized
- All content from the various legacy folders have been moved into the workspace and applied document profiles.
- Document profiles have been created and minimized, allowing custom properties to be included to better identify documents without complicating publishing
- Approval routing was set up and verified to some extent
- Roles were distributed throughout the department to both secure content in each folder, and facilitate making rapid changes to security settings and applying new security changes as required by the team

Now that the underlying work in terms of preparing the folder structure, addressing security, putting the workspace in place, and so on has been addressed, the Training department is ready for the next step—preparing the dashboard site. The team will meet over the next several days to work out details regarding layout, features of the home page, adding and configuring specific Web Parts that will add value for them, and more. The team looks forward to this phase of the project, realizing that the tedious work is behind them now.

21

From start to finish, just over three weeks have elapsed between the time that the Training department head met with his IT liaison, and the trainers within the department were provided access to their full-featured SharePoint Portal Server document management solution. SmallTime is well on their way to taking advantage of documentation management big time!

COLLABORATING AT SMALLTIME

How an organization might implement SharePoint Portal Server to not only enhance document management, but allow real-time collaboration, is discussed here. SmallTime's Marketing organization could really benefit from a collaboration process or system—new folks have recently been added to the Marketing team, and are amazed that anything actually gets done in their group. There are marketing programs and support requirements for some 50 different product lines, and reinventing the wheel seems to be business as usual. Documents reside everywhere—personal desktops, miscellaneous file servers, a couple of Lotus Notes databases, and so on—and cover the gamut of file types.

Users tend to create content as a group, but revision control has never been a strength of the organization, and therefore the task of completing much of the work falls on only a few overburdened team leaders. As Marketing tends to "touch" many of the other organizations within SmallTime, they have become well aware of other groups successfully sharing and managing data via Microsoft's SharePoint Portal Server product.

It is hoped that a similar project for the benefit of Marketing will kick off in the near future. The Marketing group vice president has pushed for including his organizations' needs into a larger enterprise-wide SharePoint framework, but others fail to grasp his vision. In the end, he approves an intra-group project to analyze their own needs, and subsequently recommend and install a SharePoint Portal Server solution. Eventually, perhaps, they can tie this into the other document management, search, and collaboration activities occurring in parallel throughout SmallTime.

The group VP's Senior IT liaison is ecstatic. Through regular meetings with his IT colleagues throughout the company, he is already quite aware of the value that may be gained in these SharePoint deployments. He also already has a keen understanding of the steps required to actually implement and configure SharePoint Portal Server. And given their late start compared to other internal organizations, he has a host of technical guides, documentation, implementation plans, configuration standards, and practical experience to guide him through a successful deployment.

His mission—to help his fellow employees share ideas and expertise as they develop marketing strategies and programs, analyze their competitors strengths and weaknesses, and promote their products across the country. This will be accomplished through a SharePoint Portal Server deployment geared toward document management and collaboration.

BUSINESS PROBLEM TO BE SOLVED

It is hoped that a document management and collaboration approach will help streamline business processes that have gone awry. As indicated above, the Marketing group produces a large number and variety of documents supporting a host of programs and products, and is having nothing but problems organizing all of this activity. Many people start working out on the same document, but tracking versions of documents falls apart after a few revisions, and the team leads wind up finishing up much of the work themselves—they believe this a better "solution" than accidentally overwriting each other's documents, which was common practice in the past.

An enormous and complicated folder structure exists on a number of servers, but other data seems to disappear into a black hole of databases and personal email accounts. The group lacks control over who accesses content. Communication is hit-and-miss. There exists no cohesive approach to document management, and no hope of doing any better without some kind of framework, standard approach, and toolset.

BUSINESS GOALS AND REQUIREMENTS

Group collaboration is the goal, plain and simple, as illustrated in Figure 21.5. It is expected that the SharePoint group collaboration deployment will provide document management and collaboration capabilities that will assist them in the following ways:

- Provide a framework for document processes
- Help the team work more efficiently on projects
- Help the team more effectively share the work load
- Allow the team to share information with coworkers
- Allow different users in the group to work on the same document
- Refine the current publishing process by using approvals

Figure 21.5
SPS provides the collaboration environment that the Marketing organization needs to meet its business goals.

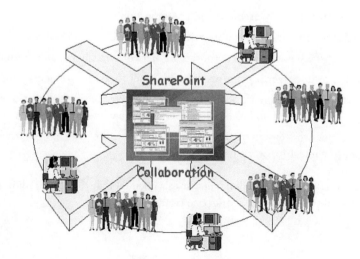

21

Other goals include the ability to automate existing publication processes, create a system for verifying document version control, and simply provide an easy and consistent communication vehicle throughout the Marketing group. Further, as alluded to above, it is hoped that some kind of approval process will allow the various Marketing authors to route a document through one or more approval levels before eventually, and automatically, publishing the document for general consumption. Finally, they are anxious to implement the check-in and check-out document version control features they have seen at work in sister organizations, leveraging the power of SharePoint-based solutions.

SUPPORT ORGANIZATION CONSIDERATIONS

SharePoint Portal Server delivers the document management and access control required by Marketing, while facilitating version control and more in a ready-to-use Web site. But it doesn't happen without both planning and a good support organization! Fortunately, the Marketing IT liaison is in a good position to be successful, armed with the knowledge of how other organizations within SmallTime deployed SharePoint Portal Server-based solutions.

After a brief kick-off meeting and review of the lessons-learned documents shared by his colleagues, he got busy designing a server and infrastructure solution to support the Marketing organization's business goals. Like the sister organizations, he will leverage the infrastructure, operations, and systems management support provided by Central IT, taking advantage of standard and procedures in place today at SmallTime. And with his deep knowledge of the Marketing group's uptime and availability requirements, balancing availability with budget constraints would be easily justified.

SOLUTIONS ARCHITECTURE

At the conclusion of his research, our IT liaison determined that a single server deployment would be adequate, and the following task list was drafted:

- Server hardware procurement and configuration
- Install the prerequisite software required by SharePoint Portal Server
- Connect the servers to the corporate IT network backbone, and the public net
- Work out the server backup/restore and duplication requirements with Central IT
- Determine how many workspaces to start with on the single server, keeping in mind the limitations on the number of workspaces that may be configured per server
- Determine who should be the workspace contact, the primary individual acting as the point of contact for workspace-related issues

Given the relatively small deployment, it was decided that the server administrator—the IT liaison—would double as the workspace contact.

Other potential configuration scenarios and potential issues were considered as well. For example, there was no reason to install SharePoint Portal Server to coexist on the same server with another application or software package.

Also, thought was given to the growth that the Marketing organization was experiencing, especially scalability requirements. It was concluded that if the organization grew another 50%, scaling to meet the expected increase in document management and collaboration could be met easily by adding an additional server. In the meantime, modifications based on increasing the number of workspaces would be more appropriate.

Much thought was given to the Simple Mail Transfer Protocol (SMTP) server, however, that must be accessible to the SharePoint Portal Server. Without the SMTP server, for example, approval emails cannot be received by SharePoint. It was learned that if the dashboard site associated with each workspace was to be used for subscriptions, the SMTP server must be set up to receive subscription notification email.

Also, the solution needed to be configured to "talk" to Lotus Notes and other database sources.

Finally, though characterized as a "collaboration scenario," some crawling of content sources will also occur in this deployment. Of course, the scope and number of crawl sources will be nothing like those seen in the Search Services deployment at SmallTime. That is, end users will use SharePoint Portal Server largely for document management, and only secondarily for search capabilities. Users will leverage these search features, though, from the dashboard site, primarily to search for documents stored in one of the local server's workspaces.

WORKSPACE CONSIDERATIONS

The first workspace is created at the end of the server installation procedure, via the New Workspace Wizard. Then, by using SharePoint Portal Server Administration, four additional workspaces are created. For each workspace, the workspace contact is configured as a Coordinator on the workspace node, again by using SharePoint Portal Server Administration.

The workspace contact can now configure SharePoint Portal Server roles on the folders in the workspace. In addition, the workspace contact can perform other Coordinator tasks such as customizing the dashboard site, specifying the category structure, and specifying approval routing on folders.

FOLDER STRUCTURE CONSIDERATIONS

Before going any further, the folder structure to be employed for marketing must be designed. Questions like the following need to be posed to the Marketing user community:

- How many documents exist today?
- Where are these documents?
- How are documented currently organized?

21

- Which users have permission to create, edit, and remove documents?

- What additional descriptive information or properties would help users sort and find documents?

- What processes are employed today, or should be employed, to promote a document from draft to "published"?

The IT liaison discovers *enhanced folders*, or folders capable of supporting many of SPS's document management features, during his research, and is especially pleased with the ability to enable users to check-in and check-out documents. The version control feature looks compelling, too. These features would prove quite useful for collaboration activities, where more than one person works on the same document. For example, checking out a document will ensure that only one person at a time will be in a position to edit the master document. And the versioning feature will track each subsequent draft, making one and only one (the latest) version of the document available for check-out. These features will without a doubt help meet the organization's business goals.

The IT liaison works with the users next, to deduct where enhanced folders would best benefit the organization. Together, they identify a number of folders that make sense, and these are copied into the first workspace, dubbed the MarketingSW workspace. Given his Coordinator role, the IT liaison then specifies attributes and properties like folder policy and security, and during a "test" verifies that everything works as advertised. Afterward, the team decides the structure and layout of all other folders.

INSTALLING CLIENT COMPONENTS

With the SharePoint Portal Server solution ready for more configuration by additional technical folks, the IT liaison ensures that everyone is clear on how to install the client components needed by additional Coordinators and other delegated users, if they're not running Office XP already.

Once the client components are installed where required on each collaboration user's computer, each user must add a Web folder that points to the workspace.

PUBLICATION PROCESS DETAILS

Currently, the Marketing group employs the traditional three-step process for publishing their documents: writing, technical review or QA, and publication. To construct this process with SharePoint Portal Server, questions like the following as posed:

- Who will create, review, read, and delete documents?

- Who needs to review a document before it is published?

- What kind of timelines should be promoted for each of these tasks, and how should they be enforced or monitored?

John, a marketing manager with SmallTime, manages all documents related to SmallTime's two largest competitors, ABC Company and Global Corporation. John typically has many folks working on documents that must then be approved by him prior to publishing. John is also one of the primary proponents of instituting an improved publishing process, favoring automated approval routings over manual processes. He is a logical choice to work with the IT liaison to answer the questions above. Before we go further, though, it must be noted that the publishing process as it exists today breaks down into

- An author creates a document
- The document is mailed or faxed to a list of specific people who review the document for completeness and accuracy
- Feedback is again provided via mail or fax back to the author
- The process repeats itself until the document has been approved by all parties

While the process itself is simple, it is neither complete nor automated. John likes the idea of supporting SharePoint Portal's review process, called approval routing. The people who review and approve documents are termed *approvers*. Any Coordinator can add approval routing to any enhanced folder, thereby automatically forcing the document to be routed from a specific author to an approver for that specific author. Best of all, with approval routing in effect, each approver will automatically receive an email notification when a document for which they are responsible needs to be reviewed.

And approval routings are not required in all cases. For example, senior authors may be set up for limited approvals or no approval at all. In the latter case, their documents would immediately move from draft/checked-out to published, once checked back in.

ADDING WEB DISCUSSIONS FEATURES

Another area where collaboration would prove valuable is in the process of editing final revisions of documents. In these cases, rather than faxing or emailing suggestions back and forth between a number of parties, the document is discussed via a Web discussion, which is simply a feature of Microsoft Office 2000 and above. John is a big proponent of this feature as well. Web discussions allow for collaboration and review, and are directly supported by SharePoint Portal Server. In this way, approvers or anyone else with an opinion can view a document and, without modifying it, simultaneously make online comments. The discussions are threaded, with replies to comments appearing directly underneath the original comment. Also, multiple discussions may occur at the same time for the same document. The authors and other end users polled in regard to this feature decide that this process will provide another piece of a comprehensive collaboration solution for their group, and endorse its inclusion into the project scope.

CREATING PROFILES

As discussed in previous SmallTime SharePoint Portal Server deployments, the ability to add additional descriptive data to each document stored in the workspace is compelling. Document profiles are immediately embraced by the Marketing team, as a way to easily add an incremental set of searchable properties to a document. New properties are added to the default Author, Title, and Description properties.

21

Note that all document folders must be associated with at least one document profile. Thus, it must be decided how many document profiles will be created, and which one best fits each folder.

MOVING CONTENT INTO MARKETINGSW

At this point, all enhanced and standard folders have been created via a structured approach driven by the Marketing user community. Once all document profiles are created and assigned to appropriate folders, documents may finally be moved into the workspace. Fortunately, drag and drop is supported in cases where the folder structure remained the same as on the miscellaneous file servers and local disks.

The IT liaison looks to John to serve as a "test bed" for solidifying the process of moving bulk data and publishing. All existing ABC Company and Global Corporation folder contents will be moved "as is" from the old file server to the corresponding workspace folders. To make it easy on John, they will be published in this case without the current approval routing.

So before moving the documents, the approval routing assigned to the two folders are temporarily disabled. This allows all of the documents to be published without requiring John's email approval.

Once the existing content from the file server is moved to the appropriate workspace folder, a check-in form appears as expected. The IT liaison adds a short remark, just to prove that the version control feature works as advertised. Note that if desired, he could also choose a specific document profile to assign. As simple as that, the content is checked in and published!

SECURITY CONSIDERATIONS

To control access to workspace content, SharePoint Portal Server draws on three roles to establish security:

- Coordinator
- author
- reader

Coordinators can specify folder policy and modify security, while authors can add or modify documents. Readers can search for and read any published versions of documents, but cannot modify documents, publish, or modify policies or security.

The IT liaison works with the Marketing management team and various team leaders to determine who should be assigned to author role for each folder. Afterward, a security policy is applied by modifying the Properties page of each folder. Finally, to ensure that everyone in the Marketing organization can at least read any published documents, the entire Windows 2000 user group is designated as a reader on all workspace folders.

DASHBOARD CONSIDERATIONS

A nice feature of SharePoint Portal Server is the fact that it automatically installs the appropriate dashboard site when a workspace is created. The address of the dashboard site is `http://server_name/workspace_name`. A user can then use the dashboard site for document management features and for searching without having to install client components on his or her computer—the dashboard site allows everyone to easily find and read content with Microsoft Internet Explorer. However, as stated previously, for performing Coordinator functions such as configuring security and creating document profiles, either the client components, or Microsoft Office XP, are required.

So, in addition to using Microsoft Office and Windows Explorer to read or manage documents, the Marketing organization can also leverage the dashboard site to access content in the MarketingSW workspace. And now that the workspace has been prepared, it is time to customize the dashboard site!

CUSTOMIZING THE DASHBOARD SITE

The Web site, called the dashboard site, can be customized to increase the dashboard site's usefulness for a specific organization, in terms of content, Web Parts, and general appearance.

Like every default SharePoint Portal Server home page, the dashboard site features four default Web Parts—Announcements, Quick Links, News, and Subscription Summary—which are customized for the Marketing organization. For example, the IT liaison adds links to the ABC Company and the Global Corporation Web sites under Quick Links, and a link to the Product Group's legacy Web site. As a reminder, he also posts the next Marketing-sponsored conference meeting under Announcements. And the usual company name and logo are added to the dashboard via the Settings management page.

GO-LIVE AND SUMMARY

At this point, the following has been performed and the SharePoint Portal Server solution is ready for go-live:

- Documents reside in the new folder structure under the MarketingSW workspace
- Document profiles are implemented, thereby facilitating the search process
- Check-in, check-out, versioning, and approval are all configured and operational
- Users are assigned to Coordinator, author, and reader roles as necessary
- Approval routings have been configured as needed
- Web discussion capabilities have been put into operation
- The dashboard site has been customized for the organization

The workspace structure and processes are in place, the content is available to be checked out and back in, and the dashboard site is ready to go. Chalk up an SPS collaboration victory at SmallTime!

21

SUMMARY

In the preceding pages, we focused on a number of SharePoint deployments at SmallTime, and how the various business goals drove completely different implementations. We drilled down into using Team Services to support a temporary project team, looked closely at search and document sharing scenarios, and spent quite a bit of time implementing document management and collaboration solutions in two organizations. Throughout this time, our focus has been strictly on creating single business unit SharePoint solutions.

An interesting phenomena occurs in these single business unit or department-wide SharePoint deployments—once the initial SharePoint Portal Server production system begins providing value, it quickly becomes apparent that other organizations would benefit from the same type of solution. This is how many SBU Portal environments tend to "grow up" into enterprise-wide implementations. More end users and more business units are added, dashboards are linked together, and an enterprise solution is born.

Another common SharePoint Portal Server growth driver includes adding incremental or new functionality. For example, as you realize the benefits of simply sharing data, the advantages of document management and even group collaboration become apparent. New group dashboard sites facilitating these functions are developed, and the SBU Portal continues to grow ever more valuable.

As you discover new uses for your SharePoint Portal implementation, and bring on new business units, it becomes quite important to begin coordinating your efforts and the efforts of your sister groups throughout the company. That is, economies of scale, common interests and standards, and investments in back-end supporting infrastructure and resources should be leveraged for the benefit of the company. Maintaining your own deployment over time ensures its effectiveness over time, and aids in integrating it into other SharePoint implementations, while reducing future integration headaches. Eventually, it should be expected that even the smallest of Portal deployments will one day become enterprise vehicles for sharing data. We saw in this chapter that SmallTime was well on their way in this regard.

In any case, both the framework and approaches to managing your SBU Portal can pay off in big ways down the road, as the portal grows in value to its user community. In the next chapter, we cover in detail the special challenges inherent to these larger and usually more complex enterprise-wide SharePoint Portal Server implementations.

EXAMPLE SCENARIO 3— ENTERPRISE-WIDE SOLUTION

In this chapter

22

DEPLOYING SHAREPOINT PORTAL SERVER ENTERPRISE-WIDE

In this chapter, we discuss the implementation of an enterprise-wide SharePoint Portal Server solution. To make the application of the following more meaningful, we are approaching this chapter in such a way as to walk Global Corporation (or "Global," another fictional entity) through planning and deploying a SharePoint Portal Server environment to support their entire company's search, data sharing, document management, and collaboration needs.

DETAILS ON GLOBAL

Global Corporation employs more than 90,000 employees across 100 sites in 20 countries. As a manufacturer and assembler of various electronics components, they require much in the way of a sophisticated document management system. Version and revision management is crucial to what must become a powerful search and collaboration vehicle as well, and transparent rollback to any stage of work is key. Engineering, marketing, accounting, and research and development groups are expected to make up the bulk of the online/active users, sharing and collaborating on both Microsoft-based and non-Microsoft-based documents. There is also an emphasis on crawling content sources both inside and outside their corporate firewall-protected resources.

Finally, the current needs of the company have been tagged at more than 18 terabytes of data spread out over three key Data Center sites, growing at an expected incremental 3 terabytes a year for at least the next two years (see Figure 22.1 for details). Much of this data resides on expensive and nonstandard hardware platforms, and as such benefit from very little consistency site-to-site. Fortunately for Global, and key to selecting SharePoint Portal Server for their portal needs, they have recently upgraded half of their 70,000 end-user clients across the enterprise to Windows 2000/SP1, and have implemented Office XP as well. The remaining clients will be phased out in favor of the new standard within the next six months.

CHALLENGES DEPLOYING ENTERPRISE-WIDE

As we have seen in previous chapters, sound deployment planning is critical in terms of successfully implementing SharePoint Portal Server. Deploying Microsoft SharePoint Server—regardless of enterprise, departmental, or small business unit scope—requires addressing the same umbrella of activities we identified previously, including

- Business goals and requirements
- Building the technical support organization
- Hardware vendor selection
- Solutions architecture
- Security plan development

- Developing the workspace(s)
- Preparing the dashboard site(s)
- Addressing change management
- Preparing for Go-Live
- Planning for post Go-Live support

Figure 22.1
Global Corporation is indeed "global," with large Data Centers in three countries, and other Information Technology (IT) support functions distributed across additional locations.

Information Technology

Key Global Corp End-User and Data Center (※) Locations

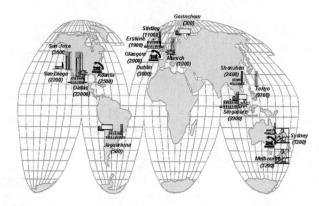

To compound matters, though, an enterprise-wide deployment implies another level of complexity, and exacerbates the previous challenges to an already daunting deployment with the following considerations:

- More than one approach to enterprise deployments
- Incremental technical support organization challenges
- Fundamental solutions architecture challenges
- Greater functional/organizational challenges
- Additional physical challenges
- Enormous data challenges

We will now drill down into the preceding challenges from the perspective of our deployment planning strategy.

→ To read in more detail about creating a deployment plan for SPS, **see** "Planning a Deployment for ABC Company" **p. 520**.

HOW TO APPROACH AN ENTERPRISE DEPLOYMENT

While Global's enterprise portal goals are many, such a huge enterprise undertaking must still start with a single footstep toward planning. An infinite number of approaches are of course available. Many enterprise deployments actually start out as successful department-wide or small-business-unit deployments. However, in the case of new-implementation methodologies to deployment planning for enterprise portal applications, two approaches stand out (see Figure 22.2).

Figure 22.2
Experience shows that large portal implementations are best accomplished in increments.

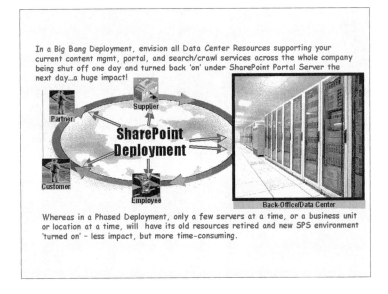

In a Big Bang Deployment, envision all Data Center Resources supporting your current content mgmt, portal, and search/crawl services across the whole company being shut off one day and turned back 'on' under SharePoint Portal Server the next day...a huge impact!

Supplier
Partner

SharePoint Deployment

Customer
Employee

Back-Office/Data Center

Whereas in a Phased Deployment, only a few servers at a time, or a business unit or location at a time, will have its old resources retired and new SPS environment 'turned on' – less impact, but more time-consuming.

Requirements for the portal tend to evolve along with the business, so it only makes sense that new subject areas, capabilities, and dimensions be added incrementally, hence the term *deploy as you go*.

THE PHASED DEPLOYMENT APPROACH

The first, a "Phased Deployment," refers to rolling out the new Portal application across one or a few business units or geographies, and is sometimes called a "deploy as you go" strategy. This allows for a relatively rapid implementation of at least part of the overall Portal solution, but also requires that legacy systems remain available to address features or needs not yet handled by the new solution. As such, this is a good way to go when it is important to show ROI quickly, but this method also requires a longer overall deployment time than the next option.

THE BIG BANG APPROACH

The second approach, the "Big Bang," requires a much longer development phase and more complicated roll-out phase, but allows the entire organization to benefit from immediate access to the same system. This second approach allows legacy systems to be retired much more quickly, reducing and possibly eliminating the time required for "parallel operations." The Big Bang, however, also tends to suffer more from scope and version-creep, and therefore must be managed aggressively to stay on target. Plus, it's a riskier approach overall, given the potential impact a failed implementation may pose. However, to its greatest benefit, the Big Bang approach to enterprise deployments tends to roll out faster than a similar Phased Deployment approach, where downtime is required to support the addition of new capabilities related to each phase.

GLOBAL AND THE PHASED DEPLOYMENT APPROACH

First off, for Global, the timing on a number of different fronts was such that it made more sense to go with a phased approach. That is, quite a few of the business units were in a position to leverage a SharePoint Portal Server solution, given that half of the end-user clients were recently upgraded to new technology. Second, a number of these business groups would benefit tremendously from simple search capabilities, of which they had none. In fact, the end users of one of the largest manufacturing facilities—MANX—were especially anxious to actually leverage the well-publicized capabilities of Office XP combined with SharePoint Portal Server! Third, given that two of the three Data Centers were in a position to terminate leases of proprietary and nonstandard DMS computing gear in the next two months, timing was considered ideal for supporting the architecture, design, and installation of new servers and infrastructure underpinning the SharePoint project. And finally, anything but a phased approach seemed just too risky, and too inclined to suffer from scope-creep, in such a large company spread out across the globe.

GLOBAL'S MANX PILOT

Given the previous, and a corporate mandate to "make it happen," the Project Steering Committee (consisting of business group executive representatives and a preliminary technical support organization) made a strategic decision to get the ball rolling quickly. An initial pilot project supporting the large MANX facility made sense to everyone, and a general budget figure was nailed down. Consisting of 1,000 users, it was by no means a small pilot, but it would represent a critical "win" once productive. And such a large body of eager end users would prove key to making the overall project successful, as well as providing a wonderful test-bed for demonstrating SharePoint Portal Server's capabilities and real-world limitations and challenges.

The extensibility of an initial SharePoint Portal Server deployment was one factor not mentioned beforehand that was also especially appealing to the business folks. That is, they knew that the initial SharePoint Portal Server deployment would provide great value for the MANX organization, but they also believed that they would quickly discover additional uses for SPS not yet envisioned. Features like the ability to add and customize workspaces for different groups, or to facilitate the creation of a corporate dashboard site linking what would eventually become many business group dashboard sites, held great promise for the initial pilot. They knew that consolidating their data and information sources and leveraging

SharePoint Portal's document management capabilities would not only change the way they managed projects, but also how they simply worked together to achieve the company's goals.

SOLUTIONS ARCHITECTURE CHALLENGES

Central to driving an enterprise Portal implementation is understanding and addressing the sheer level of solutions-stack complexities, from network infrastructure to server and disk subsystem infrastructure, up through the operating system, database, SharePoint Portal Server, potential integration points, client requirements, and more. In the next few pages, we look at some of the more critical staffing and technical challenges in detail (see Figure 22.3).

Figure 22.3
Some of the concerns and requirements of implementing a large SPS Pilot project are illustrated here.

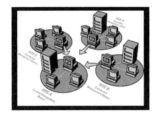

MANX: A pilot supporting 1000 users must be architected from the beginning to be scalable and available, and then stress-tested prior to Go-Live

Designed for Growth: With proper forethought, SPS scales from small environments to the 24x7 multi-site, multi-continent enterprise

Distributed: Network and systems management across SPS sites and workspaces supporting Global becomes a must

STAFFING CHALLENGES

Before a single business need can be addressed, or a technical challenge be conquered, a staffing plan must be created and filled by Global. Global, like most companies, is constrained in terms of availability of high-end business and IT folks. That is, the good ones tend to already be consumed by other key projects. However, the Project Steering Committee felt like it was more important to identify the roles that needed to be filled, and to worry about how to actually fill them later. In terms of an approach, it made sense for the Global Steering Committee folks to "whiteboard" the SPS solution stack, and start assigning priorities and responsibilities. After a quick hour, the following technical support organization for implementing SPS became clear (see Figure 22.4):

Figure 22.4
Global's technical support organization addresses both business and technology roles, and provides management and leadership to both of these areas individually and as a project team.

Global Corporation SPS Project

The pilot SPS technical support organization is composed of many roles, functional areas, and both business/functional and technology focal points.

- An SPS Pilot Project Manager was needed, to put the project into the hands of a capable resource with knowledge and experience in project management, as well as sheer bandwidth, to make the pilot a success.

- Two to three business representatives, tasked with riding out the entire SPS Pilot project, were identified as critical success factors. That is, the project would only be a win if business needs were indeed addressed.

- A senior collaboration/document management solutions architect would be required, and would in many ways help the PM to lead the other IT specialists assigned to the project.

- Various IT specialists would obviously be required, including folks skilled in designing highly available IT solutions, server and disk subsystem hardware, the Windows 2000 operating system environment, network infrastructure, client/desktop configurations, system security, and of course SharePoint Portal Server installation and configuration.

- To reduce the burden of day-to-day administrative tasks like time-keeping, scheduling, expense tracking, setting up client and business-focused data collection interviews, and so on, a Project Coordinator was also deemed critical.

It quickly became apparent to Global that they could not wait for the best internal resources to become available. Thus, the budget was "grown" to allow for bringing in consultants and other contractors into key positions that could not be filled in a timely manner with Global folks. The one position everyone on the Steering Committee agreed could not be outsourced was the Project Manager, though. In the end, the Solutions Architect and a few of the technical specialists were brought in from a Microsoft Solutions Provider skilled in deploying SharePoint Portal Server across complex enterprises.

22

CAUTION

Don't be tempted to outsource a Project Coordinator. Such a role is best served by a long-time employee of the company, someone intimately familiar with how to get things done inside the company, such as how to work around the red tape found inside even the most efficient of institutions.

CONNECTIVITY ARCHITECTURE CHALLENGES

Not only does traditional data center–centric network infrastructure come into play in regard to solutions architecture, so does simple browser or client access. In other words, both back-end and front-end network requirements must be addressed in a successful SPS deployment. High availability can be achieved back at the data center, typically through redundancy. In terms of client access, though, speed more than strict availability is emphasized. Front-end accessibility is no less critical, though, for without it, the Portal ceases to serve any purpose.

CLIENT/BROWSER REQUIREMENTS

Accessibility refers to simply being able to access data from a browser or client perspective. Fortunately for Global's pilot project, everyone is running a supported release of Internet Explorer. And by the time the SharePoint Portal Server implementation has truly "gone global," the remaining Global Corporation users will also be enjoying their new SharePoint-supported client environment.

Most Portal implementations will not be so fortunate from a client perspective. In these cases, subprojects geared at elevating client installations to a minimum-supported level will be both required and customary.

→ For minimum client requirements, refer to "System Requirements for Clients," **p. 37**.

Note that access through a SharePoint Portal Server dashboard site does not require the SPS client install, but rather consists of a minimum version of Internet Explorer. Global determined that this access mechanism, a browser-based strategy, would be employed for the bulk of SPS Pilot users.

UPGRADE VERSUS NEW CLIENT PURCHASE

One rule of thumb for many IT support organizations is that client upgrades (desktops, laptops, whatever) do not pass the "ROI" test if more than 3–4 hours must be spent performing services related to upgrades. In those cases, it makes better financial sense to simply deploy a new client complete with Windows 2000 Professional or newer, Office 2000 or (preferably) Office XP, Internet Explorer 5x+, and so on.

Think about it. These upgrade services include tasks related to identifying hardware and software revisions, mapping these to the minimum requirements mentioned previously, and performing the actual hardware or software upgrades (including scripting, or creating SMS or similar "automated" installation/upgrade packages). A typical hard-disk upgrade, therefore, almost immediately warrants a new client installation.

CONNECTIVITY TO THE PORTAL

Finally, enterprise accessibility means having connectivity—that is, a network link—that enables productive use of the Portal. This becomes such a huge issue for enterprise deployments—where perhaps hundreds or thousands of users are network-bandwidth constrained—that we have dedicated a section later in this chapter for "physical challenges" related to network connectivity.

AVAILABILITY/HIGH—AVAILABILITY REQUIREMENTS

In a small workgroup or departmental solution, it is likely that the Production system consists of one or two servers and a small number of disk drives and other resources set up to provide a certain level of high—availability, such as 99% or so uptime. Windows of planned downtime are usually quite abundant in these cases—perhaps 8 hours every evening, and 48 hours of planned downtime every weekend, might be available each week!

ENTERPRISE AVAILABILITY

An enterprise solution will tend to have more stringent uptime requirements than its departmental or small business unit colleague, due to the following:

- Greater number of users or business groups tends to force smaller windows of planned downtime.

- Users across multiple time zones force even smaller windows of planned downtime. The sun never sets on quite a few worldwide Production Portal implementations.

At the same time, other forces are at work:

- Larger data requirements tend to push backup times out longer, typically shrinking the time available for users to access the data.

- Large data stores underscore the importance of the data itself and therefore emphasize the ability to restore it quickly should the need (or a disaster!) occur.

- Large data stores drive larger indexes, and therefore tend to inherently slow down access to the data in the Portal.

- SharePoint Portal Server does not support Microsoft Cluster Server as of this writing. Therefore, the highest levels of availability must be pursued through other technical product/configuration means.

The net effect of the preceding is that great importance is placed on the system in terms of when it is actually available to be used. Thus, driving maximum availability is essential. To that end, proper change control is paramount. By the same token, great weight should be given to protecting the data that resides on the Portal. Duplicating each Production portal becomes a minimum requirement, as does providing a minimum level of data protection at a

22

hardware level. For example, RAID-protected data and OS drives should be a minimum requirement for Production-level SharePoint Portal Servers. The fact that SharePoint Portal Server does not support Microsoft's clustering technology should not read as an admission on Microsoft's part that high availability is not important. Instead, this fact should only serve to reduce the number of high availability alternatives; many others exist, from cloning disk drives, to maintaining off-site server duplicates, to utilizing third-party clustering technologies. In the end, an exercise in the cost of downtime is all that is required to determine your specific needs, driving your options accordingly.

PERFORMANCE REQUIREMENTS

Selecting an appropriate server platform is an extremely important step in a successful portal deployment. Leveraging your hardware vendor's Microsoft product expertise (especially SharePoint, Exchange, and SQL) can make a huge difference in the success of your Portal project. Of course, the key individual server hardware requirements are related to CPU speed, RAM, and hard disk space, but assistance in designing servers for specific server roles (such as Portal servers dedicated to server crawling, Index servers, corporate vs business unit searching, or other servers dedicated to Exchange, SQL2000, Active Directory Domain Servers, and so on) will assist you in budgeting, planning for, and installing each of these components.

THE SIZING QUESTIONNAIRE

To intelligently configure a Portal solution, details regarding areas like the following must be determined or estimated. Prior to Global selecting their hardware partner for the SPS Pilot project, a hardware-vendor–provided questionnaire covering these areas or questions will be obtained. Most questionnaires drive what is commonly called *user-based sizing*. That is, once Global completes the questions in the questionnaire, each vendor will take a shot a putting together a sizing, or proposal, describing what the overall SPS landscape should look like. User-based questionnaires seek to understand the number and nature of end users ultimately using the production (and/or test, or sandbox, or development, and so on) system during the peak hour of the peak month or season, so as to estimate "operations per second," and include

- Number of users—The total number of users who will ultimately use the site. In the case of Global Corporation, it is expected that 70,000 of the 90,000 total employees will be end users. However, for the purpose of the pilot, 700 of the 1,000 identified MANX personnel will actively use the SPS pilot.

- Percent of active users each day—This percentage represents the total number of specific dashboard users on any given day, and therefore must represent all dashboards across the enterprise. In many enterprise Portal deployments, it is not unusual to see perhaps 20–30% percent of all users actually "active." Sometimes, this is called the number of *concurrent users*. However, this number varies by implementation, business group, region, and other factors. Take special care to be conservative but at the same time to not grossly overestimate this number of concurrent users, as it drives sizing calculations in a big way.

- Number of operations per active user per day—Perhaps the most difficult data to capture, this represents the number of operations that a typical user performs from each dashboard over the course of a typical day. An operation could be many things—searching, retrieving, or editing documents; browsing a Web site or the home portal page; and so on. This number usually ranges from 1 to 10, and should consist of page views as opposed to site hits. Note that one simple method of collecting this kind of data is to collect page views from the Web server log of a pilot portal or other existing portal implementation.

- Number of hours per day—This is the number of hours during which the system is planned to be available. This number ranges between 8 and 24 hours, depending on the specific customer-driven requirements. In the case of Global Corporation, the system is planned for 24-hour uptime/availability requirements, with the exception of a bi-weekly four-hour "maintenance" window every other Saturday morning (which, for those interested, equates to 98.8% "availability").

- Peak factor—This number represents the delta between the average dashboard throughput vs the expected peak. While sometimes expressed as a percentage, it is more commonly depicted as a number ranging from 1 to 5.

- Breakdown of types of users—Many hardware vendors or systems integrators try to characterize SPS users into different classes. For example, certain workers might be deemed "power users" and therefore be assumed to consume a certain percentage of server resources. Other users might be termed "casual users," and consist of users performing an occasional bit of document management or searching activities. In the end, characterizing users is an inexact science, subject to interpretation by the various hardware and software vendors in the SPS market.

CAUTION

> It is imperative that each vendor or systems integrator tasked with sizing the portal be provided the same data. That is, Global must share the same data with all of its partners, to facilitate a true "apples-to-apples" comparison once each partner generates a sizing or proposal. And Global must also ensure that terms like power users and casual users are understood by all parties, so as to be consistent across different vendors.

In the end, capturing the previous data seeks to address the following formula, and provides us with a "peak throughput" number measured in operations per second:

Number of users × percent of active users per day × number of operations per active user per day × peak factor

It is with this peak "operations/second" that we can go to the various hardware and solutions vendors and request solution designs (sizings) for Microsoft SharePoint Portal Server implementations.

22

CPU and RAM Sizing

Sufficient CPU and RAM resources are required to provide an acceptable user response time. Sizing for CPU and RAM becomes critical when a large number of users is expected during a peak usage period. In this case, characterizing the users to determine an average number of "active" or "concurrent" users—users performing work—as well as an average number of operations per second—is important. With this information and business information regarding peak days and hours, it is possible to plan around the "peak" hour for which a productive solution will need to be sized. Note that if insufficient CPU or RAM resources are available, users will experience unacceptable server response times during these peak periods, and the solution will likely be deemed a failure by anyone trying to perform work at this time, regardless of how well the system performs during non-peak periods.

Pagefile Sizing

Though CPU and RAM are critical to response time, hard disks play a huge role in overall response times as well. The first role that disks play is in the form of the Pagefile. Pagefile sizing tends to be an art form for many, but the following are generally agreed upon rules:

- The total Pagefile size should be 2–3 times the size of physical RAM in each of the Portal servers.

- The Pagefile should actually be split across two disk partitions, residing on two different physical drives. Usually, one Pagefile resides on the C: drive (to capture memory dumps, if desired), and another Pagefile resides on another drive *not* busy servicing other disk requests. For example, in addition to a pair of mirrored drives for the operating system, oftentimes a separate pair of drives may be added to a server specifically for the Pagefile and bulk of the SPS application executables.

- The Pagefile should *never* reside on disks dedicated for logs, such as the Property Store log files, or the Web Storage System database log. By definition, logs are very write intensive. So, too, is the Pagefile, as it busily accepts pages in RAM that are deemed no longer valuable.

- By the same token, the Pagefile should never reside on disks dedicated to the various SharePoint data documents. This is because the Pagefile would detract from the overall read/write performance of the data drives, and the busy data drives would impede write performance of the Pagefile. Thus, any database or storage drives are off-limits to Pagefiles, too.

In the next section, we will take a look at Global's general disk space requirements, and how they will approach sizing and configuration.

Disk Space General Requirements

Another critical factor concerning hard disk sizing regards simple disk space—if there is insufficient hard disk space, end users will simply not be able to save additional documents. In fact, a lack of disk space could also impede document search capabilities.

RAID 1 VERSUS RAID 5

Finally, with regard to sizing, the performance of the overall data-serving functionality of the SharePoint Portal Server is most impacted by the configuration of the disk drives earmarked for logs, or to store the data.

In all cases, the performance of RAID 1 (mirrored) drives, or RAID 0+1 (a set of drives with data striped across them, mirrored to a similar set of drives) surpasses the performance of a RAID 5 set (striping data across all drives, with parity across all drives as well) in terms of both reads and writes. In many cases, in fact, a RAID 1 configuration will provide a 30–40% performance gain in reads over a similar RAID 5 configuration. And in RAID 0+1 or 1+0 configurations (depending on your hardware partner's implementation of this combination of "striping" and "mirroring"), write performance may be 3× that observed in a similarly configured RAID 5 solution. These are potentially huge numbers, and represent huge deltas in obtainable performance (see Figure 22.5).

BLOCKSIZE SELECTION

Another huge area affecting disk performance regards the operating system *blocksize* selected for the data and log files. As you're probably aware, when a new Windows 2000 disk partition is created under NTFS, the default blocksize is 4 kilobytes, or 4KB. The blocksize is actually the increment of data used in file transfers. So, reading a 64KB file involves 16 discrete disk reads, or I/Os (input/output activity). Some of the fastest disk controllers can do about 20,000 I/Os per second, so if you do the math, you see that eventually the disk controller can simply move no more data. At this point, the disk controller becomes a *bottleneck*—only the elimination of the bottleneck will speed up the system. That is, a true disk controller bottleneck will not be solved by adding more RAM or processing power.

Figure 22.5
Depending on the disk drives, controllers, and hardware-vendor specifics, RAID 1 typically exceeds RAID 5 read performance by 1–30%, and write performance by 20–300%, at a cost of approximately 2× in terms of drives, controllers, and storage system requirements.

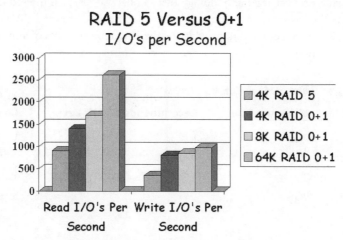

Fortunately, today's high-speed disk controllers and drives are not only fast, but also optimized for larger block sizes. By leveraging large blocks to move data, the following benefits are realized:

- A fewer number of disk I/Os is required to move the same amount of data.

- The result is an increase in the number of megabytes (MB) per second that the disk controller effectively moves.

Thus, if we look again at our previous example, it becomes quickly apparent that we can move the same 64KB of data in fewer disk I/Os if we increase the blocksize. Reformatting the drive housing our data to an 8KB blocksize reduces the number of I/Os to only 8. And reformatting for 64KB blocksizes lets us move our data in a single I/O! It is no wonder that software and hardware vendors alike, including Microsoft, Compaq, Hewlett-Packard, and more, typically recommend 64KB blocksizes for SharePoint Portal Server data and log files.

CAUTION

> Changing blocksizes requires reformatting the drive. Thus, all data is lost. To keep your data, back up all files to disk or tape. Once the drive is reformatted, restore the backup to the new drive.

DISK CONFIGURATION AND LAYOUT

While performance and availability are both important, the cost of the solution must also be weighed. Disk configuration is driven by two fundamental needs:

- The need to provide a robust system that can also be rapidly restored in the event of hardware or software failure.

- The need to maximize the I/O of the database and operating system by segregating these activities on dedicated disk sets.

One disk subsystem sizing methodology that Global was exposed to used the following table to illustrate the base configuration requirements. The disk sizes and RAID levels indicated (see Table 22.1) are designed to provide for the base requirements of a minimal productive system installation.

TABLE 22.1 DISK SIZES AND RAID LEVELS

Volume	Minimum Size	Recommended RAID Level	Contents
1	9GB	1	W2K Operating System Operating System PageFile
2	9GB	1	SPS Executables
3	9GB	1	SPS Log Files
4	27GB	5 (RAID 0+1 preferred)	SPS Data/Database Tables

The OS, Pagefile, SPS Executables, and Log Files should *always* reside on a RAID 1 volume, regardless of cost. Note that a RAID 1 solution always costs more than a comparable RAID 5 solution, but that a RAID 1 solution can lose multiple mirrors, or *copies*, of the data, so long as at least one mirror remains intact.

RAID 5, on the other hand, is typically utilized for the data volume(s) when the cost of additional drives/controllers/storage systems is as much a consideration as raw I/O performance—it represents an excellent balance between cost and overall performance. With RAID 5, the equivalent of one drive (in a set of drives) is lost to maintain parity. Thus, a set of four 9GB drives in a RAID 5 configuration does not equal 36GB. Instead, it is 27GB, as expressed in the following formula:

(# drives * size of each drive) – (1 * size of each drive) = total usable SPS space

A RAID 5 solution may "lose" a single drive, therefore, and still remain operational. That is, the parity information striped across all of the drives allows for determining the data (by block) that would have been on the drive, so for all intents and purposes the system is up and available even when a drive has failed. Once a second drive in the array fails, though, you are in trouble!

MORE ON THE DISK CONTROLLER

Not only are the RAID levels selected or drive configurations important for disk subsystem performance—the Disk Controller itself is equally, if not more, critical. For it is the Disk Controller that supports the ability to create high-performance and highly-available RAID sets in the first place.

NOTE

> Do not be tempted to implement RAID at an OS-level for any enterprise-wide Portal implementation, as this robs the OS of CPU resources. Sure, it works, but only at the expense of performance. Operating system–based RAID incurs a layer of overhead that directly impacts the performance of all applications running on top of the OS. Protecting your data is best left to hardware-based controllers dedicated to the task.

Many Disk Controllers also support caching at the controller level. The best controllers provide battery-backed cache and configurable read/write caches, so as to assist you in both safeguarding and tuning your SharePoint Portal Server (see Figure 22.6). Check with your hardware vendor prior to buying—and ensure an apples-to-apples sizing/capabilities comparison when two or more vendors are being considered.

CAUTION

> Be wary of using array controllers with write cache that is *not* battery-backed. Such controllers run the risk of losing or corrupting your data in the event of a power failure. That is, any writes still sitting in the write cache that have not actually been posted to the physical disk drives represent data that will be lost when the server loses power, if not backed up by a battery on the controller.

Figure 22.6
This high performance Disk Array Controller is worthy of an SPS production implementation, as it includes battery-backed read and write cache. In this way, no data is ever lost in the event of a power failure.

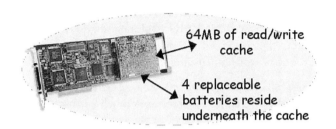

64MB of read/write cache

4 replaceable batteries reside underneath the cache

LOG FILE OPTIMAL DISK CONFIGURATION

For the two primary log types, then—the log files for the Web Storage System, and the log files associated with the property store—a pair of dedicated mirrored drives represents an optimal configuration. These files are shared across all workspaces, and therefore represent a potential bottleneck if not addressed properly in the first place. In systems requiring the highest levels of performance, dedicated disk controllers for the logs ensure that disk activity elsewhere does not interfere with log writing.

DATA STORE OPTIMAL DISK CONFIGURATION

Sizing a disk subsystem to support the Microsoft Web Storage System Database, Streaming Database, and Property Store is more complicated that the log disk configuration. For many companies, the cost of a RAID 1 or 0+1 configuration, where only 50% of the physical disk space being purchased is indeed available, is prohibitive. For others, though, like Global, the inherent performance gains that cannot be realized in a RAID 5 configuration dictate going with the more expensive approach. Work with your hardware vendor to best determine a configuration that meets your performance, availability, and scalability needs. And keep in mind that changing the layout and configuration of a disk subsystem in production is not a trivial task—get it right the first time!

SCALABILITY REQUIREMENTS

Given the nature of an enterprise deployment, and the variety of roles that individual solution components may play—for example, dedicated search servers, crawling servers, and so on—the lack of scalability of each component may quickly become a limiting factor should the scope of the solution change. Such changes might include supporting new business groups, adding loads of new users across the enterprise, configuring tens of thousands of additional crawl sites, or adding specialized capabilities like search and collaboration. Scalability is all about changing the functions or scope of the solution, adding perhaps incremental hardware or software resources, and still maintaining acceptable performance. Scalability is about not having to toss out the current Portal and force a redesign from the ground up after requirements change.

In Global's case, planning for scalability means taking into account a bit of scope-creep as well as planning for post-pilot growth, both in the number of users and scope of the pilot. Thus, servers that can be scaled up in terms of disk storage, RAM, number of network cards, and number of processors makes a lot of sense for Global.

WHAT SCALABILITY IS NOT

What is really important to note is that scalability does *not* correlate to spikes in activity resulting from periods of peak activity. For example, month-end close should not exercise the scalability of the SharePoint Portal Server solution. Month-end close will only tax the sizing of the solution, proving that the system was either adequately sized or not. Remember, the sizing process seeks to determine the peak load that must be addressed by the Portal.

Configuring a Microsoft SharePoint Portal Server solution for scalability only *starts* with the sizing process. Once a server configuration (including the number and type of servers, and the RAM, CPU, network card, disk controller, and other hardware resources required for each server) capable of addressing the business needs is designed, the configuration must then be looked at with an eye toward *redesigning* it for appropriate levels of scalability, high availability, manageability, and more.

PLANNING FOR SCALABILITY AT GLOBAL CORPORATION

Global Corporation's SharePoint Portal Server pilot project sizing exercise identified the need for three crawling servers to cover North America. But once reviewed for scalability, it became clear that four dedicated crawling servers would provide not only the capability needed immediately, but also the headroom—the scalability—to allow unanticipated true growth in core business requirements. This approach also coincidentally addressed Global's needs for high-availability, via the commonly employed "n+1" approach. That is, losing one of the North America crawling servers would not actually impact the Portal's abilities to crawl the expected number of sites—from our sizing exercise, we know that only three crawl servers are actually required.

ROLLING UPGRADES AND MAINTENANCE CYCLES

The n+1 approach illustrated previously also afforded Global another valuable benefit—the ability to bring each redundant server offline (one at a time) so as to perform system updates, OS upgrades, and so on. This capability allows for future planned maintenance or upgrades, usually described as a "rolling" maintenance cycle or "rolling" upgrade. And the n+1 tactic does so without impacting the availability and capability of the Portal solution overall. Planning for scalability truly lends itself to solving these other business problems!

Similar tactics can be employed in regard to other SharePoint Portal Server technical limitations or business needs. The fact that the number of indexes that may be propagated is effectively limited to four per dedicated search-server may be handled in a similar manner as the previous—Global can plan to implement an additional search server, and reap the benefits of rolling upgrades here too. In the same manner, the practical limitation of 15 workspaces per server also lends itself to this methodology—plan on implementing an additional server, and should unexpected downtime occur, a duplicate of the workspaces on the down server may be hosted across the remaining available servers.

STRESS-TESTING FOR PROOF-OF-CONCEPT

Even with all of the support and expertise brought to bear on their pilot, Global's SPS project steering committee still had questions about the raw performance of the solution. Risks were weighed against costs in terms of pilot failure, and another $50,000 was budgeted for a comprehensive customized stress test (also often referred to as a load test). The goal was simple—to measure the performance impact that would be typical of what the production system would bear during a peak period of activity.

Like any company that endured the sizing and characterization process and accurately completed the various sizing questionnaires, Global was able to leverage this data to identify the number of end users and types of transactions or activities that each would be performing during a peak period. At that point, it was believed that it was only a matter of scripting these business transactions, and then "playing" them back (and measuring performance) on the system that would eventually become the production environment. The following considerations quickly became apparent:

- A scripting tool would be required to script the business activities and other transactions.

- One or more technical specialists would be needed to head up and complete the stress test.

- Business and other functional specialists would need to be made available to the aforementioned technical specialists, to ensure that the business activity was scripted realistically.

- A method would need to be found to execute the scripts so as to represent 1,000 actual end users.

- Sample data and other resources would need to be made available to support the scripted activities, including documents to be managed, workspaces created, category structures created, Web sites made available to support crawling/searching, and so on.

- An approach to monitoring the performance of the end-to-SPS solution would need to be drafted and utilized to measure critical performance criteria like online response times, average crawl times, overall disk performance, and more.

After nearly a two-day meeting between the Senior Solutions Architect and his Team Leads, it was determined that the Server Team Lead would manage the stress testing engagement as well. With his background in lab-based server and disk subsystem analysis and testing tools, it was determined that he was a good fit for driving the stress test to completion. He immediately turned to his hardware vendor and Microsoft, to put together a short list of tools and approaches that addressed all of the considerations outlined previously. In the end, he spent half of his budget on a partner/consultant experienced with toolsets capable of supporting virtual Web users, and spent another $10,000 on temporary licenses for the testing tool.

After two weeks of working with the business folks and developing initial scripts, and another two weeks fine-tuning the scripts for virtual user support (as opposed to requiring 1,000 physical desktops on which to run the various tests), Global was ready to start executing test runs against the soon-to-be production SPS pilot environment. The system was tuned between runs, and by the end of the second day of testing, it was clear that the production system was undersized for peak loads. Additional RAM was added, as were additional disks, and the disk subsystems supporting the DMS were tuned throughout the solution stack. Another round of tests then demonstrated that the system was CPU-bound when performing searches, and another pair of processors were added to the search servers.

After this, things looked really good overall, and the steering committee was notified of this fact. They were also made privy to the following lessons learned, shared throughout the entire project team:

- The amount and variety of data impacted overall performance substantially. That is, with very little data loaded, most everything ran out of the disk controller's cache and therefore artificially inflated the performance numbers. Only when a more realistic amount of data was loaded did it become apparent that the disk subsystem was in need of both an upgrade and incremental tuning.

- Ramping up the 1,000 virtual end users over a 15 minute period was time-consuming but absolutely critical. This required creating a random number generator based on the unique machine name of each individual virtual user, and then staggering when each virtual user would log in to the SPS system based on this random number. Otherwise, all users would attempt to log in at about the same time, and crater the system.

- The Stress Test environment used for the testing was subject to changes and modifications throughout the month of actual script development and testing. As such, the scripts themselves had to be continually fine-tuned and adjusted, just to simply continue to work a week after they were created. In the future, the stress test system would be "locked down" for the duration of testing.

- *Scope Creep* nearly became a problem, as the business and other functional users continued to add more business processes and activities to the agreed-upon list of activities to be scripted. The Senior Solutions Architect and Project Manager addressed this early on, and froze changes in this regard by the end of the first week of script development.

- Finally, not all scripting tools (nor the companies that write these often full-featured and therefore potentially complex testing suites) are created equal. Tools should be selected based not only on price, but also in ease of access to support people, should assistance be needed at the last minute. This is especially true of testing tools that support virtual users, for it is much more difficult to troubleshoot these types of scenarios. Plus, it must be noted that a lot of horsepower is required to actually emulate 1,000 clients—Global initially brought in two quad-CPU/2.5GB RAM servers, each to service 500 virtual users, but actually wound up adding another two servers in this regard.

22

As we can see, stress testing is by no means a trivial task. It is complex, time-consuming, and subject to scope creep like any other project. But it is also an insurance policy, and as such represents an excellent investment when the cost of not meeting your SharePoint Portal Server performance or scalability requirements outweighs the cost of the stress test itself.

SECURITY REQUIREMENTS

At a basic level, security is indispensable both for document management tasks and for maintaining search capability integrity at Global. Regarding document management, access to sensitive data must be restricted—some end users will be responsible only for viewing certain documents, while others might take part in creating, modifying, and approving these documents in preparation for a larger audience. In search scenarios, on the other hand, it is critical that *all* end users view only the results of searches for which they have explicit access. All of this remains essentially true regardless of the scope—enterprise or other—of a Microsoft SharePoint Portal Server deployment; however, the challenges facing larger organizations, with perhaps multiple corporate-wide and business-unit–specific Search servers and millions of documents, is intimidating indeed.

In a large portal deployment like Global's pilot, where folder hierarchy and category structure may vary greatly between geographies or sites, a single security policy will be inadequate. Users may hold different roles for different folders in the same workspace, for example; not to mention different roles in separate workspaces. Furthermore, security policies to be implemented after building every workspace (presumably supporting different business units across the enterprise) will need to address quite a few areas:

- Security must be mapped into each workspace. This can be a daunting task in and of itself for large implementations.

- If external content is key, then specifying content sources is required. In an enterprise implementation, access to external content is almost always necessary. This access to external content may subsequently drive changes in the company's firewall or DMZ implementations.

- Users must be assigned to appropriate roles, which can also represent a great amount of planning and work in large implementations.

- Folder Coordinators must not only be assigned, but must also be specifically "designated." While not a challenge in SBU deployments, larger deployments benefit from more elegant approaches (such as shared resources across multiple folders and workspaces, perhaps depending upon functional role or group).

- Approval routes must be identified and implemented. Complex approval routes may be generated in large organizations.

- Best Bets must be identified (and managed!) over time. That is, how many users are given specific authority to update the Properties page for each file so as to identify it as a Best Bet, and how this capability is managed, must be addressed.

At a higher level within the enterprise, each server in the Portal solution must be covered by the overall company-wide security and domain/directory models. If secure transactions over an extranet or the Internet are required, support for SSL should be enabled as well. And as the Portal evolves, consideration must be given to providing additional Coordinators access to manage security profiles and monitor security infractions.

Microsoft provides the general security tools and approaches required to manage the enterprise environment, but the real challenge is in simplifying the security model or security approach whenever possible. One method of doing this is by leveraging roles. Remember, a role identifies a specific set of permissions at a folder level (with a few exceptions) for Coordinators, Authors, and Readers.

→ To read more about the three SPS roles, **see** "Workspace Overview," **p. 48**.

The best way to illustrate potential security simplification is by taking a look at Global Corporation's planned security approach.

Global's initial architecture dictates 16 discrete workspaces, hosted across the three primary data center sites. We assume that five workspaces will be installed at two locations, and six at another. If we create a master Coordinator User ID and use this for each of the three Portal installations, we then only need to concern ourselves with mapping, assigning, and managing this one ID. SharePoint Portal Server automatically assigns this user ID—the one used to create each workspace at the three different sites—to the Coordinator role at the workspace level, as well as on all of its folders.

BENEFITS OF A SINGLE INSTALLATION USER ID

The benefits are many. For instance, a single user ID may not only carry out the purposes illustrated above, but may also be leveraged for easily creating indexes and automatically scheduling index updates when warranted. A site-wide or enterprise-wide document checkout or publishing process may also be facilitated more easily in this manner. And the usual process of adding Authors and Readers to each workspace/folder is still unchanged, though now the default workspace contact is quite apparent. As the portal is eventually customized and deployed after the installation, a new and valid workspace contact will be identified. In the meantime, though, all communications directed to each individual workspace (via the email address assigned for the workspace contact) will "roll up" to a Global Coordinator, thereby facilitating consistency and accountability in cross-workspace deployment planning issues.

ADMINISTRATION REQUIREMENTS

Administration across the board is much more challenging for an enterprise-wide deployment than a departmental-based Portal solution for one primary reason—complexity. The number of servers, roles of those servers, and the specific or custom hardware and software configurations deployed drive administration complexity. The Active Directory design, and inclusion of each server into this design, also presents challenges to administration, especially in highly distributed solutions.

22

THE NEED FOR GREATER MANAGEABILITY

Enterprise-wide SharePoint Portal Server implementations leveraging structured processes require greater management capabilities over their information. They need capabilities like formal publishing processes and the capability to search on different file formats or from multiple data stores. Here, manageability refers to managing the data as opposed to managing the solution from an IT perspective.

Custom Web Parts may play a role in assisting users to better manage their data, too. Web Parts can be developed that facilitate improved data organization across the Portal. Data related to general administrative tasks, for example, may be accessed via the enterprise Portal's home page, while administrative tasks specific to a business group may be accessed only from a custom Web Part configured to display a Web page with links specific to the group.

→ To read more about deploying and customizing Web Parts, **see** "Dashboards and Web Parts," **p. 344**.

Other specific administration challenges related to enterprise-wide SharePoint Portal Server deployments may be found in the following sections.

INDEX MANAGEMENT AND OTHER SEARCH SERVICES

Index management becomes more and more critical as smaller Portal solutions grow. The time required to propagate indexes to other servers from index workspaces, not to mention performing full index updates, can become considerable.

Supporting other search-related services quickly becomes daunting tasks in and of themselves. Creating and managing categories, supporting multiple workspaces, and maintaining subscription services are two potentially time-consuming examples.

MODIFYING THE THESAURUS

Modifying the thesaurus for large enterprise-wide implementations becomes a critical task as well, especially as multiple languages/dialects are addressed by the Portal, or additional business groups leverage the Portal, each with their own "definition" of business-specific terms and group-specific vernacular. And the fact that an administrator may affect search ranking by assigning weights to specific words or acronyms adds to his workload as well.

CONFIGURING CRAWLING

The sheer number of documents in a large implementation could easily force the inclusion of several to many dedicated crawl servers, similar to what we have seen at Global. Microsoft published numbers indicating that a Portal server can crawl approximately 3,500,000 documents. However, this would be prohibitive in a single-server productive system where the Portal Server might be addressing searching and other functions. The solution is to spread out the crawling among a number of servers, then, such that the system is capable of crawling the number of documents expected to be crawled on a daily basis in say, a year or two from now. Another approach would be to plan on adding incremental servers once the number of crawls surpasses perhaps 2,000,000—this approach requires "going back to the well" for budget money, however, and simply may not be an option.

THE IMPORTANCE OF IFILTERS

Installing and registering IFilters is required when using proprietary file extensions. The "unknown" that an enterprise-wide implementation may introduce is simply the variety of data formats that could be managed by the Portal in a year or two.

OTHER ADMINISTRATION REQUIREMENTS

Miscellaneous challenges will serve as potential administrative stumbling blocks throughout the project lifecycle, unless addressed early on and in a regular manner throughout the Portal lifecycle. These include areas like

- Licenses per Server—Estimating the number of licensed users that each server within a complex Portal solution can support is difficult indeed. For many deployment scenarios, whether large department or worldwide multi-site organizations, supporting 10,000 licensed users per single SharePoint Portal Server computer is not uncommon.

- Enabling "Best Bets" —Though easy to enable, Best Bets can become cumbersome and ineffective as an organization adds users and groups with different Authors and therefore varying "definitions." Over time, these varying definitions will have to be addressed—documentation standards ease this pain!

- Documents per Server—Microsoft has indicated that one million document versions may be stored by a single SharePoint Portal Server computer. Choices regarding deployment details like the extent of the category hierarchy must be determined before a number specific to your Portal implementation can be determined.

- Documents per Index —A single SharePoint Portal Server computer can crawl something in the neighborhood of 3.5 million documents. Of course, when all of this data finds its ways into an index, the real challenge of managing and sifting through large indexes becomes a key challenge to an enterprise Portal deployment.

TECHNICAL SUPPORT ORGANIZATION CHALLENGES

While the organization supporting a Microsoft SharePoint Portal implementation must possess a robust set of capabilities and regularly perform and test a number of mission-critical services, additional requirements regarding enterprise-wide implementations are noted in the following sections.

The technical support organization must be ultra flexible. That is, the organization initially crafted to support the Portal deployment will not have their arms around the scope of the project until deep into the business requirements analysis and subsequent architecture process. It is not uncommon, then, to incrementally add technical personnel to the technical support organization with "new" skillsets specific to areas like high availability or storage-area-network design (for example) halfway into the architecture process.

22

The technical support organization will probably be lacking in end-to-end content management experience. The quickest and most effective way to jump-start this shortcoming is by leveraging a SharePoint-experienced consultant or consulting organization, as mentioned previously. Then, by carefully managing knowledge transfer between the consultant and the other team members, and taking advantage of formal and supplementary training opportunities, the technical support organization will mature into a capable SPS-support team.

Security will play a bigger role, and therefore present a more complex challenge, in an enterprise-wide Portal implementation. One common way to address this challenge is by creating a combined business unit/IT subgroup focused on security considerations.

Change management will be the wax that holds the entire production solution, and indeed system landscape, together. Without sound yet flexible processes for introducing change into the production environment, a complex business-driven IT solution like SharePoint Portal Server will implode within months of go-live.

People committed to all phases of the project will be necessary. An enterprise-wide Portal deployment will exercise creative minds, and demand creative solutions and implementation specialists—though perhaps not from an IT perspective so much as from a business collaboration and data management perspective.

FUNCTIONAL/ORGANIZATIONAL CHALLENGES

Representing perhaps one of the more insidious challenges to an enterprise-wide Portal deployment, functional and other organizational challenges will pose everything from political threats to driving huge subprojects underpinning the Portal project itself. Ultimately, people are more difficult to manage and plan for than any technology implementation. Differing functional goals like team collaboration, corporate search capabilities, and the need for both business unit and divisional workspaces will present certain organizational challenges.

Other goals of each organization within the scope of the project—goals driven by virtue of a business unit's role in an org chart, for instance—will provide new challenges. Financial and accounting groups, for example, will have different needs and different expectations than marketing and manufacturing groups. Finally, language barriers will present special problems across the board! Below, we address some of these functional and organizational challenges in more detail.

MANAGING DISPARATE BUSINESS GOALS

To say that different business groups have different goals seems quite self-explanatory. To actually manage the development of the enterprise portal such that individual business unit goals are reflected in the workspaces actually deployed is another matter altogether, though.

In our illustration with Global Corporation, nearly all of the business units require intra-corporation search capabilities. A few units also require the ability to push searches out to the Internet. In the same way, most organizations have a need for sharing documents. Some need to collaborate on the creation of new documents, though. And this latter group will also require sound revision management, a tight security model to protect data not ready for "prime time," and the capability to automatically route documents to particular reviewers.

So, the issue boils down to how to manage these disparate business goals and needs, so as to ensure that they are indeed met by the SharePoint Portal Server implementation. Global, with the help of a third-party consulting partner experienced in SharePoint deployments, has focused on gathering these needs via a simple Microsoft Excel-based matrix (see Figure 22.7). Each business group is listed in the left-most column, and various Portal capabilities, attributes, and properties are listed across the top, with their own column headings. A simple X indicates that the business group needs the capability. In this way, needs that cross all organizational boundaries are quickly identified, and "one-off" requirements are easily recognized as well.

A ready-to-edit sample matrix is included as Figure 22.7:

Figure 22.7
This sample illustration serves as an excellent vehicle for mapping business groups to their goals, needs, and other requirements.

Organization	Search Capabilities	Document Sharing	Document Management	Collaboration	Web Discussions	Version Control	Categories	Best Bets	etc...
HQ	X	X	X	X		X			
Corporate Finance					X		X	X	
Corporate Marketing				X					
Corporate HR	X	X	X						
Product Support	X								
Product Engineering	X	X		X					
Product Marketing	X		X	X					
SW Manufacturing	X	X	X	X	X	X	X	X	
SW Marketing	X	X	X	X	X	X	X	X	
NE Manufacturing	X	X							
NE Marketing					X				

NEED FOR BOTH DETAILED AND SUMMARY DATA

Once the enterprise's goals and needs are identified, the level of data detail required to support the goals must be determined. Some departments or business units may need access to the most granular of data, for example. Most business organizations focused on financial matters require this level of detail. Others, however, find the greatest value only through summarized reports or high-level roll-ups of this otherwise detailed data, including planning and executive teams. Finally, still other organizations (such as Auditing organizations) demand access to both detailed and summary data.

22

TIP

> A challenge for any SPS deployment planning team is how to obtain and retain the data needed by everyone. That is, it is critical that details remain "available" to business groups that need this data, for whatever retention period is required, in the format and level of detail required.

DIFFERING FUNCTIONAL GOALS AND THE LANGUAGE BARRIER

Like we discussed previously, a basic challenge to implementing SharePoint Portal server across the enterprise regards meeting the diverse needs of the individual organizations. Language barriers only exacerbate these differences. Imagine needing to maintain the same document in multiple languages, or provide search capabilities across German, English, and Thai SharePoint Portal Server installations! We will address just this situation in more detail in the following sections as we uncover basic data challenges. Suffice it to say, though, that neither functional goals nor business goals will ever be completely realized in multinational organizations without accounting for language barriers.

GETTING TO YOUR DATA—PHYSICAL CHALLENGES

Another area underscoring the differences between department-wide and enterprise-wide deployments concerns the ability to actually access the data. Termed "physical challenges," these special considerations apply to the client side of the Portal implementation—GUI and network access—as well as to considerations related to where the data resides from a geographical perspective.

In the next few sections, we will take a closer look at these considerations, and how an enterprise-wide deployment could seek to effectively mitigate or minimize the impact that physical challenges represent on the usability of the SharePoint Portal Server solution.

CLIENT AND GUI ACCESSIBILITY REQUIREMENTS

A larger number of end users implies a more diverse workforce. As such, the technical support organization tasked with delivering Portal services needs to be prepared to present accessibility services for the deaf or sight-impaired, moderately sight-impaired, those end users handicapped by the loss of an arm or hand, those with other mobility-related impairments, and so on.

Accessibility starts with the ability to access and effectively use the Portal Client GUI, of course. The fastest network in the world, or speediest and most available disk subsystem for storing data, means nothing if an end user cannot get past the limitations of the desktop! And even beyond this, inability to access technical or customer support services regarding the client—for example, Internet Explorer—also exacerbates this quandary.

To this end, Microsoft offers a host of services aimed at assisting the disabled. Microsoft Knowledge Base article Q165486 should be reviewed, explaining how to customize Windows-based operating systems for users with disabilities. Additionally, your hardware vendor can provide you with keyboards leveraging one of the three Dvorak layouts, thereby improving accessibility for two-handed, only-left-handed, or only-right-handed users.

NOTE

For more information on Microsoft's services for the disabled, refer to the Microsoft Accessibility and Disabilities Web site, at `http://www.microsoft.com/enable`.

As for customer support, the enterprise-wide technical support organization should be prepared to offer product and customer services support via text telephone (TTY/TDD) services. Microsoft does! Complete access to Microsoft's tech support organization is available for deaf and hard-of-hearing customers. The enterprise organization, like Global Corporation, should strive to provide the same level of commitment and service.

INSTALLING AND USING THE GUI

Once basic accessibility to the desktop is achieved, users may access most SharePoint Portal Server features via the dashboard and a browser. There is actually *no* requirement to load SharePoint client components on every end user's desktop or laptop computer. The dashboard site allows all end users the ability to perform the functions commonly associated with any portal, facilitating search functions as well as document management. Only end users tasked with actually managing a workspace must install the client components—in this case, on an OS like Microsoft Windows 2000 or later—so as to enable complete workspace management functions. The client components allow specific end users to configure security, create and manage content sources, and so on. One important note, though—any user wishing to access SharePoint Portal Server Help must install the client components, too.

PHYSICAL LOCATION OF END USERS

Once physical access to the desktop client/browser is enabled, and the GUI or SharePoint client components are loaded, the next accessibility challenge is gaining access to the site(s) hosting the SharePoint Portal Server resources. Hard-wired network connections and dial-up services still tend to remain the most common method of providing this level of access; however, wireless devices and networks, including phones, Palms and iPAQs, BlackBerries, and more, continue to push the accessibility envelope. Regardless of client device, only the TCP/IP protocol is supported.

Another key challenge particular to an enterprise-wide deployment of SharePoint Portal Server is (usually) the presence of slow wide-area-network (WAN) links connecting various physical sites together into a single network. Even worse, slower dial-up end users may still be connecting via modems at less than 28.8Kb/sec in many parts of the world, including much of the United States. VPN solutions leveraging DSL and a variety of cable modems are growing in popularity, but the number of end users behind these speedy network solutions will probably be minimal in an enterprise deployment.

A sound SharePoint architecture and deployment model therefore seeks to minimize the amount of data and GUI-based traffic that must be moved back and forth over these slow TCP/IP-based network links. This idea is discussed further in the next section.

THE PHYSICAL LOCATION OF DATA

Data comes in all shapes and sizes—half-megabyte Excel spreadsheets, 10MB PowerPoint presentations, 200MB personal SQL or access databases, multi-terabyte SQL2000 and Oracle databases, and so on. In a perfect world, all data would reside in one place, and that site would support a huge network pipe back to your desktop computer. Or perhaps all data would just sit on your computer (we all know users like that!)—regardless, the classic battle struggle between data and physical location can be summed up as this:

- If the data sits out on the enterprise network, users are often constrained in terms of the time it takes to *get* to the data. This promulgates maintaining pointers or even multiple copies of this data at different "local" sites.

- If the data sits out on the local network, it is more quickly accessed and better safe-guarded, but subsequently consumes much more disk space, administration time, and backup resources than otherwise required.

If we turn back to Global Corporation's particular constraints, they are running three differ-ent sites with many different workspaces. Each site satisfies perhaps the majority of local end-user search and collaboration requirements. But each site also hosts documents that cross geographical boundaries yet represent similar functional interests. For example, the Enterprise Marketing groups in all three geographies share and collaborate in terms of cre-ating marketing collateral. True, languages differ, but themes, ideas, and certainly financial models and products in most cases remain quite consistent. And each site facilitates cross-site corporate search mechanisms, too.

So the trade-off becomes "What will minimize my user's frustrations in downloading or moving large quantities of data?" versus "What makes budgetary sense?" How do you keep your customers happy without breaking the bank?...

In Global's case, favorable economics surrounding the cost per gigabyte of disk space drove their initial decision to maintain a data "staging" drive array in each of the three data center locations. This staging array was designed to hold the very largest or most-often accessed documents, providing the fastest read and write access. All data was also compressed on this drive. But this was not enough. Global also created a custom Web Part for a number of cross-geography organizations, like Marketing, such that a directory of documents—includ-ing properties and metadata related to each document or link—was readily available to be reviewed. This served to minimize inadvertently moving large files across the "big ponds." And it also coincidentally aided in better version and revision control.

Finally, Global reviewed the network links between major sites, and analyzed the Web/HTTP traffic that was expected to be generated between major functional groups and across geographies. Their findings suggested that upgrading a single trunk would add substantially to network response time between two large hubs of users. And by pushing VPN access within their internal network environments supporting home-based users, they facilitated the adoption of DSL and cable modems where available. Within a year, in fact, they expected that nearly half of their home-based or remote-office users would be in a position to leverage these newer technologies, allowing older dial-up modem farms to be retired faster than expected. The reduction in the latter hardware resources, support costs, and maintenance costs would more than offset the costs associated with providing VPN access for Global—in essence, many of the users would benefit from greater network throughput capabilities without incremental cost to the IT organization or business groups!

BASIC DATA CHALLENGES

While much of the discussion of this chapter has centered around data and access to data, there exist basic or inherent constraints that drive enterprise-wide SharePoint deployments in one manner or another. Some of these constraints include

- Sources of data, including sensitive internal documents, subscription service-based data, stock quote feeds, and so on, drive multi-dashboard management requirements.

- The impact of proxy servers on accessibility and security drives client configuration and support costs.

- The raw scope of data servicing different needs of the enterprise organization can overwhelm unprepared workspace Coordinators.

- The variety of data formats, like Word documents, Excel and other spreadsheets, PowerPoint presentations, Adobe PDFs, CorelDraw documents, and more can also overwhelm the workspace Coordinators.

- Language requirements, and how these drive data stores, search capabilities, and so on, must be addressed.

- Backing up and safeguarding all of this data!

SOURCES OF DATA

Mapping the standard Web Parts, or creating custom Web Parts linking various sources of data, is perhaps the most common method of "integrating" various sources of data into a cohesive portal whole. Four Web Parts ship with the SharePoint Portal by default. These are

- News
- Announcements
- Subscription Summary
- Quick Links

22

At Global, the News Web Part displays links or stories of general interest. For example, company-related news articles and stories "hot off the wire" find themselves featured here. Other news services, like press releases, are also displayed here.

The Announcements Web Part is used for company-wide announcements, business unit events, and so on. At Global, the Announcements Web Part for Marketing included a reminder regarding a deadline for the introduction of new-product literature into the sales channel.

The Subscription Summary Web Part affords a summary of the end user's various subscriptions. The inclusion of a "Subscription Notifications" Web Part makes great sense at high-level functional or perhaps corporate-wide Portal implementations—if a set of search results is found useful, the end user can easily subscribe to the related content, relying on notifications from SharePoint Portal Server as to changes or new relevant documents.

The Quick Links Web Part displays links to other areas of interest, much like a My Favorites" approach. At Global, the Quick Links Web Part in the dashboard site of the Marketing group contained links to just-announced and new-product road maps and associated collateral.

MORE ON WEB PARTS

Web Parts may be drafted that support collaboration tools like Microsoft NetMeeting, or facilitate high-level services like providing directions and maps to various company locations. As mentioned previously, Global Corporation created a custom Web Part that highlighted often used or especially large documents, including metadata properties. A special Search Web Part was also added to Global's enterprise SharePoint Portal dashboard, facilitating maximum search capability across the organization.

In any case, the point here is that a huge variety of data sources and document types dictate much in the way of management. The opportunity to share enterprise-wide data is both real and compelling, but represents a challenge in terms of information overload, and may even promote pushing out stale and inaccurate information if dashboards are not well maintained.

CREATING CUSTOM WEB PARTS SUPPORTING ENTERPRISE DEPLOYMENT

To create Web Parts supporting multiple environments, such as those inherent to complex enterprise implementations, the following approach is generally recommended:

- Leverage relative URLs in all ASP, HTML, and VBScript files—it makes the transition from Development to Test to Production much easier, not to mention more consistent.
- For any links within your Web Part, generate your own relative links (refrain from coding absolute URLs to a NetBIOS name—relative links also support fully qualified domain names both internally and externally).

SECURITY OF DATA AND THE PROXY SERVER

As stated previously, the impact that proxy servers have on the enterprise in terms of accessibility and security drives client configuration and support costs. A proxy server enhances the security of your intranet by preventing unauthorized access by someone on the Internet. A proxy server may enhance SharePoint Portal Server performance by caching recently accessed Web pages and therefore minimizing network traffic/download time, but they also add complexity. The proxy server must now be analyzed under the same constraints and high-availability requirements as those that drove the Portal configuration in the first place.

Proxy server technical ramifications are many:

- Where the proxy server resides in relation to the other SharePoint servers must be considered—proxy servers can break down index propagation if the proxy sits between the server responsible for creating/updating the index and dedicated search servers (the proxy server may be configured to allow Windows file share access to get around this, however).

- Proxy servers must be configured specifically to support and pass a few critical verbs—SharePoint Portal Server uses HTTP, DAV, and INVOKE, the last a custom SharePoint Portal Server verb.

- The proxy setting for Internet Explorer on the desktop or laptop client will impact how the client/dashboard site HTTP-based communication will occur, if at all.

- Per Microsoft, the dashboard site leverages a unique server-side object called ServerXMLHTTP to make HTTP requests, and as such maintains its own proxy settings. Thus, if the dashboard site is behind a proxy server, the proxy settings for the ServerXMLHTTP object must be specifically configured (via the proxycfg.exe utility).

→ For more information on proxy servers, refer to "Proxy Server Options," **p. 198**.

Note that while proxy servers may be deployed in both very small and enterprise-wide implementations, they are more typical in the latter. The improvements in performance and the security benefits of proxies usually outweigh the implementation and support costs in these larger deployments.

THE SCOPE OF ENTERPRISE-WIDE DATA

The raw scope of data found in enterprise-wide SharePoint Portal Server deployments can overwhelm unprepared workspace Coordinators. Other challenges include managing the same document name found in multiple servers/locations, the impact of many files on the size and propagation of indexes, the pure number of links and pointers that might be required from the dashboard or workspace, and so on. Good access to data that is spread out or distributed across many servers and updated frequently requires regular crawling. In many cases, dedicated crawl servers are eventually if not initially deployed.

Firewalls may also present a unique challenge to crawling. That is, if you wish to crawl only internal sites but want to refrain from creating lots of rules (such as excluding searching anything that ends in ".com", ".net", ".edu", and so on), any proxy server that is also hosting index workspaces (if so configured) may need to be disabled.

THE VARIETY OF DATA FORMATS

Yet another enterprise-specific challenge to deployment lies in the number and types of data formats—documents created in Word, Excel, PowerPoint, and so on are pretty common. Documents created in Adobe PDF or CorelDraw formats may be less common, though. The key here is not so much in the absolute variety than in identifying the formats in the first place.

For example, at Global Corporation, it was determined early on that nearly all documents to be managed under the MANX Pilot's cross-functional general workspace consisted of the standard Microsoft Office Suite of document types. It was never envisioned that another format even existed. As it turned out, Lotus Notes was the preferred package of choice for maintaining email and drawing documents for one of the larger high-visibility organizations. This after-the-fact observation underscored the importance of determining *all* data types up front—had this been more than a pilot, valuable collaboration opportunities as well as a huge source of raw data would have been overlooked. And the political ramifications of "missing" an organization's key data repository would have reduced the credibility of the entire project, not to mention the project sponsors.

One last point: Identifying the varieties of document formats also allows inclusion of the appropriate IFilters. As users pull down various files and documents and attempt to actually open them, the IFilter is used to determine which desktop application to invoke. It can then facilitate opening the document in its native format, as well as offer the ability to filter the document into its innate text while also identifying properties.

Thus, determining document formats up front clarifies where information is stored, and how the data will ultimately be used. This in turn helps crystallize deployment goals, both promoting cleaner enterprise integration and improving collaboration opportunities across the company.

DATA AND LANGUAGE CHALLENGES

We previously touched upon some of the language issues inherent to enterprise-wide SharePoint Portal Server deployments. The fact that not all documents residing in a particular geography may reside in the same language, and that search/best bet functionality may fade, are a few of the more obvious issues. Another is the fact that subscription notifications are generated only in the workspace language—there is no support for separate client languages.

Not so obvious issues, though, are the benefits that exist like the following:

- SharePoint Portal Server, by virtue of its support for six client-component languages (English, Japanese, German, French, Spanish, and Italian) provides great opportunities for collaborating across enterprise-wide deployments.

- Support for content in any language (except bidirectional languages like Arabic) offers huge corporate search potential. For example, SharePoint Portal Server provides noise word files and thesaurus files for languages as diverse as Chinese-Simplified, Chinese-Traditional, Dutch, English-International, English-US, French, German, Italian, Japanese, Korean, Spanish, Swedish, and Thai.

- SharePoint natively supports creating, say, a German version of SharePoint Portal Server on top of an English operating system installation.

- Furthermore, in your German workspace you may create and maintain Japanese folders.

- Japanese and other non-German content may be added to the dashboard site, too!

- To really make things easy, Microsoft also made it possible to access the workspace using the client components of any of the six languages above. Thus, Americans can access the German workspace by using the English client components.

- And finally, any user with the appropriate role can add folders, categories, document profiles, and other content in any content language.

So what's the problem? Simple—a site can quickly become so language-neutral as to present ongoing management and maintenance challenges. It is therefore recommended that as few languages as appropriate to facilitate good collaboration and effective searching be employed wherever possible.

BACKING UP AND SAFEGUARDING YOUR DATA

A number of years ago, after designing and discussing a very large database implementation with a potential customer, my client remarked, "Nice design. But how do I back up those multiple terabytes of data?" Excellent question! He understood the essence of the good news/bad news issue at once—plentiful data may be a great asset to your company, but without the facilities to protect it, back it up, and restore it if necessary, the data will begin to look more and more like a liability.

The enormous amounts of data that may be generated and managed underneath the guise of a "portal" is staggering. Think about the revisions of all of the documents being managed under the umbrella of version control, for example. And then there is all of the data mapped into multiple languages. And the copies of large data sets sitting in separate staging arrays to facilitate rapid retrieval. And the copies of documents downloaded to various client devices. In the end, all of this should be backed up and safeguarded.

LITTLE ROOM FOR ERROR

One may argue that not all versions of a document with a long version history need be backed up again and again. Or one could make a case as to why operating system drive backups may be "skipped" once committed to tape. One day when you need to fall back to a known valid release of a critical operating procedure, though, or realize that a service-packed or patched OS was never actually backed up again, and the primary drive corrupted the mirror when it died, you will begin to understand the importance of backing up everything regularly.

22

You will not have the time to realize this until much later, of course, as you scramble to keep your job and re-create your precious data in some other manner…but there will be hope.

FULL BACKUPS ON THE RISE

In any case, both technology and falling prices are driving the decision to back up data disks more frequently, and to do so more often in "full" rather than incremental modes (see Figure 22.8). The cost of tape drives, disk drives, and tape cartridges continues to drop. And the speed of tape drives has picked up considerably over the last 12 months as well.

Figure 22.8

Global adopted a 28-day backup cycle at each of their three large data centers, and leveraged best practices like rotating tapes offsite and performing regular backups of all disk partitions—OS, SPS executables, logs, and data.

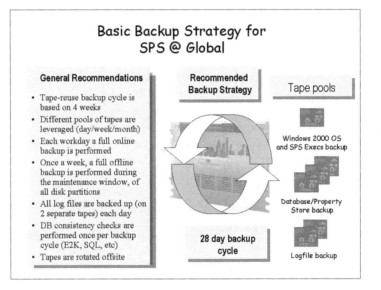

Today, the question to back up, and how often, and in what manner, is still ROI-based as always. In the case of our fictional company, Global Corporation, backups of all data partitions occur as a natural function of data center operations—each server is completely backed up to tape at least once a week. And all production resources undergo a full backup nightly. This diligence was a function of an easy ROI exercise—it was determined that adding the SharePoint Portal Server production servers to the data center standard backup solution (an SAN-based enterprise tape library running Veritas Netbackup, in this case) cost the same as losing 72 hours worth of work. That is, the combined costs of a fibre Host Bus Adapter for each production server, a port in the switched fabric, SuperDLT tape to cover all SharePoint data resources, software licenses, and administrative overhead was less over the next three years than the average cost that would be associated with lost productivity over a 72-hour period. The business units were simply unwilling to lose 72 hours of work, and funding was developed at that point to cover the backup solution.

DUPLICATING SERVERS FOR DISASTER TOLERANCE

Global did not have to go to a lot of trouble to safeguard their complete SharePoint Portal Server solution, though. By using the backup and restore scripts that SharePoint Portal Server automatically installs during the installation, the process to perform these key functions amounted to very little. In the end, they leveraged these scripts and automated them, so as to actually create duplicates of each server on another available disk partition within the data center. They also tested the ability to duplicate a copy of their master SharePoint Portal Server across their network to one of the other data centers, and found the process flawless though slow. Until budget money is available to perform this server duplication process more often, Global will plan on performing and testing remote duplicate copies for all three data centers on a monthly basis at minimum. The process is straightforward:

- From Data Center A, back up the master server to a remote disk partition located in Data Center B.
- From Data Center B, restore from the backup image just created to a standby server (sometime called their *DR*, or Disaster Recovery, server), also residing at Data Center B.

The same two steps are then performed for Data Centers B and C, and again for C and A. The standby server at each site is actually a server in the Development environment for the particular SharePoint Portal Server deployment/system landscape, having been previously "super-sized" to a certain extent in terms of RAM and CPU, so as to be capable of supporting the Production-level load.

During the month, Global also rotates and tests the ability to restore tapes across the three data centers, thereby providing yet another level of recoverability should one of the data centers be lost to a natural or man-made disaster. They test their escalation process that defines when, how, and by whose authority the decision is made to move SPS from its production infrastructure to an "unplanned downtime" status, to finally a new environment (DR site/solution).

Global understands that disaster tolerance is only as good as its last DR test, and strives therefore to prove on a scheduled basis that these processes and procedures are indeed effective. They simulate an actual disaster—the loss of a complete data center—each quarter. And to really push the limits of their DR plan, they randomly "kill off" a key member of the team responsible for failing the data center operations over to another site. In this way, Global ensures that their staff is cross-trained in DR and really prepared in an emergency to fail over (and afterward fail-back!) with a moment's notice.

SUMMARY

Whether your deployment goal is building a corporate enterprise dashboard site to consolidate your information services, or creating a series of workspaces to assist a geographically dispersed business group to collaborate on and manage its documents, you will find SharePoint Portal Server a versatile solution. A SharePoint-based solution may be scaled

22

from a single dashboard site to a network of organizational and departmental dashboards providing great functionality across an entire enterprise. Specific solutions components—search, crawl, index, workspace, and so on—may be scaled out, thereby providing a platform from which to grow as additional uses for SharePoint Portal Server are identified and implemented.

As always, it is important to coordinate your SharePoint Portal Server planning, development, and deployment efforts with other stakeholders in the company. Communication of business goals and needs is key to designing a system capable of meeting the productivity needs of the organization. The right approach to deploying the Portal must be determined as well, as must incremental technical support organization requirements.

Underpinning any successful business-driven IT project is a fundamental understanding of the data, its uses, its locations, and overall accessibility. Functional and organizational issues and challenges regarding the data, and goals of the folks using the data, must be identified, with an eye toward maximizing collaborative and information-sharing capabilities.

Finally, maintaining, administering, and safeguarding the enterprise-wide SharePoint deployment requires a greater level of commitment than simpler implementations, and benefits from a holistic approach to information management. Disaster recovery and backup/restore practices must be put into place. And just as important, these critical services must also be tested and verified.

TROUBLESHOOTING

TROUBLESHOOTING

In this chapter

23

THE SHAREPOINT SOLUTION STACKS

While troubleshooting tips and techniques may be found dispersed throughout this book, here we capture both an approach to troubleshooting, and the most common (or unusual!) issues with implementing a SharePoint Portal Server solution. Note that issues relating specifically to SharePoint Team Services are not covered herein, save for issues associated with coexisting or integrating with SharePoint Portal Server.

As SharePoint Portal Server consists of server-based and client-based solution stacks, it makes sense to approach troubleshooting in a manner that initially maintains a separation between the two. Later, we will analyze the entire end-to-end solution, including integration points. In effect, though, by verifying that the individual solution stack layers are sound, we create a foundation upon which to base additional analysis.

So, what is a solution stack? Simply put, it is the "layers" of technology that sit one on top of the other in support of a solution. Generally speaking, this might include the following:

- Hardware layer
- Firmware layer
- Operating system
- OS Service Pack(s)/OS drivers layer
- Database layer
- Application layer
- Internet-enabling layer

Of course, each of these could be further broken down into even more detailed layers. For example, hardware is usually broken down into the individual servers supporting SPS (for example, two dedicated indexing servers configured a particular way, and two dedicated crawling servers configured another way, on perhaps another server platform), as well as the disk subsystem supporting each server.

Further, multiple stacks typically exist. For example, the general SPS client solution stack might consist of an HP desktop running Microsoft Windows XP, HP's OS client drivers version 4.4, Internet Explorer 6.x, and so on. The general SPS 2001 server solution stack, on the other hand, might consist of a Compaq DL760 server with firmware and OS drivers from SmartStart 5.3, running Windows 2000 Advanced Server with Service Pack 2, and SharePoint Portal Server with Service Pack 1.

One of the keys to a sound technology solution is assembling a solution stack that is supported by all of the various technology firms involved in the solution. Assembling such a supported configuration is not trivial! This is one of the reasons why so much time is put into vendor and overall solution selection—minimizing the number of technology players while bringing together an end-to-end solution is the ultimate goal.

Here, we are interested in SharePoint Portal Server's solution stack, but you can apply this same approach to any technology or solution. That is, Exchange 2000 has its own unique solution stack, as does an Oracle iProcurement solution or an SAP R/3 on SQL Server 2000 solution. The solution might differ, and the solution stack will certainly differ, but the approach to building a supported and well-performing solution remains constant.

The solution stacks for the server and client components look like this:

SharePoint Solution Stack

Client components/browser

Various integration points

SharePoint features/functionality

SharePoint dashboard

SharePoint workspace

SharePoint Portal Server install

SharePoint prerequisites installs

DB-specific updates

Database engine

HW-specific drivers

OS service packs/patches

Operating system

Disk subsystem firmware

Disk subsystem hardware

Server firmware

Server/CPU/RAM hardware

Network infrastructure

Cooling infrastructure

Power infrastructure

TROUBLESHOOTING AND THE PHASES OF IMPLEMENTATION

Breaking down our troubleshooting methodology into *phases* of an implementation also makes sense. In most cases, these high-level phases look something like the following:

- Server installation
- Server configuration
- Client components installation
- Workspace configuration
- Dashboard customization
- Integration points

23

Each of these phases may be further broken down into subphases as appropriate. For example, server installation typically consists of hardware sizing, hardware installation, hardware configuration, applying firmware updates, operating system installation, application of service packs/patches, installation of a Web browser, and so on...before SharePoint Portal Server is ever even loaded. Obviously, the input and outcome of each one of these subphases impacts the next phase—the solution stack builds upon itself, and becomes increasingly complex. A number of significant points become clear:

- A near infinite number of combinations of hardware, firmware, operating systems, drivers, and so on exists.

- Only a finite number of combinations of the above actually work together in terms of providing an end-to-end supported solution!

Later in this chapter we will look at each of these, and drill down into greater detail. First, however, we need to spend a few minutes looking at our general approach to troubleshooting.

GENERAL TROUBLESHOOTING APPROACH

The way in which we approach a problem, whether SharePoint Portal Server–related or otherwise, is vital to actually solving the problem. Our approach recommended here is nothing short of common sense, backed up by best practices, and includes the following:

- Identify and document the problem or issue, sometimes termed the *mode of failure*, or MOF

- Address the problem in terms of general troubleshooting before escalating

- Compare the MOF with known problems/issues

- Verify the solution stack(s) as appropriate, focusing on supported combinations of both hardware and software

- Verify that changes to the solution stack have been promoted through appropriate "change control" throughout the system landscape (see note)

- Verify the integration points as appropriate (see note)

NOTE

Change control refers to the practice of first testing a suggested or potential change to a production system in a technical sandbox or other SPS environment. Eventually, after a period of perhaps a few days to a few months, the change (such as the application of a new Service Pack for Windows 2000 Advanced Server) is *promoted*, or applied, to the next system in the system landscape, like a test, or development, or training system (see Figure 23.1).

It should be noted that by the time a change is finally promoted through the entire landscape to the actual production environment, it has been thoroughly tested for an extended period of time in environments as near identical to the production environment as possible. This, combined with other best-practice approaches to managing change, allows for a world-class production SPS system in terms of stability and minimal unplanned downtime.

Figure 23.1
A sample SharePoint Portal Server five-system landscape, depicting Development, Test, Training, Production, and a Disaster Recovery environment.

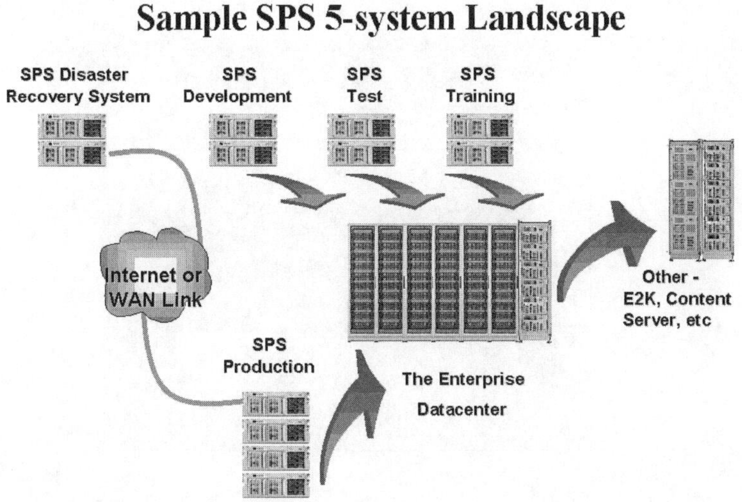

Sample SPS 5-system Landscape

NOTE

Integration points simply refer to where the solution stack layers "touch" or communicate with each other. In fact, integration points are sometimes referred to as touch points.

A discussion around the SPS client components makes for a good example. The client components are extensions to Microsoft Windows Explorer and various Microsoft Office applications. As such, these extensions represent the integration points between SharePoint Portal Server and Windows Explorer and the MS Office applications. See Figure 23.2 for an illustration of a typical high-level solution stack, as well as some of the integration points common to SharePoint Portal Server.

DOCUMENTING THE ISSUE

An excellent starting point or approach to troubleshooting is simply to document the problem and ensure that the problem itself is clear to the technical team that will work toward resolving it. Only when a complex problem can be adequately and clearly explained is there hope for a resolution. Think about your experiences with various technical support organizations, and it will quickly become evident that identifying or documenting the issue is usually the first step taken to resolve it.

Figure 23.2
SharePoint Portal Server and SPS clients exhibit a number of integration or touch points.

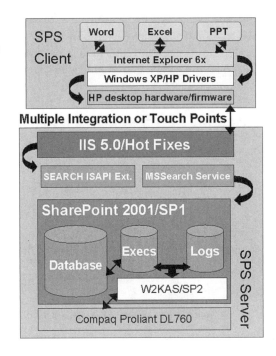

PERFORM GENERAL TROUBLESHOOTING

This section addresses potential problems associated with Microsoft SharePoint Portal Server 2001, as well as possible solutions. Use the following list of general troubleshooting steps as a standard approach to solving problems:

- Maintain careful notes of the installation process and of any unexpected errors or attempts to correct problems that may have occurred.

- Review your notes, and the notes of your colleagues performing similar tasks, whenever a new problem occurs, looking back to see if you have seen and resolved this issue in the past.

- Even if the problem is new to you, the methods you employed to solve previous problems might still be of use.

- Continue taking excellent notes as you persist in troubleshooting and taking steps to try to resolve the issue. Worse case, you can leverage these if a call to a technical support organization is required. And clear notes are of great value in the middle of the night, after you have tried a multitude of fixes and are still struggling with a problem. In this case, your notes will be critical in terms of keeping the team on the right path, and helping to avoid repeating troubleshooting tasks that are of no value.

Further, the more complex your systems environment has become, the greater importance a good internal knowledge base plays in helping you to resolve a problem. We have all been in a position where we find ourselves saying "didn't we see a problem like this six months ago?" Maintaining a knowledge base helps us answer that question with a solution.

It is also often very helpful to step back at times, and start looking over the more obvious causes of system failures. For example, you might perform or check the following, so as to quickly rule out these easy fixes as potential culprits (see Figure 23.3 for an illustration of some of these common and easy "quick fixes"):

- Verify you have power. Really, do it!

- Check all other physical connections and then restart the server, verifying whether the problem still occurs.

- Review the event log—Microsoft Windows 2000's Event Viewer can be extremely helpful in pinpointing problem areas, even if the events in the log are only really symptoms of a bigger problem.

- When unknown errors occur, check that the network connections between computers are actually functioning before proceeding with further troubleshooting. Utilize the ping utility to test whether client and server computers are connected (for example, ping 200.200.100.1 to ensure a response, and then ping the host name to ensure name resolution works). You might also ping -a 200.200.100.1, so as to check reverse name lookup as well.

- Refer to the SharePoint Portal Server Readme, other help files, and similar technical support resources to determine whether the problem you are experiencing is a known issue.

- Refer to the Microsoft Product Support Services Web site at http://support.microsoft.com/. And leverage experienced consulting resources you may already have on staff or within your local organization.

- Check your enterprise management application, like HP Openview or Compaq Insight Manager, for obvious hardware, software, or other failures.

- Gather information from the Server Installation Logs, such as the errorlog.txt file and the eventlog.txt file, by viewing them with a text editor.

- Review the setup.log file. This file is located in Program Files\Microsoft Integration\SharePoint Portal Server\Logs.

- Review the spsclisrv.log file. This file is located in Program Files\Microsoft Integration\SharePoint Portal Server\Logs for successful server installations.

- Review the Exchange Server Setup Progress.log file, if applicable. This file is located at the root of the operating system drive. This log clearly indicates whether the Web Storage System installed correctly, helping you identify some common problems such as

    A server name has an illegal character.

    IIS 5 is not installed, so the Web Storage System cannot be installed.

    The SMTP service is not installed.

Figure 23.3
Never forget to turn to and rule out the "quick fixes" before moving forward with more complex troubleshooting.

Quick Fixes include...

Leverage experienced consulting resources

Check connections and power

Review your notes and log files

Bring in an internal colleague

Check your enterprise management application, like HP Openview or CIM

Ping the server or SPS client

When you finally must call someone outside of your organization, whether it is a Product Support specialist, a technical support organization, your management team or other escalation team, or simply one of your remote colleagues, be prepared to answer the following questions:

- What is the problem?
- What is the last thing that you changed before you started seeing the problem?
- How often is it recurring? Only when something else occurs first?
- Can you reproduce the problem? Often the solution is found when you try to re–create the problem in a testing environment.
- Is more than one server affected?
- Is more than one user affected?
- Can you characterize the problem? That is, does the problem seem to be related to authentication, content, access, or personalization? Try to isolate the problem.

VERIFY KNOWN ISSUES

Next, leverage known issues, or other pockets of information to determine whether the problem at hand—your MOF—is actually a common problem that has been seen and rectified in the past. Like stated above, your own technical notes or the notes of your colleagues who perform similar tasks may be a good place to start.

An excellent example of one of these pockets of information, and a generally good place to start troubleshooting once the easy fixes are ruled out, is Microsoft's TechNet resource.

TechNet has been called by some the Microsoft Bible—like the real thing, it provides rules and gives us great examples that we can emulate, so as to keep our Microsoft solutions alive and well. A CD-based version has existed for years. More recently, though, TechNet has been made available as a Web-based resource. See `http://www.microsoft.com/technet/ sharepoint` for help on deploying, supporting, and maintaining SharePoint Portal Server.

Other valuable pockets of information exist, too, and include similar or related online toolsets by various Microsoft hardware and software partners. Examples could be

- Your server or disk subsystem hardware vendors' online toolsets
- Your hardware vendor's technical support organizations
- Microsoft's technical support organizations (specific to OS and product)
- Your SharePoint Portal Server systems integrator
- Other systems integrator toolsets and approaches available to you
- Other large and capable systems integrators, such as Compaq Global Services, Microsoft Consulting Services, IBM Global Services, and so on.

It should be noted that if your technical team can justify the time and cost, one or more individuals should be made responsible for "keeping an eye out" for new SPS issues, patches, and other updates from the various vendors that play a supporting role in your particular SPS solution stacks.

VERIFY THE SOLUTION STACKS

Should the problem at hand not easily fall into the convenient categories of easy fixes or known issues, we find ourselves in new territory. At this point, it makes sense to thoroughly verify that the solution stack foundation itself is indeed sound. This is especially important if we find ourselves with a problem cropping up after changes, however minute, have been made to the solution. Any changes may be related to, and usually ultimately are, the root cause. Even if the change itself is seemingly benign, the impact that the change has in terms of integration points may be detrimental. For example, a tape drive OS driver may continue to function apparently well even when upgraded to a new version, but the performance of the tape drive might be horrendous if a firmware upgrade is not also performed. Note that this example represents a classic case of creating an unsupported configuration out of a stable solution. Sound change control practices minimize these kinds of problems in productive SPS implementations, but issues still manage to crop up from time to time. In our tape drive example, though, even if our change control process fails, we still have the hardware vendor(s), Microsoft, and any number of systems integrators to fall back on for support.

VERIFY CHANGE CONTROL

This brings us to our next approach—verifying that any changes to the environment performed after the initial installation, but prior to the solution going live, actually underwent sound change control processes. In many cases, troubles arise simply because a change never actually was tested in a customer's enterprise environment. The smallest of changes—a firmware upgrade to a system board, or a post-Service Pack driver update—may cause a seemingly robust solution to crater.

→   To read more about change control, also commonly referred to as change management, **see** "Addressing Change Management," **p. 536**.

Suffice it to say that not enough can be said about testing the impact of a change *before* implementing it into your production portal. This means first testing potential changes in your technical sandbox, or test system, or elsewhere—see Figure 23.4 for a simple three-system landscape "Promote to Production" change management process used by many organizations running SPS. Successful testing implies that the solution stack remains stable, and therefore testing is critical across the board. Only once we know we have a stable production-ready foundation—a sound solution stack—can we proceed into more detailed troubleshooting and analysis.

Figure 23.4
This simple three-system landscape illustrates the "Promote to Production" change management process used by many organizations that have deployed SharePoint Portal Server.

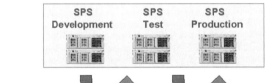

Change Management "Promote to Production"

All changes are first implemented in Development...

...and a week later, are promoted to Test...

...and finally another week later are promoted to Production...

VERIFY INTEGRATION POINTS

Another common problem area in a SharePoint Portal Server installation is the "touch points," or integration points, that many installations require simply to provide a business solution. That is, touch points from SharePoint Portal Server to Exchange Server 2000 public folders, SQL Server 2000 or Lotus Notes databases, network file servers, proxy servers, other Web servers, and more are often required to actually create a productive SPS solution, one that solves the business problems for which SPS is being implemented. No SharePoint Portal Server is an island.

Yet another layer of integration exists within the local SharePoint installation, too—SharePoint resides on top of the operating system and stores data in a Web-based database, for example. Additionally, a particular solution may have been architected to provide greater server availability or redundancy—two servers may be providing substantially the same services under the guise of one SharePoint solution. Similarly, servers dedicated to specific functions may exist in the environment, tied together both logically at an application layer, and physically from a network infrastructure perspective. An example might be a heavy-duty enterprise search solution, where multiple search servers and multiple crawl servers are configured for maximum performance, availability, and high levels of scalability, yet represent a single productive system.

USING THE PROXYCFG.EXE TOOL

If you wish to use SharePoint Portal Server with fully qualified domain names, or FQDNs, you must run the proxycfg.exe tool. Access to this tool is available via the SharePoint Portal Server \Bin directory. The proxycfg.exe tool is used to exclude access to an SPS server through the proxy server. Simply type `proxycfg` at a command prompt to view the current proxy settings.

To configure the proxy settings, type

```
proxycfg -d -p proxy_name:port_number "bypass_address"
```

where *proxy_name* is the name of your proxy server, and *port_number* is the port number used on the proxy server.

bypass_address is a mask for all of the addresses not using the specified proxy server. The bypass address is of the form *domain, such as *microsoft.com. You can use <local> as the bypass address to specify all intranet addresses. You can separate multiple bypass addresses with a semicolon.

If you are using fully qualified domain names (FQDNs) on your intranet, do not use <local>. Instead, you must use the form *domain to specify each address that the dashboard site accesses without going through the proxy server.

OUR DETAILED TROUBLESHOOTING APPROACH

In this section, we consider the SharePoint Portal Server solution stack in more detail, and uncover some of the more common—as well as unusual—SharePoint Portal Server issues and challenges. These include verifying or determining

- Minimum SharePoint Portal Server prerequisites
- SharePoint Portal Server limitations
- Minimum client components prerequisites
- Workspace configuration
- Index updating and propagation
- Dashboard customization
- Integration points

We also look at special steps and care that should be taken to troubleshoot a productive SharePoint Portal Server system, with the understanding that such a system does not lend itself to the offline testing and trial-by-error approach that might be employed on a new SPS technical sandbox server, for example.

TIP

> For frequently asked questions and other good information regarding SharePoint Portal Server installation, including troubleshooting steps and known issues, see Q290734, `http://support.microsoft.com/default.aspx?scid=kb;en-us;Q290734.`

MINIMUM SHAREPOINT PORTAL SERVER PREREQUISITES

The system requirements for SharePoint Portal Server include the following:

- Intel Pentium III or comparable AMD processor, minimum 500MHz or faster
- 256 megabytes (MB) of RAM minimum recommended
- 550MB minimum available disk space
- All disk drives must be formatted for NTFS
- Microsoft Windows 2000 Server or Windows 2000 Advanced Server operating system, with Windows 2000 Service Pack 1 (SP1) or later
- Internet Information Services (IIS) 5.0 (more details will be covered later in this chapter)
- Simple Mail Transfer Protocol (SMTP) Service, a Windows 2000 Server component (under IIS)

As per Microsoft, installing SharePoint Portal Server on a Windows 2000 or XP server that has been upgraded from Microsoft Windows NT 4 can cause SharePoint installation failures. It is therefore recommended that SharePoint Portal Server be installed only on a "clean" Windows 2000 Server. As a workaround, though, if you are installing on a Windows 2000 system that was upgraded from Windows NT 4, manually register the Oledb32.dll file before starting the installation to avoid an installation failure. To register this DLL, go to the Program Files\Common Files\System\Ole DB folder via a CMD prompt, and type `regsvr32 oledb32.dll` to register the DLL.

In addition to the minimum requirements listed previously, be sure to also install the following Windows 2000 updates before installing SharePoint Portal Server. These updates are available at `http://support.microsoft.com/`, and are expected to be addressed in Windows 2000 service packs published after SP2.

If you are installing on Windows 2000 Server with Service Pack 1, install the following updates:

- Windows 2000 Patch: Token Handle Leak in LSASS. Note that this new version of the hotfix replaces the previous hotfix (Q288861) release. For this hotfix, see Q291340: Token Handle Leak in LSASS Using Basic Authentication.

- Windows 2000 Patch: GetEffectiveRightsFromAcl Causes ERROR_NO_SUCH_DOMAIN. Addresses a problem that can cause subscription notifications to fail when the access control list (ACL) on a document contains a Domain global group. For this hotfix, see Q286360: GetEffectiveRightsFromAcl() Function Causes "ERROR_NO_SUCH_DOMAIN" Error Message.

If you are installing on Windows 2000 Server with Service Pack 2, install the following update:

- Windows 2000 Patch: Token Handle Leak in LSASS. Note that this new version of the hotfix replaces the previous hotfix (Q288861) release. For this hotfix, see Q291340: Token Handle Leak in LSASS Using Basic Authentication.

The following prerequisites must be met before installing SharePoint Portal Server:

- Windows 2000 Hotfix (Pre-SP2) Q269862 *must not* be installed on the computer. If it is installed, remove it prior to installing SharePoint Portal Server.

- The Windows Remote Registry service must be running. This service is started by default. To start the service manually

  1. On the taskbar, click Start, point to Programs, point to Administrative Tools, and then click Services.
  2. Right-click Remote Registry Service, and then click Start.

- IIS configuration: Ensure that World Wide Web Publishing Service (W3SVC/1), the default Web site in IIS, is started. SharePoint Portal Server setup performs a test to warn of potentially invalid IIS settings—this test checks the configuration of W3SVC/1 to ensure that the Web Site Identification TCP Port is 80 with IP Address "(All unassigned)". If multiple entries were configured in Advanced Settings, setup will check only the first entry. Other configurations may be valid, as long as localhost on port 80 is a valid way to connect to W3SVC/1 (the Default Web Site) on the computer. If necessary, alter the configuration by opening Internet Services Manager under Administrative Tools, and selecting Properties on the Default Web Site.

- SharePoint Portal Server requires the default Web site in IIS to use port 80 as the TCP port for localhost. Before installing SharePoint Portal Server, ensure that you specify 80 as the TCP port. In addition, do not change the port to an alternative HTTP port (such as 8080) after installation. Ensure that port 80 is specified and remains as the primary port for the server.

SHAREPOINT PORTAL SERVER GENERAL LIMITATIONS

The following software does not coexist well, if at all, with SharePoint Portal Server:

- Exchange 2000 Enterprise Server
- Microsoft Exchange Server version 5.5 and earlier
- Microsoft Site Server (any version)
- Microsoft Office Server Extensions

23

SharePoint Portal Server setup checks for the existence of this software and fails if it is already installed. If you install this software after installing SharePoint Portal Server, SharePoint Portal Server will stop functioning properly as well.

> **TIP**
>
> To keep up-to-date on programs and applications that are not supported with SPS, refer to Microsoft's Q Article Q295012, `http://support.microsoft.com/default.aspx?scid=kb;en-us;Q295012`.

Microsoft Cluster Service:

- SharePoint Portal Server is *not* supported in an MSCS (Microsoft Cluster Service or Server) clustered environment. Further, SharePoint Portal Server may not be installed in a clustered environment, nor may any SharePoint Portal Server be added to a clustered environment.

SharePoint Portal Server and Microsoft SQL Server:

- If SharePoint Portal Server is installed on a computer running SQL Server 7 or SQL Server 2000, SharePoint Portal Server will upgrade the existing Microsoft Search (MSSearch) service—during setup, a message is displayed indicating that the service will be upgraded.
- In addition, SharePoint Portal Server upgrades the full-text index format of all of the existing indexes on that computer the next time that MSSearch starts. For the upgrade to succeed, there must be enough disk space on the computer to accommodate 120 percent of the size of the largest full-text index on the drive. Upgrading the full-text index format will take several hours, too, depending on the number and size of the existing indexes.
- Because SharePoint Portal Server upgrades MSSearch and full-text indexes, do not install SharePoint Portal Server on a server that participates in a SQL Server clustering environment, or add a computer running SharePoint Portal Server to a clustered environment.

- SQL Server may be installed on a computer already running SharePoint Portal Server, however. In this case, SQL Server uses the MSSearch already installed by SharePoint Portal Server. Keep in mind that if you remove SharePoint Portal Server from a computer that has SQL Server installed, SharePoint Portal Server will not remove the upgraded MSSearch because it is a shared service with SQL Server. Also, while this solution is supported per se, in most cases and for most customers, it does not represent the best way to deploy either product.

SharePoint Portal Server and SharePoint Team Services:

- Do *not* install SharePoint Team Services on the same computer as SharePoint Portal Server. The documentation that originally shipped with SPS incorrectly discussed a sequence of events that should be followed, and a registry key that must be deleted (HKEY_LOCAL_MACHINE\Software\Microsoft\Office\9.0\Web Server) to make these two products work together on the same server. Article Q295012 explains this mistake, though, and wraps up this issue by stating that "conflicts caused by overlapping functionality" are the root cause, and that the two products will work together well if implemented on *different* servers.

CAUTION

> Incorrectly editing the registry may severely damage your system. Back up the current version of the registry, as well as any valuable data residing on the server, before making any changes to the registry.

Installing SharePoint Portal Server on a domain controller:

If you install SharePoint Portal Server on a domain controller, the following will occur:

- There will be no local Administrators group. Consequently, only users assigned to the coordinator role will be able to specify security on folders. If a coordinator makes an error, there is no possibility for a local administrator to resolve it.
- You may need to reboot the domain controller after installing SharePoint Portal Server.

Renaming a SharePoint Portal Server computer:

- You can rename a SharePoint Portal Server computer at any time. After renaming the server, you must reboot it, however. In addition, SharePoint Portal Server Administration prompts for authentication and displays an error before opening. To remedy this situation, manually add the SharePoint Portal Server snap-in back to the Microsoft Management Console (MMC). This may be accomplished by

  1. Click the Start menu, then Run.
  2. Type MMC and press Enter—the Microsoft Management Console (MMC) is started.
  3. From the MMC, click Console.
  4. Select the Add/Remove Snap-in option.

5. Select the Add button, and then choose the option for Microsoft SharePoint Portal Server.

6. Click Close, then OK, and note the addition of SPS to the MMC.

When opening SharePoint Portal Server Administration, you may see an error message stating that the server could not be opened. If this message appears, do the following:

- Ensure that your computer is connected to the network.
- Check the proxy settings for your browser. Configure the browser proxy settings to bypass the proxy server for local addresses.

Failed services on SharePoint Portal Server:

- If other server applications on the same server share services that SharePoint Portal Server requires, the services may fail to start because the other server applications have or were stopped.
- Services will also fail to start after the SharePoint Portal Server Beta 2 evaluation period has expired. The evaluation period expired on 15 April 2001, at 00:00:00. For example, Msdmserv and MSSearch will no longer start. There will be a message in the event log that clearly indicates that the product evaluation period has expired.

MSSearch may stop functioning:

- This may be because the location of the property store log files was changed.
- If MSSearch stops functioning, check to verify that the location of the property store log files was not changed to the *root* of a directory (for example, E:\). MSSearch does not function if the files are on a directory root. To resolve this, simply change the location to a subdirectory rather than the root directory (for example, change the location to E:\Logs).

The setup process fails due to "no free drive available":

- This can occur during either an installation or a repair. The install/repair process requires at least one free network drive letter on the server. If this drive letter is not available, setup fails. The Exchange Server Setup Progress.log file notes that no free drive was available.

If Setup is really slow, or fails after a long period of apparent inactivity, consider the following:

- Setup may slow due to insufficient memory or excessive network traffic.
- A slow CD-ROM–based installation could be the culprit.
- Your server may not meet the recommended processor and RAM requirements.
- Your network, if installing from a share over the network, may be degraded or otherwise slow.

TIP

> In these cases, it would be prudent to remove SPS. Refer to Microsoft's Q295704 article for detailed instructions on removing SPS manually, at `http://support.microsoft.com/default.aspx?scid=kb;en-us;Q295704`.

MINIMUM CLIENT COMPONENTS PREREQUISITES

A client of some means is required to access the dashboard site, which is actually a Web-based view of the SharePoint Portal Server workspace. Using a Web browser is the simplest means, though with limitations and specific end-user requirements. In the next few pages, we cover these limitations and other details.

DETAILED CLIENT SYSTEM REQUIREMENTS

The following comprise the minimum requirements for each end-user computer running the *client components* of SharePoint Portal Server (see Figure 23.5):

- Intel Pentium-compatible 200 megahertz (MHz) or faster
- 64MB of RAM minimum
- 30MB of available disk space on Windows 2000 systems; 50MB of available disk space on all other systems
- Microsoft Windows 98, Microsoft Windows Millennium Edition, Microsoft Windows NT version 4.0 with SP6A, or Windows 2000 Professional, Server, or Advanced Server—note that Coordinator functions require Windows 2000 Professional, Server, or Advanced Server, however
- Microsoft Internet Explorer 5 or later—Visual Basic Scripting support is required, which is included in the default installation of Internet Explorer 5
- Microsoft Outlook Express 5.01 or later
- SharePoint Portal Server Office Extensions require Microsoft Office 2000 or later

Figure 23.5
SharePoint Portal Server minimum client requirements are illustrated here.

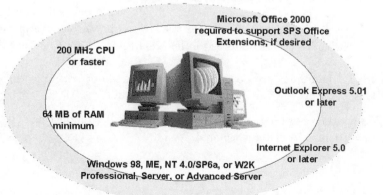

SPS Minimum Client Requirements

Microsoft Office 2000 required to support SPS Office Extensions, if desired

200 MHz CPU or faster

Outlook Express 5.01 or later

64 MB of RAM minimum

Internet Explorer 5.0 or later

Windows 98, ME, NT 4.0/SP6a, or W2K Professional, Server, or Advanced Server

ACCESSING THE DASHBOARD VIA A BROWSER

Accessing SharePoint Portal Server through the dashboard site does not require the user to install the client components. For Windows operating systems, the following browsers are supported:

- Internet Explorer 4.01 or later
- Netscape Navigator 4.51 or later (for Italian and Spanish versions of SharePoint Portal Server)
- Netscape Navigator 4.75 or later (for English, French, German, and Japanese versions of SharePoint Portal Server)

In addition to the previous, Microsoft JScript or Netscape JavaScript support must be enabled as well on the client.

> **NOTE**
>
> The Macintosh and Solaris operating systems are not supported, per the Microsoft SharePoint Portal Server 2001 Resource Kit.

COMMON CLIENT ISSUES AND RESOLUTIONS

Although the most common client-related issues tend to be related to not meeting minimum requirements, other issues crop up from time to time. Some of these include

- SharePoint Portal Server client extensions will not function correctly on a computer that was originally loaded with Windows 98 and later upgraded to Windows 2000.
- Windows 98, Windows Millennium Edition, and Windows NT 4.x computers do not support coordinator functions such as scheduling updates and configuring content sources, tasks performed by using MMC, or Web views. In addition, on computers running Windows 98 or Windows NT 4.x, you cannot access User's Help from the workspace by using F1 or the Help menu. To access User's Help when using these operating systems, click the User's Help page in the workspace, and then click the User's Help link on that page.
- To use the dashboard site with Netscape Navigator, Internet Services Manager must be used to enable Basic authentication for the workspace node on the default Web site. To enable discussions to work when the browser is Netscape Navigator, you must further enable Basic authentication for the MSOffice node on the default Web site.

In case these are not obvious, the following may be of assistance when a client installation fails:

- Is Microsoft Internet Explorer 5 or later installed on the client computer? Internet Explorer 5 or later is required.

- Is Microsoft Outlook Express 5 (OE5) or later installed on the client computer? Outlook Express 5 or later is required. This could prove critical to organizations that have removed OE5 from their standard desktop build. Note the following error message when trying to connect to SPS using a Web folder shortcut or via and Office application: "You have attempted to connect to a SharePoint Portal Server. To use the document management features of SharePoint Portal Server, you must install Outlook Express 5 (or later). See Q283990 for more details, at `http://support.microsoft.com/default.aspx?scid=kb;en-us;Q283990`."

- Are you attempting to install the client components of SharePoint Portal Server on Microsoft Windows 95? This is not supported.

- If you are attempting to install the client components on Windows NT version 4.0, do you have SP6A or later installed? SP6A is required.

- Are you an administrator on this client computer?

WORKSPACE CONFIGURATION ISSUES

After installing Microsoft SharePoint Portal Server, the creation of an initial workspace is facilitated. You create additional workspaces, or delete them, by using SharePoint Portal Server Administration. This section addresses problems encountered in creating or deleting a workspace.

Workspace creation could fail for the following reasons:

- Only 15 workspaces per server are supported—you must install another server to go beyond 15 workspaces, due to a significant CPU load placed on the server by so many workspaces.

- Duplicate name—you cannot use a workspace name that is the same as another workspace name on the server, the same as another workspace name on the destination workspace (for an index workspace), or the same as an existing IIS virtual directory.

- Illegal characters in the proposed workspace name—many special characters are simply not allowed in a workplace name. Workspace names can consist of characters from lower ASCII (characters with codes 32–127) except for the following:
  `# : \ ? * < > % / | " { } ~ [ ] Space ! ( ) = ; . , @ & +`

- Insufficient disk space—you need 550MB minimum to do the install, but you need additional disk space to create new workspaces.

- Servers cannot be in different domains if you are creating an index workspace—both the server dedicated to creating and updating indexes and the destination server must be in Windows 2000 domains; that is if you want to use fully qualified domain names and index workspace propagation together.

- Errors may be seen when anti-virus software is running during the workspace installation—stop all anti-virus software before running SharePoint Portal Server setup. If anti-virus software is running, the workspace creation that occurs at the end of the setup process will probably fail.

As for workspace deletion, if this process fails, review the following:

- The workspace, that is an index or other workspace, must actually exist.

- The destination server should be powered up and online. Actually, the destination workspace *can* be unavailable at the time the index workspace is deleted—you will simply be notified of this, and prompted to continue. If you choose to continue, the index workspace deletion succeeds. However, to actually delete the propagated index from the destination server, the process outlined in the ToolsHowTo.txt file on the SharePoint Portal Server CD must be followed.

ISSUES WITH PROPAGATING AND UPDATING INDEXES

This section addresses issues with propagating and updating indexes, both of which are facilitated via SharePoint Portal Server Administration.

TROUBLESHOOT UPDATING AN INDEX

If unable to start a full, incremental, or adaptive update

- You can start an update only if the index status is Idle. You can view the index status either from the Index tab on the Properties page of the workspace node, or in the details pane in SharePoint Portal Server Administration in MMC.

If the power to the server is interrupted during an update

- The update continues after power is restored. The index is in the initializing state for a period of time depending on the amount of content being crawled. The index is available for queries during this time, and the crawl resumes after it finishes initializing.

If the index update has stopped unexpectedly, explore the following:

- Check the status of the update in SharePoint Portal Server Administration or in the Content Sources folder, located in the Management folder in the workspace. The status display will indicate whether the update has paused due to low resources.

- Is the server out of disk space? If so, free up an appropriate amount of disk space based on the expected size of the index, and start the update again.

If crawling a content source fails, verify the following:

- Is access denied? If so, this could point to the expiration of the content access account.

- Otherwise, perhaps you are not using the default content access account, or your account has expired.

- If the account is valid and access is still denied, perhaps you have permissions problems with accessing the content.

- Is the file simply not found? If so, check the URL for your content source, and try accessing the URL from your Web browser while logged on as the specified access account.

If crawling a Lotus Notes content source fails, verify the following:

- Have you configured the Lotus Notes protocol handler by running the Lotus Notes Index Setup Wizard? If running the wizard fails for any reason, you must restart MSSearch before attempting to run the wizard again.

- Does the protocol handler need to be reconfigured? Reconfiguration of the protocol handler is required if the Lotus Notes installation changes or if Lotus Notes security changes (if you add, change, or remove user records, or if you switch user IDs). Furthermore, if you change the security mapping, you must stop and start the MSSearch service for the changes to be effective.

- Has the Lotus Notes administrator changed the port number that the Lotus Notes server uses? If so, then you must fully update that content source.

- Does the Lotus Notes server name contain a space (for example, "lotus server1")? SharePoint Portal Server cannot crawl a Lotus Notes server that contains a space in the computer name.

If crawling an Exchange Server 5.5 content source fails, or search results are not as expected, check out the following:

- Is Outlook installed on the SharePoint Portal Server computer?

- If so, is the optional Collaboration Data Objects (CDO) feature included with Outlook installed on the server? You must install CDO on the SharePoint Portal Server computer/server.

- It is recommended that Outlook be the only mail client installed on the server—verify this by reviewing the various services running on the server (via Control Panel) or programs available to be run (via the Start menu, Programs).

- Does the administrator account specified on the Exchange 5.5 tab of the server node's Properties page have permissions on the site and site configuration containers of the computer running Exchange Server? The administrator account must have permissions on both the site and site configuration containers.

- Have you changed the administrator account? If you change this account or password in Windows NT 4.0 or Windows 2000, you must immediately update this account in SharePoint Portal Server Administration.

- After you update the account in SharePoint Portal Server Administration, you must stop and restart MSSearch for the change to be effective. Be careful, though. If MSSearch is shared with Exchange 2000 Server or SQL Server on the same server, stopping and restarting MSSearch may adversely affect the operation of those applications.

23

TROUBLESHOOT PROPAGATING AN INDEX

Before continuing, know that you may propagate an index only from an index workspace to a destination workspace. If propagation fails other than related to this, verify the following:

- Is there enough disk space on the destination server?
- Is there network connectivity between the server dedicated to indexing and the server dedicated to searching?
- Did the password expire on the propagation access account?

To verify a successful propagation

- Check the event logs on the SharePoint Portal Server computer dedicated to indexing, and on the SharePoint Portal Server dedicated to searching.
- Check the event log on the server dedicated to indexing—to confirm that propagation is successful, SharePoint Portal Server logs the following event on the server dedicated to indexing:

  Event ID: 7016
  Source: Microsoft Search
  Category: Indexer
  Type: information
  Message: Catalog propagation to search server dashboard_site_computer_name succeeded.

- Check the event log on the server dedicated to searching—to confirm that propagation is successful, SharePoint Portal Server logs the following event on the server dedicated to searching:

  Event ID: 7029
  Source: Microsoft Search
  Category: Search Service
  Type: information
  Message: Catalog propagation was successfully accepted.

- On the computer dedicated to searching, SharePoint Portal Server creates and stores a search-only index in the following directory for SharePoint Portal Server:

  \Data\FTData\SharePointPortalServer\Projects\workspace_name\search\index_name

- For each propagation cycle, SharePoint Portal Server switches between the index names index0 and index1, so the mode is unknown—it may be in either state, depending on how many times you have propagated.

Regarding the network connectivity point above, verify that you do *not* see the following event, which is only displayed when the server dedicated to indexing cannot connect to the server dedicated to searching to begin propagating the index:

Event ID: 7012
Source: Microsoft Search
Category: Indexer
Type: error
Message: An error occurred during propagation to search server servername.
Details: 0x80070043 - the network name cannot be found

If you see this error, verify that the server dedicated to searching is online. That is, ensure that the server dedicated to indexing can successfully ping the server dedicated to searching, and resolve its name through the Domain Name System (DNS) or use of the hosts file.

If a connection is lost during propagation, for example it starts successfully but the connection is lost during propagation, SharePoint Portal Server will log the following event:

Event ID: 7012

Source: Microsoft Search

Category: Indexer

Type: error

Message: An error occurred during propagation to search server servername.

Details: 0x80070035 - the network path was not found

If you observe this error, ensure that the network connection is not lost. Also, verify that excessive network traffic is not preventing file copy from occurring. Note that when this error occurs, SharePoint Portal Server will retry propagation every 60 seconds, indefinitely.

DASHBOARD AND CUSTOMIZATION ISSUES

One of the more difficult to troubleshoot components of a SharePoint solution is the dashboard, not because it is especially complex, cumbersome, or prone to error, but because it touches everything. Clients access it directly, the various workspaces are tied directly to it, proxy servers need to communicate with it, and so on. The various errors, conditions, and issues that follow provide an excellent feel for the pure troubleshooting variety that may occur supporting the dashboard.

Server Access Denied:

- If you simply cannot access the server, ensure that you have specified security on the new Web site. Until you specify either Anonymous access or Basic authentication, you cannot access the server from an extranet, for example.

Error 401:

- If you have specified Anonymous access on a new Web site, you may receive error 401 (unauthorized access) when attempting to access the dashboard site. If this happens, ensure that the Internet Guest Access account is a reader on the hidden portal folder in the workspace.

23

Error 424 —if this is received when attempting to access the dashboard site, attempt the following:

- Restart the IIS Admin Service or restart the SharePoint Portal Server computer. One possible cause of a 424 error is that you failed to restart the server after configuring the proxy settings.

- Ensure that you are typing the proper address—`http://external_FQDN/workspace_name` (or `https://` if SSL is enabled). Another possible cause of a 424 error is that you are typing `http://localhost/workspace_name` for the URL—by default, SharePoint Portal Server does not support `localhost` out of the box.

- You also may receive error 424 when trying to navigate to the dashboard site by using HTTPS, though it is not unusual to receive this error when using just HTTP. In this case, on the dashboard Web site, ensure that you specify "low" IIS Application Protection for the virtual directory for the workspace.

Error 500:

- If you receive error 500 (internal server error) on the dashboard site, ensure that you have not selected the Check That File Exists check box when configuring the Public and YourWorkspace virtual directories on the new Web site. If the Check That File Exists check box is selected, clear it, and then restart the IIS Admin Service.

Error 503:

- If you attempt to access the dashboard site and you receive error 503 (service unavailable), the server is likely restarting and the services have simply not yet started. Wait several minutes and try accessing the dashboard site again. Otherwise, verify that all prerequisite and SharePoint Portal Server services are indeed started. Check the Event Viewer if one or more are stopped, in an effort to determine why they stopped or failed.

Dashboard site settings cannot be saved:

- If you cannot save settings on the dashboard site, you probably do not have write permissions on the workspace. To specify write permissions

  1. On the Start menu, go to Programs, then Administrative Tools, and then click Internet Services Manager.
  2. Expand the node for the SharePoint Portal Server computer.
  3. Expand the node for the new Web site you created.
  4. For the *YourWorkspace* virtual directory on the Web site that you created, where *YourWorkspace* is the name of the virtual directory for your workspace, perform the following:

     Right-click the virtual directory, and then click on Properties.

     On the Virtual Directory tab, select the Write check box.

Click Apply.

Click OK to close the Properties page.

A blank page displays:

- If a blank page displays when you attempt to access the dashboard site from an extranet, the proxy server may simply be offline.
- You probably need to map the internal static IP address and the external static IP address on the proxy server, in this case.

The dashboard site appears incomplete after enabling SSL:

- Bottom line—You must restart the server after enabling SSL. When accessed, the dashboard site may appear complete when you use the HTTP protocol but incomplete when you use the HTTPS protocol, even after just enabling SSL. If you have previously accessed the site by using `http://external_FQDN/workspace_name` and then you enable SSL (so that you access the site using `https://`), the dashboard site could open with no style sheet applied (this is apparent if the background is white) and with broken links. To fix this problem, restart the server.

Internet Explorer 5 Office Online Collaboration Toolbar causes links on dashboard site to malfunction:

- If you are using Internet Explorer 5 to access the dashboard site, and have enabled the Office Online Collaboration Toolbar to discuss a document, certain links on the dashboard site (for instance, the Search, Publish, and Subscribe links) may not function properly. To avoid this problem, you must close the Office Online Collaboration Toolbar before you use dashboard site links.

Troubleshooting Freedoc properties issues:

- The dashboard site may display different values for the Author and Title properties for Freedoc documents, depending on whether they are crawled from a Microsoft Exchange 2000 server or an Exchange 5.5 server. When an Exchange 5.5 server is crawled to include a Freedoc document in the index, the Subject and Sender properties are stored as Office#Title and Office#Author, respectively, instead of the FreeDoc Title and Author. In contrast, when an Exchange 2000 server is crawled, the document's title and author are included normally.

Dashboard site stops functioning after running the Internet Server Security tool:

- Your dashboard site may stop functioning altogether if you attempt to secure your server by running the Windows 2000 Internet Server Security Tool (available for download from `http://www.microsoft.com/TechNet/security/tools.asp`). For the latest information about implementing IIS security configurations to secure your SPS servers, refer to `http://www.microsoft.com/SharePoint/`.

Internet Explorer 5 Back button does not work:

- Using the Back button on Internet Explorer to return to a document in the dashboard site opened by clicking on the Discuss link under the Document title does not function as expected.

- After you are finished discussing a document via Internet Explorer, click on the inverted triangle control immediately next to the Back arrow on the toolbar. This displays a drop-down list of the most recently accessed browser pages. You can then select the item in the list that corresponds to the location from which you opened the document for discussion.

Cannot delete a dashboard in Netscape Navigator and non-English language servers:

- Deleting a dashboard using Netscape Navigator on non-English language computers may result in an error. Use Internet Explorer to delete the dashboard, or browse the workspace using Web folders to delete the dashboard.

Difficulty deleting Web discussions:

- Although Web discussions are usually managed from the Management dashboard of the dashboard site, you may have difficulty deleting discussions for the following types of documents:

  Those stored outside the workspace.

  Those created by using the Online Collaboration toolbar accessed from Internet Explorer.

  Those created from Microsoft Office applications for documents with high-ASCII (above 127) or DBCS URLs.

- To delete these discussions, an administrator must use the installable file system (IFS) to access the Web storage system drive. The administrator can use the IFS via Windows Explorer on the SharePoint Portal Server computer. SPS will map IFS to network drive M, unless a mapping for M already exists. It should be noted that users other than the administrator will have only read access to documents residing on the IFS.

Multi-word values for the Keywords field on the dashboard site:

- As indicated in the SharePoint Portal Server readme file, the Keywords property is a multi-valued property. From Web folders and Office applications, it is possible to enter values that consist of more than one word. Any multi-word values added from the dashboard site, however, are converted into single words. For example, if you enter "red apple; yellow banana" for the Keywords property on the dashboard site, SharePoint Portal Server stores the values as "red; apple; yellow; banana." This problem only affects the Keywords property when the following conditions are met:

You check in a document on the dashboard site.

The document is an Office document that supports promotion and demotion of values.

TROUBLESHOOTING OTHER INTEGRATION POINTS

While quite a few integration points have been already discussed—mainly in regard to integration/installation with the various workspaces or dashboards, including Exchange 2000, Exchange 5.5, SQL Server, Team Services, Lotus Notes, Proxy Servers, and so on—other integration points exist as well. For example, redundant server components like dual crawl servers and dual search servers might play a role in your SPS deployment. Multiple SharePoint Portal Servers would require integration, too, in the case of an SPS solution required to support more than 15 workspaces.

APPROACH TO TROUBLESHOOTING INTEGRATION POINTS

The key is to troubleshoot these types of installations by minimizing or eliminating (temporarily!) the redundant servers—in this way, if a particular feature or function is in question, it can be quickly verified "good" or "suspect." The feature should work identically on either server, assuming sound change control, and therefore a sound solution stack. A difference, or delta, would then likely indicate a problem specific to the server's workspace configuration, not to the overall solution—the hardware, OS, basic SharePoint Portal Server installation, and so on would not be in question.

Once this is performed, if the issue still exists, it will become necessary to pull in expertise in regard to the general technology area or perhaps specific feature set central to the issue. Such an issue might include problems with crawling particular content sources, for example. In this case, once all other troubleshooting discussed herein had been exhausted, it would be appropriate (if not before this) to introduce a subject matter expert, or SME, into our crawling problem.

SAMPLE INTEGRATION POINT ISSUES

Next, let us look at a couple of examples of troubleshooting complex integration points. A really pertinent example of troubleshooting an integration point not easy to classify is the following: Server Timeout before All Documents Crawled:

- In some cases, documents from an Exchange 2000 Server or a remote SharePoint Portal Server solution may not be crawled due to a server timeout error. If this occurs, the Build log includes an error message (Error Fetching URL, 80072ee2—The Operation Timed Out) for each failed URL. Review the log.

- To resolve this, the SharePoint Portal Server Administrator might need to increase the Connection/Acknowledgement timeout, and optionally, reduce the Server Hit Frequency by adding appropriate Site Hit Frequency Rules. Once these changes have been made, perform an incremental crawl.

Another example illustrates the technical depth and complexity inherent to troubleshooting key integration points—Subscriptions do not honor Exchange Server 5.5 security:

- The Subscriptions feature of SharePoint Portal Server does not honor the security settings for content that is crawled on an Exchange 5.5 server. Regardless of their permissions, Exchange 5.5 users receive subscription notifications for all Exchange 5.5 uniform resource locators (URLs).

- To work around this, you may modify a registry key to allow subscription notifications for all Exchange 5.5 URLs. The key blocks all subscription hits for content crawled on an Exchange 5.5 server by default. Perform the following:

    1. Click the Start menu, and then click Run.

    2. Type regedit, and then click OK.

    3. In the Registry Editor, locate the following registry key:
       HKEY_LOCAL_MACHINE\SOFTWARE\Microsoft\SharePoint Portal Server.

    4. Right-click AllowUnsecureExchange55Subscriptions.

    5. Click Modify.

    6. Under Value data, type 1, and then click OK.

    7. Close the Registry Editor.

    8. Restart Microsoft Search (MSSearch) via Control Panel, Services.

TROUBLESHOOTING FUNCTIONAL ISSUES

Whole chapters could be devoted to troubleshooting SharePoint Portal Server from a functional perspective because the topic is so broad! Yet that is exactly how so many issues and problems are ultimately characterized—as functional issues.

Examples of functional or content-focused issues abound throughout SharePoint documentation, from the User's Guide, to the readme on the installation CD, to issues posted online:

- Thesaurus weighting does not function as described in documentation
- Content source names limited to 150 characters
- Search on certain surnames returns unexpected results
- Incomplete procedure for Internet and extranet scenarios
- Manually register TIFF iFilter
- Incomplete list of circumstances that affect subscription notifications
- Inconsistent font sizes when English and ChS characters are mixed
- Web discussions problem on Japanese SharePoint Portal Server

- Recommended number of categories limited to 500
- Subscriptions created using similar words may be treated as duplicates
- Fails to report error for local Administrators group

The point is simply this—get comfortable with your online support and other technical support search tools, and remember to take advantage of partnerships with your hardware and software vendors and systems integrators when time is of the essence. Functional issues are rarely easy to solve, and are more difficult to quantify into search criteria. Furthermore, they often relate directly to limits or inconsistencies or permissions regarding the data—the content within the workspaces, the folder structure employed to organize the data, features used to find the data, and so on. Be patient when troubleshooting functional issues, and whenever possible leverage your technical sandbox to perform functional testing.

One last point—unfortunately, much of the functional troubleshooting you will perform will be on the production SharePoint Portal Server system, where downtime is a luxury and users need you to solve their problems *now*. In the following section, we address the special flavor of troubleshooting required in such scenarios.

TROUBLESHOOTING A PRODUCTION SPS SYSTEM

While it is easy and usually not too inconvenient to troubleshoot a non-production machine or a new installation, eventually the production system will require some level of performance analysis and troubleshooting. Perhaps a performance issue will manifest itself over time. Or maybe a piece of the solution will simply stop working one day. In any case, a prepared SharePoint Portal Server Administrator will be better positioned for quickly working through and determining the problem without incurring unnecessary downtime if the following are considered:

- Before ever installing SharePoint Portal Server, create a plan for system maintenance.
- Monitor the performance of your servers on a regular basis, leveraging a baseline from which to measure changes in response times, disk queue lengths, index creation and propagation timelines, and other performance indicators.
- Use performance counters and the Windows Performance Monitor (PerfMon) to assist you in troubleshooting, capacity planning, and simply monitoring overall performance. A specific list of counters, performance objects related to services and hardware subsystems, and instances/properties must be developed. It is also a good idea to create and save a standard performance monitoring .MSC file, such as SPSperfmon.msc, once a comprehensive list of objects has been developed. This will save time in the future, and will help ensure that all pertinent objects are indeed monitored consistently by all administrators on your SPS support team.
- SharePoint Portal Server Administrators should also maintain and use historical copies of the gatherer log to collect statistics and perform basic as well as more detailed trend analysis.

NOTE

A gatherer log file is created for the workspace each time SharePoint Portal Server updates an index. The gatherer file contains data on the URLs that are accessed while SharePoint Portal Server creates an index. You may specify that you want to log successful accesses, documents excluded by rules, the number of days to keep log files, and more by using SharePoint Portal Server Administration.

SUMMARY

While not wholly inclusive, we hope that this chapter has provided you with a sound approach to troubleshooting typical SharePoint Portal Server issues. To summarize, we recommend that a SharePoint Portal Server Administrator start by identifying and documenting the issue at hand, and then move into performing general troubleshooting, covering all of the most common issues/bases before escalating. Next, the Administrator should examine the various lists of known problems and issues, and then verify that the solution stack is indeed sound. The solution stack should, in particular, be viewed with a cautious eye—all changes to the solution stack should be completely documented and go through the proper change management processes. Finally, verifying that all of the various integration points are operating as expected, and that functional issues are addressed, is required.

Leverage your partners: Microsoft, your hardware partner or systems integrator, your SharePoint development partners, internal colleagues and so on. And leverage the many online toolsets and other applications available from these same folks.

Nearly as important as the approach we provided, we also anticipate that the various common and more puzzling issues covered herein will assist you in installing and supporting your SharePoint Portal Server system in the years ahead. For additional troubleshooting assistance outside the scope of this chapter, consult Microsoft's SharePoint Portal Server Administrator's Guide, the User's Guide, and the SharePoint Portal Server Resource Kit.

INDEX